THEORIES OF ETHNICITY

Theories of Ethnicity

A Classical Reader

Edited by

Werner Sollors

Henry B. and Anne M. Cabot Professor of English Literature, and
Professor of Afro-American Studies
Harvard University
Massachusetts

First published 1996 by
MACMILLAN PRESS LTD
Houndmills, Basingstoke, Hampshire RG21 6XS
and London
Companies and representatives
throughout the world

ISBN 0–333–64295–3 hardcover
ISBN 0–333–64296–1 paperback

A catalogue record for this book is available
from the British Library.

10 9 8 7 6 5 4 3 2 1
05 04 03 02 01 00 99 98 97 96

Printed in Great Britain by
The Ipswich Book Company Ltd
Ipswich, Suffolk

Contents

Preface

In the past decades the interest of students and scholars from various disciplines as well as of many general readers has been increasingly focused on 'ethnicity,' a word first used in its modern sense by W. Lloyd Warner during the Second World War. What exactly does 'ethnicity' mean in various fields of knowledge? When did 'ethnicity' grow so important as an area of cultural expression and identification, but also as a sign of existential connectedness that it has made people ready to kill – and to die – for it? Why has it become so central a term at a time that modernization continues to create the sense of one single world economy and a more and more widely shared global culture? Is the stress on 'ethnic diversity' a form of resistance to, or a feature of, modernity? Who are the thinkers who have been most important in the building up of a grammar in which such terms as 'ethnic community,' 'identity,' or 'cultural pluralism' have become universally disseminated? Which theoretical perspectives of the twentieth century might be helpful for an understanding of 'ethnicity' and for future thinking on the subject?

The present collection, *Theories of Ethnicity: A Classical Reader*, makes available some of the most probing and frequently cited considerations of such topics as the concept of ethnicity, melting pot and pluralism, race and race problems, migration and marginality, identity, assimilation and transnationalism, intermarriage (from 'connubium' to 'miscegenation'), generations, insiders and outsiders, kinship and religion, ethnic emergence, boundary-construction and maintenance, symbolic ethnicity, and the important role of power relations for ethnicity. *Theories of Ethnicity: A Classical Reader* includes pioneering work by sociologists (several with a sociology of knowledge perspective), anthropologists, psychologists, historians, philosophers, and literary authors from the United States, Great Britain, Norway, Sweden, Germany, Switzerland, and France. The chapters, many of which have set the intellectual agenda of what is now called 'ethnic studies,' often investigate polyethnic cultures, and among them most especially the United States, on the example of which many contributions are particularly focused.

Among the thinkers of the first half of the century are William James, Georg Simmel, Max Weber, Karl Mannheim, Robert Park, Carl Gustav

Jung, Margaret Mead, and Erik Erikson whose attempts at theorizing have done much to shape the various conceptualizations of ethnicity in the twentieth century. Among the more recent scholarly contributions are crucial works which offer such different perspectives on the subject as David Schneider's model of kinship and religion, Fredrik Barth's famous essay on the boundary, Abner Cohen's reflections on ethnicity and power, and Herbert Gans' influential concept of 'symbolic ethnicity.' Traditions of thinking emerge in the collection from the endeavours undertaken by Horace Kallen and Randolph Bourne at developing a positively conceived and viable 'transnationalism,' to the ideas of cultural reciprocity formulated speculatively and somewhat amusingly by Carl Gustav Jung and further developed by Ulf Hannerz; from Max Weber's 'negative' and Georg Simmel's notion of group affiliations to George Devereux's post-Holocaust critique of the troubling 'dissociative' character of ethnic identification; from Georg Simmel's 'Stranger' to Robert Park's reflections on migration and the marginal man; from William James' observation of a certain human blindness to Robert Merton's thinking on 'insiders' and 'outsiders;' from Karl Mannheim's investigation of the concept of the 'generation' to Marcus Lee Hansen's notion of numbered immigrant generations, Margaret Mead's generalization of the 'third generation,' and Vladimir Nahirny and Joshua Fishman's model of migration and marginality in immigrant generations; and through the pervasive stress on the modernity of ethnicity that receives particular treatment in Jean Toomer (who draws on anthropologists) or Herbert Gans, and that also becomes apparent in Philip Gleason's treatment of the surprisingly recent history of the term 'identity,' a word brought into circulation by Erik Erikson. Max Weber's self-conscious discussion of 'ethnic groups' and his use of the term 'symbolic' show the pioneering role of his theories, whereas the fact that he thought that Switzerland was no nation – while for Horace Kallen it was the pluralist model nation – also indicates the extent of disagreement found in the volume as a whole. This is also the case in the heterogeneous views of 'grandfathers' articulated by Kallen, Marcus Lee Hansen, and Margaret Mead, or in the dramatically different visions of the future of ethnic relations offered by Charles Chesnutt, Randolph Bourne, or by Herbert Gans whose new epilogue to 'Symbolic Ethnicity is published here for the first time.

Most of the essays included here have been read widely and debated either within their various disciplines or in the larger intellectual community. Many of the arguments refer to each other, at times critically, and thus help to generate discussions; some provide theoretical

access to whole areas of inquiry connected with the ethnicity complex; others are provocative in their own right. It is hoped that the
availability of a large sampling of ethnic theory of the twentieth century in a single volume will offer welcome theoretical perspectives to
general readers as well as to specialists engaged in ongoing practical
work, and that it will lead to further and more fully historically based
theorizations in the future.

WERNER SOLLORS

Foreword: Theories of American Ethnicity

Werner Sollors*

The vast literature on ethnicity has clustered around certain recurring topics. I have here selected six central aspects in the theoretical discussion of American ethnicity: 'Ethnicity as Peoplehood,' 'Ethnicity and Class,' 'Content and Meaning of Modern Ethnic Identification,' 'Ethnic Nuclei and Boundaries,' 'Assimilation and Pluralism,' and 'Race and Ethnicity.'[1]

ETHNICITY AS PEOPLEHOOD AND OTHERNESS

The word 'ethnicity' is of modern origin.[2] In America it appears to have been used for the first time in *Yankee City Series*, the first volume of which was published in 1941. The early uses of 'ethnicity' in W. Lloyd Warner and Paul S. Lunt's *The Social Life of a Modern Community* (1941), and in the same authors' volume *The Status System of a Modern Community* (1942), foreshadow some of the paradoxes that have appeared in later attempts at defining and discussing ethnicity.[3] Studying the stratification of Newburyport, Massachusetts, Warner was in need of a noun to parallel the categories of age, sex, religion, and class; a noun that would help to conceptualize ethnic group differentiation on a broader basis than 'national origin' (which does not include Negroes and presents problems with native-born descendants of immigrants). 'Race' was discredited by the emergence of fascism.[4] Warner used 'ethnicity' in the sense of a trait that 'separates the individual from some classes and identifies him with others.' Though Warner's term 'ethnic' often did not include natives, or Yankees, his 'ethnicity' became a concept within which Yankee identity could also be discussed. Warner's ambiguous attitude toward Yankee as an ethnic group reflects the ambiguity of the Greek noun *ethnos* (nation, people),

---

* From 'Theory of American Ethnicity, or: S ETHNIC?/TI AND AMERICANITI, DE OR, UNITED (W) STATES S S1 AND THEOR?', *American Quarterly*, 33(3) (Bibliography) (1981), pp. 257–83.

which was used to refer to people in general, but also to 'others.'

In 'ethnicity,' the double sense of general peoplehood (shared by all Americans) and of otherness (different from the 'mainstream' culture) lives on. Victor Borge once told the story of a musician who said, 'I have twelve children,' and added with pride, '*all* boys and girls!' One cannot help but feel a similar response to the sense of pride which is sometimes expressed about ethnicity, if ethnicity is, indeed, a general category (in which case the citizens of Newburyport cannot *escape* having it). It makes as much sense as displaying pride about belonging to *any* social class or to *any* age group.[5] Yet the phrase 'ethnics all!' can be heard as a battle cry. One cannot imagine a European government encouraging its people to engage in 'class-oriented activities,' to celebrate their aristocratic, bourgeois, and proletarian identities with the consciousness of pride that they had such diverse class identities. Yet in America, ethnicity can be conceived as deviation *and* as norm, as characteristic of minorities and as typical of the country. Philip Gleason's essay in the *Harvard Encyclopedia of American Ethnic Groups* (1980) (henceforth cited as *HEAEG*) and, in greater detail, his 'Americans All: Ethnicity, Ideology, and American Identity in the Era of World War II' (1980), have convincingly shown that the popular American character studies, 'as part of the broader American studies movement that grew up in the postwar years,' conceptualized the ethnic as 'a prototypically American figure, not because of any distinctiveness of cultural heritage, but for exactly the opposite reason, because the ethnic exhibited in an extreme degree the "character structure" produced by the American experience of change, mobility, and loss of contact with the past.' From Margaret Mead's *And Keep Your Powder Dry* (1942) and Geoffrey Gorer's *The American People: A Study in National Character* (1948), to Erik H. Erikson's 'Reflections on the American Identity' (1950), the anthropologist's, the cultural critic's, and the psychologist's assessments nicely corresponded to immigration historian Oscar Handlin's statement in the introduction to *The Uprooted* (1952): 'Once I thought to write a history of the immigrants in America. Then I discovered that the immigrants *were* American history.'[6]

In America, as Sacvan Bercovitch said in 'Fusion and Fragmentation: The American Identity' (1980), the 'conjunction of opposites' has reigned and multiplicity has become 'a chief argument for the basic unity of design.' A paradox is at the very root of American ethnicity, which makes it the incorporation of un-American Americanness.[7]

It is not surprising, then, that it has been difficult to 'define' ethnicity.

If Wsevolod Isajiw's survey of 'Definitions of Ethnicity' (1974) is accurate, four out of five social scientists and anthropologists simply prefer to leave the term undefined.[8] R. A. Schermerhorn has given the following definition of ethnic groups in what is – together with E. K. Francis, *Interethnic Relations: An Essay in Sociological Theory* (1976) – the best systematic, comparative, comprehensive, and theoretical approach to ethnicity, his *Comparative Ethnic Relations: A Framework for Theory and Research* (1970, 1978):

> An ethnic group is . . . a collectivity within a larger society having real or putative common ancestry, memories of a shared historical past, and a cultural focus on one or more symbolic elements defined as the epitome of their peoplehood. Examples of such symbolic elements are: kinship patterns, physical contiguity (as in localism or sectionalism), religious affiliation, language or dialect forms, tribal affiliation, nationality, phenotypal features, or any combination of these. A necessary accompaniment is some consciousness of kind among members of the group.[9]

Other comprehensive and pragmatic definitions are given in the introduction to *HEAEG* (vi) and in the first issue of the journal *Ethnicity* (1974, iii). Typically, such definitions focus on the external (objective, involuntary) and internal (subjective, voluntary) dimensions of ethnicity. Most commonly, however, ethnicity is not defined and discussed 'as such,' but in relation to other concepts and terms; and quite prominent among those are 'class' and 'modernity.'

ETHNICITY AND CLASS

One of the frequently expressed axioms in the literature on ethnicity is that *ethnicity is not class.* Whether scholars view this axiom with sympathy or regret, they still see the relationship of class and ethnicity as crucial. Daniel Bell, for example, in his essay on 'Ethnicity and Social Change' (1975), states that most influential ideologies in the last years have not been those based on class: 'The reduction of class sentiment is one of the factors one associates with the rise of ethnic identification.' Bell argues that compared with class, ethnicity 'has become more salient because it can combine interest with an effective tie. Ethnicity provides a tangible set of common identifications – in language, food, music, names – when other social roles become more abstract and impersonal.' Writing in *Commentary* (October 1974), and in the introduction to their book, *Ethnicity: Theory and Experience* (1975), Glazer and Moynihan echo Bell: 'As against class-based forms of social identification and conflict – which of course continue to exist – we have been surprised by the persistence and salience of ethnic-based forms of social identification and conflict.' The more 'salient' ethnicity becomes, the more obsolete are political philosophies of social class, Moynihan argues. Only our contemporary preoccupation with 'issues such as capitalism, socialism, and Communism,' he writes in the *Atlantic Monthly* (August 1968), keeps us from seeing 'that the turbulence of these times here and abroad has had far more to do with ethnic, racial, and religious affiliation than with these other issues.'[10]

Even writers less eager to forget about 'these other issues' agree that ethnicity is not class. Yet whereas Bell, Glazer, and Moynihan assume that ethnicity is more important than class, Myrdal, Howe, and Hacker think that it is rather less significant. In 'The Case Against Romantic Ethnicity' (1974), Gunnar Myrdal argues that the debate about ethnicity 'serves conservative and, in fact, reactionary interests' and explains: 'Its adversarial tone attracts some liberals and radicals, but since it does not raise the crucial problems of power and money, it does not really disturb the conservatives.' Along the same lines, Irving Howe maintains in 'The Limits of Ethnicity' (1977) that 'the turn to ethnicity . . . misreads or ignores the realities of power in America,' among which he lists economic policy, social rule and class relations.[11]

'Ethnicity,' in this view, is nothing but the new clothes for the emperor class provided by conservative tailors: talking about snazzy ethnicity instead of naked class is a symptom of confusion which breeds further confusion. Reviewing Glazer and Moynihan's *Ethnicity* in *The New York Review of Books*, Andrew Hacker makes this point very directly:

> If you cut the cake ethnically, classes become less apparent . . . It is no coincidence that the publicists of ethnicity all tend toward the conservative side in their politics . . . They would prefer not to have wage-earning Americans define themselves as working class, for that has hostile overtones toward management.

Hacker sees not just the promotion of ethnicity – by, for example Michael Novak's *Rise of the Unmeltable Ethnics: Politics and Culture in the Seventies* (1972) – but even the scholarly interest in the subject as an expression of a conservative policy. Reviewing *HEAEG* in *The New York Times Book Review*, Hacker sees the encyclopedia as an expression of 'conservatism's answer to the Marxian proletariat,' though he surprisingly and miraculously also interprets the reference work as

'Harvard's expression of atonement' for not welcoming ethnic Americans in its 'palmier days.'[12]

Apart from Herbert Gans, who has written illuminatingly about the way in which 'ethnicity' functions as a semantic substitute for 'class' in America, the battle between proponents of 'ethnicity' and partisans of 'class' seems to be a by-product of the feud between *Commentary* and *New York Review of Books* intellectuals.[13] Discussions inevitably focus on working-class ethnicity, implying that other classes do not 'have' ethnicity; they also suggest that American workers are faced with a choice whether to identify themselves by class or by ethnicity.

Glazer and Moynihan use a characteristic illustration for their contention that ethnic differences '*are* differences,' though 'Marxists thought they would disappear.' They ask ironically: 'Why on earth would one wish to be a Pole when one could be a worker?' Hacker replies, in 'Cutting Classes,' that 'to regard a person as, say, "Polish–American" is to regard him primarily as a cultural performer rather than as someone involved in a system of power.' The person faced with such a choice (or with a cultural critic who is ready to make it for him) is inevitably thought of as a worker. As early as 1940, Caroline F. Ware recognized this limitation in immigration studies, when she observed in *The Cultural Approach to History*: 'The Polish–American doctor or businessman is an "American," the Polish–American worker remains a "Polack."' Whether we imagine a worker who happens to be Polish or a Polish American who happens to be a worker, we ignore the relationship of class and ethnicity outside of the working class.[14]

Milton M. Gordon, in his classic study *Assimilation in American Life: The Role of Race, Religion, and National Origins* (1964), has offered the concept of the 'ethclass,' with the help of which alternatives in group identification can be understood across all classes and ethnic groups. According to Gordon, the type of social identification which can be summarized by the sentence, 'These are the people I feel at home with and can relax with,' is usually an attachment 'to those persons with whom one participates frequently and shares close behavioral similarities.' Gordon's hypothesis continues, 'these persons are likely to be of the same ethnic group *and* social class.' Looking at the social determinants of such an 'ethclass' one may emphasize the vertical stratifications of ethnicity or the horizontal stratifications of social class; the ethclass, however, lies at the very intersection of these coordinates. 'Thus a person's *ethclass* might be,' Gordon elaborates, 'upper-middle class white Protestant, or lower-middle class white Irish Catholic, or upper-lower class Negro Protestant, and so on.' With the help of Gordon's model we may say that ethnicity and class are different ways of looking at the composite identity form of the ethclass.[15]

Anthropologist Abner Cohen sees ethnicity as part of a power system. 'One need not be a Marxist,' Cohen writes in the preface to his *Urban Ethnicity* (1974), 'in order to recognize the fact that the earning of livelihood, the struggle for a larger share of income from the economic system, including the struggle for housing, for higher education, and for other benefits, and similar issues constitute an important variable significantly related to ethnicity. Admittedly it is not the only relevant variable' (xv).

Cohen also sees ethnicity in a larger framework of power relations, as a symbol system operating on all class levels. Cohen first developed his theory at the conclusion of a case study of *Custom and Politics in Urban Africa: A Study of Hausa Migrants in Yoruba Towns* (1969) which, in Timothy Smith's words, 'sparked a quantum leap in the sophistication of anthropological inquiry into ethnicity.' Taking Nathan Glazer and Daniel Patrick Moynihan, *Beyond the Melting Pot: The Negroes, Puerto Ricans, Jews, Italians, and Irish of New York City* (1963) as a point of departure, Cohen writes that American 'ethnic groups are not a survival from the age of mass immigration, but new social forms. In many cases members who are third or more generation immigrants, have lost their original language and many of their indigenous customs. But they have continuously re-created their distinctiveness in different ways, not because of conservatism, but because these ethnic groups are in fact interest groupings whose members share some common economic and political interests and who, therefore, stand together in the continuous competition for power with other groups.'[16]

Cohen's work *The Politics of Elite Culture: Explorations in the Dramaturgy of Power in a Modern African Society* (1981) is concerned with the cultural mystique in the articulation of elite organization. Cohen theorizes that 'symbolic action is always bivocal, being both moral and utilitarian, steeped in the human psyche, yet greatly conditioned by the power order. This is why it is the very essence of symbols that they are ambiguous, and hence manipulable and mystifying.' This approach could fruitfully be applied to American ethnicity.[17]

CONTENT AND MEANING OF MODERN ETHNIC IDENTIFICATION

In his useful survey essay, 'Ethnic Pluralism in Industrial Societies: A Special Case?' (1976), Pierre van den Berghe assesses the 'traditional' opinion about the relationship of modernization and ethnicity:

> When functionalism dominated North American sociological think-
> ing up to a decade ago, a number of phenomena was held to be
> incompatible with, or at best, to be lingering residues in our sup-
> posedly universalistic, achievement oriented, 'modern' industrial
> societies. Prominent among them were attachments to such 'obsol-
> ete' ascriptive groups as castes, 'races' and ethnic groups. Then, the
> intellectual reaction set in, and everybody began to talk of the 're-
> vival' of ethnicity.[18]

Now Nathan Glazer, in a perceptive essay on the 'Universalisation of Ethnicity' (1975), goes so far as to ascribe the process of increasing ethnic identification – which he terms 'ethnicisation' – to the very conditions of modernization. 'In the modern world,' Glazer writes,

> there is a loss of traditional and primordial identities because of the
> trends of modernisation. This means: urbanisation, new occupations,
> mass education transmitting general and abstract information, mass
> media presenting a general and universal culture. Now all this *should*
> make original ethnic identities – tribal, linguistic, regional, and the
> like, all the 'primordial' identities – weaker. However . . . in mass
> society there is the need in the individual for some kind of identity
> – smaller than the State, larger than the family, something akin to
> 'familistic allegiance.'[19]

It would be a theoretical shortcut to assume that the rise of a more uniform world economy and of technological progress leads to the disappearance of ethnic boundaries. The worldwide marketing of the Singer sewing machine, for example, as Peter Marzio has vividly illustrated in *A Nation of Nations: The People Who Came to America as Seen Through Objects and Documents Exhibited at the Smithsonian Institution* (1976), facilitated the 'making of intricately ornamented folk costumes' in different countries. Abner Cohen has brilliantly argued in 'Drama and Politics in the Development of a London Carnival' (1980) that the oil shipments to the West Indies in forty-four- and fifty-five-litre drums during the 1940s permitted the invention of the Trinidadian steelband, which has become the backbone of ethnic celebrations. The

development of computerized data-bases may well serve ethnic purposes, such as the establishment of Mormon genealogies. At this very
moment somebody may be writing an ethnocentric novel on a computerized word processor.[20]

But what is the content of modern ethnic identification? The answer
we get from American proponents of the new ethnicity is that *the content of ethnicity is elusive*. Novak places the ethnic content into the
instinctive and unmeasurable realm when he argues, in *The Rise of the
Unmeltable Ethnics*, that

> Emotions, instincts, memory, imagination, passions, and ways of
> perceiving are passed on to us in ways we do not choose, and in
> ways so thick with life that they lie far beyond the power of con-
> sciousness (let alone of analytic and verbal reason) thoroughly to
> master, totally to alter.[21]

Amen! if, however, analytic reason does get closer to the content of
ethnicity, the results may be no more revealing than Novak's invoca-
tions. In a beautifully positivistic exercise, which is included in Glazer
and Moynihan's *Ethnicity* book and in Andrew M. Greeley's *Ethnicity
in the United States: A Preliminary Reconnaissance*, Greeley and William
C. McCready set out to measure the differences in 'trust,' 'fatalism,'
'authoritarianism,' 'anxiety,' 'conformity,' 'moralistic' [sic], and 'independence for children' among Anglo-Saxon, Irish, and Italian respondents.
Asking questions such as 'How frequently do you find yourself anxious
or worrying about something?' (to measure 'anxiety'), or 'Do you think
most people can be trusted?' (to measure, yes, 'trust'), the researchers
found out that, indeed, the 'knowledge of the cultural heritage of an
immigrant group helps us understand its present behaviour,' and that
this behavior is often different from what we would expect. While the
'Italians turn out to be less fatalistic than the Irish,' the 'Irish are,
despite our hypothesis, significantly less "anxious" and "authoritarian,"
and more "trusting"' than the Anglo-Saxons. However, the most important statement appears in a footnote. 'Ought one to be concerned
about the possibility,' Greeley and McCready ask their readers (after
just having given them all the data about Anglo-Saxon/Irish differences).

> that the Irish may be more 'cute' (to use their word) in answering
> questions than other respondents? May it be possible that among
> the cultural traits that have survived the immigration is the facility
> at blarney, which has been defined as the capacity never to mean
> what one says and never to say what one means? Anyone who has

attempted to get a straight answer when wandering through the west of Ireland must be at least alive to this possibility.[22]

We know where we stand: however much we measure ethnic content, we have to rely on the unfathomable and on shared experience in order to make sense of our findings.

Gans has pointed to a general problem in 'measuring' ethnicity: 'Attitude studies probably overstate interest in ethnicity, if only because it is easier for a respondent to say that he or she favors participating in Polish life than to actually do so.' This challenges not only the question concerning content, but the very assertion that there is a new and strong concern for ethnicity in America. Glazer and Moynihan disagree with Greeley's sense of cultural differences among different ethnics when they say that 'the cultural *content* of each ethnic group, in the United States, seems to have become very similar to that of others, but the emotional significance of attachments to the ethnic group seems to persist.' The fact of ethnicity, then, does not lie in its content but in the importance that individuals ascribe to it.[23]

It is commonplace in the scholarly literature to concur with G. James Patterson, 'A Critique of "The New Ethnicity"' (1979), that American ethnic groups, because they are lacking 'first-hand knowledge of the culture, . . . tend to see relatively minor deviations from the American norm in the ethnic group as major cultural differences.' Drawing on David M. Schneider, Talcott Parsons argues in his contribution to Glazer and Moynihan's *Ethnicity* that 'however strongly affirmative these ethnic identifications are, the ethnic status is conspicuously devoid of "social content."' Schneider's most influential works are his *American Kinship: A Cultural Account* (1968), and 'Kinship, Religion and Nationality,' (1977). Parsons's own development is not without interest for ethnic theory.[24]

In 1966 Parsons maintained that 'the universalistic norms of society have applied more and more widely' whereas 'particularistic solidarities,' such as those based on ethnicity, were waning. In 1975, however, Parsons contributed 'Some Theoretical Considerations on the Nature and Trends of Change of Ethnicity' to Glazer and Moynihan's *Ethnicity* collection, in which he argued that 'full assimilation, in the sense that ethnic identification has virtually disappeared and become absorbed within the single category of "American," is very little the case.' Why the change?[25]

Parsons's new theory gives us ample evidence that his shift is a shift in *emphasis*, made possible by his use of Schneider. Parsons now emphasizes the 'optional and voluntary component of ethnic identification,' and says that the 'marks of identity are in a very important sense "empty symbols" ... [The] symbolization of ethnic identification is primarily focused on style of life distinctiveness within the larger framework of much more nearly uniform American social structure.' In other words, 'the universalistic norms' of Parsons's earlier essay have continued to apply more and more widely; however, their emanation has taken an increasingly particularistic and ethnic shape. In the terms of our fairy tale, Parsons views modern ethnicity as the emperor universalism's new clothes. Thus, when Novak seems to be saying that a spectre is going around America, the spectre of ethnicity, then Glazer or Parsons reminds us that under modern conditions ethnic groups have, in fact, become 'ghost nations.' Are ethnics merely Americans who are separated from each other by the same culture?[26]

In 'Sexuality as Symbolic Form: Performance and Anxiety in America' (1977), David S. Kemnitzer draws on Schneider as well as on Janet L. Dolgin's significant *Jewish Identity and the JDL* (1977) and describes the ideological formation of 'mediate identities,' according to which

> one does not exist solely as an individual and as a citizen or a member of a species; the gap between the two is filled by other group memberships of a particular sort: families, ethnic groups, and so on, to which one is recruited (which is *by blood*: a sharing of substance, of being between people), and voluntary organizations of which one is a member because of the kind of person one is.

This is analogous to Schneider's terms 'relationship as natural substance' and 'relationship as code for conduct,' and reminiscent of Glazer's term 'familistic allegiance.'[27]

I think that these distinctions can be pushed even further and applied to the loyalty conflict between American and ethnic identities which is so often expressed in the literature of ethnicity. Since American citizenship 'was created in the American Revolution as each inhabitant placed his consent in republican government, by that voluntary act approving its sovereignty and binding its allegiance to it,'[28] it may symbolically function as a 'relationship as code for conduct' in Schneider's sense. American identity alone thus takes the place of a relationship 'in law' (like 'husband, wife, step-, -in-law, etc.'), leaving ethnicity to fill the place of relationships 'in nature' ('the natural child, the illegitimate child, the natural mother, etc.') and 'by blood' ('father, mother, brother, sister, uncle, aunt, etc.'). In American social symbolism, as I see it, ethnicity functions as a relationship of 'blood' and 'nature,' whereas national identity may be relegated to 'the order of law.' In this terminology, one *leitmotif* among ethnicity advocates from Horace Kallen to Michael Novak makes sense. The central emotional part of ethnic rhetoric comes as a clear antithesis in Kallen's formulation: 'Men change their clothes, their politics, their wives, their religions, their philosophies, to a greater or lesser extent: they cannot change their grandfathers.' 'Grandfathers' are imagined as 'blood,' 'wives' are viewed as 'law.' In America, we may feel 'filiopietism,' but we pledge 'allegiance' to the country. To say it as bluntly as possible: 'American identity is like marriage, ethnicity is like ancestry.[29]

This kinship theory of the symbolic relationship of ethnicity and American identity has considerable explicatory power. It helps us conceptualize the symbolic interplay of citizenship and group membership. It explains why it 'is possible to be simultaneously a loyal citizen of the state, a part of the superordinate political unit, and a member of an ethnic minority.' It gives us a fresh perspective on how problems must arise when the two become 'mutually antagonistic' (as for German Americans in World War I). It helps us make sense of a statement that to be without ethnicity, without 'a sense of continuity is to be faced with one's own death.'[30]

All of this is, of course, in Kemnitzer's terms,' 'an ideological formation' (in itself a construction of law, not of nature, we might say). From a sociological point of view, ethnic identity is merely 'one kind of social identity, albeit a most important one,' as Frank A. Salamone and Charles H. Swanson conclude in 'Identity and ethnicity: ethnic groups and interactions in a multi-ethnic society' (1979), an essay that draws on Ralph Linton's role theory and Ward Goodenough's concept of the social persona.[31] If we construct an identity without ethnicity (in the sense of historical continuity through lineage) we may feel 'dead,' but if we define ourselves exclusively in ethnic terms we are equally in trouble.

In 'Ethnic Identity: Its Logical Foundations and Its Dysfunctions' George Devereux writes that

> the moment A insists on being only and ostentatiously an X, 24 hours a day, all those aspects of his behavior which cannot be correlated with his ethnic identity are deprived of any organizing and stabilizing framework ... As a result, there tends to appear, side by side with what little structuring of his behavior his ethnic identity ('being an X') provides – even when it is asserted mainly dissociatively

('not being a Y') – a logically untenable and operationally fraudulent incorporation into the ethnic identity of ideologies based on
principles which are, in essence, not only non-ethnic, but outright
anti-ethnic.[32]

Devereux convincingly locates the frequently invoked fascist implications of ethnic movements in this reduction of authentic identity to
one-dimensionality in the name of ethnicity. Focusing on the sinister
side of exclusive ethnic identity, Devereux sees the results of this identification in the dehumanization of politics and consciousness: 'Under
the Nazis,' Devereux argues, 'the Jews were gradually stripped of all
their relevant . . . identities, save only their Jewish identity, and in the
process were denied a personal identity.' This reduction applied to
victim and murderer: 'The Nazi SS member who pleaded that in performing atrocities he only obeyed commands implicitly affirmed that
his SS status took precedence over all this other group identities, including his membership in the human estate.'[33] Although the sinister
dimensions of ethnicity do underlie some American ethnic theory, they
are not always spelled out that clearly. In a superb essay on 'The
Revolt against Americanism: Cultural Pluralism and Cultural Relativ-
ism as an Ideology of Liberation' (1970), Fred H. Matthews points
out that

> for American intellectuals, folk romanticism tended to lead not to
> hatred of 'outsiders' and a lust to purge them from the nation, but
> rather to a sense of guilt about their own society's exploitation of
> the strangers, and to the desire to protect them from the aggressive
> majority. In the American context, alienated romanticism created not
> xenophobia but xenophilia.[34]

Thus, American critics continue to invoke the 'life' of ethnic 'nuclei'
as a positive asset, which, they hope, may *reduce* ethnic friction.

ETHNIC NUCLEI AND BOUNDARIES

In *Send These To Me: Jews and Other Immigrants in Urban America*
(1975), John Higham speculates that 'a very large part of the ferment
in contemporary ethnic life aims at revitalizing the nuclei of ethnic
groups that have needed new symbols and new leadership.' Seeing
this development as crucial to Black Power, Black Studies, and the
Chicago and Indian movements, Higham concludes: 'In a society as

fluid as ours – a society moreover in which so much that is crucial transcends ethnic categories – the quality of ethnic life depends to a very large extent on the quality of the nuclei. Pluralistic integration implies that the invigoration of the nuclei can relieve the defense of ethnic boundaries.' To a certain extent, this seems to be the way Higham can circumvent the dilemma that ethnic confrontation is bad, whereas ethnic consciousness is seen as potentially a good thing. Can we concentrate on the nuclei, the *centers* of ethnic cultures, without being ethnocentric in the sinister sense?[35]

In the introduction to his very influential collection, *Ethnic Groups and Boundaries: The Social Organization of Culture Difference* (1969), anthropologist Fredrik Barth states his different assumptions in plain antithesis to many American discussions of ethnicity (though with a certain affinity to Milton Gordon). It is, Barth says, 'the ethnic *boundary* that defines the group, not the cultural stuff that it encloses.' 'If a group maintains its identity when members interact with others, this entails criteria for determining membership and ways of signalling membership and exclusion.' Previous anthropologists (and, we might add, historians and sociologists) have tended to think about ethnicity 'in terms of different peoples, with different histories and cultures, coming together and accommodating themselves to each other'; instead, Barth suggests, we should 'ask ourselves what is needed to make ethnic distinctions *emerge* in an area.' In any event, 'a drastic reduction of cultural differences between ethnic groups does not correlate in any simple way with a reduction in the organizational relevance of ethnic identities, or a breakdown in boundary-maintaining processes.' With a statement that runs against the grain of much ethnic historiography, Barth argues that

> when one traces the history of an ethnic group through time, one is *not* simultaneously, in the same sense, tracing the history of 'a culture': the elements of the present culture of that ethnic group have not sprung from the particular set that constituted the group's culture at a previous time, whereas the group has a continual organizational existence with boundaries (criteria of membership) that despite modifications have marked off a continuing unit.[36]

Barth's focus on *boundaries* may appear scandalously heretical to some, but it does suggest new interpretations of the 'poly-ethnic' United States. (Barth uses this term instead of the more common Graeco-Roman mixture 'multi-ethnic' – to maintain boundaries in etymology) Barth's theory can easily integrate the observation that ethnic groups in the United States have relatively little cultural differentiation, that the cultural *content* of ethnicity (the stuff which Barth's boundaries enclose) is largely interchangeable and rarely historically authenticated. The black 'natural' hair-do ('Afro') in the wake of the Black Power movement or the clenched fist symbol of the Jewish Defense League are, of course, 'modern' and 'non-ethnic' symbols which could be (and were) easily interchanged; but when seen as symbolic markers of Barth's boundaries, their emergence can be better explained than by their denunciation as 'inauthentic.'

To take another example, the strengthening of ethnic consciousness often coincides with the rise of agitation against marginal men and disloyal group members. 'They're white inside' was the common cultural verdict about marginal Afro-Americans ('oreos'), Indians ('apples'), Mexican Americans ('coconuts') and Asians ('bananas'), in jokes that were popular during the ethnic revival. This is not merely the product of uneducated prejudice. One of America's foremost cultural critics, a Columbia-educated intellectual, similarly wrote that 'it is not the self-conscious cultural nuclei that sap at our American life, but these fringes. It is not the Jew who sticks proudly to the faith of his fathers and boasts of that venerable culture of his who is dangerous to America, but the Jew who has lost the Jewish fire and become a mere elementary, grasping animal.' The excerpt comes from Randolph Bourne's celebrated essay 'Trans-National America' (1916). According to Christopher Lasch, Bourne's essay implied 'not the ethnic pluralism advocated by recent spokesmen of the "ethnic revival" but a culture beyond ethnicity; not a glorification of ethnic consciousness in its existing state of parochialism but a genuine cosmopolitanism.' Perhaps; but Bourne undoubtedly did resort to a sinister rhetorical strategy that would strengthen boundaries. As Barth observes: 'just as both sexes ridicule the male who is feminine, and all classes punish the proletarian who puts on airs, so also can members of all ethnic groups in a poly-ethnic society act to maintain dichotomies and differences.'[37]

Barth's concept does not only explain the folk and the scholarly rhetoric directed against marginal individuals, it also helps us understand why so much energy in the writing on ethnicity is directed against the melting pot (a concept which stands, after all, for the melting down of partition walls and boundaries). As Richard Basham and David DeGroot have pointed out in 'Current Approaches to Urban and Complex Societies' (1977), 'a virtual academic industry has emerged to counter this metaphor' of the melting pot, while the importance of ethnicity 'seems greatly exaggerated by the recent trend to rush the slightest symbols of ethnic distinctiveness into print to prove that we have not really blended into a common pot.' In Barth's terms these scholars, just like other people, are working to build boundaries. If good boundaries make good ethnic scholars, then concepts like the melting pot which threaten to dissolve boundaries, must be ritualistically sacrificed.[38]

Among American scholars who have used Fredrik Barth's concept of ethnic boundaries is Andrew W. Greeley, who quotes Barth extensively in *Ethnicity in the United States*.

Ulf Hannerz has very convincingly applied Barth's theory of boundaries to American ethnicity in 'Some Comments on the Anthropology of Ethnicity in the United States' (1976). Hannerz uses as one illustration the book *Blues People* by LeRoi Jones (Amiri Baraka), who suggests 'that black music has been undergoing a continuous revitalization as a reaction to the equally continuous assimilation of its forms into mainstream music.' This example leads Hannerz to the hypothesis 'that the desire to maintain ethnic boundaries despite cultural diffusion may be a source of cultural vitality in a multiethnic society.' Another observation Hannerz makes is that 'the notion of what is characteristically Jewish has changed considerably at least in some circles in the last half-century as members of the group have been mobile between niches in the American social structure.' What this means theoretically can be seen in Herbert J. Gans's seminal essay on 'Symbolic Ethnicity: The Future of Ethnic Groups and Cultures in America' (1979), where Gans illustrates some of these changes:

> Jews have abstracted *rites de passage* and individual holidays out of the traditional religion and given them greater importance, such as the *bar mitzyah* and *bas mitzyah* (the parallel ceremony for thirteen-year-old girls that was actually invented in America). Similarly, Chanukah, a minor holiday in the religious calendar, has become a major one in popular practice, partly since it lends itself to impressing Jewish identity upon the children.

'Americans,' Gans concludes, 'increasingly perceive themselves as undergoing cultural homogenization, and whether or not this perception is justified, they are constantly looking for new ways to establish their differences from each other.'[39]

The strength of Barth's position has been made clear. Barth's formalism suggests that there is no emperor, there are only clothes. Yet as Louis Dumont has pointed out in a subtle critique of Barth's study of the Pathans of Swat (North Pakistan): 'The main thing is to *understand*, and therefore ideas and values cannot be separated from "structure."'[40]

Abner Cohen similarly criticizes Barth:

His separation between 'vessel' and 'content' makes it difficult to appreciate the dynamic nature of ethnicity. It also assumes an inflexible structure of the human psyche and implicitly denies that personality is an open system given to modifications through continual socialization under changing socio-cultural conditions.

A detailed critique which places Barth in the tradition of Hobbes was also presented by Talal Asad in 'Market Model, Class Structure and Consent: A Reconsideration of Swat Political Organisation' (1972).[41]

Barth's theory does leave us guessing about the reasons why people want to maintain boundaries. Is it a primordial trait according to which human beings want to distance themselves from others, create and maintain boundaries, even when the area that's enclosed by these boundaries appears to be, at least from a structural view, identical?

In his essay on 'Language and Ethnicity' (1977), an essay that also evaluates much theory of ethnicity, Joshua A. Fishman carefully concludes: 'If there can be no heartland without boundaries, however distant they may be, there can also be no boundaries unless there is a heartland.'[42]

ASSIMILATION AND PLURALISM

The two most popular terms used to discuss American ethnicity have also been enmeshed in the most confusing and paradoxical interpretations of American identity. Philip Gleason has directed his attention to the interrelationship between assimilation and pluralism which tend to become aspects of each other. Harold Abramson has thoughtfully developed this interdependence in an excellent image:

Each has its own dynamic evolutionary nature, but each has a correspondence to the other. It is in this sense that the assimilationist and pluralist perspectives resemble the image of the glass of water that is either half full or half empty.

If we look at Abramson's image in the light of the religious distinction between secular and sacred time, we may have a clue to the persistence of ambiguity in the study of American ethnicity.[43] *Sub specie aeternitatis*, in the fullness of time, we are all one and therefore constantly on the way not just to assimilation but to unity. Here and now, however, there are distinctions between us and between assimilation and pluralism, too. These distinctions, however, can be understood – when the belief in an American civil religion effectively blurs the sacred and the secular into the American – as an aspect of ultimate unity.[44]

Americans have conceptualized opposing models of the nature of their peoplehood for a long time. Crèvecœur's theory of an American identity that is derived from poly-ethnic backgrounds is familiar; his discourse on 'What is an American?' from the third of his *Letters of an American Farmer* (1782) is a stock element of much scholarly literature on American ethnicity: 'He becomes an American by being received in the broad lap of our great *Alma Mater*. Here individuals of all races are melted into a new race of men, whose labours and posterity will one day cause great changes in the world. 'Translated into social science, this concept is rendered as 'A + B + C = D' in William Newman, *American Pluralism: A Study of Minority Groups and Social Theory* (1973). It is the concept of assimilation more popularly known by the title of Israel Zangwill's play *The Melting-Pot* (1908).

The equally interesting opposite theory was developed by a less well-known contemporary of Crèvecœur's, a writer who used the pen name 'Celadon' (singer). His sixteen-page work, *The Golden Age: or, Future Glory of North-America Discovered by an Angel to Celadon in Several Entertaining Visions* (1785), is a rather complex formulation of what we now conceptualize as 'A + B + C = A + B + C,' a formula that can only poorly render Celadon's rapture as he turned his face westward and contemplated the future of America when

> the Angel recalled my attention by a gentle touch on my side, and pointing his finger a little to the south-west, Celadon, says he, do you see yonder long valley . . . That whole region you may call Savagenia: It being designed for the future habitation of your now troublesome Indians – And that other valley . . . It lies toward the north-west . . . This you may call Nigrania: It being allotted for the Negroes to dwell there, when the term of their vassalage is come to a period. And in all those vast spaces westward to the great ocean, there may be scats hereafter for sundry foreign nations. There may be a French, a Spanish, a Dutch, an Irish, an English, &c. yea, a Jewish State here in process of time. And all of them united in brotherly affection, will at last form the most potent empire on the face of the earth.[45]

What the angel has revealed to Celadon (who was only really surprised at the prospect of a Jewish state in America), reemerged – without the territorial implications – as Horace M. Kallen's metaphoric vision of

America as a pluralistic federal republic of nationalities in 'Democracy Versus the Melting-Pot,' a concept Kallen termed 'cultural pluralism' in 1924.[46]

The battles between the assimilationist and the pluralist perspectives are largely symbolic. The melting pot perspective often emphasized the importance of diversity for the birth of the new, and the currently more fashionable pluralistic perspective has, as John Higham has persuasively shown, 'unconsciously relied on the assimilative process which it seemed to repudiate.' Celadon and Crévecœur shared a faith in America's mission; both steered away from imagining either a nation really divided or a republic of melting pot clones. Yet the current debate polarizes these concepts to such an extent that we may find Kallen cast as a pluralist culture hero and Zangwill denounced as melting pot villain. That such debates have little to do with the actual characters to whom they attach themselves becomes clear when one compares Kallen's and Zangwill's attitudes toward 'race.' Though Zangwill's melting pot concept is sometimes denounced as 'racist,' Zangwill took pains to make clear that he always envisioned all races as part of the American melting pot: for those readers who missed the references to 'black and yellow' and 'America, where all races and nations come to labour and look forward' in *The Melting-Pot*, he added an afterword in 1914 in which he developed this theme at length. Kallen, on the other hand, was taken to task by Higham for relegating Negroes to a footnote in which he argued that their relationship to Kallen's federation of nationalities deserved separate discussion. Gleason emphasized that Kallen's notion of pluralism relied on 'inborn racial qualities whose origin and nature were obscure ... Race, culture, family socialization, and nationality were all blurred together in Kallen's discussion.' As Kallen's letters to Barrett Wendell also suggest, America's prime theoretician of pluralism was somewhat less than enlightened on the question of race.[47]

Milton Gordon has outlined pluralist and assimilationist concepts in his *Assimilation in American Life* and separated assimilation into 'melting pot' and what he terms 'Anglo-conformity.' This latter concept 'demanded the complete renunciation of the immigrant's ancestral culture in favor of the behavior and values of the Anglo-Saxon core group,' Gordon explains. In Newman's formula, this means: A + B + C = A. In common usage, 'melting pot' could stand for both of these concepts. The resulting ambiguity – did melting pot translate into A + B + C = D or into A + B + C = A – further contributed to make this image the perfect fall guy in maddeningly circular debates about ethnicity. As 'D' it could be denounced from a boundary-constructing ethnic point of view. If the reminder of commitments to what Orlando Patterson has referred to as 'the universal culture' made this position embarrassing, the denunciation could shift grounds by positing an identity of 'D' and 'A': melting pot or amalgamation was denounced as a mere smoke screen for Anglo-conformity (or, in a variant, for racism). The most persistent rhetorical feature of American discussions of the melting pot is therefore a contradictory rejection that asserts ethnicity against $A + B + C = D$ and then recoils to defend universalism against $A + B + C = A$. 'Refuting' the melting pot – an activity American writers and scholars never seem to cease finding delight in – allows us to have the ethnic cake and eat universalism, too, to construct symbolic ethnic boundaries in the name of universalism, and to denounce universalism as a veiled form of 'Anglo-conformity' at the same time.[48]

Gordon's model has remained a classic conceptualization, although Greeley has slightly touched it up and added a rather intricate 'ethnogenesis' perspective in his *Ethnicity* book. Gordon himself has adapted his triangulation of 'Anglo-conformity,' 'melting-pot,' and 'pluralism' to incorporate the theoretical approaches by Blalock, van den Berghe, and Schermerhorn (though not those by Barth, Schneider, or Cohen). In 'Toward a General Theory of Racial and Ethnic Group Relations,' included in Gordon's collection *Human Nature, Class, and Ethnicity* (1978), he noticeably makes more room for the dimensions of power and conflict to enter his model; he also emphasizes more strongly than before that the nation-state was the historical and numerical exception and that most 'nations in the world either are now or are becoming pluralistic in nature.'[49] It should be pointed out, too, that Gordon introduced the useful concept of 'structural assimilation' in his earlier work; this allowed him to conceive of a nonprimordial, noncultural modern ethnicity under assimilative conditions. A bridge could be built from Gordon's 'structural assimilation' to Barth's boundaries, as is suggested by Higham's question (asked in response to Gordon): 'Suppose pluralism turns out to preserve social barriers while ethnic cultures disintegrate?' This may well be what is at the root of the 'new ethnicity.'[50]

Finally, reminiscent of Barth's concern with the emergence of ethnic groups, Donald L. Horowitz adds some new formulae to describe processes of differentiation (sometimes called dissimilation in marked contrast to assimilation). In his essay on 'Ethnic Identity' for Glazer and Moynihan's *Ethnicity*, Horowitz refers to melting pot as 'amalgamation' and to 'Anglo-conformity' as 'incorporation.' Under the category 'differentiation' he distinguishes 'division' ('A → B + C') and 'proliferation' ('A → A + B' or 'A + B → A + B + C'). These models are useful for understanding groups such as 'Southerners' or 'Mormons' (see *HEAEG*).[51]

RACE AND ETHNICITY

The origins of the term 'race' are disputed; and theories of its etymology range from such words as Latin 'generatio,' 'ratio,' 'natio,' and 'radix' to Spanish and Castilian 'raza,' Italian 'razza,' and Old French 'haraz,' with such diverse meanings as generation, root, nobility of blood, patch of threadbare or defective cloth, taint and contamination, or horse-breeding.[52] Whether it stems from the idea of a 'taint' pertaining to those descended from Jews and Moors in the Spanish Inquisition or from the Italian adaptation of an Old French word for breeding horses, the word 'race' is several centuries older than 'ethnicity,' the term that was intended to substitute for 'race' at a time that the older word had become deeply compromised by 'racism,' a word coined, perhaps, by Magnus Hirschfeld in 1938.[53]

If 'ethnicity' was invented as a substitute for the much older term 'race,' why has 'ethnicity' not come to replace 'race' completely? This question opens a line of theoretical disagreement in discussions of ethnicity. Is 'race' an aspect of 'ethnicity'? Or does 'race' conceptually differ from 'ethnicity'? And if so, is it a difference in degree or in kind? For scholarly practice, should 'race' and 'ethnicity' be understood as aspects of the same set of phenomena, in relationship to each other, or individually? Do they deserve to be discussed together, comparatively, or as separate issues? What is to be gained, what lost, if one adopts one of these positions? Let me start with arguments for a conceptual interrelationship of 'race' and 'ethnicity,' followed by opposing views, and then offer a tentative conclusion.

Nathan Glazer maintained in 'Blacks and Ethnic Groups: The Difference and the Political Difference It Makes' (1971) that 'race' and 'ethnicity'

> form part of a single family of social identities – a family which, in addition to races and ethnic groups, includes religions (as in Holland), language groups (as in Belgium), and all of which can be included in the most general term, ethnic groups, groups defined by descent, real or mythical, and sharing a common history and experience.[54]

Glazer's metaphor of the family of social identities in which racial identification is one among many members suggests most directly that there is a relationship. His examples illustrate the possibilities of international comparisons that are opened up when one proceeds from the assumption that the differences between 'race' and 'ethnicity' are at best differences in degree, not in kind.

In *The Scope of Sociology* (1988) Milton M. Gordon argued similarly, though he takes a different approach. For Gordon, 'the term "ethnic group" is broad enough to include racial groups.' The inclusive quality of the term 'ethnic group' becomes apparent in usage, for 'all races, whatever cautious and flexible term we shall give to the term, are ethnic groups. But all ethnic groups, as conventionally defined, are not races.' Ironically, it is thus the inclusive quality of 'ethnicity' that separates it somewhat from 'race.' Gordon specifically states it: 'The larger phenomenon, then, is not race but ethnicity which, as a sociological concept, includes race.' Hence he speaks of 'races and many other types of ethnic groups.' Yet their difference should not be exaggerated, as it is 'a matter of degree rather than of kind.' Most importantly, scholars should not be led to believe that conflicts based on 'racial' difference are inevitably more serious than those based on 'ethnic' distinctions.

> [T]he most momentous and catastrophic forms of ethnic conflict in some cases rent on the perception of differences that are physical and externally visible, and in other cases on differences that are cultural and ideological, no matter how the latter differences are phrased by the participants or perpetrators.[55]

For Gordon, both the 'physical' differences (often associated with 'race') and the 'cultural' differences (of 'ethnicity') rest on 'perception,' a point to which I shall return.

In *Racial Formation in the United States* (1986) Michael Omi and Howard Winant take the opposing view. For them what they call the 'ethnicity model' tends to ignore different historical experiences, leading to the possibility of lending support to the strategy of 'blaming the victim.' The authors believe that a conceptual differentiation between race and ethnicity would, by contrast, be able to lead to a better understanding why, because of race, group distinctiveness is not altered by long-standing adoption of majority norms and culture (making it more compatible with a pluralist than an assimilationist model). Finally, the distinction would open up more scholarly interest in, for example, ethnicity *among* blacks.[56] Omi and Winant argue, partly on political grounds, that any 'true' sociological concept could also conceivably be put to bad political ends. It is also not necessary to believe that scholars who see a family relationship between race and ethnicity are therefore guided by an assimilationist bias. Omi and Winant's last point, however, is well taken. Gordon's maxim that all races are ethnic groups could be misunderstood as inviting a method of regarding all blacks as only *one* ethnic group, because they are also a 'race.' Races may be, and often are, ethnically differentiated (African Americans and Jamaicans in the United States), just as ethnic groups may be racially differentiated (Hispanics – who 'may be of any race,' as census takers know). Omi and Winant's argument supports the need for a careful examination of the relationships of 'visible' and 'cultural' modes of group construction in specific cases, but not the assumption that there is an absolute dualism between 'race' and 'ethnicity,' and a deep rift between them.

This, however, is exactly what Benjamin B. Ringer and Elinor R. Lawless claim in *Race-Ethnicity and Society* (1989):

> The they-ness imputed to racial minorities by the dominant American society has been qualitatively different from the they-ness imputed to white ethnic minorities . . . So imprinted has this differential treatment [of racial minorities in the United States] been onto the very foundations of the American society from the colonial period onward that we have constructed a theory of duality to account for this differential treatment.

Unlike Glazer's and Gordon's comparative approach this 'theory of duality' may ultimately be a local, US-based way of studying American group identification while ignoring ethnic conflicts that are, according to a US definition, 'intraracial' – as in Ireland, the Near East, the Balkans, or Rwanda and Burundi – and that have certainly taken place in the United States as well. And, describing their practice, Ringer and Lawless add a very important qualification: 'Accordingly we shall keep the two terms separate, although on occasion when we shall be looking at matters common to both racial and ethnic groups we may for the sake of simplicity use the term 'ethnicity' only.'[57] The language rule they apply could have been written by Milton Gordon, as it effectively makes ethnicity the superordinate category.

The most systematic brief in favor of a distinction between 'race' and 'ethnicity' may be the one advanced by Pierre L. van den Berghe in *Race and Racism* (1967), a work comparing the United States and South Africa. He argues that four principal connotations of 'race' make it confusing. First, there is the dated and no longer tenable context of

physical anthropology that once classified all human beings into customarily three to five races, that is evoked when scholars now speak
of 'race.' Second, the term has been and still is applied to numerous
groups such as the 'French race' or the 'Jewish race' – and in these
cases, van den Berghe recommends the use of the terms 'ethnicity' or
'ethnic groups' as synonym to only this meaning of 'race.' Third, the
polysemous word is also synonymous with 'species' when one says,
'the human race.' Only the fourth sense of 'race' is the one van den
Berghe proposes we should use; it refers, as employed by social scientists,
to a 'human group that defines itself and/or is defined by other groups
as different from other groups by virtue of innate and immutable physical
characteristics.' This differentiation leaves two meanings of 'race' to
be discarded, one to be replaced by 'ethnicity,' and the remaining instance
of 'race' defined on the ground of the distinction Gordon also suggested
between 'visible,' 'physical' (for van den Berghe also 'innate' and
'immutable') distinctions and 'cultural' ones. (Schermerhorn's definition
of ethnicity was broad enough to include cultural *and* physical – he
says, 'phenotypal' – features.) This brings us back, however, to the
point made by Gordon that 'physical' distinctions are also a matter of
'perception,' an issue addressed by van den Berghe's point that 'physical'
distinctions depend on external or internal definitions – which sets up
a tension. The terms 'physical,' 'phenotypal,' 'innate,' and 'immutable'
suggest a fixed, objectively measurable difference; the notion of 'visibility' (which could be complemented by Hannah Arendt's point that
there are 'audible' ethnic groups as well as visible ones, and by the
fact that the olfactory sense is also often invoked in setting up ethnic
boundaries) rests on culturally shaped sensory 'perception,' hence *not*
on 'objective' factors. In fact, van den Berghe acknowledges this problem
to the extent that he feels compelled to add a qualification to his distinction between 'race' and 'ethnicity':

> In practice, the distinction between a racial and an ethnic group is
> sometimes blurred by several facts. Cultural traits are often regarded
> as genetic and inherited (e.g., body odor, which is a function of
> diet, cosmetics, and other cultural items); physical appearance can
> be culturally changed (by scarification, surgery, and cosmetics); and
> the sensory perception of physical differences is affected by cultural
> perceptions of race (e.g. a rich Negro may be seen as lighter than
> an equally dark poor Negro, as suggested by the Brazilian proverb:
> 'Money bleaches'). However, the distinction between race and ethnicity
> remains analytically useful.[58]

In other words, van den Berghe's demarcation between race and ethnicity may rest on what is really a blurry and dynamic line at best. It is a matter of a relationship and of a difference in degree, of 'perception' more than of 'objective' difference.

In *Racist Culture* (1993), David Theo Goldberg extends these reflections and complicates them even more. He writes: 'The influential distinction drawn by Pierre van den Berghe between an ethnic group as 'socially defined on the basis of cultural criteria' and a race as "socially defined but on the basis of physical criteria" collapses in favor of the former.' This is so, Goldberg says, because that assignation of significance to 'physical' criteria is in itself the result of a 'cultural' choice that has been made differently in different countries and times. Goldberg reminds us that what he terms 'ethnoraces' (echoing Gordon's 'ethclasses') may also be formed 'by consent or domination by others.' Goldberg concludes: 'Ethnicity . . . tends to emphasize a rhetoric of cultural content, whereas race tends to resort to rhetoric of descent.'[59] Yet it is a matter of a 'tendency,' not of an absolute distinction.

One area in which one can see this tendential divergence in operation in the United States is in the different rules of self-definition for ethnically mixed and for racially mixed individuals that has been the subject of Mary Waters's fascinating research in *Ethnic Options* (1990). She found that not all persons from dual backgrounds have the same options for identification:

> Certain ancestries take precedence over others in the societal rules on descent and ancestry reckoning. If one believes one is part English and part German and identifies as German, one is not in danger of being accused of trying to 'pass' as non-English and of being 'redefined' English . . . But if one were part African and part German, one's self-identification as German would be highly suspect and probably not accepted if one 'looked' black according to the prevailing social norms.[60]

The Afrocentrist scholar Molefi Kete Asante took an example quite similar to the one Mary Waters analyzed in order to argue against a racially mixed identity in America: to claim, for example, a partly German heritage for black Americans, he writes, may be 'a correct statement of biological history but is of no practical value in the American political and social context. There is neither a political nor a social definition within the American society for such a masquerade.'[61] What Waters describes as a social norm, Asante tries to enforce by considering a person's real ancestry 'of no practical value' for identification, and the claiming of a parent's ethnicity merely a 'masquerade.' Those types of ancestry that are colloquially associated in the United States with the term 'race' rather than 'ethnicity' may deny a descendant the legitimate possibility of identifying with certain other forms of his or her ancestry (even though 'ancestry' may mean one parent, three grandparents, or an even higher proportion of ancestors further removed). The 'one-drop rule' and the social phenomenon of 'passing' that were subjected to scrutiny by F. James Davis, *Who Is Black?* (1991) also throw into question the notion that 'race' rests on 'physical' features or that such features are visible – since 'passing' implies that people who 'look white' may be considered to be 'really' black.[62] From a stronger theoretical probing of the issue of 'mixed race' the concept of 'race' as a 'physically based' ethnic distinction may be fundamentally questioned, as Naomi Zack's work *Race and Mixed Race* (1993) demonstrates. Naomi Zack has subjected the dualistic racial axioms to logical scrutiny and delineated the following schema:

> An individual, Jay, is black if Jay has one black forebear, any number of generations back. An individual, Kay, is white if Kay has no black forebears, any number of generations back.
>
> There is no other condition for racial blackness that applies to every black individual; there is no other condition for racial whiteness that applies to every white individual.
>
> This schema is asymmetrical as to black and white inheritance. It logically precludes the possibility of mixed race because cases of mixed race, in which individuals have both black and white forebears, are automatically designated as cases of black race.[63]

The one-drop rule may be more characteristic of contemporary practice than of past models of classification. It will be interesting to follow the theoretical and practical debates about the still prevalent denials of biracial and interracial identifications in the years to come.

Some contemporary scholars would like to consider 'race' a special 'objective' category that cannot be meaningfully discussed as a part of 'ethnicity.'[64] Yet it seems that, upon closer scrutiny, the belief in a deep divide between race and ethnicity that justifies a dualistic procedure runs against the problem that the distinction between ethnicity and race is simply not a distinction between culture and nature. Few if any scholars manage to sustain a completely dualistic procedure, and even fewer advocate abstaining from any comparisons between 'racial' and 'ethnic' groups. What seems to be the case then is that in societies that cherish racial and ethnic distinctions, ethnicity and race will interact in complex ways, and that in some societies the belief that they are completely separable will emerge so that certain ethnic conflicts can come to be understood as 'racial.'

If the theory of the Spanish origin of the term is true, then the problem with 'race' goes back to its beginnings. It was used in Castilian, as I mentioned, to describe (and expel from Spain) people 'tainted' by Jewish and Moorish blood – hence 'race' in the 'physical' and 'visible' sense, we might think. Yet the list of people to which the doctrine of purity of blood (*limpieza de sangre*) was applied went on and included descendants of heretics and of '*penitenciados* (those condemned by the Inquisition).'[65] Thus at this terrible beginning, 'race' was hardly based on the perception of 'phenotypal' difference but on a religiously and politically, hence 'culturally,' defined distinction that was legislated to be hereditary, innate, and immutable. It was what we would now call an 'ethnic' distinction, as defined by Nathan Glazer as well as by Pierre van den Berghe. Stuart Hall said memorably that race and ethnicity play hide-and-seek with each other.[66] A categorical refusal to find any possible relationship between ethnicity and race – even if that relationship should turn out to make 'race' an aspect of 'ethnicity' – does not seem promising as a program of scholarship.

Notes

1. This introductory essay consists of five sections of an essay that was originally published in the bibliography issue of *American Quarterly* 33.3 (1981): 257–283. The sections have been abridged and a few small corrections and very minor changes have been made. The section on 'Race and Ethnicity' has been added and is published here for the first time. For bibliographic guidance, see Rudolph J. Vecoli, 'Ethnicity: A Neglected Dimension of American History,' in Herbert J. Bass (ed.), *The State of American History* (Chicago: Quadrangle, 1970), 70–88; 'The Resurgence of American Immigration History,' *American Studies International*, 17 (Winter 1979), 46–66.

   Several of the relevant entries in Stephan Thernstrom, Ann Orlov, and Oscar Handlin (eds), *Harvard Encyclopedia of American Ethnic Groups* (thereafter referred to as *HEAEG*) (Cambridge: Harvard Univesity Press, 1980) end with useful bibliographic essays (e.g., 57–58, 160, and 242). *HEAEG* is an excellent reference tool for the group histories of 106 ethnic groups and includes essays on theoretical topics such as 'American Identity and Americanization,' 'Assimilation and Pluralism,' 'Concepts of Ethnicity,' 'Pluralism,' 'Politics,' 'Prejudice and Discrimination,' and

'Religion.' The work of 120 scholarly contributors has been carefully edited: its comprehensiveness, informative value and reliability, make *HEAEG* by far the most important research resource for the student of American ethnicity.

The special issue of *International Journal of Group Tensions*, 7, Nos. 3–4 (1977) is a rich and exhaustive survey of theoretical and practical approaches to ethnicity. It includes essays on definitions of ethnicity as well as on perspectives from political science, economics, anthropology, and sociology.

Volume 454 (March 1981) of *The Annals of the American Academy* is a special issue on 'America as a Multicultural Society,' and includes an essay by Milton Gordon on 'Models of Pluralism' (178–88).

Several publication series contain materials of interest. Among them are the *Ethnic Bibliographic Guides* (eds) Francesco Cordasco and William Brickmann (New York: Burt Franklin), the *Ethnic History Series* (Tacoma: Washington State American Revolution Bicentennial Commission); the *Ethnic Chronology Series* (Dobbs Ferry, N.Y.: Oceana Publishers); and the series published by R and E Research Associates (San Francisco).

An extremely useful guide to the fields is provided by Richard Kolm's *Bibliography of Ethnicity and Ethnic Groups* (Rockville, Md.: National Institute of Mental Health, 1973), which carefully annotates 451 books, articles, and lists, and which includes, without annotation, another 1,194 items. Unfortunately, the majority of the 64 books listed in the 1980–1981 *Subject Guide to Books in Print* under 'Ethnic Attitudes,' 'Ethnic Groups,' and 'Ethnicity' appeared after Kolm's *Bibliography* as well as after Jack F. Kinton's *American Ethnic Groups and the Revival of Cultural Pluralism: Evaluative Sourcebook for the 1970s* (Aurora, Ill.: Social Science and Sociological Resources, 1974), 4th rev. edn. An excellent listing of major texts, periodicals, research centers, and publishers of ethnic studies series, it also has a brief theoretical introduction.

John D. Buenker and Nicholas Burckel (eds), *Immigration and Ethnicity: A Guide to Information Sources* (Detroit: Gale Research, 1977) is a massive volume which carefully annotates over 1,300 books, essays, government reports, and other sources (1–24 and 173–225 on general and theoretical topics).

Josef J. Barton, *Brief Ethnic Bibliography: An Annotated Guide to the Ethnic Experience in the United States* (Cambridge, Mass.: Langdon Associates, 1976) has a concise, well-annotated and shrewdly selected section on 'General Works' (5–9).

Leonard Dinnerstein and David M. Reimers, *Ethnic Americans: A History of Immigration and Assimilation* (New York: Dodd, Mead, 1975) has a useful bibliographic essay (157–160).

William G. Lockwood has published a bibliography that is specifically concerned with our subject in the narrower sense. Ambitiously entitled. *Toward a Theory of Ethnicity: A Working Bibliography on Ethnic Groups and Interethnic Relations in Cross-Cultural Perspective, with Supplemental References to Caste, Nationalism, 'Tribe,' and 'Race'* (Monticello, Ill.: Council of Planning Librarians Exchange Bibliography, 1296, 1977), this 22-page pamphlet turns out to be an unannotated, alphabetical listing, which the editor describes in his brief preface as 'very eclectic, selective, and idiosyncratic' (2).

More voluminous is Wayne Charles Miller *et al.*, *A Comprehensive Bibliography for the Study of American Minorities*, 2 vols (New York: New York University Press, 1976), in which most literature of a theoretical and general nature appears under the heading 'Multi-Group Studies' and without any comments (955–70).

Further bibliographic references can be obtained from the section on 'Immigration and Ethnicity' in Frank Freidel's *Harvard Guide to American History* (Cambridge: Harvard University Press, 1974), I, 450–82, and from the *Ethnic Studies Bibliography*, 2 vols. (Pittsburgh: University Center for International Studies, 1975–1976). Journals such as *Antioch Review* (Fall 1971), *Soundings* (Spring 1973), and *Center Magazine* (July/Aug. 1974) have brought out special ethnicity issues; and a growing number of periodicals are exclusively or predominantly concerned with research on ethnicity: *Ethnicity, Ethnic and Racial Studies, Ethnic Studies, Ethnic Groups, Journal of American Ethnic History* (in preparation), *MELUS. Journal of Ethnic Studies* (two under this title), *Polyphony, Migration Today, Spectrum, Novak Report, International Migration Review*, and the *Immigration History Newsletter* of the Immigration History Society.

2. I am grateful to David Riesman, Milton Gordon, Leo Srole, and Everett Hughes for directing my attention to W. Lloyd Warner for possible earlier occurrences of the word than David Riesman's essay 'Some Observations on Intellectual Freedom,' *American Scholar*, 23 (Winter 1953–54), 15, which is customarily credited for the introduction of 'ethnicity.' The novelty of Warner's term can be measured by his occasional use of quotation marks (see *Yankee City Series* [1942], 73) and by the fact that C. Wright Mills, in reviewing *The Social Life of a Modern Community*, avoids the word 'ethnicity' and speaks instead of 'various categories such as age and sex, ethnic and "class"' (see *Power, Politics, and People* [New York: Oxford Unversity Press, 1963], 50). In *The More Perfect Union* (New York: Macmillan, 1948), 271, group relations specialist Robert M. MacIver made the telling statement that 'there is no English noun corresponding to the adjective "ethnic,"' suggesting that Warner's innovation had not yet been widely received. The two earliest uses of 'ethnicity,' reported by Einar Haugen and Joshua Fishman, which appeared in the *American Sociological Review*, 15 (1950), 196, n. 9,624, are, however, directly influenced by Warner. See Fishman, 'Language and Ethnicity,' in *Language, Ethnicity and Intergroup Relations* (ed.) Howard Giles (London, New York and San Francisco: Academic Press, 1977).

The adjective 'ethnic,' first documented by the *Oxford English Dictionary* in 1851, became increasingly popular after the publication of William Graham Sumner's *Folkways* (1906), with its famous section on 'ethnocentrism' (13). The term 'ethnic group' can be found in Isaac B. Berkson, *Theories of Americanization: A Critical Study With Special Reference to the Jewish Group* (New York: Teachers College Press, 1920), 79; Horace M. Kallen, *Culture and Democracy in the United States* (New York: Boni and Liveright, 1924), 63; and in the title of T. J. Woofter's *Races and Ethnic Groups in American Life* (New York and London: McGraw-Hill, 1933).

3. *The Social Life of a Modern Community* (New Haven: Yale University Press, 1941), 212, 220; *The Status System of a Modern Community* (New Haven: Yale University Press, 1942), 5, 66, 73; i.e., *Yankee City Series*, Vols I and II. An excerpt from this appears on Chapter 2 of *Theories of Ethnicity*.

4. The disappearance of 'race' in scholarly literature – under the influence of anthropologist Franz Boas – is discussed in Thomas F. Gossett, *Race: The History of an Idea in America* (New York: Schocken, 1965), 409–30. The substitution of 'ethnic' for 'racial' was a Pyrrhic victory, as Egal Feldman reports in a letter to the editor of *Commentary*, January 1975, 8:

> As an undergraduate . . . I recall being cautioned by my professors to avoid using the word 'race' unless I knew precisely what I meant by that term. The implication was that I could employ the term 'ethnic' even if I didn't know the exact meaning. The reason was obvious: in the imagination of that age, genocide was employed against a 'race,' not against an 'ethnic' group.

> 'Race' is now often understood as 'the most salient ethnic factor' as (Harold J. Abramson, put it in *Ethnic Diversity in Catholic America* (New York: Wiley, 1973), 175 and 183, n. 2). Among major theorists, however, Pierre L. van den Berghe and E. K. Francis employ 'race' as a category separate from, and not included in, 'ethnicity.' I shall return to this issue in the section on 'Race and Ethnicity.'

5. Quentin Anderson's work on American claims to establish a self without the aid of family or society is especially suggestive in this context. See his 'Sweet Democratic Poet,' *New Republic*, 22 November 1980, 29, as well as 'Practical and Visionary Americans,' *American Scholar*, 45 (1976), 405–18; 'Property and Vision in Nineteenth Century America,' *Virginia Quarterly* (Summer 1978); and 'John Dewey's American Democrat,' *Daedalus*, 108 (1979), 145–59.

6. 'American Identity and Americanization,' *HEAEG*, 31–58; 'Americans All,' *The American Identity: Fusion and Fragmentation* (ed.) Robert Kroes (Amsterdam: n.p., 1980), 235–64; *HEAEG*, 48, 49–50; *And Keep Your Powder Dry* (New York: Morrow, 1942); *The American People* (New York: Norton, 1948); 'Reflections on the American Identity,' *Childhood and Society* (ed.) Erik H. Erikson (New York: Norton, 1950); *The Uprooted* (Boston: Little, Brown, 1952), 3. Margaret Mead's section from *And Keep your Powder Dry* and Erik Erikson's essay are Chapters 14 & 15 (respectively) of *Theories of Ethnicity*.

7. 'Fusion and Fragmentation,' in Kroes (ed.), *The American Identity*, 19–45.

8. 'Definitions of Ethnicity,' *Ethnicity*, 1 (1974), 111.

9. *Interethnic Relations* (New York, Oxford, Amsterdam: Elsevier, 1976); *Comparative Ethnic Relations* (Chicago: University of Chicago Press, 1970, 1978), 12.

10. 'Ethnicity and Social Change,' in Glazer and Moynihan (eds), *Ethnicity: Theory and Experience* (Cambridge: Harvard University Press, 1975), 157, 169; *Commentary*, October 1974, 33; and *Ethnicity*, 7; 'The New Racialism,' *Atlantic Monthly*, August 1968, 36.

11. 'The Case Against Romantic Ethnicity,' *Center Magazine*, July/August 1974, 30; 'The Limits of Ethnicity,' *New Republic*, 25 June 1977, 19.
12. 'Cutting Classes,' *New York Review of Books*, 4 March 1976, 17–18: *Rise of the Unmeltable Ethnics* (New York: Macmillan, 1972); *New York Times Book Review*, 1 February 1981, 29.
13. Gans, Foreword, in Neil C. Sandberg's *Ethnic Identity and Assimilation* (New York: Praeger, 1974).
14. Ethnicity, 15; 'Cutting Classes,' 17; *The Cultural Approach to History* (New York: Columbia University Press, 1940), 64.
15. *Assimilation in American Life* (New York: Oxford University Press, 1964), 53, 51.
16. Preface, *Urban Ethnicity* (London: Tavistock, 1974), xv; *Custom and Politics in Urban Africa* (Berkeley: University of California Press, 1969), 191–92; 'Religion and Ethnicity in America,' *American Historical Review*, 83 (1978), 1159; Beyond the Melting Pot (Cambridge: MIT Press, 1963). Abner Cohen's essay 'The Lessons of Ethnicity' from his *Urban Ethnicity* is Chapter 20 in *Theories of Ethnicity*.
17. *The Politics of Elite Culture* (Berkeley: University of California Press, 1981), 219. See also Abner Cohen, 'Variables in Ethnicity,' in *Ethnic Change*, (ed.) Charles Keyes (Seattle: Washington University Press, 1981), 30–31.

    Hubert M. Blalock, Jr., *Toward a Theory of Minority-Group Relations* (New York: Wiley, 1967) emphasizes power relations and deductively develops theoretical propositions for black-white relations (many of which are not applicable to immigrant groups). For criticism of Blalock's approach (whose very use of 'minority relations' shows that his concerns date from the preethnicity era), see Stanley Lieberson, *American Journal of Sociology*, 74 (July 1968), 83; and R. A. Schermerhorn, *Annals of the American Academy*, 376 (March 1968), 199. Discussions of ethnicity and politics have not been central to political scientists, according to Lawrence G. Flood, 'Ethnic Politics and Political Science: A Survey of Leading Journals,' *Ethnicity*, 7 (March 1980), 96–101. If Edward R. Kantowicz, 'Politics,' *HEAEG*, 803–13; and Mark R. Levy and Michael S. Kramer, *The Ethnic Factor: How American Minorities Decide Elections* (New York: Simon and Schuster, 1972) are representative, political scientists have been preoccupied with 'voting patterns' when approaching ethnicity. Interesting departures from this preoccupation can be found in *Ethnicity and U.S. Foreign Policy*, (ed.) Abdul Aziz Said (New York: Praeger, 1977); in *Ethnic Leadership in America*, (ed.) John Higham (Baltimore and London: Johns Hopkins University Press, 1978); and in Joseph Rothschild, *Ethnopolitics: A Conceptual Framework* (New York: Columbia University Press, 1981).
18. 'Ethnic Pluralism in Industrial Societies,' *Ethnicity*, 3 (1976), 242.
19. 'Universalisation of Ethnicity,' *Encounter*, 2 (1975), 16.
20. *A Nation of Nations* (New York: Harper & Row, 1976), 530–35; 'Drama and Politics in the Development of a London Carnival,' *Man*, 15 (1980) 65–87.
21. *The Rise of the Unmeltable Ethnics: Politics and Culture in the Seventies* (New York: Macmillan, 1972), xvi.
22. Greeley and McCready, in *Ethnicity*, 216–17, n. 6.
23. Gans, Foreword, *Ethnic Identity*, vii; *Ethnicity*, 8.

xl   *Foreword: Theories of Ethnicity*

24. 'A Critique of the New Ethnicity,' *American Anthropologist,* 81 (1979) 104; *Ethnicity,* 65; *American Kinship* (Englewood Cliffs, NJ: Prentice-Hall, 1968); 'Kinship, Religion, and Nationality,' *Symbolic Anthropology: A Reader in the Study of Symbols and Meanings,* (ed.) Janet L. Dolgin, David S. Kemnitzer, and David M. Schneider (New York: Columbia University Press, 1977) [now Chapter 17 in this volume].
25. *The Negro American,* (ed.) Talcott Parsons and Kenneth B. Clark (Boston: Houghton Mifflin, 1966), 739; 'Some Theoretical Considerations on . . . Ethnicity,' in *Ethnicity,* 63–64.
26. 'Some Theoretical Considerations . . .,' 64, 65; *Ethnicity,* 8, n. 3.
27. 'Sexuality as Symbolic Form,' *Symbolic Anthropology,* 301; *Jewish Identity and the JDL* (Princeton: Princeton University Press, 1977); Schneider, *Symbolic Anthropology,* 65–66.
28. Reed Ueda, 'Naturalization and Citizenship,' *HEAEG,* 748.
29. Schneider, *Symbolic Anthropology,* 65–66; Kallen, *Culture and Democracy,* 122.
30. George de Vos and Lola Romanucci-Ross, 'Ethnicity: Vessel of Meaning and Emblem of Contrast,' *Ethnic Identity: Cultural Continuities and Change* (Palo Alto, Calif.: Mayfield, 1975), 368, 364. For a further discussion of the German Americans in World War I, see *HEAEG,* 422–23, 684–86.
31. 'Identity and ethnicity,' *Ethnic Groups,* 2 (1979) 172. For an intricate model on a different nature, see Daniel Glaser, 'Dynamics of Ethnic Identification,' *American Sociological Review,* 23 (1958), 31–40. See also Vladimir C. Nahirny and Joshua A. Fishman, 'American Immigrant Groups: Ethnic Identification and the Problem of Generations,' *Sociological Review,* N.S., 13 (1965), 311–26, now Chapter 16.

   For problems with external ethnic identification see Martin Plax, 'On Studying Ethnicity,' *Public Opinion Quarterly,* 36 (1972), 99–104; as well as Charles A. Price, 'Methods of Estimating the Size of Groups,' *HEAEG,* 1033–44; and James D. Wright, Peter H. Rossi, and Thomas F. Juravich, 'Survey Research,' *HEAEG,* 954–71.

   Karen I. Blu has made some excellent contributions to the anthropology of ethnic identity: 'Kinship and Culture: Affinity and the Role of the Father in the Trobriands,' *Symbolic Anthropology,* 47–62; 'Varieties of Ethnic Identity: Anglo-Saxons, Blacks, Indians, and Jews in a Southern County,' *Ethnicity,* 4 (1977), 263–86; and 'Race and Ethnicity – Changing Symbols of Dominance and Hierarchy in the United States,' *Anthropological Quarterly* (April 1979), 77–85.
32. 'Ethnic Identity' in de Vos and Romanucci-Ross (eds), *Ethnic Identity,* 66–67.
33. *Ibid.,* 66–67.
34. 'The Revolt against Americanism,' *Canadian Review of American Studies,* 1 (1970), 4–31 [9].
35. *Send These To Me* (New York: Atheneum, 1975), 246.
36. Introduction, *Ethnic Groups and Boundaries* (Boston: Little, Brown, 1969), 15, 17, 32–33, 38.
37. 'Trans-National America' (1916: reprinted in Randolph Bourne, *The Radical Will: Selected Writings 1911–1918,* (ed.) Olaf Hansen, preface by Christopher Lasch [New York: Urizen Books, 1977]), 254, 11 [now Chapter

8 in this volume]; Barth, *Ethnic Groups*, 18.

38. 'Current Approaches,' *American Anthropologist*, 79 (1977), 423.

39. 'Some Comments on the Anthropology of Ethnicity,' *Ethnicity in the Americas*, (ed.) Frances Henry (The Hague and Paris: Mouton, 1976), 435 [now Chapter 22 in this volume]: 'Symbolic Ethnicity,' *On the Making of Americans: Five Essays in Honor of David Riesman*, (ed.) Herbert J. Gans *et al.* (Philadelphia: University of Pennsylvania Press, 1979), 205, 215 [now Chapter 23 in this volume]. See also Gans's earlier essay, 'American Jewry: Present and Future,' *Commentary*, May 1956, 422–30, in which he speaks of 'symbolic Judaism.'

40. 'Caste: A Phenomenon of Social Structure or an Aspect of Indian Culture?' *Caste and Race: Comparative Approaches*, (ed.) Anthony de Reuck and Julie Knight (Boston: Little, Brown, 1967), 31.

41. *Urban Ethnicity*, xv; 'Market Model, Class Structure and Consent,' *Man*, 7 (March 1972), 74 ff.

42. 'Language and Ethnicity,' *Language, Ethnicity and Intergroup Relations*, (ed.) Howard Giles (London: Academic Press, 1977), 27.

43. Gleason, *HEAG*, 31–58; Abramson, *HEAEG*, 150.

44. Carlton J. Hayes has interpreted the sacred dimensions of group cohesion in *Nationalism: A Religion* (New York: Macmillan, 1960), 164–81; a thesis he presented as early as 1926 in *Essays on Nationalism* (New York: Macmillan, 1926), 92–125. Harold J. Abramson interestingly divides his entry on 'Religion' in *HEAEG* into 'The Ethnic Side of Religion' and 'The Religious Side of Ethnicity' (869–75). Timothy L. Smith, 'Religion and Ethnicity,' *American Historical Review*, 83 (1978), 1155–85, fascinatingly connects a religious approach to ethnicity with sociology, anthropology, psychology, and history and argues that 'migration was often a theologizing experience' (1175). The most popular conceptualization of the relationship of religion and ethnicity may still be Will Herberg, *Protestant – Catholic – Jew* (Garden City, N.Y.: Doubleday, 1955), although Herberg's thesis that American ethnic differences would disappear while the major religious differences would remain has been refuted. Harold J. Abramson has called attention to the persistence of ethnic differences *within* religious groups, especially in *Ethnic Diversity in Catholic America* (New York: Wiley, 1973); and a letter by the American bishops frankly acknowledged 'acrimonious relations among ethnic groups in the Catholic Church in the United States,' *Boston Globe*, 5 January 1981, 23.

45. *American Pluralism* (New York: Harper & Row, 1973), 63, 67; *The Golden Age* (n.p.: n.p., 1785), 11–12.

46. 'Democracy Versus the Melting Pot,' 18, 25 February 1915, esp. 220, 43 [now Chapter 7 in this volume].

47. *Send These To Me*, 198; *The Melting Pot*, (New York: Macmillan, 1910), 199; *The Melting-Pot*, rev. edn (New York: Macmillan, 1914), 204–07; *Send These To Me*, 208; *HEAEG*, 44; Kallen to Wendell, 22 October, 12 November 1907, and 2 May 1908.

48. *Assimilation in American Life*, 84–114; Patterson, *Ethnic Chauvinism: The Reactionary Impulse* (New York: Stein and Day, 1977).

The melting pot was definitively discussed in two indispensable essays by Philip Gleason: 'The Melting Pot: Symbol of Fusion or Confusion,'

American Quarterly, 16 (1964), 20–46, and 'Confusion Compounded: The Melting Pot in the 1960s and 1970s,' *Ethnicity*, 6 (1979), 10–20. I came to 'A Defence of the Melting Pot,' in *The American Identity*, (ed.) Kroes, 181–214.

49. Greeley, *Ethnicity*, 309; *Human Nature, Class, and Ethnicity* (New York: Oxford University Press, 1978), 93.

Gordon's statement is characteristic of a new focus on comparative approaches to ethnicity. According to Schermerhorn, *Comparative Ethnic Relations*, the percentage of intergroup research done exclusively in the United States was 99 percent in 1947, 84 percent in 1957, and up again at 89 percent in 1964 (9). Against this backdrop of provincialism, most of the recent major works in ethnicity have emphasized comparative studies and approaches, and broadened the comparisons to include not only the United States and European nation-states, but also poly-ethnic societies around the globe. Among the recent books that have supported or adhered to comparative methods are the works by E. K. Francis, Schermerhorn, and van den Berghe, as well as Tamotsu Shibutani and Kian M. Kwan, *Ethnic Stratification: A Comparative Approach* (New York: Macmillan, 1965), a solid and thorough survey of much ethnic theory and many case studies. Essay collections have followed suit, as is indicated by *Ethnicity and Resource Competition in Plural Societies*, (ed.) L. A. Despres (The Hague: Mouton 1975) – which explicitly asks for a theoretical framework for comparative ethnic studies (191) – and by *Ethnic Identity*, (ed.) de Vos and Romanucci-Ross – which includes Margaret Mead's statement that 'comparison is the basic method of anthropological work' in her interesting essay on 'Ethnicity and Anthropology in America' (173–97). Arthur Mann, 'Ethnicity in a Comparative Context,' is a well-written, concise and informative summary of these developments, which further enhances the usefulness of his richly detailed and highly readable book, *The One and the Many: Reflections on the American Identity* (Chicago and London: University of Chicago Press, 1979), 149–54.

50. *Send These To Me*, 225.

51. 'Ethnic Identity,' *Ethnicity*, 116; *HEAEG*, 720, 948.

52. Leo Spitzer, 'Wortgeschichtliches,' *Zeitschrift für romanische Philologie*, 53, 3–4 (July 1933), 300–301, *Essays in Historical Semantics* (New York, 1948), 147–169, and *American Journal of Philology*, 52 (1941), 129–143, advocated a development from Latin 'ratio' to 'razza.' Benvenuto Terracini, *Nueva revista de filología hispánica*, 5 (1951): 424–430, offered some critical comments on Spitzer. Gianfranco Contini, 'I piú antichi esempi di "Razza",' *Studi di Filologia Italiana*, 17 (1959): 319–327, and Francesco Sabatini, 'Conferme per l'etimologia di *razza* dal francese antico *haraz*,' *Studi di Filologia Italiana*, 20 (1962): 365–382, found very early evidence for the origin of 'race' in the Old French word for horse-breeding 'haraz' to Italian 'razza' in a case of 1362, or even 1267. G. Merk, *Travaux de Linguistique et de Littérature*, published by Centre de Philologie et de Littératures Romanes de l'Université de Strasbourg VII, 1 (1969), 177–188, viewed French 'race' as 'le produit d'une contamination sémantique et phonétique de *generatio* avec *ratio* et, secondairement, avec *natio*.'

Verena Stolcke, 'Invaded Women: Gender, Race, and Class in the Formation of Colonial Society,' in *Women, 'Race,' and Writing in the Early
Modern Period*, (eds) Margo Hendricks and Patricia Parker (London and
New York: Routledge, 1994), 272–286, here 276–277, has stressed that
raza, the Spanish word for 'race' had different meanings: it stood for
'the succession of generations (*de raza en raza*) as well as all the members of a given generation;' it often took a close connection of 'quality'
and 'nobility of blood;' yet it was also 'confused in the middle of the
fifteenth century with the old Castilian *raza* which meant "a patch of
threadbare or defective cloth," or, simply, "defect, guilt",' obtaining a
meaning exactly opposite to 'nobility,' namely, 'taint' and 'contamination.' See also Adriano Prospero, 'Tra natura e cultura: Dall'intolleranza
religiosa alla discriminazione per sangue,' in *Il Razzismo e le sue storie*,
(ed.) Girolamo Imbruglia (Napoli: Edizioni Scientifiche Italiane, 1992),
113–129. As Rosario Coluccia, 'Ancora sull'etimologia di "razza":
Discussione chiusa o aperta?,' *Studi di Filologia Italiana* 30 (1972), 325–
330, argues, more research and more evidence is needed.

53. According to Robert Miles, *Racism* (London: Routledge, 1989), 42, citing Hirschfeld's still fascinating book *Racism* (London: Victor Gollancz,
1938).
54. 'Blacks and Ethnic Groups: The Difference and the Political Difference It
Makes,' *Social Problems*, 18 (Spring 1971): 444–461; here 447.
55. *The Scope of Sociology* (New York: Oxford University Press, 1988), 119,
130, 131.
56. *Racial Formation in the United States* (London and New York: Routledge,
1986), 21ff.
57. *Race-Ethnicity and Society* (London and New York: Routledge, 1989),
27.
58. Pierre L. van den Berghe, *Race and Racism: A Comparative Perspective*
(New York: Wiley, 1967), 9–10.
59. David Theo Goldberg, *Racist Culture* (Oxford: Blackwell, 1993), 75–76,
60. Mary C. Waters, *Ethnic Options: Choosing Identities in America* (Berkeley:
University of California Press, 1990), 18–19.
61. 'Racism, Consciousness, and Afrocentricity,' in Gerald Early (ed.), *Lure
and Loathing: Essays on Race, Identity, and the Ambivalence of Assimilation* (New York: Allen Lane, The Penguin Press, 1993), 142.
62. See F. James Davis. *Who Is Black? One Nation's Definition* (University
Park: Pennsylvania State University Press), 1991.
63. *Race and Mixed Race* (Philadelphia: Temple University Press, 1993), 5.
64. See, for example, M. G. Smith, 'Ethnicity and Ethnic Groups in America:
The View from Harvard,' *Ethnic and Racial Studies*, 5 (1982), 1–22.
Ronald Takaki, *A Different Mirror: A History of Multicultural America*
(Boston: Little Brown, 1993), 10, argued more subtly that race 'has been
a social construction that has historically set apart racial minorities from
European immigrant groups. Contrary to the notions of scholars like Nathan
Glazer and Thomas Sowell, race in America has not been the same as
ethnicity.' Yet he does not draw the conclusion from this assessment that
'race' and 'ethnicity' should not be compared. Most page references to

what is indexed as 'ethnicity' in Takaki's book actually refer to discussions of Jewish immigration.

65. Stolcke, 'Invaded Women,' 276–7.
66. Stuart Hall, 'Ethnicity,' W. E. B. Du Bois lecture, Harvard University, 1994.

Acknowledgements

The editor is grateful to Valarie Moses and Tanya Ponton for wideranging bibliographic and biographical searches, to Breda O'Keeffe for energetic research and proofreading assistance at all stages of this project, to Niko Pfund and Annabella Buckley for their support, to Barbara Docherty and Keith Povey for copy-editing the manuscript, and to Larry Benson, Leo Damrosch, Derek Pearsall and the Hyder E. Rollins Publication Fund at Harvard University for defraying a substantial part of the permission fees.

The editor and publishers wish to thank the following for permission to reproduce copyright material:

Oxford University Press, for the extracts from the *Oxford English Dictionary* (1961) and its *Supplement* (1972) in Chapter 1.

Dictionnaires le Robert, for the extract from *Grand Robert* (1985) in Chapter 1.

Yale University Press, for W. Lloyd Warner and Paul S. Lunt, 'Ethnicity', pp. 72–3 in Warner and Lunt, *The Status System of a Modern Community* (1942) in Chapter 2.

Boston Evening Transcript and *Melus Forum*, for Charles W. Chesnutt, 'The Future American' (1900) in Chapter 3.

Holt, for the extract from William James, 'On a Certain Blindness in Human Beings', in William James, *Talks to Teachers on Psychology: and to Students on Some of Life's Ideals* (1900) in Chapter 4.

Free Press, for the extract from Georg Simmel, 'The Stranger', Chapter 3 in Kurt H. Wolff (trans), *The Sociology of Georg Simmel* (1950) in Chapter 5. and for the extract from Georg Simmel, 'The Web of Group Affiliations', in Reinhard Bendix (trans), *Conflict* and *The Web of Group Affiliations* (1955) in Chapter 5.

University of California Press and J.C.B. Mohr, for Max Weber, 'Ethnic Groups', Chapter V in Guenther Roth and Claus Wittich (eds), *Economy and Society* (1978) in Chapter 6.

The Nation, for Horace M. Kallen, 'Democracy Versus the Melting-Pot: A Study of American Nationality' (February 18 and 25 1915) in Chapter 7.

Atlantic Monthly, for Randolph S. Bourne, 'Trans-National America' (July 1916) in Chapter 8.

ITPS (Routledge), for 'The Problem of Generations', Chapter VII in Paul Kecskemeti (ed.), *Essays on the Sociology of Knowledge* (1952) in Chapter 9.

The American Journal of Sociology, for Robert E. Park, 'Human Migration and the Marginal Man' (May 1928) in Chapter 10.

D. Van Nostrand, for 'Race Problems and Modern Society', Chapter in Baker Brownwell (ed.), *Problems of Civilization* (1929) in Chapter 11.

The Forum and Princeton University Press, for Carl Gustav Jung, 'Your Negroid and Indian Behavior' (April 1930) in Chapter 12.

Augustuna Historical Society Publications, for Marcus Lee Hansen, 'The Problem of the Third Generation Immigrant' (1938) in Chapter 13.

William Morrow, for Margaret Mead, 'We Are All Third Generation', Chapter III in *And Keep Your Powder Dry: An Anthropologist Looks at America* (1949) in Chapter 14.

W.W. Norton, for Erik H. Erikson, 'Reflections on the American Identity', Chapter 8 in Erik H. Erikson, *Childhood and Society* (1963) in Chapter 15.

Sociological Review and Joshua Fishman, for Vladimir C. Nahirny and Joshua A. Fishman, 'American Immigrant Groups: Ethnic Identification and the Problem of Generations' (1965) in Chapter 16.

American Ethnological Society, Tulane University, for David M. Schneider, 'Kinship, Nationality and Religion in American Culture: Toward a Definition of Kinship', in Victor Turner (ed.), *Forms of Symbolic Action* (1969) in Chapter 17.

Universitetsforlag, Little, Brown and the author, for Fredrik Barth, 'Ethnic Groups and Boundaries', 'Introduction' in Fredrik Barth, *Ethnic Groups and Boundaries: The Social Organization of Culture Difference* (1969) in Chapter 18.

The American Journal of Sociology, The University of Chicago Press and the author, for Robert K. Merton, 'Insiders and Outsiders: A Chapter in the Sociology of Knowledge' (1972) in Chapter 19.

Tavistock Publications and the author, for Abner Cohen, 'The Lesson of Ethnicity', from 'Introduction: The Lesson of Ethnicity', in Abner Cohen (ed.), *Urban Ethnicity* (1974) in Chapter 20.

Mayfield and Lola Romanucci-Ross, for George Devereux, 'Ethnic Identity: Its Logical Foundations and its Dysfunctions', Chapter 2 in George de Vos and Lola Romanucci-Ross, *Ethnic Identities: Cultural Continuities and Change* (1975) in Chapter 21.

Mouton and the author, for Ulf Hannerz, 'Some Comments on the Anthropology of Ethnicity in the United States', Chapter in Frances Henry (ed.), *Ethnicity in the Americas* (1976) in Chapter 22.

University of Pennsylvania Press and the author, for Herbert J. Gans, 'Symbolic Ethnicity: The Future of Ethnic Groups and Cultures in America', in Herbert Gans *et al.* (eds), *On the Making of Americans: Essays in Honor of David Riesman* (1979) in Chapter 23. Epilogue © Herbert Gans 1996.

The Journal of American History and the author, for Philip Gleason, 'Identifying Identity: A Semantic History' (1983) in Chapter 24.

American Quarterly (Johns Hopkins University Press), for the extracts from Werner Sollors, 'Theory of American Ethnicity' (1981) in the Foreword.

Notes on the Contributors

Fredrik Barth was born in 1928 at Leipzig, Germany. He was educated at the University of Chicago (M.A. 1949) and Cambridge University (Ph.D. 1957). He has been a professor at University of Bergen, Norway, and at the University of Oslo, Norway. His works include *Political Leadership among Swat Pathans* (1959), *Ethnic Groups and Boundaries* (1969), *Cosmologies in the Making* (1987), and *Balinese Worlds* (1993).

Randolph S. Bourne (1886–1918) was born in Bloomfield, NJ, and was educated at Columbia University. His liberal interests led to vigorous advocacy of many causes, notably progressive education, pacifism and political and social reform. He contributed to such journals as *Columbia Monthly*, *Atlantic Monthly*, *New Republic* and *Dial*. His works include *Youth and Life* (1913), *The Gary Schools* (1916), and *Education and Living* (1917). Many of his essays have been collected in *The Radical Will*.

Charles W. Chesnutt (1858–1932) was born in Cleveland, OH, and was educated there. He taught for nine years in the public schools of North Carolina, ending his teaching career as the principal of the State Normal School at Fayetteville, North Carolina. In 1887 he returned to Ohio to practise law and to write. His best-known literary works include the short story collections *The Conjure Woman* and *The Wife of His Youth* (both 1899), and the novels *The House Behind the Cedars* (1900), *The Marrow of Tradition* (1901), and *The Colonel's Dream* (1905). He also published several essays in which he reflected on the meaning of race. In 1928, he was awarded the Spingarn Medal by the National Association for the Advancement of Colored People (NAACP) for his eminence as a literary artist depicting the struggles of African-Americans.

Abner Cohen studied at the Universities of London, BA (Hons Philosophy), MA (Sociology), and Manchester, Ph.D. (Social Anthropology). He has been a Research Associate at the University of Manchester, 1956–61. At the University of London (SOAS), he has been a Research Fellow, 1961–64, a lecturer in African Sociology, 1964–70, a reader in African Anthropology, 1970–72, and Professor of Anthropology since 1972. He is now Emeritus Professor and Senior Research Associate, Queen Elizabeth House, University of Oxford. He has done field research in the Near East, 1958–59, Nigeria, 1962–63, Sierra Leone, 1969–70, and Britain. His works include *Arab Border Villages in Israel* (1965, 1972), *Custom and Politics in Urban Africa* (1969), *Two Dimensional Man* (1974), *The Politics of Elite Culture* (1981), and *Masquerade Politics* (1993).

George Devereux (1908–85) was born in Lugos, Hungary, and attended the University of Paris, the University of California of Berkeley (Ph.D., 1935) and is a graduate of Topeka Institute for Psychoanalysis. He has been the director of research at Winter Veterans Administration Hospital in Topeka (1946–53) and at Devereux Foundation in Devon, PA (1953–5). He was an associate professor (1956) and a professor of research in ethnopsychiatry (1956–63) at Temple University, and a professor of ethnopsychiatry at Ecole des Hautes Etudes en Sciences Sociales, Paris, France (1963–77). He is the author of many publications, including *Reality and Dream: The Psychotherapy of a Plains Indian* (1951), *A Study of Abortion in Primitive Societies* (1955), *Culture and Mental Disorder* (1956), *Dreams in Greek Tragedy* (1976), and *Basic Problems of Ethnopsychiatry* (1980). He also contributed about 230 articles to scientific journals.

Erik H. Erikson (1902–94), an American psychoanalyst, was born in Frankfurt, Germany. In 1933, he graduated from the Vienna Psychoanalytic Institute. He taught at Harvard and Yale Universities and at the University of California at Berkeley. He is best known for his ideas on how human beings develop a sense of identity, and for his studies of adolescence. He expressed his central ideas in the books *Childhood and Society* (1950) and *Identity: Youth and Crisis* (1968).

Joshua A. Fishman (1926–) was born in Philadelphia, was educated at the University of Pennsylvania, BS, and MS 1948, Columbia University, Ph.D., 1953. He was a teacher in elementary and secondary Jewish schools (1945–1950), lecturer at City College (1955–57), professor of psychology at University of Pennsylvania, Yeshiva University, and Ferkauf Graduate School of Education. His works include *Yiddish in America* (1965), *Language and Nationalism* (1972), *Never Say Die: A Thousand Years of Yiddish* (1981), and *Language and Ethnicity* (1989).

Herbert J. Gans (1927–) was born in Cologne, Germany, received his Ph.B. in 1947 and MA in 1950, both from the University of Chicago, and took his Ph.D. in 1957 at the University of Pennsylvania. After teaching at Pennsylvania, Teachers College, Columbia University, and the Massachusetts Institute of Technology, he joined the Department of Sociology at Columbia in 1971, and is now its Robert S. Lynd Professor of Sociology. He is the author of nine books, among them *The Urban Villagers* (1962, 1982); *The Levittowners* (1967, 1982); *Popular Culture and High Culture* (1974); *Deciding What's News* (1979); *Middle American Individualism* (1988, 1991); and, most recently, *The War Against the Poor: The Underclass and Antipoverty Policy* (1995). He is a past president of the Eastern Sociological Society and of the American Sociological Association.

Philip Gleason (1927–), received his BS in Education at the University of Dayton, 1951; MA 1955, and Ph.D. 1960, at the University of Notre Dame. He has special interest in the convergence of American intellectual history, religious and immigration history. He is the author of *The Conservative Reformers: German–American Catholics and the Social Order* (1968), *Concepts of Ethnicity*, with William Petersen and Michael Novak (1982), *Speaking of Diversity: Language and Ethnicity in Twentieth Century America* (1992), and *Contending with Modernity: Catholic Higher Education in the Twentieth Century* (1996).

Ulf Hannerz (1942–) is Professor of Social Anthropology at Stockholm University. He is especially interested in the social organization of complex cultures, not least in transnational culture. He has conducted field studies in the USA, the Caribbean, and Nigeria, and is the author of *Soulside* (1969), *Exploring the City* (1980), *Cultural Complexity* (1992), *Transnational Connections* (1996), and several other books. He is a member of the Royal Swedish Academy of Sciences and the American Academy of Arts and Sciences and Chair of the European Association of Social Anthropologists (EASA).

Marcus Lee Hansen (1892–1938) was a doctoral student of Frederick Jackson Turner at Harvard (Ph.D. 1924), and a professor of history at the University of Illinois from 1928 to 1938. Hansen wrote the first comprehensive histories of European immigration to the United States. His best-known works, all published posthumously, include *The Atlantic Migration, 1607–1860* (1940), *The Mingling of the Canadian and American Peoples* (1940), and *The Immigrant in American History* (1940).

William James (1842–1910) was the most widely read American philosopher at the turn of the century. The brother of the novelist Henry James, William was born in New York City. As a medical student at Harvard University, he studied anatomy and physiology under the naturalist Louis Agassiz. James wrote the famous essay 'The Will to Believe' (1896). His many other works includes *Varieties of Religious Experience* (1902), *Pragmatism* (1907), and *The Nearing of Truth* (1909).

Carl Gustav Jung (1875–1961) was a Swiss psychiatrist and psychologist who developed the field of analytical psychology. His teachings extended beyond psychology and influenced other fields, including anthropology, philosophy, and theology. Jung challenged many of the psychoanalytical theories proposed by Sigmund Freud. Jung, the son of a minister, was born in Basel. In 1895, Jung entered the University of Basel to study archaeology. He graduated as a physician from the University of Zurich in 1902 and began to practice psychiatry in Zurich. Jung became a professor of medical psychology at the University of Basel in 1943. He published books and papers on psychoanalysis and psychology which are included in *The Collected Works of C. G. Jung* (1953–1979).

Horace M. Kallen (1882–1974) was the American philosopher who coined the term 'cultural pluralism' in his best-known book, *Culture and Democracy in the United States: Studies in the Group Psychology of the American Peoples* (1924). Kallen was born in Berenstadt, Silesia, Germany. He came to the United States in 1887, graduated from Harvard University in 1903 (AB) where he studied with William James, Josiah Royce, George Santayana, and Barrett Wendell, and received his Ph.D. from Harvard in 1909. He also studied at Princeton University, Oxford University, and at the Sorbonne. He was an instructor in logic at Clark College, and taught psychology and philosophy at University of Wisconsin, Madison. He cofounded the New School for Social Research in 1919 and was a member of the faculty until 1952, and professor emeritus until his death in 1974. His works include *Why Religion* (1927), *Patterns of Progress* (1950) and *Utopians at Bay* (1959). He also edited many works including William James' *Some Problems of Philosophy: A Beginning of an Introduction to Philosophy* (1911), and *Freedom in the Modern World* (1928).

Paul S. Lunt coauthored two volumes of the Yankee City series with W. Lloyd Warner, *The Social Life of a Modern Community* (1941) and *The Status System of a Modern Community* (1942) and published for the Human Relations Area Files at Johns Hopkins University the books *Algeria* (1956), *Morocco* (1956), and *Tunisia* (1956).

Karl Mannheim (1893–1947) was a Hungarian-born sociologist. Influenced by Marxist thought, Mannheim fled to Germany after the fall of the radical Béla Kun government (1919). After teaching sociology at Frankfurt (from 1926) he was forced to flee, again, after the Nazis came to power (1933), and served as a professor at the University of London from 1933 to 1947. His major work, *Ideology and Utopia* (1929), was a pioneering study in the sociology of knowledge. He also wrote *Man and Society in an Age of Reconstruction* (1935) and *Diagnosis of Our Time* (1943).

Margaret Mead (1901–78) was an American anthropologist known for her studies of how culture influences the development of personality. Mead was born in Philadelphia, PA. She graduated from Barnard College and received a Ph.D. degree in Anthropology from Columbia University. From 1926 to 1969, she was a curator of ethnology at the American Museum of Natural History in New York City. Mead's best-known book, *Coming of Age in Samoa* (1928) compares the lives of adolescents in a Samoan village and in Western societies. Her other books include *Growing Up in New Guinea* (1930), *Sex and Temperament in Three Primitive Societies* (1935), *Male and Female* (1949), and *Culture and Commitment* (1970).

Robert K. Merton (1910–) is an American sociologist best known for his integration of social theory and empirical research in the form of 'theories of the middle range' and for having founded the specialty known as the sociology of science.

Vladimir C. Nahirny (1928–94) was Associate Professor of Sociology at Hunter College, City University of New York, and the author of *The Russian Intelligentsia: From Torment to Silence* (1983). When he wrote the paper (together with Joshua A. Fishman) reprinted in this volume, he was a research associate on the project which resulted in the volume *Language Loyalty in the United States* (1966) to which he contributed several chapters, foremost among them the one on Ukrainians in the USA.

Robert E. Park (1864–1944) was born in Harveyville, PA. He worked as a journalist and then took his Ph.D. in Germany with a dissertation on *The Crowd*. He became one of the founders of the Chicago School of Sociology, and an advisor of Tuskegee Institute. His works include *Race and Culture: 1913–1944* (1950) and *Introduction to the Science of Sociology* (1921) with Ernest Burgess.

David M. Schneider was born in New York City. He is a professor of anthropology at University of Chicago. He wrote *American Kinship: A Cultural Account* (1968) and co-authored *Class Differences in Sex Roles in American Kinship and Family Structure* (1973). His other books include *Matrilineal Kinship* (1961) and *Symbolic Anthropology: A Reader in the Study of Symbols and Meanings* (1977).

Georg Simmel (1858–1918) was a German sociologist and essayist. He studied at the University of Berlin (Ph.D. 1881) where, as a Jew, he was denied a university chair until 1914. He lectured at the university essentially as an unaffiliated scholar. He was a founding member of the German Sociological Association in 1910. He was considered a pioneer in the sociology of human emotions, while he wrote on a large variety of topics, from art and culture to religion and metaphysics. He was the author of *Philosophy of Money* (1900). Four essays written between 1890 and 1918 appeared in English as *Georg Simmel: On Women, Sexuality, and Love* (1984).

Werner Sollors is Henry B. and Anne M. Cabot Professor of English Literature and Professor of Afro-American Studies at Harvard University. He has taught English, Comparative Literature and Afro-American Studies at Berlin, Columbia University and the Università degli Studi di Venezia. He wrote *Beyond Ethnicity: Consent and Descent in American Culture*, has completed the study *Neither Black Nor White and Yet Both: Thematic Explorations of Interracial Literature*, and is working on *Panorama of the Twentieth Century*, a cultural history of the modern literature of the United States. He has also edited *The Invention of Ethnicity*, *The Life Stories of Undistinguished Americans as Told by Themselves*, *The Return of Thematic Criticism* and *Blacks at Harvard*.

Jean Toomer (1894–1967) was born in Washington, DC. He was educated in the public schools of Washington, and studied various fields at the University of Wisconsin, at the City College of New York, and at other universities. With the publication of *Cane* (1923) he emerged as a major figure of the Harlem Renaissance. Despite much critical praise, *Cane* sold only 500 copies on publication and remained largely unread until the 1960s. He studied with the Russian mystic Gurdjieff and eventually established a Gurdjieff Institute in Wisconson. Selections of his many unpublished literary works and non-fiction writings appear in *The Wayward and the Seeking* (1980) and in *A Jean Toomer Reader* (1993).

William Lloyd Warner (1898–1970) was born in Redlands, Cal. He received his BA from the University of California at Berkeley, and undertook postgraduate study at Harvard University, 1929–31. He was an instructor and assistant professor at Harvard University and Radcliffe College (1929–35), a professor of anthropology and sociology at University of Chicago, and professor of Social Research at Michigan State University. His works include the community study of Newburyport, the *Yankee City* series, as well as *Who Shall Be Educated?* (1945) with Robert H. Havighurst and Martin B. Loeb, *Structure of American Life* (1952), and *The Family of God* (1961).

Max Weber (1864–1920) was a German social scientist and one of the founders of modern sociology. Weber was born in Erfurt, Germany, studied at the universities of Berlin, Göttingen, and Heidelberg, and was appointed professor at the University of Freiburg (1894) and then at the University of Heidelberg (1896). His works include the influential books *The Protestant Ethic and the Spirit of Capitalism* (1904–05), *Economy and Society* (1922), and *Methodology of the Social Sciences* (1922). Important works by Weber have been collected in English translation in *From Max Weber: Essays in Sociology* and *The Theory of Social and Economic Organization*.

Part I
Etymology

1 'Ethnic, ethnical, ethnicity, *ethnie, ethnique*': Entries from *Oxford English Dictionary* (1961) and *Supplement* (1972), and *Grand Robert* (1985)*

OXFORD ENGLISH DICTIONARY

Ethnic (e·pnik), *a.* and *sb.* Forms: 4–6 ethnyke, 5–7 ethnik(e, 6–8 ethnick(e, (6 æth-, ethenicke, etneke), 7 ethnique, (ethnycke), 6– ethnic. [ad. Gr. ἐθνικ–ός heathen, f. ἔθνος nation; in the LXX, hence in N. T. and the Fathers, τὰ ἔθνη = the nations, Gentiles (rendering Heb. גוֹיִם *gōyīm*, pl. of גּוֹי *gōy*, nation, esp. non-Israelitish or 'Gentile' nation).

The Gr. ἔθνος was formerly often imagined to be the source of Eng. HEATHEN; hence the confused forms *hethnic*, HEATHENIC, which might be regarded as corrupt variants of this word.]

A. *adj.*

1. Pertaining to nations not Christian or Jewish; Gentile, heathen, pagan.

c **1470** HARDING *Chron.* Printer's Pref.ix, The bible bookes of Iudges and Kynges .. farre surmounting all ethnike dooynges. **1545** UDALL *Erasm. Par.* Pref. 3 An ethnike and a pagane kyng. **1581** MARBECK *Bk. of Notes* 61 That all composition is against the nature of God even the Ethnicke Philosophers perceived. **1611** SPEED *Hist. Gt. Brit.* VI. xlix. § 171 Professing himselfe to be a Christian, and withall protesting that he would not be a soueraigne ouer an Ethnike Empire. **1651** HOBBES *Leviath.* III. xlii. 281 Exhorted their Converts to obey their then Ethnique Princes. **1804** MOORE *Epist.* III. iii. 45 All the charm that ethnic fancy gave To blessed arbours o'er the western wave. **18..**

* Extracts from the *Oxford English Dictionary* (1961), p. 313–14. *Oxford English Dictionary*, Supplement (1972), p. 979–80; and *Grand Robert* (1985), p. 188–9.

LONGF. *Drinking Song* vii, These are ancient ethnic revels Of a faith long since forsaken. **1851** CARLYLE *Sterling* I. vii. (1872) 45, I find at this time his religion is as good as altogether Ethnic, Greekish. **1873** LOWELL *Among my Bks.* Ser. II. 107 There is first the ethnic forecourt, then the purgatorial middle-space.

2. Pertaining to race; peculiar to a race or nation; ethnological.

1851 D. WILSON *Preh. Ann.* (1863) I. ix. 229 That ethnic stock which embraced all existing European races. **1865** *Reader* II Feb. 163/1 The slight development of ethnic peculiarities in childhood. **1875** LIGHTFOOT *Comm. Col.* (1886) 133 Heresies are at best ethnic: truth is essentially catholic.

† **B.** *sb.* One who is not a Christian or a Jew; a Gentile, heathen, pagan. *Obs.*

c **1375** *Sc. Leg. Saints, Barnabas* 161 A part of It [the temple] fel done & mad a gret distruccione Of ethnykis. *c* **1534** tr. *Pol. Verg. Eng. Hist.* (Camd. Soc.) I. 169 Beinge on all sides beesett with the Tracherie of these rude æthenickes, hee was sodainlie slayne. **1588** ALLEN *Admon.* 37 Yf he.. heare not the Churche, let him be taken for an Ethnike. **1625** B. JONSON *Staple of N.* II. iv, A kind of Mule! That's half an Ethnick, half a Christian! **1664** EVELYN *Sylva* (1776) 614 The Ethnics do still repute all great trees to be divine. **1728** MORGAN *Algiers* I. iv. 77 They look upon them [the Jews] as several degrees beneath.. Heathens, Ethnicks, Pagans, and Idolaters.

Ethnical (e·þnikăl), *a.* [f. prec. + –AL.]

† **1.** Of an ethnic nature or character; heathenish.

1547 BP. HOOPER *Declar. Christ* v. D iij, What .. blasphemy of God, and Et[h]nycall idolatrie is this. **1577** NORTHBROOKE *Dicing* (1843) 67 Ethnical sportes and pastimes. **1634** SIR T. HERBERT *Trav.* 195 The Religion of the Peguans is Ethnicall, knowing many but false Gods. **1702** C. MATHER *Magn. Chr.* III. II. xx. (1852) 447 The custom of preaching at funerals may seem ethnical in its origin.

† **b.** Pagan; = ETHNIC A. I. *Obs.*

a **1638** MEDE *Wks.* III. viii. 643 The Woman which escaped the fury of the Ethnical Dragon. **1659** W. BROUGH *Sacr. Princ.* 548 Should not .. Ethnical Rome be lesse Babylon then the Christian. **1762** J. BROWN *Poetry & Mus.* xiii. (1763) 237 The Subjects of the narrative .. may be drawn .. either from ethnical or sacred Story.

2. Of or pertaining to race or races, their origin, and characteristics. Cf. ETHNIC A. 2.

1846 GROTE *Greece* II. i. II. 308 Purely upon geographical not upon ethnical considerations. **1871** FREEMAN *Hist. Ess.* Ser. I. iii 58 As far as ethnical connexion is concerned, this analogy will hold good.

3. Pertaining to the science of races; = ETHNOLOGICAL 2.

1862 D. WILSON *Preh. Man* i. (1865 4 Here then are materials full of promise for the ethnical student. **1884** *Publisher & Bookbuyer's Jrnl.* 15 Nov. 11/2 The confused character of the prevailing ethnical literature dealing with the Sudan.

Ethnically (e·þnikăli), *adv.* [f. prec. + –LY².]

† **1.** In an 'ethnical' or heathenish ma ner. *Obs.*

1563–87 FOXE *A. & M.* (1596) 117/2 This pope .. mainteined the filthie idolatrie of images .. commanding them most ethnicallie to be incensed.

2. As regards race; 'racially'.

1847 GROTE *Greece* II. xxii. III. 464 The Œnotrians were ethnically akin to the primitive population of Rome. **1876** GLADSTONE *Synchr. Homer.* 65 No one can suppose Trojan and Hellene to have been .. ethnically one, though both were probably of the Aryan stock.

Ethnicism (e·þnisiz'm). [f. ETHNIC + –ISM.]

† **a.** Heathenism, paganism; heathenish superstition; an instance of this (*obs*). **b.** In mod. use without reproachful implication: The religions of the Gentile nations of antiquity; the common characteristics of these as contrasted with Hebraism and Christianity.

1613 PURCHAS *Pilgr.* IX. v. § 3 (R.) Certaine Brasilians .. had set vp a new sect of Christian ethnicisme, or mungrell-Christianity. **1625** JACKSON *Orig. Vnbeliefe* xxiii. 226 Feigned relations of a new starres appearance or other like Ethnicismes. **1667** WATERHOUSE *Fire Lond.* 111 In darkness of errour and in the shadow of death through Ethnicism. **1849** tr. *Nitzsch's Chr. Doctr.* Pref. 7 The two great directions of religio-historical development, Ethnicism and Revelation. **1851** CARLYLE *Sterling* i. ix. (1872) 54 A mind .. occupied .. with mere Ethnicism, Radicalism and revolutionary tumult.

Ethnicist (e·þnisist). *rare.* [f. as prec. + –IST.] = ETHNOLOGIST.

1846 *Times* 15 May 4/5 'Smith' has been proved by .. an American ethnicist and philologist to be nothing more nor less than Shemita, or a descendant of Shem.

† **Ethnicity.** *Obs. rare*⁻¹. [f. as prec. + –ITY.] Heathendom, heathen superstition.

1772 NUGENT tr. *Hist. Friar Gerund* I. 332 From the curling spume of the celebrated Egean waves fabulous ethnicity feigned Venus their idolatress conceived.

† **Ethnicize**, *v. Obs. rare*⁻¹. [f. as prec. + –IZE.] *intr.* To act, speak, etc. like an 'ethnic' or heathen.

1663 J. SPENCER *Prodigies* (1665) 247 Whereas both Tacitus and Josephus relate the sudden opening of the doors of the Temple, etc... they appear to me very much to Ethnicize in all these stories.

† **E·thnish,** *a. Obs.* [f. Gr. ἔθνος (see ETHNIC) + –ISH.] = HEATHENISH.

1550 BECON *Fortr. Faithful* Prol., Walowing in al kind of wealthe like Ethnysh Epicures. **1563** *Homilies* 11. *Idolatry* (1859) 187 Helene .. worshipped the King, and not the wood .. for that is an ethnish error.

Ethnize (e·þnəiz), *v. rare.* [f. Gr. ἔθν–ος (τὰ ἔθνη the nations, Gentiles: see ETHNIC) + –IZE.] *intr.* To favour Gentile or heathen views or practices. Hence **Ethnizing** *vbl. sb.*, in quot. *attrib.*

1847 BUCH tr. *Hagenbach's Hist. Doctr.* I. 42 The earliest heresies of which we have any trustworthy account, appear either as judaizing, or as ethnizing (hellenizing) tendencies.

Ethnodicy (eþnǫ·disi). *rare.* [mod. f. Gr. ἔθνο–ς nation + –δικία administration of justice, f. δίκη justice.] Comparative jurisprudence as a branch of ethnology.

1889 *Athenæum* 21 Sept. 391/3 The labours of the [Ethnographical] Congress are organized in six sections, viz. general ethnology; ethics, ethnodicy, and sociology.

Ethnogenic (eþnoɩdʒe·nik), *a.* [f. next + –IC.] Pertaining to ethnogeny.

Ethnogeny (eþnǫ·dʒĭni). [mod. f. Gr. ἔθνο–ς nation + –γενεια birth.] That branch of ethnology which treats of the origin of races, nations, and peoples. In mod. Dicts.

Ethnographer (eþnǫ·grăfəɹ). [f. ETHNOGRAPH-Y (or Gr. ἔθνο–ς nation + –γραφ–ος writer) + –ER[1].] One who treats descriptively of the races of mankind; one who is versed in the science of ethnography.

1854 H. MILLER *Sch. & Schm.* x. (1857) 202 An evidence, the ethnographer might perhaps say, of its purely Celtic origin. **1865** TYLOR *Early Hist. Man.* viii. 202 The Ethnographer, who has studied the stone implements of Europe. **1884** A. M. FAIRBAIRN in *Congregationalist* Apr. 280 The greatest ethnographers, that is, the men who have most extensively studied the customs, the manners, the beliefs of men.

ethnic, *a. and sb.* Add: **A.** *adj.* **2.** Also, pertaining to or having common racial, cultural, religious, or linguistic characteristics, esp. designating a racial or other group within a larger system; hence (*U.S. colloq.*), foreign, exotic.

1935 HUXLEY & HADDON *We Europeans* iv. 136 Nowhere does a human group now exist which corresponds closely to a systematic sub-species in animals, since various original sub-species have crossed repeatedly and constantly. For existing populations, the non-committal term *ethnic group* should be used. *Ibid.* vi. 181 The special type of ethnic grouping of which the Jews form the best-known example. **1936** *Discovery* June 167 [In Africa] linguistic divisions are a very fair indication of ethnic groups. **1939** C. S. COON *Races of Europe* xi. 444 The Jews are an ethnic unit, although one which has little regard for spatial considerations. Like other ethnic units, the Jews have their own standard racial character. **1964** *Listener* 6 Feb. 233/2 There are many grouping of people, ethnic units, population aggregates – call them what you will – that may be distinguished from each other. **1965** *Sun* 6 Dec. 7/6 Ethnic .. has come to mean foreign, or un-American or plain quaint. **1969** *New Yorker* 30 Aug. 76/2 Its hopelessly reactionary nature is best exemplified not .. even by the ethnic comedians. **1970** *Daily Tel.* 16 Apr. 18 The situation is fast becoming greatly complicated by the presence in Cambodia of large numbers, put at 400,000 to 500,000, of 'ethnic' Vietnamese.

B. *sb.* **2.** *Greek Antiq.* An epithet denoting nationality, derived from or corresponding to the name of a people or city [= ἐθνικόν (Steph. Byz.)]. Also *gen.*

1828 J. A. CRAMER *Anc. Greece* III. Index p. i, The Greek ethnic of each town or place has been subjoined where there was authority for it. **1902** D. G. HOGARTH *Nearer East* 194 Where the 'Arab' (to use the ethnic widely) lives under conditions similar to the Greek, he resembles him. **1921** C. T. SELTMAN *Temple Coins Olympia* 103 The dies .. upon which the full ethnic ΓΑΛΕΙΩΝ appears. **1921** *Brit. Mus. Return* 79 The ethnics of Damastium and Pelagia. **1959** A. G. WOODHEAD *Study Gk. Inscriptions* 44 Sometimes the single name, without further elaboration, sometimes with patronymic and demotic or ethnic, or with one of the two.

3. A member of an ethnic group or minority. orig. *U.S.*

1945 WARNER & SROLE *Social Syst. Amer. Ethnic Groups* (Yankee City Ser. III) v. 68 The Irish .. had their origins largely in the peasant stratum . . . The Jews were of the burgher class . . . These differences in the ethnics' social-class backgrounds will be seen later to have important bearing on their adaptation. *Ibid.* 93 The ethnics have conspicuously succeeded in 'getting ahead' in the Yankee City social hierarchy. **1961** *Times Lit. Suppl.* 17 Nov. 828/4 The former 'ethnics', a polite term for Jews, Italians, and other lesser breeds just inside the law. **1963** T. & P. MORRIS *Pentonville* iii. 62 It is the general view of the prison staff that the majority of 'coloureds' and 'ethnics' are West Indians. **1964** S. M. MILLER in I. L. Horowitz *New Sociology*

297 As the white ethnics – first the Irish, later the Jews, and still more recently the Italians .. gained strength.

ethnicity. Restrict † *Obs. rare* to sense in Dict. and add: **2.** Ethnic character or peculiarity.

1953 D. RIESMAN in *Amer. Scholar* XXIII. I. 15 The groups who, by reason of rural or small-town location, ethnicity, or other parochialism, feel threatened by the better educated upper-middle-class people. **1964** P. WORSLEY in I. L. Horowitz *New Sociology* 384 Existing barriers of ethnicity imported into office could thus be removed. **1970** *Oxf. Univ. Gaz.* C. Suppl. VI. 14 In Hilary Term Dr. Leslie Palmier .. gave a series of lectures entitled 'Ethnicity in Indonesia'.

ethnobotany (eþnobǫ·tăni). orig. *U.S.* [f. Gr. ἔθνο–ς nation + BOTANY.] The traditional knowledge and customs of a people concerning plants; the scientific study or description of such knowledge and customs. Hence, **e:thnobota·nical** *a.*, **ethnobo·tanist**.

1896 J. W. HARSHBERGER in *Bot. Gaz.* XXI. 146 The study of ethnobotany aids in elucidating the cultural position of the tribes who used the plants for food, shelter or clothing. **1899** *Smithsonian Rep.* 65 Dr. Walter Hough was detailed to carry on ethno-botanical researches in Mexico. **1934** *N. & Q.* CLXVII. 129/1 The importance of ethnobotany has long been understood by systematic anthropologists. *Ibid.*, An ethno-botanical note on *Datura Metel.* **1934** WEBSTER, Ethnobotanist. **1955** *Times* 3 Aug. 7/4 Its distinguished American ethnobotanist.

ethnocentric (eþnose·ntrik), *a.* [f. Gr. ἔθνο–ς nation + CENTRIC *a.*] Regarding one's own race or ethnic group as of supreme importance. So **ethnoce·ntrism, e:thnocentri·city**.

1900 W. J. McGEE in *Ann. Rep. Bur. Amer. Ethnol. 1897*–98 931 In primitive culture the epocentric and ethnocentric views are ever-present and always-dominant factors of both mentation and action. **1907** W. G. SUMNER *Folkways* i. 13 *Ethnocentrism* is the technical name for this view of things in which one's own group is the center of everything, and all others are scaled and rated with reference to it. *Ibid.* 15 The state .. became the object of that group vanity and antagonism which had been ethnocentric. **1951** E. E. EVANS-PRITCHARD *Social Anthrop.* vi. 127 This ethnocentric attitude has to be abandoned if we are to appreciate the rich variety of human culture and social life. **1957** W. S. ALLEN *Ling. Stud. Lang.* 8 Mar. 7 A familiarity with many languages .. may do much to reduce the ethnocentrism with which, as native speakers of a language, we are inevitably burdened. **1959** *Listener* 1 Jan. 27/2 Is it really necessary to resuscitate the white man's burden at the very time when so much depends upon our getting rid of this form of ethnocentricity? **1964** I. L. HOROWITZ *New Sociology* 34 The present ethnocentricity reflects a fascination with machines at the expense of minds. **1964** M. CRITCHLEY *Developmental Dyslexia* xii. 70 The age at which a child normally begins to read with facility is also the age at which .. he turns from an autistic, egocentric individual, to a societal, ethnocentric being.

ethnohistory (eþnohi·stŏri). [f. Gr. ἔθνο–ς nation + HISTORY *sb.*] The study of the history of races or cultures, esp. non-Western races or cultures. So **e:thnohisto·rian**, a student or expert in ethnohistory; **e:thnohisto·rical** *a.*, of or pertaining to ethnohistory.

1936 *Times Lit. Suppl.* 2 May 378/2 Each of us must have within reach five hundred ethnohistorians. **1936** L. P. WEAVER tr. *Székely's Cosmos, Man & Soc.* 12 Hitherto ethnohistorical research has depended on three sources: archæological documents, linguistic documents and authentic writing. **1952** *Amer. Anthropologist* LIV. 331 Ethnohistory is blessed with an abundance of source materials. **1965** *Language* XLI. 203 Evidence that the ethnohistorian must use. **1966** *New Statesman* 13 May 710/2 (Advt.), The study .. of internal change within the non-Western societies (i.e. ethnohistory).

ethnolinguistic (e:þnoliŋgwi·stik), *a.* [f. Gr. ἔθνο–ς nation + LINGUISTIC *a.*] Of or pertaining to ethnolinguistics.

1950 D. L. OLMSTED *Ethnolinguistics So Far* iv. 10 The frequency of morphemes in a given ethnolinguistic situation is of importance in determining the relations between talk and action. **1964** E. A. NIDA *Toward Sci. Transl.* vii. 148 One important element in this ethnolinguistic model of translation is the nature of the response implied.

ethnolinguistics (e:þnoliŋgwi·stiks). [f. as prec.] The study of the relations between linguistic and cultural behaviour.

1950 D. L. OLMSTED *Ethnolinguistics So Far* 1 The word *ethnolinguistics* has been used in a number of contexts by social scientists. **1964** R. H. ROBINS *Gen. Linguistics* ix. 352 The specific study of the interdisciplinary links .. between anthropology and linguistics has been called *ethnolinguistics*.

ethnomusicology (e:þnomiūzikǫ·lŏdʒi). [f. Gr. ἔθνο–ς nation + *MU-SICOLOGY.] The scientific study of the music of a culture or sub-culture, considered either as a combination of sounds or as an aspect of socio-cultural behaviour; also, the comparative study of the music of more than one culture. Hence **e:thnomusicolo·gical** *a.*, pertaining to this study; **e:thnomusico·logist**, a student of or expert in ethnomusicology.

1950 J. KUNST *Musicologica* Pref., It is intended as a general introduction to ethno-musicology, before going on to the study of the forms of separate music-cultures. **1951** *Africa* Jan. 319 This work fulfilled a long-standing need by ethnomusicologists. **1958** *Listener* 15 May 824/3 The book reflects the present state of ethnomusicological studies, **1959** *Times Lit. Suppl.* 5 June 332/1 The new subject of ethnomusicology has emerged in no more than a generation to put system into a mass of authentic material gathered from all parts of the globe. **1967** W. P. MALM *Music Cultures of Pacific* i. 9 An ethnomusicologist should be a man of many viewpoints if he is to appreciate fully the meaning of music in a given culture. **1970** *Daily Tel.* 30 Sept. 10/5 Dr Frank Harrison, Reader in the History of Music at Oxford University.., has been appointed to the Chair of Ethnomusicology at Amsterdam University.

ethnoscience (eþnosəi·ĕns). [f. Gr. ἔθνο–ς nation + SCIENCE.] The study of races or cultures; ethnography.

1964 E. A. NIDA *Toward Sci. Transl.* iii. 38 B. N. Colby in an unpublished paper, entitled 'Eidos, Semantics and Ethnoscience', has dealt extensively with a number of these approaches to studies of semantic fields. **1964** *Language* XL. 230 The terminology which is now appearing in anthropological literature devoted to ethnoscience.

ETHNIE [ɛtni] n. f. – 1896, Vacher de la Pouge; dér. sav. du grec *ethnos* ≪peuple, nation≫.

♦ **Didact.** Ensemble d'individus que rapprochent un certain nombre de caractères de civilisation, notamment la communauté de langue et de culture (alors que la *race* dépend de caractères anatomiques). On trouve aussi *ethnos*.

1 On réserve le nom de races à ceux (*les groupements humains*) établis d'après un ensemble de caractères physiques (. . .) On sait, d'autre part, quo'on appelle *nation* ou *état* ceux qui correspondent

à une communauté politique. Viennent enfin ceux basés sur des caractères de civilisation, en particulier une langue ou un groupe de langues identiques; on a créé pour eux un terme qui tend de plus en plus à s'imposer, ce sont les *ethnies* (...) Dès qu'on aborde les grandes masses qui peuplent la majeure partie des continents, les races, les ethnies et les frontières politiques s'enchevêtrent à qui mieux mieux.

Henri-V. VALLOIS, les Races humaines, p. 8.

2 Entre les races ou entre les civilisations, entre les ethnies, pensait Spenhler, il y a des murs infranchissables. Les communications et les télécommunications font qu'ils s'écroulent, malgré les oppositions encore tenaces de la Russie, de la Chine, des patriotismes paradoxaux de tous ces gens dont le but était justement de favoriser l'internationalisation.

IONESCO, Journal en miettes, pp. 60–61.

ETHNIQUE [εtnik] adj. – 1541; *etnique*, XIIIe; lat. sav. *ethnicus*, du grec *ethnikos*, de *ethnos* «peuple».

♦ **1.** Didact. (hist: antiq. chrétienne). Qui appartient au paganisme. ⇒ **Gentil, idolâtre, païen.** *Superstition ethnique.*

♦ **2.** (1752). Didact. Qui sert à désigner une population. – Ling. *Mot ethnique:* mot dérivé d'un mot désignant un lieu (pays, région, etc.) et servant à signifier l'appartenance d'un sujet à celui-ci. «*Français*» *est un nom ethnique.*

N. m. (1864). Dénomination d'un peuple. *L'ethnique de France est «français».*

1 Les populations indigènes de l'Afrique du Nord (...) sont ordinairement désignées sous le nom de Berbères; ce n'est pas un ethnique datant d'une époque lointaine (...)

Agustin BERNARD, l'Algérie, p. 81 (→ Berbère, cit. 1).

♦ **3.** (1871). Didact. (mais plus cour.). Relatif à l'etnie, à une ethnie. ⇒ **Racial.** *Caractères ethniques,* propres à une ethnie. *Différences ethniques. Groupes ethniques.*

2 L'idée d'une différence de races dans la population de la France, si évidente chez Grégoire de Tours, ne se présente à aucun degré chez les écrivains et les poètes français postérieurs à Hugues Capet. La différence du noble et du vilain est aussi accentuée que possi-

ble; mais la différence de l'un à l'autre n'est en rien une différence ethnique (. . .)

RENAN, Qu'est-ce qu'une nation?, 11 mars 1882, Œuvres, t. 1, p. 891.

3 (. . .) les hommes qui l'habitent (*la France*) constituent un mélange ethnique et psychologique d'une complexité et d'une qualité singulières, dont les éléments se complètent et se tempèrent les uns aux autres, depuis des siècles, par leur coexistence, leurs commerces, leurs conflits, leurs expériences et leurs malheurs communs.

VALÉRY, Regards sur le monde actuel, p. 180.

4 Sur un fond autochtone, la formation ethnique du peuple russe résulte surtout de deux séries d'invasions.

André SIEGFRIED, L'Ame des peuples, VI, II.

ETHNOGRAPHIE [ɛtnɔgʀafi] n. f. – 1819, Boiste; donné comme rare ou inusité par les dict. de la première moitié du xixᵉ; de *ethno-*, et *-graphie*.

Didactique.

♦ **1.** Vx. Classement des peuples d'après leurs langues.

Quant au mot *ethnographie*, il signifiait au commencement du siècle (*le XIXᵉ*) tout simplement le classement des peuples d'après leurs langues; c'était un terme linguistique introduit par Balbi (1826).

J. DENIKER, *in* Grande Encyclopédie (BERTHELOT), art. *Ethnographie*.

♦ **2.** Mod. Étude descriptive des divers groupes humains, notamment des ethnies vivant dans une civilisation pré-industrielle, de leurs caractères anthropologiques, sociaux, etc. *Ethnographie et ethnologie**.

L'ethnographie, telle qu'elle existe actuellement est en somme un complément de l'anthropologie. Cette dernière s'occupe surtout de l'homme au point de vue physique, tandis que la première le considère au point de vue social. Elle recherche quels sont les éléments constitutifs d'une population donnée, en s'aidant des renseignements que lui fournit l'anthropologie, en ce qui concerne les caractères anatoiques et physiologiques; la linguistique en ce qui concerne les langues; la géographie en ce qui concerne l'influence du milieu; l'histoire et l'archéologie (historique et préhistorique) en ce qui concerne les données sur le passé des groupes ethniques, sur leur composition et décomposition, etc.

J. DENIKER, *in* Grande Encyclopédie (BERTHELOT), art. *Ethnographie*.

L'ethnographie étudie les usages de tous genres des groupes d'hommes vivant en société.

Ch. SEIGNOBOS, Hist. sincère de la nation franç., 1, p. 7.

Dans notre quête de l'homme comme dans notre monde de l'art, le plus étranger rejoint le plus ancien: les sociétés que l'on appelait sauvages, nous les appelons primitives. De l'histoire des civilisations mortes, comme de l'ethnographie des peuples mourants, nous attendons qu'elles nous enseignent ce qu'est l'homme lorsqu'il ne nous ressemble pas.

MALRAUX, la Métamorphose des dieux, p. 32.

DÉR. Ethnographe, ethnographique.

2 'Ethnicity' (1942)
W. Lloyd Warner and
Paul S. Lunt*

In this chapter we shall examine first the participation of the ten ethnic groups in the social system of Yankee City. The volume in the Yankee City Series called *The Social Systems of American Ethnic Groups* is largely concerned with the study of the internal organization and changing functions of the several ethnic groups. The present chapter is not directly interested in these problems; it is concerned with questions of how, where, and why ethnic individuals are members of the whole status system of Yankee City. A mass of observable variations in social usage distinguishes ethnic groups from that part of the community which has inherited and developed Yankee customs. In some cases the observable differences are biologically as well as culturally determined. Since the individuals who compose the several ethnic groups function as interacting members of the larger society it is necessary – if one is to understand the place of ethnics in the community – to take account of them as members of the status system.

For this purpose we shall look upon 'ethnicity' as one of the several characteristics which modify the social system and are modified by it. The other characteristics to be considered are age, sex, and religion. From one point of view each is a *trait* possessed by the individuals who compose the interactive units of the social aggregate. Each characteristic (by the classification and evaluation of the members of the community) separates the individual from some classes of individuals and identifies him with others.

Sex and age can be reduced to primarily biological facts which, when evaluated by the group, fit into a social context. Ethnicity may be evaluated almost entirely upon a biological basis or upon purely social characteristics. Negroes tend to be at the first extreme, since they are most physically variant of all groups in the community, and the Irish at the other extreme, since they are most like the native white stock. The Yankee City Negro's culture comes from a Yankee

* From W. Lloyd Warner and Paul S. Lunt, *The Status* 1942, p. 13. *System of a Modern Community* (New Haven: Yale University Press, 1942), pp. 72–3.

tradition, but the group's biological differences provide a symbol around which social differences are defined and evaluated. The Irish maintain certain social usages which differentiate them in varying degrees from the whole community. The other groups fall in between these two extremes.

Part II
Essays

3 The Future American (1900)

Charles W. Chesnutt*

FIRST ARTICLE

The future American race is a popular theme for essayists, and has been much discussed. Most expressions upon the subject, however, have been characterized by a conscious or unconscious evasion of some of the main elements of the problem involved in the formation of a future American race, or, to put it perhaps more correctly, a future ethnic type that shall inhabit the northern part of the western continent. Some of these obvious omissions will be touched upon in these articles; and if the writer has any preconceived opinions that would affect his judgment, they are at least not the hackneyed prejudices of the past – if they lead to false conclusions, they at least furnish a new point of view, from which, taken with other widely differing views, the judicious reader may establish a parallax that will enable him to approximate the truth.

The popular theory is that the future American race will consist of a harmonious fusion of the various European elements which now make up our heterogeneous population. The result is to be something infinitely superior to the best of the component elements. This perfection of type – for no good American could for a moment doubt that it will be as perfect as everything else American – is to be brought about by a combination of all the best characteristics of the different European races, and the elimination, by some strange alchemy, of all their undesirable traits – for even a good American will admit that European races, now and then, have some undesirable traits when they first come over. It is a beautiful, a hopeful, and to the eye of faith, a thrilling prospect. The defect of the argument, however, lies in the incompleteness of the premises, and its obliviousness of certain facts of human nature and human history.

---

* From Sallyaan H. Ferguson, *Melus Forum* (1900), pp. 96–107; originally published in the *Boston Evening Transcript* (August 18, 1900), p. 29; (August 25, 1900), p. 15; (September 1, 1900) p. 24.

Before putting forward any theory upon the subject, it may be well enough to remark that recent scientific research has swept away many hoary anthropological fallacies. It has been demonstrated that the shape or size of the head has little or nothing to do with the civilization or average intelligence of a race; that language, so recently lauded as an infallible test of racial origin is of absolutely no value in this connection, its distribution being dependent upon other conditions than race. Even color, upon which the social structure of the United States is so largely based, has been proved no test of race. The conception of a pure Aryan, Indo-European race has been abandoned in scientific circles, and the secret of the progress of Europe has been found in racial heterogeneity, rather than in racial purity. The theory that the Jews are a pure race has been exploded, and their peculiar type explained upon a different and much more satisfactory hypothesis. To illustrate the change of opinion and the growth of liberality in scientific circles, imagine the reception which would have been accorded to this proposition, if laid down by an American writer fifty or sixty years ago: 'The European races, as a whole, show signs of a secondary or derived origin; certain characteristics, especially the texture of the hair, lead us to class them as intermediate between the extreme primary types of the Asiatic and Negro races respectively' (Professor Ripley's *Races of Europe*, p. 457, New York, 1899). This is put forward by the author, not as a mere hypothesis, but as a proposition fairly susceptible of proof, and is supported by an elaborate argument based upon microscopical comparisons, to which numerous authorities are cited. If this fact be borne in mind it will simplify in some degree our conception of a future American ethnic type.

By modern research the unity of the human race has been proved (if it needed any proof to the careful or fair-minded observer), and the differentiation of races by selection and environment has been so stated as to prove itself. Greater emphasis has been placed upon environment as a factor in ethnic development, and what has been called 'the vulgar theory of race,' as accounting for progress and culture, has been relegated to the limbo of exploded dogmas. One of the most perspicuous and forceful presentations of these modern conclusions of anthropology is found in the volume above quoted, a book which owes its origin to a Boston scholar.

Proceeding then upon the firm basis laid down by science and the historic parallel, it ought to be quite clear that the future American race – the future American ethnic type – will be formed of a mingling, in a yet to be ascertained proportion, of the various racial varieties which make up the present population of the United States; or, to extend the area a little farther, of the various peoples of the northern hemisphere of the western continent; for, if certain recent tendencies are an index of the future, it is not safe to fix the boundaries of the future United States anywhere short of the Arctic Ocean on the north and the Isthmus of Panama on the south. But, even with the continuance of the present political divisions, conditions of trade and ease of travel are likely to gradually assimilate to one type all the countries of the hemisphere. Assuming that the country is so well settled that no great disturbance of ratios is likely to result from immigration, or any serious conflict of races, we may safely build our theory of a future American race upon the present population of the country. I use the word 'race' here in its popular sense – that of a people who look substantially alike, and are moulded by the same culture and dominated by the same ideals.

––––

By the eleventh census, the ratios of which will probably not be changed materially by the census now under way, the total population of the United States was about 65,000,000, of which about seven million were black and colored, and something over 200,000 were of Indian blood. It is then in the three broad types – white, black and Indian – that the future American race will find the material for its formation. Any dream of a pure white race, of the Anglo-Saxon type, for the United States, may as well be abandoned as impossible, even if desirable. That such future race will be predominantly white may well be granted – unless climate in the course of time should modify existing types; that it will call itself white is reasonably sure; that it will conform closely to the white type is likely; but that it will have absorbed and assimilated the blood of the other two races mentioned is as certain as the operation of any law well can be that deals with so uncertain a quantity as the human race.

There are no natural obstacles to such an amalgamation. The unity of the race is not only conceded but demonstrated by actual crossing. Any theory of sterility due to race crossing may as well be abandoned; it is founded mainly on prejudice and cannot be proved by the facts. If it come from Northern or European sources, it is likely to be weakened by lack of knowledge; if from Southern sources, it is sure to be colored by prejudice. My own observation is that in a majority of cases people of mixed blood are very prolific and very long-lived.

The admixture of races in the United States has never taken place under conditions likely to produce the best results; but there have nevertheless been enough conspicuous instances to the contrary in this country, to say nothing of a long and honorable list in other lands, to disprove the theory that people of mixed blood, other things being equal, are less virile, prolific or able than those of purer strains. But whether this be true or not is apart from this argument. Admitting that races may mix, and that they are thrown together under conditions which permit their admixture, the controlling motive will be not abstract considerations with regard to a remote posterity, but present interest and inclination.

The Indian element in the United States proper is so small proportionally – about one in three hundred – and the conditions for its amalgamation so favorable, that it would of itself require scarcely any consideration in this argument. There is no prejudice against the Indian blood, in solution. A half or quarter-breed, removed from the tribal environment, is freely received among white people. After the second or third remove he may even boast of his Indian descent; it gives him a sort of distinction, and involves no social disability. The distribution of the Indian race, however, tends to make the question largely a local one, and the survival of tribal relation may postpone the results for some little time. It will be, however, the fault of the United States Indian himself if he be not speedily amalgamated with the white population.

The Indian element, however, looms up larger when we include Mexico and Central America in our field of discussion. By the census of Mexico just completed, over eighty per cent of the population is composed of mixed and Indian races. The remainder is presumably of pure Spanish, or European blood, with a dash of Negro along the coast. The population is something over twelve millions, thus adding nine millions of Indians and Mestizos to be taken into account. Add several millions of similar descent in Central America, a million in Porto Rico, who are said to have an aboriginal strain, and it may safely be figured that the Indian element will be quite considerable in the future American race. Its amalgamation will involve no great difficulty, however; it has been going on peacefully in the countries south of us for several centuries, and is likely to continue along similar lines. The peculiar disposition of the American to overlook mixed blood in a foreigner will simplify the gradual absorption of these Southern races.

———

The real problem, then, the only hard problem in connection with the future American race, lies in the Negro element of our population. As

I have said before, I believe it is destined to play its part in the formation of this new type. The process by which this will take place will be no sudden and wholesale amalgamation – a thing certainly not to be expected, and hardly to be desired. If it were held desirable, and one could imagine a government sufficiently autocratic to enforce its behests, it would be no great task to mix the races mechanically, leaving to time merely the fixing of the resultant type.

Let us for curiosity outline the process. To start with, the Negroes are already considerably mixed – many of them in large proportion, and most of them in some degree – and the white people, as I shall endeavor to show later on, are many of them slightly mixed with the Negro. But we will assume, for the sake of the argument, that the two races are absolutely pure. We will assume, too, that the laws of the whole country were as favorable to this amalgamation as the laws of most Southern States are at present against it; i.e., that it were made a misdemeanor for two white or two colored persons to marry, so long as it was possible to obtain a mate of the other race – this would be even more favorable than the Southern rule, which makes no such exception. Taking the population as one-eighth Negro, this eighth, married to an equal number of whites, would give in the next generation a population of which one-fourth would be mulattoes. Mating these in turn with white persons, the next generation would be composed one-half of quadroons, or persons one-fourth Negro. In the third generation, applying the same rule, the entire population would be composed of octoroons, or persons only one-eighth Negro, who would probably call themselves white, if by this time there remained any particular advantage in being so considered. Thus in three generations the pure whites would be entirely eliminated, and there would be no perceptible trace of the blacks left.

The mechanical mixture would be complete; as it would probably be put, the white race would have absorbed the black. There would be no inferior race to domineer over; there would be no superior race to oppress those who differed from them in racial externals. The inevitable social struggle, which in one form or another, seems to be one of the conditions of progress, would proceed along other lines than those of race. If now and then, for a few generations, an occasional trace of the black ancestor should crop out, no one would care, for all would be tarred with the same stick. This is already the case in South America, parts of Mexico and to a large extent in the West Indies. From a negroid nation, which ours is already, we would have become a composite and homogeneous people, and the elements of racial discord which have troubled our civil life so gravely and still threaten our free institutions, would have been entirely eliminated.

But this will never happen. The same result will be brought about slowly and obscurely, and, if the processes of nature are not too violently interrupted by the hand of man, in such a manner as to produce the best results with the least disturbance of natural laws. In another article I shall endeavor to show that this process has been taking place with greater rapidity than is generally supposed, and that the results have been such as to encourage the belief that the formation of a uniform type out of our present racial elements will take place within a measurably near period.

SECOND ARTICLE

I have said that the formation of the new American race type will take place slowly and obscurely for some time to come, after the manner of all healthy changes in nature. I may go further and say that this process has already been going on ever since the various races in the Western world have been brought into juxtaposition. Slavery was a rich soil for the production of a mixed race, and one need only read the literature and laws of the past two generations to see how steadily, albeit slowly and insidiously, the stream of dark blood has insinuated itself into the veins of the dominant, or, as a Southern critic recently described it in a paragraph that came under my eye, the 'domineering' race. The Creole stories of Mr. Cable and other writers were not mere figments of the imagination; the beautiful octoroon was a corporeal fact; it is more than likely that she had brothers of the same complexion, though curiously enough the male octoroon has cut no figure in fiction, except in the case of the melancholy Honoré Grandissime, f.m.c. [i.e., free men of color]; and that she and her brothers often crossed the invisible but rigid color line was an historical fact that only an ostrich-like prejudice could deny.

Grace King's 'Story of New Orleans' makes the significant statement that the quadroon women of that city preferred white fathers for their children, in order that these latter might become white and thereby be qualified to enter the world of opportunity. More than one of the best families of Louisiana has a dark ancestral strain. A conspicuous American family of Southwestern extraction, which recently contributed a party to a brilliant international marriage, is known, by the well-informed, to be just exactly five generations removed from a Negro ancestor.

One member of this family, a distinguished society leader, has been known, upon occasion, when some question of the rights or privileges of the colored race came up, to show a very noble sympathy for her distant kinsmen. If American prejudice permitted her and others to speak freely of her pedigree, what a tower of strength her name and influence would be to a despised and struggling race!

A distinguished American man of letters, now resident in Europe, who spent many years in North Carolina, has said to the writer that he had noted, in the course of a long life, at least a thousand instances of white persons known or suspected to possess a strain of Negro blood. An amusing instance of this sort occurred a year or two ago. It was announced through the newspapers, whose omniscience of course no one would question, that a certain great merchant of Chicago was a mulatto. This gentleman had a large dry goods trade in the South, notably in Texas. Shortly after the publication of the item reflecting on the immaculateness of the merchant's descent, there appeared in the Texas newspapers, among the advertising matter, a statement from the Chicago merchant characterizing the rumor as a malicious falsehood, concocted by his rivals in business, and incidentally calling attention to the excellent bargains offered to retailers and jobbers at his great emporium. A counter-illustration is found in the case of a certain bishop, recently elected, of the African Methodist Episcopal Church, who is accused of being a white man. A colored editor who possesses the saving grace of humor, along with other talents of a high order, gravely observed, in discussing this rumor, that 'the poor man could not help it, even if he were white, and that a fact for which he was in no wise responsible should not be allowed to stand in the way of his advancement.'

During a residence in North Carolina in my youth and early manhood I noted many curious phases of the race problem. I have in mind a family of three sisters so aggressively white that the old popular Southern legend that they were the unacknowledged children of white parents was current concerning them. There was absolutely not the slightest earmark of the Negro about them. It may be stated here, as another race fallacy, that the 'telltale mark at the root of the nails,' supposed to be an infallible test of Negro blood, is a delusion and a snare, and of no value whatever as a test of race. It belongs with the gruesome superstition that a woman apparently white may give birth to a coal-black child by a white father. Another instance that came under my eye was that of a very beautiful girl with soft, wavy brown hair, who is now living in a Far Western State as the wife of a white husband.

A typical case was that of a family in which the tradition of Negro origin had persisted long after all trace of it had disappeared. The family took its origin from a white ancestress, and had consequently been free for several generations. The father of the first colored child, counting the family in the female line – the only way it could be counted – was a mulatto. A second infusion of white blood, this time on the paternal side, resulted in offspring not distinguishable from pure white. One child of this generation emigrated to what was then the Far West, married a white woman and reared a large family, whose descendants, now in the fourth or fifth remove from the Negro, are in all probability wholly unaware of their origin. A sister of this pioneer emigrant remained in the place of her birth and formed an irregular union with a white man of means, with whom she lived for many years and for whom she bore a large number of children, who became about evenly divided between white and colored, fixing their status by the marriages they made. One of the daughters, for instance, married a white man and reared in a neighboring county a family of white children, who, in all probability, were as active as any one else in the recent ferocious red-shirt campaign to disfranchise the Negroes.

In this same town there was stationed once, before the war, at the Federal arsenal there located, an officer who fell in love with a 'white Negro' girl, as our Southern friends impartially dub them. This officer subsequently left the army, and carried away with him to the North the whole family of his inamorata. He married the woman, and their descendants, who live in a large Western city, are not known at all as persons of color, and show no trace of their dark origin.

Two notable bishops of the Roman Catholic communion in the United States are known to be the sons of a slave mother and a white father, who, departing from the usual American rule, gave his sons freedom, education and a chance in life, instead of sending them to the auction block. Colonel T. W. Higginson, in his 'Cheerful Yesterdays,' related the story of a white colored woman whom he assisted in her escape from slavery or its consequences, who married a white man in the vicinity of Boston and lost her identity with the colored race. How many others there must be who know of similar instances! Grace King, in her 'Story of New Orleans,' to which I have referred, in speaking of a Louisiana law which required the public records, when dealing with persons of color, always to specify the fact of color, in order, so far had the admixture of races gone, to distinguish them from whites, says: 'But the officers of the law could be bribed, and the qualification once dropped acted, inversely, as a patent of pure blood.'

A certain well-known Shakspearean actress has a strain of Negro blood, and a popular leading man under a well-known manager is similarly gifted. It would be interesting to give their names, but would probably only injure them. If they could themselves speak of their origin, without any unpleasant consequences, it would be a handsome thing for the colored race. That they do not is no reproach to them; they are white to all intents and purposes, even by the curious laws of the curious States from which they derived their origin, and are in all conscience entitled to any advantage accompanying this status.

Anyone at all familiar with the hopes and aspirations of the colored race, as expressed, for instance, in their prolific newspaper literature, must have perceived the wonderful inspiration which they have drawn from the career of a few distinguished Europeans of partial Negro ancestry, who have felt no call, by way of social prejudice, to deny or conceal their origin, or to refuse their sympathy to those who need it so much. Pushkin, the Russian Shakspeare, had a black ancestor. One of the chief editors of the London Times, who died a few years ago, was a West Indian colored man, who had no interest in concealing the fact. One of the generals of the British army is similarly favored, although the fact is not often referred to. General Alfred Dodds, the ranking general of the French army, now in command in China, is a quadroon. The poet, Robert Browning, was of West Indian origin, and some of his intimate personal friends maintained and proved to their own satisfaction that he was partly of Negro descent. Mr. Browning always said that he did not know; that there was no family tradition to that effect; but if it could be demonstrated he would admit it freely enough, if it would reflect any credit upon a race who needed it so badly.

The most conspicuous of the Eurafricans (to coin a word) were the Dumas family, who were distinguished for three generations. The mulatto, General Dumas, won distinction in the wars under the Revolution. His son, the famous Alexandre Dumas père, has delighted several generations with his novels, and founded a school of fiction. His son, Alexandre fils, novelist and dramatist, was as supreme in his own line as his father had been in his. Old Alexandre gives his pedigree in detail in his memoirs; and the Negro origin of the family is set out in every encyclopaedia. Nevertheless, in a literary magazine of recent date, published in New York, it was gravely stated by a writer that 'there was a rumor, probably not well founded, that the author of "Monte Christo" had a very distant strain of Negro blood.' If this had been written with reference to some living American of obscure origin, its point might be appreciated; but such extreme delicacy in stating so widely known a fact appeals to one's sense of humor.

These European gentlemen could be outspoken about their origin, because it carried with it no social stigma or disability whatever. When such a state of public opinion exists in the United States, there may be a surprising revision of pedigrees!

A little incident that occurred not long ago near Boston will illustrate the complexity of these race relations. Three light-colored men, brothers, by the name, we will say, of Green, living in a Boston suburb, married respectively a white, a brown and a black woman. The woman with the white mother became known as white, and associated with white people. The others were frankly colored. By a not unlikely coincidence, in the course of time the children of the three families found themselves in the same public school. Curiously enough, one afternoon the three sets of Green children – the white Greens, the brown Greens and the black Greens – were detained after school, and were all directed to report to a certain schoolroom, where they were assigned certain tasks at the blackboards about the large room. Still more curiously, most of the teachers of the school happened to have business in this particular room on that particular afternoon, and all of them seemed greatly interested in the Green children.

'Well, well, did you ever! Just think of it! And they are all first cousins!' was remarked audibly.

The children were small, but they lived in Boston, and were, of course, as became Boston children, preternaturally intelligent for their years. They reported to their parents the incident and a number of remarks of a similar tenor to the one above quoted. The result was a complaint to the school authorities, and a reprimand to several teachers. A curious feature of the affair lay in the source from which the complaint emanated. One might suppose it to have come from the white Greens; but no, they were willing that the incident should pass unnoticed and be promptly forgotten; publicity would only advertise a fact which would work to their social injury. The dark Greens rather enjoyed the affair; they had nothing to lose; they had no objections to being known as the cousins of the others, and experienced a certain not unnatural pleasure in their discomfiture. The complaint came from the brown Greens. The reader can figure out the psychology of it for himself.

A more certain proof of the fact that Negro blood is widely distributed among the white people may be found in the laws and judicial decisions of the various States. Laws, as a rule, are not made until demanded by a sufficient number of specific cases to call for a general rule; and judicial decisions of course are never announced except as the result of litigation over contested facts. There is no better index of the character and genius of a people than their laws.

In North Carolina, marriage between white persons and free persons of color was lawful until 1830. By the Missouri code of 1855, the color line was drawn at one-fourth of Negro blood, and persons of only one-eighth were legally white. The same rule was laid down by the Mississippi code of 1880. Under the old code noir of Louisiana, the descendant of a white and a quadroon was white. Under these laws many persons currently known as 'colored,' or, more recently as 'Negro,' would be legally white if they chose to claim and exercise the privilege. In Ohio, before the civil war, a person more than half-white was legally entitled to all the rights of a white man. In South Carolina, the line of cleavage was left somewhat indefinite; the color line was drawn tentatively at one-fourth of Negro blood, but this was not held conclusive.

'The term "mulatto",' said the Supreme Court of that State in a reported case, 'is not invariably applicable to every [admixture] of African blood with the European, nor is one having all the features of a white to be ranked with the degraded class designated by the laws of the State as persons of color, because of some remote taint of the Negro race.... The question whether persons are colored or white, where color or feature is doubtful, is for the jury to determine by reputation, by reception into society, and by their exercises of the privileges of a white man, as well as by admixture of blood.'

It is well known that this liberality of view grew out of widespread conditions in the State, which these decisions in their turn tended to emphasize. They were probably due to the large preponderance of colored people in the State, which rendered the whites the more willing to augment their own number. There are many interesting color-line decisions in the reports of the Southern courts, which space will not permit the mention of.

In another article I shall consider certain conditions which retard the development of the future American race type which I have suggested, as well as certain other tendencies which are likely to promote it.

THIRD ARTICLE

I have endeavored in two former letters to set out the reasons why it seems likely that the future American ethnic type will be formed by a fusion of all the various races now peopling this continent, and to show that this process has been under way, slowly but surely, like all evolutionary movements, for several hundred years. I wish now to consider some of the conditions which will retard this fusion, as well as certain other facts which tend to promote it.

The Indian phase of the problem, so far at least as the United States is concerned has been practically disposed of in what has already been said. The absorption of the Indians will be delayed so long as the tribal relations continue, and so long as the Indians are treated as wards of the Government, instead of being given their rights once for all, and placed upon the footing of other citizens. It is to be presumed that this will come about as the wilder Indians are educated and by the development of the country brought into closer contact with civilization, which must happen before a very great while. As has been stated, there is no very strong prejudice against the Indian blood; a well-stocked farm or a comfortable fortune will secure a white husband for a comely Indian girl any day, with some latitude, and there is no evidence of any such strong race instinct or organization as will make the Indians of the future wish to perpetuate themselves as a small but insignificant class in a great population, thus emphasizing distinctions which would be overlooked in the case of the individual.

The Indian will fade into the white population as soon as he chooses, and in the United States proper the slender Indian strain will ere long leave no trace discoverable by anyone but the anthopological expert. In New Mexico and Central America, on the contrary, the chances seem to be that the Indian will first absorb the non-indigenous elements, unless, which is not unlikely, European immigration shall increase the white contingent.

The Negro element remains, then, the only one which seems likely to present any difficulty of assimilation. The main obstacle that retards the absorption of the Negro into the general population is the apparently intense prejudice against color which prevails in the United States. This prejudice loses much of its importance, however, when it is borne in mind that it is almost purely local and does not exist in quite the same form anywhere else in the world, except among the Boers of

South Africa, where it prevails in an even more aggravated form; and, as I shall endeavor to show, this prejudice in the United States is more apparent than real, and is a caste prejudice which is merely accentuated by differences of race. At present, however, I wish to consider it merely as a deterrent to amalgamation.

This prejudice finds forcible expression in the laws which prevail in all the Southern States, without exception, forbidding the intermarriage of white persons and persons of color – these last being generally defined within certain degrees. While it is evident that such laws alone will not prevent the intermingling of races, which goes merrily on in spite of them, it is equally apparent that this placing of mixed marriages beyond the pale of the law is a powerful deterrent to any honest or dignified amalgamation. Add to this legal restriction, which is enforced by severe penalties, the social odium accruing to the white party to such a union, and it may safely be predicted that so long as present conditions prevail in the South, there will be little marrying or giving in marriage between persons of different race. So ferocious is this sentiment against intermarriage, that in a recent Missouri case, where a colored man ran away with and married a young white woman, the man was pursued by a 'posse' – a word which is rapidly being debased from its proper meaning by its use in the attempt to dignify the character of lawless Southern mobs – and shot to death; the woman was tried and convicted of the 'crime' of miscegenation – another honest word which the South degrades along with the Negro.

Another obstacle to race fusion lies in the drastic and increasing proscriptive legislation by which the South attempts to keep the white and colored races apart in every place where their joint presence might be taken to imply equality; or, to put it more directly, the persistent effort to degrade the Negro to a distinctly and permanently inferior caste. This is undertaken by means of separate schools, separate railroad and street cars, political disfranchisement, debasing and abhorrent prison systems, and an unflagging campaign of calumny, by which the vices and shortcomings of the Negroes are grossly magnified and their virtues practically lost sight of. The popular argument that the Negro ought to develop his own civilization, and has no right to share in that of the white race, unless by favor, comes with poor grace from those who are forcing their civilization upon others at the cannon's mouth; it is, moreover, uncandid and unfair. The white people of the present generation did not make their civilization; they inherited it ready-made, and much of the wealth which is so strong a factor in their power was created by the unpaid labor of the colored people. The present generation has, however, brought to a high state of development one distinctively American institution, for which it is entitled to such credit as it may wish to claim; I refer to the custom of lynching, with its attendant horrors.

The principal deterrent to race admixture, however, is the low industrial and social efficiency of the colored race. If it be conceded that these are the result of environment, then their cause is not far to seek, and the cure is also in sight. Their poverty, their ignorance and their servile estate render them as yet largely ineligible for social fusion with a race whose pride is fed not only by the record of its achievements but by a constant comparison with a less developed and less fortunate race, which it has held so long in subjection.

The forces that tend to future absorption of the black race are, however, vastly stronger than those arrayed against it. As experience has demonstrated, slavery was favorable to the mixing of the races. The growth, under healthy civil conditions, of a large and self-respecting colored citizenship would doubtless tend to lessen the clandestine association of the two races; but the effort to degrade the Negro may result, if successful, in a partial restoration of the old status. But, assuming that the present anti-Negro legislation is but a temporary reaction, then the steady progress of the colored race in wealth and culture and social efficiency will, in the course of time, materially soften the asperities of racial prejudice and permit them to approach the whites more closely, until, in time, the prejudice against intermarriage shall have been overcome by other considerations.

It is safe to say that the possession of a million dollars, with the ability to use it to the best advantage, would throw such a golden glow over a dark complexion as to override anything but a very obdurate prejudice. Mr. Spahr, in his well-studied and impartial book on 'America's Working People,' states as his conclusion, after a careful study of conditions in the South, that the most advanced third of the Negroes of that section has already, in one generation of limited opportunity, passed in the race of life the least advanced third of the whites. To pass the next third will prove a more difficult task, no doubt, but the Negroes will have the impetus of their forward movement to push them ahead.

The outbreaks of race prejudice in recent years are the surest evidence of the Negro's progress. No effort is required to keep down a race which manifests no desire nor ability to rise; but with each new forward movement of the colored race it is brought into contact with the whites at some fresh point, which evokes a new manifestation of prejudice until custom has adjusted things to the new condition. When all Negroes were poor and ignorant they could be denied their rights with impunity. As they grow in knowledge and in wealth they become self-assertive, and make it correspondingly troublesome for those who would ignore their claims. It is much easier, by a supreme effort, as recently attempted with temporary success in North Carolina, to knock the race down and rob it of its rights once for all, than to repeat the process from day to day and with each individual; it saves wear and tear on the conscience, and makes it easy to maintain a superiority which it might in the course of a short time require some little effort to keep up.

This very proscription, however, political and civil in the South, social all over the country, varying somewhat in degree, will, unless very soon relaxed, prove a powerful factor in the mixture of the races. If it is only by becoming white that colored people and their children are to enjoy the rights and dignities of citizenship, they will have every incentive to 'lighten the breed,' to use a current phrase, that they may claim the white man's privileges as soon as possible. That this motive is already at work may be seen in the enormous extent to which certain 'face bleachers' and 'hair straighteners' are advertised in the newspapers printed for circulation among the colored people. The most powerful factor in achieving any result is the wish to bring it about. The only thing that ever succeeded in keeping two races separated when living on the same soil – the only true ground of caste – is religion, and as has been alluded to in the case of the Jews, this is only superficially successful. The colored people are the same as the whites in religion; they have the same standards and mediums of culture, the same ideals, and the presence of the successful white race as a constant incentive to their ambition. The ultimate result is not difficult to foresee. The races will be quite as effectively amalgamated by lightening the Negroes as they would be by darkening the whites. It is only a social fiction, indeed, which makes of a person seven-eighths white a Negro; he is really much more a white man.

The hope of the Negro, so far as the field of moral sympathy and support in his aspirations is concerned, lies, as always, chiefly in the North. There the forces which tend to his elevation are, in the main, allowed their natural operation. The exaggerated zeal with which the South is rushing to degrade the Negro is likely to result, as in the case of slavery, in making more friends for him at the North; and if the North shall not see fit to interfere forcibly with Southern legislation, it may at least feel disposed to emphasize, by its own liberality, its disapproval of Southern injustice and barbarity.

An interesting instance of the difference between the North and the South in regard to colored people, may be found in two cases which only last year came up for trial in two adjoining border States. A colored man living in Maryland went over to Washington and married a white woman. The marriage was legal in Washington. When they returned to their Maryland home they were arrested for the crime of 'miscegenation' – or perhaps it is only a misdemeanor in Maryland – and sentenced to fine and imprisonment, the penalty of extra-judicial death not extending so far North. The same month a couple, one white and one colored, were arrested in New Jersey for living in adultery. They were found guilty by the court, but punishment was withheld upon a promise that they would marry immediately; or, as some cynic would undoubtedly say, the punishment was commuted from imprisonment to matrimony.

The adding to our territories of large areas populated by dark races, some of them already liberally dowered with Negro blood, will enhance the relative importance of the non-Caucasian elements of the population, and largely increase the flow of dark blood toward the white race, until the time shall come when distinctions of color shall lose their importance, which will be but the prelude to a complete racial fusion.

The formation of this future American race is not a pressing problem. Because of the conditions under which it must take place, it is likely to be extremely slow – much slower, indeed, in our temperate climate and highly organized society, than in the American tropics and subtropics, where it is already well under way, if not a fait accompli. That it must come in the United States, sooner or later, seems to be a foregone conclusion, as the result of natural law – lex dura, sed tamen lex – a hard pill, but one which must be swallowed. There can manifestly be no such thing as a peaceful and progressive civilization in a nation divided by two warring races, and homogeneity of type, at least in externals, is a necessary condition of harmonious social progress.

If this, then, must come, the development and progress of all the constituent elements of the future American race is of the utmost importance as bearing upon the quality of the resultant type. The white race is still susceptible of some improvement; and if, in time, the more objectionable Negro traits are eliminated, and his better qualities correspondingly developed, his part in the future American race may well be an important and valuable one.

4 On a Certain Blindness in Human Beings (1900)

William James*

Our judgments concerning the worth of things, big or little, depend
on the *feelings* the things arouse in us. Where we judge a thing to be
precious in consequence of the *idea* we frame of it, this is only because the idea is itself associated already with a feeling. If we were
radically feelingless, and if ideas were the only things our mind could
entertain, we should lose all our likes and dislikes at a stroke, and be
unable to point to any one situation or experience in life more valuable or significant than any other.

Now the blindness in human beings, of which this discourse will
treat, is the blindness with which we all are afflicted in regard to the
feelings of creatures and people different from ourselves.

We are practical beings, each of us with limited functions and duties to perform. Each is bound to feel intensely the importance of his
own duties and the significance of the situations that call these forth.
But this feeling is in each of us a vital secret, for sympathy with
which we vainly look to others. The others are too much absorbed in
their own vital secrets to take an interest in ours. Hence the stupidity
and injustice of our opinions, so far as they deal with the significance
of alien lives. Hence the falsity of our judgments, so far as they presume to decide in an absolute way on the value of other persons'
conditions or ideals.

Take our dogs and ourselves, connected as we are by a tie more
intimate than most ties this world; and yet, outside of that tie of friendly
fondness, how insensible, each of us, to all that makes life significant
for the other! – we to the rapture of bones under hedges, or smells of
trees and lamp-posts, they to the delights of literature and art. As you
sit reading the most moving romance you ever fell upon, what sort of
a judge is your fox-terrier of your behavior? With all his good will
toward you, the nature of your conduct is absolutely excluded from
his comprehension. To sit there like a senseless statue, when you might

---

* From Chapter II in William James, *Talks to Teachers on Psychology: and to Students on Some of Life's Ideals* (New York: Holt, 1900), pp. 229–34 (beginning only).

be taking him to walk and throwing sticks for him to catch! What queer disease is this that comes over you every day, of holding things and staring at them like that for hours together, paralyzed of motion and vacant of all conscious life? The African savages came nearer the truth; but they, too, missed it, when they gathered wonderingly round one of our American travellers who, in the interior, had just come into possession of a stray copy of the New York *Commercial Advertiser*, and was devouring it column by column. When he got through, they offered him a high price for the mysterious object; and, being asked for what they wanted it, they said: 'For an eye medicine' – that being the only reason they could conceive of for the protracted bath which he had given his eyes upon its surface.

The spectator's judgment is sure to miss the root of the matter, and to possess no truth. The subject judged knows a part of the world of reality which the judging spectator fails to see, knows more while the spectator knows less; and, wherever there is conflict of opinion and difference of vision, we are bound to believe that the truer side is the side that feels the more, and not the side that feels the less.

Let me take a personal example of the kind that befalls each one of us daily:

Some years ago, while journeying in the mountains of North Carolina, I passed by a large number of 'coves,' as they call them there, or heads of small valleys between the hills, which had been newly cleared and planted. The impression on my mind was one of unmitigated squalor. The settler had in every case cut down the more manageable trees, and left their charred stumps standing. The larger trees he had girdled and killed, in order that their foliage should not cast a shade. He had then built a log cabin, plastering its chinks with clay, and had set up a tall zigzag rail fence around the scene of his havoc, to keep the pigs and cattle out. Finally, he had irregularly planted the intervals between the stumps and trees with Indian corn, which grew among the chips; and there he dwelt with his wife and babes – an axe, a gun, a few utensils, and some pigs and chickens feeding in the woods, being the sum total of his possessions.

The forest had been destroyed; and what had 'improved' it out of existence was hideous, a sort of ulcer, without a single element of artificial grace to make up for the loss of Nature's beauty. Ugly, indeed, seemed the life of the squatter, scudding, as the sailors say, under bare poles, beginning again away back where our first ancestors started, and by hardly a single item the better off for all the achievements of the intervening generations.

Talk about going back to nature! I said to myself, oppressed by the dreariness, as I drove by. Talk of a country life for one's old age and for one's children! Never thus, with nothing but the bare ground and one's bare hands to fight the battle! Never, without the best spoils of culture woven in! The beauties and commodities gained by the centuries are sacred. They are our heritage and birthright. No modern person ought to be willing to live a day in such a state of rudimentariness and denudation.

Then I said to the mountaineer who was driving me, 'What sort of people are they who have to make these new clearings?' 'All of us,' he replied. 'Why, we ain't happy here, unless we are getting one of these coves under cultivation.' I instantly felt that I had been losing the whole inward significance of the situation. Because to me the clearings spoke of naught but denudation, I thought that to those whose sturdy arms and obedient axes had made them they could tell no other story. But, when *they* looked on the hideous stumps, what they thought of was personal victory. The chips, the girdled trees, and the vile split rails spoke of honest sweat, persistent toil and final reward. The cabin was a warrant of safety for self and wife and babes. In short, the clearing, which to me was a mere ugly picture on the retina, was to them a symbol redolent with moral memories and sang a very paean of duty, struggle, and success.

I had been as blind to the peculiar ideality of their conditions as they certainly would also have been to the ideality of mine, had they had a peep at my strange indoor academic ways of life at Cambridge.

5 The Stranger (1908) and The Web of Group Affiliations (1908)

Georg Simmel*

THE STRANGER

If wandering is the liberation from every given point in space, and thus the conceptional opposite to fixation at such a point, the sociological form of the 'stranger' presents the unity, as it were, of these two characteristics. This phenomenon too, however, reveals that spatial relations are only the condition, on the one hand, and the symbol, on the other, of human relations. The stranger is thus being discussed here, not in the sense often touched upon in the past, as the wanderer who comes today and goes tomorrow, but rather as the person who comes today and stays tomorrow. He is, so to speak, the *potential* wanderer: although he has not moved on, he has not quite overcome the freedom of coming and going. He is fixed within a particular spatial group, or within a group whose boundaries are similar to spatial boundaries. But his position in this group is determined, essentially, by the fact that he has not belonged to it from the beginning, that he imports qualities into it, which do not and cannot stem from the group itself.

The unity of nearness and remoteness involved in every human relation is organized, in the phenomenon of the stranger, in a way which may be most briefly formulated by saying that in the relationship to him, distance means that he, who is close by, is far, and strangeness means that he, who also is far, is actually near. For, to be a stranger is naturally a very positive relation; it is a specific form of interaction. The inhabitants of Sirius are not really strangers to us, at least not in any sociologically relevant sense: they do not exist for us at all; they are beyond far and near. The stranger, like the poor and like

* From *Der Fremde* (1908), Chapter 3 in Kurt H. Wolff (trans), *The Sociology of Georg Simmel* (Glencoe Ill.: Free Press, 1950), pp. 402–8; *Die Kreuzung sozialer Kreise* (in Reinhard Bendix (trans), *Conflict* and *The Web of Group Affiliations* (New York: Free Press, 1955), pp. 150–61.

sundry 'inner enemies,' is an element of the group itself. His position as a full-fledged member involves both being outside it and confronting it. The following statements, which are by no means intended as exhaustive, indicate how elements which increase distance and repel, in the relations of and with the stranger produce a pattern of coordination and consistent interaction.

Throughout the history of economics the stranger everywhere appears as the trader, or the trader as stranger. As long as economy is essentially self-sufficient, or products are exchanged within a spatially narrow group, it needs no middleman: a trader is only required for products that originate outside the group. Insofar as members do not leave the circle in order to buy these necessities – in which case *they* are the 'strange' merchants in that outside territory – the trader *must* be a stranger, since nobody else has a chance to make a living.

This position of the stranger stands out more sharply if he settles down in the place of his activity, instead of leaving it again: in innumerable cases even this is possible only if he can live by intermediate trade. Once an economy is somehow closed, the land is divided up, and handicrafts are established that satisfy the demand for them, the trader, too, can find his existence. For in trade, which alone makes possible unlimited combinations, intelligence always finds expansions and new territories, an achievement which is very difficult to attain for the original producer with his lesser mobility and his dependence upon a circle of customers that can be increased only slowly. Trade can always absorb more people than primary production; it is, therefore, the sphere indicated for the stranger, who intrudes as a supernumerary, so to speak, into a group in which the economic positions are actually occupied – the classical example is the history of European Jews. The stranger is by nature no 'owner of soil' – soil not only in the physical, but also in the figurative sense of a life-substance which is fixed, if not in a point in space, at least in an ideal point of the social environment. Although in more intimate relations, he may develop all kinds of charm and significance, as long as he is considered a stranger in the eyes of the other, he is not an 'owner of soil.' Restriction to intermediary trade, and often (as though sublimated from it) to pure finance, gives him the specific character of *mobility*. If mobility takes place within a closed group, it embodies that synthesis of nearness and distance which constitutes the formal position of the stranger. For, the fundamentally mobile person comes in contact, at one time or another, with every individual, but is not organically connected, through established ties of kinship, locality, and occupation, with any single one.

Another expression of this constellation lies in the objectivity of the stranger. He is not radically committed to the unique ingredients and peculiar tendencies of the group, and therefore approaches them with the specific attitude of 'objectivity.' But objectivity does not simply involve passivity and detachment; it is a particular structure composed of distance and nearness, indifference and involvement. I refer to the discussion (in the chapter on 'Superordination and Subordination') of the dominating positions of the person who is a stranger in the group; its most typical instance was the practice of those Italian cities to call their judges from the outside, because no native was free from entanglement in family and party interests.

With the objectivity of the stranger is connected, also, the phenomenon touched upon above,[1] although it is chiefly (but not exclusively) true of the stranger who moves on. This is the fact that he often receives the most surprising openness – confidences which sometimes have the character of a confessional and which would be carefully withheld from a more closely related person. Objectivity is by no means non-participation (which is altogether outside both subjective and objective, interaction), but a positive and specific kind of participation – just as the objectivity of a theoretical observation does not refer to the mind as a passive *tabula rasa* on which things inscribe their qualities, but on the contrary, to its full activity that operates according to its own laws, and to the elimination, thereby, of accidental dislocations and emphases, whose individual and subjective differences would produce different pictures of the same object.

Objectivity may also be defined as freedom: the objective individual is bound by no commitments which could prejudice his perception, understanding, and evaluation of the given. The freedom, however, which allows the stranger to experience and treat even his close relationships as though from a bird's-eye view, contains many dangerous possibilities. In uprisings of all sorts, the party attacked has claimed, from the beginning of things, that provocation has come from the outside, through emissaries and instigators. Insofar as this is true, it is an exaggeration of the specific role of the stranger: he is freer, practically and theoretically; he surveys conditions with less prejudice; his criteria for them are more general and more objective ideals; he is not tied down in his action by habit, piety, and precedent.[2]

Finally, the proportion of nearness and remoteness which gives the stranger the character of objectivity, also finds practical expression in the more *abstract nature* of the relation to him. That is, with the stranger one has only certain *more general* qualities in common, whereas the relation to more organically connected persons is based on the commonness of specific differences from merely general features. In fact, all somehow personal relations follow this scheme in various patterns. They are determined not only by the circumstance that certain common features exist among the individuals, along with individual differences, which either influence the relationship or remain outside of it. For, the common features themselves are basically determined in their effect upon the relation by the question whether they exist only between the participants in this particular relationship, and thus are quite general in regard to this relation, but are specific and incomparable in regard to everything outside of it – or whether the participants feel that these features are common to them because they are common to a group, a type, or mankind in general. In the case of the second alternative, the effectiveness of the common features becomes diluted in proportion to the size of the group composed of members who are similar in this sense. Although the commonness functions as their unifying basis, it does not make *these* particular persons interdependent on one another, because it could as easily connect everyone of them with all kinds of outside individual other than the members of his group. This, too, evidently, is a way in which a relationship includes both nearness and distance at the same time: to the extent to which the common features are general, they add, to the warmth of the relation founded on them, an element of coolness, a feeling of the contingency of precisely *this* relation – the connecting forces have lost their specific and centripetal character.

In the relation to the stranger, it seems to me, this constellation has an extraordinary and basic preponderance over the individual elements that are exclusive with the particular relationship. The stranger is close to us, insofar as we feel between him and ourselves common features of a national, social, occupational, or generally human, nature. He is far from us, insofar as these common features extend beyond him or us, and connect us only because they connect a great many people.

A trace of strangeness in this sense easily enters even the most intimate relationships. In the stage of first passion, erotic relations strongly reject any thought of generalization: the lovers think that there has never been a love like theirs; that nothing can be compared either to the person loved or to the feelings for that person. An estrangement – whether as cause or as consequence it is difficult to decide – usually comes at the moment when this feeling of uniqueness vanishes from the relationship. A certain skepticism in regard to its value, in itself and for them, attaches to the very thought that in their relation, after all, they carry out only a generally human destiny; that they experience an experience that has occurred a thousand times before; that, had they not accidentally met their particular partner, they would have found the same significance in another person.

Something of this feeling is probably not absent in any relation, however close, because what is common to two is never common to them alone, but is subsumed under a general idea which includes much else besides, many *possibilities* of commonness. No matter how little these possibilities become real and how often we forget them, here and there, nevertheless, they thrust themselves between us like shadows, like a mist which escapes every word noted, but which must coagulate into a solid bodily form before it can be called jealousy. In some cases, perhaps the more general, at least the more unsurmountable, strangeness is not due to different and ununderstandable matters. It is rather caused by the fact that similarity, harmony, and nearness are accompanied by the feeling that they are not really the unique property of this particular relationship: they are something more general, something which potentially prevails between the partners and an indeterminate number of others, and therefore gives the relation, which alone was realized, no inner and exclusive necessity.

On the other hand, there is a kind of 'strangeness' that rejects the very commonness based on something more general which embraces the parties. The relation of the Greeks to the Barbarians is perhaps typical here, as are all cases in which it is precisely general attributes, felt to be specifically and purely human, that are disallowed to the other. But 'stranger,' here, has no positive meaning; the relation to him is a non-relation; he is not what is relevant here, a member of the group itself.

As a group member, rather, he is near and far *at the same time*, as is characteristic of relations founded only on generally human commonness. But between nearness and distance, there arises a specific tension when the consciousness that only the quite general is common, stresses that which is not common. In the case of the person who is a stranger to the country, the city, the race, etc., however, this non-common element is once more nothing individual, but merely the strangeness of origin, which is or could be common to many strangers. For this reason, strangers are not really conceived as individuals, but as strangers of a particular type: the element of distance is no less general in regard to them than the element of nearness.

This form is the basis of such a special case, for instance, as the tax levied in Frankfort and elsewhere upon medieval Jews. Whereas the *Beede* (tax) paid by the Christian citizen changed with the changes of his fortune, it was fixed once for all for every single Jew. This fixity rested on the fact that the Jew had his social position as a *Jew*, not as the individual bearer of certain objective contents. Every other citizen was the owner of a particular amount of property, and his tax followed its fluctuations. But the Jew as a taxpayer was, in the first place, a Jew, and thus his tax situation had an invariable element. This same position appears most strongly, of course, once even these individual characterizations (limited though they were by rigid invariance) are omitted, and all strangers pay an altogether equal head-tax.

In spite of being inorganically appended to it, the stranger is yet an organic member of the group. Its uniform life includes the specific conditions of this element. Only we do not know how to designate the peculiar unity of this position other than by saying that it is composed of certain measures of nearness and distance. Although some quantities of them characterize all relationships, a *special* proportion and reciprocal tension produce the particular, formal relation to the 'stranger.'

THE WEB OF GROUP AFFILIATIONS

Individualism and Multiple Group Affiliation

The modern pattern differs sharply from the concentric pattern of group-affiliations as far as a person's achievements are concerned. Today someone may belong, aside from his occupational position, to a scientific association, he may sit on a board of directors of a corporation and occupy an honorific position in the city government. Such a person will be more clearly determined sociologically, the less his participation in one group by itself enjoins upon him participation in another. He is determined sociologically in the sense that the groups 'intersect' in his person by virtue of his affiliation with them. Whether or not the fact that a person who performs several functions reveals a characteristic combination of his talents, a special breadth of activity depends not only on his participation in several offices and institutions but naturally on the extent of their division of labor. In this way, the objective structure of a society provides a frame work within which an individual's non-interchangeable and singular characteristics may develop and find expression depending on the greater or lesser possibilities which that structure allows.

In England, it was long customary to staff a number of quite different administrative bodies with the same personnel. Already in the Middle Ages one and the same person could be a circuit judge and a justice in Ireland, a member of the Treasury and a Baron of the Exchequer, a member of the King's court of justice and a Justice in Banco. As the same group of persons formed so many different official boards, it is apparent that none of these persons were especially characterized by the mere fact of their participation on these boards. The objective functions of each person could not be differentiated sufficiently under these circumstances. And, therefore, his performance of several functions could not be an essential rationale of his individuality, nor could a knowledge of these functions provide a sufficient clue in this respect.

The individual may add affiliations with new groups to the single affiliation which has hitherto influenced him in a pervasive and one-sided manner. The mere fact that he does so is sufficient, quite apart from the nature of the groups involved, to give him a stronger awareness of individuality in general, and at least to counteract the tendency of taking his initial group's affiliations for granted. For this reason, representatives of the groups with which an individual is affiliated, are already opposed to the mere formality of a new affiliation, even if the purpose of the latter does not involve any competition with the previous group affiliations.

In the twelfth and thirteenth centuries the frequent imperial prohibitions of alliances between German towns were probably designed to meet real dangers. But in the Frankish, and at first also in the German, empire it was much more a matter of abstract principle that the government and the Church were opposed to the guilds. This was a case of an association based on free choice [guilds], the principle of which permitted an unlimited increase of associations; such associations were necessarily rivals of the powers exercised by existing associations. The mere fact of multiple group-affiliations enabled the person to achieve for himself an individualized situation in which the groups had to be oriented towards the individual. In the earlier situation the individual was wholly absorbed by, and remained oriented toward, the group.

Opportunities for individualization proliferate into infinity also because the same person can occupy positions of different rank in the various groups to which he belongs. This is already important with regard to familial relationships. The dissolution of the primitive Germanic class-organization was furthered greatly because consideration was given to the relatives of the wife as well as to all in-law relations. Thus one could belong to different kinship-groups at the same time. The rights and duties of each of these groups conflicted with those of every other so effectively that it has been said that only relatives existed but no kinship-associations. However, this result would not have come about, indeed the entire situation could not have arisen to this extent, if the individual had occupied the same position with regard to each line of relatives. But the individual occupied a central position in one group of relatives, while his position was peripheral in another; he had an authoritative position in the one group, but in the other his position made him the equal of many other relatives. In one situation the individual's economic interests would be involved, in another his involvement would be significant only in a personal sense. The structure of these connections excluded the possibility that a second individual would occupy exactly the same position within the same context.

Under these conditions of unilateral kinship the individual would have been born into a fixed position. And the accent of importance remained ever on the position which dominated the individual because kinship unilaterally determined that position. On the other hand, if the relations between kinship groups were multilateral, then it was the individual who brought about the contact of one line of relatives with another. Within the family such positions and their individual combinations could arise by themselves, as it were.

But each new group-formation produces immediately, and in a more deliberate way than the family, a certain inequality, a differentiation between the leaders and the led. If, as in the case of the humanists mentioned above, a common interest established a bond between persons of high and of low status, then this made inoperative such differences as divided them otherwise. Yet, new differences between high and low arose within this community of scholars according to criteria that were germane to it but that were out of keeping with the criteria of high and low, which prevailed in the other groups with which the humanists were affiliated. In this manner the personality of each individual was determined, in a more characteristic and many-sided way than would be the case otherwise.

However, the same result can also be achieved, if equality prevails within a newly formed group, while its members occupy and retain positions of greatly varied rank in those groups with which they have been affiliated hitherto. Such a case is a highly significant sociological type in the sense that both the individual who ranks low in his original group and another who ranks high in his group, are now equals in a social sense. Medieval knighthood worked in this way, for example. Under its rules, the ministerial vassals of a Princely Court were members of an association of peers to which the prince, and even the emperor, belonged. All members of this association were equals in matters relating to the knighthood. This gave the ministerial vassal a position which had nothing to do with his duties of office, and rights which did not stem from his lord. The differences of birth between nobility, freemen, and vassals were not thereby eliminated. But these differences were 'intersected' by a new line of division which was established by the association of all those who were bound together as equals in accordance with the rights and customs of knighthood. To be sure this association did not establish a real community but one which was effective through a common ideal; but as such this community maintained *one* standard of judgment for all. Any person, although he was affiliated with groups in which he stood either high or low, was at the same time part of a group in which he was the 'equal' of every other. This was a combination of group-affiliation of a singular kind, which determined and enriched the vitality of the individual as a social being.

One and the same person may occupy positions of different rank in different groups. Since these positions are completely independent of one another, strange combinations of group-affiliations can arise. Thus, an intellectually and socially prominent man has to subordinate himself to a non-commissioned officer in countries with universal military training. Or take the beggar's guild in Paris which elects a 'king,' who was originally a beggar like all the others, and who, as far as I know, remains one, but who is given truly princely honors and privileges. This is perhaps the most remarkable and individualizing combination of low rank in one and high rank in another social position.

This overlapping may also take place within one and the same situation as soon as this includes a multiplicity of relationships – as for example in the case of the private tutor or even more so the earlier tutors of aristocratic youths. The tutor of princes is to be superior to his charge, he is to dominate and direct him – and yet he is, on the other hand, a servant, while his charge is the master. Another case: a corporal in Cromwell's army, who was well versed in the Bible, could deliver a moralizing sermon to his major, while he obeyed him without reservation in matters of military service. Finally, the content of these multiple relationships has decisive consequences for the individual the more they are a part of his personal life. There is, for example, the characteristic phenomenon of the aristocrat with liberal sentiments, of the man of the world who has distinctly religious tendencies, of the scholars, who seek their social contacts exclusively among men of affairs.

Multiple Group-Affiliations Within a Single Group

A typical example of multiple group-affiliations within a single group is the competition among persons who show their solidarity in other respects. On the one hand the merchant joins other merchants in a group which has a great number of common interests: legislation on issues of economic policy, the social prestige of business, representation of business-interests, joint action as over against the general public in order to maintain certain prices, and many others. All of these concern the world of commerce as such and make it appear to others as a unified group. On the other hand, each merchant is in competition with many others. To enter this occupation creates for him at one and the same time association and isolation, equalization and particularization. He pursues his interests by means of the most bitter competition with those with whom he must often unite closely for the sake of common interests. This inner contrast is probably most pronounced in the area of commerce, but it is present in some way in all other areas as well, down to the ephemeral socializing of an evening party.

An infinite range of individualizing combinations is made possible by the fact that the individual belongs to a multiplicity of groups, in which the relationship between competition and socialization varies greatly. It is a trivial observation that the instinctive needs of man prompt him to act in these mutually conflicting ways: he feels and acts *with* others but also *against* others. A certain measure of the one and the other, and a certain proportion between them, is a purely formal necessity for man, which he meets in the most manifold ways. Often this occurs in a manner, which makes an individual's action understandable not on the basis of its objective meanings, but on the basis of the satisfaction which it affords to the formal drives mentioned above. Individuality is characterized, both in regard to its natural striving and its historical development, by that proportion between socialization and competition which is decisive for it.

And the reverse tendency arises on the same basis: the individual's need for a clearer articulation and for a more unambiguous development of his personality, forces him to select certain groups. And from their combination he gains his maximum of individuality – the one group offering him opportunities for socialization, the other opportunities for competition. Thus, the members of a group in which keen competition prevails will gladly seek out such other groups as are lacking in competition as much as possible. As a result businessmen have a decided preference for social clubs. The estate-consciousness of the aristocrat, on the other hand, rather excludes competition within his own circle; hence, it makes supplementations of that sort (i.e., social clubs) largely superfluous. This suggests forms of socialization to the aristocrat which contain stronger competitive elements-for example, those clubs which are held together by a common interest in sports.

Finally, I shall mention here the frequent discrepancies which arise because an individual or a group are controlled by interests that are opposed to each other. This may permit individuals and groups to belong at the same time to parties which are opposed to each other. Individuals are likely to become affiliated with conflicting groups, if in a many-sided culture the political parties are intensely active. Under such conditions it usually happens that the political parties also represent the different viewpoints on those questions which have nothing at all to do with politics. Thus, a certain tendency in literature, art, religion, etc., is associated with one party, an opposite tendency with another. The dividing line which separates the parties is, thereby, extended throughout the entire range of human interests. Obviously, an individual who will not surrender completely to the dictates of the party, will join a group, say on the basis of his esthetic or religious convictions, which is amalgamated with his political enemies. He will be affiliated with two groups which regard each other as opponents.

Religion as a Factor in Multiple Group-Affiliations

Religious affiliation is the most important and at the same time the most characteristic example (of individualization) ever since religion has been emancipated from racial, national, or local ties, a world-historical fact of immeasurable significance. Either the religious community embraces the civic community in terms of its other essential or comprehensive interests, or the religious community is entirely free of all solidarity with whatever is *not* religion. The nature of religion is completely expressed in both of these sociological types, though in a different language or at another level of development in each case.

It is understandable that the co-existence and the sharing of human interests is not possible with people who do not share one's faith. The deeply justified need for unity was satisfied, *a priori* so to speak, in all of ancient civilization, in the Semitic as well as the Graeco-Roman world. Religion was made an affair of the tribe or the state. With a few exceptions, the deity was identified with the interests of the political group, and the duties toward Him were identical with the all-embracing duties toward the latter.

Yet the power of religious motivation is equally apparent, where it is independent of all social ties originating from other motives, and where it is strong enough to bring together believers adhering to the same creed, in spite of all the differences between them which arise out of their other affiliations. This form of religious organization is obviously a highly individualistic one. The religious temper has lost the support which it had obtained from its integration with the entire, complex of social ties. Now religious experience is based upon the soul of the individual and it is his responsibility; on that basis the individual seeks to establish a bond with others who are similarly qualified in terms of their religious experience, but perhaps in no other respect. Christianity in its pure sense is an entirely individualistic religion, and this has made possible its diffusion throughout the manifold of national and local groups.[3] The Christian was conscious of the fact that he took with him his church-affiliation into every community of his choosing, regardless of the psychological influences and the duties which such a community exerted and made incumbent upon him. This consciousness must have created a feeling of individual determination and self-confidence.

This sociological significance of religion reflects its dual relationship to life. On the one hand, religion stands in contrast to the whole substance of human life; it is the counterpart and the equivalent of life itself, aloof from its secular movements and interests. On the other hand, religion takes sides among the parties in the secular life, though it had elevated itself above the world of affairs as a matter of principle. As such religion is an element of secular life alongside all its other elements; it becomes involved in the multitude of changing relationships though at the same time it rejects this involvement. As a result a remarkable involution occurs. The disavowal of all social ties, which is evidence of a deep religiosity, allows the individual and his religious group to coming contact with any number of other groups with whose members they do not snare any common interests. And the relationships again serve to distinguish and to determine the individuals concerned as well as the religious groups.

This pattern is repeated in many specific religious situations and in the peculiar intertwining between the religious and the other interests of individuals. In the quarrels between France and Spain, the Huguenots placed themselves at one time at the service of the king, when the struggles turned against Catholic Spain and its friends in France. On another occasion, when they were oppressed by the king, they joined Spain directly. The cruel suppression of the Irish Catholics by England revealed a dual position of another type. One day the Protestants of England and Ireland would feel united against a common religious enemy without regard for their fellow countrymen; the next day the Protestants and Catholics of Ireland would be united against the suppressor of their common fatherland without consideration of religious differences. By way of contrast the European states intervened in Asia to defend Chinese or Turkish Christians; but this action seemed quite outrageous and incomprehensible to people like the Chinese, among whom the primitive identity of religious and political group-affiliation is still unbroken.

But where this unity has been broken as much as in Switzerland, the abstract nature of religion – which because of this abstract quality occupies a definite position in relation to all other interests – brings about immediately very characteristic patterns of group-affiliation. Because of the enormous differences between its cantons, Switzerland does not have a system of political parties such that politically like-minded people in the various cantons would divide themselves into major parties with regard to the national government. Only the *ultramontane people of all cantons*, (i.e., Catholics who follow the Papal authority in all questions of secular and ecclesiastical policy) form a joint group in political affairs.

One can assume without question that this emancipation of religious from political ties has also consequences in the opposite direction, in that it will make possible political mergers which would have been frustrated by the continuing unity of both. The most striking example is perhaps the union between Scotland and England in 1707. For both countries the advantages of becoming a *single* state were bound up with the continued existence of the two churches. Up to that time political and religious concepts had been closely interrelated in both countries. Only the separation of Church and State made the amalgamation of political interests between the two countries possible; otherwise the ecclesiastical interests would not have tolerated it. It was said of the two countries that they could preserve harmony only by agreeing to differ. Once this solution, together with its consequences for group-affiliation, had taken place, then it was no longer possible to abolish the freedom which had been gained. Hence the principle: *cuius regio eius religio*, is valid only if it does not need to be stated explicitly, but instead reflects the existence of a naive and undifferentiated condition in which Church and State are at one.

It is quite remarkable when the religious point of view overcomes all other bases of separation and amalgamates persons and interests despite their natural differentiation. Yet, this religious unity is thought of as quite parallel to those (other cases of organized solidarity) which arise merely on the basis of an objective differentiation. Thus in 1896 the Jewish workers of Manchester came together in an organization which was to include *all* categories of workers (mainly these were tailors, shoemakers, and bakers) and which intended to make common cause with the other trade unions in regard to the interests of labor. But the other trade unions were organized in accordance with the *objective* differences between types of work. This principle of organization was so important that the Trade Unions could not be induced to amalgamate with the International, because the latter was constituted without regard for the type of work in which its members were engaged. Although the case of the Jewish workers seems to go back to the undifferentiated community of interests in the religious as well as the social and economic sense, it reveals nevertheless the separation of these interests, at least on principle. The voluntary coordination of the Jewish workers with trade-unions organized on a purely objective basis [namely the division of labor] reveals that their organization was based on a practical purpose (rather than in accordance with religious belief).

The situation is manifestly different in the case of the Catholic trade unions of Germany, because of their great scope, because of the political significance of Catholicism in Germany, and because their religion does not place the Catholic workers in as conspicuous a position as the Jewish workers, (For example, in Germany the religious differentiation has produced special workers' associations within the general Catholic organizations. In Aachen a number of years ago, weavers, spinners, finishers, needlemakers, metal workers and construction workers were organized in this way.) Catholic organizations are large enough to allow for this division without involving an overlapping of group-affiliations such that each of these special associations would join with non-Catholic workers in the same trade. Still, this latter development has already occurred on occasion and that inner division is apparently the first step in this direction.

Notes

1. On pp. 500–502 of the same chapter from which the present '*Exkurs*' is taken (IX, '*Der Raum und die räumlichen Ordnungen der Gesellschaft,*' Space and the Spatial Organization of Society). The chapter itself is not included in this volume. – Tr.

2. But where the attacked make the assertion falsely, they do so from the tendency of those in higher position to exculpate inferiors, who, up to the rebellion, have been in a consistently close relation with them. For, by creating the fiction that the rebels were not really guilty, but only instigated, and that the rebellion did not really start with *them*, they exonerate themselves, inasmuch as they altogether deny all real grounds for the uprising.

3. In this respect Christianity is surpassed only by Buddhism in its original form, although Buddhism is not a religion in the real sense of that word, since it teaches that salvation can be won only in an absolutely personal way, without any transcendental meditation.

6 Ethnic Groups (1922)
Max Weber*

1 'RACE' MEMBERSHIP[1]*

A much more problematic source of social action than the sources analyzed above is 'race identity' common inherited and inheritable traits that actually derive from common descent. Of course, race creates a 'group' only when it is subjectively perceived as a common trait: this happens only when a neighborhood or the mere proximity of racially different persons is the basis of joint (mostly political) action, or conversely, when some common experiences of members of the same race are linked to some antagonism against members of an *obviously* different group. The resulting social action is usually merely negative: those who are obviously different are avoided and despised or, conversely, viewed with superstitious awe. Persons who are externally different are simply despised irrespective of what they accomplish or what they are, or they are venerated superstitiously if they are too powerful in the long run. In this case antipathy is the primary normal reaction. However, this antipathy is shared not just by persons with anthropological similarities, and its extent is by no means determined by the degree of anthropological relatedness; furthermore, this antipathy is linked not only to inherited traits but just as much to other visible differences.

If the degree of objective racial difference can be determined, among other things, purely physiologically by establishing whether hybrids reproduce themselves at approximately normal rates, the subjective aspects, the reciprocal racial attraction and repulsion, might be measured by finding out whether sexual relations are preferred or rare between two groups, and whether they are carried on permanently or temporarily and irregularly. In all groups with a developed 'ethnic' consciousness the existence or absence of intermarriage (*connubium*) would then be

* From Chapter V in Guenther Roth and Claus Wittich (eds), *Economy and Society* (Berkeley: University of California Press, 1978), pp. 385–98, originally published in 1922 but written before 1914.

a normal consequence of racial attraction or segregation. Serious research on the sexual attraction and repulsion between different ethnic groups is only incipient, but there is not the slightest doubt that racial factors, that means, common descent, influence the incidence of sexual relations and of marriage, sometimes decisively. However, the existence of several million mulattoes in the United States speaks clearly against the assumption of a 'natural' racial antipathy, even among quite different races. Apart from the laws against biracial marriages in the Southern states, sexual relations between the two races are now abhorred by both sides, but this development began only with the Emancipation and resulted from the Negroes' demand for equal civil rights. Hence this abhorrence on the part of the Whites is socially determined by the previously sketched tendency toward the monopolization of social power and honor, a tendency which in this case happens to be linked to race.

The *connubium* itself, that means, the fact that the offspring from a permanent sexual relationship can share in the activities and advantages of the father's political, economic or status group, depends on many circumstances. Under undiminished patriarchal powers, which we treat elsewhere, the father was free to grant equal rights to his children from slaves. Moreover, the glorification of abduction by the hero made racial mixing a normal event within the ruling strata. However, patriarchal discretion was progressively curtailed with the monopolistic closure, by now familiar to us, of political, status or other groups and with the monopolization of marriage opportunities; these tendencies restricted the *connubium* to the offspring from a permanent sexual union within the given political, religious, economic and status group. This also produced a high incidence of inbreeding. The 'endogamy' of a group is probably everywhere a secondary product of such tendencies, if we define it not merely as the fact that a permanent sexual union occurs primarily on the basis of joint membership in some association, but as a process of social action in which only endogamous children are accepted as full members. (The term 'sib endogamy' should not be used; there is no such thing unless we want to refer to the levirate marriage and arrangements in which daughters have the right to succession, but these have secondary, religious and political origins.) 'Pure' anthropological types are often a secondary consequence of such closure; examples are sects (as in India) as well as pariah peoples, that means, groups that are socially despised yet wanted as neighbors because they have monopolized indispensable skills.

Reasons other than actual racial kinship influence the degree to which blood relationship is taken into account. In the United States the smallest admixture of Negro blood disqualifies a person unconditionally, whereas very considerable admixtures of Indian blood do not. Doubtlessly, it is important that Negroes appear esthetically even more alien than Indians but it remains very significant that Negroes were slaves and hence disqualified in the status hierarchy. The conventional *connubium* is far less impeded by anthropological differences than by status differences, that means, differences due to socialization and upbringing (*Bildung* in the widest sense of the word). Mere anthropological differences account for little, except in cases of extreme esthetic antipathy.

2   THE BELIEF IN COMMON ETHNICITY: ITS MULTIPLE SOCIAL ORIGINS AND THEORETICAL AMBIGUITIES

The question of whether conspicuous 'racial' differences are based on biological heredity or on tradition is usually of no importance as far as their effect on mutual attraction or repulsion is concerned. This is true of the development of endogamous conjugal groups, and even more so of attraction and repulsion in other kinds of social intercourse, i.e., whether all sorts of friendly, companionable, or economic relationships between such groups are established easily and on the footing of mutual trust and respect, or whether such relationships are established with difficulty a with precautions that betray mistrust.

The more or less easy emergence of social circles in the broadest sense of the word (*soziale Verkehrsgemeinschaft*) may be linked to the most superficial features of historically accidental habits just as much as to inherited racial characteristics. That the different custom is not understood in its subjective meaning since the cultural key to it is lacking, is almost as decisive as the peculiarity of the custom as such. But, as we shall soon see, not all repulsion is attributable to the absence of a 'consensual group.' Differences in the styles of beard and hairdo, clothes, food and eating habits, division of labor between the sexes, and all kinds of other visible differences can, in a given case, give rise to repulsion and contempt, but the actual extent of these differences is irrelevant for the emotional impact, as is illustrated by primitive travel descriptions, the Histories of Herodotus or the older prescientific ethnography. Seen from their positive aspect, however, these differences may give rise to consciousness of kind, which may become as easily the bearer of group relationships as groups ranging from the household and neighborhood to political and religious communities are usually the bearers of shared customs. All differences of customs can sustain a specific sense of honor or dignity in their practitioners. The original motives or reasons for the inception of different habits of life are forgotten and the contrasts are then perpetuated as conventions. In this manner, any group can create customs, and it can also effect, in certain circumstances very decisively, the selection of anthropological types. This it can do by providing favorable chances of survival and reproduction for certain hereditary qualities and traits. This holds both for internal assimilation and for external differentiation.

Any cultural trait, no matter how superficial, can serve as a starting point for the familiar tendency to monopolistic closure. However, the universal force of imitation has the general effect of only gradually changing the traditional customs and usages, just as anthropological types are changed only gradually by racial mixing. But if there are sharp boundaries between areas of observable styles of life, they are due to conscious monopolistic closure, which started from small differences that were then cultivated and intensified; or they are due to the peaceful or warlike migrations of groups that previously lived far from each other and had accommodated themselves to their heterogeneous conditions of existence. Similarly, strikingly different racial types, bred in isolation, may live in sharply segregated proximity to one another either because of monopolistic closure or because of migration. We can conclude then that similarity and contrast of physical type and custom, regardless of whether they are biologically inherited or culturally transmitted, are subject to the same conditions of group life, in origin as well as in effectiveness, and identical in their potential for group formation. The difference lies partly in the differential instability of type and custom, partly in the fixed (though often unknown) limit to engendering new hereditary qualities. Compared to this, the scope for assimilation of new customs is incomparably greater, although there are considerable variations in the transmissibility of traditions.

Almost any kind of similarity or contrast of physical type and of habits can induce the belief that affinity or disaffinity exists between groups that attract or repel each other. Not every belief in tribal affinity, however, is founded on the resemblance of customs or of physical type. But in spite of great variations in this area, such a belief can exist and can develop group-forming powers when it is buttressed by a memory of an actual migration, be it colonization or individual migration. The persistent effect of the old ways and of childhood reminiscences continues as a source of native-country sentiment (*Heimatsgefühl*) among emigrants even when they have become so thoroughly adjusted to the new country that return to their homeland would be intolerable (this being the case of most German-Americans, for example).

In colonies, the attachment to the colonists' homeland survives despite considerable mixing with the inhabitants of the colonial land and despite profound changes in tradition and hereditary type as well. In case of political colonization, the decisive factor is the need for political support. In general, the continuation of relationships created by marriage is important, and so are the market relationships, provided that the 'customs' remained unchanged. These market relationships between the homeland and the colony may be very close, as long as the consumer standards remain similar, and especially when colonies are in an almost absolutely alien environment and within an alien political territory.

The belief in group affinity, regardless of whether it has any objective foundation, can have important consequences especially for the formation of a political community. We shall call 'ethnic groups' those human groups that entertain a subjective belief in their common descent because of similarities of physical type or of customs or both, or because of memories of colonization and migration; this belief must be important for the propagation of group formation; conversely, it does not matter whether or not an objective blood relationship exists. Ethnic membership (*Gemeinsamkeit*) differs from the kinship group precisely by being a presumed identity, not a group with concrete social action, like the latter. In our sense, ethnic membership does not constitute a group; it only facilitates group formation of any kind, particularly in the political sphere. On the other hand, it is primarily the political community, no matter how artificially organized, that inspires the belief in common ethnicity. This belief tends to persist even after the disintegration of the political community, unless drastic differences in the custom, physical type, or, above all, language exist among its members.

This artificial origin of the belief in common ethnicity follows the previously described pattern [. . .] of rational association turning into personal relationships. If rationally regulated action is not widespread, almost any association, even the most rational one, creates an overarching communal consciousness; this takes the form of a brotherhood on the basis of the belief in common ethnicity. As late as the Greek city state, even the most arbitrary division of the polis became for the member an association with at least a common cult and often a common fictitious ancestor. The twelve tribes of Israel were subdivisions of a political community, and they alternated in performing certain functions on a monthly basis. The same holds for the Greek tribes (*phylai*) and their subdivisions; the latter, too, were regarded as units of common ethnic descent. It is true that the original division may have been induced by political or actual ethnic differences, but the effect was the same when such a division was made quite rationally and schematically, after the break-up of old groups and relinquishment of local cohesion, as it was done by Cleisthenes. It does not follow, therefore, that the Greek polis was actually or originally a tribal or lineage state, but that ethnic fictions were a sign of the rather low degree of rationalization of Greek political life. Conversely, it is a symptom of the greater rationalization of Rome that its old schematic subdivisions (*curiae*) took on religious importance, with a pretense to ethnic origin, to only a small degree.

The belief in common ethnicity often delimits 'social circles,' which in turn are not always identical with endogamous connubial groups, for greatly varying numbers of persons may be encompassed by both. Their similarity rests on the belief in a specific 'honor' of their members, not shared by the outsiders, that is, the sense of 'ethnic honor' (a phenomenon closely related to status honor, which will be discussed later). These few remarks must suffice at this point. A specialized sociological study of ethnicity would have to make a finer distinction between these concepts than we have done for our limited purposes.

Groups, in turn, can engender sentiments of likeness which will persist even after their demise and will have an 'ethnic' connotation. The political community in particular can produce such an effect. But most directly, such an effect is created by the *language group*, which is the bearer of a specific 'cultural possession of the masses' (*Massenkulturgut*) and makes mutual understanding (*Verstehen*) possible or easier.

Wherever the memory of the origin of a community by peaceful secession or emigration ('colony,' *ver sacrum*, and the like) from a mother community remains for some reason alive, there undoubtedly exists a very specific and often extremely powerful sense of ethnic identity, which is determined by several factors: shared political memories or, even more importantly in early times, persistent ties with the old cult, or the strengthening of kinship and other groups, both in the old and the new community, or other persistent relationships. Where these ties are lacking, or once they cease to exist, the sense of ethnic group membership is absent, regardless of how close the kinship may be.

Apart from the community of language, which may or may not coincide with objective, or subjectively believed, consanguinity, and apart from common religious belief, which is also independent of consanguinity, the ethnic differences that remain are, on the one hand, esthetically conspicuous differences of the physical appearance (as mentioned before) and, on the other hand and of equal weight, the perceptible differences in the *conduct of everyday life*. Of special importance are precisely those items which may otherwise seem to be of small social relevance, since when ethnic differentiation is concerned it is always the conspicuous differences that come into play.

Common language and the ritual regulation of life, as determined by shared religious beliefs, everywhere are conducive to feelings of ethnic affinity, especially since the intelligibility of the behavior of others is the most fundamental presupposition of group formation. But since we shall not consider these two elements in the present context, we ask: what is it that remains? It must be admitted that palpable differences in dialect and differences of religion in themselves do not exclude sentiments of common ethnicity. Next to pronounced differences in the economic way of life, the belief in ethnic affinity has at all times been affected by outward differences in clothes, in the style of housing, food and eating habits, the division of labor between the sexes and between the free and the unfree. That is to say, these things concern one's conception of what is correct and proper and, above all, of what affects the individual's sense of honor and dignity. All those things we shall find later on as objects of specific differences between status groups. The conviction of the excellence of ones own customs and the inferiority of alien ones, a conviction which sustains the sense of ethnic honor, is actually quite analogous to the sense of honor of distinctive status groups.

The sense of ethnic honor is a specific honor of the masses (*Massenehre*), for it is accessible to anybody who belongs to the subjectively believed community of descent. The 'poor white trash,' i.e., the propertyless and, in the absence of job opportunities, very often destitute white inhabitants of the southern states of the United States of America in the period of slavery, were the actual bearers of racial antipathy, which was quite foreign to the planters. This was so because the social honor of the 'poor whites' was dependent upon the social *déclassement* of the Negroes.

And behind all ethnic diversities there is somehow naturally the notion of the 'chosen people,' which is merely a counterpart of status differentiation translated into the plane of horizontal co-existence. The idea of a chosen people derives its popularity from the fact that it can be claimed to an equal degree by any and every member of the mutually despising groups, in contrast to status differentiation which always rests on subordination. Consequently, ethnic repulsion may take hold of all conceivable differences among the notions of propriety and transform them into 'ethnic conventions.'

Besides the previously mentioned elements, which were still more or less closely related to the economic order, conventionalization (a term expounded elsewhere) may take hold of such things as a hairdo or style of beard and the like. The differences thereof have an 'ethnically' repulsive effect, because they are thought of as symbols of ethnic membership. Of course, the repulsion is not always based merely on the 'symbolic' character of the distinguishing traits. The fact that the Scythian women oiled their hair with butter, which then gave off a rancid odor, while Greek women used perfumed oil to achieve the same purpose, thwarted – according to an ancient report – all attempts at social intercourse between the aristocratic ladies of these two groups. The smell of butter certainly had a more compelling effect than even the most prominent racial differences, or – as far as I could see – the 'Negro odor,' of which so many fables are told. In general, racial qualities are effective only as limiting factors with regard to the belief in common ethnicity, such as in case of an excessively heterogeneous and esthetically unaccepted physical type; they are not positively group-forming.

Pronounced differences of custom, which play a role equal to that of inherited physical type in the creation of feelings of common ethnicity and notions of kinship, are usually caused, in addition to linguistic and religious differences, by the diverse economic and political conditions of various social groups. If we ignore cases of clear-cut linguistic boundaries and sharply demarcated political or religious communities as a basis of differences of custom – and these in fact are lacking in wide areas of the African and South American continents – then there are only gradual transitions of custom and no immutable ethnic frontiers, except those due to gross geographical differences. The sharp demarcations of areas wherein ethnically relevant customs predominate, which were not conditioned either by political or economic or religious factors, usually came into existence by way of migration or expansion, when groups of people that had previously lived in complete or partial isolation from each other and became accommodated to heterogeneous conditions of existence came to live side by side. As a result, the obvious contrast usually evokes, on both sides, the idea of blood disaffinity (*Blutsfremdheit*), regardless of the objective state of affairs.

It is understandably difficult to determine in general – and even in a concrete individual case – what influence specific ethnic factors (i.e., the belief in a blood relationship, or its opposite, which rests on similarities, or differences, of a person's physical appearance and style of life) have on the formation of a group.

There is no difference between the ethnically relevant customs and customs in general, as far as their effect is concerned. The belief in common descent, in combination with a similarity of customs, is likely to promote the spread of the activities of one part of an ethnic group among the rest, since the awareness of ethnic identity furthers imitation. This is especially true of the propaganda of religious groups.

It is not feasible to go beyond these vague generalizations. The content of joint activities that are possible on an ethnic basis remains indefinite. There is a corresponding ambiguity of concepts denoting ethnically determined action, that means, determined by the belief in blood relationship. Such concepts are *Völkerschaft, Stamm* (tribe), *Volk* (people), each of which is ordinarily used in the sense of an ethnic subdivision of the following one (although the first two may be used in reversed order). Using such terms, one usually implies either the existence of a contemporary political community, no matter how loosely organized, or memories of an extinct political community, such as they are preserved in epic tales and legends; or the existence of a linguistic or dialect group; or, finally, of a religious group. In the past, cults in particular were the typical concomitant of a tribal or *Volk* consciousness. But in the absence of the political community, contemporary or past, the external delimitation of the group was usually indistinct. The cult communities of Germanic tribes, as late as the Burgundian period (6th century A.D.), were probably rudiments of political communities and therefore pretty well defined. By contrast, the Delphian oracle, the undoubted cultic symbol of Hellenism, also revealed information to the barbarians and accepted their veneration, and it was an organized cult only among some Greek segments, excluding the most powerful cities. The cult as an exponent of ethnic identity is thus generally either a remnant of a largely political community which once existed but was destroyed by disunion and colonization, or it is – as in the case of the Delphian Apollo – a product of a *Kulturgemeinschaft* brought about by other than purely ethnic conditions, but which in turn gives rise to the belief in blood relationship. All history shows how easily political action can give rise to the belief in blood relationship, unless gross differences of anthropological type impede it.

3 TRIBE AND POLITICAL COMMUNITY: THE DISUTILITY OF THE NOTION OF 'ETHNIC GROUP'

The tribe is clearly delimited when it is a subdivision of a polity, which, in fact, often establishes it. In this case, the artificial origin is revealed by the round numbers in which tribes usually appear, for example, the previously mentioned division of the people of Israel into twelve tribes, the three Doric *phylai* and the various *phylai* of the other Hellenes. When a political community was newly established or reorganized, the population was newly divided. Hence the tribe is here a political artifact, even though it soon adopts the whole symbolism of blood-relationship and particularly a tribal cult. Even today it is not rare that political artifacts develop a sense of affinity akin to that of blood relationship. Very schematic constructs such as those states of the United States that were made into squares according to their latitude have a strong sense of identity; it is also not rare that families travel from New York to Richmond to make an expected child a 'Virginian.'

Such artificiality does not preclude the possibility that the Hellenic *phylai*, for example, were at one time independent and that the polis used them schematically when they were merged into a political association. However, tribes that existed before the *polis* were either identical with the corresponding political groups which were subsequently associated into a *polis*, and in this case they were called *ethnos*, not *phyle*; or, as it probably happened many times, the politically unorganized tribe, as a presumed 'blood community,' lived from the memory that it once engaged in joint political action, typically a single conquest or defense, and then such political memories constituted the tribe. Thus, the fact that tribal consciousness was primarily formed by common political experiences and not by common descent appears to have been a frequent source of the belief in common ethnicity.

Of course, this was not the only source: Common customs may have diverse origins. Ultimately, they derive largely from adaptation to natural conditions and the imitation of neighbors. In practice, however, tribal consciousness usually has a political meaning: in case of military danger or opportunity, it easily provides the basis for joint political action on the part of tribal members or *Volksgenossen* who consider one another as blood relatives. The eruption of a drive to political action is thus one of the major potentialities inherent in the rather ambiguous notions of tribe and people. Such intermittent political action may easily develop into the moral duty of all members of tribe or people (*Volk*) to support one another in case of a military attack, even if there is no corresponding political association, violators of this solidarity may suffer the fate of the (Germanic, pro-Roman) sibs of Segestes and Inguiomer – expulsion from the tribal territory –, even if the tribe has no organized government. If the tribe has reached this stage, it has indeed become a continuous political community, no matter how inactive in peacetime, and hence unstable, it may be. However, even under favorable conditions the transition from the habitual to the customary and therefore obligatory is very fluid. All in all, the notion of 'ethnically' determined social action subjective phenomena that a rigorous sociological analysis – as we do not attempt it here – would have to distinguish carefully: the actual subjective effect of those customs conditioned by heredity and those determined by tradition; the differential impact of the varying content of custom; the influence of common language, religion and political action, past and present, upon the formation of customs; the extent to which such factors create attraction and repulsion, and especially the belief in affinity or disaffinity of blood; the consequences of this belief for social action in general, and specifically for action on the basis of shared custom or blood relationship, for diverse sexual relations, etc. – all of this would have to be studied in detail. It is certain that in this process the collective term 'ethnic' would be abandoned, for it is unsuitable for a really rigorous analysis. However, we do not pursue sociology for its own sake and therefore limit ourselves to showing briefly the diverse factors that are hidden behind this seemingly uniform phenomenon.

The concept of the 'ethnic' group, which dissolves if we define our terms exactly, corresponds in this regard to one of the most vexing, since emotionally charged concepts: the *nation*, as soon as we attempt a sociological definition.

4   NATIONALITY AND CULTURAL PRESTIGE[2]

The concept of 'nationality' shares with that of the 'people' (*Volk*) – in the 'ethnic' sense – the vague connotation that whatever is felt to be distinctively common must derive from common descent. In reality, of course, persons who consider themselves members of the same nationality are often much less related by common descent than are persons belonging to different and hostile nationalities. Differences of nationality may exist even among groups closely related by common descent, merely because they have different religious persuasions, as in the case of Serbs and Croats. The concrete reasons for the belief in joint nationality and for the resulting social action vary greatly.

Today, in the age of language conflicts, a shared common language is pre-eminently considered the normal basis of nationality. Whatever the 'nation' means beyond a mere 'language group' can be found in the specific objective of its social action, and this can only be the *autonomous polity*. Indeed, 'nation state' has become conceptually identical with 'state' based on common language. In reality, however, such modern nation states exist next to many others that comprise several language groups, even though these others usually have one official language. A common language is also insufficient in sustaining a sense of national identity (*Nationalgefühl*) – a concept which we will leave undefined for the present. Aside from the examples of the Serbs and Croats, this is demonstrated by the Irish, the Swiss and the German-speaking Alsatians; these groups do not consider themselves as members, at least not as full members, of the 'nation' associated with their language. Conversely, language differences do not necessarily preclude a sense of joint nationality: The German-speaking Alsatians considered themselves – and most of them still do – as part of the French 'nation,' even though not in the same sense as French-speaking nationals. Hence there are qualitative degrees of the belief in common nationality.

Many German-speaking Alsatians feel a sense of community with the French because they share certain customs and some of their 'sensual culture' (*Sinnenkultur*) – as Wittich in particular has pointed out – and also because of common political experiences. This can be understood by any visitor who walks through the museum in Colmar, which is rich in relics such as tricolors, *pompier* and military helmets, edicts by Louis Philippe and especially memorabilia from the French Revolution; these may appear trivial to the outsider, but they have sentimental value for the Alsatians.[3] This sense of community came into being by virtue of common political and, indirectly, social experiences which are highly valued by the masses as symbols of the destruction of feudalism, and the story of these events takes the place of the heroic legends of primitive peoples. *La grande nation* was the liberator from feudal servitude, she was the bearer of civilization (*Kultur*), her language was *the* civilized language; German appeared as a dialect suitable for everyday communication. Hence the attachment to those who speak the language of civilization is an obvious parallel to the sense of community based on common language, but the two phenomena are not identical; rather, we deal here with an attitude that derives from a partial sharing of the same culture and from shared political experiences.

Until a short time ago most Poles in Upper Silesia had no strongly developed sense of Polish nationality that was antagonistic to the Prussian state, which is based essentially on the German language. The Poles were loyal if passive 'Prussians,' but they were not 'Germans' interested in the existence of the *Reich*; the majority did not feel a conscious or a strong need to segregate themselves from German-speaking fellow-citizens. Hence, in this case there was no sense of nationality based on common language, and there was no *Kulturgemeinschaft* in view of the lack of cultural development.

Among the Baltic Germans we find neither much of a sense of nationality amounting to a high valuation of the language bonds with the' Germans, nor a desire for political union with the *Reich*; in fact, most of them would abhor such a unification. However, they segregate themselves rigorously from the Slavic environment, and especially from the Russians, primarily because of status considerations and partly because both sides have different customs and cultural values which are mutually unintelligible and disdained. This segregation exists in spite of, and partly because of, the fact that the Baltic Germans are intensely loyal vassals of the Tsar and have been as interested as any 'national' Russian (*Nationalrusse*) in the predominance of the Imperial Russian system, which they provide with officials and which in turn maintains their descendants. Hence, here too we do not find any sense of nationality in the modern meaning of the term (oriented toward a common language and culture). The case is similar to that of the purely proletarian Poles: loyalty toward the state is combined with a sense of group identity that is limited to a common language group within this larger community and strongly modified by status factors. Of course, the Baltic Germans are no longer a cohesive status group, even though the differences are not as extreme as within the white population of the American South.

Finally, there are cases for which the term nationality does not seem to be quite fitting; witness the sense of identity shared by the Swiss and the Belgians or the inhabitants of Luxemburg and Liechtenstein. We hesitate to call them 'nations,' not because of their relative smallness – the Dutch appear to us as a nation – but because these neutralized states have purposively forsaken power. The Swiss are not a nation if we take as criteria common language or common literature and art. Yet they have a strong sense of community despite some recent disintegrative tendencies. This sense of identity is not only sustained by loyalty toward the body politic but also by what are perceived to be common customs (irrespective of actual differences). These customs are largely shaped by the differences in social structure between Switzerland and Germany, but also all other big and hence militaristic powers. Because of the impact of bigness on the internal power structure, it appears to the Swiss that their customs can be preserved only by a separate political existence.

The loyalty of the French Canadians toward the English polity is today determined above all by the deep antipathy against the economic and social structure, and the way of life, of the neighboring United States; hence membership in the Dominion of Canada appears as a guarantee of their own traditions.

This classification could easily be enlarged, as every rigorous sociological investigation would have to do. It turns out that feelings of identity subsumed under the term 'national' are not uniform but may derive from diverse sources: Differences in the economic and social structure and in the internal power structure, with its impact on the customs, may play a role, but within the German *Reich* customs are very diverse; shared political memories, religion, language and, finally, racial features may be source of the sense of nationality. Racial factors often have a peculiar impact. From the viewpoint of the Whites in the United States, Negroes and Whites are not united by a common sense of nationality, but the Negroes have a sense of American nationality at least by claiming a right to it. On the other hand, the pride of the Swiss in their own distinctiveness, and their willingness to defend it vigorously, is neither qualitatively different nor less widespread than the same attitudes in any 'great' and powerful 'nation.' Time and again we find that the concept 'nation' directs us to political power. Hence, the concept seems to refer – if it refers at all to a uniform phenomenon – to a specific kind of pathos which is linked to the idea of a powerful political community of people who share a common language, or religion, or common customs, or political memories; such a state may already exist or it may be desired. The more power is emphasized, the closer appears to be the link between nation and state. This pathetic pride in the power of one's own community, or this longing for it, may be much more widespread in relatively small language groups such as the Hungarians, Czechs or Greeks than in a similar but much larger community such as the Germans 150 years ago, when they were essentially a language group without pretensions to national power.

Notes

1. On race and civilization, see also Weber's polemical speech against A. Ploetz at the first meeting of the German Sociological Association, Frankfurt, 1910, in *GAzSS*, 456–62. Two years later, at the second meeting of the Association in Berlin, Weber took the floor again after a presentation by Franz Oppenheimer. Among other things, Weber said (*op. cit.*, 489):

   > With race theories you can prove and disprove anything you want. It is a scientific crime to attempt the circumvention, by the uncritical use of completely unclarified racial hypotheses, of the sociological study of Antiquity, which of course is much more difficult, but by no means without hope of success; after all, we can no longer find out to what extent the qualities of the Hellenes and Romans rested on inherited dispositions. The problem of such relationships has not yet been solved by the most careful and toilsome investigations of living subjects, even if undertaken in the laboratory and with the means of exact experimentation.

2. Cf. the related section on 'The Nation' in ch. IX: 5 of Roth and Wiltich (eds), *Economy and Society* (Berkeley 1978).
3. See Werner Wittich, *Deutsche und französische Kultur im Elsass* (Strassburg: Schlesier und Schweikhardt, 1900), 38ff; for a French transl., see 'Le génie national des races française et allemande en Alsace.' *Revue internationale de Sociologie*, vol. X, 1902, 777–824 and 857–907, esp. 814ff. Cf. also Weber, *GAzRS*, I, 25, n. 1; *GAzSS*, 484. 'Outsiders,' in contrast to the pre-1914 custodian who showed Weber his greatest treasures, cherish the Colmar museum for one of the most powerful works of art of the late Middle Ages, Grünewald's 'Isenheim Altar.'

7 Democracy versus the Melting-Pot: A Study of American Nationality (1915)

Horace M. Kallen*

PART ONE

It was, I think, an eminent lawyer who, backed by a ripe experience of inequalities before the law, pronounced our Declaration of Independence to be a collection of 'glittering generalities.' Yet it cannot be that the implied slur was deserved. There is hardly room to doubt that the equally eminent gentlemen over whose signatures this orotund synthesis of the social and political philosophy of the eighteenth century appears conceived that they were subscribing to anything but the dull and sober truth when they underwrote the doctrine that God had created all men equal and had endowed them with certain inalienable rights, among these being life, liberty, and the pursuit of happiness. That this doctrine did not describe a condition, that it even contradicted conditions, that many of the signatories owned other men and bought and sold them, that many were eminent by birth, many by wealth, and only a few by merit – all this is acknowledged. Indeed, they were aware of these inequalities; they would probably have fought their abolition. But they did not regard them as incompatible with the Declaration of Independence. For to them the Declaration was neither a pronouncement of abstract principles nor an exercise in formal logic. It was an instrument in a political and economic conflict, a weapon of offence and defence. The doctrine of 'natural rights' which is its essence was formulated to shield social orders against tho aggrandizement of persons acting under the doctrine of 'divine right': its function was to afford sanction for refusing customary obedience to traditional superiority. Such also was the function of the Declaration. Across the

---

* From *The Nation*, 100 (2590) (February 18 1915), pp. 190–4; 100 (2591) (February 25 1915), pp. 217–20.

water, in England, certain powers had laid claim to the acknowledgment of their traditional superiority to the colonists in America. Whereupon the colonists, through their representatives, the signatories to the Declaration, replied that they were quite as good as their traditional betters, and that no one should take from them certain possessions which were theirs.

To-day the descendants of the colonists are reformulating a declaration of independence. Again, as in 1776, Americans of British ancestry find that certain possessions of theirs, which may be lumped under the word 'Americanism,' are in jeopardy. This is the situation which Mr. Ross's book,[1] in common with many others, describes. The danger comes once more, from a force across the water, but the force is this time regarded not as superior, but as inferior. The relationships of 1776 are, consequently, reversed. To conserve the inalienable rights of the colonists of 1776, it was necessary to declare all men equal; to conserve the inalienable rights of their descendants in 1914, it becomes necessary to declare all men unequal. In 1776 all men were as good as their betters; in 1914 men are permanently worse than their betters. 'A nation may reason,' writes Mr. Ross, 'why burden ourselves with the rearing of children? Let them perish unborn in the womb of time. The immigrants will keep up the population. A people that has no more respect for its ancestors and no more pride of race than this deserves the extinction that surely awaits it.'

I

Respect for ancestors, pride of race! Time was when these would have been repudiated as the enemies of democracy, as the antithesis of the fundamentals of our republic, with its belief that 'a man's a man for a' that.' And now they are being invoked in defence of democracy, against the 'melting-pot,' by a sociological protagonist of the 'democratic idea'! How conscious their invocation is cannot be said. But that they have unconsciously colored much of the social and political thinking of this country from the days of the Cincinnati on, seems to me unquestionable, and even more unquestionable that this apparently sudden and explicit conscious expression of them is the effect of an actual, felt menace. Mr. Ross, in a word, is no voice crying in a wilderness. He simply utters aloud and in his own peculiar manner what is felt and spoken wherever Americans of British ancestry congregate thoughtfully. He is the most recent phase of the operation of these forces in the social and economic history of the United States; a voice and instrument of theirs. Being so, he has neither taken account of them nor observed them, but has reacted in terms of them to the social situation which constitutes the theme of his book. The reaction is secondary, the situation is secondary. The standards alone are really primary and, perhaps, ultimate. Fully to understand the place and function of 'the old world in the new,' and the attitude of the 'new world' towards the old, demands an appreciation of the influence of these primary and ultimate standards upon all the peoples who are citizens of the country.

II

In 1776 the mass of white men in the colonies *were* actually, with respect to one another, rather free and rather equal. I refer, not so much to the absence of great differences in wealth, as to the fact that the whites were *like-minded*. They were possessed of ethnic and cultural unity; they were homogeneous with respect to ancestry and ideals. Their century-and-a-half-old tradition as Americans was continuous with their immemorially older tradition as Britons. They did not, until the economic-political quarrel with the mother country arose, regard themselves as other than Englishmen, sharing England's dangers and England's glories. When the quarrel came they remembered how they have left the mother country in search of religious liberty for themselves; how they had left Holland, where they had found this liberty, for fear of losing their ethnic and cultural identity, and what hardships they had borne for the sake of conserving both the liberty and the identity. Upon these they grafted that political liberty the love of which was innate, perhaps, but the expression of which was occasioned by the economic warfare with the merchants of England. This grafting was not, of course, conscious. The continuity established itself rather as a mood than as an articulate idea. The economic situation *was* only an occasion, and not a cause. The cause lay in the homogeneity of the people, their *like-mindedness*, and in their *self-consciousness*.

Now, it happens that the preservation and development of any given type of civilization rests upon these two conditions – like-mindedness and self-consciousness. Without them art, literature – culture in any of its nobler forms – is impossible: and colonial America had a culture – chiefly of New England – but representative enough of the whole British–American life of the period. Within the area of what we now call the United States this life was not, however, the only life. Similarly animated groups of Frenchmen and Germans, in Louisiana and in

Pennsylvania, regarded themselves as the cultural peers of the British, and because of their own common ancestry, their like-mindedness and self-consciousness, they have retained a large measure of their individuality and spiritual autonomy to this day, after generations of unrestricted and mobile contact and a century of political union with the dominant British populations.

In the course of time the state, which began to be with the Declaration of Independence, became possessed of all the United States. French and Germans in Louisiana and Pennsylvania remained at home; but the descendants of the British colonists trekked across the continent, leaving tiny self-conscious nuclei of population in their wake, and so established ethnic and cultural standards for the whole country. Had the increase of these settlements borne the same proportion to the unit of population that it bore between 1810 and 1820, the Americans of British stock would have numbered today over 100,000,000. The inhabitants of the country do number over 100,000,000; but they are not the children of the colonists and pioneers: they are immigrants and the children of immigrants, and they are not British, but of all the other European stocks.

First came the Irish, integral to the polity of Great Britain, but ethnically different, Catholic in religion, fleeing from economic and political oppression, and self-conscious and rebellious. They came seeking food and freedom, and revenge against the oppressors on the other side. Their area of settlement is chiefly the East. There they were not met with open arms. Historically only semi-alien, their appearance aroused, none the less, both fear and active opposition. Their diversity in religion was outstanding, their gregarious politics disturbing. Opposition, organized, religious, political, and social, stimulated their natural gregariousness into action. They organized, in their turn, religiously and politically. Slowly they made their way, slowly they came to power, establishing themselves in many modes as potent forces in the life of America. Mr. Ross thinks that they have their virtue still to prove; how he does not say. To the common-sense of the country they constitute an approved ethnic unity of the white American population.

Behind the Irish came the great mass of the Germans, quite diverse in speech and customs, culturally and economically far better off than the Irish, and self-conscious, as well through oppression and political aspiration as for these other reasons. They settled inland, over a stretch of relatively continuous territory extending from western New York to the Mississippi, from Buffalo to Minneapolis, and from Minneapolis to St. Louis. Spiritually, these Germans were more akin to the American settlers than the Irish, and, indeed, although social misprision pursued them also, they were less coldly received and with less difficulty tolerated. As they made their way, greater and greater numbers of the peasant stock joined them in the Western nuclei of population, so that between the Great Lakes and the Mississippi Valley they constitute the dominant ethnic type.

Beyond them, in Minnesota, their near neighbors, the Scandinavians, prevail, and beyond these, in the mountain and mining regions, the central and eastern and southern Europeans – Slavs of various stocks, Magyars, Finns, Italians. Beyond the Rockies, cut off from the rest of the country by this natural barrier, a stratum of Americans of British ancestry balances the thinnish stratum on the Atlantic sea-coast; flanked on the south by Latins and scattering groups of Asiatics, and on the north by Scandinavians. The distribution of the population upon the two coasts is not dissimilar; that upon the Atlantic littoral is only less homogeneous. There French-Canadians, Irish, Italians, Slavs, and Jews alternate with the American population and each other, while in the West the Americans lie between and surround the Italians, Asiatics, Germans, and Scandinavians.

Now, of all these immigrant peoples the greater part are peasants, vastly illiterate, living their lives at fighting weight, a minimum of food and a maximum of toil. Mr. Ross thinks that their coming to America was determined by no spiritual urge; only the urge of steamship agencies and economic need or greed. However generally true this opinion may be, he ignores, curiously enough, three significant and one notable exception to it. The significant exceptions are the Poles, the Finns, the Bohemians – the subjugated Slavic nationalities generally. Political and religious and cultural persecution plays no small role in the movement of the masses of them. The notable exception is the Jews. The Jews come far more with the attitude of the earliest settlers than any of the other peoples; for they more than any other present-day immigrant group are in flight from persecution and disaster; in search of economic opportunity, liberty of conscience, civic rights. They have settled chiefly in the Northeast, with New York city as the centre of greatest concentration. Among them, as among the Puritans, the Pennsylvania Germans, the French of Louisiana, self-consciousness and like-mindedness are intense and articulate. But they differ from the subjugated Slavic peoples in that the latter look backward and forward to *actual*, even if enslaved, home lands; the Jews, in the mass, have thus far looked to America as their home land.

In sum, when we consider that portion of our population which has taken root, we see that it has not stippled the country in small units of diverse ethnic groups. It forms rather a series of stripes or layers of varying sizes, moving east to west along the central axis of settlement, where towns are thickest; i.e., from New York and Philadelphia, through Chicago and St. Louis, to San Francisco and Seattle. Stippling is absent even in the towns, where the variety of population is generally greater. Probably 90 per cent of that population is either foreign-born or of foreign stock; yet even so, the towns are aggregations, not units. Broadly divided into the sections inhabited by the rich and those inhabited by the poor, this economic division does not abolish, it only crosses, the ethnic one. There are rich and poor little Italys, Irelands, Hungarys, Germanys, and rich and poor Ghettoes. The *common* city life, which depends upon like-mindedness, is not inward, corporate, and inevitable, but external, inarticulate, and incidental, a reaction to the need of amusement and the need of protection, not the expression of a unity of heritage, mentality, and interest. Politics and education in our cities thus present the phenomenon of ethnic compromises not unknown in Austria-Hungary; concessions and appeals to 'the Irish vote,' 'the Jewish vote,' 'the German vote'; compromise school committees where members represent each ethnic faction, until, as in Boston, one group grows strong enough to dominate the entire situation.

South of Mason and Dixon's line the cities exhibit a greater homogeneity. Outside of certain regions in Texas the descendants of the native white stock, often degenerate and backward, prevail among the whites, but the whites as a whole constitute a relatively weaker proportion of the population. They live among nine million negroes, whose own mode of living tends, by its mere massiveness, to standardize the 'mind' of the proletarian South in speech, manner, and the other values of social organization.

III

All the immigrants and their offspring are in the way of becoming 'Americanized,' if they remain in one place in the country long enough – say, six or seven years. The general notion, 'Americanization,' appears to denote the adoption of English speech, of American clothes and manners, of the American attitude in politics. It connotes the fusion of the various bloods, and a transmutation by 'the miracle of assimilation' of Jews, Slavs, Poles, Frenchmen, Germans, Hindus, Scandinavians into beings similar in background, tradition, outlook, and spirit to the descendants of the British colonists, the Anglo-Saxon stock. Broadly speaking, the elements of Americanism are somewhat external, the effect of environment; larger internal, the effect of heredity. Our economic individualism, our traditional *laissez-faire* policy, is largely the effect of environment: where nature offers more than enough wealth to go round, there is no immediate need for regulating distribution. What poverty and unemployment exist among us is the result of unskilled and wasteful social housekeeping, not of any actual natural barrenness. And until the disparity between our economic resources and our population becomes equalized, so that the country shall attain an approximate economic equilibrium, this will always be the case. With our individualism go our optimism and our other 'pioneer' virtues: they are purely reactions to our unexploited natural wealth, and, as such, moods which characterize all societies in which the relation between population and resource is similar. The predominance of the 'new freedom' over the 'new nationalism' is a potent political expression of this relationship, and the overwhelming concern of both novelties with the economic situation rather than with the cultural or spiritual is a still stronger one. That these last alone justify or condemn this or that economic condition or programme is a commonplace: 'by their fruits shall ye know the soils and the roots.'

The fruits in this case are those of New England. Eliminate from our roster Whittier, Longfellow, Lowell, Hawthorne, Emerson, Howells, and what have we left? Outstanding are Poe and Whitman, and the necromantic mysticism of the former is only a sick-minded version of the naturalistic mysticism of the latter, while the general mood of both is that of Emerson, who in his way expresses the culmination of that movement in mysticism from the agonized conscience of colonial and Puritan New England – to which Hawthorne gives voice – to serene and optimistic assurance. In religion this spirit of Puritan New England non-conformity culminates similarly: in Christian Science when it is superstitious and magical; in Unitarianism when it is rationalistic: in both cases, over against the personal individualism, there is the cosmic unity. For New England, religious, political, and literary interests remained coordinate and indivisible; and New England gave the tone to and established the standards for the rest of the American state. Save for the very early political writers, the 'solid South' remains unexpressed, while the march of the pioneer across the continent is permanently marked by Mark Twain for the Middle West, and by Bret Harte for the Pacific slope. Both these men carry something of the tone and spirit of New England, and with them the 'great tradition' of America, the America of the 'Anglo-Saxon,' comes to an end. There remains nothing large or significant that is unexpressed, and no unmentioned writer who is so completely representative.

The background, tradition, spirit, and outlook of the whole of the America of the 'Anglo-Saxon,' then, find their spiritual expression in the New England school, Poe, Whitman, Mark Twain, Bret Harte. They realize an individual who has passed from the agonized to the optimistic conscience, a person of the solid and homely virtues tempered by mystic certainty of his destiny, his election, hence always ready to take risks, and always willing to face dangers. From the agony of Arthur Dimmesdale to the smug industrial and social rise of Silas Lapham, from the irresponsible kindliness or Huck Finn to the 'Luck of Roaring Camp,' the movement is the same, though on different social levels. In regions supernal its coordinate is the movement from the God of Jonathan Edwards to the Oversoul of Emerson and the Divinity of Mrs. Eddy. It is summed up in the contemporary representative 'average' American of British stock – an individualist, English-speaking, interested in getting on, kind, neighborly, not too scrupulous in business, indulgent to his women, optimistically devoted *laissez-faire* in economics and politics, very respectable in private life, tending to liberalism and mysticism in religion, and moved, where his economic interests are unaffected, by formulas rather than ideas. He typifies the aristocracy of America. From among his fellows are recruited her foremost protagonists in politics, religion, art, and learning. He constitutes, in virtue of being heir of the oldest *rooted* economic settlement and spiritual tradition of the white man in America, the measure and the standard of Americanism that the newcomer is to attain.

Other things being equal, a democratic society which should be a realization of the assumptions of the Declaration of Independence, supposing them to be true, would be a levelling society such that all persons become alike, either on the lowest or the highest plane. The outcome of free social contacts should, according to the laws of imitation, establish 'equality' on the highest plane; for imitation is of the higher by the lower, so that the cut of a Paris gown at $1,000 becomes imitated in department stores at $17.50, and the play of the rich becomes the vice of the poor. This process of levelling up through imitation is facilitated by the so-called 'standardization' of externals. In these days of ready-made clothes, factory-made goods, refrigerating plants, it is almost impossible that the mass of the inhabitants of this country should wear other than uniform clothes, use other than uniform furniture or utensils, or eat anything but the same kind of food. In these days of rapid transit and industrial mobility it must seem impossible that any stratification of population should be permanent. Hardly anybody seems to have been born where he lives, or to live where he has been born. The teetering of demand and supply in industry and commerce keeps large masses of population constantly mobile; so that many people no longer can be said to have homes. This mobility reinforces the use of English – for a *lingua franca*, intelligible everywhere, becomes indispensable – by immigrants. And ideals that are felt to belong with the language tend to become 'standardized,' widespread, uniform, through the devices of the telegraph and the telephone, the syndication of 'literature,' the cheap newspaper and the cheap novel, the vaudeville circuit, the 'movie,' and the star system. Even more significantly, mobility leads to the propinquity of the different stocks, thus promoting intermarriage and pointing to the coming of a new 'American race' – a blend of at least all the European stocks (for there seems to be some difference of opinion as to whether negroes also should constitute an element in this blend) into a newer and better being whose qualities and ideals shall be the qualities and ideals of the contemporary American of British ancestry. Apart from the unintentional impulsion towards this end, of the conditions I have just enumerated, there exists the instrument especially devised for this purpose which we call the public school – and to some extent there is the State university. That the end has been and is being attained, we have the biographical testimony of Jacob Riis, of Steiner, and of Mary Antin – a Dane and two Jews, intermarried, assimilated even in religion, and more excessively and self-consciously American than the Americans. And another Jew, Mr. Israel Zangwill, of London, profitably promulgates it as a principle and an aspiration, to the admiring approval of American audiences, under the device, 'the melting-pot.'

IV

All is not, however, fact, because it is hope; nor is the biography of an individual, particularly of a literary individual, the history of a *group*. The Riises and Steiners and Antins protest too much, they are too self-conscious and self-centred, their 'Americanization' appears too much like an achievement, a *tour de force*, too little like a growth. As for Zangwill, at best he is the obverse of Dickens, at worst he is a Jew making a special plea. It is the work of the Americanized writers that is really significant, and in that one senses, underneath the excellent writing, a dualism and the strain to overcome it. The same dualism is apparent in different form among the Americans, and the strain to overcome it seems even stronger. These appear to have been most explicit at the high-water marks of periods of immigration: the Know Nothing party was one early expression it; the organization, in the '80s, of the patriotic societies – the Sons and the Daughters of the American Revolution, later on of the Colonial Dames, and so on – another. Since the Spanish War it has shown itself in the continual, if uneven, growth of the political conscience, first as a muckraking magazine propaganda, then as a nationwide attack on the corruption of politics by plutocracy, finally as the altogether respectable and evangelical Progressive party, with its slogan of 'Human rights against property rights.'

In this process, however, the non-British American or Continental immigrant has not been a fundamental protagonist. He has been an occasion rather than a force. What has been causal has been 'American.' Consider the personnel and history of the Progressive party by way of demonstration: it is composed largely of the professional groups and of the 'solid' and 'upper' middle class; as a spirit it has survived in Kansas, which by an historic accident happens to be the one Middle Western State predominantly Yankee, as a victorious party it has survived in California, one of the few States outstandingly 'American' in population. What is significant in it, as in every other form of the political conscience, is the fact that it is a response to a feeling of 'something out of gear,' and naturally the attention seeks the cause, first of all, outside of the self, not within. Hence the interest in economico-political reconstruction. But the maladjustment in that region is really external. And the political conscience is seeking by a mere change in outward condition to abolish an inward disparity. 'Human rights versus property rights' is merely the modern version of the Declaration of Independence, still assuming that men are men merely, as like as marbles and destined under uniformity of conditions to uniformity of spirit. The course of our economic history since the Civil War shows aptly enough how shrewd were, other things being equal, Marx's generalizations concerning the tendencies of capital towards concentration in the hands of a few. Attention consequently has fixed itself more and more upon the equalization of the distribution of wealth – not socialistically, of course. And this would really abolish the dualism if the economic dualism of rich and poor were the fundamental one. It happens merely that it isn't.

The Anglo-Saxon American, constituting as he does the economic upper class, would hardly have reacted to economic disparity as he has if that had been the only disparity. In point of fact it is the ethnic disparity that troubles him. His activity as entrepreneur has crowded our cities with progressively cheaper laborers of Continental stock, all consecrated to the industrial machine, and towns like Gary, Lawrence, Chicago, Pittsburgh, have become industrial camps of foreign mercenaries. His undertakings have brought into being the terrible autocracies of Pullman and of Lead, North Dakota. They have created a mass of casual laborers numbering 5,000,000, and of work-children to the number of 1,500,000 (the latter chiefly in the South, where the purely 'American' white predominates). They have done all this because the greed of the entrepreneur has displaced high-demanding labor by cheaper labor, and has brought into being the unnecessary problem of unemployment. In all things greed has set the standard, so that the working ideal of the people is to get rich, to live, and to think as the rich, to subordinate government to the service of wealth, making the actual government 'invisible.' *Per contra* it has generated 'labor unrest,' the First World War, the civil war in Colorado.

Because the great mass of the laborers happen to be of Continental and not British ancestry, and because they are late-comers, Mr. Ross blames them for this perversion of our public life and social ideals. Ignoring the degenerate farming stock of New England, the 'poor whites' of the South, the negroes, he fears the anthropological as well as the economic effects of the 'fusion' of these Continental Europeans, Slavs, and Italians and Jews, with the native stock, and grows anxious over the fate of American institutions at their hands. Nothing could better illustrate the fact that the dualism is primarily ethnic and not economic. Under the *laissez-faire* policy, the economic process would have been the same, of whatever race the rich, and whatever race the poor. Only race prejudice, primitive, spontaneous, and unconscious, could have caused a trained economist to ignore the so obvious fact that in a capitalistic industrial society labor is useless and helpless without capital; that hence the external dangers of immigration are in the greed of the capitalist and the indifference of the Government. The restriction of immigration can naturally succeed only with the restriction of the entrepreneur's greed which is its cause. But the abolition of immigration and the restoration of the supremacy of 'human rights' over 'property rights' will not abolish the fundamental ethnic dualism; it may aggravate it.

The reason is obvious. That like-mindedness in virtue of which men are as nearly as is possible in fact 'free and equal' is not primarily the result of a constant set of external conditions. Its pre-potent cause is an intrinsic similarity which, for America, has its roots in that ethnic and cultural unity of which our fundamental institutions are the most durable expression. Similar environments, similar occupations, do, of course, generate similarities: 'American' is an adjective of similarity applied to Anglo-Saxons, Irish, Jews, Germans, Italians, and so on. But the similarity is one of place and institution, acquired, not inherited, and hence not transmitted. Each generation has, in fact, to become 'Americanized' afresh, and, withal, inherited nature has a way of redirecting nurture, of which our public schools give only too much evidence. If the inhabitants of the United States are stratified economically as 'rich' and 'poor,' they are stratified ethnically as Germans, Scandinavians, Jews, Irish, and although the two stratifications cross more frequently than they are coincident, they interfere with each other far less than is hopefully supposed. The history of the 'International' in recent years, the present *débâcle* in Europe, are indications of how little 'class-consciousness' modifies national consciousness. To the dominant nationality in America nationality, in the European sense, has had no meaning; for it had set the country's standards and had been assimilating others to itself. Now that the process seems to be slowing down, it finds itself confronted with the *problem* of nationality, just as do the Irish, the Poles, the Bohemians, the Czechs, and the other oppressed nationalities in Europe. 'We are submerged,' writes a great American man of letters, who has better than any one I know interpreted the American spirit to the world, 'we are submerged beneath a conquest so complete that the very name of us means something not ourselves . . . I feel as I should think an Indian might feel, in the face of ourselves that were.'

The fact is that similarity of class rests upon no inevitable external condition, while similarity of nationality is inevitably intrinsic. Hence the poor of two different peoples tend to be less like-minded than the poor and the rich of the same peoples. At his core no human being, even in 'a state of nature,' is a mere mathematical unit of action like the 'economic man.' Behind him in time and tremendously in him in quality are his ancestors; around him in space are his relatives and kin, looking back with him to a remoter common ancestry. In all these he lives and moves and has his being. They constitute his, literally, *natio*, and in Europe every inch of his non-human environment wears the effects of their action upon it and breathes their spirit. The America he comes to, beside Europe, is nature virgin and inviolate: it does not guide him with ancestral blazings: externally he is cut off from the past. Not so internally: whatever else he changes, he cannot change his grandfather. Moreover, he comes rarely alone; he comes companioned with his fellow-nationals; and he comes to no strangers, but to kin

and friend who have gone before. If he is able to excel, he soon achieves
a local habitation. There he encounters the native American to whom
he is a Dutchman, a Frenchy, a Mick, a wop, a dago, a hunky, or a
sheeny, and he encounters these others who are unlike him, dealing
with him as a lower and outlandish creature. Then, be he even the
rudest and most primeval peasant, heretofore totally unconscious of
his nationality, of his categorical difference from other men, he must
inevitably become conscious of it. Thus, in our industrial and congested
towns where there are real and large contacts between immigrant
nationalities the first effect appears to be an intensification of spiritual
dissimilarities, always to the disadvantage of the dissimilarities.

The second generation, consequently, devotes itself feverishly to
the attainment of similarity. The older social tradition is lost by attrition
or thrown off for advantage. The merest externals of the new one are
acquired – *via* the public school. But as the public school imparts it,
or as the settlement imparts it, it is not really a *life*, it is an abstraction,
an arrangement of words. America is a word: as an historic fact, a
democratic ideal of life, it is not realized at all. At best and at worst
– now that the captains of industry are becoming disturbed by the
mess they have made, and 'vocational training' is becoming a part of
the educational programme – the prospective American learns a trade,
acquiring at his most impressionable age the habit of being a cog in
the industrial machine. And this he learns, moreover, from the sons
and daughters of earlier immigrants, themselves essentially uneducated
and nearly illiterate, with what spontaneity and teaching power they
have squeezed out in the 'normal' schools by the application of that
Pecksniffian 'efficiency'-press called pedagogy.

But life, the expression of emotion and realization of desire, the
prospective American learns from the yellow press, which has set itself
explicitly the task of appealing to his capacities. He learns of the
wealth, the luxuries, the extravagances, and the immoralities of specific
rich persons. He learns to want to be like them. As that is impossible
in the mass, their amusements become his crimes or vices. Or suppose
him to be strong enough to emerge from the proletarian into the middle
class, to achieve economic competence and social respectability. He
remains still the Slav, the Jew, the German, or the Irish citizen of the
American commonwealth. Again, in the mass, neither he nor his children nor his children's children lose their ethnic individuality. For
marriage is determined by sexual selection and by propinquity, and
the larger the town, the lesser the likelihood of mixed marriage. Although
the gross number of such marriages is greater than it was fifty years

ago, the relative proportions, in terms of variant units of population, tends, I think, to be significantly less. As the stratification of the towns echoes and stresses the stratification of the country as a whole, the likelihood of a new 'American' race is remote enough, and the fear of it unnecessary. But equally remote also is the possibility of a universalization of the inwardness of the old American life. Only the externals succeed in passing over.

It took over two hundred years of settled life in one place for the New England school to emerge, and it emerged in a community in which like-mindedness was very strong, and in which the whole ethnic group performed all the tasks, economic and social, which the community required. How when ethnic and industrial groups are coincident? When ethnic and social groups are coincident? For there is a marked tendency in this country for the industrial and social stratification to follow ethnic lines. The first comers in the land constitute its aristocracy, are its chief protagonists of the pride of blood as well as of the pride of pelf, its formers and leaders of opinion, the standardizers of its culture. Primacy in time has given them primacy in status, like all 'first-born,' so that what we call the tradition and spirit of America is theirs. The non-British elements of the population are practically voiceless, but they are massive, 'barbarian hordes,' if you will, and the effect, the unconscious and spontaneous effect of their pressure, has been the throwing back of the Anglo-American upon his ancestry and ancestral ideals. This has taken two forms: (1) the 'patriotic' societies – not, of course, the Cincinnati or the Artillery Company, but those that have arisen with the great migrations, the Sons and Daughters of the American Revolution, the Colonial Dames; and (2) the specific clan or tribal organizations consisting of families looking back to the same colonial ancestry – the societies of the descendants of John Alden. etc., etc. The ancient hatred for England is completely gone. Wherever possible, the ancestral line is traced across the water to England; old ancestral homes are bought; and those of the forebears of national heroes like John Harvard or George Washington become converted into shrines. More and more public emphasis has been placed upon the unity of the English and American stock – the common interests of the 'Anglo-Saxon' nations, and of 'Anglo-Saxon' civilization, the unity of the political, literary, and social tradition. If all that is not ethnic nationality returned to consciousness, what is it?

Next in general estimation come the Germans and the Irish, with the Jews a close third, although the position of the last involves some abnormalities. Then come the Slavs and Italians and other central and south Europeans; finally, the Asiatics. The Germans, as Mr. Ross points out, have largely a monopoly of brewing and baking and cabinet-making. The Irish shine in no particular industries unless it be those carried on by municipalities and public-service corporations. The Jews mass in the garment-making industries, tobacco manufacture, and in the 'learned professions.' The Scandinavians appear to be on the same level as the Jews in the general estimation, and going up. They are farmers, mostly, and outdoor men. The Slavs are miners, metal-workers, and packers. The Italians tend to fall with the negroes into the 'pick and shovel brigade.' Such a country-wide and urban industrial and social stratification is no more likely than the geographical and sectional stratification to facilitate the coming of the 'American race'! And as our political and 'reforming' action is directed upon symptoms rather than fundamental causes, the stratification, as the country moves towards the inevitable equilibrium between wealth and population, will tend to grow more rigid rather than less. Thus far the pressure of immigration alone has kept the strata from hardening. Eliminate that, and we may be headed for a caste system based on ethnic divirsity and mitigated to only a negligible degree by economic differences.

PART TWO

V

The array of forces for and against that like-mindedness which is the stuff and essence of nationality aligns itself as follows: For it make social imitation of the upper by the lower classes, the facility of communications, the national pastimes of baseball and motion-picture, the mobility of population, the cheapness of printing, and the public schools. Against it make the primary ethnic differences with which the population starts, its stratification over an enormous extent of country, its industrial and economic stratification. We are an English-speaking country, but in no intimate and inevitable way, as is New Zealand or Australia, or even Canada. English is to us what Latin was to the Roman provinces and to the middle ages – the language of the upper and dominant class, the vehicle and symbol of culture: for the mass of our population it is a sort of Esperanto or Ido, a *lingua franca* necessary less in the spiritual than the economic contacts of the daily life. This mass is composed of elementals, peasants – Mr. Ross speaks of their menacing American life with 'peasantism' – the proletarian foundation material of all forms of civilization. Their self-consciousness as groups is comparatively weak. This is a factor which favors their 'assimilation,' for the more cultivated a group is, the more it is aware of its individuality, and the less willing it is to surrender that individuality. One need think only of the Puritans themselves, leaving Holland for fear of absorption into the Dutch population; of the Creoles and Pennsylvania Germans of this country, or of the Jews, anywhere. In his judgment of the assimilability of various stocks Mr. Ross neglects this important point altogether, probably because his attention is fixed on existing contrasts rather than potential similarities. Peasants, however, having nothing much to surrender in taking over a new culture, feel no necessary break, and find the transition easy. It is the shock of confrontation with other ethnic groups and the feeling of aliency that generates in them an intenser self-consciousness, which then militates against Americanization in spirit by reinforcing the two factors to which the spiritual expression of the proletarian has been largely confined. These factors are language and religion. Religion is, of course, no more a 'universal' than language. The history of Christianity makes evident enough how religion is modified, even inverted, by race, place, and time. It becomes a principle of separation, often the sole repository of the national spirit, almost always the conservator of the national language and of the tradition that is passed on with the language to succeeding generations. Among immigrants, hence, religion and language tend to be coordinate: a single expression of the spontaneous and instinctive mental life of the masses, and the primary inward factors making against assimilation. Mr. Ross, I note, tends to grow shrill over the competition of the parochial school with the public school, at the same time that he belittles the fact 'that on Sundays Norwegian is preached in more churches in America than in Norway.'

And Mr. Ross's anxiety would, I think, be more than justified were it not that religion in these cases always does more than it intends. For it conserves the inward aspect of nationality rather than mere religion, and tends to become the centre of exfoliation of a higher type of personality among the peasants in the natural terms of their own *natio*. This *natio*, reaching consciousness first in a reaction against America, then as an effect of the competition with Americanization, assumes spiritual forms other than religious: the parochial school, to hold its own with the public school, gets secularized while remaining national. *Natio* is what underlies the vehemence of the 'Americanized' and the spiritual and political unrest of the Americans. It is the fundamental fact of American life to-day, and in the light of it Mr. Wilson's resentment of the 'hyphenated' American is both righteous and pathetic. But a hyphen attaches, in things of the spirit, also to the 'pure' English American. His cultural mastery tends to be retrospective rather than prospective. At the present time there is no dominant American mind. Our spirit is inarticulate, not a voice, but a chorus of many voices each singing a rather different tune. How to get order out of this ca-cophony is the question for all those who are concerned about those things which alone justify wealth and power, concerned about justice, the arts, literature, philosophy, science. What must, what *shall* this cacophony become – a unison or a harmony?

For decidedly the older America, whose voice and whose spirit was New England, is gone beyond recall. Americans still are the artists and thinkers of the land, but they work, each for himself, without common vision or ideals. The older tradition has passed from a life into a memory, and the newer one, so far as it has an Anglo-Saxon base, is holding its own beside more and more formidable rivals, the expression in appropriate form of the national inheritances of the various populations concentrated in the various States of the Union, populations of whom their national self-consciousness is perhaps the chief spiritual asset. Think of the Creoles in the South and the French-Canadians in the North, clinging to french for so many generations and maintaining, however weekly, spiritual and social contacts with the mother-country; of the Germans, with their *Deutschthum*, their *Männerchöre*, *Turnvereine*, and *Schützenfeste*; of the universally separate Jews; of the intensely nationalistic Irish; of the Pennsylvania Germans; of the indomitable Poles, and even more indomitable Bohemians; of the 30,000 Belgians in Wisconsin, with their 'Belgian' language, a mixture of Walloon and Flemish welded by reaction to a strange social environment. Except in such cases as the town of Lead, South Dakota, the great ethnic groups of proletarians, thrown upon themselves in a new environment, generate from among themselves the other social classes which Mr. Ross misses so sadly among hem: their shopkeepers, their physicians, their attorneys, their journalists, and their national and political leaders, who form the links between them and the greater American society. They develop their own literature, or become conscious of that of the mother-country. As they grow more prosperous and 'Americanized,' as they become freed from the stigma of 'foreigner,' they develop group self-respect: the 'wop' changes into a proud Italian, the 'hunky' into an intensely nationalist Slav. They learn, or they recall, the spiritual heritage of their nationality. Their cultural abjectness gives way to cultural pride and the public schools, the libraries, and the clubs become beset with demands for texts in the national language and literature.

The Poles are an instance worth dwelling upon. Mr. Ross's summary of them is as striking as it is premonitory. There are over a million of them in the country, a backward people, prolific, brutal, priest-ridden – a menace to American institutions. Yet the urge that carries them in such numbers to America is not unlike that which carried the Pilgrim Fathers. Next to the Jews, whom their brethren in their Polish home are hounding to death, the unhappiest people in Europe, exploited by both their own upper classes and the Russian conqueror, they have resisted extinction at a great cost. They have clung to their religion because it was a mark of difference between them and their conquerors; because they love liberty, they have made their language of literary importance in Europe. Their aspiration, impersonal, disinterested, as it must be in America, to free Poland, to conserve the Polish spirit, is the most hopeful and American thing about them – the one thing that stands actually between them and brutalization through complete economic degradation. It lifts them higher than anything that, in fact, America offers them. The same thing is true for the Bohemians, 17,000 of them, workingmen in Chicago, paying a proportion of their wage to maintain schools in the Bohemian tongue and free thought; the same thing is true of many other groups.

How true it is may be observed from a comparison of the vernacular dailies and weeklies with the yellow American press which is concocted expressly for the great American masses. The content of the former, when the local news is deducted, is a mass of information, political, social, scientific; often translations into the vernacular of standard English writing, often original work of high literary quality. The latter, when the news is deducted, consists of the sporting page and the editorial page. Both pander rather than awaken, so that it is no wonder that in fact the intellectual and spiritual pabulum of the great masses consists of the vernacular papers in the national tongue. With them go also the vernacular drama, and the thousand and one other phenomena which make a distinctive culture, the outward expression of that fundamental like-mindedness wherein men are truly 'free and equal.' This, beginning for the dumb peasant masses in language and religion, emerges in the other forms of life and art and tends to make smaller or larger ethnic groups autonomous, self-sufficient, and reacting as spiritual units to the residuum of America.

What is the cultural outcome likely to be, under these conditions? Surely not the melting-pot. Rather something that has become more and more distinct in the changing State and city life of the last two decades, and which is most articulate and apparent among just those peoples whom Mr. Ross praises most – the Scandinavians, the Germans, the Irish, the Jews.

It is in the area where Scandinavians are most concentrated that Norwegian is preached on Sunday in more churches than in Norway. That area is Minnesota, not unlike Scandinavia in climate and character. There, if the newspapers are to be trusted, the 'foreign language' taught in an increasingly larger number of high schools is Scandinavian. The Constitution of the State resembles in many respects the famous Norwegian Constitution of 1813. The largest city has been chosen as the 'spiritual capital,' if I may say so, the seat of the Scandinavian 'house of life,' which the Scandinavian Society in America is reported to be planning to build as a centre from which there is to spread through the land Scandinavian culture and ideals.

The eastern neighbor of Minnesota is Wisconsin, a region of great concentration of Germans. Is it merely a political accident that the centralization of State authority and control has been possible there to a degree heretofore unknown in this country? That the Socialist organization is the most powerful in the land, able under ordinary conditions to have elected the Mayor of a large city and a Congressman, and kept out of power only by coalition of the other parties? That German is the overwhelmingly predominant 'foreign language' in the public schools and in the university? Or that the fragrance of *Deutschthum* pervades the life of the whole State? The earliest German immigrants to America were group conscious to a high degree. They brought with them a cultural tradition and political aspiration. They wanted to found a State. If a State is to be regarded as a mode of life of the mind, they have succeeded. Their language is the predominant 'foreign' one throughout the Middle West. The teaching of it is required by law in many place, southern Ohio and Indianapolis, for example. Their national institutions, even to cooking, are as widespread as they are. They are organized into a great national society, the German-American Alliance, which is dedicated to the advancement of German culture and ideals. They encourage and make possible a close and more intimate contact with the fatherland. They endow Germanic museums, they encourage and provide for exchange professorships, erect monuments to German heroes, and disseminate translations of the German classics. And there are, of course, the very excellent German vernacular press, the German theatre, the German club, the German organization of life.

Similar are the Irish, living in strength in Massachusetts and New

York. When they began to come to this country they were far less well off and far more passionately self-conscious than the Germans. For numbers of them America was and has remained just a centre from which to plot for th freedom of Ireland. For most it was an opportunity to escape both exploitation and starvation. The way they made was made against both race and religious prejudice: in the course of it they lost much that was attractive as well as much that was unpleasant. But Americanization brought the mass of them also spiritual self-respect, and their growing prosperity both here and in Ireland is what lies behind the more inward phases of Irish Nationalism – the Gaelic movement, the Irish theatre, the Irish Art Society. I omit consideration of such organized bodies as the Ancient Order of Hibernians. All these movements alike indicate the conversion of the negative nationalism of the hatred of England to the positive nationalism of the loving care and development of the cultural values of the Celtic spirit. A significant phase of it is the voting of Irish history into the curriculum of the high schools of Boston. In sum, once the Irish body had been fed and erected, the Irish mind demanded and generated its own peculiar form of self-realization and satisfaction.

And, finally, the Jews. Their attitude towards America is different in a fundamental respect from that of other immigrant nationalities. They do not come to the United States from truly native lands, lands of their proper natio and culture. They come from lands of sojourn, where they have been for ages treated as foreigners, at most as semi-citizens, subject to disabilities and persecutions. They come with no political aspirations against the peace of other states such as move the Irish, the Poles, the Bohemians. They come with the intention to be completely incorporated into the body-politic of the state. They alone, as Mr. H. G. Wells notes, of all the immigrant peoples have made spontaneously conscious and organized efforts to prepare themselves and their brethren for the responsibilities of American citizenship. There is hardly a considerable municipality in the land, where Jews inhabit, that has not its Hebrew Institute, or its Educational Alliance, or its Young Men's Hebrew Association, or its Community House, especially dedicated to this task. They show the highest percentage of naturalization, according to Mr. Ross's tables, and he concedes that they have benefited politics. Yet of all self-conscious peoples they are the most self-conscious. Of all immigrants they have the oldest civilized tradition, they are longest accustomed to living under law, and are at the outset the most eager and the most successful in eliminating the external differences between themselves and their social environment. Even their religion

is flexible and accommodating, as that of the Christian sectaries is not
for change involves no change in doctrine, only in mode of life.

Yet, once the wolf is driven from the door and the Jewish immigrant
takes his place in our society a free man and an American, he tends
to become all the more a Jew. The cultural unity of his race, history,
and background is only continued by the new life under the new
conditions. Mr. H. G. Wells calls the Jewish quarter in New York a
city within a city, and with more justice than other quarters because,
although it is far more in tune with Americanism than the other quarters,
it is also far more autonomous in spirit and self-conscious in culture.
It has its sectaries, its radicals, its artists, its literati; its press, its literature, its theatre, its Yiddish and its Hebrew, its Talmudical colleges
and its Hebrew schools, its charities and its vanities, and its coordinating
organization, the Kehilla, all more or less duplicated wherever Jews
congregate in mass. Here not religion alone, but the whole world of
radical thinking, carries the mother-tongue and the father-tongue, with
all that they imply. Unlike the parochial schools, their separate schools,
being national, do not displace the public schools; they supplement
the public schools. The Jewish ardor for pure learning is notorious.
And, again, as was the case with the Scandinavians, the Germans, the
Irish, democracy applied to education has given the Jews their will
that Hebrew shall be coordinate with French and German in the regent's
examination. On a national scale of organization there is the American
Jewish Committee, the Jewish Historical Society, the Jewish Publication
Society. Rurally, there is the model Association of Jewish Farmers,
with their cooperative organization for agriculture and for agricultural
education. In sum, the most eagerly American of the immigrant groups
are also the most autonomous and self-conscious in spirit and culture.

VI

Immigrants appear to pass through four phases in the course of being
Americanized. In the first phase they exhibit economic eagerness, the
greed of the unfed. Since external differences are a handicap in the economic struggle, they 'assimilate,' seeking thus to facilitate the attainment of economic independence. Once the proletarian level of such
independence is reached, the process of assimilation slows down and
tends to come to a stop. The immigrant group is still a national group,
modified, sometimes improved, by environmental influences, but
otherwise a solitary spiritual unit, which is seeking to find its way out
on its own social level. This search brings to light permanent group

distinctions, and the immigrant, like the Anglo-Saxon American, is thrown back upon himself and his ancestry. Then a process of dissimilation begins. The arts, life, and ideals of the nationality become central and paramount: ethnic and national differences change in status from disadvantages to distinctions. All the while the immigrant has been using the English language and behaving like an American in matters economic and political, and continues to do so. The institutions of the Republic have become the liberating cause and the background for the rise of the cultural consciousness and social autonomy of the immigrant Irishman, German, Scandinavian, Jew, Pole, or Bohemian. On the whole, Americanization has not repressed nationality. Americanization has liberated nationality.

Hence, what troubles Mr. Ross and so many other Anglo-Saxon Americans is not really inequality; what troubles them is *difference*. Only things that are alike in fact and not abstractly, and only men that are alike in origin and in spirit and not abstractly, can be truly 'equal' and maintain that inward unanimity of action and outlook which make a national life. The writers of the Declaration of Independence and of the Constitution were not confronted by the practical fact of ethnic dissimilarity among the whites of the country. Their descendants are confronted by it. Its existence, acceptance, and development provide one of the inevitable consequences of the democratic principle on which our theory of government is based, and the result at the present writing is to many worthies very unpleasant. Democratism and the Federal principle have worked together with economic greed and ethnic snobbishness to people the land with all the nationalities of Europe, and to convert the early American nation into the present American state. For in effect we are in the process of becoming a true federal state, such a state as men hope for as the outcome of the European war, a great republic consisting of a federation or commonwealth of nationalities.

Given, in the economic order, the principle of *laissez-faire* applied to a capitalistic society, in contrast with the manorial and guild systems of the past and the Socialist utopias of the future, the economic consequences are the same, whether in America, full of all Europe, or in England, full of the English, Scotch, and Welsh. Given, in the political order, the principle that all men are equal and that each, consequently, under the law at least, shall have the opportunity to make the most of himself, the control of the machinery of government by the plutocracy is a foregone conclusion. *Laissez-faire* and unprecedentedly bountiful natural resources have turned the mind of the state to wealth alone, and in the haste to accumulate wealth considerations of human quality have been neglected and forgotten, the action of government has been remedial rather than constructive, and Mr. Ross's 'peasantism,' i.e., the growth of an expropriated, degraded industrial class, dependent on the factory rather than on land, has been rapid and vexatious.

The problems which these conditions give rise to are important, but not primarily important. Although they have occupied the minds of all our political theorists, they are problems of means, of instruments, not of ends. They concern the conditions of life, not the *kind of life*, and there appears to have been a general assumption that only one kind of human life is possible in America. But the same democracy which underlies the evils of the economic order underlies also the evils – and the promise – of the ethnic order. Because no individual is merely an individual, the political autonomy of the individual has meant and is beginning to realize in these United States the spiritual autonomy of his group. The process is as yet far from fruition. We are, in fact, at the parting of the ways. A genuine social alternative is before us, either of which parts we may realize if we will. In social construction the will is father is to the fact, for the fact is nothing more than the concord or conflict of wills. What do we will to make of the United States – a unison, singing the old Anglo-Saxon theme 'America,' the America of the New England school, or a harmony, in which that theme shall be dominant, perhaps, among others, but one among many, not the only one?

The mind reverts helplessly to the historic attempts at unison in Europe – the heroic failure of the pan-Hellenists, of the Romans, the disintegration and the diversification of the Christian Church, for a time the most successful unison in history; the present-day failures of Germany and of Russia. Here, however, the whole social situation is favorable, as it has never been at any time elsewhere – everything is favorable but the basic law of America itself, and the spirit of American institutions. To achieve unison – it can be achieved – would be to violate these. For the end determines the means, and this end would involve no other means than those used by Germany in Poland, in Schleswig-Holstein, and Alsace-Lorraine; by Russia in the Pale, in Poland, in Finland. Fundamentally it would require the complete nationalization of education, the abolition of every form of parochial and private school, the abolition of instruction in other tongues than English and the concentration of the teaching of history and literature upon the English tradition. The other institutions of society would require treatment analogous to that administered by Germany to her

European acquisitions. And all of this, even if meeting with no resistance, would not completely guarantee the survival as a unison of the older Americanism. For the programme would be applied to diverse ethnic types, and the reconstruction that, with the best will, they might spontaneously make of the tradition would more likely than not be a far cry from the original. It is, already.

The notion that the programme might be realized by radical and even enforced miscegenation, by the creation of the melting-pot by law, and thus by the development of the new 'American race,' is, as Mr. Ross points out, as mystically optimistic as it is ignorant. In historic times, so far as we know, no new ethnic types have originated, and what we know of breeding gives us no assurance of the disappearance of the old types in favor of the new, only the addition of a new type, if it succeeds in surviving, to the already existing older ones. Biologically, life does not unify; biologically, life diversifies; and it is sheer ignorance to apply social analogies to biological processes. In any event, we know what the qualities and capacities of existing types are; we know how by education to do something towards the repression of what is evil in them and the conservation of what is good. The 'American race' is a totally unknown thing; to presume that it will be better because (if we like to persist in the illusion that it is coming) it will be later, is no different from imagining that, because contemporary, Russia is better than ancient Greece. There is nothing more to be said to the pious stupidity that identifies recency with goodness. The unison to be achieved cannot be a unison of ethnic types. It must be, if it is to be at all, a unison of social and historic interests, established by the complete cutting off of the ancestral memories of our populations, the enforced, exclusive use of the English language and English and American history in the schools and in the daily life.

The attainment of the other alternative, a harmony, also requires concerted public action. But the action would do no violence to our fundamental law and the spirit of our institutions, nor to the qualities of men. It would seek simply to eliminate the waste and the stupidity of our social organization, by way of freeing and strenthening the strong forces actually in operation. Starting with our existing ethnic and cultural groups, it would seek to provide conditions under which each may attain the perfection that is proper to its kind. The provision of such conditions is the primary intent of our fundamental law and the function of our institutions. And the various nationalities which compose our commonwealth must learn first of all this fact, which is perhaps, to most minds, the outstanding ideal content of 'Americanism'

– that democracy means self-realization through self-control, self-government, and that one is impossible without the other. For the application of this principle, which is realized in a harmony of societies, there are European analogies also. I omit Austria and Turkey, for the union of nationalities is there based more on inadequate force than on consent, and the form of their organization is alien to ours. I think of England and of Switzerland. England is a state of four nationalities – the English, Welsh, Scotch, and Irish (if one considers the Empire, of many more), and while English history is not unmarred by attempts at unison, both the home policy and the imperial policy have, since the Boer War, been realized more and more in the application of the principle of harmony: the strength of the kingdom and the empire have been posited more and more upon the voluntary and autonomous cooperation of the component nationalities. Switzerland is a state of three nationalities, a republic as the Untied States is, far more democratically governed, concentrated in an area not much different in size, I suspect, from New York City, with a population not far from it in total. Yet Switzerland has the most loyal citizens in Europe. Their language, literary and spiritual traditions are on the one side German, on another Italian, on a third side French. And in terms of social organization, of economic prosperity, of public education, of the general level of culture, Switzerland is the most successful democracy in the world. It conserves and encourages individuality.

The reason lies, I think, in the fact that in Switzerland the conception of 'natural right' operates, consciously or unconsciously, as a generalization from the unalterable data of human nature. What is inalienable in the life of mankind is its intrinsic positive quality – its psychophysical inheritance. Men may change their clothes, their politics, their wives, their religions, their philosophies, to a greater or lesser extent: they cannot change their grandfathers. Jews or Poles or Anglo-Saxons, in order to cease being Jews or Poles or Anglo-Saxons, would have to cease to be. The selfhood which is inalienable in them, and for th realization of which they require 'inalienable' liberty, is ancestrally determined, and the happiness which they pursue has its form implied in ancestral endowment. This is what, actually, democracy in operation assumes. There are human capacities which it is the function of the state to liberate and to protect; and the failure of the state as a government means its abolition. Government, the state, under the democratic conception, is merely an instrument, not an end. That it is often an abused instrument, that it is often seized by the powers that prey, that it makes frequent mistakes and considers only secondary ends, surface needs, which vary from moment to moment, is, of course, obvious: hence our social and political chaos. But that it is an instrument, flexibly adjustable to changing life, changing opinion, and needs, our whole electoral organization and party system declare. And as intelligence and wisdom prevail over 'politics' and special interests, as the steady and continuous pressure of the inalienable qualities and purposes of human groups more and more dominate the confusion of our common life, the outlines of a possible great and truly democratic commonwealth become discernible.

Its form is that of the Federal republic; its substance a democracy of nationalities, cooperating voluntarily and autonomously in the enterprise of self-realization through the perfection of men according to their kind. The common language of the commonwealth, the language of its great political tradition, is English, but each nationality expresses its emotional and voluntary life in its own language, in its own inevitable aesthetic and intellectual forms. The common life of the commonwealth is politico-economic, and serves as the foundation and background for the realization of the distinctive individuality of each natio that composes it. Thus 'American civilization,' may come to mean the perfection of the cooperative harmonies of 'European civilization,' the waste, the squalor, and the distress of Europe being eliminated – a multiplicity in a unity, an orchestration of mankind. As in an orchestra, every type of instrument has its specific timbre and tonality, founded in its substance and form; as every type has its appropriate theme and melody in the whole symphony, so in society each ethnic group is the natural instrument, it spirit and culture are its theme and melody and the harmony and dissonances and discords of them all make the symphony of civilization, with this difference: a musical symphony is written before it is played; in the symphony of civilization the playing is the writing, so that there is nothing so fixed and inevitable about its progressions as in music, so that within the limits set by nature they may vary at will, and the range and variety of the harmonies may become wider and richer and more beautiful.

But the question is, do the dominant classes in America want such a society?

Note

1. Edward Alsworth Ross, *The Old World in the New* (New York: The Century Co.)

8 Trans-National America (1916)

Randolph S. Bourne*

No reverberatory effect of the great war has caused American public opinion more solicitude than the failure of the 'melting-pot.' The discovery of diverse nationalistic feelings among our great alien population has come to most people as an intense shock. It has brought out the unpleasant inconsistencies of our traditional beliefs. We have had to watch hard-hearted old Brahmins virtuously indignant at the spectacle of the immigrant refusing to be melted, while they jeer at patriots like Mary Antin who write about 'our forefathers.' We have had to listen to publicists who express themselves as stunned by the evidence of vigorous nationalistic and cultural movements in this country among Germans, Scandinavians, Bohemians, and Poles, while in the same breath they insist that the alien shall be forcibly assimilated to that Anglo-Saxon tradition which they unquestioningly label 'American.'

As the unpleasant truth has come upon us that assimilation in this country was proceeding on lines very different from those we had marked out for it, we found ourselves inclined to blame those who were thwarting our prophecies. The truth became culpable. We blamed the war, we blamed the Germans. And then we discovered with a moral shock that these movements has been making great headway before the war ever began. We found that the tendency, reprehensible and paradoxical as it might be, has been for the national clusters of immigrants, as they became more and more firmly established and more and more prosperous, to cultivate more and more assiduously the literatures and cultural traditions of their homelands. Assimilation, in other words, instead of washing out the memories of Europe, made them more and more intensely real. Just as these clusters became more and more objectively American, did they become more and more German or Scandinavian or Bohemian or Polish.

To face the fact that our aliens are already strong enough to take a share in the direction of their own destiny, and that the strong cultural movements represented by the foreign press, schools, and colonies

* From *Atlantic Monthly*, 118 (July 1916), pp. 86–97.

are a challenge to our facile attempts, is not, however, to admit the
failure of Americanization. It is not to fear the failure of democracy.
It is rather to urge us to an investigation of what Americanism may
rightly mean. It is to ask ourselves whether our ideal has been broad
or narrow – whether perhaps the time has not come to assert a higher
ideal than the 'melting-pot.' Surely we cannot be certain of our spiritual democracy when, claiming to melt the nations within us to a
comprehension of our free and democratic institutions, we fly into
panic at the first sign of their own will and tendency. We act as if we
wanted Americanization to take place only on our own terms, and not
by the consent of the governed. All our elaborate machinery of settlement and school and union, of social and political naturalization, however, will move with friction just in so far as it neglects to take into
account this strong and virile insistence that American shall be what
the immigrant will have a hand in making it, and not what a ruling
class, descendant of those British stocks which were the first permanent immigrants, decide that America shall be made. This is the condition which confronts us, and which demands a clear and general
readjustment of our attitude and our ideal.

I

Mary Antin is right when she looks upon our foreign-born as the people
who missed the Mayflower and came over on the first boat they could
find. But she forgets that when they did come it was not upon other
Mayflowers, but upon a 'Maiblume,' a 'Fleur de Mai,' a 'Fior di Maggio,'
a 'Majblomst.' These people were not mere arrivals from the same
family, to be welcomed as understood and long-loved, but strangers
to the neighborhood, with whom a long process of settling down had
to take place. For they brought with them their national and racial
characters, and each new national quota had to wear slowly away the
contempt with which its mere alienness got itself greeted. Each had
to make its way slowly from the lowest strata of unskilled labor up to
a level where it satisfied the accredited norms of social success.

We are all foreign-born or the descendants of foreign-born, and if
distinctions are to be made between us they should rightly be on some
other ground than indigenousness. The early colonists came over with
motives no less colonial than the later. They did not come to be assimilated in an American melting-pot. They did not come to adopt the
culture of the American Indian. They had not the smallest intention of

'giving themselves without reservation' to the new country. They came to get freedom to live as they wanted to. They came to escape from the stifling air and chaos of the old world; they came to make their fortune in a new land. They invented no new social framework. Rather they brought over bodily the old ways to which they had been accustomed. Tightly concentrated on a hostile frontier, they were conservative beyond belief. Their pioneer daring was reserved for the objective conquest of material resources. In their folkways, in their social and political institutions, they were, like every colonial people, slavishly imitative of the mother country. So that, in spite of the 'Revolution,' our whole legal and political system remained more English than the English, petrified and unchanging, while in England law developed to meet the needs of the changing times.

It is just this English-American conservatism that has been our chief obstacle to social advance. We have needed the new peoples – the order of the German and Scandinavian, the turbulence of the Slav and Hun – to save us from our own stagnation. I do not mean that the illiterate Slav is now the equal of the New Englander of pure descent. He is raw material to be educated, not into a New Englander, but into a socialized American along such lines as those thirty nationalities are being educated in the amazing schools of Gary. I do not believe that this process is to be one of decades of evolution. The spectacle of Japan's sudden jump from mediævalism to post-modernism should have destroyed that superstition. We are not dealing with individuals who are to 'evolve.' 'We are dealing with their children, who, with that education we are about to have, will start level with all of us. Let us cease to think of ideals like democracy as magical qualities inherent in certain peoples. Let us speak, not of inferior races, but of inferior civilizations. We are all to educate and to be educated. These peoples in America are in a common enterprise. It is not what we are now that concerns us, but what this plastic next generation may become in the light of a new cosmopolitan ideal.

We are not dealing with static factors, but with fluid and dynamic generations. To contrast the older and the newer immigrants and see the one class as democratically motivated by love of liberty, and the other by mere money-getting, is not to illuminate the future. To think of earlier nationalities as culturally assimilated to America, while we picture the later as a sodden and resistive mass, makes only for bitterness and misunderstanding. There may be a difference between these earlier and these later stocks, but it lies neither in motive for coming nor in strength of cultural allegiance to the homeland. The truth is that no more tenacious cultural allegiance to the mother country has been shown by any alien nation than by the ruling class of Anglo-Saxon descendants in these American States. English snobberies, English religion, English literary styles, English literary reverences and canons, English ethics,; English superiorities, have been the cultural food that we have drunk in from our mothers' breasts. The distinctively American spirit – pioneer, as distinguished from the reminiscently English – that appears in Whitman and Emerson and James, has had to exist on sufferance alongside of this other cult, unconsciously belittled by our cultural makers of opinion. No country has perhaps had so great indigenous genius which had so little influence on the country's traditions and expressions. The unpopular and dreaded German-American of the present day is a beginning amateur in comparison with those foolish Anglophiles of Boston and New York and Philadelphia whose reversion to cultural type sees uncritically in England's cause the cause of Civilization, and, under the guise of ethical independence of thought, carries along European traditions which are no more 'American' than the German categories themselves.

It speaks well for German-American innocence of heart or else for its lack of imagination that it has not turned the hyphen stigma into a 'Tu quoque!' If there were to be any hyphens scattered about, clearly they should be affixed to those English descendants who had had centuries of time to be made American where the German had had only half a century. Most significantly has the war brought out of them this alien virus, showing them still loving English things, owing allegiance to the English Kultur, moved by English shibboleths and prejudice. It is only because it has been the ruling class in this country that bestowed the epithets that we have not heard copiously and scornfully of 'hyphenated English Americans.' But even our quarrels with England have had the bad temper, the extravagance, of family quarrels. The Englishman of to-day nags us and dislikes us in that personal, peculiarly intimate way in which he dislikes the Australian, or as we may dislike our younger brothers. He still thinks of us incorrigibly as 'colonials.' America – official, controlling, literary, political America – is still, as a writer recently expressed it, 'culturally speaking, a self-governing dominion of the British Empire.'

The non-English American can scarcely be blamed if he sometimes thinks of the Anglo-Saxon predominance in America as little more than a predominance of priority. The Anglo-Saxon was merely the first immigrant, the first to found a colony. He has never really ceased to be the descendant of immigrants, nor has he ever succeeded in transforming that colony into a real nation, with a tenacious, richly woven fabric of native culture. Colonials from the other nations have come and settled down beside him. They found no definite native culture which should startle them out of their colonialism, and consequently they looked back to their mother-country, as the earlier Anglo-Saxon immigrant was looking back to his. What has been offered the new-comer has been the chance to learn English, to become a citizen, to salute the flag. And those elements of our ruling classes who are re-sponsible for the public schools, the settlements, all the organizations for amelioration in the cities, have every reason to be proud of the care and labor which they have devoted to absorbing the immigrant. His opportunities the immigrant has taken to gladly, with almost a pathetic eagerness to make his way in the new land without friction or disturbance. The common language has made not only for the necessary communication, but for all the amenities of life.

If freedom means the right to do pretty much as one pleases, so long as one does not interfere with others, the immigrant has found freedom, and the ruling element has been singularly liberal in its treatment of the invading hordes. But if freedom means a democratic coopera-tion in determining the ideals and purposes and industrial and social institutions of a country, then the immigrant has not been free, and the Anglo-Saxon element is guilty of just what every dominant race is guilty of in every European country: the imposition of its own culture upon the minority peoples. The fact that this imposition has been so mild and, indeed, semi-conscious does not alter its quality. And the war has brought just the degree to which that purpose of 'Americaniz-ing,' that is, 'Anglo- Saxonizing,' the immigrant has failed.

For the Anglo-Saxon now in his bitterness to turn upon the other peoples, talk about their 'arrogance,' scold them for not being melted in a pot which never existed, is to betray the unconscious purpose which lay at the bottom of his heart. It betrays too the possession of a racial jealousy similar to that of which he is now accusing the so-called 'hyphenates.' Let the Anglo-Saxon be proud enough of the her-oic toil and heroic sacrifices which moulded the nation. But let him ask himself, if he had had to depend on the English descendants, where he would have been living to-day. To those of us who see in the ex-ploitation of unskilled labor the strident red *leit-motif* of our civiliza-tion, the settling of the country presents a great social drama as the waves of immigration broke over it.

Let the Anglo-Saxon ask himself where he would have been if these races had not come? Let those who feel the inferiority of the non-Anglo-Saxon immigrant contemplate that region of the States which has remained the most distinctively 'American,' the South. Let him ask himself whether he would really like to see the foreign hordes Americanized into such an Americanization. Let him ask himself how superior this native civilization is to the great 'alien ' states of Wisconsin and Minnesota, where Scandinavians, Poles, and Germans have self-consciously labored to preserve their traditional culture, while being outwardly and satisfactorily American. Let him ask himself how much more wisdom, intelligence, industry and social leadership has come out of these alien states than out of all the truly American ones. The South, in fact, while this vast Northern development has gone on, still remains an English colony, stagnant and complacent, having progressed culturally scarcely beyond the early Victorian era. It is culturally sterile because it has had no advantage of cross-fertilization like the Northern states. What has happened in states such as Wisconsin and Minnesota is that strong foreign cultures have struck root in a new and fertile soil. America has meant liberation, and German and Scandinavian political ideas and social energies have expanded to a new potency. The process has not been at all the fancied 'assimilation' of the Scandinavian or Teuton. Rather has it beer a process of their assimilation of us – I speak as an Anglo-Saxon. The foreign cultures, have not been melted down or run together, made into some homogeneous Americanism, but have regained distinct but cooperating to the greater glory and benefit, not only of themselves but of all the native 'Americanism' around them.

What we emphatically do not want is that these distinctive qualities should be washed out into a tasteless, colorless fluid of uniformity. Already we have far too much of this insipidity, masses of people who are cultural half-breeds, neither assimilated Anglo-Saxons nor nationals of another culture. Each national colony in this country seems to retain in its foreign press, its vernacular literature, its schools, its intellectual and patriotic leaders, a central cultural nucleus. From this nucleus the colony extends out by imperceptible gradations to a fringe where national characteristics are all but lost. Our cities are filled with these half-breeds who retain their foreign names but have lost the foreign savor. This does not mean that they have actually been changed into New Englanders or Middle Westerners. It does not mean that they have been really Americanized. It means that, letting slip from them whatever native culture they had, they have substituted for it only the most rudimentary American – the American culture of the cheap newspaper, the 'movies,' the popular song, the ubiquitous automobile. The unthinking who survey this class call them assimilated, Americanized. The great American public school has done its work. With these people our institutions are safe. We may thrill with dread at the aggressive hyphenate, but this tame flabbiness is accepted as Americanization. The same moulders of opinion whose ideal is to melt the different races into Anglo-Saxon gold hail this poor product as the satisfying result of their alchemy.

Yet a truer cultural sense would have told us that it is not the self-conscious cultural nuclei that sap at our American life, but those fringes. It is not the Jew who sticks proudly to the faith of his fathers and boasts of that venerable culture of his who is dangerous to America, but the Jew who has lost the Jewish fire and become a mere elementary, grasping animal. It is not the Bohemian who supports the Bohemian schools in Chicago whose influence is sinister, but the Bohemian who has made money and has got into ward politics. Just so surely as we tend to disintegrate these nuclei of nationalistic culture do we tend to create hordes of men and women without a spiritual country, cultural outlaws, without taste, without standards but those of the mob. We sentence them to live on the most rudimentary planes of American life. The influences at the centre of the nuclei are centripetal. They make for the intelligence and the social values which mean an enhancement of life. And just because the foreign-born retains this expressiveness is he likely to be a better citizen of the American community. The influences at the fringe, however, are centrifugal, anarchical. They make for detached fragments of peoples. Those who came to find liberty achieve only license. They become the flotsam and jetsam of American life, the downward under tow of our civilization with its leering cheapness and falseness of taste and spiritual outlook, the absence of mind and sincere feeling which we see in our slovenly towns, our vapid moving pictures, our popular novels, and in the vacuous faces of the crowds on the city street. This is the cultural wreckage of our time, and it is from the fringes of the Anglo-Saxon as well as the other stocks that it falls. America has as yet no impelling integrating force. It makes too easily for this detritus of cultures. In our loose, free country, no constraining national purpose, no tenacious folk-tradition and folk-style hold the people to a line.

The war has shown us that not in any magical formula will this purpose be found. No intense nationalism of the European plan can be ours. But do we not begin to see a new and more adventurous ideal? Do we not see how the national colonies in America, deriving power from the deep cultural heart of Europe and yet living here in mutual toleration, freed from the age long tangles of races, creeds, and dynasties, may work out a federated ideal? America is transplanted Europe, but a Europe that has not been disintegrated and scattered in the transplanting as in some Dispersion. Its colonies live here inextricably mingled, yet not homogeneous. They merge but they do not fuse.

America is a unique sociological fabric, and it bespeaks poverty of imagination not to be thrilled at the incalculable potentialities of so novel a union of men. To seek no other, goal than the weary old nationalism – belligerent, exclusive, inbreeding, the poison of which we are witnessing now in Europe, – is to make patriotism a hollow sham, and to declare that, in spite of our boastings, America must ever be a follower and not a leader of nations.

II

If we come to find this point of view plausible, we shall have to give up the search for our native 'American' culture. With the exception of the South and that New England which, like the Red Indian, seems to be passing into solemn oblivion, there is no distinctively American culture. It is apparently our lot rather to be a federation of cultures. This we have been for half a century, and the war has made it ever more evident that this is what we are destined to remain. This will not mean, however, that there are not expressions of indigenous genius that could not have sprung from any other soil. Music, poetry, philosophy, have been singularly fertile and new. Strangely enough, American genius has flared forth just in those directions which are least understood of the people. If the American note is bigness, action, the objective as contrasted with the reflective life, where is the epic expression of this spirit? Our drama and our fiction, the peculiar fields for the expression of action and objectivity, are somehow exactly the fields of the spirit which remain poor and mediocre. American materialism is in some way inhibited from getting into impressive artistic form its own energy with which it bursts. Nor is it any better in architecture, the least romantic and subjective of all the arts. We are inarticulate of the very values which we profess to idealize. But in the finer forms – music, verse, the essay, philosophy – the American genius puts forth work equal to any of its contemporaries. Just in so far as our American genius has expressed the pioneer spirit, the adventurous, forward-looking drive of a colonial empire, is it representative of that whole America of the many races and peoples, and not of any partial or traditional enthusiasm. And only as that pioneer note is sounded can we really speak of the American culture. As long as we thought of Americanism in terms of the 'melting-pot,' our American cultural tradition lay in the past. It was something to which the new Americans were to be moulded. In the light of our changing ideal of Americanism, we must perpetrate the paradox that our American cultural tradition lies in the future. It will be what we all together make out of this incomparable opportunity of attacking the future with a new key.

Whatever American nationalism turns out to be, it is certain to become something utterly different from the nationalisms of twentieth-century Europe. This wave of reactionary enthusiasm to play the orthodox nationalistic game which is passing over the country is scarcely vital enough to last. We cannot swagger and thrill to the same national self-feeling. We must give new edges to our pride. We must be content to avoid the unnumbered woes that national patriotism has brought in Europe, and that fiercely heightened pride and self-consciousness. Alluring as this is, we must allow our imaginations to transcend this scarcely veiled belligerency. We can be serenely too proud to fight if our pride embraces the, creative forces of civilization which armed contest nullifies. We can be too proud to fight if our code of honor transcends that of the schoolboy on the playground surrounded by his jeering mates. Our honor must be positive and creative, and not the mere jealous and negative protectiveness against metaphysical violations of our technical rights. When the doctrine is put forth that in one American flows the mystic blood of all our country's sacred honor, freedom, and prosperity, so that an injury to him is to be the signal for turning our whole nation into that clan-feud of horror and reprisal which would be war, then we find ourselves back among the musty schoolmen of the Middle Ages, and not in any pragmatic and realistic America of the twentieth century.

We should hold our gaze to what America has done, not what mediaeval codes of dueling she has failed to observe. We have transplanted European modernity to our soil, without the spirit that inflames it and turns all its energy into mutual destruction. Out of these foreign peoples there has somehow been squeezed the poison. An America, 'hyphenated' to bitterness, is somehow non-explosive. For, even if we all hark back in sympathy to a European nation, even if the war has set every one vibrating to some emotional string twanged on the other side of the Atlantic, the effect has been one of almost dramatic harmlessness.

What we have really been witnessing, however unappreciatively, in this country has been a thrilling and bloodless battle of Kulturs. In that arena of friction which has been the most dramatic – between the hyphenated German-American and the hyphenated English-American – there have emerged rivalries of philosophies which show up deep traditional attitudes, points of view which accurately reflect the gigantic issues of the war. America has mirrored the spiritual issues. The vicarious struggle has been played out peacefully here in the mind. We have seen the stout resistiveness of the old moral interpretation of history on which Victorian England thrived and made itself great in its own esteem. The clean and immensely satisfying vision of the war as a contest between right and wrong; the enthusiastic support of the Allies as the incarnation of virtue-on-a-rampage; the fierce envisaging of their selfish national purposes as the ideals of justice, freedom and democracy – all this has been thrown with intensest force against the German realistic interpretations in terms of the struggle for power and the virility of the integrated State. America has been the intellectual battle ground of the nations.

III

The failure of the melting-pot, far from closing the great American democratic experiment, means that it has only just begun. Whatever American nationalism turns out to be, we see already that it will have a color richer and more exciting than our ideal has hitherto encompassed. In a world which has dreamed of internationalism, we find that we have all unawares been building up the first international nation. The voices which have cried for a tight and jealous nationalism of the European pattern are failing. From that ideal, however valiantly and disinterestedly it has been set for us, time and tendency have moved us further and further away. What we have achieved has been rather a cosmopolitan federation of national colonies, of foreign cultures, from whom the sting of devastating competition has been removed. America is already the world federation in miniature, the continent where for the first time in history has been achieved that miracle of hope, the peaceful living side by side, with character substantially preserved, of the most heterogeneous peoples under the sun. Nowhere else has such contiguity been anything but the breeder of misery. Here, notwithstanding our tragic failures of adjustment, the outlines are already too clear not to give us a new vision and a new orientation of the American mind in the world.

It is for the American of the younger generation to accept this cosmopolitanism, and carry it along with self- conscious and fruitful purpose. In his colleges, he is already getting, with the study of modern history and politics, the modern literatures, economic geography, the privilege of a cosmopolitan outlook such as the people of no other nation of to-day in Europe can possibly secure. If he is still a colonial, he is no longer the colonial of one partial culture, but of many. He is a colonial of the world. Colonialism has grown into cosmopolitanism, and his motherland is no one nation, but all who have anything life-enhancing to offer to the spirit. That vague sympathy which the France of ten years ago was feeling for the world – a sympathy which was drowned in the terrible reality of war – may be the modern American's, and that in a positive and aggressive sense. If the American is parochial, it is in sheer wantonness or cowardice. His provincialism is the measure of his fear of bogies or the defect of his imagination.

Indeed, it is not uncommon for the eager Anglo-Saxon who goes to a vivid American university to-day to find his true friends not among his own race but among the acclimatized German or Austrian, the acclimatized Jew, the acclimatized Scandinavian or Italian. In them he finds the cosmopolitan note. In these youths, foreign-born or the children of foreign-born parents, he is likely to find many of his old inbred morbid problems washed away. These friends are oblivious to the repressions of that tight little society in which he so provincially grew up. He has a pleasurable sense of liberation from the stale and familiar attitudes of those whose ingrowing culture has scarcely created anything vital for his America of to-day. He breathes a larger air. In his new enthusiasms for continental literature, for unplumbed Russian depths, for French clarity of thought, for Teuton philosophies of power, he feels himself citizen of larger world. He may be absurdly superficial, his outward-reaching wonder may ignore all the stiller and homelier virtues of his Anglo-Saxon home, but he has at least found the clue to that international mind which will be essential to all men and women of good-will if they are ever to save this Western world of ours from suicide. His new friends have gone through a similar evolution. America has burned most of the baser metal also from them. Meeting now with this common American background, all of them may yet retain that distinctiveness of their native cultures and their national spiritual slants. They are more valuable and interesting to each other for being different, yet that difference could not be creative were it not for this new cosmopolitan outlook which America has given them and which they all equally possess.

A college where such a spirit is possible even to the smallest degree, has within itself already the seeds of this international intellectual world of the future. It suggests that the contribution of America will be an intellectual internationalism which goes far beyond the mere exchange of scientific ideas and discoveries and the cold recording of facts. It will be an intellectual sympathy which is not satisfied until it has got at the heart of the different cultural expressions, and felt as they feel. It may have immense preferences, but it will make understanding and not indignation its end. Such a sympathy will unite and not divide.

Against the thinly disguised panic which calls itself 'patriotism' and the thinly disguised militarism which calls itself 'preparedness' the cosmopolitan ideal is set. This does not mean that those who hold it are for a policy of drift. They, too, long passionately for an integrated and disciplined America. But they do not want one which is integrated only for domestic economic exploitation of the workers or for predatory economic imperialism among the weaker peoples. They do not want one that is integrated by coercion or militarism, or for the truculent assertion of a mediaeval code of honor and of doubtful rights. They believe that the most effective integration will be one which coordinates the diverse elements and turns them consciously toward working out together the place of America in the world-situation. They demand for integration a genuine integrity, a wholeness and soundness of enthusiasm and purpose which can only come when no national colony within our America feels that it is being discriminated against or that its cultural case is being prejudged. This strength of cooperation, this feeling that all who are here may have a hand in the destiny of America, will make for a finer spirit of integration than any narrow 'Americanism' or forced chauvinism.

In this effort we may have to accept some form of that dual citizenship which meets with so much articulate horror among us. Dual citizenship we may have to recognize as the rudimentary form of that international citizenship to which, if our words mean anything, we aspire. We have assumed unquestioningly that mere participation in the political life of the United States must cut the new citizen off from all sympathy with his old allegiance. Anything but a bodily transfer of devotion from one sovereignty to another has been viewed as a sort of moral treason against the Republic. We have insisted that the immigrant whom we welcomed escaping from the very exclusive nationalism of his European home shall forthwith adopt a nationalism just as exclusive, just as narrow, and even less legitimate because it is founded on no warm traditions of his own. Yet a nation like France is said to permit a formal and legal dual citizenship even at the present time.

Though a citizen of hers may pretend to cast of his allegiance in favor of some other sovereignty, he is still subject to her laws when he returns. Once a citizen, always a citizen, no matter how many new citizenships he may embrace. And such a dual citizenship seems to us sound and right. For it recognizes that, although the Frenchman may accept the formal institutional framework of his new country and indeed become intensely loyal to it, yet his Frenchness he will never lose. What makes up the fabric of his soul will always be of this Frenchness, so that unless he becomes utterly degenerate he will always to some degree dwell still in his native environment.

Indeed, does not the cultivated American who goes to Europe practice a dual citizenship, which, if not formal, is no less real? The American who lives abroad may be the least expatriate of men. If he falls in love with French ways and French thinking and French democracy and seeks to saturate himself with the new spirit, he is guilty of at least a dual spiritual citizenship. He may be still American, yet he feels himself through sympathy also a Frenchman. And he finds that this expansion involves no shameful conflict within him, no surrender of his native attitude. He has rather for the first time caught a glimpse of the cosmopolitan spirit. And after wandering about through many races and civilizations he may return to America to find them all here living vividly and crudely, seeking the same adjustment that he made. He sees the new peoples here with a new vision. They are no longer masses of aliens, waiting to be 'assimilated,' waiting to be melted down into the indistinguishable dough of Anglo-Saxonism. They are rather threads of living and potent cultures, blindly striving to weave themselves into a novel international nation, the first the world has seen. In an Austria-Hungary or a Prussia the stronger of these cultures would be moving almost instinctively to subjugate the weaker. But in America those wills-to-power are turned in a different direction into learning how to live together.

Along with dual citizenship we shall have to accept, I think, that free and mobile passage of the immigrant between America and his native land again which now arouses so much prejudice among us. We shall have to accept the immigrant's return for the same reason that we consider justified our own flitting about the earth. To stigmatize the alien who works in America for a few years and returns to his own land, only perhaps to seek American fortune again, is to think in narrow nationalistic terms. It is to ignore the cosmopolitan significance of this migration. It is to ignore the fact that the returning immigrant is often a missionary to an inferior civilization.

This migratory habit has been especially common with the unskilled laborers who have been pouring into the United States in the last dozen years from every country in southeastern Europe. Many of them return to spend their earnings in their own country or to serve their country in war. But they return with an entirely new critical outlook, and a sense of the superiority of American organization to the primitive living around them. This continued passage to and fro has already raised the material standard of living in many regions of these backward countries. For these regions are thus endowed with exactly what they need, the capital for the exploitation of their natural resources, and the spirit of enterprise. America is thus educating these laggard peoples from the very bottom of society up, awaking vast masses to a new-born hope for the future. In the migratory Greek, therefore, we have not the parasitic alien, the doubtful American asset, but a symbol of that cosmopolitan interchange which is coming, in spite of all war and national exclusiveness.

Only America, by reason of the unique liberty of opportunity and traditional isolation for which she seems to stand, can lead in this cosmopolitan enterprise. Only the American – and in this category I include the migratory alien who has lived with us and caught the pioneer spirit and a sense of new social vistas – has the chance to become that citizen of the world. America is coming to be, not a nationality but a trans-nationality, a weaving back and forth, with the other lands, of many threads of all sizes and colors. Any movement which attempts to thwart this weaving, or to dye the fabric any one color, or disentangle the threads of the strands, is false to this cosmopolitan vision. I do not mean that we shall necessarily glut ourselves with the raw product of humanity. It would be folly to absorb the nations faster than we could weave them. We have no duty either to admit or reject. It is purely a question of expediency. What concerns us is the fact that the strands are here. We must have a policy and an ideal for an actual situation. Our question is, What shall we do with our America? How are we likely to get the more creative America – by confining our imaginations to the ideal of the melting-pot, or broadening them to some such cosmopolitan conception as I have been vaguely sketching?

The war has shown America to be unable, though isolated geographically and politically from a European world-situation, to remain aloof and irresponsible. She is a wandering star in a sky dominated by two colossal constellations of states. Can she not work out some position of her own, some life of being in, yet not quite of, this seething and embroiled European world? This is her only hope and promise. A trans-nationality of all the nations, it is spiritually impossible for her to pass into the orbit of any one. It will be folly to hurry herself into a premature and sentimental nationalism, or to emulate Europe and play fast and loose with the forces that drag into war. No Americanization will fulfill this vision which does not recognize the uniqueness of this trans-nationalism of ours. The Anglo-Saxon attempt to fuse will only create enmity and distrust. The crusade against 'hyphenates' will only inflame the partial patriotism of transnationals, and cause them to assert their European traditions in strident and unwholesome ways. But the attempt to weave a wholly novel international nation out of our chaotic America will liberate and harmonize the creative power of all these peoples and give them the new spiritual citizenship, as so many individuals have already been given, of a world.

Is it a wild hope that the undertow of opposition to metaphysics in international relations, opposition to militarism, is less a cowardly provincialism than a groping for this higher cosmopolitan ideal? One can understand the irritated restlessness with which our proud pro-British colonists contemplate a heroic conflict across the seas in which they have no part. It was inevitable that our necessary inaction should evolve in their minds into the bogey of national shame and dishonor. But let us be careful about accepting their sensitiveness as final arbiter. Let us look at our reluctance rather as the first crude beginnings of assertion on the part of certain strands in our nationality that they have a right to a voice in the construction of the American ideal. Let us face realistically the America we have around us. Let us work with the forces that are at work. Let us make something of this trans-national spirit instead of outlawing it. Already we are living this cosmopolitan America. What we need is everywhere a vivid consciousness of the new ideal. Deliberate headway must be made against the survivals of the melting-pot ideal for the promise of American life.

We cannot Americanize America worthily by sentimentalizing and mortalizing history. When the best schools are expressly renouncing the questionable duty of teaching patriotism by means of history, it is not the time to force shibboleth upon the immigrant. This form of Americanization has been heard because it appealed to the vestiges of our old sentimentalized and moralized patriotism. This has so far held the field as the expression of the new American's new devotion. The inflections of other voices have been drowned. They must be heard. We must see if the lesson of the war has not been for hundreds of these later Americans a vivid realization of their trans-nationality, a new consciousness of what America meant to them as a citizenship in the world. It is the vague historic idealisms which have provided the fuel for the European flame. Our American ideal can make no progress until we do away with this romantic gilding of the past.

All our idealisms must be those of future social goals in which all can participate, the good life of personality lived in the environment of the Beloved Community. No mere doubtful triumphs of the past, which redound to the glory of only one of our transnationalities, can satisfy us. It must be a future America, on which all can unite, which pulls us irresistibly toward it, as we understand each other more warmly.

To make real this striving amid dangers and apathies is work for a younger *intelligentsia* of America. Here is an enterprise of integration into which we can all pour ourselves, of a spiritual welding which should make us, if the final menace ever came, not weaker, but infinitely strong.

9 The Problem of Generations (1928)

Karl Mannheim*

I HOW THE PROBLEM STANDS AT THE MOMENT

A The Positivist Formulation of the Problem

The first task of the sociologist is to review the general state of investigation into his problem. All too often it falls to his lot to deal with stray problems to which all the sciences in turn have made their individual contribution without anyone having ever paid any attention to the continuity of the investigation as a whole. We shall need to do more, however, than give a mere survey of past contributions to the problem of generations. We must try to give a critical evaluation of the present stage of discussion (in Part I); this will help us in our own analysis of the problem (in Part II).

Two approaches to the problem have been worked out in the past: a 'positivist' and a 'romantic-historical' one. These two schools represent two antagonistic types of attitudes towards reality, and the different ways in which they approach the problem reflect this contrast of basic attitudes. The methodical ideal of the Positivists consisted in reducing their problems to quantitative terms; they sought a quantitative formulation of factors ultimately determining human existence. The second school adopted a qualitative approach, firmly eschewing the clear day light of mathematics, and introverting the whole problem.

To begin with the former. The Positivist is attracted by the problem of generations because it gives him the feeling that here he has achieved contact with some of the ultimate factors of human existence as such. There is life and death; a definite, measurable span of life; generation follows generation at regular intervals. Here, thinks the Positivist, is the framework of human destiny in comprehensible, even measurable form. All other data are conditioned within the process of life itself:

* From *Das Problem der Generationen* (1928), Chapter VII in Paul Kecskemeti (ed.), *Essays on the Sociology of Knowledge* (New York: Oxford University Press, 1952), pp. 276–322.

they are only the expression of particular relationships. They can disappear, and their disappearance means only the loss of one of many possible forms of historical being. But if the ultimate human relationships are changed, the existence of man as we have come to understand it must cease altogether – culture, creativeness, tradition must all disappear, or must at least appear in a totally different light.

Hume actually experimented with the idea of a modification of such ultimate data. Suppose, he said, the type of succession of human generations to be completely altered to resemble that of a butterfly or caterpillar, so that the older generation disappears at one stroke and the new one is born all at once. Further, suppose man to be of such a high degree of mental development as to be capable of choosing rationally the form of government most suitable for himself. (This, of course, was the main problem of Hume's time.) These conditions given, he said, it would be both possible and proper for each generation, without reference to the ways of its ancestors, to choose afresh its own particular form of state. Only because mankind is as it is – generation following generation in a continuous stream, so that whenever one person dies off, another is born to replace him – do we find it necessary to preserve the continuity of our forms of government. Hume thus translates the principle of political continuity into terms of the biological continuity of generations.

Comte[1] too toyed with a similar idea: he tried to elucidate the nature and tempo of progress (the central problem of his time) by assuming a change in the basic data of the succession of generations and of the average length of life. If the average span of life of every individual were either shortened or lengthened, he said, the tempo of progress would also change. To lengthen the life-span of the individual would mean slowing up the tempo of progress, whereas to reduce the present duration of life by half or a quarter would correspondingly accelerate the tempo, because the restrictive, conservative, 'go-slow' influence of the older generation would operate for a longer time, should they live longer, and for a shorter time, should they disappear more quickly.

An excessively retarded pace was harmful, but there was also danger that too great an acceleration might result in shallowness, the potentialities of life never being really exhausted. Without wishing to imply that our world is the best of all possible worlds, Comte nevertheless thought that our span of life average generation period 30 years were necessary correlatives of our organism, and that further, the slow progress of mankind was directly related to this organic limitation.

The tempo of progress and the presence of conservative as well as reforming forces in society are thus directly attributed to biological factors. This is, indeed, how the problem looks in broad daylight. Everything is almost mathematically clear: everything is capable of analysis into its constituent elements, the constructive imagination of the thinker celebrates its triumph; by freely combining the available data, he has succeeded in grasping the ultimate, constant elements of human existence, and the secret of History lies almost fully revealed before us.

The rationalism of positivism is a direct continuation of classical rationalism, and it shows the French at work in its own domain. In fact, the important contributors to the problem are for the most part French. Comte, Cournot, J. Dromel, Mentré, and others outside Germany are positivists or, at any rate, have come under their influence. Ferrari, the Italian, and O. Lorenz, the Austrian historian, all worked at a time when the positivist wave encompassed all Europe.[2]

Their formulations of the problem had something in common. They all were anxious to find a general law to express the rhythm of historical development, based on the biological law of the limited life-span of man and the overlap of new and old generations. The aim was to understand the changing patterns of intellectual and social currents directly in biological terms, to construct the curve of the progress of the human species in terms of its vital substructure. In the process, everything, so far as possible, was simplified: a schematic psychology provided that the parents should always be a conservative force.

Presented in this light, the history of ideas reduced to a chronological table. The core of the problem, after this simplification, appears to be to find the average period of time taken for the older generation to be superseded by the new in public life, and principally, to find the natural starting-point in history from which to reckon a new period. The duration of a generation is very variously estimated – many assessing it at 15 years (e.g. Dromel), but most taking it to mean 30 years, on the ground that during the first 30 years of life people are still learning, that individual creativeness on an average begins only at that age, and that at 60 a man quits public life.[3] Even more difficult is it to find the natural beginning of the generation series, because birth and death in society as a whole follow continuously one upon the other, and full intervals exist only in the individual family where there is a definite period before children attain marriageable age.

This constitutes the core of this approach to the problem: the rest represents mere applications of the principle to concrete instances found in history. But the analytical mind remains at work all the time, and brings to light many important ramifications of the problem while working on the historical material.

Mentré[4] in particular, who first reviewed the problem historically, placed the whole formulation on a more solid basis.[5] He takes up the analysis of the problem of generations in the human family after a discussion of the same phenomenon among animals, based on the work of Espinas (*'Les Sociétés Animales'*, Paris, 1877). It is only after having investigated these elementary aspects of the problem that he takes up more complex aspects, such as the question of social and intellectual generations.

We also must take into account a refinement of the problem due to Mentré which flows from the distinction he makes (in common with Lévy-Bruhl) between 'institutions' and *'séries libres'*. A rhythm in the sequence of generations is far more apparent in the realm of the *'séries'* – free human groupings such as salons and literary circles – than in the realm of the institutions which for the most part lay down a lasting pattern behaviour either by prescriptions or by the organisation of collective understandings, thus preventing the new generation from its originality. An essential part of his work is concerned with the question as to whether there is what he calls a *pre-eminent sphere* in history (for example, politics, science, law, art, economics, etc.) which determines all others. He comes to the conclusion that there is no such dominant sphere imposing its own rhythm of development upon the others, since all alike are embedded in the general stream of history,[6] although the aesthetic sphere is perhaps the most appropriate to reflect overall changes of mental climate. An analysis of the history of this sphere in France since the 16th century led him to the view that essential changes had come about at intervals of 30 years.

Mentré's book is useful as the first comprehensive survey of the problem, although in reality it yields little, considering its volume, and fails to probe deeply enough or to formulate the problem in systematic terms. That the French recently became so interested in the problem of change from one generation to another was largely due to the fact that they witnessed the sudden eclipse of liberal cosmopolitanism as a result of the arrival of a nationalistically-minded young generation. The change of generations appeared as an immediately given datum and also as a problem extending far outside the academic field, a problem whose impact upon real life could be observed in concrete fashion, for example, by issuing questionnaires.[7]

Although Mentré occasionally makes remarks which point beyond a purely quantitative approach, we may consider him as a positivist whose treatment of the problem of generations thus far represents the last word of the school on this subject.

We must now turn our attention to the alternative romantic historical approach.

B The Romantic – Historical Formulation of the Problem

We find ourselves in a quite different atmosphere if we turn to Germany and trace the development of the problem there. It would be difficult to find better proof of the thesis that ways of formulating problems and modes or thought differ from country to country and from epoch to epoch, depending on dominant political trends than the contrasting solutions offered to our problem in the various countries at different times. It is true that Rümelin, who attacked the problem from the statistical viewpoint, and O. Lorenz, who used genealogical research data as his starting-point, both remained faithful to the positivist spirit of their epoch. But the whole problem of generations took on a specifically 'German' character when Dilthey tackled it. All the traditions and impulses which once inspired the romantic-historical school were revived in Dilthey's work; in Dilthey we witness the sudden re-emergence, in revised form, of problems and categories which in their original, romantic-historicist setting helped found the social and historical sciences in Germany.

In Germany and France, the predominating trends of thought in the last epoch emerged closely related with their respective historical and political structures.

In France a positivist type of thought, deriving directly from the tradition of the Enlightenment, prevailed. It tended to dominate not merely the natural but also the cultural sciences. It not only inspired progressive and oppositional groups, but even those professing Conservatism and traditionalism. In Germany, on the other hand, the position was just the reverse – the romantic and historical schools supported by a strong conservative impulse always held sway. Only the natural sciences were able to develop in the positivist tradition: the cultural sciences were based entirely on the romantic-historical attitude, and positivism gained ground only sporadically, in so far as from time to time it was sponsored by oppositional groups.

Although the antithesis must not be exaggerated, it is nevertheless true that it provided rallying points in the struggle which was conducted round practically every logical category; and the problem of

generations itself constituted merely one stage in the development of
this much wider campaign. Unless we put this antithesis between French
positivism and German romanticism into its wider context, we cannot
hope to understand it in relation to the narrower problem of generations.

For the liberal positivist type, especially at home, as stated, in France,
the problem of generations serves above all as evidence in favour of
its unilinear conception of progress.

This type of thought, arising out of modern liberal impulses, from
the outset adopted a mechanistic, externalised concept of time, and
attempted to use it as an objective measure unilinear progress by virtue of its expressibility in quantitative terms. Even the succession of
generations was considered as something which articulated rather than
broke the unilinear continuity of time. The most important thing about
generations from this point was that they constituted one of the essential driving forces of progress.

It is this concept of progress, on the other hand, that is challenged
by the romantic and historicist German mind which, relying on data
furnished by a conservative technique of observation, points to the
problem of generations precisely as evidence against the concept of
unilinear development in history.[8] The problem of generations is seen
here as the problem of the existence of an interior time that cannot be
measured but only experienced in purely qualitative terms.

The relative novelty of Dilthey's work consists in just this distinction which he made between the qualitative and quantitative concept
of time. Dilthey is interested in the problem of generations primarily
because, as he puts it, the adoption of the 'generation' as a temporal
unit of the history of intellectual evolution makes it possible to replace
such purely external units as hours, months, years, decades, etc., by a
concept of measure operating from within (*eine von innen abmessende
Vorstellung*). The use of generations as units makes it possible to appraise intellectual movements by an intuitive process of re-enactment.[9]

The second conclusion to which Dilthey comes in connection with
the phenomenon of generations is that not merely is the succession of
one after another important, but also that their *co-existence* is of more
than mere chronological significance. The same dominant influences
deriving from the prevailing intellectual, social, and political circumstances are experienced by contemporary individuals, both in their early,
formative, and in their later years. They are contemporaries, they constitute one generation, just because they are subject to common influences. This idea that, from the point of view of the history of ideas,
contemporaneity means a state of being subjected to similar influences

rather than a mere chronological datum, shifts the discussion from a plane on which it risked degenerating into a kind of arithmetical mysticism to the sphere of interior time which can be grasped by intuitive understanding.

Thus, a problem open to quantitative, mathematical treatment only is replaced by a qualitative one, centred about the notion of something which is not quantifiable, but capable only of being experienced. The time-interval separating generations becomes subjectively experienceable time; and contemporaneity becomes a subjective condition of having been submitted to the same determining influences.

From here it is only one step to the phenomenological position of Heidegger, who gives a very profound interpretation of this qualitative relationship – for him, the very stuff and substance of Fate. 'Fate is not the sum of individual destinies, any more than togetherness can be understood as a mere appearing together of several subjects. Togetherness in the same world, and the consequent preparedness for a distinct set of possibilities, determines the direction of individual destinies in advance. The power of Fate is then unleashed in the peaceful intercourse and the conflict of social life. The inescapable fate of living in and with one's generation completes the full drama of individual human existence.'[10]

The qualitative concept of time upon which, as we have seen, Dilthey's approach was based, also underlies the formulation given the problem by the art historian Pinder.[11] Dilthey with a happy restraint is never led to develop any but genuine possibilities opened up by the romantic-qualitative approach. As a matter of fact, he was able to learn also from positivism. Pinder, on the other hand, becomes thoroughly enmeshed in all the confusions of romanticism. He gives many deep insights, but does not know how to avoid the natural excesses of romanticism. '*The non-contemporaneity of the contemporaneous*' is what interests Pinder most in relation to generations. Different generations live at the same time. But since experienced time is the only real time, they must all in fact be living in qualitatively quite different subjective eras. 'Everyone lives with people of the same and of different ages, with a variety of possibilities of experience facing them all alike. But for each the 'same time' is a different time – that is, it represents a different *period of his self*, which he can only share with people of his own age.'[12]

Every moment of time is therefore in reality more than a point-like event – it is a temporal volume having more than one dimension, because it is always experienced by several generations at various stages of development.[13] To quote a musical simile employed by Pinder: the thinking of each epoch is polyphonous. At any given point in time we must always sort out the individual voices of the various generations, each attaining that point in time in its own way.

A further idea suggested by Pinder is that each generation builds up an 'entelechy' of its own by which means alone it can really become a qualitative unity. Although Dilthey believed the inner unity of a generation to exist in the community of determining influences of an intellectual and social kind, the link of contemporaneity as such did not assume a purely qualitative form in his analysis. Heidegger tried to remedy this with his concept of 'fate' as the primary factor producing unity; Pinder, then, in the tradition of modern art history, suggested the concept of 'entelechy'.

According to him, the entelechy of a generation is the expression of the unity of its 'inner aim' – of its inborn way of experiencing life and the world. Viewed within the tradition of German art history, this concept of 'entelechy' represents the transfer of Riegl's concept of the 'art motive' (*Kunstwollen*)[14] from the phenomenon of unity of artistic styles to that of the unity of generations, in the same way as the concept of the 'art motive' itself resulted from the rejuvenation and fructification, under the influence of positivism, of the morphological tendency already inherent in the historicist concept of the '*Spirit of a people*' (*Volksgeist*).

The concept of a '*spirit of the age*' (*Zeitgeist*) with which one had hitherto principally worked, now turns out to be – to take another of Pinder's favourite[15] musical analogies – an accidental chord, an apparent harmony, produced by the vertical coincidence of notes which in fact owe a primary horizontal allegiance to the different parts (i.e. the generation-entelechies) of a fugue. The generation-entelechies thus serve to destroy the purely temporal concepts of an epoch over-emphasized in the past (e.g. Spirit of the age or epoch). The epoch as a unit has no homogeneous driving impulse, no homogeneous principle of form – no entelechy. Its unity consists at most in the related nature of the means which the period makes available for the fulfilment of the different historical tasks of the generations living in it. Periods have their characteristic colour – 'such colours do in fact exist, but somewhat as the colour-tone of a varnish through which one can look at the many colours of the different generations and age-groups'.[16]

Although this denial of the existence of an entelechy peculiar to each epoch means that epochs can no longer serve as units in historical analysis and that the concept of *Zeitgeist* becomes inapplicable and relativized, other terms customarily used as units in the history of ideas are left valid. According to Pinder, in addition to entelechies of generations, there exist entelechies of art, language, and style; entelechies of nations and tribes – even an entelechy of Europe; and finally, entelechies of the individuals themselves.

What then, according to Pinder, constitutes the historical process? The interplay of constant and transient factors. The constant factors are civilization, nation, tribe, family, individuality, and type; the transient factors are the entelechies already mentioned. 'It is maintained that growth is more important than experience ('influences', 'relationships'). It is maintained that the life of art, as seen by the historian, consists in the interactions of *determining* entelechies, *born* of mysterious processes of nature, with the equally essential frictions, influences, and relations *experienced* in the actual development of these entelechies.[17] What is immediately striking here is that the social factor is not even alluded to in this enumeration of determining factors.

This romantic tendency in Germany completely obscured the fact that between the natural or physical and the mental spheres there is a level of existence at which social forces operate. Either a completely spiritualistic attitude is maintained and everything is deduced from entelechies (the existence of which, however, is not to be denied), or there is a feeling of obligation to introduce some element of realism, and then some crude biological data like race and generation (which, again, must be admitted to exist) are counted upon to produce cultural facts by a 'mysterious natural process'. Undoubtedly, there are mysteries in the world in any case, but we should use them as explanatory principles in their proper place, rather than at points where it is still perfectly possible to understand the agglomeration of forces in terms of social processes. Intellectual and cultural history is surely shaped, among other things, by social relations in which men get originally confronted with each other, by groups within which they find mutual stimulus, where concrete struggle produces entelechies and thereby also influences and to a large extent shapes art, religion, and so on. Perhaps it would also be fruitful to ask ourselves whether society in fact can produce nothing more than 'influences' and 'relationships', or whether, on the contrary, social factors also possess a certain creative energy, a formative power, a social entelechy of their own. Is it not perhaps possible that this energy, arising from the interplay of social forces, constitutes the link between the other entelechies of art, style, generation, etc., which would otherwise only accidentally cross paths or come together? If one refuses to look at this matter from this point of view, and assumes a direct relationship between the spiritual and the vital without any sociological and historical factors mediating between them, he will be too easily tempted to conclude that especially productive generations are the 'chance products of nature',[18] and 'the problem of the times of birth will point towards the far more difficult and mysterious one of the times of death'.[19] How much more sober, how much more in tune with the genuine impulses of research, is the following sentence in which Dilthey, so to speak, disposed of such speculations in advance 'For the time being, the most natural assumption would appear to be that on the whole, both the degree and the distribution of ability are the same for each generation, the level of efficiency within the national society being constant, so that two other groups of conditions[20] would explain both the distribution and the intensity of achievement.'

Valuable, even a stroke of genius, is Pinder's idea of the 'non-contemporaneity of the contemporaneous', as well as his concept of entelechies – both the result of the romantic-historical approach and both undoubtedly unattainable by positivism. But his procedure becomes dangerously inimical to the scientific spirit where he chooses to make use of the method of analogy. This mode of thought, which actually derives from speculations about the philosophy of nature current during the Renaissance, was revived and blown up to grotesque proportions by the Romantics; it is used currently by Pinder whenever he tries to work out a biological world-rhythm. His ultimate aim also is to establish measurable intervals in history (although somewhat more flexibly than usual), and to use this magical formula of generations in order to discover birth cycles exercising a decisive influence on history. Joel,[21] otherwise an eminent scholar, indulges in even more unwarranted constructions in this field. His latest publication on the secular rhythm in history reminds the reader immediately of the romantic speculations.

It is a complete misconception to suppose, as do most investigators, that a real problem of generations exists only in so far as a rhythm of generations, recurring at unchanging intervals, can be established. Even if it proved impossible to establish such intervals, the problem of generations would nevertheless remain a fruitful and important field of research.

We do not yet know – perhaps there is a secular rhythm at work in history, and perhaps it will one day be discovered. But we must definitely repudiate any attempt to find it through imaginative speculations, particularly when this speculation – whether biological or spiritual in its character – is simply used as a pretext for avoiding research into the nearer and more transparent fabric of social processes and their influence on the phenomenon of generations. Any biological rhythm must work itself out through the medium of social events: and if this important group of formative factors is left unexamined, and everything is derived directly from vital factors, all the fruitful potentialities in the original formulation of the problem[22] are liable to be jettisoned in the manner of its solution.

II THE SOCIOLOGICAL PROBLEM OF GENERATIONS

The problem of generations is important enough to merit serious consideration. It is one of the indispensable guides to an understanding of the structure of social and intellectual movements. Its practical importance becomes clear as soon as one tries to obtain a more exact understanding of the accelerated pace of social change characteristic of our time. It would be regrettable if extra-scientific methods were permanently to conceal elements of the problem capable of immediate investigation.

It is clear from the foregoing survey of the problem as it stands today that a commonly accepted approach to it does not exist. The social sciences in various countries only sporadically take account of the achievements of their neighbours. In particular, German research into the problem of generations has ignored results obtained abroad. Moreover, the problem has been tackled by specialists in many different sciences in succession; thus, we possess a number of interesting sidelights on the problem as well as contributions to an overall solution, but no consciously directed research on the basis of a clear formulation of the problem as a whole.

The multiplicity of points of view, resulting both from the peculiarities of the intellectual traditions of various nations and from those of the individual sciences, is both attractive and fruitful; and there can be no doubt that such a wide problem can only be solved as a result of co-operation between the most diverse disciplines and nationalities. However, the co-operation must somehow be planned and directed from an organic centre. The present status of the problem of generations thus affords a striking illustration of the anarchy in the social and cultural sciences, where everyone starts out afresh from his own point of view (to a certain extent, of course, this is both necessary and fruitful), never pausing to consider the various aspects as part of a single general problem, so that the contributions of the various disciplines to the collective solution could be planned.

Any attempt at over-organization of the social and cultural sciences is naturally undesirable: but it is at least worth considering whether there is not perhaps one discipline – according to the nature of the problem in question – which could act as the organizing centre for work on it by all the others. As far as generations are concerned, the task of sketching the layout of the problem undoubtedly falls to sociology. It seems to be the task of *Formal Sociology* to work out the simplest, but at the same time the most fundamental facts relating to the phenomenon of generations. Within the sphere of formal sociology, however, the problem lies on the borderline between the static and the dynamic types of investigation. Whereas formal sociology up to now has tended for the most part to study the social existence of man exclusively *statically*, this particular problem seems to be one of those which have to do with the ascertainment of the origin of social dynamism and of the laws governing the action of the dynamic components of the social process. Accordingly, this is the point where we have to make the transition from the formal static to the formal dynamic and from thence to applied historical sociology – all three together comprising the complete field of sociological research.

In the succeeding pages we shall attempt to work out in formal sociological terms all the most elementary facts regarding the phenomenon of generations, without the elucidation of which historical research into the problem cannot even begin. We shall try to incorporate any results of past investigations, which have proved themselves relevant, ignoring those which do not seem to be sufficiently well founded.

A Concrete Group – Social Location (*Lagerung*)

To obtain a clear idea of the basic structure of the phenomenon of generations, we must clarify the specific inter-relations of the individuals comprising a single generation-unit.

The unity of a generation does not consist primarily in a social bond of the kind that leads to the formation of a concrete group, although it may sometimes happen that a feeling for the unity of a generation is consciously developed into a basis for the formation of concrete groups, as in the case of the modern German Youth Movement.[23] But in this case, the groups are most often mere cliques, with the one distinguishing characteristic that group-formation is based upon the consciousness of belonging to one generation, rather than upon definite objectives.

Apart from such a particular case, however, it is possible in general to draw a distinction between generations as mere collective facts on the one hand, and *concrete social groups* on the other.

Organizations for specific purposes, the family, tribe, sect, are all examples of such *concrete groups*. Their common characteristic is that the individuals of which they are composed do actually *in concrete* form a group, whether the entity is based on vital, existential ties of 'proximity' or on the conscious application of the rational will. All 'community' groups (*Gemeinschaftsgebilde*), such as the family and the tribe, come under the former heading, while the latter comprises 'association' groups (*Gesellschaftsgebilde*).

The generation is not a concrete group in the sense of a community, i.e. a group which cannot exist without its members having concrete knowledge of each other, and which ceases to exist as a mental and spiritual unit as soon as physical proximity is destroyed. On the other hand, it is in no way comparable to associations such as organizations formed for a specific purpose, for the latter are characterized by a deliberate act of foundation, written statutes, and a machinery for dissolving the organization – features serving to hold the group together, even though it lacks the ties of spatial proximity and of community of life.

By a concrete group, then, we mean the union of a number of individuals through naturally developed or consciously willed ties. Although the members of a generation are undoubtedly bound together in certain ways, the ties between them have not resulted in a concrete group. How, then, can we define and understand the nature of the generation as a social phenomenon?

An answer may perhaps be found if we reflect upon the character of a different sort of social category, materially quite unlike the generation but bearing a certain structural resemblance to it – namely, the class position (*Klassenlage*) of an individual in society.

In its wider sense class-position can be defined as the common 'location' (*Lagerung*) certain individuals hold in the economic and power structure of a given society as their 'lot'. One is proletarian *entrepreneur*, or *rentier*, and he is what he is because he is constantly aware of the nature of his specific 'location' in the social structure, i.e. of the pressures or possibilities of gain resulting from that position. This place in society does not resemble membership of an organization terminable by a conscious act of will. Nor is it at all binding in the same way as membership of a community (*Gemeinschaft*) which means that a concrete group affects every aspect of an individual's existence.

It is possible to abandon one's class position through an individual or collective rise or fall in the social scale, irrespective for the moment whether this is due to personal merit, personal effort, social upheaval, or mere chance.

Membership of an organization lapses as soon as we give notice of our intention to leave it; the cohesion of the community group *ceases to exist* if the mental and spiritual dispositions on which its existence has been based cease to operate in us or in our partners; and our previous class position loses its relevance for us as soon as we acquire a new position as a result of a change in our economic and power status.

Class position is an objective fact, whether the individual in question knows his class position or not, and whether he acknowledges it or not.

Class-consciousness does not necessarily accompany a class position, although in certain social conditions the latter can give rise to the former, lending it certain features, and resulting in the formation of a 'conscious class'.[24] At the moment, however, we are only interested in the general phenomenon of social *location* as such. Besides the concrete social group, there is also the phenomenon of similar location of a number of individuals in a social structure – under which heading both classes and generations fall.

We have now taken the first step towards an analysis of the 'location' phenomenon as distinct from the phenomenon '*concrete group*', and this much at any rate is clear – viz. the unity of generations is constituted essentially by a similarity of location of a number of individuals within a social whole.

B   The Biological and Sociological Formulation of the Problem of Generations

Similarity of location can be defined only by specifying the structure within which and through which location groups emerge in historical-social reality. Class-position was based upon the existence of a changing economic and power structure in society. Generation location is based on the existence of biological rhythm in human existence – the factors of life and death, a limited span of life, and ageing. Individuals who belong to the same generation, who share the same year of birth, are endowed, to that extent, with a common location in the historical dimension of the social process.

Now, one might assume that the sociological phenomenon of location can be explained by, and deduced from, these basic biological factors. But this would be to make the mistake of all naturalistic theories which try to deduce sociological phenomena directly from natural facts, or lose sight of the social phenomenon altogether in a mass of primarily anthropological data. Anthropology and biology only help us explain the phenomena of life and death, the limited span of life, and the mental, spiritual, and physical changes accompanying ageing as such; they offer no explanation of the relevance these primary factors have for the shaping of social interrelationships in their historic flux.

The sociological phenomenon of generations is ultimately based on the biological rhythm of birth and death. But to be *based* on a factor does not necessarily mean to be *deducible* from it, or to be implied in it. If a phenomenon is *based* on another, it could not exist without the latter; however, it possesses certain characteristics peculiar to itself, characteristics in no way borrowed from the basic phenomenon. Were it not for the existence of social interaction between human beings − were there no definable social structure, no history based on a particular sort of continuity, the generation would not exist as a social location phenomenon; there would merely be birth, ageing, and death. The *sociological* problem of generations therefore begins at that point where the sociological relevance of these biological factors is discovered. Starting with the elementary phenomenon itself, then, we must first of all try to understand the generation as a particular type of social location.

C   The Tendency 'Inherent In' a Social Location

The fact of belonging to the same class, and that of belonging to the same generation or age group, have this in common, that both endow the individuals sharing in them with a common location in the social and historical process, and thereby limit them to a specific range of potential experience, predisposing them for a certain characteristic mode of thought and experience, and a characteristic type of historically relevant action. Any given location, then, excludes a large number of possible modes of thought, experience, feeling, and action, and restricts the range of self-expression open to the individual to certain circumscribed possibilities. This *negative* delimitation, however, does not exhaust the matter. Inherent in a *positive* sense in every location is a tendency pointing towards certain definite modes of behaviour, feeling, and thought.

We shall therefore speak in this sense of a tendency 'inherent in' every social location; a tendency which can be determined from the particular nature of the location as such.

For any group of individuals sharing the same class position, society always appears under the same aspect, familiarized by constantly repeated experience. It may be said in general that the experiential, intellectual, and emotional data which are available to the members of a certain society are not uniformly 'given' to all of them; the fact is rather that each class has access to only one set of those data, restricted to one particular 'aspect'. Thus, the proletarian most probably appropriates only a fraction of the cultural heritage of his society, and that in the manner of his group. Even a mental climate as rigorously uniform as that of the Catholic Middle Ages presented itself differently according to whether one were a theologizing cleric, a knight, or a monk. But even where the intellectual material is more or less uniform or at least uniformly accessible to all, the *approach* to the material, the way in which it is assimilated and applied, is determined in its direction by social factors. We usually say in such cases that the approach is deter-mined by the special traditions of the social stratum concerned. But these traditions themselves are explicable and understandable not only in terms of the history of the stratum but above all in terms of the location relationships of its members within the society. Traditions bearing in a particular direction only persist so long as the location relation-ships of the group acknowledging them remain more or less unchanged. The concrete form of an existing behaviour pattern or of a cultural product does not derive from the history of a particular tradition but ultimately from the history of the location relationships in which it originally arose and hardened itself into a tradition.

D   Fundamental Facts in Relation to Generations

According to what we have said so far, the social phenomenon 'gen-eration' represents nothing more than a particular kind of identity of location, embracing related 'age groups' embedded in a historical-social process. While the nature of class location can be explained in terms of economic and social conditions, generation location is deter-mined by the way in which certain patterns of experience and thought tend to be brought into existence by the *natural data* of the transition from one generation to another.

   The best way to appreciate which features of social life result from the existence of generations is to make the experiment of imagining what the social life of man would be like if one generation lived on for ever and none followed to replace it. In contrast to such a utopian, imaginary society, our own has the following characteristics:[25]

(*a*) new participants in the cultural process are emerging, whilst
(*b*) former participants in that process are continually disappearing;

(c) members of any one generation can participate only in a temporally limited section of the historical process, and

(d) it is therefore necessary continually to transmit the accumulated
cultural heritage;

(e) the transition from generation to generation is a continuous process.

These are the basic phenomena implied by the mere fact of the existence of generations, apart from one specific phenomenon we choose
to ignore for the moment, that of physical and mental ageing.[26] With
this as a beginning, let us then investigate the bearing of these elementary facts upon formal sociology.

(a) *The continuous emergence of new participants in the cultural process*
In contrast to the imaginary society with no generations, our own – in
which generation follows generation – is principally characterized by
the fact that cultural creation and cultural accumulation are not accomplished by the same individuals – instead, we have the continuous
emergence of new age groups.

This means, in the first place, that our culture is developed by individuals who come into contact anew with the accumulated heritage. In
the nature of our psychical make-up, a fresh contact (meeting something anew) always means a changed relationship of distance from the
object and a novel approach in assimilating, using, and developing the
proffered material. The phenomenon of 'fresh contact' is, incidentally,
of great significance in many social contexts; the problem of generations is only one among those upon which it has a bearing. Fresh
contacts play an important part in the life of the individual when he is
forced by events to leave his own social group and enter a new one –
when, for example, an adolescent leaves home, or a peasant the country-
side for the town, or when an emigrant changes his home, or a social
climber his social status or class. It is well known that in all these
cases a quite visible and striking transformation of the consciousness
of the individual in question takes place: a change, not merely in the
content of experience, but in the individual's mental and spiritual adjustment to it. In all these cases, however, the fresh contact is an event
in one individual biography, whereas in the case of generations, we
may speak of 'fresh contacts' in the sense of the addition of new psy-
cho-physical units who are in the literal sense beginning a 'new life'.
Whereas the adolescent, peasant, emigrant, and social climber can only
in a more or less restricted sense be said to begin a 'new life', in the
case of generations, the 'fresh contact' with the social and cultural

heritage is determined not by mere social change, but by fundamental biological factors. We can accordingly differentiate between two types of 'fresh contact': one based on a shift in social relations, and the other on vital factors (the change from one generation to another). The latter type is *potentially* much more radical, since with the advent of the new participant in the process of culture, the change of attitude takes place in a different individual whose attitude towards the heritage handed down by his predecessors is a novel one.

Were there no change of generation, there would be no 'fresh contact' of this biological type. If the cultural process were always carried on and developed by the same individuals, then, to be sure, 'fresh contacts' might still result from shifts in social relationships, but the more radical form of 'fresh contact' would be missing. Once established, any fundamental social pattern (attitude or intellectual trend) would probably be perpetuated – in itself an advantage, but not if we consider the dangers resulting from one-sidedness. There might be a certain compensation for the loss of fresh generations in such a utopian society only if the people living in it were possessed, as befits the denizens of a Utopia, of perfectly universal minds – minds capable of experiencing all that there was to experience and of knowing all there was to know, and enjoying an elasticity such as to make it possible at any time to start afresh. 'Fresh contacts' resulting from shifts in the historical and social situation could suffice to bring about the changes in thought and practice necessitated by changed conditions only if the individuals experiencing these fresh contacts had such a perfect 'elasticity of mind'. Thus the continuous emergence of new human beings in our own society acts as compensation for the restricted and partial nature of the individual consciousness. The continuous emergence of new human beings certainly results in some loss of accumulated cultural possessions; but, on the other hand, it alone makes a fresh selection possible when it becomes necessary; it facilitates re-evaluation of our inventory and teaches us both to forget that which is no longer useful and to covet that which has yet to be won.

(b) *The continuous withdrawal of previous participants in the process of culture*
The function of this second factor is implied in what has already been said. It serves the necessary social purpose of enabling us to forget. If society is to continue, social remembering is just as important as forgetting and action starting from scratch.

At this point we must make clear in what social form remembering manifests itself and how the cultural heritage is actually accumulated. All psychic and cultural data only really exist in so far as they are produced and reproduced in the present: hence past experience is only relevant when it exists concretely incorporated in the present. In our present context, we have to consider two ways in which past experience can be incorporated in the present:

(i) as consciously recognized models[27] on which men pattern their behaviour (for example, the majority of subsequent revolutions tended to model themselves more or less consciously on the French Revolution); or

(ii) as unconsciously 'condensed', merely 'implicit' or 'virtual' patterns; consider, for instance, how past experiences are 'virtually' contained in such specific manifestations as that of sentimentality. Every present performance operates a certain selection among handed-down data, for the most part unconsciously. That is, the traditional material is transformed to fit a prevailing new situation, or hitherto unnoticed or neglected potentialities inherent in that material are discovered in the course of developing new patterns of action:[28]

At the more primitive levels of social life, we mostly encounter unconscious selection. There the past tends to be present in a 'condensed', 'implicit', and 'virtual' form only. Even at the present level of social reality, we see this unconscious selection at work in the deeper regions of our intellectual and spiritual lives, where the tempo of transformation is of less significance. A conscious and reflective selection becomes necessary only when a semi-conscious transformation, such as can be effected by the traditionalist mind, is no longer sufficient. In general, rational elucidation and reflectiveness invade only those realms of experience which become problematic as a result of a change in the historical and social situation; where that is the case, the necessary transformation can no longer be effected without conscious reflection and its technique of de-stabilization.

We are directly aware primarily of those aspects of our culture which have become subject to reflection; and these contain only those elements which in the course of development have somehow, at some point, become problematical. This is not to say, however, that once having become conscious and reflective, they cannot again sink back into the a-problematical, untouched region of vegetative life. In any case, that form of memory which contains the past in the form of reflection is much less significant – e.g. it extends over a much more restricted range of experience – than that in which the past is only 'implicitly', 'virtually' present; and reflective elements are more often dependent on unreflective elements than *vice versa*.

Here we must make a fundamental distinction between *appropri-ated* memories and *personally acquired* memories (a distinction appli-cable both to reflective and unreflective elements). It makes a great difference whether I acquire memories for myself in the process of personal development, or whether I simply take them over from some-one else. I only really possess those 'memories' which I have created directly for myself, only that 'knowledge' I have personally gained in real situations. This is the only sort of knowledge which really 'sticks' and it alone has real binding power. Hence, although it would appear desirable that man's spiritual and intellectual possessions should con-sist of nothing but individually acquired memories, this would also involve the danger that the earlier ways of possession and acquisition will inhibit the new acquisition of knowledge. That experience goes with age is in many ways an advantage. That, on the other hand, youth lacks experience means a lightening of the ballast for the young; it facilitates their living on in a changing world. One is old primarily in so far as[29] he comes to live within a specific, individually acquired, framework of useable past experience, so that every new experience has its form and its place largely marked out for it in advance. In youth, on the other hand, where life is new, formative forces are just coming into being, and basic attitudes in the process of development can take advantage of the moulding power of new situations. Thus a human race living on for ever would have to learn to forget to com-pensate for the lack of new generations.

(c) *Members of any one generation can only participate in a temporally limited section of the historical process*
The implications of this basic fact can also be worked out in the light of what has been said so far. The first two factors, (a) and (b), were only concerned with the aspects of constant 'rejuvenation' of society. To be able to start afresh with a new life, to build a new destiny, a new framework of anticipations, upon a new set of experiences, are things which can come into the world only through the fact of new birth. All this is implied by the factor of social rejuvenation. The fac-tor we are dealing with now, however, can be adequately analysed only in terms of the category of 'similarity of location' which we have mentioned but not discussed in detail above.[30]

Members of a generation are 'similarly located', first of all, in so far as they all are exposed to the same phase of the collective process. This, however, is a merely mechanical and external criterion of the phenomenon of 'similar location'. For a deeper understanding, we must turn to the phenomenon of the 'stratification' of experience (*Erlebnisschichtung*), just as before we turned to 'memory'. The fact that people are born at the same time, or that their youth, adulthood, and old age coincide, does not in itself involve similarity of location; what does create a similar location is that they are in a position to experience the same events and data, etc., and especially that these experiences impinge upon a similarly 'stratified' consciousness. It is not difficult to see why mere chronological contemporaneity cannot of itself produce a common generation location. No one, for example, would assert that there was community of location between the young people of China and Germany about 1800. Only where contemporaries definitely are in a position to participate as an integrated group in certain common experiences can we rightly speak of community of location of a generation. Mere contemporaneity becomes sociologically significant only when it also involves participation in the same historical and social circumstances. Further, we have to take into consideration at this point the phenomenon of 'stratification', mentioned above. Some older generation groups experience certain historical processes together with the young generation and yet we cannot say that they have the same generation location. The fact that their location is a different one, however, can be explained primarily by the different 'stratification' of their lives. The human consciousness, structurally speaking, is characterized by a particular inner 'dialectic'. It is of considerable importance for the formation of the consciousness which experiences happen to make those all-important 'first impressions', 'childhood experiences – and which follow to form the second, third, and other 'strata'. Conversely, in estimating the biographical significance of a particular experience, it is important to know whether it is undergone by an individual as a decisive childhood experience, or later in life, superimposed upon other basic and early impressions. Early impressions tend to coalesce into a *natural view* of the world. All later experiences then tend to receive their meaning from this original set, whether they appear as that set's verification and fulfilment or as its negation and antithesis. Experiences are not accumulated in the course of a lifetime through a process of summation or agglomeration, but are 'dialectically' articulated in the way described. We cannot here analyse the specific forms of this dialectical articulation, which is potentially present whenever we act, think, or feel, in more detail (the relationship of 'antithesis' is only one way in which new experiences may graft themselves upon old ones). This much, however, is certain, that even if the rest of one's life consisted in one long process of negation and destruction of the natural world view acquired in youth, the determining influence of these early impressions would still be predominant. For even in negation our orientation is fundamentally centred upon that which is being negated, and we are thus still unwittingly determined by it. If we bear in mind that every concrete experience acquires its particular face and form from its relation to this primary stratum of experiences from which all others receive their meaning, we can appreciate its importance for the further development of the human consciousness. Another fact, closely related to the phenomenon just described, is that any two generations following one another always fight different opponents, both within and without. While the older people may still be combating something in themselves or in the external world in such fashion that all their feelings and efforts and even their concepts and categories of thought are determined by that adversary, for the younger people this adversary may be simply non-existent: their primary orientation is an entirely different one. That historical development does not proceed in a straight line – a feature frequently observed particularly in the cultural sphere – is largely attributed to this shifting of the 'polar' components of life, that is, to the fact that internal or external adversaries constantly disappear and are replaced by others. Now this particular dialectic, of changing generations, would be absent from our imaginary society. The only dialectical features of such a society would be those which would arise from social polarities – provided such polarities were present. The primary experiential stratum of the members of this imaginary society would simply consist of the earliest experiences of mankind; all later experience would receive its meaning from that stratum.

(d) *The necessity for constant transmission of the cultural heritage*
Some structural facts which follow from this must at least be indicated here. To mention one problem only: a utopian, immortal society would not have to face this necessity of cultural transmission, the most important aspect of which is the automatic passing on to the new generations of the traditional ways of life, feelings, and attitudes. The data transmitted by conscious teaching are of more limited importance, both quantitatively and qualitatively. All those attitudes and ideas which go on functioning satisfactorily in the new situation and serve as the basic inventory of group life are unconsciously and unwittingly handed on and transmitted: they seep in without either the teacher or pupil knowing anything about it. What is consciously learned or inculcated belongs to those things which in the course of time have somehow,

somewhere, become problematic and therefore invited conscious reflection. This is why that inventory of experience which is absorbed
by infiltration from the environment in early youth often becomes the
historically oldest stratum of consciousness, which tends to stabilize
itself as the natural view of the world.[31]

But in early childhood even many reflective elements are assimilated in the same 'a-problematical' fashion as those elements of the
basic inventory had been. The new germ of an original intellectual
and spiritual life which is latent in the new human being has by no
means as yet come into its own. The possibility of really questioning
and reflecting on things only emerges at the point where personal experimentation with life begins – round about the age of 17, sometimes
a little earlier and sometimes a little later.[32] It is only then that life's
problems begin to be located in a 'present' and are experienced as
such. That level of data and attitudes which social change has rendered problematical, and which therefore requires reflection, has now
been reached; for the first time, one lives 'in the present'. Combative
juvenile groups struggle to clarify these issues, but never realize that,
however radical they are, they are merely out to transform the upper-
most stratum of consciousness which is open to conscious reflection.
For it seems that the deeper strata are not easily de-stabilized[33] and
that when this becomes necessary, the process must start out from the
level of reflection and work down to the stratum of habits.[34] The 'up-
to-dateness' of youth therefore consists in their being closer to the
'present' problems (as a result of their 'potentially fresh contact' discussed above, pp. 125 ff.), and in the fact that they are dramatically
aware of a process of de-stabilization and take sides in it. All this
while, the older generation cling to the re-orientation that had been
the drama of *their* youth.

From this angle, we can see that an adequate education or instruction of the young (in the sense of the complete transmission of all
experiential stimuli which underlie pragmatic knowledge) would encounter a formidable difficulty in the fact that the experiential problems of the young are defined by a different set of adversaries from
those of their teachers. Thus (apart from the exact sciences), the teacher-
pupil relationship is not as between one representative of 'consciousness in general' and another, but as between one possible subjective
centre of vital orientation and another subsequent one. This tension[35]
appears incapable of solution except for one compensating factor: not
only does the teacher educate his pupil, but the pupil educates his
teacher too. Generations are in a state of constant interaction.

This leads us to our next point:

(e) *The uninterrupted generation series*

The fact that the transition from one generation to another takes place continuously tends to render this interaction smoother; in the process of this interaction, it is not the oldest who meet the youngest at once; the first contacts are made by other 'intermediary' generations, less removed from each other.

Fortunately, it is not as most students of the generation problem suggest – the thirty-year interval is not solely decisive. Actually, all intermediary groups play their part; although they cannot wipe out the biological difference between generations, they can at least mitigate its consequences. The extent to which the problems of younger generations are reflected back upon the older one becomes greater in the measure that the dynamism of society increases. Static conditions make for attitudes of piety – the younger generation tends to adapt itself to the older, even to the point of making itself appear older. With the strengthening of the social dynamic, however, the older generation becomes increasingly receptive to influences from the younger.[36] This process can be so intensified that, with an elasticity of mind won in the course of experience, the older generation may even achieve greater adaptability in certain spheres than the intermediary generations, who may not yet be in a position to relinquish their original approach.[37]

Thus, the continuous shift in objective conditions has its counterpart in a continuous shift in the oncoming new generations which are first to incorporate the changes in their behaviour system. As the tempo of change becomes faster, smaller and smaller modifications are experienced by young people as significant ones, and more and more intermediary shades of novel impulses become interpolated between the oldest and newest re-orientation systems. The underlying inventory of vital responses, which remains unaffected by the change, acts in itself as a unifying factor; constant interaction, on the other hand, mitigates the differences in the top layer where the change takes place, while the continuous nature of the transition in normal times lessens the frictions involved. To sum up: if the social process involved no change of generations, the new impulses that can originate only in new organisms could not be reflected back upon the representatives of the tradition; and if the transition between generations were not continuous, this reciprocal action could not take place without friction.

E   Generation Status, Generation as Actuality, Generation Unit

This, then, broadly constitutes those aspects of generation phenomena which can be deduced by formal analysis. They would completely determine the effects resulting from the existence of generations if they could unfold themselves in a purely biological context, or if the generation phenomenon could be understood as a mere location phenomenon. However, a generation in the sense of a location phenomenon falls short of encompassing the generation phenomenon in its full actuality.[38] The latter is something more than the former, in the same way as the mere fact of class position does not yet involve the existence of a consciously constituted class. The location as such only contains potentialities which may materialize, or be suppressed, or become embedded in other social forces and manifest themselves in modified form. When we pointed out that mere co-existence in time did not even suffice to bring about community of generation location, we came very near to making the distinction which is now claiming our attention. In order to share the same generation location, i.e. in order to be able passively to undergo or actively to use the handicaps and privileges inherent in a generation location, one must be born within the same historical and cultural region. Generation as an actuality, however, involves even more than mere co-presence in such a historical and social region. A further concrete nexus is needed to constitute generation as an actuality. This additional nexus may be described as *participation in the common destiny* of this historical and social unit.[39] This is the phenomenon we have to examine next.

We said above that, for example, young people in Prussia about 1800 did not share a common generation location with young people in China at the same period. Membership in the same historical community, then, is the widest criterion of community of generation location. But what is its narrowest criterion? Do we put the peasants, scattered as they are in remote districts and almost untouched by current upheavals, in a common actual generation group with the urban youth of the same period? Certainly not! – and precisely because they remain unaffected by the events which move the youth of the towns. We shall therefore speak of a *generation as an actuality* only where a concrete bond is created between members of a generation by their being exposed to the social and intellectual symptoms of a process of dynamic de-stabilization. Thus, the young peasants we mentioned above only share the same generation location, without, however, being members of the same generation as an actuality, with the youth of the town.

They are similarly located, in so far as they are *potentially* capable of being sucked into the vortex of social change, and, in fact, this is what happened in the wars against Napoleon, which stirred up all German classes. For these peasants' sons, a mere generation location was transformed into membership of a generation as an actuality. Individuals of the same age, they were and are, however, only united as an actual generation in so far as they participate in the characteristic social and intellectual currents of their society and period, and in so far as they have an active or passive experience of the interactions of forces which made up the new situation. At the time of the wars against Napoleon, nearly all social strata were engaged in such a process of give and take, first in a wave of war enthusiasm, and later in a movement of religious revivalism. Here, however, a new question arises. Suppose we disregard all groups which, do *not* actively participate in the process of social transformation – does this mean that all those groups which *do* so participate, constitute one generation? From 1800 on, for instance, we see two contrasting groups – one which became more and more conservative as time went on, as against a youth group tending to become rationalistic and liberal. It cannot be said that these two groups were unified by the *same* modern mentality. Can we then speak, in this case, of the same actual generation? We can, it seems, if we make a further terminological distinction. Both the romantic-conservative and liberal-rationalist youth belonged to the same actual generation, romantic-conservatism and liberal-rationalism were merely two *polar forms* of the intellectual and social response to an historical stimulus experienced by all in common. Romantic-conservative youth, and liberal-rationalist group, belong to the same actual generation but form separate 'generation units' within it. The generation unit represents a much more concrete bond than the actual generation as such. *Youth experiencing the same concrete historical problems may be said to be part of the same actual generation; while those groups within the same actual generation which work up the material of their common experiences in different specific ways, constitute separate generation units.*

F   The Origin of Generation Units

The question now arises, what produces a generation unit? In what does the greater intensity of the bond consist in this case? The first thing that strikes one on considering any particular generation unit is the great similarity in the data making up the consciousness of its members. Mental data are of sociological importance not only because of their actual content, but also because they cause the individuals sharing them to form one group – they have a socializing effect. The concept of Freedom, for example, was important for the Liberal generation-unit, not merely because of the material demands implied by it, but also because in and through it it was possible to unite individuals scattered spatially and otherwise.[40] The data such, however, are not the primary factor producing a group – this function belongs to a far greater extent to those formative forces which shape the data and give them character and direction. From the casual slogan to a reasoned system of thought, from the apparently isolated gesture to the finished work of art, the same formative tendency is often at work – the social importance of which lies in its power to bind individuals socially together. The profound emotional significance of a slogan, of an expressive gesture, or of a work of art lies in the fact that we not merely absorb them as objective data, but also as vehicles of formative tendencies and fundamental integrative attitudes, thus identifying ourselves with a set of collective strivings.

Fundamental integrative attitudes and formative principles are all-important also in the handing down of every tradition, firstly because they alone can bind groups together, secondly, and, what is perhaps even more important, they alone are really capable of becoming the basis of continuing practice. A mere statement of fact has a minimum capacity of initiating a continuing practice. Potentialities of a continued thought process, on the other hand, are contained in every thesis that has real group-forming potency; intuitions, feelings, and works of art which create a spiritual community among men also contain in themselves the potentially new manner in which the intuition, feeling, or work of art in question can be re-created, rejuvenated and reinterpreted in novel situations. That is why unambiguousness, too great clarity is not an unqualified social value; productive misunderstanding is often a condition of continuing life. Fundamental integrative attitudes and formative principles are the primary socializing forces in the history of society, and it is necessary to live them fully in order really to participate in collective life.

Modern psychology provides more and more conclusive evidence in favour of the *Gestalt* theory of human perception: even in our most elementary perceptions of objects, we do not behave as the old atomistic psychology would have us believe; that is, we do not proceed towards a global impression by the gradual summation of a number of elementary sense data, but on the contrary, we start off with a global impression of the object as a whole. Now if even sense perception is governed by the *Gestalt* principle, the same applies, to an even greater extent, to the process of intellectual interpretation. There may be a number of reasons why the functioning of human consciousness should be based on the *Gestalt* principle, but a likely factor is the relatively limited capacity of the human consciousness when confronted with the infinity of elementary data which can be dealt with only by means of the simplifying and summarizing *Gestalt* approach. Seeing things in terms of *Gestalt*, however, also has its social roots with which we must deal here. Perceptions and their linguistic expressions never exist exclusively for the isolated individual who happens to entertain them, but also for the social group which stands behind the individual. Thus, the way in which seeing in terms of *Gestalt* modifies the datum as such – partly simplifying and abbreviating it, partly elaborating and filling it out – always corresponds to the meaning which the object in question has for the social groups as a whole. We always see things already formed in a special way; we think concepts defined in terms of a specific context. Form and context depend, in any case, on the group to which we belong. To become really assimilated into a group involves more than the mere acceptance of its characteristic values– it involves the ability to see things from its particular 'aspect', to endow concepts with its particular shade of meaning, and to experience psychological and intellectual impulses in the configuration characteristic of the group. It means, further, to absorb those interpretive formative principles which enable the individual to deal with new impressions and events in a fashion broadly pre-determined by the group.

The social importance of these formative and interpretive principles is that they form a link between spatially separated individuals who may never come into personal contact at all. Whereas mere common 'location' in a generation is of only potential significance, a generation as an actuality is constituted when similarly 'located' contemporaries participate in a common destiny and in the ideas and concepts which are in some way bound up with its unfolding. Within this community of people with a common destiny there can then arise particular *generation-units*. These are characterized by the fact that they do not merely involve a loose participation by a number of individuals in a pattern of events shared by all alike though interpreted by the different individuals differently, but an identity of responses, a certain affinity in the way in which all move with and are formed by their common experiences.

Thus within any generation there can exist a number of differentiated, antagonistic generation-units. Together they constitute an 'actual' generation precisely because they art oriented toward each other, even though only in the sense of fighting one another. Those who were young about 1810 in Germany constituted one actual generation whether they adhered to the then current version of liberal or conservative ideas. But in so far as they were conservative or liberal, they belonged to different units of that actual generation.

The generation-unit tends to impose a much more concrete and binding tie on its members because of the parallelism of responses it involves. As a matter of fact, such new, overtly created, partisan integrative attitudes characterizing generation-units do not come into being spontaneously, without a personal contact among individuals, but within *concrete groups* where mutual stimulation in a close-knit vital unit inflames the participants and enables them to develop integrative attitudes which do justice to the requirements inherent in their common 'location'. Once developed in this way, however, these attitudes and formative tendencies are capable of being detached from the concrete groups of their origin and of exercising an appeal and binding force over a much wider area.

The generation-unit as we have described it is not, as such, a concrete group, although it does have as its nucleus a concrete group which has developed the most essential new conceptions which are subsequently developed by the unit. Thus, for example, the set of basic ideas which became prevalent in the development of modern German Conservatism had its origin in the concrete association '*Christlich-deutsche Tischgesellschaft*'. This association was first to take up and reformulate all irrational tendencies corresponding to the overall situation prevailing at that time, and to the particular 'location', in terms of generation, shared by the young Conservatives. Ideas which later were to have recruiting power in far wider circles originated in this particular concrete group.

The reason for the influence exercised beyond the limits of the original concrete group by such integrative attitudes originally evolved within the group is primarily that they provide a more or less adequate expression of the particular 'location' of a generation as a whole. Hence, individuals outside the narrow group but nevertheless similarly located find in them the satisfying expression of their location in the prevailing *historical configuration*. Class ideology, for example, originates in more closely knit concrete groups and can gain ground only to the extent that other individuals see in it a more or less adequate expression and interpretation of the experiences peculiar to their particular *social* location. Similarly, the basic integrative attitudes and formative principles represented by a generation-unit, which are originally evolved within such a concrete group, are only really effective and capable of expansion into wider spheres when they formulate the typical experiences of the individuals sharing a generation location. Concrete groups can become influential in this sense if they succeed in evolving a 'fresh contact' in terms of a 'stratification of experience', such as we have described above. There is, in this respect, a further analogy between the phenomenon of class and that of generation. Just as a class ideology may, in epochs favourable to it, exercise an appeal beyond the 'location' which is its proper habitat,[41] certain impulses particular to a generation may, if the trend of the times is favourable to them, also attract individual members of earlier or later age-groups.

But this is not all; it occurs very frequently that the nucleus of attitudes particular to a new generation is first evolved and practised by older people who are isolated in their own generation (forerunners),[42] just as it is often the case that the forerunners in the development of a particular class ideology belong to a quite alien class.

All this, however, does not invalidate our thesis that there are new basic impulses attributable to a particular generation location which, then, may call forth generation units. The main thing in this respect is that the proper vehicle of these new impulses is always a collectivity. The real seat of the class ideology remains the class itself, with its own typical opportunities and handicaps – even when the author of the ideology, as it may happen, belongs to a different class, or when the ideology expands and becomes influential beyond the limits of the class location. Similarly, the real seat of new impulses remains the generation location (which will selectively encourage one form of experience and eliminate others), even when they may have been fostered by other age-groups.

The most important point we have to notice is the following: not every generation location – not even every age-group – creates new collective impulses and formative principles original to itself and adequate to its particular situation. Where this does happen, we shall speak of a *realization of potentialities inherent* in the location, and it appears probable that the frequency of such realizations is closely connected with the tempo of social change.[43] When as a result of an acceleration in the tempo of social and cultural transformation basic attitudes must change so quickly that the latent, continuous adaptation and modification of traditional patterns of experience, thought, and expression is no longer possible, then the various new phases of experience are consolidated somewhere, forming a clearly distinguishable new impulse, and a new centre of configuration. We speak in such cases of the formation of a new generation style, or of a *new generation entelechy*.

Here too, we may distinguish two possibilities. On the one hand, the generation unit may produce its work and deeds unconsciously out of the new impulse evolved by itself, having an intuitive awareness of its existence as a group but failing to realize the group's character as a generation unit. On the other hand, groups may consciously experience and emphasize their character as generation units – as is the case with the contemporary German youth movement, or even to a certain extent with its forerunner, the Student's Association (*Burschenschaft*) Movement in the first half of the nineteenth century, which already manifested many of the characteristics of the modern youth movement.

The importance of the acceleration of social change for the realization of the potentialities inherent in a generation location is clearly demonstrated by the fact that largely static or very slowly changing communities like the peasantry display no such phenomenon as new generation units sharply set off from their predecessors by virtue of an individual entelechy proper to them; in such communities, the tempo of change is so gradual that new generations evolve away from their predecessors without any visible break, and all we can see is the purely biological differentiation and affinity based upon difference or identity of age. Such biological factors are effective, of course, in modern society too, youth being attracted to youth and age to age. The generation unit as we have described it, however, could not arise solely on the basis of this simple factor of attraction between members of the same age-group.

The quicker the tempo of social and cultural change is, then, the greater are the chances that particular generation location groups will react to changed situations by producing their own entelechy. On the other hand, it is conceivable that too greatly accelerated a tempo might lead to mutual destruction of the embryo entelechies. As contemporaries, we can observe, if we look closely, various finely graded patterns of response of age groups closely following upon each other and living side by side; these age groups, however, are so closely packed together that they do not succeed in achieving a fruitful new formulation of distinct generation entelechies and formative principles. Such generations, frustrated in the production of an individual entelechy, tend to attach themselves, where possible, to an earlier generation which may have achieved a satisfactory form, or to a younger generation which is capable of evolving a newer form. Crucial group experiences can act in this way as 'crystallizing agents', and it is characteristic of cultural life that unattached elements are always attracted to perfected configurations,

even when the unformed, groping impulse differs in many respects
from the configuration to which it is attracted. In this way the impulses
and trends peculiar to a generation may remain concealed because of
the existence of the clear-cut form of another generation to which they
have become attached.

From all this emerges the fact that each generation need not evolve
its own, distinctive pattern of interpreting and influencing the world;
the rhythm of successive generation locations, which is largely based
upon biological factors, need not necessarily involve a parallel rhythm
of successive motivation patterns and formative principles. Most generation theories, however, have this in common, that they try to establish a direct correlation between waves of decisive year classes of birth
– set at intervals of thirty years, and conceived in a purely naturalistic, quantifying spirit – on the one hand, and waves of cultural changes
on the other. Thus they ignore the important fact that the realization
of hidden potentialities inherent in the generation location is governed
by extra-biological factors, principally, as we have seen, by the prevailing tempo and impact of social change.

Whether a new *generation style* emerges every year, every thirty,
every hundred years, or whether it emerges rhythmically at all, depends
entirely on the trigger action of the social and cultural process. One
may ask, in this connection, whether the social dynamic operates predominantly through the agency of the economic or of one or the other
'ideological' spheres: but this is a problem which has to be examined
separately. It is immaterial in our context how this question is answered;
all we have to bear in mind is that it depends on this group of social
and cultural factors whether the impulses of a generation shall achieve
a distinctive unity of style, or whether they shall remain latent. The
biological fact of the existence of generations merely provides the
possibility that generation entelechies may emerge at all – if there
were no different generations succeeding each other, we should never
encounter the phenomenon of generation styles. But the question which
generation locations will realize the potentialities inherent in them,
finds its answer at the level of the social and cultural structure – a
level regularly skipped by the usual kind of theory which starts from
naturalism and then abruptly lands in the most extreme kind of
spiritualism.

A formal sociological clarification of the distinction between the
categories 'generation location', 'generation as actuality', and 'generation
unit', is important and indeed indispensable for any deeper analysis,
since we can never grasp the dominant factors in this field without

making that distinction. If we speak simply of 'generations' without any further differentiation, we risk jumbling together purely biological phenomena and others which are the product of social and cultural forces: thus we arrive at a sort of sociology of chronological tables (*Geschichtstabellensoziologie*), which uses its bird's-eye perspective to 'discover' fictitious generation movements to correspond to the crucial turning-points in historical chronology.

It must be admitted that biological data constitute the most basic stratum of factors determining generation phenomena; but for this very reason, we cannot observe the effect of biological factors directly; we must, instead, see how they are reflected through the medium of social and cultural forces.

As a matter of fact, the most striking feature of the historical process seems to be that the most basic biological factors operate in the most latent form, and can only be grasped in the medium of the social and historical phenomena which constitute a secondary sphere above them. In practice this means that the student of the generation problem cannot try to specify the effects attributable to the factor of generations before he has separated all the effects due to the specific dynamism of the historical and social sphere. If this intermediary sphere is skipped, one will be tempted to resort immediately to naturalistic principles, such as generation, race, or geographical situation, in explaining phenomena due to environmental or temporal influences.

The fault of this naturalistic approach lies not so much in the fact that it emphasizes the role of natural factors in human life, as in its attempt to explain *dynamic* phenomena directly by something *constant*, thus ignoring and distorting precisely that intermediate spare in which dynamism really originates. Dynamic factors operate on the basis of constant, factors – on the basis of anthropological, geographical, etc., data – but on each occasion the dynamic factors seize upon different potentialities inherent in the constant factors. If we want to understand the primary, constant factors, we must observe them in the framework of the historical and social system of forces from which they receive their shape. Natural factors, including the succession of generations, provide the basic range of potentialities for the historical and social process. *But precisely because they are constant and therefore always present in any situation, the particular features of a given process of modification cannot be explained by references to them.*

Their varying relevance (the particular way in which they can manifest themselves in this or that situation) can be clearly seen only if we pay proper attention to the formative layer of social and cultural forces.

G   The Generation in Relation to other Formative Factors in History

It has been the merit of past theorizing about generations that it has kept alive scientific interest in this undoubtedly important factor in the history of mankind. Its one-sidedness, however – this may now be said in the light of the foregoing analysis – lay in the attempt to explain the whole dynamic of history from this one factor – an excusable one-sidedness easily explained by the fact that discoverers often tend to be over-enthusiastic about phenomena they are the first to see. The innumerable theories of history which have sprung up so luxuriantly recently all manifest this one-sidedness: they all single out just one factor as the sole determinant in historical development. Theories of race, generation, 'national spirit', economic determinism, etc., suffer from this one-sidedness, but it may be said to their credit that they bring at least one partial factor into sharp focus and also direct attention to the general problem of the structural factors shaping history. In this they are definitely superior to that brand of historiography which limits itself to the ascertainment of causal connections between individual events and to the description of individual characters, and repudiates all interest in structural factors in history, an attitude which eventually had to result in the conclusion that nothing after all can be learned from history, since all of its manifestations are unique and incomparable. That this cannot be so, must be realized by anyone who takes the liberty to think about history rather than merely to collect data, and also observe in everyday life how every new departure or outstanding personality has to operate in a given field which, although in constant process of change, is capable of description in structural terms.

   If in our attempts to visualize the structure of the historical dynamic we refuse to deduce everything from a single factor, the next question is whether it is not perhaps possible to fix some sort of definite order of importance in the structural factors involved, either for a particular period or in general – for of course it cannot be assumed *a priori* that the relative importance of the various social or other factors (economy, power, race, etc.), must always be the same. We cannot here attempt to solve the whole problem: all that can be done is to examine more closely our own problem of generation in relation to the other formative factors in history.

   Petersen (1925) had the merit of breaking away from that historical monism which characterized most earlier theories of generations. In dealing with the concrete case of romanticism, he tried to treat the problem of generations in conjunction with other historical determinants such as the ethnic unit, the region, the national character, the spirit of the epoch, the social structure, etc.

But however welcome this break with monistic theory is, we cannot agree with a mere juxtaposition of these factors (apparently this is only a provisional feature of the theory); the sociologist, moreover, cannot yet feel satisfied with the treatment of the social factor, at least in its present form.

If we are speaking of the 'spirit of an epoch', for example, we must realize, as in the case of other factors, too, that this *Zeitgeist*, the mentality of a period, does not pervade the whole society at a given time. The mentality which is commonly attributed to an epoch has its proper seat in one (homogeneous or heterogeneous) social group which acquires special significance at a particular time, and is thus able to put its own intellectual stamp on all the other groups without either destroying or absorbing them.

We must try to break up the category of *Zeitgeist* in another fashion than Pinder did. With Pinder, the *Zeitgeist* as a fictitious unit was dissolved, so as to make the real units, i.e. for Pinder, the generation entelechies, visible. According to him, the *Zeitgeist* is not one organic individuality, since there is no real, organic entelechy corresponding to it. It would seem to us, too, that there is no such *Zeitgeist* entelechy which would confer organic unity on the spirit of an epoch; but in our view the real units which have to be substituted for the fictitious unit of *Zeitgeist* are entelechies of social currents giving polar tension to each temporal segment of history.

Thus the nineteenth century has no unitary *Zeitgeist*, but a composite mentality made up (if we consider its political manifestations)[44] of the mutually antagonistic conservative-traditional and liberal impulses, to which was later added the proletarian-socialist one.

We would, however, not go quite as far as Pinder does in his denial of any temporal unity, and in his determination to attribute any homogeneity found in the manifestations of an epoch to a quite accidental crossing of various otherwise separate entelechies (accidental chords). The *Zeitgeist* is a unitary entity (otherwise, It would be meaningless to speak of it), in so far as we are able to view it in a dynamic-antinomical light.

The dynamic-antinomical unity of an epoch consists in the fact that polar opposites in an epoch always interpret their world in terms of one another, and that the various and opposing political orientations only become really comprehensible if viewed as so many different attempts to master the same destiny and solve the same social and intellectual problems that go with it.[45] Thus from this point of view the spirit of an age is no accidental coincidence of contemporary entelechies (as with Pinder); nor does it constitute itself an entelechy (a unified centre of volition – or formative principle, as with Petersen) on a par with other entelechies. We conceive it, rather, as a dynamic relationship of tension which we may well scrutinize in terms of its specific character but which should never be taken as a substantial 'thing'.

Genuine entelechics are primarily displayed by the social and intellectual trends or currents of which we spoke above. Each of these trends or currents (which may well be explained in terms of the social structure) evolves certain basic attitudes which exist over and above the change of generations as enduring (though nevertheless constantly changing) formative principles underlying social and historical development. Successively emerging new generations, then, superimpose their own generation entelechies upon the more comprehensive, stable entelechies of the various polar trends; this is how entelechies of the liberal, conservative, or socialist trends come to be transformed from generation to generation. We may conclude from this: generation units are no mere constructs, since they have their own entelechies; but these entelechies cannot he grasped in and for themselves: they must be viewed within the wider framework of the trend entelechies. It follows, furthermore, that it is quite impossible either to delimit or to count intellectual generations (generation units) except as articulations of certain overall trends. The trend entelechy is prior to the generation entelechy, and the latter, can only become effective and distinguishable within the former – but this does not mean to say that every one of the conflicting trends at a given point of time will necessarily cause new generation-entelechies to arise.

It is quite wrong to assume, for example, that in the first decades of the nineteenth century there existed in Germany only one romantic-conservative generation,[46] which was succeeded later by a liberal-rationalistic one. We should say, more precisely, that in the first decades of the nineteenth century the situation was such that only that section of the younger generation which had its roots in the romantic-conserva-tive tradition was able to develop new generation-entelechies. This section alone was able to leave its own mark on the prevailing tone of the age. What happened in the thirties, then, was not that a 'new generation' emerged which somehow happened to be liberal and rationalistic – but the situation changed, and it now became possible for the first time for the other section of the younger generation to reconstitute the tradition from which it derived in such a way as to produce its own generation-entelechy. The fundamental differentiation and polarization were undoubtedly always there, and each current had its own younger generation: but the opportunity for creative development of its basic impulse was granted first to the romantic conservatives, and only later to the liberal-rationalists.

We may say in this sense, that Petersen's[47] distinction between a *leading*, a *diverted*, and a *suppressed* type of generation is both correct and important, but it is not yet expressed in a sufficiently precise form, because Petersen failed to analyse the corresponding sociological differentiation.

Petersen assumes a direct interaction between supra-temporal character types on the one hand, and the *Zeitgeist* (which he considers as an unambiguously ascertainable datum) on the other, as if the historic process consisted in these two factors struggling with each other, and the fate of the single individuals were actually determined by their reciprocal interpenetration. Let us take, as an illustration of Petersen's method, an individual of an emotional type; he would be what Petersen would call a 'romantically inclined' character. If we further suppose that this man lives in an age the spirit of which is essentially romantic, this coincidence may well result in a heightening of his romantic inclinations, so that he will belong to the 'leading type' of his generation. Another individual, however, in whom emotional and rational inclinations tended more or less to balance one another, could in similar circumstances be drawn over into the romantic camp. Thus he would represent Petersen's *diverted* type. If we take finally, a third individual who by nature was rationalistically inclined but living in a romantic epoch, he would represent the *suppressed* type. Only two alternatives would be open to him: either he could swim with the tide and, against his own inclinations, follow the romantic tendencies of his time – a course which would lead to stultifications – or, alternatively, if he insisted on maintaining his ground, he could remain isolated in his time, an epigone of a past, or the forerunner of a future generation.

Apart from the somewhat cursory way in which 'emotional' and romantically inclined' are taken as synonymous, there is something essentially correct in this classification of generation type into *leading*, *diverted*, and *suppressed*. But what occurs is no clash between supra-temporal individual dispositions existing in a supra-social realm on the one hand, and an undifferentiated unitary *Zeitgeist* (because no such thing really exists) on the other. The individual is primarily moulded by those contemporary intellectual influences and currents which are indigenous to the particular social group to which he belongs. That is to say, he is in the first instance in no way affected or attracted by the *Zeitgeist* as a whole, but only by those currents and trends of the time which are a living tradition in his particular social environment. But that just these particular trends and not others should have taken root and maintained themselves in his world is ultimately due to the fact that they afford the typical 'chances' of his life situation their most adequate expression. There is therefore no question of an undifferentiated 'spirit of the age' promoting or inhibiting the potentialities inherent in individual characters: *in concreto* the individual is always exposed to differentiated, polarized trends or currents within the 'global spirit of the age', and in particular to that trend which had found its home in his immediate environment. The individual's personality structure will be confronted, in the first place, with this particular trend.

The reason why literary historians tend to overlook the fact that most people are confined to an existence within the limits of one of the trends of their time, and that the 'spirit of the age' is always split up into a number of tendencies rather than being now exclusively romantic, now exclusively rationalistic, is that their material consists primarily of biographies of *hommes de lettres*, a social group of a very particular character.

In our society only the *hommes de lettres* exist as a relatively un-attached (*freischwebend*) group (this being, of course, a sociological determinant of their situation); hence, they alone can vacillate, joining now one trend, now another. In the first half of the nineteenth century, they tended to embrace trends supported by a young generation which, favoured by circumstances of the time, had just achieved an intellectually dominant position – i.e. trends which permitted the formation of entelechies. The period of the Restoration and the social and political weakness of the German bourgeoisie at the beginning of the nineteenth century favoured the development of entelechies at the romantic conservative pole of the younger generation, which also attracted a large part of the socially unattached *literati*. From the thirties on, the July revolution and the growing industrialization of the country favoured the development of new liberal rationalist entelechies among the younger generation; and many of the *literati* promptly joined this camp.

The behaviour of these *hommes de lettres*, then, gives the impression that at one moment the 'spirit of the age' is entirely romantic, and at the next entirely liberal-rationalist, and further that whether the spirit of the age is to be romantic or rationalist is exclusively determined by these *literati* – poets and thinkers. In actual fact, however, the decisive impulses which determine the direction of social evolution do not originate with them at all, but with the much more compact, mutually antagonistic social groups which stand behind them, polarized into antagonistic trends. This wave-like rhythm in the change of the *Zeitgeist* is merely due to the fact that – according to the prevailing conditions – now one, and then the other pole succeeds in rallying an active youth which, then, carries the 'intermediary' generations and in particular the socially unattached individuals along. We do not wish to underrate the enormous importance of these literary strata (a social group to which many of the greatest thinkers and poets belong), for indeed they alone endow the entelechies radiating from the social sphere with real depth and form. But if we pay exclusive attention to them, we shall not be able really to account for this vector structure of intellectual currents. Taking the whole historical and social process into consideration, we can say that there has never been an epoch *entirely* romantic, or *entirely* rationalist in character; at least since the nineteenth century, we clearly have to deal with a culture polarized in this respect. It may very well be asserted, however, that it is now the one, now the other of these two trends that takes the upper hand and becomes *dominant*. In sociological terms, to sum up once more, this means simply that the circumstances of the time favour the formation of a new generation-entelechy at one or the other pole, and that this new entelechy always attracts the vacillating middle strata, primarily the literary people of the time. Thus the socially attached individual (to whatever psychological 'type' he may belong) allies himself with that current which happens to prevail in his particular social circle; the socially unattached *homme de lettres* of whatever psychological type, on the other hand, generally must clarify his position with regard to the *dominant* trend of his time. The outcome for the individual of this battle between his own natural disposition, the mental attitude most appropriate to his social situation, and the dominant trend of his time, undoubtedly differs from case to case; but only a very strong personality will be in a position to maintain his individual disposition in face of the antagonistic mental attitude of the social circle of his origin, especially if his group happens to be in process of rising in the social scale. An irrationally inclined 'bourgeois' would find it as difficult to come into his own in the forties of the nineteenth century as a young aristocrat with rational inclinations to preserve this rationalism in face of the rise of romanticism and religious revivalism in his social circle. We find for the most part that the opponents of a new generation-entelechy consist mainly of people who, because of their 'location' in an older generation, are unable or unwilling to assimilate themselves into the new entelechy growing up in their midst.

The generation location always exists as a potentiality seeking realization – the medium of such realization, however, is not a unitary *Zeitgeist* but rather one or the other of the concrete trends prevailing at a given time.[48] Whether new generation-entelechies will be formed at one pole in the social vector space or another depends, as we have seen, on historical group destinies.

There remains one further factor which we have not yet considered and which must be added to the others, complicated enough as they are.

We have not yet considered the fact that a newly rising generation-entelechy has not equal possibilities of asserting itself in every field of intellectual pursuit. Some of these fields tend to promote the emergence of new entelechies; others, to hinder it. And we can grade the different fields according to the degree to which they evidence the existence of generation entelechies.

Thus, for example, the natural sciences in which factors of total orientation (*Weltanschauung*) play a less important part than in other fields, definitely tend to conceal generation-entelechies.

The sphere of 'civilization'[49] in general, by virtue of the unilinear nature of developments falling within it, tends to conceal experiential and volitional transformations to a far greater extent than does the sphere of 'culture'. And within the sphere of 'culture' itself, Pinder is certainly right in ascribing to linguistic manifestations (religion, philosophy, poetry, and letters) a role different from that played by the plastic arts and music.[50]

In this field, however, we need a finer differentiation. It will have to be shown how far the various social and generation impulses and formative principles have peculiar affinities to this or that art form, and also whether they do not in certain cases bring new art forms into existence.

We must also consider the degree to which *forms of social intercourse* show stratification according to generations. Here, too, we find that certain forms of intercourse are more adequate to one particular set of social and generation trends than others. Mentré (1920) has already shown that an association deliberately organized on the basis of written statutes is much less capable of being moulded by new generations impulses than are less formal groupings (such as literary *salons* for example). Thus, it appears that in the same way as factors in the social and historical realm exercise either a restrictive or encouraging influence on the emergence of generation-entelechies, the degree to which various cultural 'fields' lend themselves to serving as sounding-boards for a new generation cannot be exactly determined in advance. All this indicates from yet another point of view that the generation factor – which at the biological level operates with the uniformity of a natural law – becomes the most elusive one at the social and cultural level, where its effects can be ascertained only with great difficulty and by indirect methods.

The phenomenon of generations is one of the basic factors contributing to the genesis of the dynamic of historical development. The analysis of the interaction of forces in this connection is a large task in itself, without which the nature of historical development cannot be properly understood. The problem can only be solved on the basis of a strict and careful analysis of all its component elements.

The *formal sociological* analysis of the generation phenomenon can be of help in so far as we may possibly learn from it what can and what cannot be attributed to the generation factor as one of the factors impinging upon the social process.

Notes

1. For these quotations from Hume and Comte, cf. Mentré (1920), pp. 179 ff. and 66 ff.
2. The exact titles of all works referred to in this essay can be found in the References on pp. 154–5.
3. Rümelin's attempt seems to be the most scientific; he tried to assess generation periods in various nations, using purely statistical methods and ignoring all problems related to intellectual history. The two decisive factors entering into his calculations were the average age of marriage among men, and half the average period of marital fertility. The generation-period is obtained as the sum of these two quantities (which vary as between both social groups and countries). Germany was computed at 361/2, and France at 341/2 years.
4. Cf. Mentré (1920).
5. We shall discuss here in detail only those students of the problem of generations whose contributions appeared after the publication of Mentré's work.
6. Mentré (1920), p. 298.
7. Cf. also the books of Agathon (1912), Bainville (1918), Ageorges (1912), Valois (1921), E. R. Curtius (1920), and Platz (1922), also always take into consideration the factor of generations.
8. For the conservative concept of time, cf. 'Conservative Thought', to be published in a later volume.

For a repudiation of the concept of progress as used to sum up historical development, cf. for example, Pinder (1926), p. 138.

9. Cf. Dilthey (1922), pp. 36 ff.
10. Heidegger (1927), pp. 384 ff.
11. Pinder (1926), cf. especially Ch. 7.
12. Pinder (1926), p. 21. Pinder's italics.
13. Ibid., p. 20.
14. Cf. K. Mannheim, 'On the Interpretation of *Weltanschauung*,' in Paul Kecskemeti (ed.), *Essays on the Sociology of Knowledge* (New York: Oxford University Press, 1952) pp. 33 ff.
15. Pinder (1926), p. 98.
16. Pinder (1926), pp. 159 ff.
17. Pinder (1926), p. 154, Pinder's italics.
18. Pinder (1926), p. 30.
19. *Ibid.*, p. 60.
20. That is, the 'cultural situation' and 'social and political conditions'. Dilthey (1875), p. 38.
21. See Joel (1925).
22. O. Lorenz sought to substitute for the century as unit a more rationally deducible unit of three generations. Scherer emphasizes a 600-year rhythm in his *History of Literature*, pp. 18 ff. We shall have to refer to the work of the modern literary historians Kummer and Petersen, as well as L. von Wiese, in the next part of this investigation.
23. In this connection it would be desirable to work out the exact differences between modern youth movements and the age-groups of men's societies formed amongst primitive peoples, carefully described by H. Schurtz (1902).
24. It is a matter for historical and sociological research to discover at what stage in its development, and under what conditions, a class becomes class-conscious, and similarly, when individual members of a generation become conscious of their common situation and make this consciousness the basis of their group solidarity. Why have generations become so conscious of their unity to-day? This is the first question we have to answer in this context.
25. Since actual experiments are precluded by the nature of the social sciences, such a 'mental experiment' can often help to isolate the important factors.
26. Cf. Spranger (1925) on 'being young' and 'becoming old', and the intellectual and spiritual significance of these phenomena. (He also gives references to other literature on the psychology of the adolescent – whereon see also Honigsheim (1924)). Further, see A. E. Brinckmann (1925) (who proceeds by way of interpretive analysis of works of art), Jacob Grimm (1893), F. Boll (1913), Giese (1928). Literature relating to the youth movement, which constitutes a problem in itself, is not included in the biography at the end of this book.
27. This is not the place to enumerate all the many forms of social memory. We will therefore deliberately simplify the matter by limiting ourselves to two extreme alternatives. 'Consciously recognized models' include, in the wider sense, also the body of global knowledge, stored in libraries. But this sort of knowledge is only effective in so far as it is continually

actualized. This can happen in two ways – either intellectually, when it is used as a pattern or guide for action, or spontaneously, when it is 'virtually present' as condensed experience.

Instinct, as well as repressed and unconscious knowledge, as dealt with in particular by Freud, would need separate treatment.

28. This process of discovery of hidden possibilities inherent in transmitted material alone makes it clear why it is that so many revolutionary and reformist movements are able to graft their new truths on to old ones.

29. That is, if we ignore – as we said we would – the biological factors of physical and psychological ageing.

30. It must be emphasized that this 'ability to start afresh' of which we are speaking has nothing to do with 'conservative' and 'progressive' in the usual sense of these terms. Nothing is more false than the usual assumption uncritically shared by most students of generations, that the younger generation is 'progressive' and the older generation *eo ipso* conservative. Recent experiences have shown well enough that the old liberal generation tends to be more politically progressive than certain sections of the youth (e.g. the German Students' Associations – *Burschenschaften* – etc.). 'Conservative' and 'progressive' are categories of historical sociology, designed to deal with the descriptive contents of the dynamism of a historical period of history, whereas 'old' and 'young' and the concept of the 'fresh contact' of a generation are categories belonging to formal sociology. Whether youth will be conservative, reactionary, or progressive, depends (if not entirely, at least primarily) on whether or not the existing social structure and the position they occupy in it provide opportunities for the promotion of their own social and intellectual ends. Their 'being young', the 'freshness' of their contact with the world, manifest themselves in the fact that they are able to re-orient any movement they embrace, to adopt it to the total situation. (Thus, for instance, they must seek within Conservatism the particular form of this political and intellectual current best suited to the requirements of the modern situation: or within Socialism, in the same way, an up-to-date formulation.) This lends considerable support to the fundamental thesis of this essay, which will have to be further substantiated later – that biological factors (such as youth and age) do not of themselves involve a definite intellectual or practical orientation (youth cannot be automatically correlated with a progressive attitude and so on); they merely *initiate* certain formal tendencies, the actual manifestations of which will 'ultimately depend on the prevailing social and cultural context. Any attempt to establish a direct identity or correlation between biological and cultural data leads to a *quid pro quo* which can only confuse the issue.

31. It is difficult to decide just at what point this process is complete in an individual – at what point this unconscious vital inventory (which also contains the national and provincial peculiarities out of which national and provincial entelechies can develop) is stabilized. The process seems to stop once the inventory of a-problematical experience has virtually acquired its final form. The child or adolescent is always open to new influences if placed in a new *milieu*. They readily assimilate new unconscious mental attitudes and habits, and change their language or dialect.

The adult, transferred into a new environment, consciously transforms certain aspects of his modes of thought and behaviour, but never acclimatizes himself in so radical and thoroughgoing a fashion. His fundamental attitudes, his vital inventory, and, among external manifestations, his language and dialect, remain for the most part on an earlier level. It appears that language and accent offer an indirect indication as to how far the foundations of a person's consciousness are laid, his basic view of the world stabilized. If the point can be determined at which a man's language and dialect cease to change, there is at least an external criterion for the determination also of the point at which his unconscious inventory of experience ceases to accumulate. According to A. Meillet, the spoken language and dialect does not change in an individual after the age of 25 years. (A. Meillet: *Méthode dans les sciences*, Paris, Alcan, 1911; also his '*Introduction à l'étude comparative des langues indoeuropéennes*' 1903, as quoted in Mentré (1920), p. 306 ff.)

32. Spranger (1925) also assumes an important turning point about the age of 17 or so (p. 145).

33. This throws some light on the way in which 'ideas' appear to precede real social transformation. 'Ideas' are understood here in the French rather than in the Platonic sense. This 'modern Idea' has a tendency to destabilize and set in motion the social structure. It does not exist in static social units – for example, in self-contained peasant communities – which tend to draw on an unconscious, traditional way of life. In such societies, we do not find the younger generation, associated with ideas of this kind, rising against their elders. 'Being young' here is a question of biological differentiation. More on this matter later.

34. The following seems to be the sequence in which this process unfolds: first the 'conditions' change. Then concrete behaviour begins unconsciously to transform itself in the new situation. The individual seeks to react to the new situation, by instinctive, unconscious adjustment. (Even the most fanatical adherent of an orthodoxy constantly indulges in an adaptive change of his behaviour in respects which are not open to conscious observation.) If the dynamic of the situation results in too quick cultural change and the upheaval is too great, if unconscious adjustment proves inadequate and behaviour adaptations fail to 'function' in the sudden new situation, so that an aspect of reality becomes problematic, then that aspect of reality will be made conscious – on the level of either mythology, philosophy, or science, according to the stage of cultural evolution reached. From this point on, the unravelling of the deeper layers proceeds, as required by the situation.

35. L. von Wiese (1924), gives a vivid description of this father-son antagonism. Of considerable importance is the suggestion that the father is more or less forced into the role of representing 'Society' to his son (p. 196).

36. It should be noted, on the other hand, as L. von Wiese (1924, p. 197) points out, that with the modern trend towards individualism, every individual claims more than before the right to 'live his own life'.

37. This is a further proof that natural biological factors characteristic of old age can be invalidated by social forces, and that biological data can almost be turned into their opposites by social forces.

38. Up till now we have not differentiated between generation location, generation as actuality, etc. These distinctions will now be made.
39. Cf. the quotation from Heidegger, p. 115, above.
40. Mental data can both bind and differentiate socially. The same concept of Freedom, for example, had totally different meanings for the liberal and the conservative generation-unit. Thus, it is possible to obtain an indication of the extent to which a generation is divided into generation-units by analysing the different meaning given to a current idea. Cf. 'Conservative Thought' (to follow in a later volume), where the conservative concept of Freedom is analyzed in contrast to the liberal concept current at the same time.
41. In the 40s in Germany, for example, when oppositional ideas were in vogue, young men of the nobility also shared them. Cf. Karl Marx: 'Revolution and Counter-revolution in Germany' (German edition, Stuttgart, 1913, pp. 20 f. and 25).
42. For instance, Nietzsche may be considered the forerunner of the present neo-romanticism. An eminent example of the same thing in France is Taine, who under the influence of the events of 1870–71 turned towards patriotism, and so became the forerunner of a nationalistic generation. (Cf. Platz (1922), pp. 43 ff.) In such cases involving forerunners, it would be advisable to make individual case-analyses and establish in what respect the basic structure of experience in the forerunner differs from that of the new generation which actually starts at the point where the forerunner leaves off. In this connection, the history of German Conservatism contains an interesting example, i.e. that of the jurist Hugo, whom we may consider as the founder of the 'historical school'. Nevertheless, he never thought in *irrationalislic* terms as did the members of the school (e.g. Savigny) in the next generation which lived through the Napoleonic wars.
43. The speed of social change, for its part, is never influenced by the speeds of the succession of generations, since this remains constant.
44. We draw on examples deliberately from the history of political ideas, partly to counterbalance the tendency (especially evident in Germany) to study the problem of generations exclusively in the context of the history of literature or art; and partly to show that we believe that *the structural situation of decisive social impulses and also the differentiation between generations is clearest at this point.* The other entelechies and changes of style must of course be studied for their own sake independently, and cannot be derived in any way from political factors, but their reciprocal relations and affinities can best be understood and made clear from this angle. The artist certainly lives in the first instance in his artistic world with its particular traditions, but as a human being he is always linked with the driving forces of his generation even when politically indifferent, and this influence must always transform even purely artistic relations and entelechies. As a point of orientation for a survey of the whole structure, the history of political ideas seems to us to be most important. This matter will be further dealt with below.
45. From our point of view, the 'spirit of an age' is thus the outcome of the dynamic interaction of actual generations succeeding one another in a continuous series.

46. Romanticism and Conservatism did not always go together. Romanticism was originally a revolutionary movement in Germany, the same as in France.
47. Petersen (1925), pp. 146 ff.
48. This can also be observed in the modern youth movement, which is constantly in process of social and political polarization. Purely as a social phenomenon, it represents a coherent actual generation entity, but it can only be understood concretely in terms of the 'generation units' into which it is socially and intellectually differentiated.
49. Cf. A. Weber: 'Prinzipielles zur Kultursoziologie' (*Archiv für Soziale Wissenschaft und Sozial Politik*, 1920).
50. Pinder (1926), p. 156.

References

Agathon (1912) *Les jeunes gens d'aujourd'hui* (Paris: Plon Nourrit).
Ageorges (1912) *La marche montante d'une génération (1890–1910)*.
Bainville (1918) *Histoire de trois générations* (Paris: Nouvelle Librairie Nationale).
Boas, F. (1911) *Changes in Bodily Form of Descendants of Immigrants* (Washington).
Brinckmann, A. E. (1925) *Spätwerke grosser Meister* (Frankfurt).
Boll, F. (1913) *Die Lebensalter. Ein Beitrag zur antiken Ethnologie und zur Geschichte der Zahlen* (Berlin).
Cournot, A. (1872) *Considerations* (Paris: Machette).
Curtius, E. R. (1920) *Die literarischen Wegbereiter des neuen Frankreichs* (Potsdam: G. Kiepenheuer).
Dilthey, W. (1875) *Über das Studium der Geschichte der Wissenschaften vom Menschen, der Gesellschaft und dem Staat*, Abgedr. Ges. Schr. Bd. V., pp. 36–41.
Dilthey, W. (1922) *Leben Schleiermachers*, Bd. 1, 2, Aufl. (Berlin, Leipzig).
Dromel, Justin (1862) *La loi des révolutions, les générations, les nationalités, les dynasties, les réligions* (Paris: Didier & Co.).
Ferrari, G. (1874) *Teoria dei periodi politici*. (Milano: Hoepli).
Giese (1928) 'Erlebnisform des Alterns', *Deutsche Psychologie*, 5(2).
Grimm, Jakob (1893) *Über das Alter*, Reclams Universal-Bibl., No. 5311.
Heidegger, M. (1927) 'Sein und Zeit'. *Fahrbuch für Philosophie und phänomenologische Forschg.*, Bd. VIII (Halle a.d.S.), pp. 384 ff.
Herbst, F. (1823) *Ideale und Irrtümer des akademischen Lebens in unserer Zeit* (Stuttgart).
Honigsheim, P. (1924) 'Die Pubertät, *Kölner Vierteljahrshefte für Soziologie*, Jahrg. III, (Heft 4.
Joel, K. (1925) 'Der sekuläre Rhythmus der Geschichte', *Fahrbuch für Soziologie* Bd. 1.
Korschelt, E. (1924) *Lebensdauer, Altern und Tod*. 3, Aufl. (Bibliography).
Kummer, F. (1900) *Deutsche Literaturgeschichte des 19. Fahrhunderts. Dargestellt nach Generationen* (Dresden).

Landsberger, Franz (1927) 'Das Generationsproblem in der Kunstgeschichte', *Kritische Berichte*, Jahrg. 1, Heft 2.

Lorenz, O. (1886/1891) *Die Geschichtswissenschaft in Hauptrichtungen und Aufgaben kritisch erörtert* (Teil I, Berlin, 1886; Teil II, 1891).

Mentré F. (1920) *Les générations sociales*. Ed. Bossard (Paris).

Nohl, H. (1914) 'Das Verhältnis der Generationen in der Pädagogik'. *Die Tat* (Monatsschrift) (May).

Ortega y Gasset (1928) *Die Aufgabe unserer Zeit*, Introduction by E. R. Curtius (Zurich) (Chapter I, 'Der Begriff der Generation') Verl. d. Neuen Schweizer Rundschau.

Petersen, J. (1926) *Die Wesensbestimmung der deutschen Romantik* (Chapter 6, 'Generation') (Leipzig).

Pinder, W. (1926) *Kunstgeschichte nach Generationen. Zwischen Philosophie und Kunst.*, Johann Volkelt zum 100. Lehrsemester dargebracht (Leipzig).

Pinder, W. (1926) *Das Problem der Generation in der Kunstgeschichte Europas* (Berlin).

Platz, R. (1922) *Geistige Kämpfe in modernen Frankreich* (Kempten).

Rümelin, G. (1875) 'Über den Begriff und die Dauer einer Generation', *Reden und Aufsätze*, I (Tübingen).

Schurtz, H. (1902) *Altersklassen und Männerbünde. Eine Darstellung der Grundformen der Gesellschaft* (Berlin).

Spranger (1925) *Psychologie des Jugendalters* (Leipzig).

Scherer, W. (1885) *Geschichte der deutschen Literatur*, 3. Aufl. (Berlin).

Valois, G. (1921) *D'un siècle à l'autre. Chronique d'une génération (1885–1920)* (Paris: Nouvelle librairie nationale).

von Wiese, L., (1924) *Allgemeine Soziologie als Lehre von den Beziehungs-gebilden*, Teil I (Munich and Leipzig: Beziehungslehre).

von Wiese, L., 'Väter und Söhne', *Der Neue Strom*, Jahrg. I, Heft 3.

Zeuthen, H. G. (1909) 'Quelques traits de la propagation de la science de génération en génération'. *Rivista di Scienza*.

10 Human Migration and the Marginal Man (1928)

Robert E. Park*

Students of the great society, looking at mankind in the long perspective of history, have frequently been disposed to seek an explanation of existing cultural differences among races and peoples in some single dominating cause or condition. One school of thought, represented most conspicuously by Montesquieu, has found that explanation in climate and in the physical environment. Another school, identified with the name of Arthur de Gobineau, author of *The Inequality of Human Races*, has sought an explanation of divergent cultures in the innate qualities of races biologically inherited. These two theories have this in common, namely, that they both conceive civilization and society to be the result of evolutionary processes – processes by which man has acquired new inheritable traits – rather than processes by which new relations have been established between men.

In contrast to both of these, Frederick Teggart has recently restated and amplified what may be called the catastrophic theory of civilization, a theory that goes back to Hume in England, and to Turgot in France. From this point of view, climate and innate racial traits, important as they may have been in the evolution of races, have been of only minor influence in creating existing cultural differences. In fact, races and cultures, so far from being in any sense identical – or even the product of similar conditions and forces – are perhaps to be set over against one another as contrast effects, the results of antagonistic tendencies, so that civilization may be said to flourish at the expense of racial differences rather than to be conserved by them. At any rate, if it is true that races are the products of isolation and inbreeding, it is just as certain that civilization, on the other hand, is a consequence of contact and communication. The forces which have been decisive in the history of mankind are those which have brought men together in fruitful competition, conflict, and co-operation.

Among the most important of these influences have been – according to what I have called the catastrophic theory of progress – migra-

---

* From *The American Journal of Sociology*, 33(6) (May 1928), pp. 881–93.

tion and the incidental collisions, conflicts, and fusions of people and cultures which they have occasioned.

'Every advance in culture,' says Bücher, in his *Industrial Evolution*, 'commences, so to speak, with a new period of wandering,' and in support of this thesis he points out that the earlier forms of trade were migratory, that the first industries to free themselves from the household husbandry and become independent occupations were carried on itinerantly. 'The great founders of religion, the earliest poets and philosophers, the musicians and actors of past epochs, are all great wanderers. Even today, do not the inventor, the preacher of a new doctrine, and the virtuoso travel from place to place in search of adherents and admirers – notwithstanding the immense recent development in the means of communicating information?'[1]

The influences of migrations have not been limited, of course, by the changes which they have effected in existing cultures. In the long run, they have determined the racial characteristics of historical peoples. 'The whole teaching of ethnology,' as Griffith Taylor remarks, 'shows that peoples of mixed race are the rule and not the exception.'[2] Every nation, upon examination, turns out to have been a more or less successful melting-pot. To this constant sifting of races and peoples, human geographers have given the title 'the historical movement,' because, as Miss Semple says in her volume *Influences of Geographic Environment*, 'it underlies most written history and constitutes the major part of unwritten history, especially that of savage and nomadic tribes.'[3]

Changes in race, it is true, do inevitably follow, at some distance, changes in culture. The movements and mingling of peoples which bring rapid, sudden, and often catastrophic, changes in customs and habits are followed, in the course of time, as a result of interbreeding, by corresponding modifications in temperament and physique. There has probably never been an instance where races have lived together in the intimate contacts which a common economy enforces in which racial contiguity has not produced racial hybrids. However, changes in racial characteristics and in cultural traits proceed at very different rates, and it is notorious that cultural changes are not consolidated and transmitted biologically, or at least to only a very slight extent, if at all. Acquired characteristics are not biologically inherited.

Writers who emphasize the importance of migration as an agency of progress are invariably led to ascribe a similar role to war. Thus Waitz, commenting upon the role of migration as an agency of civilization, points out that migrations are 'rarely of a peaceful nature at first.' Of war he says: 'The first consequence of war is that fixed

relations are established between people, which render friendly intercourse possible, an intercourse which becomes more important from
the interchange of knowledge and experience than from the mere interchange of commodities.'[4] And then he adds:

> Whenever we see a people, of whatever degree of civilization, not
> living in contact and reciprocal action with others, we shall gener-
> ally find a certain stagnation, a mental inertness, and a want of ac-
> tivity, which render any change of social and political condition next
> to impossible. There are, in times of peace, transmitted like an ev-
> erlasting disease, and war appears then, in spite of what the apos-
> tles of peace may say, as a saving angel, who rouses the national
> spirit, and renders all forces more elastic.[5]

Among the writers who conceive the historical process in terms of
intrusions, either peaceful or hostile, of one people into the domain of
another, must be reckoned such sociologists as Gumplowicz and
Oppenheim. The former, in an effort to define the social process abstractly, has described it as the interaction of heterogeneous ethnic
groups, the resulting subordination and superordination of races constituting the social order – society, in fact.

In much the same way, Oppenheim, in his study of the sociological
origin of the state, believes he has shown that in every instance the
state has had its historical beginnings in the imposition, by conquest
and force, of the authority of a nomadic upon a sedentary and agricultural people. The facts which Oppenheim has gathered to sustain his
thesis show, at any rate, that social institutions have actually, in many
instances at least, come into existence abruptly by a mutation, rather
than by a process of evolutionary selection and the gradual accumulation of relatively slight variations.[6]

It is not at once apparent why a theory which insists upon the importance of catastrophic change in the evolution of civilization should
not at the same time take some account of revolution as a factor in
progress. If peace and stagnation, as Waitz suggests, tend to assume
the form of a social disease; if, as Sumner says, 'society needs to
have some ferment in it' to break up this stagnation and emancipate
the energies of individuals imprisoned within an existing social order;
it seems that some 'adventurous folly' like the crusades of the middle
ages, or some romantic enthusiasm like that which found expression
in the French Revolution, or in the more recent Bolshevist adventure
in Russia, might serve quite as effectively as either migration or war
to interrupt the routine of existing habit and break the cake of custom.

Revolutionary doctrines are naturally based upon a conception of catastrophic rather than of evolutionary change. Revolutionary strategy, as it has been worked out and rationalized in Sorel's *Reflections on Violence*, makes the great catastrophe, the general strike, an article of faith. As such it becomes a means of maintaining morale and enforcing discipline in the revolutionary masses.[7]

The first and most obvious difference between revolution and migration is that in migration the breakdown of social order is initiated by the impact of an invading population, and completed by the contact and fusion of native with alien peoples. In the case of the former, revolutionary ferment and the forces which have disrupted society have ordinarily had, or seem to have had, their sources and origins mainly if not wholly within, rather than without, the society affected. It is doubtful whether it can be successfully maintained that every revolution, every *Aufklärung*, every intellectual awakening and renaissance has been and will be provoked by some invading population movement or by the intrusion of some alien cultural agency. At least it seems as if some modification of this view is necessary, since with the growth of commerce and communication there is progressively and relatively more movement and less migration. Commerce, in bringing the ends of the earth together, has made travel relatively secure. Moreover, with the development of machine industry and the growth of cities, it is the commodities rather than men which circulate. The peddler, who carries his stock on his back, gives way to the traveling salesman, and the catalogue of the mail order house now reaches remote regions which even the Yankee peddler rarely if ever penetrated. With the development of a world-economy and the interpenetration of peoples, migrations, as Bücher has pointed out, have changed their character:

> The migrations occurring at the opening of the history of European peoples are migrations of whole tribes, a pushing and pressing of collective units from east to west which lasted for centuries. The migrations of the Middle Ages ever affect individual classes alone; the knights in the crusades, the merchants, the wage craftsmen, the journeymen hand-workers, the jugglers and minstrels, the villeins seeking protection within the walls of a town. Modern migrations, on the contrary, are generally a matter of private concern, the individuals being led by the most varied motives. They are almost invariably without organization. The process repeating itself daily a thousand times is united only through the one characteristic, that it

is everywhere a question of change of locality by persons seeking more favourable conditions of life.[8]

Migration, which was formerly an invasion, followed by the forcible displacement or subjugation of one people by another, has assumed the character of a peaceful penetration. Migration of peoples has, in other words, been transmuted into mobility of individuals, and the wars which these movements so frequently occasioned have assumed the character of internecine struggles, of which strikes and revolutions are to be regarded as types.

Furthermore, if one were to attempt to reckon with all the forms in which catastrophic changes take place, it would be necessary to include the changes that are effected by the sudden rise of some new religious movement like Mohammedanism or Christianity, both of which began as schismatic and sectarian movements, and which by extension and internal evolution have become independent religions. Looked at from this point of view, migration assumes a character less unique and exceptional than has hitherto been conceived by the writers whom the problem has most intrigued. It appears as one, merely, of a series of forms in which historic changes may take place. Nevertheless, regarded abstractly as a type of collective action, human migration exhibits everywhere characteristics that are sufficiently typical to make it a subject of independent investigation and study, both in respect to its form and in respect to the effects which it produces.

Migration is not, however, to be identified with mere movement. It involves, at the very least, change of residence and the breaking of home ties. The movements of gypsies and other pariah peoples, because they bring about no important changes in cultural life, are to be regarded rather as a geographical fact than a social phenomenon. Nomadic life is stabilized on the basis of movement, and even though gypsies now travel by automobile, they still maintain, comparatively unchanged, their ancient tribal organization and customs. The result is that their relation to the communities in which they may at any time be found is to be described as symbiotic rather than social. This tends to be true of any section or class of the population – the hobos, for example, and the hotel dwellers – which is unsettled and mobile.

Migration as a social phenomenon must be studied not merely in its grosser effects, as manifested in changes in custom and in the mores, but it may be envisaged in its subjective aspects as manifested in the changed type of personality which it produces. When the traditional organization of society breaks down, as a result of contact and collision with a new invading culture, the effect is, so to speak, to emancipate the individual man. Energies that were formerly controlled by custom and tradition are released. The individual is free for new adventures, but he is more or less without direction and control. Teggart's statement of the matter is as follows:

> As a result of the breakdown of customary modes of action and of thought, the individual experiences a "release" from the restraints and constraints to which he has been subject, and gives evidence of this "release" in aggressive self-assertion. The overexpression of individuality is one of the marked features of all epochs of change. On the other hand, the study of the psychological effects of collision and contact between different groups reveals the fact that the most important aspect of "release" lies not in freeing the soldier, warrior, or berserker from the restraint of conventional modes of action, but in freeing the individual judgment from the inhibitions of conventional modes of thought. It will thus be seen (he adds) that the study of the *modus operandi* of change in time gives a common focus to the efforts of political historians, of the historians of literature and of ideas, of psychologists, and of students of ethics and the theory of education.[9]

Social changes, according to Teggart, have their inception in events which 'release' the individuals out of which society is composed. Inevitably, however, this release is followed in the course of time by the reintegration of the individuals so released into a new special order. In the meantime, however, certain changes take place – at any rate they are likely to take place – in the character of the individuals themselves. They become, in the process, not merely emancipated, but enlightened.

The emancipated individual invariably becomes in a certain sense and to a certain degree a cosmopolitan. He learns to look upon the world in which he was born and bred with something of the detachment of a stranger. He acquires, in short, an intellectual bias. Simmel has described the position of the stranger in the community, and his personality, in terms of movement and migration.

'If wandering,' he says, 'considered as the liberation from every given point in space, is the conceptual opposite of fixation at any point, then surely the sociological form of the stranger presents the union of both of these specifications.' The stranger stays, but he is not settled. He is a potential wanderer. That means that he is not bound as others are by the local proprieties and conventions. 'He is the freer man, practically and theoretically. He views his relation to others with less prejudice; he submits them to more general, more objective standards, and he is not confined in his action by custom, piety or precedents.'

The effect of mobility and migration is to secularize relations which were formerly sacred. One may describe the process, in its dual aspect, perhaps, as the secularization of society and the individuation of the person. For a brief, vivid, and authentic picture of the way in which migration of the earlier sort, the migration of a people, has, in fact, brought about the destruction of an earlier civilization and liberated the peoples involved for the creation of a later, more secular, and freer society, I suggest Gilbert Murray's introduction to *The Rise of The Greek Epic*, in which he seeks to reproduce the events of the Nordic invasion of the Aegean area.

What ensued, he says, was a period of chaos:

A chaos in which an old civilization is shattered into fragments, its laws set at naught, and that intricate web of normal expectation which forms the very essence of human society torn so often and so utterly by continued disappointment that at last there ceases to be any normal expectation at all. For the fugitive settlers on the shores that were afterwards Ionia, and for parts too of Doris and Aeolis, there were no tribal gods or tribal obligations left, because there were no tribes. There were no old laws, because there was no one to administer or even to remember them; only such compulsions as the strongest power of the moment chose to enforce. Household and family life had disappeared, and all its innumerable ties with it. A man was now not living with a wife of his own race, but with a dangerous strange woman, of alien language and alien gods, a woman whose husband or father he had perhaps murdered – or, at best, whom he had bought as a slave from the murderer. The old Aryan husbandman, as we shall see hereafter, had lived with his herds in a sort of familiar connexion. He slew "his brother the ox" only under special stress or for definite religious reasons, and he expected his women to weep when the slaying was performed. But now he had left his own herds far away. They had been devoured by enemies. And he lived on the beasts of strangers whom he robbed or held in servitude. He had left the graves of his fathers, the kindly ghosts of his own blood, who took food from his hand and loved him. He was surrounded by the graves of alien dead, strange ghosts whose names he knew not, and who were beyond his power to control, whom he tried his best to placate with fear and aversion. One only concrete thing existed for him to make henceforth the centre of his allegience, to supply the place of his old family hearth, his gods, his tribal customs and sanctities. It was a circuit wall of stones, a *Polis*; the wall which he and his fellows, men of diverse tongues and worships united by a tremendous need, had built up to be the one barrier between themselves and a world of enemies.[10]

It was within the walls of the *polis* and in this mixed company that Greek civilization was born. The whole secret of ancient Greek life, its relative freedom from the grosser superstitions and from fear of the gods, is bound up, we are told, with this period of transition and chaos, in which the older primitive world perished and from which the freer, more enlightened social order sprang into existence. Thought is emancipated, philosophy is born, public opinion sets itself up as an authority as over against tradition and custom. As Guyot puts it, 'The Greek with his festivals, his songs, his poetry, seems to celebrate, in a perpetual hymn, the liberation of man from the mighty fetters of nature.'[11]

What took place in Greece first has since taken place in the rest of Europe and is now going on in America. The movement and migration of peoples, the expansion of trade and commerce, and particularly the growth, in modern times, of these vast melting-pots of races and cultures, the metropolitan cities, has loosened local bonds, destroyed the cultures of tribe and folk, and substituted for the local loyalties the freedom of the cities; for the sacred order of tribal custom, the rational organization which we call civilization.

In these great cities, where all the passions, all the energies of mankind are released, we are in position to investigate the processes of civilization, as it were, under a microscope.

It is in the cities that the old clan and kinship groups are broken up and replaced by social organization based on rational interests and temperamental predilections. It is in the cities, more particularly, that the grand division of labor is effected which permits and more or less compels the individual man to concentrate his energies and his talents on the particular task he is best fitted to perform, and in this way emancipates him and his fellows from the control of nature and circumstance which so thoroughly dominates primitive man.

It happens, however, that the process of acculturation and assimilation and the accompanying amalgamation of racial stocks does not proceed with the same ease and the same speed in all cases. Particularly where peoples who come together are of divergent cultures and widely different racial stocks, assimilation and amalgamation do not take place so rapidly as they do in other cases. All our so-called racial problems grow out of situations in which assimilation and amalgamation do not take place at all, or take place very slowly. As I have said elsewhere, the chief obstacle to the cultural assimilation of races is not their different mental, but rather their divergent physical traits. It is not because of the mentality of the Japanese that they do not so easily assimilate as do the Europeans. It is because

> the Japanese bears in his features a distinctive racial hallmark, that he wears, so to speak, a racial uniform which classifies him. He cannot become a mere individual, indistinguishable in the cosmopolitan mass of the population, as is true, for example, of the Irish, and, to a lesser extent, of some of the other immigrant races. The Japanese like the Negro, is condemned to remain among us an abstraction, a symbol – and a symbol not merely of his own race but of the Orient and of that vague, ill-defined menace we sometimes refer to as the "yellow peril."[12]

Under such circumstances peoples of different racial stocks may live side by side in a relation of symbiosis, each playing a role in a common economy, but not interbreeding to any great extent; each maintaining, like the gypsy or the pariah peoples of India, a more or less complete tribal organization or society of their own. Such was the situation of the Jew in Europe up to modern times, and a somewhat similar relation exists today between the native white and the Hindu populations in Southeast Africa and in the West Indies.

In the long run, however, peoples and races who live together, sharing in the same economy, inevitably interbreed, and in this way if in no other, the relations which were merely co-operative and economic become social and cultural. When migration leads to conquest, either economic or political, assimilation is inevitable. The conquering peoples impose their culture and their standards upon the conquered, and there follows a period of cultural endosmosis.

Sometimes relations between the conquering and the conquered peoples take the form of slavery; sometimes they assume the form, as in India, of a system of caste. But in either case the dominant and the subject peoples become, in time, integral parts of one society. Slavery and caste are merely forms of accommodation, in which the race problem finds a temporary solution. The case of the Jews was different. Jews never were a subject people, at least not in Europe. They were never reduced to the position of an inferior caste. In their ghettos in which they first elected, and then were forced, to live, they preserved their own tribal traditions and their cultural, if not their political, independence. The Jew who left the ghetto did not escape; he deserted and became that execrable object, an apostate. The relation of the ghetto Jew to the larger community in which he lived was, and to some extent still is, symbiotic rather than social.

When, however, the walls of the medieval ghetto were torn down and the Jew was permitted to participate in the cultural life of the peoples among whom he lived, there appeared a new type of personality, namely, a cultural hybrid, a man living and sharing intimately in the cultural life and traditions of two distinct peoples; never quite willing to break, even if he were permitted to do so, with his past and his traditions, and not quite accepted, because of racial prejudice, in the new society in which he now sought to find a place. He was a man on the margin of two cultures and two societies, which never completely interpenetrated and fused. The emancipated Jew was, and is, historically and typically the marginal man, the first cosmopolite and citizen of the world. He is, par excellence, the 'stranger,' whom Simmel, himself a Jew, has described with such profound insight and understanding in his *Sociologie* [see Chapter 5 in this volume]. Most if not all the characteristics of the Jew, certainly his pre-eminence as a trader and his keen intellectual interest, his sophistication, his idealism and lack of historic sense, are the characteristics of the city man, the man who ranges widely, lives preferably in a hotel – short, the cosmopolite. The autobiographies of Jewish immigrants, of which a great number have been published in America in recent years, are all different versions of the same story – the story of the marginal man; the man who, emerging from the ghetto in which he lived in Europe, is seeking to find a place in the freer, more complex and cosmopolitan life of an American city. One may learn from these autobiographies how the process of assimilation actually takes place in the individual immigrant. In the more sensitive minds its effects are as profound and as disturbing as some of the religious conversions of which William James has given us so classical an account in his *Varieties of Religious Experience*. In these immigrant autobiographies the conflict of cultures, as it takes place in the mind of the immigrant, is just the conflict of 'the divided self,' the old self and the new. And frequently there is no satisfying issue of this conflict, which often terminates in a profound disillusionment, as described, for example, in Lewisohn's autobiography *Up Stream*. But Lewisohn's restless wavering between the warm security of the ghetto, which he has abandoned, and the cold freedom of the outer world, in which he is not yet quite at home, is typical. A century earlier, Heinrich Heine, torn with the same conflicting loyalties, struggling to be at the same time a German and a Jew, enacted a similar role. It was, according to his latest biographer, the secret and the tragedy of Heine's life that circumstance condemned him to live in two worlds, in neither of which he ever quite belonged. It was this that embittered his intellectual life and gave to his writings that character of spiritual conflict and instability which, as Browne says, is evidence of 'spiritual distress.' His mind lacked the integrity which is based on conviction: 'His arms were weak' – to continue the quotation – 'because his mind was divided; his hands were nerveless because his soul was in turmoil.'

Something of the same sense of moral dichotomy and conflict is probably characteristic of every immigrant during the period of transition, when old habits are being discarded and new ones are not yet formed. It is inevitably a period of inner turmoil and intense self-consciousness.

There are no doubt periods of transition and crisis in the lives of most of us that are comparable with those which the immigrant experiences when he leaves home to seek his fortunes in a strange country. But in the case of the marginal man the period of crisis is relatively permanent. The result is that he tends to become a personality type. Ordinarily the marginal man is a mixed blood, like the Mulatto in the United States or the Eurasian in Asia, but that is apparently because the man of mixed blood is one who lives in two worlds, in both of which he is more or less of a stranger. The Christian convert in Asia or in Africa exhibits many if not most of the characteristics of the marginal man – the same spiritual instability, intensified self-consciousness, restlessness, and *malaise*.

It is in the mind of the marginal man that the moral turmoil which new cultural contacts occasion manifests itself the most obvious forms. It is in the mind of the marginal man – where the changes and fusions of culture are going on – that we can best study the processes of civilization and of progress.

Notes

1. Carl Bücher, *Industrial Evolution*, trans from 3rd German edn by S. Morley Wickett (New York: H. Holt & Co., 1907).
2. Griffith Taylor, *Environment and Race: A Study of Evolution, Migration, Settlement, and Status of the Races of Men* (London: Oxford University Press, 1927). p. 336.
3. Ellen Churchill Semple, *Influences of Geographic Environment* (New York: H. Holt & Co., 1911). p. 75.

4. Theodor Waitz, *Introduction to Anthropology*, p. 347.
5. Waitz, *Introduction*, p. 348.
6. Franz Oppenheim, *The State: Its History and Development Viewed Sociologically* (1914).
7. Georges Sorel. *Reflections on Violence* (New York. 1914).
8. Carl Bücher, *Industrial Evolution*, p. 349.
9. Frederick J. Teggart, *Theory of History*, p. 196.
10. Gilbert Murray, *The Rise of the Greek Epic*, pp. 78–9.
11. A. H. Guyot, *Earth and Man* (Boston, 1857), cited by Franklin Thomas, *The Environmental Basis of Society* (New York, 1921), p. 205.
12. 'Racial Assimilation in Secondary Groups,' *Publications of the American Sociological Society*, 8 (1914).

11 Race Problems and Modern Society (1929)

Jean Toomer*

From whatever angle one views modern society and the various forms of contemporary life, the records of flux and swift changes are everywhere evident. Even the attitude which holds that man's fundamental nature has not altered during the past ten thousand years, must admit the changes of forms and of modes which have occurred perhaps without precedent and certainly with an ever increasing rapidity during the life period of the now living generations. If the world is viewed through one or more of the various formulated interpretations of this period, or if one's estimate rests upon the comparatively inarticulate records of day to day experience, the results have the common factor of change. Let it be Spengler's *Decline of the West*, or Keyserling's *The World in the Making*, or Waldo Frank's survey of Western culture,[1] or Joseph Wood Krutch's analysis of the modern temper,[2] and there is found testimony to the effect that the principles of cohesion and crystallization are being rapidly withdrawn from the materials of old forms, with a consequent break up of these forms, a setting free of these materials, with the possibility that the principles of cohesion and crystallization will recombine the stuff of life and make new forms.

Bertrand Russell[3] has indicated the revisions of mental outlook made necessary by recent scientific and philosophic thinking. James Harvey Robinson has shown why we *must* create new forms of thinking and bring about a transformation of attitude.[4] From a different angle, the social science of the world-wide struggle between the owning and the laboring classes, clearly summarized by Scott Nearing,[5] comes to much the same conclusion, in so far as the factor of change is concerned. Again, the records of psychology bear striking witness of this factor. For though, on the one hand, there are in vogue a number of dogmas and pat formulas which assume a constant set of simple factors, and allow, say, Leonardo da Vinci to be seen at a glance, and which offer ready explanations of why, say, George Santayana writes, on the other

---

* Baker Brownell (ed.), *Problems of Civilisation* (New York: D. Van Nostrand, 1929). pp. 67–111.

168

hand, the practice of psychology discloses a surprising and bewildering flux and chaos, both in the individual and in the collective psyche. And in general, what is taking place in most fields of life is sufficiently radical for Baker Brownell to see it resulting in a new human universe.[6]

Be it the shifting forms of relation between men and women, or the revolt of youth everywhere, or the widespread emergence and concurrence of the machine, mechanical techniques, and civilized instinctive life-rhythms, or the phenomenon of the radio, or the possibility of super-power, or the 'rising tide of color' and the change of status among races, or the threat of another war, or the menace of opium, or the counter problems of degeneracy and eugenics, or the effects of mal-education and the efforts to reeducate, or the promise of a general renaissance of art and literature, or the decay of religions and the rising of new teachings and new prophets, or the forming of what appear to be new psychological types of human beings, or the increasing beliefs in vast earth-disturbances and changes – in short, wherever one is placed, and whatever aspect of the world condition he may focus on or experience, he is likely to be aware of the movement of forces that have at least in part broken from old forms and that have not yet achieved stability in new forms.

This is true, it seems, of the human world in general. Modern society is in flux. The psychology of the main peoples is the psychology of a transitional period.

And at the same time – paradoxical enough – it is also evident that there are certain forms of modern society which, at least for the time being, are not only not changing in the above sense, but are growing and strengthening as they now exist. I refer to the established economic and political systems – and their immediate by-products – of Western nations, especially of the English speaking nations. For despite the disorganized aspect of the economic situation as a consequence of the War, and as described by Keynes, it is, I think, the agreed opinion of students of Western economic and political institutions, particularly of those which obtain in the United States, that these systems, and especially the philosophy[7] which has grown up about them, have become stronger and more organized within the past thirty years. Their development during this period in the United States, for example, is suggested by these general facts: that this country now turns out, and is increasingly turning out, a surplus of both money and products; that it is sending in larger quantities this surplus into foreign fields; that since 1900 it has become a lending, instead of a borrowing nation; that Henry Ford has become a philosopher. One student of economic conditions states that within ten years all the main European boards of directors will be dominated and controlled by Americans. Thus, irrespective of all the changes suggested at the beginning of this article, irrespective of the example and influence of the Soviet Union from without, and of radical and liberal labor and political forces from within, the World War notwithstanding, and despite the protests and revolts of foreign peoples, the business, political, legal, and military organizations and expansion of Western nations have advanced. At the present time they at least appear to be more solid and crystallized than ever. And they are growing stronger. So true is this, and so dominant an influence do these systems exercise on all the other forms of life, that, should one view the modern Western nations from within the business and political worlds – and their outgrowths – one might well conclude that there were no radical changes occurring anywhere, or that at most these changes were taking place only in minor social forms and concerned only an uninfluential minority.

For the growth of business and of business technique, and the increased support that the political and legal systems give to the dominant economic practices, this growth and this increase have parallels in all the forms of life that are at all connected with these systems. Thus, wealth, and such power as wealth gives, are increasingly considered valuable: more and more men are devoting themselves to their attainment, seeing in them the end of life and the highest goal that life offers. The big businessman is the modern hero. The average man, that is, the average businessman, is already the ideal, even the idol, of millions of people; and there is a growing tendency for institutions of higher education, physicians, and psychologists to accept and affirm the average businessman as the ideal at which all people of sound sense should aim. The notions of prosperity and of necessary progress go hand in hand, and both are being elevated in the public mind. To have a larger bank-account, to live in a socially better located house, to drive a better car, to be able to discuss the stock-exchange and the servant problem – these are items which have an ever stronger appeal to an ever larger number of people. And not a bit of so-called religion is used as an aid to such fulfilment. The fact that most of us are just one step ahead of the sheriff is a thing that one mentions less and less. As our need to keep ahead of him increases, so does our optimism. Yes, crime does increase, but we are thousands of years in advance of backward peoples, and each day sees us further outdistance them. Social position is a matter of spending-power and possession of the items of prosperity. Never has aristocracy been taken so seriously. Results are looked for, and measured in terms of, silver dollars. Even sermons and poems must pass the success test before anyone considers them of merit. And all the while, the inner content of life is decreasing and rapidly losing significance. The inclination to prosperity and the inclination to suicide are somehow compatible. At any rate, both are increasing.

So that, as I have said, if one viewed the modern world from the point of view of Western economic and political systems, and their direct outgrowths, the evidence of their growth and crystallization would seem so weighty, widespread, and generally influential, that it might well be concluded that the organization and advance of old forms have precedence and power over the forces that are bringing about changes. It could be held that these changes, however radical they might be, are all tending to take place round and about the fixed points of our economic system and its by products.

Of course, within the form of big business, the materials are often unstable and the events uncertain, and there are many swift unexpected turnovers and reversals; and it may be that the very nature of this system is transient in character and capable of no long duration. But my personal experience is that the form itself is growing. And though we are no longer warranted in thinking in terms of extended periods of gradual growth only, but must think also in terms of sudden transformations, it being possible that our whole economic scheme will change, as it were, overnight, I cannot now see any signs of its break up, from within, in the immediate future. And while it is true that there is of necessity an intricate interchange occurring between the fixed factors and the factors of change, it is no less true that the dominant rhythms come from what we all concede to be our dominant institutions.

Thus, while it is a fact that modern society is in flux, it is also a fact that modern society is crystallized and formed about the solid structure of big business; and while modern psychology is the psychology of a transitional period, it is also the psychology of a stabilized big business period. It is desirable to keep both of these general facts in mind when we now turn to consider the particular matter of race problems and their relation to the other forms of the modern social order.

But now, in order to give this article focus and points of concrete reference, I shall take America, – that is, the United States – as a sufficiently representative modern society, and as a social scheme that contains a sufficiently representative class of race problems. For here in America there are changing forms and established forms; and, with the possible exception of the Soviet Union, the main features of our economic and political systems and their social outgrowths have points in common with those that obtain in other modern nations. And – again with the exception of the Soviet Union, in which, I am told, the economic and political causes of race problems either no longer exist or are being removed, the minority races and peoples being guaranteed similar rights, the children of all peoples being taught that all races are similar – American race problems have points in common with the race problems of other countries (the British and Hindu, the Eurasian, the gentile and Jew on the Continent, the whites and blacks in South Africa) and with the large number of problems everywhere – such as nationality problems – which are psychologically similar to race problems.

It will be well to note here that no serious student of race claims to know what race really is; nor do we know. Therefore the term 'race problem' is a loose sociological term, which contains a variety of vague meanings; it is subject to being used with whatever meaning one happens to give it.

Scientific opinion is in doubt as to what race is. Authorities such as Roland Dixon, Franz Boas, A. L. Kroeber, Ellsworth Huntington, and Flinders Petrie agree that from the point of view of exact knowledge, the whole subject of race is uncertain and somewhat confused. It is clear that the human race is something different from the other orders of life of the natural kingdom. It is noticeable that there are differences within the human group. But it is not admissible to define and understand race solely on the basis of an obvious variation of a single physical feature, such as color of skin; and when one seeks for a fundamental knowledge of it, then, despite the exact biological ideas of the germ-plasm and genes, and despite the exact anthropological ideas associated with measurements of physical features, the difficulties encountered tend to mount faster than one's understanding.

One may, with Professor Kroeber,[8] try to understand and use the term 'race' in its strict biological sense, and hold it to mean an hereditary subdivision of a species. I personally think that this is a much needed practice, because, among other things, it calls attention to the strictly biological aspect of race, it points to race as an organic phenomenon, and it allows the purely sociological aspects of racial matters to be distinguished and seen for what they are. Surely, there can not be much advance in the understanding of race problems, until we do clearly distinguish between their organic and social factors. But from the point of exact definition and real knowledge, the term 'hereditary subdivision of a species' is hardly better understood than the term 'race.' For again we are brought up to the questions: What is a subdivision? Upon what criteria should our ideas of a subdivision rest? Can these criteria be used to adequately define and understand race? Does anyone really know what a subdivision is? The fact is that the difficulties involved in the present ideas of, and approach to race, are causing thoughtful men to recast their data and take new directions. In some cases there is a tendency to step out of the scientific confusion by accepting the notions of race in common usage. As an example of this, I quote the following remarks[9] of Louis Wirth:

> What sort of criteria enable us to tell what constitutes a race and who belongs to it? If the present study shows anything, it indicates that the word race has been used in a great many contradictory ways, and that the physical anthropologists, with their anthropometric measurements, reduce a race to a highly variable statistical concept. A race, it may turn out, is after all not so much a clearly delimitable, homogenous biological group, as a cultural group, whose self and group consciousness is more or less attached to some clearly visible biological trait. Perhaps the old naïve notion of classifying races by skin color has, in the final analysis, more practical value than the minute and complex measurements of cephalic index, nostrility, hair shape, etc. If Dr. Herskovits's data and interpretations are correct, a race is something social rather than biological. A race, it turns out, is a group of people that we treat as if they were one. You belong to a certain race, if you feel yourself to be a member, and if others treat you as if you were.

This is a clear statement of what race is commonly taken to mean. It has a certain sound sense to recommend it. But in effect it does no more than transpose race from the confusion of science back again to the confusion of public opinion. Nor do I think we will profit by giving scientific questions also into the keeping of the 'average man.' It may be that we will have to discard the notion of race. At any rate, I consider it likely that scientific investigation will increasingly use other, and perhaps more fruitful, concepts in its future attempts to understand human differences. In view of the phenomena to be dealt with,

and also because of the now evident tendencies to think in terms of
'type,' it is possible that the conception of type, *types of men*, physico-
psychological types of men, will, among thoughtful people, largely
supplant the now prevalent notions of races. However this may be,
suffice it here to repeat that race is a somewhat confused and uncertain subject.

This being the case with the main term, how then am I to give any
real clarity to the term 'race problem'? What is it that distinguishes
race problems from all the other problems with which man is belabored?
In what real way do racial maladjustments differ from the scores of
maladjustments that burden men's psyche? Just how are sociological
debates about race different from the endless series of debates on all
possible subjects that men are continually engaging in? In another place[10]
I have pursued an investigation of race problems that gives these questions
a more detailed treatment than is possible here. And in the same work
I have indicated, among other things, that the answer which is often
given, namely, that biological race-differences explain the nature of
race problems – that this answer is incorrect. For this answer is involved in the confusion between organic and social factors. Professor
Kroeber has pointed out the error of such practice. It assumes that
biological race-phenomena give rise to sociological race problems. But
the strictly racial history of man, with its repeated crossings and
recrossings of all the sub-groups of the human stock, with its great
number of intermixtures of all kinds, shows clearly that as organisms
we are noticeably free from concern with the issues that we sociologically contend with – that so-called race problems are not due to biological causes, but to the superimposed forms and controversies of our
social *milieu.*

The same conclusion is reached by both social and personal psychology. For herein it is seen that it is first necessary that we be conditioned by the factors of our social environment, before we do and
can respond in terms of racial similarities and differences. If we were
never taught and never acquired ideas, opinions, beliefs, and superstitions about race, if we were never conditioned to have feelings and
so-called instincts about these notions and beliefs, we would never
have any responses or behavior in terms of race: we would not experience race prejudice and animosity. To an unconditioned child – that
is, to a child that has not acquired racial notions and feelings from its
environment, let the child be of whatever race you will – differences
of skin color are no more and no less than differences of color of its

toys or dresses. No child has prejudice against a toy because its color is white or black. No racially unconditioned child has prejudice against a person because his color is white or black. Differences of texture of hair are similarly no more and no less than differences of texture between the hair of different animals – a shaggy dog, and a sleek cat. And so it is with all the other physical characteristics that are commonly supposed to provoke supposedly innate racial prejudices and preferences. There are no such things as innate racial antipathies. We are not born with them. Either we acquire them from our environment, or else we do not have them at all. So that, paradoxical as it may sound, the fact is that race, as such, does not give rise to race problems. The physical aspects of race do not cause the problems that center around what are called racial hatreds and prejudices. This is the conclusion of experimental psychology.[11] And biologists, those who hold no brief in favor of environment as a dominant factor in the making of adult man, are inclined to agree with this position as to the origin of race problems. 'It is only just to admit at once,' says Professor East, a geneticist, 'that many cases of racial antagonism have no biological warrant.'[12]

The meaning and the importance of the above conclusion consists in this: since race problems are social and psychological in origin, they can be fundamentally dealt with – they can be radically changed and even eliminated – by use of the proper social and psychological instruments. It is possible for man and society to constructively handle the racial situation. I shall return to this matter and treat it more in detail in a short while.

So then, race problems are sociological and psychological both in cause and in character. When we deal with them, we are entirely in the field of socio-psychological phenomena. Thus, if you could, so to speak, cut away man's psyche, leaving him to exist as a straight organic product, you would by that act eliminate, not only race problems, but most of the other so-called human problems as well. But I do not propose this method as a solution of race problems. Though if I did, I would not be in want of support. Many are now trying to do substantially just this thing. The attempts variously go under the guise, sometimes of education, sometimes psychology, liquor, opium, while the principle of cutting, interpreted as killing, and applied now to the body instead of to the psyche, would win half the world, as the last war showed, to its support. But this is another matter.

In telling what race problems are not, I suggested what they are. A race problem is any form of behavior, be it a scientific problem, a maladjustment, or a debate or discussion, which is associated with ideas opinions, beliefs, etc., about races. Once we leave the sphere of science, the fact that we do not know what races are does not prevent our having notions, beliefs, preferences, and prejudices about them. On the contrary, since it is never knowledge but the lack of it that provides the most fruitful condition for racial animosities, our lack of understanding supplies the very best circumstance for racial maladjustments to multiply and continue from generation to generation. Let a person be once conditioned to respond in terms of notions and beliefs about race, and his prejudice will stand in direct proportion to his misinformation, while the stress of his prejudice, animosity, etc., will determine the acuteness of his problem.

In considering race problems, we may, I think, for the present purpose divide them into three classes. First, there is the class of race problems which falls in the domain of scientific investigation. These consist of the racial matters dealt with in biology, anthropology, and psychology. They have to do with man's biological and cultural make up and behavior. They involve the attempt to ascertain the facts and understand the principles of human organic, social, and psychological existence – in so far as these are particularly concerned with matters of race. They include the aim of applying the knowledge thus gained for the best possible regulation of human affairs.

Second, there are race problems that take the form of discussion and debate. There are serious discussions of the race question. These discussions often draw upon the data of science, and, pressing beyond prejudice and petty issues, they also aim to arrive at a theoretically sound understanding of racial matters, and at practical conclusions that can be relied upon to guide men in the developing of intelligence, character, and ability. These discussions are frequently reducible to the question of interbreeding – of intermarriage. Sometimes they get entangled in arguments about heredity and environment, about superiority and inferiority. Too often they get lost in a maze of unconscious assumptions in favor of one's own type of life, one's own standards. As often as not they tend to lose sense of genuine values. The race-theme can compel the partial or total eclipse of all else. They are sometimes too solemn, too serious; too seldom does a good laugh relieve the tenseness. And now and again, I am afraid, the people who engage in these discussions are taken in by the humbug of education and civilization. In these cases the serious discussions of race fall far below the intelligence displayed by creative thinking in other fields.

At their best, however, they do lead to clarification, and to the taking of measures for increasing constructive racial life and interracial relationships.

Then there are all manner of absurd and sometimes explosive remarks and debates over racial issues. These range all the way from parlor and backyard gossip about 'niggers,' 'crackers,' 'kikes,' 'wops,' etc., through naïve verbal releases for hurt emotions, to propagandist and pathological speeches, articles and books. Debates of this type are particularly notable in that they usually repeat what has already been said to no profit thousands of times, and in that they take place in shameless ignorance of new and constructive ideas and attitudes.

Then, third, there is the class of race problems which arise from, or, better, which *are* the actual day to day experiences of maladjustments due to factors of a racial character. These include experiences caused by the drawing of the color line; by fights – physical, legal, and otherwise – between the races; by all manner of racial aggressions, resistances, oppositions, oppressions, fears, prejudices, hatreds; and by the occasional stoning and burning of houses, riots, lynchings.

Race problems of the scientific class and of the serious discussion class are decidedly in the minority. They comprise but a small portion of the total behavior concerned with race. Indeed, in common use, the term 'race problem' does not include them. For race problems, in the popular mind, are those associated with racial animosities and prejudices. Race problems of the social gossip, propagandist, and pathological debate class, and those of the actual maladjustment class, are by far the most numerous. They comprise the bulk of the racial situation. Soon I shall give a brief social description of this situation. For the present it is enough to remark in general that it is spreading to involve all of America, and that it is, it seems, rapidly growing more acute.

Having made the above groupings, I am now able to indicate what seems to me to be the true relation of these classes of race problems to the other forms of our social order. With this relationship established, I will then review some of the more important questions of the race issue, and at least suggest tentative answers.

What explanations are there for the persistence and increase of the kind of race problems which intelligent opinion considers negative, undesirable, to be eliminated? How comes it that in this age of increasing scientific knowledge, these negative aspects of life also increase? Why is it that in the midst of such radical changes as we noted at the beginning of this article, race problems, in their established forms, are becoming more crystallized? Since everyone who is sincerely interested in an intelligent and constructive regulation of human life wishes that race problems be fundamentally solved, since these problems can be basically dealt with by taking the proper social and psychological measures, since there is a sufficient knowledge to begin this work, why is it that we have not devised and applied the proper instruments? In what now follows we will see the situation that gives rise to these and other important questions, particularly to the question: What is to be done about it?

Recalling what was said as to the existence in modern society of two classes of forms, one of which was undergoing radical changes, one of which was becoming more crystallized, we may now ask, Into which class of forms do race problems fall? It is probable, and I think it is accurate to say that race problems of the scientific and of the serious discussion type belong to the changing category. They are among the forms that are undergoing radical changes. For not only are they in touch with the forces and factors they are in general producing new intellectual and conscious outlooks, but they are also being strongly influenced by the particular discovery of new racial data and of new methods of dealing with race. Though the science of man shows less striking revolutions than the science of physics, it is nevertheless certain that its progress has caused the forming of new attitudes and of new approaches to racial phenomena. From the scientific point of view, the whole matter of race is something different – perhaps quite different – from what it was twenty or thirty years ago. But race problems of this type comprise only a small fraction of the racial situation.

The bulk of racial behavior belongs to the established crystallizing category. Most race problems, in their given forms, are tending not to radically change, but to crystallize. By far the larger part of our racial situation, with its already given patterns and tendencies, is rapidly growing more acute. These facts, if such they be, will be brought out if we note with what other social forms race problems are most closely associated, and if we see some of the main patterns and tendencies.

There is no need to present new facts to support the statement that race problems are closely associated with our economic and political systems, and that they are most distant from the intellectual and cultural activities that now manifest marked changes. It is well known that whenever two or more races (or nationalities) meet in conditions that are mainly determined by acquisitive interests, race problems arise as by products of economic issues. The desire for land, the wish to exploit natural resources, the wish for cheap labor – wherever these motives have dominated a situation involving different races, whether the races are set in rivalry, or with one dominant and the other dominated, race problems also have sprung up. Just this is the situation in China, India, South Africa, Europe, and in different sections of the United States. The economic and political causes of race problems in these places are too well known to need more than bare statement.

In America, the 'acquisitive urge' for land, natural resources, and cheap labor variously gave rise to the problems of the whites and the Indians, the whites and the negroes, the whites and the Asiatics, the old stock and the immigrants. The Indian problem began over land deals, and, in so far as it still exists, it is still a matter of white men desiring Indian territory for economic profit. Political and legal devices have all tended to be in the service of this interest. The Asiatic problem is obviously economic, and its 'solution' is always seen with an eye to the economic situation. Immigrant problems are the direct outgrowth of demands for cheap labor, and of the circumstances attending the immigrant's economic condition after he arrives in this country. While the way in which the negro problem has been and still is tied up with our economic and political systems, and their social outgrowths, is even more evident. This is not to say that economic causes and factors are the only ones giving rise to race problems; there are certainly other causes and factors, while the basic cause of all of man's negative problems must be sought, I think, in some abnormal feature of man's fundamental make up. Here I am simply indicating the relationship between the organized expressions of man's acquisitive urge, namely, between our economic and political systems, and race problems. In addition to the various historical and social science studies that show this relationship, it can be clearly seen if one has the patience to go over the *Congressional Records* that bear on this subject. And there recently appeared in *Harper's Magazine* an article[13] dealing with the future of America, written by an eminent biologist, wherein much that is relevant to the present point, and indeed to the general trend of this paper, is considered.

Just as race problems are closely associated with our economic and political systems, so are they with one of the main outgrowths of these system – our social scheme of caste distinctions. No small measure of racial animosity is due to this scheme. This scheme is crystallizing. The economic and political systems are increasing. And so are race problems. How could it be otherwise than that the things which are causing an increased anti-Americanism abroad, and an increase of crime and degeneracy, and a decrease of intelligence at home, also cause more and more race antagonism.

Certain factors of American race problems, particularly certain of the factors involved in the race problems of the whites and negroes, were modified by the Civil War. Many more factors were added then, and have been added since then. But the main forms of these problems, namely, the sharp sociological divisions between the white and colored people, have persisted from the beginning of American history, and they have steadily become more and more fixed and crystallized. They have grown up, so to speak, with the growth of our economic, political, and social systems. And the probability is that they will continue to increase with the increase of these systems. Scientific liberal opinion, and intelligent humanism, will tend to have as much, and no more influence on the character of race problems as they have on the character of big business and on the characters of Republican and Democratic party politics.

So much, then, by way of indicating the relation between race problems and the other main forms of our social order. Now to see that racial situation, its main patterns and tendencies.

Many accounts of race problems in the United States might well lead a reader to the conclusion that everywhere about our streets he would see race problems enacted day after day. The impression is often given that race issues are to be met with as frequently and as tangibly as one meets newsboys selling papers. Whereas the fact is that our towns and streets, of whatever section, are often so noticeably without any race behavior, that one wonders, sometimes, where are all these problems the books tells us America is burdened with. Again, books frequently treat race problems as if they existed only in books, in theory, abstracted from the psyche of living men. From what I have written thus far, one might get the impression that race issues assemble in and about 'systems' and 'institutions.' Of course they don't. Race problems, where they do exist, and are manifest in living men, and nowhere else. And, of course, they do obtain in some quantity. But their forms and manifestations often have very little in common with what is written about them. It is difficult to treat, in a well balanced and reasoned way, a subject which in nature is irrational. And it is particularly difficult to do this when one must meet the requirements of a short exposition.

The South – that is, the southern section of the United States – is particularly open to strange descriptions. Reports of the South would have it that white Southerners are always indefatigably engaged on the one hand, in keeping the negro in his place, and, on the other, in prying into the family closets of their white economic, political, and social enemies, with the intent of discovering there some trace of dark blood with which to stigmatize and break these enemies. Doubtless such things do happen. I am told that occasionally it is somehow discovered that some white family of hitherto high repute has indeed a drop of negro blood – whereon this family is likely to fall below the social level of prosperous negroes. And there are reports of ingenious tests devised and used for detecting the presence of dark blood in those who otherwise would pass for pure white. This is similar to the assertion that some people in Vienna wish to make blood tests compulsory for every school child, in order that any trace of Semitic blood may be detected. Doubtless there are such tests, or wishes for such tests, in both places. And, of course, in our South there are lynchings, peonage, false legal trials, and no court procedure at all, political disfranchisement, segregation, and, on the social level, a rigid maintenance of caste distinctions. And, among negroes, there is a sizable amount of discontent, fear, hatred, and an effort to get better conditions. Certainly both races are enslaved by the situation. But there are, on the other hand, intelligent attempts on the part of both white and colored men to constructively deal with the existing factors.[14] And there are thousands of both whites and blacks who from day to day experience no active form of race problem, but who are, like masses of people everywhere, sufficiently content to go their way and live their life, counting their day lucky if, without working them too hard, it has given them the means to eat and sleep and reproduce their kind.

There is no doubt, however, that the race problem is at least a latent problem with almost everyone, not only in the South, but everywhere within the United States. For America is a nation in name only. In point of fact, she is a social form containing racial, national, and cultural groups which the existing economic, political, and social systems tend to keep divided and repellent. Moreover, each group is left to feel, and often taught and urged to feel, that some other group is the cause of its misfortune. Against the actual and potential antagonisms thus caused, many of our churches and other orders of so-called brotherhood and good will do no more than make feeble, and, often enough, hypocritical gestures.

Below the sociological level, all the races and stocks present in

America – and almost all of the main peoples in some numbers are assembled here – have met and mingled their bloods. Biologically, what has taken place here somewhat justifies the name 'melting pot'. But it is thus everywhere where people meet. Let people meet – and they mingle. This is biology, the reproductive urge within man, acting with no thought of sociological differences, acting even in the face of social prohibitions and restraint of all sorts. These organic acts are fundamental in human biology. This mingling of bloods has been recognized and formulated as a maxim by anthropology.[15] Subject to the influence of the American environment, the different peoples and stocks have to intermixed here, that – among others, and notably – Dr. Ales Hrdlicka sees the forming of a distinct racial type, which he calls the American type. But the consciousness of most so-called Americans lags far behind the organic process.

When we view the scene sociologically, then, as I have said, we everywhere see strong tendencies to form separatist and repellent groups. On the social level, the term 'melting pot' is somewhat of a mismoner. Of so-called racial divisions and antagonisms, there is the nation wide separation of the white and colored groups. Jews and gentiles tend to remain apart. The bewildering number of nationalistic groups – English, German, French, Italians, Greeks, Russians, etc., etc. – tend to do likewise. And it sometimes happens that those of Northern and Southern European descent are as prejudiced against each other, or against newly arrived technical citizens, as they are against negroes. Negroes do not care too much for foreigners. There are a number of fairly defined prejudices within each of the several groups; while the lines drawn, and the animosities aroused, by differences of sectional, fraternal, business, political, social, artistic, religious, and scientific allegiance are quite considerable. So that, all in all, it is rare indeed to find anyone who is genuinely conscious of being an American. We have slogans: one hundred per cent American; America first; etc. But they do not mean much. The character of perhaps the greatest American – Walt Whitman – is as antipathetic to the conduct of the majority of those who dwell here, as the ideals of liberty and union, and the high values that have ever been and still are somehow present in the spirit of this country, are antipathetic to this same conduct.

Just as separatism has everywhere increased since the War, so the above mentioned separatistic tendencies have here increased since then.

The World War and its consequences gave a decided turn to the racial situation within the negro group. But this turn was not, and is not, in a radically new direction. Rather, it has resulted in a strengthening of certain of the forces and factors implicit in the form that has existed since the Civil War, and indeed ever since the introduction of negroes into America – the form, namely, which in its main outline divides white from black. And thus this form itself has become further strengthened and crystallized. A number of factors, among which are greater pressure from without, increased organization and articulateness within the group, and, as a result of the World War, a deeper seated disillusion as regards the promises of the dominant white American – these, together with other factors, have caused an intensification of negro race consciousness. And with this there has come an increased aggressiveness – more fight. It is no small factor in favor of this fighting attitude that it is being recognized and affirmed by other American minority groups. It is remarked, for instance, that whereas the Indians are hopeless because they do not try to fight for and help themselves, the negroes demand and therefore deserve better conditions. There is more bitterness, an ever increasing absorption and concern with race issues; very few intelligent negroes are permitted to be interested in anything else. Within the negro world there has come about a parallel growth and organization of economic and professional activities, and, consequently, an increased group independence and the emergence of a fairly well defined middle class, a tendency to deliberately withdraw from attempts to participate as Americans in the general life of the United States, a greater attempt to participate as negroes in the general life, a stronger demand, from some, for social equality, and from others, for economic and educational opportunity, some spread of proletarian class consciousness, some activity in art and literature.

From the point of view of deliberate intention, it would seem that the new negro is much more negro and much less American than was the old negro of fifty years ago. From the point of view of sociological types, the types which are arising among negroes, such as the business man, the politician, the educator, the professional person, the college student, the writer, the propagandist, the movie enthusiast, the bootlegger, the taxi driver, etc. – these types among negroes are more and more approaching the corresponding white types. But, just as certain as it is that this increasing correspondence of types makes the drawing of distinctions supposedly based on skin color or blood composition appear more and more ridiculous, so it is true that the lines are being drawn with more force between the colored and white groups. Negroes are themselves now drawing these lines. Interbreeding and intermarriage, for instance, are becoming as taboo among negroes as among whites.

A similar increase of separatism is to be seen among Nordics. There are those who, with greater urgency than ever, are aiming toward an inviolate white aristocracy. Their already fixed inclination toward a Western modification of the caste system is stimulated, and sometimes over stimulated, by the threat that the rising tide of Southern and darker peoples may cause them to lose control. They tend to see all virtue menaced by this rising tide. They increasingly tend to feel and think that not only their own souls, but also the very spirit of America, and even in the world, would be violated, should any save those of their own stock exercise decisive influence. And there are some whites who would like to see the darker peoples, particularly the negroes, either deported, or sterilized, or swept off by a pestilence.

There are Jews who are more and more emphasizing the actuality and distinction of the Jewish race. They would have the Jews remain strictly as they are, preserving and transmitting their character and culture in more or less isolation from the other peoples of America.

While the Indian, still being pressed off his land and increasingly compelled to attend United States schools, holds aloof so far as possible from the white man, and sometimes indicates the white man's presence in America by a symbolic of tin cans.

The main tendencies toward separatism are observed and given a brilliant record in André Siegfried's *America Comes of Age*. And therein will also be found an excellent summary, from one point of view, of the deadlock existing in the American racial situation. For despite the movement above suggested, the situation is indeed in deadlock. The races cannot draw nearer together; nor can they draw much farther apart – and still remain races in America. But they will undoubtedly push away from one another, until they completely occupied what small room for withdrawal is still left. For, as I have indicated, the strongest forces now active are tending to intensify and crystallize the very patterns, tendencies, and conditions that brought about the present situation.

Thus, from a racial point of view, and, to my mind, from several other points of view, America, which set out to be a land of the free, has become instead a social trap. The dominant forms of her social life – her economic, political, educational, social, and racial forms – compel her people to exist and meet in just the ways most conducive to the maintenance of this trap. All Americans are in it – the whites no less than the black, the black no more than the red, the Jew no more than the gentile. It is sometimes thought, both by themselves and by others, that the dominant white Protestant holds the keys to the situation, and could, by a simple turn of the hand, unlock it if he wished to. But this is not fact – it is fiction. The dominant white is just as much a victim of his form as is the negro of his; while both are equally held by the major American customs and institutions. This is sound social science and it is sound psychology. And until all parties recognize it to be so, and stop berating one another, and get down to work to bring about basic constructive changes, it is romance to talk about solving race problems. As it is, both white and colored people share the same stupidity; for both see no other way out than by intensifying the very attitudes which entrapped them. And so, Americans of all colors and of most descriptions are crawling about their social person, which is still called Democracy. They are unable to see, and indeed they do not suspect, what it is that holds them; perhaps they do not realize that they are held, so busy are they with their by now habitual rivalries, fears, egotisms, hatreds, and illusions.

But perhaps it is premature to call the prevalent racial tendencies stupid and short sighted. It may be that a solution does lie in the direction which calls for an increase to bursting point of the existing conditions. Circumstances have been known to change as a result of the accentuation of their negative factors. But as often as not, the change, when summed up, is seen to have consisted of no more than a complete disappearance of all positive factors. However this may be, there is no doubt that race prejudice, and all associated with it, is tending to carry the entire body of America toward some such climax. Much of the writing about Nordics and negroes, and much of the talk as to who is superior and who is inferior and who is equal, and all the other nonsense about race, is just so much verbal fanfare accompanying the actual march.

Too often the very agencies and instruments that might turn its course, or even change its character, are themselves either no more than adjuncts of the prevalent economic, social, and racial forms, or else the force of these forms tends to render them helpless. Thus our churches, our schools, colleges, universities, newspapers, large lecture platforms, are frequently just so many systematized parts of the machine itself; while even the science of anthropology is sometimes constrained to use the language of popular opinion and prejudice. And, as I have said before, liberal opinion and intelligent humanism affect the race question just about as much as they affect the practice of big business and the politics of the Republican and Democratic parties.

But no description of the situation in America is faithful to the entire scene, which fails to notice and consider the positive possibilities contained in the emergence of a large number of the type of people who cannot be classified as separatist and racial. These people are truly synthetic and human. They exist all over America. And though they may not be so defined and articulate as the separatist type, and though they are less in numbers, it is quite possible that their qualitative significance will exercise the greater influence in shaping the future of this country. M. Siegfried and others failed either to note this type or to give due weight to it, with the consequence that their pictures of the American situation are, to say the least, incomplete.

There are present here individuals, and even groups, drawn from all fields of life – business, the crafts, the professions, the arts and sciences – who, in the first place, and in general, affirm truly human values, and sincerely strive that life may contain the greatest possible positive meaning, and who, in the second place, actually do something toward bringing about a worth-while day to day existence. When people of this type face the racial situation, they either have no prejudices or antagonisms, or else they press beyond them, in order to apply the standards of intelligence, character, and ability to this aspect of life also. And it is generally agreed that both individual growth and the development of America as a whole are intimately concerned with achieving a creative synthesis of the best elements here present.

Putting aside the matter of type for the moment, I would like to quote in this connection the following passage:

> I can see no reasonable excuse for oppression and discrimination on a color line basis. I have no sympathy with a regimen of repression on the part of the whites, and no sympathy with the militant aggressiveness of such organizations as the Association for the Advancement of the Colored People, which lobby and threaten, to gain the acceptance of ill advised programs. There is no reason for trying to make university-men either of all negroes or of all whites. To give the ballot to morons and illiterates of either race is foolish. But it does seem to me that many of the unpleasant elements of the situation can be eliminated by approaching all matters from the individualistic rather than the racial point of view. I am inclined to believe that even the strictly genetic phases of the matter can be settled on this basis. It is a question of eugenics ideals. An aristocracy of brains is difficult to establish and still more difficult to maintain. There is too much variability everywhere. Each individual must stand on his own merits.

This is the well considered position of Edward M. East, who approaches the subject from the genetic point of view. I do not give it as being representative of the type mentioned above – some will think it a bit conservative. But I do give it as a sign of intelligent liberal opinion, and as a sign that real values are beginning to displace petty issues in racial matters. The various forms of contemporary literature contain numerous examples of the same tendency.

But the greater number of people of the expanding type are not articulate. They are confused and scattered. Their psychology partakes of the transitional transforming aspects of this age. They are not sure of themselves. They do not as yet feel certain of their position. They are not sufficiently conscious of their type. Often they exist isolate and nebulous, and come to feel, because of the contrary conduct all around them, either that they must be wrong, or else that they must hide their real selves and deny their true values. Often they have been so compelled, and are now so accustomed, to use the dominant, which is to them an alien, language, that they can find no words for even talking to themselves, much less to others. When it comes to the particular matter of race and race problems, this type of American, though never actively participating in the various clashes and controversies, oppressions and protests against oppressions, are frequently drawn into a passive participation in narrow racial, social, and cultural issues, simply because they can find no opportunity for positive action in what really concerns them. For seldom do the various race programs and propagandists speak in their terms. Hardly ever are they directly appealed to by and for aims to which they can genuinely respond. Too seldom is there possibility for them to align themselves with a constructive human undertaking. For most racial programs, like most political programs, are alien to this type. But it is, I think , this type of American who must and will provide the unprejudiced energy, the intelligence, and the clean vision necessary for the solution of what, even to the most narrow minded, is a distressing racial situation.

Race problems can be solved. In so far as they are sociological in character – and we established the fact earlier in this paper that most so-called race problems are of this character – they can be constructively dealt with by using the proper social and psychological means. These means are available. We have enough of the right kind of tools for beginning work. Modern psychology, and particularly the behavioristic method worked out by Doctor Watson, provides the means for rightly conditioning children, and for gradually rightly reconditioning adults. New and better methods of teaching are to be had for the general training of young and coming generations. History and social science show us where our large systems and institutions are at fault, and theoretically at least the way is open for constructive changes. The science of man has enough sound data about race, so that no one need ever be misinformed in ways that lead to prejudice and antagonism. Human values have a sufficiently clear definition, so that everyone can recognize what they are. In short, in so far as race problems are environmental, we have the means to understand our job and set about it.

And there is enough knowledge of biology and genetics to enable us to make a similar start at solving the organic problems of race.

Stripped to its essentials, the positive aspect of the race problem can be expressed thus: how to bring about a selective fusion of the racial and cultural factors of America, in order that the best possible stock and culture may be produced. This implies the need and desirability of breeding on the basis of biological fitness. It implies the need and desirability of existing and exchanging on the basis of intelligence, character, and ability. It means that the process of racial and cultural amalgamation should be guided by these standards.

We have, as I have said, enough knowledge to start solving this problem. Why don't we do something? Why do we, instead, let the negative features of the racial situation run on and intensify? How comes it that in this age of increasing general scientific knowledge, these and other undesirable aspects of life also increase? Why is it that in the midst of such radical changes as we noted at the beginning of this article, race problems, in their established forms, are becoming more crystallized?

There is the obvious answer that all of this is so because race problems are closely associated with the other main forms of our social order, which are also increasing, namely, with our economic, political, and social systems. These systems express and stimulate acquisitive passion for money power, antisocial urges; and since it is their nature to arouse and maintain all kinds of antagonisms, it is only natural that they also stimulate and feed racial animosities. Socially constructive forms of activity, being less powerful and in the minority, can make but little impression upon and headway against them. Put differently, the most influential men and women of our age and nation are so committed to practices that are against intelligence and hostile to well being, that they either consciously or unconsciously do not favor and are often opposed to the use of those agencies and instruments that could bring about constructive changes. These men and women are sufficiently powerful in their hostility to good measures to prevent their being tried. Men and women of sound sense and good conscience are comparatively helpless. Essentialized, this means that man, the destructive being, still is stronger than man, the intelligent being. The destructive part of us increasing, even while our intelligence expands. These parts are in vital contest. It is a critical struggle for supremacy in its most fundamental aspect. Thus far, the negative has proven stronger than the positive. This is the explanation that is given not only to tell why race problems are unsolved, but also to explain the presence among us of war, degeneracy, and most of the other ills of man.

As regards racial animosities, I should like to add two other brief considerations. For one: all that has to do with race prejudice and beliefs about race, falls into the class of opinions and feelings which James Harvey Robinson has shown to stubbornly resist and resent questioning and change under any conditions. Prejudices and superstitions of all kinds are among the stubborn decorations of man's psyche. It is regrettable – more, it is shameful, but it is no cause for wonder – that they throw us, far more often than we successfully contend with them.

For another: our psychological posture is prostrate. With much activity outside, our spirit is strangely inactive. We are so habituated to living miserably, that it is hard for most of us to realize that we contain within us the possibility of living otherwise. It is difficult for people born and reared in prison to envisage and wish for a free life. We have lied and cheated so much and so long, that we have become cynical as to the existence of real virtue. Too much routine and cheap pleasure, and perhaps an overdose of book learning, have dulled our sense of potentialities. Too little meaning too long in life has led us to doubt that life has any real significance. When men are in psychological states of these kinds, it is difficult for positive appeals to energize them. They are inclined not to see or recognize good means when these are offered them. They are inclined to let the best of tools lie useless. And thus we face the possibility that we, who have almost enough knowledge to separate the atom, may fail to separate men from their antagonisms.

Notes

1. A series of articles by Waldo Frank, in *The New Republic*, 1927–28.
2. Articles by Joseph Wood Krutch, in *The Atlantic Monthly*, 1927–28.

3. *Philosophy*, by Bertrand Russell.
4. *The Mind in the Making*, by James Harvey Robinson.
5. *Where is Civilization Going?* by Scott Nearing.
6. *The New Universe*, by Baker Brownell.
7. See Chapter VII, 'The Sickness of an Acquisitive Society', in *The Mind in the Making*.
8. See *Anthropology*, by A. L. Kroeber. Particularly the first five chapters.
9. Taken from a review of *The American Negro*, by Melville J. Herskovits. This review appeared in the *Chicago Evening Post Literary Review*, March 23, 1928.
10. *The Crock of Problems*, by Jean Toomer.
11. General psychological facts bearing on this conclusion will be found in *Behaviorism*, by John B. Watson.
12. *Heredity aud Human Affairs*, by Edward M. East, page 184.
13. 'The Future of America, A Biological Forecast,' anonymous, in *Harper's Magazine*, April, 1928.
14. In this connection, see *The Advancing South*, by Edwin Mims.
15. For a concise statement of this maxim, together with data to this effect drawn from a study of racial crossing in America, see *The American Negro*, by Melville J. Herskovits.

12 Your Negroid and Indian Behaviour (1930)

Carl Gustav Jung*

I

It would never occur to the naïve European to regard the psychology of the average American as particularly complicated or sophisticated. On the contrary, he is rather impressed by the simplicity and straight-forwardness of American thought and manners. He likes to think of Americans as being a very active, businesslike, and astonishingly effi-cient people, concentrated upon a single goal – the Yellow God – and a bit handicapped by what certain English magazines call 'Ameri-cana' – something on the borderline of a mild insanity: 'Colonial people are likely to be a bit odd, don't know, like our South African cousins.'

Thus, when I have something serious to say about Americans and their particular psychology, my European audience, while not exactly shocked, is at all events somewhat puzzled and inclined to disapprove. What Americans will think about my ideas remains to be seen.

In 1909 I paid my first short visit to the United States. This way my first impression of the American people as a whole; before that I had known individuals only. I remember walking through the streets of Buffalo and seeing hundreds of workmen leaving a factory. Being a naïve European, I could not help remarking to my American com-panion: 'I really had no idea there was such an amazing amount of Indian blood in your people.'

'What!' said he. 'Indian blood?' I bet there is not one drop of it in this whole crowd.'

I replied : 'But don't you see their faces? They are more Indian than European.' Whereupon I was informed that most of these work-men were of Irish, Scotch, and German extraction. I was puzzled and half incredulous, but later I came to see how ridiculous my hypoth-esis had been. Nevertheless, my impression remained firm, and the years have only strenghtened it.

When I returned from America, I carried away with me that peculiarly

* From *The Forum*, 83(4) (April 1930), pp. 193–9.

dissatisfied feeling of one who has somehow missed the point. I had to confess that I was unable to 'size them up.' I only knew that a subtle difference existed between the American and the European – a difference like that between the Australian and South African. It is not so much in the anatomical features as in the general behavior, both physical and mental. One finds it in the language, the gestires, the mentality, in the movements of the body, and in certain things even more nebulous than these. You can say many witty and clever things about that difference and still be unable to analyze it.

But another impression also stuck in my mind. I had not noticed it at first, but it kept coming back as things will when they possess a certain importance and yet have not been understood. I was once the guest of a stiff and solemn New England family whose respectability was almost terrifying. It felt almost like home, for there are very conservative and highly respectable folk in Switzerland too. But there were Negro servants waiting on the table, and they made me feel as if I were eating lunch in a circus. I found myself cautiously scrutinizing the dishes, looking for imprints of those black fingers. A solemnity brooded over the meal for which I could see no reason; but I suppose it was the solemnity of great virtue or something like that. At all events, nobody laughed. Everyone was just too nice and too polite.

At last I could stand it no longer, and for better or worse I began to crack jokes. Though these were greeted with condescending smiles, I could not arouse that hearty and generous American laugh which I love and admire. 'Well,' I thought, 'Indian blood, wooden faces, camouflaged Mongols. Why not try some Chinese on them?' So I came to my last story – really a good one – and no sooner had I finished than right behind my chair an enormous avalanche of laughter broke loose. It was the Negro servant, and it was the real American laughter – that grand, unrestrained, unsophisticated laughter revealing rows of teeth, tongue, palate, everything.

I loved that African brother!

II

The American laugh is most impressive. Laughing is a very important emotional expression and one learns a lot about character through careful observation of the way people laugh. There are some folk who suffer from a crippled laughter. It is just painful to see them laugh, and the sound of that shrill, evil, compressed rattle almost makes you sick.

America as a nation can laugh. This means a lot: it means that there is still childlikeness, a soundness of emotion, an immediate rapport with fellow beings.

This laughter goes hand in hand with a remarkable vivacity and great ease of expression. Americans are great talkers. Gossip even extends into monstrously big newspapers, so that the talking goes on even when you are reading. The style of 'good' American writing is a talking style. When it is not too flat, it is just as refreshing and exhilarating to us Europeans as your laughter. But often, alas, it is just chattering – the noise of the big ant heap.

One of the greatest advantages of the American language is its slang. I am far from sniffing at American slang; on the contrary, I like it profoundly. Slang means a language in the making, a thing fully alive. Its pictures are not worm-eaten metaphors, pale images hallowed by immemorial age, smooth, correct and concise conversions; they are figures full of life, carrying all the stamina of their earthly origin and the incomparable flavor of a strange and new country. In America one feels this new current of a strange life in the flow of the old English language, and Englishmen often wonder where it comes from. Is it the new country only? I doubt it, and will shortly give my reason.

The way the American moves shows a strong tendency towards nonchalance. It is evident in the way he walks, how he wears his hat, how he holds his cigar, and how he speaks. Americans move with loose joints and swaying hips. This characteristic of primitive Negro women is frequently seen in American women, while the swinging gait of the men is fairly usual.

The most amazing feature of American life is its boundless publicity. Everybody has to meet everybody else, and they seem to enjoy doing it. To a Central European like myself the lack of distance between people, the absence of hedges and fences round the gardens, the belief in popularity, the gossip columns in the newspapers, the open doors in the houses (from the street one can look right through the sitting room and the adjoining bedroom into the backyard) – all this is more than disgusting; it is directly terrifying. You are immediately swallowed up by a hot and all-engulfing wave of emotional incontinence which knows no restraint. You see it in the eagerness and the hustling of everyday life, in all sorts of enthusiasms such as orgiastic sectarian outbursts, and in the violence of public admiration and reproval.

This overwhelming influence of collective emotions spreads into everything. It easily goes too far and leads people into situations which

individual deliberation would hardly ever have chosen. It has a decidedly flattening influence upon American psychology. You see this
particularly in the sex problem as it has developed since the war.
There is a marked tendency to promiscuity, which not only shows
itself in the frequency of divorces, but more especially still in the
younger generation's peculiar freedom from sex prejudices.

As an inevitable consequence, the individual rapport between the
sexes will suffer from it. Easy access never calls forth, and therefore
never develops, the values of character, because it forestalls any deep
mutual understanding. Such an understanding, without which no real
love can exist, can only be reached by overcoming all the difficulties
that arise from the psychological difference between the sexes. Promiscuity paralyzes all these efforts so that individual rapport seems quite
superfluous. Thus, the more so-called unprejudiced freedom and easy
promiscuity prevail, the more love becomes flat; it degenerates into
transitory sex interludes.

All American life seems to be the life of the big settlement – real
town life. Even the smallest community denies to itself the character
of a village and tends to become a city. It seems as though everything
were collective and standardized, for the town rules the whole style
of living, even in the country. Once, on a visit to a so-called camp
with so-called country life, a European friend who was travelling with
me whispered: 'I bet they even have a textbook on how to camp.'
And lo! – there it was, glistening in red and gold on the shelf.

The country is admirable – nay, just divine – with the faint per-
fume of unhistorical eternity in the air. The crickets are not yet shy
of man, and the bullfrog talks in the night with his prehistoric boom-
ing voice. Beautiful, immense nights, and days blessed with sunshine.
Yes, there is *real* country – and nobody seems to be up to it, least all
that hustling, noisily chattering, motoring townfolk. They are not even
down to it as the red Indians are. Among the Indians one feels peculiarly content, for they are obviously under their country and not on
top of it; so there, at last, is a peace of God.

III

I know the mother nations of North America pretty well, but if I relied solely on the theory of heredity, I should be completely at a loss
to explain how the Americans descending from European stock have
arrived at their striking peculiarities. One might suppose that some of

these characteristics are survivals of the old pioneer attitude, but I fail to see any connection between the particular qualities I have mentioned and the character of the early farmer-colonists. There is, indeed, a much better hypothesis to explain the American temperament, and it lies in the fact that the United States are pervaded by that most striking and suggestive figure – the Negro. Some states are more than half black – a fact that may astonish the naïve. European who thinks of America as a white nation. It is not wholly white, if you please; it is partly colored. It can not be helped; it is so.

Now what is more contagious than to live side by side with a rather primitive people? Go to Africa and see what happens. When the effect is so very obvious that you stumble over it, then you call it 'going black.' But if it is not so obvious, then it is explained as 'the sun.' (In India it is always the sun.) In reality it is a partial going black, counterbalanced by a particularly stiff-necked conventionality (with its subdivisions of righteousness and conspicuous respectability). With such conventionality people simply dry up, though they may make the sun responsible for it.

It is much easier for us Europeans to be a trifle immoral, or at least a bit lax, because we do not have to hold the moral standard against the heavy downward pull of primitive life. The inferior man exercises a tremendous pull upon civilised beings who are forced to live with him, because he fascinates the inferior layers of our psyche, which has lived through untold ages of similar conditions. *On revient toujours à ses premiers amours.* To our subconscious mind contact with primitives recalls not only our childhood, but also our prehistory; and with the Germanic races this means a harking back of only about twelve hundred years. The barbarous man in us is still wonderfully strong and he easily yields to the lure of his youthful memories. Therefore he needs very definite defenses. The Latin peoples, being older, don't need to be so much on their guard; hence their attitude toward the Negro is different from that of the Nordics.

But the defenses of the Germanic man reach only as far as consciousness reaches. Below the threshold of consciousness the contagion meets little resistance. Since the Negro lives within your cities and even within your houses, he also lives within your skin, subconsciously. Naturally it works both ways. Just as every Jew has a Christ complex, so every Negro has a white complex, and every white American a Negro Complex. The Negro, generally speaking, would give anything to change his skin; so too, the white man hates to admit that he has been touched by the black.

What, then, about American laughter? What about the boundless, noisy sociality? The pleasure in movement and in stunts of all sorts? The loose-jointed walk, the Negroid dance and music? (Incidentally, the rhythm of jazz is the same as the *n'goma* – the African dance. To an accompaniment of jazz music you can dance the *n'goma* perfectly, with all its jumping and rocking and its swinging of shoulders and hips. American music is most obviously pervaded by the African rhythm and the African melody.)

It would be difficult not to see that the Negro, with his primitive motility, his expressive emotionality, his childlike immediacy, his sense of music and rhythm, his funny and picturesque language, has infected American behavior. As every psychologist and every doctor knows, nothing is more contagious than tics, stammering, choreic movements, and signs of emotions – particularly laughing and peculiarities of speech. Even if you don't understand a joke in a foreign language, you can't help smiling when everybody else smiles. Stammering, too, can be of the most infectious quality, so that one can be of the most infectious quality, so that one can hardly refrain from imitating it involuntarily. Melody and rhythm are also most insinuating; they can obsess you for days. And as for language, it is always disturbing how its pronunciation and metaphors affect you; you begin with an apologetic quotation, 'as they say,' and soon you find yourself unconsciously adopting the new pronunciation or the new metaphor because you can't help it.

The white man is a terrific problem to the Negro, and whenever you affect somebody profoundly, then in a mysterious way something comes back from him to yourself. The Negro, by his mere presence in America, is a source of temperamental and mimetic infection which the European can't help noticing, for he sees the hopeless gap between the American and the African Negro.

Such racial infection is a very serious mental and moral problem wherever a primitive race outnumbers the white man. America has this problem only in a relative degree, since, throughout the country as a whole, the whites, far outnumber the blacks. The whites apparently, can assimilate the primitive influence with little risk to themselves. Still, even a casual visitor soon learns that there is such a thing as 'the Negro question' in the States.

I am quite convinced, therefore that some American peculiarities can be traced to the Negro directly, while others result from a compensatory defence against this laxity. But these things remain more externals, leaving the inner quick of American character untouched –

which would not be true if America represented a full-fledged example of 'going black'.

IV

Since I am not a behaviorist, I allow myself to suppose that you are still far off from the real man when you merely observe his behavior. I regard behaviour as nothing more than a shell which conceals the really living substance within. Thus, under the slightly Negroid mannerisms of the American, I discern pretty clearly the essential white man within, and my question is: Is this American white man just a simple white, or is he in any way different from the European representatives of the species? I believe there is a marked difference between them within as well as without; and this brings us to the second part of my theory.

It may seem mysterious and unbelievable, yet it is a fact observable throughout history, that man can be assimilated by a country. In the air and soil of a country there is an x and y which slowly permeate man and mold him to the type of the aboriginal inhabitant, even to the point of slightly remodeling his physical features. To state such an overwhelmingly obvious fact in terms of exact measurements is, I admit, extremely difficult. Yet there are many things that escape all our means of exact scientific verification despite their most obvious and indubitable character. For example, think of the subtleties of expression in eyes, gesture, and intonation. In practice everybody goes by them and no idiot could misunderstand them, yet to prepare an absolutely scientific description of them would be a most ticklish task.

Let us, then, accept the fact that there are these subtle indications in man, Sometimes they lurk in the lines of his face, sometimes in his gestures or the look of his eyes, and sometimes in his soul that shines forth through the transparent veil of his body. From such indications it is often possible to tell in what country a man has been born. I know quite a number of instances where children of purely European parents were born in exotic countries and exhibited the marks of their birthplaces, either in the imponderabilia of their appearance or in their mental make-up, or in both; and to such a degree that not only I myself, but other people who were entirely ignorant of the circumstances, could make the diagnosis. I remember particularly seeing in New York a family of German immigrants. Three of the children had been born in Germany and four in America. The first three were clearly

Germans, while the others were unmistakable Americans.

Somehow a foreign country gets under the skin of those born in it. Certain very primitive tribes are convinced that it is not feasible to usurp foreign territory, because the children born there would inherit the wrong ancestor spirits dwelling in the trees, rocks, and water of the strange country. There seems to be a subtle truth in this primitive intuition. It would mean that the spirit of the Indian gets at the American within and without. Indeed, there is often an astonishing likeness between the cast of the American face and that of the red Indian – more, I think, in the men's faces than in the women's. But women are always the more conservative element, in spite of their conspicuous affectation of modernity. This is a paradox, certainly – one of the many paradoxes of human nature.

The external assimilation of man to the peculiarities of a country is a thing one could almost expect. There is nothing astonishing in it. But the external influence is feeble in comparison with the less visible, but all the more intense, influence on the mind. It is probable that long before the body reacts, the mind has undergone considerable changes – changes that are not obvious to the individual himself or to his immediate circle, though they may be apparent to an outsider. Thus, I would not expect the average American, who has not lived for a couple of years in Europe, to realize how different his mental attitude is from the European's; nor would I expect the average European to discern his difference from the American. That is the reason why so many things that are really characteristic of a foreign country seem to be merely odd or ridiculous: the conditions from which they spring are either not known or not understood. They would not seem odd or ridiculous if one could feel the local atmosphere to which they belong, and which makes them perfectly comprehensible and logical.

Almost every great country has its collective attitude, which one might call its genius, or *spiritus loci*. Sometimes you can catch it in a formula; again it is more evasive; yet always it is indescribably present as a sort of air that permeates everything – the aspect of people, their speech, gestures, clothing, interests, ideals, politics, philosophy, art, and even religion. In a well-defined civilization with a solid historical background, such as French civilization, you can easily find the keynote of the national spirit. In France it is *la gloire*, which is a marked prestige psychology in its noblest as well as its most ridiculous forms. You notice it in the speech, gestures, convictions, in the style of everything, in politics and even in science.

In Germany it is the Idea, and it is impersonated by everybody.

There are no ordinary human beings; you are either *Herr Professor* or *Herr Gebeimrath, Herr Oberrechnungsrat,* and even longer things than that. Sometimes the German Idea is right, and sometimes it is wrong; but it never ceases to be an idea, whether it belongs to the highest philosophy or merely a foolish bias.

England's innermost truth, and at the same time her most valuable contribution to the assets of the human family, is the Gentleman. Rescued from the dusty knighthood of the early Middle Ages, the code of the gentleman now reaches down into the smallest corner of modern English life. It is an ultimate principle, never failing in its convincing weight – at once the shining armor of the perfect knight in soul and body, and the miserable coffin of poor natural feelings.

But can you "size up" other countries like Italy, Austria, Spain, Holland, Switzerland just as easily? They are all very characteristic countries, yet their spirit is more difficult to catch. You cannot seize it in one word; it requires at least a couple of sentences. America is also one of those countries whose heart can not be pierced by one shot. European prejudice would say Money; but the only people who can think like that are those who have no idea what money means to Americans. Yes, if they themselves were American, it *would* be money; but America is not as simple as that.

Of course there is any amount of ordinary materialism in America, just as elsewhere; but there is also an admirable idealism which hardly finds its equal anywhere else. To us Europeans, money still carries with it something of the old taboo dating from the times when every business was dishonest without exception. That is why it is still good form with us to hush up money matters. The American, unhampered by the burden of historical conditions, can take and spend money for what it is worth. For this reason America is peculiarly free from the spell of money, although she makes a lot of it.

V

America, then, has a principle or ideal or attitude, but it is surely not money. Often in searching through the conscious and the unconscious minds of American patients and pupils, I have found something which I can only describe as a sort of heroic ideal. Your most idealistic effort is concerned in bringing out the best in every man. When you find a good man, you naturally support him and push him on, until at last he is liable to collapse from sheer exertion, success, and triumph.

It is done in every family, where ambitious mothers lead boys on with the idea that they must be hereos of some sort. You find it in the factory, where the whole system is designed to get the best man into the best place. And again in the schools, where every child is trained to be brave, courageous, efficient, and " a good sport" – in short, a hero.

In America there is no record that people will not kill themselves to break. The moving pictures abound with heroes of every description. American applause holds the world's record. The 'great' and 'famous' man, no matter what he may be 'great' in, gets drowned in euthusiastic crowds. In Germany you are great if your titles are two yards long; in England if you are a gentleman; in France if your prestige coincides with that of the country. In small countries, as a rule, there is no greatness alive because things need to be small; therefore greatness is usually posthumous. America is perhaps the only country where 'greatness' is unrestricted, because this limitless concept of greatness expresses the most fundamental hopes and convictions of the nation.

To an American all this seems to be part of the nature of things. Not so, however, to a European. Many Europeans are infected with a feeling of inferiority when they come into contact with America and her heroic ideal. As a rule they don't admit it, so they boast of Europe all the louder and ridicule the many things in America which are open to criticism, such as her roughness, brutality, and primitivity. Often they get their first and decisive shock at the customs house, so that their appetite is ruined at the start. It is inevitable, of course, that the heroic attitude should be coupled with a sort of primitiveness; it always has been the ideal of a somewhat sporty and primitive society. And this is where the real historical spirit of the Red Man enters the game.

Look at your sports! They are the roughest, the most reckless, and the most efficient in the world. The idea of play has practically disappeared from them. Your sport demands a training that is almost cruel and an application that is almost inhuman. Your sportsmen are gladiators, every inch of them; and the excitement of the spectators derives from ancient instincts that are akin to bloodthirst.

Your students go through initiations and form secret societies like the best among barbarous tribes. In fact, secret societies of every description abound all over the country, from the Ku Klux Klan to the Knights of Columbus, and their rites are analogous to those of all primitive, mystery religions. America has resuscitated the ghosts of

Spiritualism, of which she is the orignal home, and cures diseases by Christian Science, which has more to do with the shaman's mental healing than with any kind of science. Moreover, it is proving fairly effectual - as, indeed, were the shaman's cures.

And have you ever compared the skyline of New York or any other great American city with that of a pueblo like Taos? Have you noticed how the houses pile up in towers toward the center? Without conscious imitation America instinctively molds herself to the spectral outline of the Red Man's temperament.

There is nothing miraculous about it. It has always been so. The conqueror overcomes the old inhabitant in the body, and succumbs to his spirit. Rome at the zenith of her power contained within her walls all the mystery cults of the East, and the spirit of the humblests among them – a Jewish mystery society – transformed the greatest of all cities from top to bottom. The conqueror gets the wrong ancestor spirits, the primitives would say. I like this picturesque way of putting it. It is short and expresses every implication.

People rarely want to know what a thing is in itself; they want to know whether it is favorable or unfavorable, advisable or inadvisable – as if there were indubitably good or bad things. They are as we take them. Moreover, anything that moves is a risk. Thus a nation in the making is naturally a big risk – to itself as well as to other nations. It is surely not my task to play the role of a prophet or that of a ridiculous adviser of nations; for there is nothing to give advice about. Facts are neither favorable nor unfavorable. They are merely interesting. And the most interesting fact about America is that this childlike, impetuous, 'naive' people has probably the most complicated psychology of all nations.

13 The Problem of the Third Generation Immigrant (1938)

Marcus Lee Hansen*

By long established custom whoever speaks of immigration must refer to it as a 'problem.' It was a problem to the first English pioneers in the New World scattered up and down the Atlantic coast. Whenever a vessel anchored in the James River and a few score weary and emaciated gentlemen, worn out by three months upon the Atlantic, stumbled up the bank, the veterans who had survived Nature's rigorous 'seasoning' looked at one another in despair and asked: 'Who is to feed them? Who is to teach them to fight the Indians, or grow tobacco, or clear the marshy lands and build a home in the malaria-infested swamps? These immigrants certainly are a problem.' And three hundred years later when in the course of a summer more than a million Europeans walked down the gangplanks of the ocean greyhounds into the large reception halls built to receive them, government officials, social workers, journalists said: 'How are these people from the peasant farms of the Mediterranean going to adjust themselves to the routine of mines and industries, and how are they going to live in a country where the language is strange, and how are they, former subjects of monarchs and lords, going to partake in the business of governing themselves? These immigrants certainly are a problem.'

They certainly were. The adventurers (call them colonists or immigrants) who transferred civilization across the Atlantic numbered more than forty million souls. Every one of them was a problem to his family and himself, to the officials and landlords from whom he parted, to the officials and landlords whom he joined. On every mile of the journey, on land and on sea, they caused concern to someone. The public authorities at the ports of embarkation sighed the traditional sigh of relief when the emigrant vessel was warped away from the dock and stood out to the open sea carrying the bewildered persons

---

* From *Augustana Historical Society Publications* (Rock Island, Ill.: Augustana Historical Society, 1938), pp. 5–20.

who for a week or more had wandered about the streets; the captain of that vessel was happy when the last of his passengers who had complained of everything from food to weather said good-bye – often with a clenched fist; and the officers of New York and Baltimore were no less happy when the newly-arrived American set out for the West. How much of a problem the forty million actually were will not be known until their history is written with realism as well as sympathy.

The problem of the immigrant was not solved; it disappeared. Foreign-born to the number of almost fifteen million are still part of the American population, but they are no longer immigrants. By one adjustment after the other they have accommodated themselves and reconciled themselves to the surrounding world of society, and when they became what the natives called 'Americanized' (which was often nothing but a treaty of peace with society) they ceased to be a problem. This was the normal evolution of an individual, but as long as the group classified as immigrants was being constantly recruited by the continual influx of Europeans the problem remained. The quota law of 1924 erected the first dam against the current and the depression of 1929 cut off the stream entirely. Statistics reveal what has happened. During the year ended June 30, 1936, there were admitted as immigrants only 36,329 aliens. During the same period 35,817 aliens left the United States for permanent residence abroad – a net gain of only 512. But this was the first year since 1931 that there had been any gain at all. The great historic westward tide of Europeans has come to an end and there is no indication in American conditions or sentiment that it will ever be revived.

Thus there has been removed from the pages of magazines, from the debates in Congress and from the thoughts of social workers the well-known expression: the problem of the immigrant. Its going has foreshadowed the disappearance of a related matter of concern which was almost as troublesome as the first, a rather uncertain worry which was called 'the problem of the second generation.'

The sons and the daughters of the immigrants were really in a most uncomfortable position. They were subjected to the criticism and taunts of the native Americans and to the criticism and taunts of their elders as well. All who exercised any authority over them found fault with the response. Too often in the schoolroom the Yankee schoolmistress regarded them as mere dullards hardly worthy of her valuable attention. Thus neglected they strayed about the streets where the truant officer picked them up and reported them as incorrigible. The delinquency of the second generation was talked about so incessantly that finally little

Fritz and little Hans became convinced that they were not like the children from the other side of the tracks. They were not slow in comprehending the source of all their woes: it lay in the strange dualism into which they had been born.

Life at home was hardly more pleasant. Whereas in the schoolroom they were too foreign, at home they were too American. Even the immigrant father who compromised most willingly in adjusting his outside affairs to the realities that surrounded him insisted that family life, at least, should retain the pattern that he had known as a boy. Language, religion, customs and parental authority were not to be modified simply because the home had been moved four or five thousand miles to the westward. When the son and the daughter refused to conform, their action was considered a rebellion of ungrateful children for whom so many advantages had been provided. The gap between the two generations was widened and the family spirit was embittered by repeated misunderstanding. How to inhabit two worlds at the same time was the problem of the second generation.

That problem was solved by escape. As soon as he was free economically, an independence that usually came several years before he was free legally, the son struck out for himself. He wanted to forget everything: the foreign language that left an unmistakable trace in his English speech, the religion that continually recalled childhood struggles, the family customs that should have been the happiest of all memories. He wanted to be away from all physical reminders of early days, in an environment so different, so American, that all associates naturally assumed that he was as American as they. This picture has been deliberately overdrawn, but who will deny that the second generation wanted to forget, and even when the ties of family affection were strong, wanted to lose as many of the evidences of foreign origin as they could shuffle off?

Most easy to lose was that which, if retained, might have meant the most to the civilization of the American republic. The immigrant brought with him European culture. This does not mean that the man who wielded the pickaxe was really a Michael Angelo or that the one who took to house painting was in fact an unrecognized Rembrandt. They brought a popular though uncritical appreciation of art and music; they felt at home in an environment where such aspects of culture were taken for granted and (what is not to be overlooked in any consideration of the development of American life) they did not subscribe to the prevailing American sentiment that it was not quite moral for a strong, able-bodied man to earn his living by playing a fiddle. If they did not

come in loaded down with culture, at least they were plentifully supplied with the seeds of culture that, scattered in a fertile soil, could
flourish mightily.

The soil was not fertile. Americans of the nineteenth century were
not entirely unfriendly to a little art now and then if it were limited to
the front parlor and restricted to the women. Even a man might play a
little, sing a little and paint a little if he did it in a straightforward,
wholesome way and for relaxation only. But these foreigners, most of
whom had been in Paris and set up what they called a studio where
they dawdled away the hours, day and night, were not to be trusted.
Let them earn their living by doing a man's work instead of singing
arias at the meetings of the womans club in the middle of the afternoon
or giving piano lessons to the young girls, thereby taking away the
source of livelihood from the village spinster who also gave lessons
and willingly sang for nothing. The second generation was entirely
aware of the contempt in which such activities were held and they
hastened to prove that they knew nothing about casts, symphonies or
canvas. Nothing was more Yankee than a Yankeeized person of foreign
descent.

The leaders among the natives proclaimed loudly: It is wonderful
how these young people catch the spirit of American institutions. The
leaders among the foreign-born sighed and said to themselves: This
apostasy means nothing good. It is not good for the sons and daughters
who give up a heritage richer than farm acres and city lots; it is not
good for this uncouth pioneer nation which has spent its time chopping
down trees and rolling stones and has never learned how the genius of
one might brighten the life of many and satisfy some human longings
that corn bread and apple pie can never appease. Blind, stupid America,
they said, the one nation of the globe which has had offered to it the
rich girls that every people of Europe brought and laid at its feet and
it spurned them all. The immigrants, perhaps, may be excused. Their
thoughts and efforts were taken up with material cares and they were
naturally under some suspicion. But nothing can absolve the traitors
of the second generation who deliberately threw away what had been
preserved in the home. When they are gone all the hope will be lost
and the immigration of the nineteenth century will have contributed
nothing to the development of America but what came out of the strong
muscles of a few million patient plodders.

These pessimists were wrong. All has not been lost. After the second
generation comes the third and with the third appears a new force and
a new opportunity which, if recognized in time, can not only do a

good job of salvaging but probably can accomplish more than either the first or the second could ever have achieved.

Anyone who has the courage to codify the laws of history must include what can be designated 'the principle of third generation interest.' The principle is applicable in all fields of historical study. It explains the recurrence of movements that seemingly are dead; it is a factor that should be kept in mind particularly in literary or cultural history; it makes it possible for the present to know something about the future.

The theory is derived from the almost universal phenomenon that what the son wishes to forget the grandson wishes to remember. The tendency might be illustrated by a hundred examples. The case of the Civil War may be cited. The Southerners who survived the four years of that struggle never forgot. In politics and in conversation the 'lost cause' was an endless theme. Those who listened became weary and the sons of the Confederate veterans were among them. *That* second generation made little effort to justify the action of their fathers. Their expressed opinion was that, after all, the result was inevitable and undoubtedly for the best. These sons went North and won success in every field of business and in every branch of learning. But now the grandsons of the Confederates rule in the place of the sons and there is no apologizing for the events of 1861; instead there is a belligerency that asserts the moral and constitutional justice of their grandfathers' policy. The South has been revived. Its history is taught with a fervid patriotism in the universities and schools. Recently there has been formed the Southern Historical Association as an evidence of the growing interest. The great novel of the Civil War and Reconstruction era was not written by one who had participated in the events or witnessed the scenes. It did not come from the pen of one who had listened to a father's reminiscences. *Gone with the Wind* was written by a granddaughter of the Confederacy, in the year 1936, approximately sixty years after the period with which it dealt had come to an end.

Immigration not only has its history, it has its historiography. The writing of descriptions of that great epic movement began almost as early as the movement itself. Every immigrant letter written from new shores was history, very personal and very uncritical. Every sheaf of reminiscences written by one of the participants in his later years was also history, a little more uncritical. There was much to be recounted and since sons would not listen the grayheaded participants got together and, organized as pioneer societies, they told one another of the glorious deeds that they had seen and sometimes performed and listened to the reading of the obituaries of the giants that had fallen. When the last of them had joined his ancestors the pioneer society automatically disbanded leaving behind as the first chapter of immigrant historiography a conglomerate mass of literature, much and often most of it useless. All of it seemed useless to the son who cleared out his father's desk and he resolved not to waste any of his time on such pointless pursuits.

As a broad generalization it may be said that the second generation is not interested in and does not write any history. That is just another aspect of their policy of forgetting. Then, however, appears the 'third generation.' They have no reason to feel any inferiority when they look about them. They are American born. Their speech is the same as that of those with whom they associate. Their material wealth is the average possession of the typical citizen. When anyone speaks to him about immigrants he always makes it clear that he has in mind the more recent hordes that have been pouring through the gates and any suggestion that the onrush should be stemmed is usually prefaced with the remark that recent immigrants are not so desirable as the pioneers that arrived in earlier times. It is in an attitude of pride that the substantial landowner or merchant looks about him and says: 'This prosperity is our achievement, that of myself and of my fathers; it is a sign of the hardy stock from which we have sprung; who were they and why did they come?' And so their curiosity is projected back into the family beginnings. Those who are acquainted with the universities of the Middle West, where a large proportion of the students are grandchildren and greatgrandchildren of the nineteenth century immigrants can sense this attitude of inquiry and can not escape the feeling of pride in which they study the history and culture of the nations from which their ancestors came.

To show how universal this spirit has been we can retrace some periodic resurgences of national spirit and relate them to the time of immigration. There were Irishmen in America before the Revolution but there is no reason to question the generalization that until 1840 two-thirds of the emigrants from Ireland were the so-called Scotch–Irish. In the 1830s their influx was particularly large; in fact, the great proportion of Ulstermen who came to America arrived in the course of that decade. Sixty years later (at the time of the third generation) a renaissance of Scotch–Irish sentiment in the United States was strikingly apparent. Local societies were formed that met in monthly or quarterly conclave to sing the praises of their forebears and to glory in the achievements of the Presbyterian Church. Beginning in 1889 and continuing for more than a decade representatives of these societies met in an annual national meeting called a 'Scotch–Irish Congress.' Then the movement lost its impetus. Leaders died or took up other activities; members refrained from paying dues; attendance at sessions dwindled. After 1903 no more Scotch–Irish congresses were held.

We can pass to another example. The large German immigration reached its crest in the late 1840s and early 1850s, A little over half a century later, in the first decade of the twentieth century, a breeze of historical interest stirred the German-American community. One of the number was moved to offer a prize for the best historical discussion of the contribution of the German element to American life. Not only the prize-winning work (the well-known volume by A. B. Faust) but many of the manuscripts that had been submitted in the competition were published, forming a library of German–American activity in many fields. Several local and state historical societies were formed and the study of German literature in universities and schools enjoyed an amazing popularity that later observers could ascribe only to the propaganda of an intriguing nation. The Theodore Roosevelt Professorship established at the University of Berlin in 1907 was an expression of the same revival. The war naturally put an end to this activity and obscured much of the valuable work that the investigators had performed.

The auspices under which we have met this evening suggest the next example to be cited. The large Scandinavian immigration began in the 1850s and after the interruption of the Civil War reached its culmination in the 1880s. True to expectations we find that at present the most lively interest in history of this nature is exhibited in Scandinavian circles in America. Among Scandinavians, Norwegians were pioneers and in historical research they are also a step in advance. The Swedes came a little later and an intelligent prophet of that period looking forward to the cultural development of the nationality in their new home would have said: 'About 1930 'a historical society will be formed.' It was. In June, 1930, the Augustana Historical Society was organized among the members of the Augustana Synod which so faithfully represents the more than a million people of Swedish descent who are citizens of the American republic. And now, having consumed half of the time allotted me in an introduction which is half of the paper, I come to the topic of the evening, a subject which will be interpreted in the light of the foregoing remarks. It reads: The problem of the third generation immigrant.

As problems go it is not one to cause worry or to be shunned. It has none of the bitterness or heart-breaking features of its predecessors. It is welcome. In summary form it may be stated as follows: Whenever any immigrant group reaches the third generation stage in its development a spontaneous and almost irresistible impulse arises which forces the thoughts of many people of different professions, different positions in life and different points of view to interest themselves in that one factor which they have in common: heritage – the heritage of blood. The problem is: how can this impulse be organized and directed so that the results growing therefrom will be worthy of the high instincts from which it has sprung and a dignified tribute to the pioneers and at the same time be a contribution to the history of the United States which has received all Europeans on a basis of equality and which should record their achievements in the same spirit of impartiality.

It is hardly necessary for me to remind this gathering that the Swedish stock in America is fast approaching the third generation stage. During the decade of the eighties their coming reached its height in numbers. The census of 1930 records that of the persons born in Sweden giving the date of their arrival in the country fifty-two percent landed before 1900 – and this in spite of the great mortality that the newcomers of that period have suffered. The children that crowd the Sunday school rooms of the churches of this Synod it is well known are the grandsons and granddaughters of the pioneers that built the churches; grandsons and granddaughters, I am also sure, are present in increasing numbers in the student body of this college which those same pioneers at the cost of many sacrifices, built for the sake of those who were to come after them. Among the leaders of this society are men of the first generation and of the second generation but they are the proverbial exception, or it may be better to say they are third generation in spirit. No matter how active they are in leadership the organization can succeed only if the grandchildren of the pioneers will follow.

We will assume that this will be the case; that the membership of the Augustana Historical Society will continue to increase in numbers, that the members will continue to pay their dues, that a few patrons will arise to sponsor special enterprises in research and publication. It is not my object to enlighten you on how to bring about this happy condition. We will assume that many members will carry on their own investigations, that now and then an expert can be subsidized to probe deeply into some vital aspects of Swedish–American history and that the publications will continue to be of the high standard that has already been established. My suggestions will be of a different nature and will center about another set of questions: what fields shall be investigated? Where shall the emphasis be put in research and publication? What should be the attitude in which the past, which belongs not only to the

Swedes but also to the Americans, should be approached? In attempting an answer I speak with no authority except that which comes from several years of delving into the records of most of the pioneer and historical societies of America.

Everyone accepts the premise that self-laudation is not the end in view. Nevertheless it will be hard to keep out because of the human characteristic of speaking nothing but good of the men who labored hard and have now disappeared from the earthly stage. At the first meeting of the Scotch–Irish Congress the speakers presented one paper after the other which dealt with the achievements of the Ulsterman at home and abroad, during all ages and in all spheres of human effort. Finally one of the delegates arose and made a cutting remark that only a Scotch–Irishman would dare to make. While listening to the programs he said, he had been asking himself the question: 'What on earth have the rest of creation been doing for the last eighteen hundred years?' That question should be in the mind of every writer who is tempted to generalize on the contribution of ethnic groups to the development of American life.

If not to the laudation of great men to what activities should the efforts of the society be directed? Let that question first be approached by a calm realization of the fact that the society will not live forever. The time will come when membership will dwindle, when promising subjects for research will be few in number and of little popular interest. That has been the life-course of every organization of this nature. The constituency becomes gradually thinned out as the third generation merges into the fourth and the fourth shades off into the fifth. Even societies with substantial endowments have in their later years found it difficult to continue to produce work of high scholarly quality. The final judgment rendered regarding the success or failure of this society as of others will rest upon the answer given to two pertinent inquiries: Did they, when the time was appropriate, write the history of the special group with whom they were concerned on broad impartial lines, and did they make a permanent contribution to the meaning of American history at large? A few proposals by the following of which a satisfactory reply can be given to both of those questions are now in order.

First of all let it be remembered that the history of any immigrant stock in America is far broader than the history of the particular religious organization that was predominant in the number of communicants that it could claim. The neglect of that fact was the first error made by historical writers in America. When they set out to write the story of the settlement of Englishmen in New England they centered it all about the migration of the Puritan church and neglected a hundred other factors that surrounded the coming and establishment of the colonies on that coast. In recent years some correction has been made but the traditional emphasis has been so great that in spite of the labors of many scholars and the resources of a dozen secular institutions, the history of New England is still less satisfactory than that of any other section of the older part of the country. From such a false start may the Augustana Historical Society be preserved!

Religion must certainly be a leading theme in the program. The church was the first, the most important and the most significant institution that the immigrants established. Its policies reacted upon every other phase of their existence but in turn and, in fact, first, those other phases of their existence established the conditions under which the church was planted and grew. If one should study the agriculture, the system of land purchase, the distribution of population, the state of the roads, the circulation of books and newspapers, the development of amusements he would be in a better position to appraise the situation that the church did occupy in the life of every community. In Mr. Rölvaag's stirring novel *Giants in the Earth* no episode is presented with more effect than that which recounts the coming of the clergyman and the effect is produced not by the description of the man and his mission. It is the background of dull, material routine that has preceded that gives to the brief chapter its epic quality. History had been made before the clergyman and the church appeared and to be understood they must be placed in their proper order in the sequence of events.

Moreover, for an understanding of religious development to the formation of those churches that broke with the faith of the old country relatively more attention should be given than the number of their communicants would warrant. In no other experience was the psychology of the immigrant more clearly reflected. When they said that they passed from the old world to the new many of them meant that the world should be new in all respects. When they gave up allegiance to a government it was easy to give up allegiance to a church. The secessions from the Lutheran faith can be dealt with conveniently, quickly and without embarrassment by ascribing them to the successful methods of proselyting that the well-financed American home missionary societies employed. But the immigrant met the proselyter halfway – perhaps more than halfway – and when one knows what was going on in the mind of the person who did break away from his mother church it will be easier to understand the actions of some of those who did not break away but certainly caused frictions within the church to which they remained true and created situations that could not have arisen in the old Swedish parish from which they had recently come.

Even the study of politics is not entirely foreign to an organization which has chosen as its mission the history of the Augustana Synod. The clergymen of that Synod like the clergymen of any other religious body in the republic had no intention of destroying the fundamental separation of Church and State which the fathers of the constitution had ordained, but how they itched to go into politics! How they lived to find in every Sunday's text some idea that could be applied to the decision of that burning political issue that the men in the audience had been discussing before the services had begun and which they would surely begin to discuss again as soon as the benediction had been pronounced. There is much evidence to suggest that the immigrant church had a great influence in determining the way in which the naturalized citizen would cast his vote. But not a single study has been made of church influence in any election and the results of such a study would throw as much light upon the status of the church as it would upon the political history of that election.

The church had some competitors in the matter of interest, affection and usefulness. Whatever the difficulties that attended the founding of the pioneer congregation, that of inducing the immigrant to join was hardly existent. The immigrant was an inveterate joiner – a habit which was, without question, the result of his feeling of lonesomeness. In Europe the individual was born into many groups that he had to join in America and he entered into them rather light-heartedly hoping that from all he would derive the satisfaction that no single one could yield. When some energetic spirit said to him: Come and join this fraternal organization, he went; when the suggestion of a singing society was broached he fell in with the plan; when some one undertook to line up a shooting corps he took down his gun and practiced marksmanship. All of these pursuits weakened somewhat the hold of the church and the minister was led to adopt an uncompromising attitude toward amusements that otherwise would have been held both innocent and useful. Therefore, it can be said that without a knowledge of the social environment the policy of the church can not be understood.

If these suggestions should be followed, the product would be a history of the Swedes in America that no one could accuse of being tainted with partiality. Perhaps not all the passages would be read with a glow of pride but there would be no humiliation and the pride in the achievement of what no other ethnic group in America has been willing to do would soon overcome regrets that arose out of what truth made it necessary to say. In such an accomplishment the Augustana Historical Society would achieve all that it founders had hoped for it in the field of religious history and the incidental products would give to the world a true and inspiring picture of what the Swedish pioneers had done in the task of subduing the primitive American wilderness.

Although a historical society has justified its existence when it has faithfully recorded the experiences and achievements of the particular element in the population or the particular region in the country that it was created to serve, still unless the story that is written from these records can be made to fit in as one chapter in the larger volume that is called American history the charge of antiquarianism can hardly be escaped. Men of insight who understand that it is the ultimate fate of any national group to be amalgamated into the composite American race will be reconciled to the thought that their historical activities will in time be merged with the activities of other societies of the same nature and finally with the main line of American historiography itself. How such a merging may profoundly influence the course of all national historical writing is illustrated by reference to that one group which is the most mature among the population minorities.

The Scotch–Irish Congress during the fourteen years of its existence published ten volumes of *Proceedings*. A study of the contents of these volumes reveals the widening nature of the interests growing out of the researches. The laudatory character of the contributions to the first publication has been mentioned. Such papers are not entirely absent from the last volume but there also appear titles such as these: 'Paths and Roads of our Forefathers,' 'The Colonial Defenses of Franklin County,' 'German Life and Thought in a Scotch–Irish Settlement' – substantial contributions to the pioneer history of the environment in which the group developed. It is well known that during the decade of the 1890s the character of American historical writing changed. A new emphasis appeared. Scholars looked beyond the older settlements ranged along the seaboard into the communities in the back country. A word that every schoolboy can now explain crept into the textbooks. This word and this theory now almost dominate every page in the volume. The word is 'frontier' and the theory is the 'frontier interpretation of American history.' Older students wise in the way of the classroom have been known to pass on to the younger students this piece of practical advice: 'In any examination in American history if you don't know the answer tie it up with the development of the frontier.'

This new emphasis is universally credited to Professor Frederick J. Turner. However, Turner or no Turner the frontier hypothesis was bound to come and to appear in the very decade during which he wrote his famous essay. In fact, the hypothesis may be distilled from the conglomerate mass of information and theory jumbled together in the ten volumes of Scotch–Irish proceedings. It is doubtful whether the pronouncement of one man, no matter how brilliant, could have turned the course of historical writing unless it were already veering in that direction. It is quite possible that Turner who wrote in 1893 drew upon the frontier interest that the Scotch–Irish were arousing by their studies of the part that the Ulstermen took in the movement of settlement into the West. The interest that they awakened united with the scholars that Professor Turner trained to give to American history its new and significant social interpretation.

The frontier doctrine in its original narrow statement has been overdone. We are beginning to see that the Mississippi Valley was for fifty years the frontier of Europe as well as of the eastern states and that it reacted upon England, Germany and Scandinavia with a force comparable to that which it exerted upon Atlantic America. Some historians with the orthodox professional training have recognized this fact and they are attempting, in a rather clumsy way, to analyze the operation of these influences. There is, however, one omission in their training. They know nothing about the hundreds of immigrant communities in America that formed the human connecting link between the old world and the new, nothing about the millions of personal contacts that brought humble public opinion on both sides of the Atlantic so close together.

The next stage in American historical writing will concern itself with this widened outlook. Herein lies not only the great opportunity but also the great obligation of the third generation historical activity. It alone can provide the atmosphere; it alone can uncover the sources; it alone call interpret the mentality of the millions of persons who had not entirely ceased to be Europeans and had not yet become accepted Americans. The problem of the third generation immigrant is to undertake the job that has been assigned and to perform it well.

The close of this discourse may very properly be a warning. It can be assumed too readily that the history of migration can not he anything but a desirable influence. That is not necessarily the case. Prejudice and super-nationalism may be the product. Societies organized with the laudable intention of commemorating the deeds of which any people should be proud may fall into the hands of those who will use them for instruments of propaganda. Instead of a world covered with a network of associations which will foster an appreciation of the best that each nation has produced, we may find international societies for the promotion of hatred and intolerance. Historians must recognize an obligation to guide the national curiosity to know the past along those lines which will serve the good of all.

If told as it transpired, the epic of migration can add an ideal to take the place of one of the many that recent decades have shattered. For it is a simple story of how troubled men, by courage and action, overcame their difficulties, and how people of different tongues and varied culture have managed to live together in peace.

14 We Are All Third Generation (1942)

Margaret Mead*

What then is this American character, this expression of American institutions and of American attitudes which is embodied in every American, in everyone born in this country and sometimes even in those who have come later to these shores? What is it that makes it possible to say of a group of people glimpsed from a hotel step in Soerabaja or strolling down the streets of Marseilles, 'There go some Americans,' whether they have come from Arkansas or Maine or Pennsylvania, whether they bear German or Swedish or Italian surnames? Not clothes alone, but the way they wear them, the way they walk along the street without awareness that anyone of higher status may be walking there also, the way their eyes rove as if by right over the façade of palaces and the rose windows of cathedrals, interested and unimpressed, referring what they see back to the Empire State building, the Chrysler tower, or a good-sized mountain in Montana. Not the towns they come from – Sioux City, Poughkeepsie, San Diego, Scotsdale – but the tone of voice in which they say, 'Why, I came from right near there. My home town was Evansville. Know anybody in Evansville?' And the apparently meaningless way in which the inhabitant of Uniontown warms to the inhabitant of Evansville as they name over a few names of people whom neither of them know well, about whom neither of them have thought for years, and about whom neither of them care in the least. And yet, the onlooker, taking note of the increased warmth in their voices, of the narrowing of the distance which had separated them when they first spoke, knows that something has happened, that a tie has been established[1] between two people who were lonely before, a tie which every American hopes he may be able to establish as he hopefully asks every stranger: 'What's your home town?'

Americans establish these ties by finding common points on the road that all are expected to have traveled, after their forebears came from Europe one or two or three generations ago, or from one place to

* From Chapter III in Margaret Mead, *And Keep Your Powder Dry: An Anthropologist Looks at America* (New York: Morrow, 1942, reprinted 1949), pp. 27–53.

216

another in America, resting for long enough to establish for each generation a 'home town' in which they grew up and which they leave to move on to a new town which will become the home town of their children. Whether they meet on the deck of an Atlantic steamer, in a hotel in Singapore, in New York or in San Francisco, the same expectation underlies their first contact – that both of them have moved on and are moving on and that potential intimacy lies in paths that have crossed. Europeans, even Old Americans whose pride lies not in the circumstance that their ancestors have moved often but rather in the fact that they have not moved for some time, find themselves eternally puzzled by this 'home town business.' Many Europeans fail to find out that in nine cases out of ten the 'home town' is not where one lives but where one did live; they mistake the sentimental tone in which an American invokes Evansville and Centerville and Unionville for a desire to live there again; they miss entirely the symbolic significance of the question and answer which say diagrammatically, 'Are you the same kind of person I am? Good, how about a coke?'

Back of that query lies the remembrance and the purposeful forgetting of European ancestry. For a generation, they cluster together in the Little Italies, in the Czech section or around the Polish Church, new immigrants clinging together so as to be able to chatter in their own tongue and buy their own kind of red peppers, but later there is a scattering to the suburbs and the small towns, to an 'American' way of life, and this is dramatized by an over acceptance of what looks, to any European, as the most meaningless sort of residence – on a numbered street in Chicago or the Bronx. No garden, no fruit trees, no ties to the earth, often no ties to the neighbors, just a number on a street, just a number of a house for which the rent is $10 more than the rent in the old foreign district from which they moved – how can it mean anything? But it does.

For life has ceased to be expressed in static, spatial terms as it was in Europe, where generation after generation tied their security to the same plot of ground, or if they moved to a city, acted as if the house there, with its window plants, was still a plot of ground anchored, by fruit trees. On a plot of ground a man looks around him, looks at the filled spaces in the corner of the garden. There used to be plum trees there, but father cut them down, when he was a child; now he has planted young peaches – the plot is filled up again. And he can lean over the wall and talk to the neighbor who has planted plums again – they are the same kind of people, with the same origins and the same future. Having the same origins and the same future, they can dwell in the present which is assumed to be part of one continuous way of life.

But for two Americans, chance met on a train or at adjacent desks in a big office building, working in a road gang or a munition plant or on the same ground crew at an airport, there are no such common origins or common expectations. It is assumed, and not mentioned, that grandparents likely were of different nationality, different religion, different political faith, may have fought on opposite sides of the same battles – that great-great-grandparents may have burned each other at the stake. 'My name – Sack. Yes, I know that you know that it was likely something else, likely something you couldn't pronounce, but it's Sack now, see? I was born in Waynesboro.' 'Your name – Green. I don't even stop to think whether that is a changed name. Too many Greens. An American name. Maybe it had a second syllable before. Did you say you had an uncle in Waynesboro? Well, I declare! Isn't life full of coincidences!' And the president of a national scientific society in making his inaugural address, takes five minutes to mention that the president of another great national society who made *his* inaugural address last week, actually came from the same county and went to the same high school – many years later, of course. 'Never' – and his voice, which has just been dealing in fulsome phrases with the role of his profession in the war, now breaks for the first time – 'never has such a thing happened before in America.' Each and every American has followed a long and winding road; if the roads started in the same spot in Europe, best forget that – that tie leads backwards to the past which is best left behind. But if the roads touched here, in this vast country where everyone is always moving, that is a miracle which brings men close together.

In our behavior, however many generations we may actually boast of in this country, however real our lack of ties in the old world may be, we are all third generation,[2] our European ancestry tucked away and half forgotten, the recent steps in our wanderings over America immortalized and over-emphasized. When a rising man is given an administrative job and a chance to choose men for other jobs, he does not, if he is an American, fill those jobs with members of his family – such conduct is left to those who have never left their foreign neighborhoods, or to the first generation. He does not fill them exclusively with members of his own class; his own class is an accidental cross-section which wouldn't contain enough skills. He can't depend upon his golfing mates or this year's neighbors to provide him with the men he needs. Instead, he fills the jobs with men from somewhere along the road he has traveled, his home town, his home state, his college, his former company. They give him the same kind of assurance that a first-generation Hollywood producer felt when he put his cousins in charge of the accounts – their past and his past are one – at one spot anyway – just as in a kin-oriented society common blood assures men of each other's allegiance. The secretary, trying to shield her boss from the importunities of the office seeker, knows it's no use trying to turn away a man from that little North Dakota college that the boss went to. The door is always open to them, any one of them, any day. And a newspaper headline screams: 'Rocks of Chickamauga blood still flows in soldiers' veins.'

European social scientists look at this picture of American intimacy and fail to understand it. In the first place, they cannot get inside it. An Englishman, who has never been in America before, arriving in Indianapolis and trying to establish relationships with an American who has never been in England, finds himself up against what seems to be a blank wall. He meets hearty greetings, eager hospitality, an excessive attempt to tie the visitor to the local scene by taking him rapidly over its civic wonders, an equally excessive attempt to tie in Uncle Josiah's trip to India with the fact that the guest was reared in the Punjab – and then blankness. But if the Englishman then takes a tour in the Northwest, spends a week in the town where his Indiana host lived as a boy and then returns to Indianapolis, he will find a very different greeting awaiting him, which he may mistakenly put down to the fact that this is a second meeting. Only if he is a very astute observer will he notice how the path he has taken across the United States has the power to thaw out any number of hosts at any number of dinner parties.

The wife of the European scientist, now living as a faculty wife in a small university town in Colorado, will find herself similarly puzzled. She doesn't seem to get anywhere with the other faculty wives. Their husbands and her husband have the same status, the same salary, perhaps the same degree of world-wide reputation. She has learned their standards of conspicuous consumption; she can make exactly the same kind of appetizers, set a bridge table out with prizes just as they do – and yet, there is no intimacy. Only when both have children can she and some faculty wife really get together. She thinks it is the common interest in the children which forms the tie; actually it is the common experience of the children, who have something in common which the two women will never have in the same way – the same home town, which provides the necessary link, so fragile, and from a European point of view so meaningless and contentless, and yet, for an American, so essential. Later, even if they have lived childlessly beside each other, should they meet again in Alaska or Mississippi, they would be friends – with no real accession of common interests that the European wife could see. For she does not realize that to Americans only the past can give intimacy, nor can she conceive how such an incredibly empty contact in the past can be enough.

A group of people travel together from Australia to San Francisco: a manufacturer from Kansas City; a nurse from Sydney; a missionary from India; a young English stockbroker temporarily resident in New York; and a jobber from Perth. They form a fair enough table group on the boat, dance together, go ashore together, and separate on the dock without a shadow of regret. Then, to the amazement of the Englishman, he begins to get letters from the Kansas City manufacturer, reporting on the whereabouts and doings of every one of the ill-assorted group. The man actually keeps up with them – these people who shared three uneventful weeks on an ocean liner.

But it is impossible for all Americans who must work or play together to have a bit of identical past, to have lived, even in such rapidly shifting lives, within a few miles of the spot where the others have lived, at some different period for some different reason. Thin and empty as is the 'home town' tie, substitutes for it must be found; other still more tenuous symbols must be invoked. And here we find the enthusiastic preferences for the same movie actor, the same brand of peaches, the same way of mixing a drink. Superficially it makes no sense at all that preference for one brand of cigarette over another may call forth the same kind of enthusiasm that one might expect if two people discovered that they had both found poetry through Keats or both nearly committed suicide on account of the same girl. Only by placing these light preferences against a background of idiosyncratic experience – by realizing that every American's life is different from every other American's; that nowhere, except in parts of the Deep South and similar pockets, can one find people whose lives and backgrounds are both identical or even similar – only then do these feverish grabs at a common theme make sense. English or Dutch residents in the colonies will spend hours sighing over the names of the shops or drinks of their respective Bond Streets, creating in their nostalgia a past atmosphere which they miss in the harsh tropical landscape about them. Americans, in a sense colonials in every part of America, but colonials who have come to have no other home, also create a common atmosphere within which to bask in the present as they criticize or approve the same radio program or moving picture actor.

There is also that other American method of forming ties, the association – the lodge, fraternity, club which is such a prominent feature
of American life. Lloyd Warner[3] has described our societies of veterans of past wars as comparable to a cult of the dead which binds a
community together, with the veterans of the most distant war lowest
in the social scale. Seen from the point of view which I have been
discussing, each war creates a magnificent common past for large numbers
of men. It is not surprising that those who have the fewest ties among
themselves – those whose poverty-stricken way of life admits of few
associations – cling longest to this common experience.

Social scientists have observed with mild wonder that among American
Indians, ranging the Great Plains before the coming of the white man,
there was the same efflorescence of associations,[4] that Blackfoot and
Omaha Indians were also joiners. But Blackfoot and Omaha, like the
inhabitants of Kansas City and Fort Worth, were also newcomers. They
came from a wooded land where the rituals of their lives were localized
and particularized to the great undifferentiated open spaces where men
had not lived before. Like the Palefaces who came later, they needed
new ties and based them upon new patterns of group relationship; and
those new patterns served at least as a bulwark against loneliness, in a
land so great that the myths are full of stories of groups of playing
children who wandered away and were never found until they were
grown. So the white man, having left his brothers – in Sicily and
Bohemia, in New York and Boston and Chicago – rapidly creates new
patterns of social kinship, trying to compensate by rigidness of the
ritual for the extemporized quality of the organization, so that men
who have no common past may share symbolic adoption into the same
fraternal society.

Social scientists, taking their cues from Eastern colleges or from
Sinclair Lewis, have been inclined to sneer at the American habit of
'joining,' at the endless meetings, the clasp of fellowship, the songs,
the allegedly pseudo-enthusiasm with which 'brothers' greet each other.
Safe on the eminence of available intellectual ties and able to gossip
together about the famous names and the scandals of their professions,
they have failed to appreciate that these associational ties give not the
pseudo-security which some European philosopher feels he would get
out of them if he had to share in them, but very real security. Not
until he has been marooned – his train missed, no taxi available – and
driven sixty miles across bad roads in the middle of the night by someone
who belongs to another chapter of the same national organization does
he begin to realize that the tie of common membership, flat and without

content as it is, bolstered up by sentimental songs which no one really likes to sing but which everyone would miss if they weren't sung, has an intensity of its own; an intensity measured against the loneliness which each member would feel if there were no such society.

If this then, this third-generation American, always moving on, always, in his hopes, moving up, leaving behind him all that was his past and greeting with enthusiasm any echo of that past when he meets it in the life of another, represents one typical theme of the American character structure, how is this theme reflected in the form of the family, in the upbringing of the American child? For to the family we must turn for an understanding of the American character structure. We may describe the adult American, and for descriptive purposes we may refer his behavior to the American scene, to the European past, to the state of American industry, to any other set of events which we wish; but to understand the regularity of this behavior we must investigate the family within which the child is reared. Only so can we learn how the newborn child, at birth potentially a Chinaman or an American, a Pole or an Irishman, becomes an American. By referring his character to the family we do not say that the family is the cause of his character and that the pace of American industry or the distribution of population in America are secondary effects, but merely that all the great configuration of American culture is mediated to the child by his parents, his siblings,[5] his near relatives, and his nurses. He meets American law first in the warning note of his mother's voice: 'Stop digging, here comes a cop.' He meets American economics when he finds his mother unimpressed by his offer to buy another copy of the wedding gift he has just smashed: 'At the 5 and 10 cent store, can't we?' His first encounter with puritan standards may come through his mother's 'If you don't eat your vegetables you can't have any dessert.' He learns the paramount importance of distinguishing between vice and virtue; that it is only a matter of which comes first, the pleasure or the pain.[6] All his great lessons come through his mother's voice, through his father's laughter, or the tilt of his father's cigar when a business deal goes right. Just as one way of understanding a machine is to understand how it is made, so one way of understanding the typical character structure of a culture is to follow step by step the way in which it is built into the growing child. Our assumption when we look at the American family will be that each experience of early childhood is contributing to make the growing individual 'all of a piece,' is guiding him towards consistent and specifically American inconsistency in his habits and view of the world.

What kind of parents are these 'third generation' Americans? These people who are always moving, always readjusting, always hoping to buy a better car and a better radio, and even in the years of Depression orienting their behavior to their 'failure' to buy a better car or a better radio. Present or absent, the better car, the better house, the better radio are key points in family life. In the first place, the American parent expects his child to leave him, leave him physically, go to another town, another state; leave him in terms of occupation, embrace a different calling, learn a different skill; leave him socially, travel if possible with a different crowd. Even where a family has reached the top and actually stayed there for two or three generations, there are, for all but the very, very few, still larger cities or foreign courts to be stormed. Those American families which settle back to maintain a position of having reached the top in most cases moulder there for lack of occupation, ladder-climbers gone stale from sitting too long on the top step, giving a poor imitation of the aristocracy of other lands. At the bottom, too, there are some without hope, but very few. Studies of modern youth dwell with anxiety upon the disproportion between the daydreams of the under-privileged young people and the actuality which confronts them in terms of job opportunities. In that very daydream the break is expressed. The daughter who says to her hard-working mother: 'You don't know. I may be going to be a great writer,' is playing upon a note in her mother's mind which accepts the possibility that even if her daughter does not become famous, she will at least go places that she, the mother, has never gone.

In old societies such as those from which their grandparents and great-grandparents came (and it is important to remember that Americans are oriented towards the Europe from which their ancestors emigrated not to the Europe which exists today) parents had performed an act of singular finality when they married, before ever a child was born. They had defined its probable place in the sun. If they maintained the same status throughout the child's growing life, kept the necessary bit of ground or inheritance to start him off as befitted him, reared him to act and feel and believe in a way appropriate to 'that state of life to which it has pleased God to call him,' the parents had done their share. Their service to their child was majorly the maintenance of their own place in the world. His care, his food, his shelter, his education – all of these were by-products of the parents' position. But in America, such an attitude, such a concentration on one's own position make one, in most cases, a bad parent. One is not just restaking the same old claim for one's child, nor can one stake out the child's new claim for him. All one can do is to make him strong and well equipped to go prospecting for himself. For proper behavior *in* that state of life to which it has pleased God to call one, is substituted proper behavior *towards* that state of life to which God, if given enough assistance, may call one's son and daughter. Europeans laugh at the way in which parents pick for their newborn babies colleges which they have never seen. It does, of course, make sense to plan one's affairs so that one's son goes to the same school one went to oneself; but this fantastic new choice – for a squirming bit of humanity which may after all not have the brains to get through the third grade – is inexplicable. Parenthood in America has become a very special thing, and parents see themselves not as giving their children final status and place, rooting them firmly for life in a dependable social structure, but merely as training them for a race which they will run alone.

With this orientation towards a different future for the child comes also the expectation that the child will pass beyond his parents and leave their standards behind him. Educators exclaim impatiently over the paradox that Americans believe in change, believe in progress and yet do their best – or so it seems – to retard their children, to bind them to parental ways, to inoculate them against the new ways to which they give lip service. But here is a point where the proof of the pudding lies in the eating. If the parents were really behaving as the impatient educators claim they are, really strangling and hobbling their children's attempts to embrace the changing fashions in manners or morals, we would not have the rapid social change which is so characteristic of our modern life. We would not go in twenty years from fig leaves on Greek statues to models of unborn babies in our public museums. It is necessary to distinguish between ritual and ceremonial resistances and real resistances. Among primitive peoples, we find those in which generation after generation there is a mock battle between the young men and the old men: generation after generation the old men lose. An observer from our society, with an unresolved conflict with his father on his mind, might watch that battle in terror, feeling the outcome was in doubt. But the members of the tribe who are fighting the mock battle consciously or unconsciously know the outcome and fight with no less display of zeal for the knowing of it. The mock battle is no less important because the issue is certain.

Similarly, on the island of Bali, it is unthinkable that a father or a brother should plan to give a daughter of the house to some outsider. Only when a marriage is arranged between cousins, both of whose fathers are members of the same paternal line, can consent be appropriately given. Yet there flourishes, and has flourished probably for hundreds of years, a notion among Balinese young people that it is more fun to marry someone who is not a cousin. So, generation after generation, young men carry off the daughters of other men, and these daughters, their consent given in advance, nevertheless shriek and protest noisily if there are witnesses by. It is a staged abduction, in which no one believes, neither the boy nor the girl nor their relatives. Once in a while, some neurotic youth misunderstands and tries to abduct a girl who has not given her consent, and as a result the whole society is plunged into endless confusion, recrimination, and litigation.

So it is in American society. American parents, to the extent that they are Americans, expect their children to live in a different world, to clothe their moral ideas in different trappings, to court in automobiles although their forebears courted, with an equal sense of excitement and moral trepidation, on horsehair sofas. As the parents' course was uncharted when they were young – for they too had gone a step beyond their parents and transgressed every day some boundary which their parents had temporarily accepted as absolute – so also the parents know that their children are sailing uncharted seas. And so it comes about that American parents lack the sure hand on the rudder which parents in other societies display, and that they go in for a great deal of conventional and superficial grumbling. To the traditional attitudes characteristic of all oldsters who find the young a deteriorated version of themselves, Americans add the mixture of hope and envy and anxiety which comes from knowing that their children are not deteriorated versions of themselves, but actually – very actually – manage a car better than father ever did. This is trying; sometimes very trying. The neurotic father, like the neurotic lover in Bali, will misunderstand the license to grumble, and will make such a fuss over his son or daughter when they behave as all of their age are behaving, that the son or daughter has to be very unneurotic indeed not to take the fuss as something serious, not to believe that he or she is breaking father's heart. Similarly, a neurotic son or daughter will mistake the ceremonial grumbling for the real thing, and break their spirits in a futile attempt to live up to the voiced parental standards. To the average child the parents' resistance is a stimulus.

On the east coast, people grumble about the coming of winter, lament over the wild geranium which marks the end of spring, and shudder noisily away from the winter that they would not do without. Occasionally, someone takes this seasonal grumbling seriously and moves to Southern California; but for most people, born and bred in a north temperate climate, the zest and tang of the too cold winter is as essential a part of life as the sultry heat and wilting flowers of the too hot summer. If one were to do a series of interviews among immigrants to Southern California, one would go away convinced that Americans had but one aim, to escape from the dreadful rigors of the north temperate zone into the endless health-giving, but eventless balminess, of a Riviera climate. This would be quite wrong. It would be equally wrong to suppose the Southern Californian insincere in his passionate climatophilism. Just as the flight from the bruising effects of winter to the soothing effects of no winter at all is a part of the American scene, so each generation of Americans produces a certain number of fathers and sons who make personal tragedies out of the changing character of the American scene; tragedies which have their own language, music and folklore, and are an inalienable part of that American scene.

By and large, the American father has an attitude towards his children which may be loosely classified as autumnal. They are his for a brief and passing season, and in a very short while they will be operating gadgets which he does not understand and cockily talking a language to which he has no clue. He does his best to keep ahead of his son, takes a superior tone as long as he can, and knows that in nine cases out of ten he will lose. If the boy goes into his father's profession, of course, it will take him a time to catch up. He finds out that the old man knows a trick or two; that experience counts as over against this new-fangled nonsense. But the American boy solves that one very neatly: he typically does not go into his father's profession, nor take up land next to his father where his father can come over and criticize his plowing. He goes somewhere else, either in space or in occupation. And his father, who did the same thing and expects that his son will, is at heart terrifically disappointed if the son accedes to his ritual request that he docilely follow in his father's footsteps and secretly suspects the imitative son of being a milksop. He knows he is a milksop – so he think – because he himself would have been a milksop if he had wanted to do just what his father did.

This is an attitude which reaches its most complete expression in the third-generation American. His grandfather left home, rebelled against a parent who did not expect final rebellion, left a land where everyone ex-pected him to stay. Come to this country, his rebellious adventuring cooled off by success, he begins to relent a little, to think perhaps the strength of his ardor to leave home was overdone. When his sons grow up, he is torn between his desire to have, them succeed in this new country – which means that they must be more American than he, must lose entirely their foreign names and every trace of allegiance to a foreign way of life – and his own guilt towards the parents and the fatherland which he has denied. So he puts on the heat, alternately punishing the child whose low marks in school suggest that he is not going to be a successful American and berating him for his American ways and his disrespect for his father and his father's friends from the old country. When that son leaves home, he throws himself with an intensity which his children will not know into the American way of life; he eats American, talks American, dresses American, he will be American or nothing. In making his way of life consistent, he inevitably makes it thin; the overtones of the family meal on which strange, delicious, rejected European dishes were set, and about which low words in a foreign tongue wove the atmosphere of home, must all be dropped out. His speech has a certain emptiness; he rejects the roots of words – roots lead back, and he is going forward – and comes to handle language in terms of surfaces and clichés. He rejects half of his life in order to make the other half self-consistent and complete. And by and large he succeeds. Almost miraculously, the sons of the Polish day laborer and the Italian fruit grower, the Finnish miner and the Russian garment worker become Americans.

Second generation – American-born of foreign-born parents – they set part of the tone of the American eagerness for their children to go onward. They have left their parents; left them in a way which requires more moral compensation than was necessary even for the parent generation who left Europe. The immigrant left his land, his parents, his fruit trees, and the little village street behind him. He cut the ties of military service; he flouted the king or the emperor; he built himself a new life in a new country. The father whom he left behind was strong, a part of something terribly strong, something to be feared and respected and fled from. Something so strong that the bravest man might boast of a successful flight. He left his parents, entrenched representatives of an order which he rejected. But not so his son. He leaves his father not a part of a strong other-way of life, but bewildered on the shores of the new world, having climbed only halfway up the beach. His father's ties to the old world, his mannerisms, his broken accent, his little foreign gestures are not part parcel of something strong and different; they are signs of his failure to embrace this new way of life. Does his mother wear a kerchief over her head? He cannot see the generations of women who have worn such kerchiefs. He sees only the American women who wear hats, and he pities and rejects his mother who has failed to become – an American. And so there enters into the attitude of the second-generation American – an attitude which again is woven through our folkways, our attitude towards other languages, towards anything foreign, towards anything European – a combination of contempt and avoidance, a fear of yielding, and a sense that to yield would be weakness. His father left a father who was the representative of a way of life which had endured for a thousand years. When he leaves his father, he leaves a partial failure; a hybrid, one who represents a step towards freedom, not freedom itself. His first-generation father chose between freedom and what he saw as slavery; but when the second-generation American looks at his European father, and through him, at Europe, he sees a choice between success and failure, between potency and ignominy. He passionately rejects the halting English, the half-measures of the immigrant. He rejects with what seems to him equally good reasons 'European ties and entanglements.' This second-generation attitude which has found enormous expression in our culture especially during the last fifty years, has sometimes come to dominate it – in those parts of the country which we speak of as 'isolationist.' Intolerant of foreign language, foreign ways, vigorously determined on being themselves, they are, in attitude if not in fact, second-generation Americans.

When the third-generation boy grows up, he comes up against a father who found the task of leaving his father a comparatively simple one. The second-generation parent lacks the intensity of the first, and his son in turn fails to reflect the struggles, the first against feared strength and the second against guiltily rejected failure, which have provided the plot for his father and grandfather's maturation. He is expected to succeed; he is expected to go further than his father went; and all this is taken for granted. He is furthermore expected to feel very little respect for the past. Somewhere in his grandfather's day there was an epic struggle for liberty and freedom. His picture of that epic grandfather is a little obscured, however, by the patent fact that his father does not really respect him; he may have been a noble character, but he had a foreign accent. The grandchild is told in school, in the press, over the radio, about the founding fathers, but they were not after all *his* founding fathers; they are, in ninety-nine cases out of a hundred, somebody else's ancestors. Any time one's own father, who in his own youth had pushed his father aside and made his own way, tries to get in one's way, one can invoke the founding fathers – those ancestors of the real Americans; the Americans who got here earlier – those Americans which father worked so very hard, so slavishly, in fact, to imitate. This is a point which the European observer misses.

He hears an endless invocation of Washington and Lincoln, of Jefferson and Franklin. Obviously, Americans go in for ancestor worship, says the European. Obviously, Americans are longing for a strong father, say the psycho-analysts.[8] These observers miss the point that Washington is not the ancestor of the man who is doing the talking; Washington does not represent the past to which one belongs by birth, but the past to which one tries to belong by effort. Washington represents the thing for which grandfather left Europe at the risk of his life, and for which father rejected grandfather at the risk of his integrity. Washington is not that to which Americans passionately cling but that to which they want to belong, and fear, in the bottom of their hearts, that they cannot and do not.

This odd blending of the future and the past, in which another man's great-grandfather becomes the symbol of one's grandson's future, is an essential part of American culture. 'Americans are so conservative.' say Europeans. They lack the revolutionary spirit. Why don't they rebel? Why did President Roosevelt's suggestion of altering the structure of the Supreme Court and the Third-Term argument raise such a storm of protest? Because, in education, in attitudes, most Americans are third generation, they have just really arrived. Their attitude towards this country is that of one who has just established membership, just been elected to an exclusive club, just been initiated into the rites of an exacting religion. Almost any one of them who inspects his own ancestry, even though it goes back many more generations than three, will find a gaping hole somewhere in the family tree. Campfire girls give an honor to the girl who can name all eight great-grandparents, including the maiden names of the four great-grandmothers. Most Americans cannot get this honor. And who was that missing great-grandmother? Probably, oh, most probably, not a grandniece of Martha Washington.

We have, of course, our compensatory mythology. People who live in a land torn by earthquakes have myths of a time when the land was steady, and those whose harvest are uncertain dream of a golden age when there was no drought. Likewise, people whose lives are humdrum and placid dream of an age of famine and rapine. We have our rituals of belonging, our DAR's and our Descendants of King Philip's Wars, our little blue book of the blue-blooded Hawaiian aristocracy descended from the first missionaries, and our *Mayflower*, which is only equaled in mythological importance by the twelve named canoes which brought the Maoris to New Zealand. The mythology keeps alive the doubt. The impressive president of a patriotic society knows that she is a member by virtue of only one of the some eight routes through which membership is possible. Only one. The other seven? Well, three are lost altogether. Two ancestors were Tories. In some parts of the country she can boast of that; after all, Tories were people of substance, real 'old families.' But it doesn't quite fit. Of two of those possible lines, she has resolutely decided not to think. Tinkers and tailors and candlestick makers blend indistinctly with heaven knows what immigrants! She goes to a meeting and is very insistent about the way in which the Revolutionary War which only one-eighth of her ancestors helped to fight should be represented to the children of those whose eight ancestors were undoubtedly all somewhere else in 1776.

On top of this Old American mythology, another layer has been added, a kind of placatory offering, a gesture towards the Old World which Americans had left behind. As the fifth- and sixth- and seventh-generation Americans lost the zest which came with climbing got to the top of the pecking order[9] in their own town or city and sat, still uncertain, still knowing their credentials were shaky, on the top of the pile, the habit of wanting to belong – to really belong, to be accepted absolutely as something which one's ancestors had NOT been – became inverted. They turned towards Europe, especially towards England, towards presentation at Court, towards European feudal attitudes. And so we have had in America two reinforcements of the European class attitudes – those hold-overs of feudal caste attitudes, in the newly-come immigrant who carries class consciousness in every turn and bend of his neck, and the new feudalism, the 'old family' who has finally toppled over backwards into the lap of all that their remote ancestors left behind them.

When I say that we are most of us – whatever our origins – third-generation in character structure, I mean that we have been reared in an atmosphere which is most like that which I have described for the third generation. Father is to be outdistanced and outmoded, but not because he is a strong representative of another culture, well entrenched, not because he is a weak and ineffectual attempt to imitate the new culture; he did very well in his way, but he is out of date. He, like us, was moving forwards, moving away from something symbolized by his own ancestors, moving towards something symbolized by other people's ancestors. Father stands for the way things were done, for a direction which on the whole was a pretty good one, in its day. He was all right because he was on the right road. Therefore, we, his children, lack the mainsprings of rebellion. He was out of date; he drove an old model car which couldn't make it on the hills. Therefore it is not necessary to fight him, to knock him out of the race. It is much easier and quicker to pass him. And to pass him it is only necessary to keep on going and to see that one buys a new model every year. Only if one slackens, loses one's interest in the race towards success, does one slip back. Otherwise, it is onward and upward, *towards* the world of Washington and Lincoln; a world in which we don't fully belong, but which we feel, if we work at it, we some time may achieve.

Notes

1. I owe my understanding of the significance of these chronological ties to discussions with Kurt Lewin and John G. Pilley.
2. Mead, Margaret (1940) Conflict of Cultures in America. *Proceedings, 54th Annual Convention, Middle States Association of Colleges and Secondary Schools* (November) pp. 30–44.
3. Warner, W. L., and P. S. Lunt (1941) *The Social Life of a Modern Community* (Yankee City Series, 1) (New Haven Yale University Press).
4. Lowie, Robert H. 'Plains Indian Age-Societies: Historical and Comparative Summary', *Anthropological Papers*, American Museum of Natural History, 11 (13), pp. 877–984.
5. Sibling is a coined word used by scientists for both brothers and sisters. The English language lacks such a word.
6. Cf. Samuel Butler's definition: That vice is when the pain follows the pleasure and virtue when the pleasure follows the pain.
7. Bateson, G., and M. Mead (1942) *Balinese Character: A Photographic Analysis* (New York: New York Academy of Sciences).
8. I owe my classification of the American attitude towards the 'founding fathers' to a conversation with Dr. Ernst Kris, in which he was commenting on the way in which Americans, apparently, wanted a strong father, although, in actual fact, they always push their fathers aside.
9. Pecking order is a very convenient piece of jargon which social psychologists use to describe a group in which it is very clear to everybody in it just which bird can peck which, or which cow can butt which other cow away from the water trough. Among many living creatures these 'pecking orders' are fixed and when a newcomer enters the group he has to fight and scramble about until everybody is clear just where he belongs – below No. 8 chick, for instance, and above old No. 9.

15 Reflections on the American Identity (1950)

Erik H. Erikson*

1 POLARITIES

It is a commonplace to state that whatever one may come to consider a truly American trait can be shown to have its equally characteristic opposite. This, one suspects, is true of all 'national characters,' or (as I would prefer to call them) national identities – so true, in fact that one may begin rather than end with the proposition that a nation's identity is derived from the ways in which history has, as it were, counterpointed certain opposite potentialities; the ways in which it lifts this counterpoint to a unique style of civilization, or lets it disintegrate into mere contradiction.

This dynamic country subjects its inhabitants to more extreme contrasts and abrupt changes during a lifetime or a generation than is normally the case with other great nations. Most of her inhabitants are faced, in their own lives or within the orbit of their closest relatives, with alternatives presented by such polarities as: open roads of immigration and jealous islands of tradition; outgoing internationalism and defiant isolationism; boisterous competition and self-effacing cooperation; and many others. The influence of the resulting contradictory slogans on the development of an individual ego probably depends on the coincidence of nuclear ego stages with critical changes in the family's geographic and economic vicissitudes.

The process of American identity formation seems to support an individual's ego identity as long as he can preserve a certain element of deliberate tentativeness of autonomous choice. The individual must be able to convince himself that the next step is up to him and that no matter where he is staying or going he always has the choice of leaving or turning in the opposite direction if he chooses to do so. In this country the migrant does not want to be told to move on, nor the sedentary man to stay where he is; for the life style (and the family

---

* From Chapter 8 in Erik H. Erikson, *Childhood and Society* (New York: Norton, 1963), 2nd edn, pp. 285–325.

history) of each contains the opposite element as a potential alternative which he wishes to consider his most private and individual decision.

Thus the functioning American, as the heir of a history of extreme contrasts and abrupt changes, bases his final ego identity on some tentative combination of dynamic polarities such as migratory and sedentary, individualistic and standardized, competitive and co-operative, pious and freethinking, responsible and cynical, etc.

While we see extreme elaborations of one or the other of these poles in regional, occupational, and characterological types, analysis reveals that this extremeness (of rigidity or of vacillation) contains an inner defense against the always implied, deeply feared, or secretly hoped-for opposite extreme.

To leave his choices open, the American, on the whole, lives with two sets of 'truths': a set of religious principles or religiously pronounced political principles of a highly puritan quality, and a set of shifting slogans, which indicate what, at a given time, one may get away with on the basis of not more than a hunch, a mood, or a notion. Thus, the same child may have been exposed in succession or alternately to sudden decisions expressing the slogans 'Let's get the hell out of here' and again, 'Let's stay and keep the bastards out' – to mention only two of the most sweeping ones. Without any pretense of logic or principle, slogans are convincing enough to those involved to justify action whether within or just outside of the lofty law (in so far as it happens to be enforced or forgotten, according to changing local climate). Seemingly shiftless slogans contain time and space perspectives as ingrained as those elaborated in the Sioux or Yurok system; they are experiments in collective time-space to which individual ego defenses are co-ordinated. But they change, often radically, during one and the same childhood.

A true history of the American identity would have to correlate Parrington's observations on the continuity of formulated thought with the rich history of discontinuous American slogans which pervade public opinion in corner stores and in studies, in the courts and in the daily press. For in principles and concepts too, an invigorating polarity seems to exist on the one hand between the intellectual and political aristocracy which, always mindful of precedent, guards a measure of coherent thought and indestructible spirit, and, on the other hand, a powerful mobocracy which seems to prefer changing slogans to self-perpetuating principles. This native polarity of aristocracy and mobocracy (so admirably synthesized in Franklin D. Roosevelt) pervades American democracy more effectively than the advocates and the critics of the great American middle class seem to realize. This American middle class, decried by some as embodying an ossification of all that is mercenary and philistine in this country, may represent only a transitory series of overcompensatory attempts at settling tentatively around some Main Street, fireplace, bank account, and make of car; it does not, as a class should, preclude high mobility and a cultural potential unsure of its final identity. Status expresses a different relativity in a more mobile society: it resembles an escalator more than a platform; it is a vehicle, rather than a goal.

All countries, and especially large ones, complicate their own progress in their own way with the very premises of their beginnings. We must try to formulate the way in which self-contradictions in American history may expose her youth to an emotional and political short circuit and thus endanger her dynamic potential.

2 'MOM'

In recent years the observations and warnings of the psychiatric workers of this country have more and more converged on two concepts: the 'schizoid personality' and 'maternal rejection.' Essentially this means not only that many people fall by the wayside as a result of psychotic disengagements from reality, but also that all too many people, while not overtly sick, nevertheless seem to lack a certain ego tonus and a certain mutuality in social intercourse. One may laugh at this suggestion and point to the spirit of individualism and to the gestures of animation and of jovial friendliness characterizing much of the social life in this country; but the psychiatrists (especially after the shocking experience during the last war, of being forced to reject or to send home hundreds of thousands of 'psychoneurotics') see it differently. The streamlined smile within the perfectly tuned countenance and within the standardized ways of exhibiting self-control does not always harbor that true spontaneity which alone would keep the personality intact and flexible enough to make it a going concern.

For this the psychiatrists tend to blame 'Mom.' Case history after case history states that the patient had a cold mother, a dominant mother, a rejecting mother – or a hyperpossessive, overprotective one. They imply that the patient, as a baby, was not made to feel at home in this world except under the condition that he behave himself in certain definite ways, which were inconsistent with the timetable of an infant's needs and potentialities, and contradictory in themselves. They imply that the mother dominated the father, and that while the father offered more tenderness and understanding to the children than the mother did, he disappointed his children in the end because of what he 'took' from the mother. Gradually what had begun as a spontaneous movement in thousands of clinical files – become a manifest literary sport in books decrying the mothers of this country as 'Moms' and as a 'generation of vipers.'

Who is this 'Mom'? How did she lose her good, her simple name? How could she become an excuse for all that is rotten in the state of the nation and a subject of literary temper tantrums? *Is* Mom really to blame?

In a clinical sense, of course, to blame may mean just to point to what the informed worker sincerely considers the primary cause of the calamity. But there is in much of our psychiatric work an undertone of revengeful triumph, as if a villain had been spotted and cornered. The blame attached to the mothers in this country (namely, that they are frigid sexually, rejective of their children, and unduly dominant in their homes) has in itself a specific moralistic punitiveness. No doubt both patients and psychiatric workers were blamed too much when they were children; now they blame all mothers, because all causality has become linked with blame.

It was, of course, a vindictive injustice to give the name of 'Mom' to a certain dangerous type of mother, a type apparently characterized by a number of fatal contradictions in her motherhood. Such injustice can only be explained and justified by the journalistic habit of sensational contraposition – a part of the publicist folkways of our day. It is true that where the 'psycho-neurotic' American soldier felt inadequately prepared for life, he often implicitly and more often unconsciously blamed his mother; and that the expert felt compelled to agree with him. But it is also true that the road from Main Street to the foxhole was longer – geographically, culturally, and psychologically – than was the road to the front lines from the home towns of nations which were open to attack and had been attacked, or which had prepared themselves to attack other people's homelands and now feared for their own. It seems senseless to blame the American family for the failures, but to deny it credit for the gigantic human achievement of overcoming that distance.

'Mom,' then, like similar prototypes in other countries – see the 'German father,' to be discussed in the next chapter – is a composite image of traits, none of which could be present all at once in one single living woman. No woman consciously aspires to be such a 'Mom,' and yet she may find that her experience converges on this Gestalt, as if she were forced to assume a role. To the clinical worker, 'Mom' is something comparable to a 'classical' psychiatric syndrome which you come to use as a yardstick although you have never seen it in pure form. In cartoons she becomes a caricature, immediately convincing to all. Before analyzing 'Mom,' then, as a historical phenomenon, let us focus on her from the point of view of the pathogenic demands which she makes on her children and by which we recognize her presence in our clinical work:

1. 'Mom' is the unquestioned authority in matters of mores and morals in her home, and (through clubs) in the community; yet she permits herself to remain, in her own way, vain in her appearance, egotistical in her demands, and infantile in her emotions.

2. In any situation in which this discrepancy clashes with the respect which she demands from her children, she blames her children; she never blames herself.

3. She thus artificially maintains what Ruth Benedict would call the discontinuity between the child's and the adult's status without endowing this differentiation with the higher meaning emanating from superior example.

4. She shows a determined hostility to any free expression of the most naïve forms of sensual and sexual pleasure on the part of her children, and she makes it clear enough that the father, when sexually demanding, is a bore. Yet as she grows older she seems unwilling to sacrifice such external signs of sexual competition as too youthful dresses, frills of exhibitionism, and 'make-up.' In addition, she is avidly addicted to sexual display in books, movies, and gossip.

5. She teaches self-restraint and self-control, but she is unable to restrict her intake of calories in order to remain within the bounds of the dresses she prefers.

6. She expects her children to be hard on themselves, but she is hypochondriacally concerned with her own well-being.

7. She stands for the superior values of tradition, yet she herself does not want to become 'old.' In fact, she is mortally afraid of that status which in the past was the fruit of a rich life, namely the status of the grandmother.

This will be sufficient to indicate that 'Mom' is a woman in whose life cycle remnants of infantility join advanced senility to crowd out the middle range of mature womanhood, which thus becomes self-absorbed and stagnant. In fact, she mistrusts her own feelings as a woman and mother. Even her overconcern does not provide trust, but lasting mistrust. But let it be said that this 'Mom' – or better: any, woman who reminds herself and others of the stereotype Mom – is not happy; she does not like herself; she is ridden by the anxiety that her life was a waste. She knows that her children do not genuinely love her, despite Mother's Day offerings. 'Mom' is a victim, not a victor.

Assuming, then, that this is a 'type,' a composite image of sufficient relevance for the epidemiology of neurotic conflict in this country: to explain it would obviously call for the collaboration of historian, sociologist, and psychologist, and for a new kind of history, a kind which at the moment is admittedly in its impressionistic and sensational stages. 'Mom,' of course, is only a stereotyped caricature of existing contradictions which have emerged from intense, rapid, and as yet unintegrated changes in American history. To find its beginning, one would probably have to retrace this history back to the time when it was up to the American woman to evolve one common tradition, on the basis of many imported traditions, and to base on it the education of her children and the style of her home life; when it was up to her to establish new habits of sedentary life on a continent originally populated by men who in their countries of origin, for one reason or another, had not wanted to be 'fenced in.' Now, in fear of ever again acquiescing to an outer or inner autocracy, these men insisted on keeping their new cultural identity tentative to a point where women had to become autocratic in their demands for some order.

The American woman in frontier communities was the object of intense rivalries on the part of tough and often desperate men. At the same time, she had to become the cultural censor, the religious conscience, the aesthetic arbiter, and the teacher. In that early rough economy hewn out of hard nature it was she who contributed the finer graces of living and that spirituality without which the community falls apart. In her children she saw future men and women who would face contrasts of rigid sedentary and shifting migratory life. They must be prepared for any number of extreme opposites in milieu, and always ready to seek new goals and to fight for them in merciless competition. For, after all, worse than a sinner was a sucker.

We suggested that the mothers of the Sioux and of the Yurok were endowed with an instinctive power of adaptation which permitted them to develop child-training methods appropriate for the production of hunters and hunters' wives in a nomadic society, and of fishermen and acorn gatherers in a sedentary valley society. The American mother, I believe, reacted to the historical situation on this continent with similar unconscious adjustment when she further developed Anglo-Saxon patterns of child training which would avoid weakening potential frontiersmen by protective maternalism. In other words, I consider what is now called the American woman's 'rejective' attitude a modern fault based on a historical virtue designed for a vast new country, in which the most dominant fact was the frontier, whether you sought it, or avoided it, or tried to live it down.

From the frontier, my historian-sociologist and I would have to turn to puritanism as a decisive force in the creation of American motherhood and its modern caricature, 'Mom.' This much-maligned puritanism, we should remember, was once a system of values designed to check men and women of eruptive vitality, of strong appetites, as well as of strong individuality. In connection with primitive cultures we have discussed the fact that a living culture has its own balances which make it durable and bearable to the majority of its members. But changing history endangers the balance. During the short course of American history rapid developments fused with puritanism in such a way that they contributed to the emotional tension of mother and child. Among these were the continued migration of the native population, unchecked immigration, industrialization, urbanization, class stratification, and female emancipation. These are some of the influences which put puritanism on the defensive – and a system is apt to become rigid when it becomes defensive. Puritanism, beyond defining sexual sin for full-blooded and strong-willed people gradually extended itself to the total sphere of bodily living, compromising all sensuality – including marital relationships – and spreading its frigidity over the tasks of pregnancy, childbirth, nursing, and training. The result was that men were born who failed to learn from their mothers to love the goodness of sensuality before they learned to hate its sinful uses. Instead of hating sin, they learned to mistrust life. Many became puritans without faith or zest.

The frontier, of course, remained the decisive influence which served to establish in the American identity the extreme polarization which characterizes it. The original polarity was the cultivation of the sedentary and migratory poles. For the same families, the same mothers, were forced to prepare men and women who would take root in the community life and the gradual class stratification of the new villages and towns and at the same time to prepare these children for the possible physical hardships of homesteading on the frontiers. Towns, too, developed their sedentary existence and oriented their inward life to work bench and writing desk, fireplace and altar, while through them, on the roads and rails, strangers passed bragging of God knows what greener pastures. You had either to follow – or to stay behind and brag louder. The point is that the call of the frontier, the temptation to move on, forced those who stayed to become defensively sedentary, and defensively proud. In a world which developed the slogan, 'If you can see your neighbor's chimney, it is time to move on,' mothers had to raise sons and daughters who would be determined to ignore the call of the frontier – but who would go with equal determination once they were forced or chose to go. When they became too old, however, there was no choosing, and they remained to support the most sectarian, the most standardized adhesiveness. I think that it was the fear of becoming too old to choose which gave old age and death a bad name in this country. (Only recently have old couples found a solution, the national trailer system, which permits them to settle down to perpetual traveling and to die on wheels.)

We know how the problems of the immigrant and of the migrant, of the émigré and of the refugee, became superimposed on one another, as large areas became settled and began to have a past. To the new American, with a regional tradition of stratification, newcomers increasingly came to be characterized by the fact that they had escaped from something or other, rather than by the common values they sought; and then there were also the masses of ignorant and deceived chattels of the expanding industrial labor market. For and against all of these latter Americans, American mothers had to establish new moral standards and rigid tests of social ascendancy.

As America became the proverbial melting pot, it was the Anglo-Saxon woman's determination which assured that of all the ingredients mixed, puritanism – such as it then was – would be the most pervasive streak. The older, Anglo-Saxon type became ever more rigid, though at the same time decent and kind in its way. But the daughters of immigrants, too, frantically tried to emulate standards of conduct which they had not learned as small children. It is here, I think, that the self-made personality originated as the female counterpart of the self-made man; it is here that we find the origin of the popular American concept of a fashionable and vain 'ego' which is its own originator and arbiter. In fact, the psychoanalysis of the children of immigrants clearly reveals to what extent they, as the first real Americans in their family, become their parents' cultural parents.

This idea of a self-made ego was in turn reinforced and yet modified by industrialization and by class stratification. Industrialization, for example, brought with it mechanical child training. It was as if this new man-made world of machines, which was to replace the 'segments of nature' and the 'beasts of prey,' offered its mastery only to those who would become like it, as the Sioux 'became' buffalo, the Yurok salmon. Thus, a movement in child training began which tended to adjust the human organism from the very start to clocklike punctuality in order to make it a standardized appendix of the industrial world. This movement is by no means at an end either in this country or in countries which for the sake of industrial production want to become like us. In the pursuit of the adjustment to and mastery over the machine, American mothers (especially of the middle class) found themselves standardizing and overadjusting children who later were expected to personify that very virile individuality which in the past had been one of the outstanding characteristics of the American. The resulting danger was that of creating, instead of individualism, a mass-produced mask of individuality.

As if this were not enough, the increasing class differentiation in some not large but influential classes and regions combined with leftovers of European aristocratic models to create the ideal of the lady, the woman who not only does not need to work, but who, in fact, is much too childlike and too determinedly uninformed to even comprehend what work is all about. This image, in most parts of the country, except the South, was soon challenged by the ideal of the emancipated woman. This new ideal seemed to call for equality of opportunity; but it is well known how it came, instead, to represent often enough a pretense of sameness in equipment, a right to mannish behavior.

In her original attributes, then, the American woman was a fitting and heroic companion to the post-revolutionary man, who was possessed with the idea of freedom from any man's autocracy and haunted by the fear that the nostalgia for some homeland and the surrender to some king could ever make him give in to political slavery. Mother became 'Mom' only when Father became 'Pop' under the impact of the identical historical discontinuities. For, if you come down to it, Momism is only misplaced paternalism. American mothers stepped into the role of the grandfathers as the fathers abdicated their dominant place in the family, in the field of education, and in cultural life. The post-revolutionary descendants of the Founding Fathers forced their women to be mothers *and* fathers, while they continued to cultivate the role of freeborn sons.

I cannot try to appraise the quantity of emotional disturbance in this country. Mere statistics on severe mental disorders do not help. Our improved methods of detection and our missionary zeal expand together as we become aware of the problem, so that it would be hard to say whether today this country has bigger and better neuroses, or bigger and better ways of spotlighting them – or both. But I would, from my clinical experience, dare to formulate a specific *quality* in those who are disturbed. I would say that underneath his proud sense of autonomy and his exuberant sense of initiative the troubled American (who often looks the least troubled) blames his mother for having let him down. His father, so he claims, had not much to do with it – except in those rare cases where the father was an extraordinarily stern man on the surface, an old-fashioned individualist, a foreign paternalist, or a native 'boss.' In the psychoanalysis of an American man it usually takes considerable time to break through to the insight that there was a period early in life when the father did seem bigger and threatening. Even then, there is at first little sense of that specific rivalry for the mother as stereotyped in the oedipus complex. It is as if the mother had ceased to be an object of nostalgia and sensual attachment before the general development of initiative led to a rivalry with the 'old man.' Behind a fragmentary 'oedipus complex,' then, appears that deep-seated sense of having been abandoned and let down by the mother, which is the silent complaint behind schizoid withdrawal. The small child felt, it seems, that there was no use regressing, because there was nobody to regress to, no use investing feelings because the response was so uncertain. What remained was action and motion right up to the breaking point. Where action, too, failed, there was only withdrawal and the standardized smile, and later, psychosomatic disturbance. But wherever our methods permit us to look deeper, we find at the bottom of it all the conviction, the mortal self-accusation, that it was *the child who abandoned the mother*, because he had been in such a hurry to become independent.

American folklore highlights this complex in its original power, in the saga of the birth of John Henry, a colored spiker, who, according to the widely known ballad, later died in an attempt to show that a he-man is the equal of any machine. The saga, not equally well known, goes as follows:[1]

Now John Henry was a man, but he's long dead.

The night John Henry was born the moon was copper-colored and the sky was black. The stars wouldn't shine and the rain fell hard. Forked lightning cleaved the air and the earth trembled like a leaf. The panthers squalled in the brake like a baby and the Mississippi River ran upstream a thousand miles. John Henry weighed forty-four pounds.

They didn't know what to make of John Henry when he was born. They looked at him and then went and looked at the river.

"He got a bass voice like a preacher," his mamma said.

"He got shoulders like a cotton-rollin'' rousterbout,' his papa said.

"He got blue gums like a conjure man," the nurse woman said.

"I might preach some," said John Henry, "but I ain't gonter be no preacher. I might roll cotton on de boats, but I ain't gonter be no cotton-rollin' rousterbout. I might got blue gums like a conjure man, but I ain't gonter git familiar wid de spirits. 'Cause my name is John Henry, and when folks call me by my name, dey'll know I'm a natchal man."

"His name is John Henry," said his mamma. "Hit's a fack."

"And when you calls him by his name," said his papa, "he's a natchal man."

So about that time John Henry raised up and stretched. "Well," he said, "ain't hit about supper-time?"

"Sho hit's about supper-time," said his mamma.

"And after," said his papa.

"And long after," said the nurse woman.

"Well," said John Henry, "did de dogs had they supper?"

"They did," said his mamma.

"All de dogs," said his papa.

"Long since," said the nurse woman.

"Well, den," said John Henry, "ain't I as good as de dogs?"

And when John Henry said that he got mad. He reared back in his bed and broke out the slats. He opened his mouth and yowled, and it put out the lamp. He cleaved his tongue and spat, and it put out the fire. "Don't make me mad!" said John Henry, and the thunder rumbled and rolled. "Don't let me git mad on de day I'm bawn, 'cause I'm skeered of my ownse'f when I gits mad."

And John Henry stood up in the middle of the floor and he told them what he wanted to eat. "Bring me four ham bones and a pot full of cabbages," he said. "Bring me a bait of turnip greens tree-top tall, and season hit down wid a side er middlin'. Bring me a pone er cold cawn bread and some hot potlicker to wash hit down. Bring me two hog jowls and a kittleful er whippowill peas. Bring me a skilletful er red-hot biscuits and a big jugful er cane molasses. 'Cause my name is John Henry, and I'll see you soon."

So John Henry walked out of the house and away from the Black River Country where all good rousterbouts are born.

There are, of course, analogous stories in other countries, from Hercules to Buslaev. Yet there are specific points in this story which I feel are thoroughly American. To characterize the kind of humor employed here would demand an objective approach beyond my present means. But what we must keep in mind, for further reference, is the fact that John Henry begins with a gigantic gripe: he is thwarted in his enormous appetite; he begs, 'don't let me git mad on de day I'm bawn'; he solves the dilemma by jumping on his own feet and by boasting of the capacity of his gut; he will not commit himself to any identity as predetermined by the stigmata of birth; and he leaves to become a man who is nothing but a man before any attempt is made to provide him with what he has demanded.

3 JOHN HENRY

This same John Henry is the hero of a legend which reports how, in his very death, he demonstrated the triumph of flesh over machine:

> Cap'n says to John Henry,
> "Gonna bring me a steam drill' round,
> Gonna take that steam drill out on the job,
> Gonna whop that steel on down,
> Lawd, Lawd, gonna whop that steel on down."
> John Henry told his cap' n,
> Said, "A man ain't nothin' but a man,
> And befo' I'd let that steam drill beat me down
> I'd die with this hammer in my hand,
> Lawd, Lawd, I'd die with the hammer in my hand."[2]

The tune of this ballad, according to the Lomaxes, 'is rooted in a Scottish melody, its devices are those of medieval balladry, but its content is the courage of the common man' who believes to the end that a man counts only as a man.

John Henry thus is one of the occupational models of the stray men on the expanding frontier who faced new geographic and technological worlds as men and without a past. The last remaining model seems to be the cowboy who inherited their boasts, their gripes, their addiction to roaming, their mistrust of personal ties, their libidinal and religious concentration on the limits of endurance and audacity, their dependence on 'critters' and climates.

These workmen developed to its very emotional and societal limits the image of the man without roots, the motherless man, the womanless man. Later in this book we shall maintain that this image is only one of a particular variety of new images existing over the whole world; their common denominator is the freeborn child who becomes an emancipated adolescent and a man who refutes his father's conscience and his nostalgia for a mother, bowing only to cruel facts and to fraternal discipline. They bragged as if they had created themselves tougher than the toughest critters and harder than any forged metal:

> Raised in the backwoods, suckled by a polar bear, nine rows of jaw teeth, a double coat of hair, steel ribs, wire intestines, and a barbed wire tail, and I don't give a dang where I drag it. Whoopee- whee-a-ha![3]

They preferred to remain anonymous so that they could be the condensed product of the lowest and the highest in the universe.

> I'm shaggy as a bear, wolfish about the head, active as a cougar, and can grin like a hyena, until the bark will curl off a gum log. There's a sprinkling of all sorts in me, from the lion down to the skunk; and before the war is over, you will pronounce me an entire zoological institute, or I miss a figure in my calculation.[4]

If there is totemism in this, taken over from the Indians, there is also a commitment of tragic incongruity: for you can meet a 'segment of nature' by identifying with it, but if you try to be colder and harder than machines, if you aspire to wire guts, your intestines may let you down.

When discussing two American Indian tribes, we concluded that their particular forms of early training were well synchronized with their world images and their economic roles in them. Only in their myths, in their rituals, and in their prayers did we find references to what their particular form of expulsion from infantile paradise had cost them. In a great and diverse nation like America, is there any form of folk life which would be apt to reflect typical trends in the early relationship to the mother?

I think that the folk song is the psychological counterpart in agricultural lands to the communal prayer chants of the primitives. The primitives' songs, as we saw, are songs addressed to the Supernatural Providers: these people put all the nostalgia for the lost paradise of infancy into their songs in order to make them convincing through the magic of tears. Folk songs, however, express the nostalgia of the working men who have learned to coerce the soil with harsh tools wielded in the sweat of their brow. Their longing for a restored home is sung as recreation after work – and often as an accompaniment to it, if not as an auxiliary tool, in their work songs.

In its 'old-time love songs' American song has inherited much of the quiet depth of the European folk song: 'Black, black, black is the color of my true love's hair.' But it is primarily in the melodies that the memory of the old world's deep valleys, quiet mills, and sweet lassies survives. In its changing words the folk song in this country deliberately cultivates that 'split personality' which much later enters melody in the era of jazz. As a discrepancy between melody and word it is already attested to in the supposedly oldest American song, 'Springfield Mountain.' The sweetest melodies may serve both the goriest and the most disrespectful verses; even the love songs have a tendency to dissipate deep sentiment. 'If you look between the lines,' so the Lomaxes say, 'you cannot help but be struck by two repeatedly expressed attitudes toward love . . . Love is dangerous – 'It ain't nothing but a notion that is gone with the wind.' . . . Love is for laughter, and courtship is a comedy. Apparently these people who weren't afraid of Indians, or loneliness, or the varmints, or the woods, or freedom, or wild horses, or prairie fires, or drought, or six-guns, were afraid of love.'[5]

It is, then, in the very love songs, that we find not only the sorrow of having been abandoned (an international theme) but also the fear of committing yourself to deep emotions, lest you get caught and hurt, by 'keerless love.'

Instead of romanticism there is in much of American song a stubborn clinging to the ugly facts of poverty, loneliness, and toil on a continent that punished as it challenged. There is a special emphasis on animals which are of immediate and constant nuisance value: 'June bugs, possums, coons, roosters, geese, hound dogs, mocking birds, rattlesnakes, billy goats, razor-back hogs, liver lipped mules.' The use of animals particularly serves the class of nonsense songs and fancy word play which must half hide from the severe elders and half reveal to the young folk some kind of erotic allusions, when at 'innocent' play parties dance steps had to be avoided and yet approximated in 'play steps':

> And it's ladies to the center and it's gents
> around the row,
> And we'll rally round the canebrake and shoot
> the buffalo.

> The girls will go to school, the boys will
>   act the fool,
> Rally round the barnyard and chase the old
>   gray mule.
>
> Oh, the hawk shot the buzzard and the buzzard
>   shot the crow
> And we'll rally round the canebrake and
>   shoot the buffalo.[6]

Nonsense becomes most irreverent in its dealings with the decline and end of expendable old things. These are mostly animals – 'the old gray mare,' who 'ain't what she used to be,' or 'the old red rooster,' who 'can't crow like he uster,' or Aunt Nancy's gray goose:

> Go tell Aunt Nancy
> Her old gray goose is dead.
> The one she's been savin'
> To make her feather bed.
> The goslin's are mournin'
> 'Cause their mammy's dead.
> She only had one fe-eather,
> A-stickin' in her head.[7]

The bitter and yet gay irony in this last verse refers to the days when, according to the Lomaxes, 'a goosefeather bed was the very prime in sleeping, because it cradled you and cuddled you and almost covered you at the same time.' Sometimes, however, the gay good riddance applies undisguisedly to people:

> My wife, she died, O then, O then,
> My wife, she died, O then,
> My wife, she died,
> And I laughed till I cried,
> To think I was single again.[8]

It fits the free expression of these sentiments of 'to hell with the worn-out' and of 'don't take yourself too seriously' that so much of American song must be walked, danced, and run to, to reveal its true spirit. Here perpetual action fuses with gay references to everyday work techniques expressing the American creed, the faith in magic liberation by going places and by doing things.

Cowboy songs, reflecting one of the last forms of the unique and deviant ways of the highly specialized workmen of the frontier, show an exquisite synthesis of work pattern and emotional expression. While trying to tire a bucking bronco, careful lest he let his muscular calm be sabotaged by fear or rage, or while shoving his animals along the hot and dusty trail, careful lest he hasten or upset the cattle which must be delivered in the pink of well-fed condition, the cowboy engaged in the sing-song out of which came the purified versions of popular song. Throughout, the rhyme and reason of the 'cowboy's lament' remains the fact that for him there is no way back. There are the well-known tear-jerkers of the cowboy who will never see his mother again, nor his 'darling sister'; or who will return to a sweetheart only to find himself deceived once more. But more genuinely pervading is the strange fact that this man's man in his songs becomes something of a mother and a teacher and a nursemaid to the dogies whom he delivers to their early death:

> Your mother was raised away down in Texas
> Where the jimpson weed and the sand-burrs grow,
> So we'll fill you up on cactus and cholla,
> Until you are ready for Idaho.[9]

He sings lullabies to his dogies as they move through the early prairie night on a thousand little hoofs:

> Go slow, little dogies, stop milling around,
> For I'm tired of your roving all over the ground,
> There's grass where you're standin',
> So feed kind o'slow,
> And you don't have forever to be on the go,
> Move slow, little dogies, move slow.[10]

And although he protests; 'It's your misfortune and none of my own,' he feels identified with these little steers whom he has branded, castrated, and nursed along until they were ready to be shipped and slaughtered:

> You ain't got no father, you ain't got no mother,
> You left them behind when first you did roam,
> You ain't got no sister, you ain't got no brother,
> You're just like a cowboy, a long way from home.[11]

American song, then, in its melodies affirms the nostalgia for the old, even while in its words it often expresses a deliberate and stubborn paradox, a denial of trust in love, a denial of a need for trust. It thus becomes a more intimate declaration of independence.

In this country the image of the freeman is founded on that northern European who, having escaped feudal and religious laws, disavowed his motherland and established a country and a constitution on the prime principle of preventing the resurgence of autocracy. This image, of course, later developed along lines which were quite unforeseeable to those original settlers who merely wanted to reinstate on this continent a new England, an England with equally quaint villages, but with more elbowroom for free thought. They could not foresee the persistent wild call of a continent which had never been anybody's motherland and which, with all its excessive rigors, became an autocratic tempter. In America nature is autocratic, saying, 'I am not arguing, I am telling you.' The size and rigor of the country and the importance of the means of migration and transportation helped to create and to develop the identity of autonomy and initiative, the identity of him who is 'going places and doing things.' Historically the overdefined past was apt to be discarded for the undefined future; geographically, migration was an ever-present fact; socially, chances and opportunities lay in daring and luck, in taking full advantage of the channels of social motility.

It is no coincidence, then, that psychological analyses should find at the bottom of much specific mental discomfort the complex of having abandoned the mother and of having been abandoned by her. In general, Americans do not experience 'this country' as a 'motherland' in the soft, nostalgic sense of 'the old country.' 'This country' is loved almost bitterly and in a remarkably unromantic and realistic way. Oratory may emphasize localities; deeper loyalties are attached to voluntary associations and opportunities, signifying level of achievement rather than local belonging. Today when there is so much demand for homes in defensively overdefined, overly standardized, and over-restricted neighborhoods, many people enjoy their most relaxed moments at crossroads counters, in bars, in and around automotive vehicles, and in camps and cabins, playing that they are unconfined and free to stay, free to move on. No country's population travels farther and faster. After the war, more veterans of this than of any other nation chose to start their new lives in places other than the home town they had dreamed of in the front lines. To many Americans, then, while there is 'no place like home,' it is important that you should be able to take it with you or find its facsimile a thousand miles away. Those with the best places to stay in probably travel the most.

But in thus mastering with a vengeance the expanses of a vast continent, Americans also learned to control the second autocrat, which was unexpectedly met with by the free sons: the machine.

The autocracy of the continent and the autocracy of the machine must be understood when one undertakes to study or criticize American child-training methods which tend to make a child slightly nostalgic and yet faithful, autonomous and yet reliable, individualistic and yet predictable. That such methods begin with systematic maternal 'rejection' is in itself folklore, which must be traced to facts, born of necessity, and to fancy, born of need; for the man and the woman who would fit into the image of the self-made man and the self-made personality, and who would create and 'adjust' their ego identity as they went along, did not have much use for protective mother love. Indeed, where they received it as children, they had to repudiate it later. Where 'Mom' did not exist, she had to be invented: for such is the historical importance of 'griping' in this country that a man, to stand on his own feet in a powerfully changing world, must keep himself up by his own gripes.

Because John Henry was born after the dogs had been fed, he jumped on his feet before he had his first meal. In view of the continent before him, and of the tasks required of him, his first hours in this world were meaningful, although admittedly extreme. But what will John Henry do in a double-breasted business suit? What will happen to his 'wire guts' when he must serve machines and finds himself caught in the impersonal machinery of modern life?

4 ADOLESCENT, BOSS, AND MACHINE

Adolescence is the age of the final establishment of a dominant positive ego identity. It is then that a future within reach becomes part of the conscious life plan. It is then that the question arises whether or not the future was anticipated in earlier expectations.

The problem posed by physiological maturation has been stated forcefully by Anna Freud.[12]

> The physiological process which marks the attainment of physical sexual maturity is accompanied by a stimulation of the instinctual processes. . . . Aggressive impulses are intensified to the point of complete unruliness, hunger becomes voracity and the naughtiness of the latency-period turns into the criminal behavior of adolescence. Oral and anal interests, long submerged, come to the surface again. Habits of cleanliness, laboriously acquired during the latency-period, give place to pleasure in dirt and disorder, and instead of

modesty and sympathy we find exhibitionistic tendencies, brutality and cruelty to animals. The reaction-formations, which seemed to be firmly established in the structure of the ego, threaten to fall to pieces. At the same time, old tendencies which had disappeared come into consciousness. The Oedipus wishes are fulfilled in the form of phantasies and day-dreams, in which they have undergone but little distortion; in boys ideas of castration and in girls penis-envy once more become the center of interest. There are very few new elements in the invading forces. Their onslaught merely brings once more to the surface the familiar content of the early infantile sexuality of little children.

This is the picture in terms of the individual ego, which appears to be invaded by a newly mobilized and vastly augmented id as though from a hostile innerworld, an inner outerworld. Our interest is directed toward the quantity and quality of support the adolescent ego, thus set upon, may expect from the outer outerworld; and toward the question of whether ego defenses as well as identity fragments developed in earlier stages receive the necessary additional sustenance. What the regressing and growing, rebelling and maturing youths are now primarily concerned with is who and what they are in the eyes of a wider circle of significant people as compared with what they themselves have come to feel they are; and how to connect the dreams, idiosyncrasies, roles, and skills cultivated earlier with the occupational and sexual prototypes of the day.

The danger of this stage is role diffusion; as Biff puts it in *Death of a Salesman*: 'I just can't take hold, Mom, I can't take hold of some kind of a life.' Where such a dilemma is based on strong previous doubt as to one's ethnic and sexual identity, delinquent and outright psychotic incidents are not uncommon. Youth after youth, bewildered by his assumed role, a role forced on him by the inexorable standardization of American adolescence, runs away in one form or another: leaves schools and jobs, stays out at night, or withdraws into bizarre and inaccessible moods. Once he is 'delinquent,' his greatest need and often his only salvation is the refusal on the part of older youths, of advisers, and of judiciary personnel to type him further by pat diagnoses and social judgments which ignore the special dynamic conditions of adolescence. Their greatest service may be the refusal to 'confirm' him in his criminality.[13]

Among young Americans with early defined identities, there is a type of teen-age boy whom I will try to sketch in the setting of his milieu. My method is the clinical description of a 'type': but the boy is not a patient, far from it. In fact, he has no use for 'headshrinkers.' Maybe for this very reason, one should find a means of studying him thoughtfully: for to restrict our understanding to those who need us desperately, would mean to limit our view unduly.

The family is Anglo-Saxon, mildly Protestant, of the white-collar class. This type of boy is tall, thin, muscular in his body build. He is shy, especially with women, and emotionally retentive, as if he were saving himself for something. His occasional grin, however, indicates a basic satisfaction with himself. Among his peers, he can be rowdy and boisterous; with younger children, kind and circumspect. His goals are vaguely defined. They have something to do with action and motion. His ideal prototypes in the world of sports seem to fulfill such needs as disciplined locomotion; fairness in aggression; calm exhibitionism; and dormant masculine sexuality. Neurotic anxiety is avoided by concentration on limited goals with circumscribed laws. Psychoanalytically speaking, the dominant defense mechanism is self restriction.

His mother is somewhat of a 'Mom.' She can be harsh, loud-voiced, and punitive. More likely than not she is sexually rather frigid. His father, while exhibiting the necessary toughness in business, is shy in his intimate relationships and does not expect to be treated with much consideration at home. Such parents in our case histories are still noted down as pathogenic, while it is quite clear that they represent a cultural pattern. What they will do to a child depends on variables not covered by the existing clinical terms. As for the mother, who shows a certain contempt for male weakness, her bark is worse than her bite. She has a male ideal, derived from the history of her family; it usually comes from her father's side, and she indicates to the son that she believes that he has a chance to come close to this ideal. She is wise enough (sometimes lazy or indifferent enough) to leave it to him whether he wants to live up to this ideal or not. Most important, she is not overprotective. Unlike mothers who drive on but cannot let go (they are the pathogenic, the 'overprotective' ones), she does not overly tie the boy to herself. She gives her teen-age children the freedom of the street, of the playground, and of parties, even into the night. The father is prevailed upon not to worry and to lend his car, or rather 'the car.' It must be admitted that this mother is sure of how far the boy will go in sexual matters, because unconsciously she knows that she starved some of the original devil out of him when he was small. In his early childhood she deliberately understimulated him sexually and emotionally.

I have indicated in how far a certain determined lack of maternalism in such mothers may be historically founded, not only in religious puritanism, but in unconscious continuation of historical conditions which made it dangerous for a son to believe more in the past than in the future; dangerous to base his identity on the adherence to his child-hood home and on the exclusion of possible migration in pursuit of a better chance; dangerous ever to appear to be a 'sissy' instead of one who has learned to tolerate a certain amount of deprivation and loneliness.

We have discussed the development of the basic body feeling out of the mutual regulation of mother and infant. Parts of the body feel like 'mine' and feel 'good' to the degree in which early surroundings first took them in trust and then, with proper connotations, gradually re-leased them to the child's own care. Areas of greatest conflict remain areas abruptly disconnected from the body feeling, and later from one's identity. They remain disturbing areas in the fast-growing body of the adolescent who will be overly concerned and self-conscious about them and suffer periods of a loss of contact with his own body parts. There is no doubt that this adolescent in his most intimate feelings is de-tached from his genitals; they have been called 'private' all along, and this not in the sense that they were his private property, but rather that they were too private even for him, to touch. He has been threatened – early and almost casually – with the loss of his genitals; and in accord with the general ego restriction which is his favorite defense mechanism, he has detached himself from them. Of this he is, of course, unconscious. Vigorous exercise helps to keep his body image intact and permits him to live out his intrusiveness in the goal-mindedness of sports.

The ego quality of autonomy, as we have said, depends on a con-sistent definition of individual privilege and obligation in the nursery. In the wake of recent developments, which involve our adolescent, all kinds of influences have weakened the bonds of privileges and obliga-tions, with and against which the child may develop his autonomy. Among these are the decrease in the size of our families, and early bowel training. A large group of siblings can see to it, and does, that there is feasible equality in the apportioning of privileges and obliga-tions to the 'too young' and the 'already old enough.' A large family, if utilized for this purpose, is a good school for democracy, especially if the parents gradually learn to restrict themselves to a firm advisory capacity. Small families accentuate diversities such as sex and age. In the wake of the demand for early training in cleanliness, orderliness, and punctuality, individual mothers, in small families, often face one child at a time in a guerrilla war of wits and endurance. Our mother, then, has unhesitatingly subscribed to the scientific slogan that it is best to 'condition' the child as early as possible, *before* the matter can become an issue of his muscular ambivalence. It makes sense to her to expect that very early training will lead to automatic compliance and maximum efficiency, with a minimum of friction. After all, the method works with dogs. With the 'behaviorist' psychology of her day, she failed to consider the fact that dogs are trained to serve and die; that they will not be forced to represent to their young what their masters represented to them. Children must eventually train their own children, and any impoverishment of their impulse life, for the sake of avoiding friction, must be considered a possible liability affecting more than one lifetime. Generations will depend on the ability of every pro-creating individual to face his children with the feeling that he was able to save some vital enthusiasm from the conflicts of his childhood. Actually, such early training principles fail to work smoothly from the start because they demand too constant effort on the part of the parent: they become parent training rather than child training.

Our boy thus became 'regular,' but he also learned to associate both meals and bowels with worry and haste. His belated campaign for somatic autonomy thus started under bewildering circumstances, and this with a definite initial deficit in the boy's ability to make choices because his area of control had been invaded before he could either object or comply by reasonably free choice. I would like to suggest in all seriousness that early bowel training and other arrangements in-vented to condition the child in advance of his ability to regulate him-self may be a very questionable practice in the upbringing of individuals who later on are supposed to exert vigorous and free choice as citi-zens. It is here that the machine ideal of 'functioning without friction' invaded the democratic milieu. Much political apathy may have its origin in a general feeling that, after all, matters of apparent choice have probably been fixed in advance – a state of affairs which be-comes fact, indeed, if influential parts of the electorate acquiesce in it because they have learned to view the world as a place where grown-ups talk of choice, but 'fix' things so as to avoid overt friction.

As for the so-called oedipus stage when 'the child identifies with the superego of the parents,' it is most important that this superego should make a maximum of collective sense in terms of the ideals of the day. The superego is bad enough as a mere institution, because it perpetuates internally the relation of the big-and-angry adult and the small-but-bad child. The patriarchal era exploited the universal evolu-tionary fact of an internalized and unconscious moral 'governor' in certain definite ways, while other eras have exploited it in other ways. The paternal exploitation apparently leads to suppressed guilt feelings and fear of castration as a result of rebellion against the father; the maternal one focuses on feelings of mutual destruction and mutual abandonment of mother and child. Each age, then, must find its own way of dealing with the superego as a universally given potentiality for the inner, automatic survival of a universal outer chasm between adult and child. The more idiosyncratic this relationship and the less adequate the parent in reflecting changing cultural prototypes and institutions, the deeper the conflict between ego identity and superego will be.

Self-restriction, however, saves our boy much moral wear and tear. He seems to be on reasonably good terms with his superego and remains so in puberty and adolescence because of an ingenious arrangement in American life which diffuses the father ideal. The boy's male ideal is rarely attached to his father, as lived with in daily life. It is usually an uncle or friend of the family, if not his grandfather, as presented to him (often unconsciously) by his mother.

The grandfather, a powerful and powerfully driven man – according to a once widely prevailing American pattern, another composite of fact and myth – sought new and challenging engineering tasks in widely separated regions. When the initial challenge was met, he handed the task over to others, and moved on. His wife saw him only for an occasional impregnation. His sons could not keep pace with him and were left as respectable settlers by the wayside; only his daughter was and looked like him. Her very masculine identification, however, did not permit her to take a husband as strong as her powerful father. She married what seemed, in comparison, a weak but safe man and settled down. In many ways, however, she talks like the grandfather. She does not know how she persistently belittles the sedentary father and decries the family's lack of mobility, geographic and social. Thus she establishes in the boy a conflict between the sedentary habits which she insists on, and the reckless habits she dares him to develop. At any rate, the early 'oedipus' image, the image of the overpoweringly bigger and greater father and possessor of the mother, who must be emulated or defeated, becomes associated with the myth of the grandfather. Both become deeply unconscious and remain so under the dominant necessity of learning how to be a fair brother, restricted and restricting, and yet healthy and encouraging. The father goes relatively free of his boys' resentment, unless, of course, he happens to be 'old-fashioned,' obviously alien, or a man of the 'boss type.' Otherwise he too becomes more of a big brother. Much of sexual rivalry, like sexuality in general, has been excluded from awareness.

The boys I have in mind, already in early adolescence, are tall, often taller than their fathers. About this they make slightly condescending jokes. In fact, it seems that something akin to the Indians' 'joking relationship' is developing between father and son in this country. This joking is often applied to that marginal area where one may hope 'to get away with something' – i.e., elude the mother's watchful eye. This establishes a mutual identification which helps to avoid any direct opposition, and any clear conflict of wills. The boys' dreams indicate that their physical prowess and their independent identity arouses anxiety in them: for once, when they were small boys, they were afraid of these same fathers who then seemed so wise and so potent. It is as if these boys were balancing on a tightrope. Only if they are stronger than or different from the real father will they live up to their secret ideals, or indeed, to their mother's expectations; but only if they somehow demonstrate that they are weaker than the omnipotent father (or grandfather) image of their childhood will they be free of anxiety. Thus, while they become boastful and ruthless in many respects, they can be astonishingly kind and apologetic in others.

Where the son's initiative is concerned, convention urges the father, too, to restrain any tendency he may have to challenge the son. To this purpose the future is emphasized as against the past. If the sons in their group behavior seem to be organized in the pursuit of one further degree of Americanization, it is the fatherly obligation to let the children proceed in their own way. In fact, because of their greater affinity with the tempo and with the technical problems of the immediate future, the children are in a sense 'wiser' than the parents; and indeed, many children are more mature in their outlook on problems of daily living. The father of such boys does not hide his relative weakness behind a mask of inflated patriarchal claims. If he shares with the son an admiration for an ideal type, be he baseball player or industrial leader, comedian, scientist, or rodeo artist, the need to become like the ideal is emphasized without burdening it with a problem of the father's defeat. If the father plays baseball with his son, it is not in order to impress him with the fact that he, the father, comes closer to the perfection of a common ideal type – for he probably does not – but rather that they play together at identifying with that type, and that there is always the chance, hoped for by both, that the boy may more nearly approach the ideal than the father did.

All of this by no means excludes the fact that the father is potentially quite a man, but he shows it more away from home, in business, on camping trips, and in his club. As the son becomes aware of this, a new, almost astonished respect is added to his affection. There are real friendships between fathers and sons.

Fraternal images, boldly or gingerly, thus step into the gaps left by decaying paternalism; fathers and sons are unconsciously working on the development of a fraternal pattern which will forestall the reactionary return of more patriarchal oedipus patterns without, on the other hand, leading to a general impoverishment of the father-son relationship.[14]

How does his home train this boy for democracy? If taken too literally, one may hardly dare to ask that question. The boy has no political sense whatsoever. The 'dignity of man' has never occurred to him. In fact, he does not even know any kind of indignation in the positive sense of becoming acutely aware of the violation of a principle, with the exception of *unfairness*. In early life this takes the form of feeling cheated out of a birthright, when bigger and smaller siblings, on the basis of their superiority or inferiority, demand special privileges. Painfully learning a measure of obligation and privilege as related to strength and weakness, he becomes an advocate of fairness – unfairness, primarily in sports, is probably the only subject which would cause a facsimile of indignation – and then, of course, bossiness of any kind. 'No one can do this to me' is the slogan of such indignation. It is the counterpart of other countries' more heroic honor or honneur, droit or fair play. While this boy may grinningly join in some casual references to a lower race or class, he is not really intolerant: for the most part his life is too protected and 'restricted' to bring him up against an individual decision in this matter. Where he is up against it, he decides on the basis of friendship, not citizenship. It is his privilege, not his duty, to accept a pal of whatever kind. As far as 'general citizenship' is concerned, he catches on to the school's concept of behavior which goes by this name, but he does not connect it with politics. Otherwise, he more or less somnambulistically moves in a maze of undefined privileges, licenses, commitments, and responsibilities. He wants a vague, general success, and he is glad if he can get it in fairness, or while being unaware of unfairness. In this connection it must be said that our boy, mostly by default and because of restricted vision, and often out of carelessness, causes great harm to his less fortunate age mates of darker shades, whom he excludes from his home, his clique, and himself, because to see and to face them as actual human beings might cause vague discomfort. He ignores them, although he might have furthered their participation in the American identity by taking more seriously the simple social principle that what nobody can do to me, nobody should do to anybody else either.

But I submit that this boy's family life harbors more democracy than meets the eye. It may not reflect the democracy of the history books and the newspaper editorials, but it reflects a number of trends characterizing, for better or worse, the democratic process as it is, and as it must expand. I must point here to one of those configurational analogies between family life and national mores which are hard to fit into a theoretical pattern but seem of utmost relevance:

'Now it is an unwritten but firm rule of Congress that no important bloc shall ever be voted down – under normal circumstances – on any matter which touches its own vital interests.'[15] This statement refers, of course, to political interest groups (the farm bloc, the silver bloc, the friends of labor, etc.) which utilize in a powerful, yet unofficial way, the official two-party polarization – and are utilized by it. At times they contribute positive legislation, but more often – and what is sometimes more important – they prevent unwelcome legislation. What ensues of positive legislation may be good legislation, but it must, first of all, not be unacceptable to any of the major blocs (just as a candidate for president *may* be a potentially great man, but *must* be a man not unacceptable to any large block of voters). This principle not only keeps any one group from complete domination, but it also saves each group from being completely dominated.

The American family, similarly, tends to guard the right of the individual member – parents included – not to be dominated. In fact, each member, as he grows and changes, reflects a variety of outside groups and their changing interests and needs: the father's occupational group, the mother's club, the adolescent's clique, and the children's first friends. These interest groups determine the individual's privileges in his family; it is they who judge the family. The sensitive receptor of changing styles in the community and the sensitive arbiter of their clash within the home is, of course, the mother; and I think that this necessity to function as arbiter is one more reason why the American mother instinctively hesitates to lavish on her children the kind of naïve animal love which, in all its naïveté, can be so very selective and unjust; and which, above all, may weaken the child in his determination to seek in his peers what the family cannot and should not give him. The mother remains, in a sense, above the parties and interests; it is as if she had to see to it that each party and interest develops as vigorously as possible – up to the point where she must put in a veto in the interest of another individual or of the family as a whole. Here, then, we must expect to find the inner rationale for a variety of activities and inactivities: they represent not so much what everybody wants to do, but rather what, of all the available things to do, is least unacceptable to anybody concerned. Such an inner arrangement, of course, is easily upset by any show of vested interest, or special interest, or minority interest: and it is for this reason that there is a great amount of apparently petty bickering whenever interests clash. The family is successful if the matter is settled to the point of 'majority concurrence,' even if this is reluctantly given; it is gradually undermined by frequent decisions in favor of one interest group, be it the parents or the babies. This give-and-take cuts down to an extraordinary degree the division of the family into unequal partners who can claim privileges on the basis of age, strength, weakness, or goodness. Instead, the family becomes a training ground in the tolerance of different *interests* – not of different *beings*; liking and loving has little to do with it. In fact, both overt loving and overt hating are kept on a low key, for either might weaken the balance of the family and the chances of the individual member: for the over-all important thing is to accrue claims for future privilege justifiable on the basis of one's past concessions.

The meaning of it all is, of course, an automatic prevention of autocracy and inequality. It breeds, on the whole, undogmatic people, people ready to drive a bargain and then to compromise. It makes complete irresponsibility impossible, and it makes open hate and warfare in families rare. It also makes it quite impossible for the American adolescent to become what his brothers and sisters in other large countries become so easily, uncompromising ideologists. Nobody can be sure he is right, but everybody must compromise – for the sake of his future chance.

The analogy here to the two-party system is clear: American politics is not, as is that of Europe, 'a prelude to civil war', it cannot become either entirely irresponsible or entirely dogmatic; and it must not try to be logical. It is a rocking sea of checks and balances in which uncompromising absolutes must drown. The danger is that such absolutes may be drowned in all-around acceptable banalities, rather than in productive compromise.

In the family, the corresponding danger is that the interests which are not unacceptable to the whole family become areas so devoid of real issues that family life becomes an institution for parallel day-dreaming where each member is tuned in on his favorite radio program, or withdrawn behind the magazine representing his interests. A general low tonus of mutual responsibility may empty the pattern of majority concurrence of its original indignation, and thus of its dignity.

Where in Europe then, adolescence would lead to a conflict with the father, and the necessity of either rebelling or submitting (or, as we shall see in the chapter on Germany, first rebelling and then submitting) there is, on the whole, no necessity for such exertion in the American family. The adolescent swings of the American youth do not overtly concern the father, nor the matter of authority, but focus rather on his peers. The boy has a delinquent streak, as had his grandfather in the days when laws were absent or not enforced. This may express itself in surprising acts of dangerous driving or careless destruction and waste, an individual counterpart to the mass plundering of the continent. This stands in surprising contrast to the defense mechanisms of ascetic self-restriction – until one realizes that occasional utter carelessness is the necessary counterpart and safety-valve of self-restriction. Both carelessness and self-restriction 'feel' self-initiated; they underscore the fact that there is no boss – and that there need be little thought.

Our boy is anti-intellectual. Anybody who thinks or feels too much seems 'queer' to him. This objection to feeling and thinking is, to some extent, derived from an early mistrust of sensuality. It signifies some atrophy in this sphere, and then again, it is representative of a general tentativeness, of a wish not to meditate and not to make up his mind until the free exploration by action of a number of chances may force him to think.

If this boy attends church, and as I suggested he is Protestant, he finds a milieu which makes no great demands on his ability to surrender to moods of damnation or salvation or even of simple piety. In church life he must prove himself by overt behavior which demonstrates discipline by self-restriction, thus earning the fellowship of all those whose good and fair fortunes on earth God obviously legitimizes. Church membership, then, makes things ever so much easier, since at the same time it provides a clearer definition of one's social and credit status in the community. Here again, sociologists, in their somewhat naïve and literal criticism of the 'American class system,' seem sometimes to overlook the historic necessity in America of finding in community and church life a scope for activities which are acceptable to all the individuals concerned. This calls for some initial principle of selection, for some uniformity. Without it, democracy would not have begun to work in this country. But the sociologists are right in pointing out that all too often membership of lesser or greater exclusiveness, sectarianism, and faddism leads to a mere shell of fraternal congregation where the habits of family life are further indulged rather than brought to any political or spiritual fruit. The church community becomes a frigid and punitive Mom; God a Pop who in view of public pressure cannot avoid providing for those of his children who prove worthy by self-restricted conduct and proper appearance; while the brethren have the prime obligation of proving their creditworthiness by being moderate in dealing with one another and by diverting more energetic tactics to 'outsiders.'

The type of adolescent I am discussing here is not and will never be a true individualist. But then it would be hard to point out any true individualist within the orbit of his experience – unless it be the myth of the mother's father. But this image becomes buried in self-constriction or is, at the most, held in abeyance for the day when, as grown men, they may become the 'bosses' of something or other.

With this individualistic core in him, complicated as it is by the transmission through the mother, our adolescent is allergic to the professional kinds of individualism displayed by writers and politicians. He mistrusts both – they make him feel uncomfortable, as if they reminded him that there is something that he should be or should do but that he cannot remember. He has experienced, or rather faced, no autocracy except that of his mother, who by now has become Mom, in the original and kinder sense, to him. If he resents her he tries to forget it.

He is aware that his older sister, slim, trim, and poised, on occasion seems to get almost physically upset in the mother's presence. The boy cannot see why; but then, this belongs to the general area of women's whims which he carefully circumnavigates. He does not know, he does not want to know, the burden which the sister must carry in becoming a woman and a mother without becoming like the woman who is her mother. For she must be the self-made woman of *her* period; she must work on herself, in competitive companionship with all the other girls who make and are made by the new standards. Margaret Mead has impressively described the difficult job which these girls share, namely, the necessity of saving a full measure of warmth and sexual responsiveness through the years of calculated appearances when even naturalness on occasion must be affected.[16] The sister's crisis will come when she becomes a mother and when the vicissitudes of child training will perforce bring to the fore the infantile identification with her mother. There is much less of 'Mom' in her than there was in her mother; whether this remnant will be decisive depends on region, class, and kind of husband.

This American adolescent, then, is faced, as are the adolescents of all countries who have centered or are entering the machine age, with the question: freedom for what, and at what price? The American feels so rich in his opportunities for free expression that he often no longer knows what it is he is free from. Neither does he know where he is not free; he does not recognize his native autocrats when he sees them. He is too immediately occupied with being efficient and being decent.

This adolescent will make an efficient and decent leader in a circumscribed job, a good manager or professional worker and a good officer, and will most enjoy his recreation with 'the boys' in the organizations to which he belongs. As a specimen, he illustrates the fact that in war or in peace, the fruit of American education is to be found in a combination of native mechanical ability, managerial autonomy, personalized leadership, and unobtrusive tolerance. These young men truly are the backbone of the nation.

But are they, as men, not strangely disinterested in the running of the nation? Are these freeborn sons not apt to be remarkably naïve, overly optimistic, and morbidly self-restrained in their dealings with the men who run them? They know how to accept a circumscribed task; they can be boisterous when on a spree; but on the whole, they respectfully shy away from all bigness, whether it is dollars or loud words. They (theoretically) hate autocrats, but they tolerate bossism because they usually cannot differentiate between a boss and 'bosses.' We have repeatedly mentioned this category of 'boss,' and it is time to state explicitly that there is a boss and a 'boss,' just as there is a Mom and a 'Mom.' We use both words without quotation marks in their more colloquial and more affectionate sense, in the sense of *my Mom*, and *my boss*; while we designate with quotation marks the 'Moms' who make for Momism as discussed above and the 'bosses' that constitute the bossism to which we must now make reference.

For the old autocrats have disappeared, and the new ones know how to hide behind the ambiguity of language, which fills the legislatures and the daily press, industrial strife and organized entertainment. 'Bosses' are self-made autocrats and, therefore, consider themselves and one another the crown of democracy. As far as is necessary, a 'boss' stays within the law, and as far as is possible he enters boldly into the vacuum left by the emancipated sons in their endeavor to restrict themselves in fairness to others. He looks for areas where the law has been deliberately uncharted (in order to leave room for checks, balances, and amendments) and tries to use it and abuse it for his own purposes. He is the one who – to speak in highway terms – passes and cuts in where others leave a little space for decency's and safety's sake.

Here it is not a matter of taste or mere principle which makes me join those who decry the danger of bossism. I approach the matter from the point of view of psychological economy. 'Bosses' and 'machines,' I have learned, are a danger to the American identity, and thus to the mental health of the nation. For they present to the emancipated generations, to the generations with tentative identities, the ideal of an autocracy of irresponsibility. In them is seen the apparently successful model, 'he who measures himself solely by what 'works,' by what he can get away with and by what he can appear to be.' They make 'functioning' itself a value above all other values. In their positions of autocratic power in legislation, in industry, in the press, and in the entertainment world, they knowingly and unknowingly use superior machinery to put something over on the naïve sons of democracy. They thrive on the complication of 'machinery' – a machinery kept deliberately complicated in order that it may remain dependent on the hard-bitten professional and expert of the 'inside track.' That these men run themselves like machinery is a matter for their doctor, psychiatrist, or undertaker. That they view the world and run the people as machinery becomes a danger to man.

Consider our adolescent boy. In his early childhood he was faced with a training which tended to make him machinelike and clocklike. Thus standardized, he found chances, in his later childhood, to develop autonomy, initiative, and industry, with the implied promise that decency in human relations, skill in technical details, and knowledge of facts would permit him freedom of choice in his pursuits, that the identity of free choice would balance his self-coercion. As an adolescent and man, however, he finds himself confronted with superior machines, complicated, incomprehensible, and impersonally dictatorial in their power to standardize his pursuits and tastes. These machines do their powerful best to convert him into a consumer idiot, a fun egotist, and an efficiency slave – and this by offering him what he seems to demand. Often he remains untouched and keeps his course: this will largely depend on the wife whom he – as the saying goes – chooses. Otherwise, what else can he become but a childish joiner, or a cynical little boss, trying to get in on some big boss' 'inside track' – or a neurotic character, a psychosomatic case?

For the sake of its emotional health, then, a democracy cannot afford to let matters develop to a point where intelligent youth, proud in its independence and burning with initiative, must leave matters of legislation, law, and international affairs, not to speak of war and peace, to 'insiders' and 'bosses.' American youth can gain the full measure of its identity and of its vitality only by being fully aware of autocratic trends in this and in any other land as they repeatedly emerge from changing history. And this not only because political conscience cannot regress without catastrophic consequences, but also because political ideals are part and parcel of an evolution in conscience structure which, if ignored, must lead to illness.

As we consider what consequences must arise from the particular dangers threatening the emotional state of the nation, our attention is drawn to Momism and to bossism, the two trends which have usurped the place of paternalism: Momism in alliance with the autocratic rigor of a new continent, and bossism with the autocracy of the machine and the 'machines.'

Psychiatric enlightenment has begun to debunk the superstition that to manage a machine you must become a machine, and that to raise masters of the machine you must mechanize the impulses of childhood. But let it be clear that the humanization of early childhood – as pioneered by enlightened obstetricians and pediatricians – must have its counterpart in a political rejuvenation. Men and women in power must make a concerted effort to overcome the rooted conception that man, for his own good, must be subject to 'machines' either in politics, business, education, or entertainment. American adolescents believe deeply in truly free enterprise; they prefer one big chance in a hundred little ones to an average-sized certainty. The very fact that for this same reason they do not contemplate rebellion (as those seem to fear who would gag their sources of information) obligates us to protect youth against a state of affairs which may make their gestures of free men seem hollow and their faith in man illusory and ineffective.

The question of our time is, How can our sons preserve their freedom and share it with those whom, on the basis of a new technology and of a more universal identity, they must consider equals? This makes it necessary for men and women in power to give absolute priority over precedent and circumstance, convention and privilege, to the one effort which can keep a democratic country healthy: the effort to 'summon forth the potential intelligence of the younger generation' (Parrington).

I have sketched some of the dilemma of the grandsons of self-made men, themselves the grandsons of rebels. In other countries youth is still involved in the first phases of revolution against autocracy. Let us turn to some of their historical problems.[17]

Notes

1. Roark Bradford, *John Henry* (New York: Harper Bros., 1931).
2. J. A. Lomax and A. Lomax (eds.), *Folksong U.S.A.* (New York: Duell, Sloan and Pearce, 1947).
3. Alfred Henry Lewis, *Wolfville Days* (New York: Frederic A. Stokes Co., 1902). Quoted in B. A. Botkin, *A Treasury of American Folklore* (New York: Crown Publishers, 1944).
4. *Colonel Crockett's Exploits and Adventures in Texas*, Written by Himself (1836).
5. Lomax and Lomax *Folksong USA*.
6. Lomax and Lomax *Folksong USA*.
7. Lomax and Lomax *Folksong USA*.
8. Lomax and Lomax *Folksong USA*.
9. M. and T. Johnson, *Early American Songs* (New York: Associated Music Publishers, Inc., 1943).
10. From *Singing America*, used by permission of the National Recreation Association, copyright owners, and C. C. Birchard and Co., publishers.
11. Johnson and Johnson, *Early American Song*.
12. Anna Freud, *The Ego and the Mechanisms of Defense* (London: The Hogarth Press and the Institute of Psycho-Analysis, 1937).
13. See E. H. and K. T. Erikson, 'The Confirmation of the Delinquent,' *Chicago Review* (Winter 1957).
14. In psychoanalytic patients the overwhelming importance of the grandfather is often apparent. He may have been a blacksmith of the old world or a railroad builder of the new, an as yet proud Jew or an unreconstructed Southerner. What these grandfathers have in common is the fact that they were the last representatives of a more homogeneous world, masterly and cruel with good conscience, disciplined and pious without loss of self-esteem. Their world invented bigger and better machinery like gigantic playthings which were not expected to challenge the social values of the men who made them. Their mastery persists in their grandsons as a stubborn, an angry sense of superiority. Overtly inhibited, they yet can accept others only on terms of prearranged privilege.
15. John Fischer, 'Unwritten Rules of American Politics,' *Harper's Magazine*, 197 (November 1948), pp. 27–36.
16. Margaret Mead, *Male and Female* (New York: William Morrow & Co., 1949).
17. What did I dread in some of the now more obscure passages of this chapter? I think it is the inner split between the morality of daily existence, the ideologies of political life, and the neutral dictates of modern super-organization. The bosses are, at least in this country, about to be absorbed in the smoother teams of managerial power. In other and newer nation states (which repeat a century of our history in decades), a variety of revolutionary ideologies are bringing to power the bosses of party machines, of military and industrial machineries, of labor organizations etc. The frequent display of the ethical bewilderment of middle age charged with the management of unforeseen changes forces much of youth into apathetic conformity or cynical detachment. The moral is that the iden-

tity gain of successful revolts against aging systems does not in itself guarantee the generative values necessary for an ethics of mature power. If man permits his ethics to depend on the machineries he can set in motion, forgetting to integrate childhood and society, he may find himself helplessly harnessed to the designs of total destruction along with those of total production. (For a discussion of the moral, the ideological, and the ethical sense in human development, see 'The Golden Rule and the Cycle of Life,' *Harvard Medical Alumni Bulletin*, December 1962.) [Erikson's note of 1963 edn.]

16 American Immigrant Groups: Ethnic Identification and the Problem of Generations (1965)

Vladimir C. Nahirny and
Joshua A. Fishman*

A half century of inquiry and discussion on American immigrant groups has given currency to a handful of such concepts as 'Anglo-conformity', 'cultural pluralism', 'the third generation interest', 'behavioural assimilation' and 'structural assimilation'. This essay attempts to take another look at ethnic identification and ethnic continuity in the United States in the hope that this meagre arsenal of commonly accepted formulations can be enriched. Its vantage point will be a recently completed study of language maintenance among immigrant groups in which several topics in the sociology of language were explored at the nationwide, community and family levels of analysis.[1]

Basic to this essay is the view that the erosion of ethnicity and ethnic identity experienced by most (but not all) American ethnic groups takes place in the course of three generations; it involves, in other words, the immigrant fathers, their sons and their grandsons. Contrary to the widely prevalent opinion that there ensues some kind of a return to the fold of ethnicity, whenever any immigrant group reaches the third generation stage of its development',[2] we hold that the ethnic heritage, including the ethnic mother tongue, usually ceases to play any viable role in the life of the third generation. Hansen's claim to the effect that 'Anyone who has the courage to codify the laws of history must include what can be designated as the principle of the third generation interest',[3] stems largely from a misreading of the contrastive pattern involved. For he seemed to have come upon the idea

* From *Sociological Review*, NS 13 (1965), pp. 311–26.

of the 'returning grandsons' against the background of the 'fleeing sons'. To cite him again: 'The theory is derived from the almost universal phenomenon that what the son wishes to forget the grandson wishes to remember. This tendency might be illustrated by a hundred examples.'[4] The resurgent interest of the grandsons in ethnicity is thus relative to the determination of the sons to forget it. Viewed in this light, the revival of 'third generation interest' may actually portend little more than a somewhat appreciative or even indifferent orientation of the grandsons in comparison to that of the sons. The very violence with which some of the sons dissociated themselves from their ethnic heritage expressed the extent to which it had taken hold of them. The very attempt of some of these sons to cut loose all the ties that bound them to the ethnic community reflected their manifold involvement in it. Even instances of highly negative responses testify to the impact of ethnicity upon the attitudes and actions of the sons. The grandsons, in turn, find it possible to become interested in their ethnic heritage precisely because they have been left largely untouched by it. They need not forget the ethnic ways since these have scarcely been known to them. They need not unlearn the language of their immigrant grandfathers since they have never mastered it. They need not emphasize their Americanism by dissociating from ethnicity because their Americanism is unstrained and their ethnicity attenuated. The sons, still deeply involved in ethnicity, tend to depreciate it for the strength of its claims is a hindrance to them; the grandsons, only slightly affected by ethnicity, tend to appreciate it for the weakness of its claims upon them removes all hindrances. If it be granted, then, that this is the case, Hansen's principle of the 'third generation interest' may forestall not only the end of ethnicity but its vital role in the lives of grandsons as well.

The foregoing comments raise a series of issues that need urgent reappraisal. One of them is the murky concept of ethnic identification. To suggest that immigrant fathers and grandsons are more positive toward or less inimical to ethnicity than the sons, is usually taken to imply that the concept of ethnic identification lends itself to analysis along a unidimensional attitudinal continuum, i.e. that we are merely dealing with 'more' and 'less' of the same 'thing'. Once this dubious assumption is made, the next logical step is to construct scales capable of measuring the positiveness or the intensity of identification with ethnicity. In fact, this has been one of the standard procedures employed by students of ethnic groups in the United States. A careful perusal of the diverse and *ad hoc* selected criteria for gauging ethnic identification makes painfully evident the simplistic character of this procedure.[5] It ignores the central fact that the fathers, sons and grandsons may differ among themselves not only in the *degree* but also in the *nature* of their identification with ethnicity.

It has been long thought that the generational conflict between immigrant fathers and their song represents the first major blow to the continuity of ethnic groups and their cultures in the United States. On the one hand, it has been observed that most immigrant fathers desperately tried to instill in their sons their own (i.e. the fathers') love for and allegiance to the ethnic heritage; on the other hand, most of the sons of these immigrant fathers were found determined to forget everything – the mother tongue that left (or was rumoured to leave) so many traces in their speech, the 'strange' customs that they were forced to practice at home, in church, or even in more public places, etc.[6] In many a case, as Hansen observed, 'Nothing was more Yankee than a Yankeeized person of foreign descent.'[7] How general this revolt might have been is only of minor concern here; what deserves careful scrutiny is the limited extent to which most immigrant fathers could ever have led any of their sons to appreciate or to identify with ethnicity in the same manner as they themselves did. To those immigrant fathers of pre-World War I days who were of rural background, ethnicity represented a particular way of life inseparably bound up with the daily round of activities within the village community. On the whole, this way of life was steeped in intimacy and immediacy to such an extent that both the human and nonhuman worlds within it were highly individualized and scarcely transferable. Rural inhabitants throughout Europe tended to endow separate strips of their soil with unique attributes and names. Mere reference to any of these strips evoked specific images and attitudes. Likewise, the domesticated animals they so intimately knew possessed individual qualities and names.[8]

Consonant with the character of this primeval world was ethnicity, since it was equally rendered immanent and parochial. Folks songs and folk costumes, local festivities and dialects – all these and other elements of ethnicity – possessed idiosyncratic characteristics within this milieu. Where trained linquists distinguished only several regional dialects, peasant immigrants readily recognized many differentiating features between their own local speech and that current a few miles away from their native village. And it was precisely this parochial tongue – the speech of their kin and dear ones, rather than the national language, that the peasant immigrants appeared to have been attached to. Like poets, they responded to the particular with no reference to the general; unlike poets, they were hardly cognizant of the fact that this same particular might encompass, in some way, the general. So abiding was this particularized attachment to ethnicity among some that the very establishment of 'national' ethnic organizations in the United States was considerably hindered by it. In some Lithuanian churches, for example, the singing of religious hymns had to be discontinued because 'some singers tried to sing them according to their dialect and the other singers were opposed to that version'.[9]

The point made above deserves additional attention if only because *ethnic identification* has been commonly defined as 'a person's use of racial, national or religious terms to identify himself, and thereby, to relate himself to others'.[10] These national terms or general categories allegedly provide a universalistic framework for ordering social relationships. *Ethnic orientation*, therefore, has been defined as 'those features of a person's feeling and action towards others which are a function of the ethnic category by which he identifies himself.'[11] To appreciate the difficulty posed by such definitions of ethnic identification and orientation, it may suffice to note that many peasant immigrants – be they of Finnish, Italian, Lithuanian, Norwegian, Slovak, Ukrainian or even of Polish or German origins – were hardly responsive to such comprehensive categories. The very mode of orientation toward ethnicity largely barred most immigrant fathers from being sensitive to general ethnic categories. Being an outgrowth of past personal experience, the ethnic identification of the immigrant fathers constituted something deeply subjective and concrete; that is to say, it was hardly externalized or expressed in general symbolic terms. So much was this the case that many of them were simply ignorant of their national identity. According to one of the foremost students of rural life in Poland, many Polish peasants continued to be utterly confused with regard to their national identity as late as the first decade of this century.

> There are still many people in the village of *Zmiaca* as well as in the neighbouring villages who identify their nationality by saying that they are either Catholics . . . or peasants or, finally, that they are Kaiser's people (cysarskimi). If one endeavours to convince them that they are Poles they become disturbed and avoid discussing it altogether.[12]

But what is salient in this context is not so much whether peasant immigrants were aware of the existence of appropriate ethnic categories (some of them undoubtedly were) as the extent to which any of their attitudes and actions were a function of their identification with such

categories.[13] It may be argued that the establishment of so many ethnic organizations and churches by the immigrant fathers was directly
expressive of their ethnic consciousness and solidarity. Yet, it is known
that the first ethnic organizations and churches of well-nigh all immigrant groups were set up along local rather than along national ethnic
lines. The very patterns of chain migration and settlement largely proceeded along such parochial lines. Some two hundred and fifty present-
day Ukrainian organizations in the United States and Canada are still
based on such parochial loyalties and attachments. Membership in mutual
benefit societies in the 'Little Italies' tended to be almost exclusively
based on *campanilismo* (local loyalty).[14] Norwegian–American *bygdelags*
provide an additional illustration of this same phenomenon. According
to the estimate of one author, there were still fifty such *lags* in 1929,
and each year some 75,000 Norwegian–Americans came under the direct
influence of these societies.

> Immigrants from Norway who during their youth shared a common
> acquaintance with families and places find at the conventions a ready
> opportunity to meet neighbors again, refresh half-forgotten mem-
> ories and be cheered by the homelike coziness that association with
> friends of one's youth usually gives. This pre-eminently is the at-
> tracting and assembling force connected with gatherings of those
> from the same home community.[15]

The first immigrant organizations partook of the nature of communal
reunions; indeed, they provided immigrants with an *ersatz* framework
within which they did and could recreate their common past experience – from speaking and hearing their dialect to singing and dancing
local folk songs and dances. It was not a response to national symbols
that made most immigrants band together, but a highly particularized
response to many facets of their very concrete and delimited former
ways of life. Only those who had personally experienced this way of
life in the past – embedded, as it was, in the local scenery with its
fjords, orchards or white peasant huts, and replete with local traditions
and commemorations – could draw delight from and genuinely appreciate its occasional re-creation in the United States. To the extent, then,
that immigrant fathers from a given 'country of origin' were primarily
sensitive and responsive to such local pasts, they possessed *many different
ethnic pasts* rather than *one national past*. Of the latter past they were
indeed largely ignorant, as is amply evidenced by the continued popularity among them of parochial folk heroes and Robin Hoods, local
tales and stories.[16]

Sheer human sentiment was involved in the establishment of many immigrant organizations, and their primary function in this country was to foster friendly ties among former neighbours and, thereby, to keep alive the local customs and precious personal memories of their ancestral homes. Clearly enough, most immigrant mothers and fathers of pre-World War I days did not hearken back to a collective and generalized past of their respective ethnic groups; they did not endow with affective aura all Norwegian fjords, Lithuanian forests or Ukrainian orchards. In the fashion of the ancient wanderer, Odysseus, the immigrants knew only too well that a chimney and the smoke rising from it were not exclusive attributes of their ancestral homes alone; yet, the one and only smoke that they could neither easily forget nor readily find a substitute for was precisely that which had once come from their own childhood homes.

Personal experience and memory underlay this mode of identification with and attachment to ethnicity and ethnic traditions. To dismiss this as a lachrymose nostalgia for a bygone past and as nothing but another instance of *Schwaermerei* is simply to disregard the significance of concrete experiences for the continuity of personal identity. A cursory look at some immigrant folk songs, sayings and folk poems reveals the desperate quest of their authors for such a link with the past. It is worthy of note that those of the immigrant fathers who could read and write not infrequently turned into amateur versifiers; that is to say, they resorted to that particular genre which enabled them to relate themselves to the past in terms of more concrete and more permanent imagery. Most of this poetry abounds in highly singular symbols conveying the most intimate experience – from the 'grave' where 'my mother rests'[17] and 'Das Lied dass meine Mutter sang'[18] to 'each fjord' where 'the past in memories brightly gleams'.[19]

In view of the foregoing it is certainly appropriate to suggest that the immigrant fathers could scarcely transmit to their sons this kind of mnemonic orientation toward ethnicity, even when they genuinely tried to inculcate the *mores maiorum* of their ancestors. By listening to the stories told by parents or by studying ethnically related geography and history, the sons were able, as best, to respond to certain generalized attributes of the old country – be they Norwegian fjords, Finnish lakes, or Lithuanian forests. But what bearing could such acquaintance with ethnicity have on that special relationship which links the family or the individual from generation to generation? Too radical a break in the actual life patterns of generations had made the personal and concrete experiences of the immigrant fathers inaccessible to the sons.

For the fathers, the 'old ways' survived as realities, since they continued to link them meaningfully to the ancestral past as well as to the community of their immigrant contemporaries. For the sons, in turn, they stood (at best) for *ideals* to be *appreciated and cherished*. Whereas the immigrant fathers accepted ethnicity as a way of life and, to that extent, as a living tradition, the sons viewed it increasingly as the 'dead hand of the past' which they were taught to hold dear to and respect in their childhood years. Partly influenced by the dominant de-ethnicized society (with its stress on cultural novelty and on social inclusiveness), the sons turned before long to a wholesale purging of that past which they came to consider as reflecting archaic survivals. As a result, those elements of traditional ethnicity to which their parents were so intensely attached, and which were so strikingly different from those found in the dominant society, were cast off and, with time, replaced by supposedly less superstitious practices of the dominant society.[20] One uniquely differentiating quality of any ethnic group – the mother tongue – suffered the most serious blow at the hands of the sons. For it was largely upon their insistence that English was introduced into church services, ethnic organizations and ethnic publications. Ethnic parishes were not only made bilingual but were transformed into two generationally segregated congregations – one of them ethnic, comprising the immigrant fathers and mothers, the other American, comprising their sons and daughters.[21] Similar patterns of segregation along generational lines also affected local lodges of mutual benefit societies and other ethnic organizations.

The observations made above underscore the most important difference in ethnic orientation between fathers and sons. While the sons treated ethnicity as something to be evaluated, manipulated or even dispensed with at will, the fathers still continued to live by it and, in the process of doing so, imperceptibly but necessarily changed and modified it. In the case of the fathers, ethnicity retained the basic mark of any genuine tradition. In the case of the sons, it simply ceased being a complete pattern of daily life.

It is impossible to assess how many and precisely what elements of ethnicity were considered by the sons as unworthy of retention. The mother tongue was certainly one of them, since there is convincing evidence to show that in many instances the sons even vehemently disapproved of teaching it to their own children in ethnic schools.[22] Differences in this respect existed from one ethnic group to another and certainly from one second generation individual to another. There is hardly any doubt, however, that the attitude of many sons verged on outright nihilism; that is, they tended to dismiss their respective ethnic heritages *in toto*, either by equating them with ignorance and superstition, or by equating them with poverty and backwardness. Their crude attack on the ancestral tradition and on the purportedly degrading enslavement of their parents to it, although pronounced in the name of reason, closely resembled the breathless fervour of religious conversion experience.[23] To appreciate the tragic predicament in which some of the sons found themselves, it suffices to point out that the more intensely they despised their ethnic heritage the more conscious they were of their ethnic identity. The more ashamed they were of this past, and even of their parents, the more they were aware of their ethnic background. For it should be kept in mind that by suppressing ethnicity the sons also rebelled against parts of themselves. If they insisted, for example, that English be introduced in the church services and sermons, it was not primarily because they were unable to understand the mother tongue, but because they sought to eliminate it from public use. Even today, one may encounter second generation individuals who relish in protesting that they remember but a few phrases of their mother tongue. Yet it is far from surprising to find that these 'few phrases' may miraculously expand on appropriate occasions into relatively fluent command of the conversational language.

What was the nature of the sons' ethnic identification if, at the same time, they scoffed at their own ethnic heritage? In what ways did the sons relate themselves to their fathers if they disparaged or despised many personal attributes possessed by their fathers? How did the sons identify themselves with their respective ethnic groups if they were bent on eliminating the very ties that bound them to these groups? The questions posed here raise a myriad of fascinating problems bearing on individual and group identification. A relatively simple and hardly adequate answer would be to suggest that the sons simply severed all the ties (personal and organizational) binding them to their respective ethnic groups. There can be no doubt that many second generation individuals did precisely that. At the same time, there is evidence to suspect that even those sons who were most intent on eliminating or suppressing the ethnic heritage frequently retained some kind of connection with ethnicity.

One suggestive way of approaching the problem raised above is to hypothesize that the ethnic orientation of the sons did not need to be expressed only via the acceptance of such obvious and specific strains of the ancestral heritage as folk customs and traditions. Rather, it might have been expressible via identification with selected and quite abstract values and ideals that ostensibly symbolized the ancestral heritage. Drawing mainly, though not exclusively, upon Jewish sources, the few illustrations that follow should further clarify this peculiar mode of orientation toward ethnicity.

In two symposia dealing with American-Jewish intellectuals, published in *Contemporary Jewish Records*[24] and *Commentary*[25] one central and recurrent theme is readily discernible. The editor of *Commentary* somewhat tauntingly summarized this theme as follows:

> Believing . . . that the essence of Judaism is the struggle for universal justice and human brotherhood, these young intellectuals assert over and over again that anyone who fights for this ideal is to that degree more Jewish than a man who merely observes the rituals or identifies himself with the Jewish community.[26]

Some of the participants in the two symposia go so far as to claim that the more thoroughly one divests oneself from ancestral tradition the more one reaffirms the 'essence of Judaism', i.e. the more qualified one becomes to play the rôle of spokesman for 'rational social change' or for a 'rationally organized democratic world society unfettered by parochial traditions and superstitions'.[27] Even more, the very estrangement from ancestral tradition was proclaimed to be a virtue in that it fostered

> a critical sense out of rôle of detachment; it is, if you will, the assumption of the rôle of prophet . . . the one of whom the Hebrew assayist Akhad Ha-am has written: ' . . . he is a man of truth! He sees life as it is with a view unwarped by subjective feelings; and he tells you what he sees just as he sees it, unaffected by irrelevant considerations!'[28]

It is only too evident that this kind of Judaism, so eagerly embraced by some sons, was not received from their natural fathers through a process of transmission from generation to generation. It may be traced to the most diverse sources – to Amos and Maimonides, to Marx and Trotsky, or even to Hess and Buber – but hardly to the Jewishness of the Torah-centred *shtetl* of their own fathers and mothers. In fact, any of these remote ancestors could have equally linked the sons to their respective versions of Judaism. In the twenties and thirties, for example, Marx and Trotsky helped many an uprooted son along the road of return to the fold of Judaism, since they supposedly symbolized the struggle for 'universal justice' and 'human brotherhood'. Many other and widely divergent versions of Judaism were entertained by the sons.

For example, those who were more intellectually oriented eagerly reminded themselves and all who would listen that:

> Judaism remained the only culture beside the Greek which believed in learning for its own sake and which honoured the sage more than it did the plutocrat. This too was effective, for 'bourgeois standards' constituted another of our violent hatreds.[29]

It would be of little value to inquire whether any of these conceptions of Judaism are *historically valid*. What is certain is the fact that the French, Greeks, Poles, Czechs, Norwegians, Hungarians, indeed, well-nigh all ethnic groups, have unearthed in their collective pasts analogous values and ideals. Greek–American publications abound in references to the distinguished ancestors of all the Greeks; they incessantly remind their readers of such 'essential' attributes of the Greek heritage as being the 'cradle of Western culture', and first lighting the 'torch of democracy'. Poles equally pride themselves on the daring exploits of their forefathers on behalf of freedom and justice; in fact, they have long been stereotyped as perennial freedomfighters. Sister Mary Ligouri readily established the 'ideal link' between the United States and Poland in these telling words:

> The undying love of freedom in the heart of a Pole equalises him with his fellow-American who cherished liberty from the earliest days of the settlements here. The Pole will give his life for liberty whenever war is being waged for its preservation. Like the average soldier of the present day, the Pole is fighting on every battle-field. The Pole is a 'genuine' soldier. He stood the test of heroism time and time again for the world's freedom, for love of his own patria.[30]

Very similar attempts have repeatedly been made by American ethnic groups to provide themselves with a *bilateral line of descent* by tracing their origins to the American colonial past as well as to their 'classical' antiquity. Many of these groups have successfully discovered distinguished ancestors among the contemporaries of John Smith, George Washington and Abraham Lincoln. Recurrent rallies and pageants serve to reaffirm periodically the values that are avowedly associated with these ancestors. Poles delight in recalling the words of Lincoln, who is purported to have addressed Polish soldiers of the Army of the Potomac as follows:

> My friends, it has been a privilege to meet and greet everyone of you . . . in the veins of every Pole flows the blood of your heroic

ancestors – your soldierly qualities are therefore inherent... The United States has deep feeling and sympathy for Poland and the hospitality of our shores shall always be open to her sons... We shall not fail to reward those who aided us in conquering a foe who espouses slavery and would destroy our republic.[31]

Students of American ethnic groups disagree among themselves as to whether the *creators* of this kind of past are recruited from among the educated immigrant fathers, their sons, or grandsons. Some suggest that the sons could hardly be history-minded since they were much too touchy about their foreign background.[32] On the other hand, the grandsons, much more secure in their Americanness, displayed an increasing interest and pride in their ethnic origins. But what is significant in this context is not so much the generational composition of the authors as the peculiar affinity between this highly selected and transmuted past and the touchy attitude evinced by the sons and daughters of immigrants toward their ancestral background. Undoubtedly the uneasy and, at times, derogatory attitude of the sons toward the heritage of their close ancestors – their own fathers and mothers – made them prone to fall back upon the heritage of remote ancestors – from Pericles to Marx, from Columbus to Kosciusko. Similarly, the sons' hyphenated status predisposed them to define their ethnic ancestry in terms of a bilateral rule of descent, selectively American on one side and selectively ethnic on the other. These considerations strongly suggest first of all that the immigrant sons sought to disavow those *tangible* elements of traditional ethnicity to which they had been directly exposed in their parental homes. They indicate, secondly, that the more determined they were to be weaned from those aspects of ethnicity which had been transmitted to them by their natural fathers, the more inclined they were to embrace the *intangible* values attributed to the distant past of their adopted fathers. The more predisposed they were to equate the heritage of their own fathers with ignorance and provinciality the more readily they identified themselves with those ethnically related values which somehow transcended the actual heritage of their fathers. Such a mode of orientation toward ethnicity required neither attachment to nor personal involvement in the parental heritage. In this sense, indeed, the ethnic identification of the sons may be said to resemble another kind of identification, namely, that with the proletarian class. By this we mean that it is possible for some individuals to identify intensely with the proletarian class and also disavow particular proletarians of this same class. Moreover, it is possible to deride the interests of particular proletarians, or even to dismiss them individually as typical representatives of the *Lumpenproletariat*, and, at the same time, attribute to or derive from the proletarian class (as collectivity) lofty and noble values and ideals. Similarly, individuals may symbolically relate themselves to their respective ethnic groups, as many a populist has done with regard to the peasantry throughout modern history, and equally brand particular peasants as 'superstitious', 'narrow-minded', and 'ignorant'. In all these instances the mode of identification seems to be characteristically ambivalent, since it allows the individuals to pride themselves on their connection with national or social collectivities in *abstracto* and also despise and be ashamed of their association with these same people in *concreto*.

While estranged from the parental heritage, the sons, nevertheless, remained more *conscious* of their ethnic identity than were their immigrant fathers. For the ethnic identity of the fathers was so much taken for granted and accepted implicitly that they were scarcely explicitly conscious of it. On the other hand, the marginality of the sons made them acutely self-conscious and also highly sensitive to it; especially when passing through adolescence. Some of them became more 'Yankeeized' than the Yankees themselves; others turned into more ardent ethnics than their immigrant fathers had ever been. Such a bifurcated orientation toward ethnicity seems to have typically been resolved by the sons in two ways: they either completely estranged themselves from ethnicity – by changing their names or even marrying 'hundred per cent Americans' – or vehemently reasserted their loyalty to it.[33] Yet even if it be admitted that this latter mode of response led some sons to extensive involvement in organized ethnic life, helping thereby to salvage many an immigrant organization from imminent extinction, there is little evidence that the maintenance of such tangible elements of ethnicity as the mother tongue was in any way affected by it.[34]

Viewed in the light of the foregoing analysis, it should become apparent why traditional ethnicity – and the mother tongue in particular – was made virtually inaccessible to the daily life of the generation of grandsons. Of course, to the extent that the grandsons continued to be involved in ethnic organizations they could not but remain exposed to organizationally sustained vestiges of ethnicity. But such exposure was obviously selective, intermittent and limited only to narrowly circumscribed segments of life. The generational discontinuity between the formative experiences and the dominant environments of most immigrant fathers and sons rendered the family ineffective as an agency for the transmission of traditional ethnicity. So pronounced was this generational gap that by the time the sons reached adolescence the immigrant family had become transformed into two linguistic sub-groups segregated along generational lines.[35] The grandsons literally became outsiders to their ancestral heritage, even though many of them attended churches and schools established by the immigrant fathers. By then the ethnic mother tongue had come to resemble another foreign language which one studied in school as a required subject. There was no doubt about the national identity of the grandson – they were simply Americans of one particular (if not of mixed) ethnic ancestry. Neither was there any trace left of the 'wounded identity' of the sons, for in constrast to the sons, the grandsons had never experienced the full brunt of marginality. The grandsons neither sought to disavow nor rushed to embrace their ethnic past. Increasingly it came to approximate an object of cognitive orientation, something that the grandsons had to study in order to acquire 'knowledge about' it and in order to 'appreciate' it. But such knowledge and appreciation is usually kept within reasonable bounds and need have little or no relevance to daily life – from the selection of spouses to personal and organizational associations.

CONCLUDING REMARKS

In this essay we have explored the generational shift in ethnic identification. By doing so we hope to have shown how much remains to be accomplished in the way of clarifying the relevant dimensions of ethnic identification. More substantively, however, we have been primarily concerned with specifying the differences in the mode of orientation toward ethnicity between the immigrant fathers, their sons and their grandsons. A case has also been made for the contention that the very disengagement of the sons from the ethnic heritage resulted from their heightened ethnic sensitivity. Thus we came to a somewhat paradoxical conclusion that despite acculturation, as reflected in the abandonment of the ethnic mother tongue and many other ethnic patterns of behaviour – the sons continued to remain acutely conscious of their ethnic identity. It is likely that under different social conditions more of these same acculturated sons might have embraced ethnicity as a cause.

Notes

1. Joshua A. Fishman *et al.*, *Language Loyalty in the United States* (New York, Yeshiva University, 1964). (A mimeographed report in three volumes prepared under contract SAE – 8729 with the Language Research Section, US Office of Education, DHEW.)
2. M. L. Hansen, 'The Third Generation in America,' *Commentary*, (November 14, 1962), p. 496. The full text of Hansen's essay is Chapter 13 in *Theories of Ethnicity*.
3. Hansen, 'The Third Generation', p. 495; *Theories*, p. 205.
4. Hansen, 'The Third Generation', see also Nathan Glazer: 'Ethnic Groups in America: From National Culture to Ideology,' in Morroe Berger *et al.* (eds), *Freedom and Control in Modern Society* (New York: Octagon Books, Inc., 1964), p. 170.
5. See Ludwig Geismar, 'A Scale for the Measurement of Ethnic Identification', *Jewish Social Studies*, 16 (January 1954), pp. 33–60; Bernard Lazarowitz, 'Some factors in Jewish Identification', *Jewish Social Studies*, 15 (January 1953), pp. 3–24.
6. See, e.g. Irvin L. Child, *Italian or American? The Second Generation in Conflict* (New Haven: Yale University Press, 1943).
7. Hansen, 'The Third Generation', p. 494.
8. See Einar Haugen, 'The Norwegian Language in America,' I, pp. 191–232, *Names in a New World* (Philadelphia: University of Pennsylvania Press, 1953), for ample evidence that this was not purely a southern and eastern European pattern.
9. Reverend Casimir P. Sirvaitis, *Religious Folkways in Lithuania and their Conservation Among the Lithuanian Immigrants in the United States*, Ph.D. dissertation, Catholic University of America (1945), p. 661.
10. Daniel Glazer, 'Dynamics of Ethnic Identification', *American Sociological Review*, 23 (February 1958), p. 31.
11. Glazer, 'Dynamics' p. 31.
12. Franciszek Bujak, *Zmiaca – Wies Powiatu Limanowskiego: Stosunki Gospodarcze i Spoleczne* (Krakow: G. Gebethner, 1903), p. 131. For similar evidence concerning German, Hungarian and Mexican immigrants to the United States see J. A. Fishman *et al. Language Loyalty in the United States*, Chapters 15, 16, 17 and 19.
13. Underlying the symbolic–categorical approach to ethnic identification is the assumption that individuals 'act' and 'feel' ethnically to the extent to which they identify themselves with appropriate ethnic collectivities. This approach overlooks the fact that individuals may 'act' and 'feel' ethnically by simply identifying with their own mothers, fathers and neighbours, without being conscious of any ethnic category or larger collectivity. In a similar vein, of course, individuals may act and feel like working class people without ever consciously identifying with the proletarian class, or even being aware of its existence.
14. John S. Macdonald and Beatrice D. Macdonald, 'Chain Migration Ethnic Neighborhood Formation and Social Networks', *Milbank Memorial Fund Quarterly*, 42 (January 1964), p. 88.
15. Jacob Hodnefeld, 'Norwegian – American *Bygdelags* and Their Publica-

tions', *Norwegian–American Studies and Records*, 18 (1954), p. 171.

16. We know but little (in terms of empirical details or dynamic theory) about the conditions under which such plural and parochial ethnic values and symbols are transformed into or replaced by a singular set of national ones. To be sure, there is no reason to assert that any ethnic group's awareness of its 'corporate' past must necessarily swallow up its particular parochial awareness. There is, however, some historical evidence to suggest that the emergence of one national past entails the weakening of plural local pasts. At the time of the French Revolution the idea of *la patrie* symbolized one single nation and also stood in opposition to the alleged diversity of the *ancien regime*. The Jacobin nationalists vociferously attacked all local customs and traditions, probably on the assumption that the individual's commitment to central national values cannot but be weak as long as parochial attachments remain strong.

17. Iaroslav Rudnytskyi, *Materialy do Ukrainsko-Kanadiiskoi Folklorystyky i Diialektolohii* (Winnipeg, Ukrainska Vilna Akademiia Nauk, 1958), p. 424.

18. *Deutsch–Amerikanische Geschichtsblaetter*, 2 (1902), p. 34.

19. Gerald H. Thorson, *America is not Norway: The Story of the Norwegian–American Novel*, Ph.D. dissertation, Columbia University (1957), p. 20.

20. 'Language Maintenance in a Supra-Ethnic Age', in J. A. Fishman *et al.*, *Language Loyalty in the United States*, Chapter 22.

21. 'Mother Tongue Retentiveness in Ethnic Parishes', in J. A. Fishman *et al.*, *Language Loyalty in the United States*, Chapter 9.

22. 'The Ethnic Group School in the United States', in J. A. Fishman *et al.*, *Language Loyalty in the United States*, Chapter 6.

23. This kind of revolt against traditional ethnicity in the second generation has most frequently been recognized in connection with individuals of Jewish ethnic background. Usually, this phenomenon has received literary treatment only. For a more research oriented treatment see Jessie Bernard: 'Biculturality: A Study in Social Schizophrenia', in I. Graeber and S. H. Briff (eds.) *Jews in a Gentile World* (New York: Macmillan, 1942), pp. 264–293.

24. 'Under Forty: A Symposium on American Literature and the Younger Generation of American Jews', *Contemporary Jewish Record*, 7 (February 1944), pp. 3–36.

25. 'Jewishness and the Younger Intellectuals: A Symposium', *Commentary*, 31 (April 1961), pp. 306–359.

26. 'Jewishess', p. 310.

27. 'Jewishess', p. 312.

28. Daniel Bell, 'A Parable of Alienation', *The Jewish Frontier*, 13 (November 1946), p. 19.

29. Norman Podhoretz, 'Jewish Culture and the Intellectuals', *Commentary*, 19 (1955), p. 453.

30. Sister Mary Liguori, 'The Most Ideal Link Between the United States and Poland,' *Polish American Studies*, 2 (July–December 1945), p. 67.

31. 'Polish Rally to Recall Civil War', *The Christian Science Monitor* (February 1, 1963), p. 4.

32. John J. Appel, 'Hansen's Third Generation 'Law' and the Origins of the

American–Jewish Historical Society,' *Jewish Social Studies*, 23 (January 1961), p. 3.

33. This latter form of ethnic identification on the part of some sons, originally documented by I. L. Child, *Italian or American? The Second Generation in Conflict*, has recently been uncovered again by Wallace E. Lambert of McGill University. See his recent report 'A Study of the Rôle of Attitudes and Motivations in Second Language Learning' (Montreal: McGill University, 1962).

34. 'Language Maintenance Among Cultural and Organizational Leaders of Four Ethnic Groups', in J. A. Fishman *et al.*, Chapter 2.

35. 'Community and Family Dynamics of Language Maintenance', in J. A. Fishman *et al.*, *Language Loyalty in the United States*, Chapter 12.

17 Kinship, Nationality and Religion in American Culture: Toward a Definition of Kinship (1969)

David M. Schneider*

Kinship has traditionally been defined in Anthropology in terms of certain concrete elements, relations of blood and marriage, or in terms of some set of functional prerequisites to which those concrete elements are crucial. Thus Morgan deals with kinship in terms of relations of consanguinity and affinity, Malinowski in terms of how sexual relations are regulated and how the family is formed, that unit being defined as primarily concerned with the problems of reproduction, socialization and social placement. Levy, in line with Malinowski, defined kinship with reference to the facts of biological relatedness and/or sexual relations, and his view is not very different from that of Gellner in this respect (Gellner, 1957, 1960; Levy, 1965; Malinowski, 1930).

In these views the facts of biological relatedness and sexual relations are treated as scientifically demonstrable facts of life and the question that is asked centers on how the particular society organizes its cultural forms with respect to these facts of life. These facts are treated as having determinate or causal value, imposing certain sharp, clear limits on whatever forms may be posed with respect to them. Thus a tribe of Australian Aborigines, the Trobriand or Yap islanders may deny the causal link between coitus and conception in their cultural forms, but if their beliefs call a complete halt to coitus it can be shown that they could hardly survive long as a society.

Whatever the legitimacy or productivity of this way of dealing with kinship, it seemed to me that there was another view which might be worth pursuing. This view is implicit in much anthropological think-

* From Victor Turner (ed.), *Forms of Symbolic Action* (New Orleans: American Ethnological Society, Tulane University, 1969), pp. 116–25.

ing, but was made most explicitly to me by Parsons (1951). In this view culture is defined as a system of symbols and meanings. That is, any given culture is seen to consist in a system of units and their interrelations, and these contain the fundamental definitions of the nature of the world, of what life is like, of man's place in it. Instead of asking how a society is organized so as to assure its continuity over time, one asks instead of what units it is built, how these units are defined and differentiated, how they articulate one with another. And one asks what meanings such a state of affairs has and how those meanings may be spelled out into patterns for action.

Studying American kinship from this point of view yielded some results which proved to be rather different from those deriving from the traditional functional or the traditional 'consanguinity and affinity' or 'facts of biological relatedness and/or sexual relations' views. For indeed, the fundamental question was how kinship was defined in American culture, not the question of how those externally devised definitions partitioned the material of American culture.

The purpose of this paper is to ask whether the results of the study of American kinship from this point of view are of any value in helping us to understand the nature of kinship and to define it most usefully for analytic purposes.

Perhaps the most important point to be made about American kinship is that there is a fundamental distinction between the distinctive features of kinship on the one hand and the kinsman as a person on the other (Schneider, 1968). The former embodies those aspects which distinguish kinship from any other domain of American culture – the domain of kinship as distinct from commerce, politics, friendship, etc. Those features which distinguish kinship from other domains are necessarily present in any of its parts as these are further differentiated. Thus although mother, father, brother and sister are all different kinds of kinsmen, each is a kinsman as against the storekeeper, the mayor or the policeman, and as kinsmen all share the distinctive features of kinship.

The distinctive features of the domain of kinship in American culture can be abstracted from a consideration of the classification of the different kinds of relatives.

There are two kinds of relatives in American culture. There are those related 'by blood' and those related 'by marriage.'

'Blood' or blood-relationship is the outcome of a single act of sexual intercourse which brings together sperm and egg and creates a child. Mother and father are thus related to the child by the fact that they create it and that the child is created out of material substance which each contributes. 'Blood' is thus a state of shared physical substance. This shared physical substance is an 'objective fact of nature,' a natural phenomena, a concrete or substantive part of nature. And this 'objective fact of nature' cannot be terminated for it endures. A blood relationship is a relationship of identity, and those who share a blood relationship share a common identity. The phrase 'the same flesh and blood' is a statement of this.

Where 'blood' is a substance, a material thing whose constitution is whatever it is that is really in nature, and a natural entity which endures and cannot be terminated, 'marriage' is just the opposite. It is not a material thing or a substance in the same sense as biogenetic heredity is. It is not a 'natural thing' in the sense of a material object found free in nature. As a state of affairs it is of course natural, but it is not in itself a natural object. And it is terminable by death or divorce. Where blood is a natural material, marriage is not; where blood endures, marriage is terminable; and since there is no such 'thing' as blood of which marriage consists, and since there is no such material which exists free in nature, persons related by marriage are not related 'in nature.'

If relatives 'by marriage' are not related 'in nature' how are they related? They are related by 'a relationship,' that is, by the fact that they follow a particular code for conduct, a particular pattern for behavior. It is in this sense that a stepmother is not a 'real' mother, not the genetrix, but she is in a mother-child relationship to her husband's child.

The distinctive feature which defines the order of blood relatives is blood, a natural substance and blood relatives are thus 'related by nature.' This, I suggest, is but a special instance within the larger class of *the natural order* of things as defined by American culture. That is, the natural order is the way things are in nature, and one special class of things in the natural order consists in blood relatives.

Correspondingly, the feature which alone distinguishes relatives 'by marriage' or 'in law' is their relationship, the pattern for their behavior, the code for their conduct. This, I suggest, is a special instance within the larger class of *the order of law*, which is opposed to *the order of nature*. The order of law is imposed by man and consists in rules and regulations, customs and traditions. It is law in its special sense, where a foster parent who fails to care properly for a child can be brought to court, and it is law in its most general sense of law and order, custom, the rule of law, the government of action by morality and the restraint of human reason.

The domain of kinship, then, consists of two major parts, and each of these parts is but a special case of the two major orders of which the world is composed, the order of nature and the order of law. And it is this, of course, which makes sense of the fact that those who are relatives 'by marriage' are also called 'in-laws,' for they are related through the order of law, not through the order of nature.

In fact of course the complete typology of kinds of relatives distinguished by American culture is built out of these two elements; *relationship as natural substance* and *relationship as code for conduct*. These two elements combine to make three major categories as follows:

Relatives	*Nature*	*Law*
(1) **In Nature** the natural child, the illegitimate child, the natural mother, etc.	+	−
(2) **In Law** Husband, wife, step-in-law, etc.	−	+
(3) **By Blood** father, mother, brother, sister, uncle, aunt, etc. etc.	+	+

Blood is a matter of birth, birth a matter of procreation, and procreation a matter of sexual intercourse. Sexual intercourse as an act of procreation creates the blood relationship of parent and child and makes genitor and genetrix out of husband and wife. And sexual intercourse is an act in which and through which love is expressed; indeed, it is often called 'making love,' and love is an explicit cultural symbol in American kinship.

There are two kinds of love in American kinship. One can be called *conjugal love*, the other *cognatic love*. Conjugal love is erotic, having the sexual act as its concrete embodiment. Cognatic love, on the contrary is not an act but a state of affairs and marks the blood relationship, the identity of natural substance which obtains between parent and child. Cognatic love has nothing erotic about it. The conjugal love of husband and wife is the opposite of the cognatic love of parent, child and sibling. One is the union of opposites, the other the unity which identities have, the sharing of biogenetic substance.

It is the symbol of love which links conjugal and cognatic love together and relates them both to and through the symbol of sexual intercourse. Love in the sense of sexual intercourse is a natural act with natural consequences according to its cultural definition. And love in the sense of sexual intercourse at the same time stands for unity.

Finally, the contrast between home and work brings out aspects which complete the picture of the distinctive features of kinship in American culture. This can best be understood in terms of the contrast between love and money which stand from home and work. Indeed, what one does at home, it is said, one does for love, not for money, while what one does at work one does strictly for money, not for love. Money is material, it is power, it is impersonal and universalistic, unqualified by considerations of sentiment and morality. Relations of work and money are temporary, transient, contingent. Love on the other hand is highly personal and particularistic, and beset with considerations of sentiment and morality. Where love is spiritual money is material. Where love is enduring and without qualification, money is transient and contingent. And finally, it is personal considerations which are paramount in love – who the person is, not how well he performs, while with work and money it does not matter who he is, but only how well he performs his task. Money is in this sense impersonal.

The facts of biological relatedness and sexual relations play a fundamental role in American kinship, for they are symbols, culturally formulated symbols in terms of which a system of social relationships is defined and differentiated. The beliefs about the facts of biological relatedness and sexual relations constitute a model in terms of which a series of conditions about the nature of kinship or about a domain of social relationships are stated. The statement of identity in terms of flesh and blood between mother and child, whatever significance the actual biological relations may have, is at the same time a symbolic statement of the kind of social relationship between them.

Once the symbolic significance of biological relatedness and sexual relations is perceived it becomes immediately apparent that an enormous number of other symbols might operate with almost equal effect for defining the domain of kinship and for providing for the internal differentiation of elements within that system.

And if it is indeed true that whatever it is that we are calling 'kinship' might equally well be defined and differentiated in terms of any number of other symbols, we seem to have lost all hold on something we think of as 'kinship in general,' for if it could be anything how can it be something in particular?

But at this juncture there are some other important points to be made before we consider the question of definition. The problem that arises now is that of the boundary of the American kinship system. Where does kinship leave off and something else begin? Let us return to the problem with this question in mind.

The different symbols of American kinship seem to say one thing; they are all concerned with unity of some kind. The unity of those related by blood, of those joined in love, of the parent and child in the face of the child's growing up and going off to found a family of his own, of man and woman as husband and wife and so on. All of these different kinds of unity are expressed as the unity of substance or the unity required by a code for conduct.

Put somewhat differently, all of the symbols of American kinship seem to 'say' one thing; they provide for relationships of diffuse, enduring solidarity. 'Diffuse' because they are functionally diffuse rather than specific in Parsons' terms. That is, where the 'job' is to get a specific thing 'done' there is no such specific limitation on the aim or goal of any kinship relationship. Instead the goal is 'solidarity,' that is, the 'good' or 'well being' or 'benefit' of ego with alter. Whatever it is that is 'good for' the family, the spouse, the child, the relative, etc. is the 'right' thing to do. And 'enduring' in the generalized sense symbolized by 'blood'; there is no built-in termination point or termination date. Indeed, it 'is' and cannot be terminated. But although a marital relationship can be terminated by death or divorce, it is, as the saying goes, 'til death do us part,' it is supposed to endure and persevere and it is not to be regarded as transient or temporary or conditional.

The phrase 'diffuse, enduring solidarity' is mine. The natives do not use it and although some of them understand it when I explain it to them, it falls like jargon on their ears. Which it should, of course, for that is just what it is.

Yet this generalization permits us to look at American culture and ask, Is this the only domain of diffuse, enduring solidarity? and see that the obvious answer is No! There are at least two others which obviously fit that description. One is called 'nationality,' the other 'religion.'

In American culture, one is 'An American' either by birth or through a process which is called, appropriately enough, 'naturalization.' In precisely the same terms as kinship, there are the same two 'kinds of citizens,' those by birth and those by law. And indeed it would not be hard to show that the same three categories are derived from these two elements as three categories of kinsmen are derived from those elements. There is the person who is by birth an American but who has taken the citizenship of another country; there is the person who is American by naturalization but not by birth; and there is the person who by both birth and law is American.

What is the role of a national? To love his country, his father- or mother-land. Loyalty and support for his nation and all those who belong to it. Patriotism in the extreme of 'My Country Right or Wrong' is one statement of it. But even where it does not take that particular form, loyalty to and love for one's country is the most generalized expression of diffuse, enduring solidarity.

I will not pursue this in any further detail. My point is not to demonstrate incontestably that kinship and nationality are structured in identical terms, but rather to make a plausible enough case for this so that we can consider its implications for the question of how to frame a useful definition of kinship.

One argument that might be presented against the view that kinship and nationality are structured in terms of the same set of symbols is that kinship contains things like family, uncle, in-laws and so forth which do not have corresponding elements within the domain of nationality. States, counties, towns and so forth do not seem at first glance like family, uncle or in-laws etc.

This argument brings us back to the opening statement in the description of American kinship; there is a fundamental difference between the distinctive features of kinship on the one hand and the relative as a person on the other.

As I have tried to show elsewhere (1968, 57–75), the structuring of the relative as a person is the outcome of the intersection of a series of different elements from different symbol systems of which kinship, age, sex, and class are but four among others, and only one of which is 'kinship' in a 'pure' sense. For example, not only is 'father' a kinsman, but he is also male and the cultural definition of his maleness derives from the sex-identity symbol system; he is also older and those aspects of his definition as older derive from the age symbol system, and so forth.

What I am saying here is really quite simple but perhaps it appears

to be somewhat radical. I am saying that what we have heretofore
regarded as the single domain of kinship is really made up of two distinct domains. One is a 'pure' domain of kinship per se which has as
its defining element a single symbol, coitus (Schneider 1968:30–54).
The second is that domain which has traditionally been regarded as
the domain of kinship, the system of person-based definitions. I
believe that the importance of the difference between the 'pure' domain of kinship and the 'conglomerate' part has not been sufficiently
appreciated.[1]

Now let us go back to the problem which is raised by comparing
what seems at first glance to be the internal differentiation of the domains of kinship and nationality and finding them apparently quite
disparate, the one being cast in apparently genealogical terms, the other
in terms of states, cities, counties and so on.

Once the distinction between the 'pure' and the 'conglomerate' domains of kinship is appreciated, the same distinction can be applied to
nationality. It is not nationality as it applies to what makes a person a
resident of a county for purposes of meeting the relief requirements
that is at issue. It is instead the comparison of the domains of kinship
and nationality as 'pure' domains, each defined in terms of a single
symbol or a single set of closely interlocked symbols. At this level
these are internally undifferentiated domains, and it is in these terms
that their identity is being postulated.

Let us turn now to religion and consider the situation there. As a conven-
ience, and purely for the purposes of this paper, I assume that 'religion'
means the Judeo-Christian tradition. I know that this hardly exhausts
the many different beliefs that are to be found in America, not the least
of which I call 'devout atheism.' But once again my aim is not to try to
exhaust the material to show indisputably that kinship, nationality and
religion are all the same thing, but rather to build that case for what it
may suggest with regard to the problem of defining kinship.

There is a special problem, too, in that there is an historical continuity to the relationship between the Jewish and Christian traditions.
At the same time both co-exist in America and their co-existence as
well as their historical relations pose special problems.

In the tradition of Judaism nation, state and kinship group are one,
and certainly the identity between kinship and nationality in Judaism
is very clear. To be a Jew one's mother must be Jewish even if one's
father is not, and to be converted to Judaism is not an easy thing.
Thus the modern state of Israel has encountered a number of problems
which arise from this special view that anyone who is by birth a Jew

is also necessarily by nationality a Jew and correspondingly a Jew by religious definition.[2]

With Christianity, as is well known the criterion for membership shifted from birth to volition. That is, in the most general sense, one is a Christian by an act of faith and not an act of birth, and correspondingly conversion to The Faith becomes a very different matter and a real possibility since it takes only an act of will to effect.

But this view leaves out two very important facts. Being a Jew is not simply being born a Jew. There is a code for conduct which is linked to the fact of birth. What is true is that it is the act of birth which has the quality of the defining feature, and so the other element tends to be easily overlooked. And it is here that the parallel between kinship and religion in Judaism is quite clear, for in both there are those two features, relationship as substance and relationship as code for conduct; the substance element is bio-genetic, the code for conduct is one of diffuse, enduring solidarity.

Although the shift from Judaism to Christianity seems to drop the condition of substance as the defining feature and rest it entirely on the commitment to the code for conduct, this is not really so. Certainly there is a shift away from the particularistic, bio-genetic, criterion of substance as the defining features. But the shift entails a re-alignment so that commitment to the code for conduct becomes paramount as the defining feature, and the substantive element is re-defined from a material to a spiritual form. It is the triumph of the spirit over matter that is at issue here. Closely linked to this is the prominent place given to love as a symbol, to the spiritual aspects of love, and to the spiritual aspects of creation as against its rather more narrowly material or bio-genetic aspects in Judaism.

The prevalence of the symbol of 'love' in Christianity, the prevalence of the use of kinship terms in Christianity, the importance or such concepts as 'faith' and 'trust' and 'belief' all testify, to me at least, that the domain of religion may well be structured in the same terms as kinship and nationality, and the historical fact that Judaism is indeed so clearly defined as one nation, one religion, and one family suggests to me that there may be something in what I say.

Let me add one more point. If Judaism is the clearest and simplest case where kinship, religion and nationality are all a single domain, then the transformation of Christianity centers on the separation of a natural and a supernatural element, so that kinship becomes differentiated as being based on relationship as natural substance religion as relationship as supernatural (spiritual) substance. In other words, kinship and religion are more highly differentiated in Christianity than in Judaism, and this differentiation depends on a different form of the distinction between supernatural and natural.[3]

There is certainly no doubt in my mind that I am far out of my depth in this discussion. I am no theologian and have little command of this material. If I were pressed to spell this out in detail I would have to resign from the discussion. On the other hand, once again, I am merely trying to make a plausible enough case for the guess that religion (in the Judeo–Christian tradition) is defined in the same terms as kinship so that this can be taken into consideration in trying to reach a useful definition of kinship.

But once again we are faced with the problem of the double-domain, for at one level it is certainly indisputable that people tend to join the church of their parents and they are in this sense born to a church as they are born to a family, and this is hardly an act of volition at this level. And if one takes even a passing look at the bureaucratic organization of some churches or synagogues many of the highest ideals are systematically transformed into petty schismatic differences. The internal differentiation of any particular religious organization or set of beliefs is one thing; the domain of religion I would suggest quite another. There is the 'pure' domain of religion which I am comparing to that of kinship and nationality and there is the internally differentiated 'conglomerate' domain which I am not.

Let me summarize the argument briefly. From a close study of American kinship it seems clear that this particular system depends first on a distinction between the 'pure' domain of kinship, defined in terms of the symbol of coitus and differentiated into two major aspects, relationship as natural substance and relationship as code for conduct, and a 'conglomerate' domain of kinship, differentiated into 'the family' on one hand and an articulated system of person-defined statuses (genealogical?) on the other.

If we consider only the 'pure' domain of kinship and treat a system of diffuse, enduring solidarity, it seems possible that what is called 'nationality' and 'religion' are defined and structured in identical terms, namely, in terms of the dual aspects of relationship as natural substance and relationship as code for conduct, and that most if not all of the major diacritical marks which are found in kinship are also found in nationality and religion.

If this is true – and I repeat that I only offer it as a very tentative hypothesis – then it might well be that at the level of the 'pure' domain, religion, nationality and kinship are all the same thing (culturally), and that their differences arise through the kinds of combinations and permutations they enter into with other 'pure' domains, and at the level of the 'conglomerate' domain.

Thus far I speak only of American culture not from having carefully surveyed its precise boundaries, but precisely because I don't know what those boundaries are. Hence the next step is to generalize the view of American kinship, religion and nationality and ask how widely applicable this view may or may not be to other cultures. At the moment, and from but a small grasp of world ethnography, I would hazard the guess that this generalized view will obtain fairly widely, but this remains an empirical question which can only be answered by concrete studies.

Finally, if all this proves true, the question arises of the utility of any definition of 'kinship' until we have more fully explored the ways in which culture as a system of symbols and meanings is formed and its different parts articulated.

Notes

1. I have spoken here of two domains, one a 'pure' and one a 'conglomerate' domain. Perhaps it would be better to treat these as two parts of a single domain rather than as two different domains. But this is not my problem here, and so I will proceed simply as if the two domain mode of expression is adequate to the exposition here and leave to another time the question of one domain of two parts or two domains intimately linked.
2. This may be a convenient point to note that I have omitted from this paper considerations of race and racism, which cannot be omitted from any comprehensive or systematic review of this problem. I can refer the reader to Louis Dumont's brilliant discussions of this subject for its bearing on the questions before us and at the same time acknowledge the stimulus which his writings have provided for me, even when I have resisted his views. See his *Homo Hierarchicus* especially.
3. I think that I have absorbed this from Parsons somehow, but the closest form I have found the notion is in Parsons' article on Christianity (1968, 427).

References

Gellner, E. (1957) 'Ideal Language and Kinship Structure', *Philosophy of Science*, 24, pp. 235–242.

Gellner, E. (1960) 'The Concept of Kinship', *Philosophy of Science*, 27, pp. 187–204.

Levy, M. J., Jr. (1965) 'Aspects of the Analysis of Family Structure', in A. J. Coale *et al.*, *Aspects of the Analysis of Family Structure* (Princeton: Princeton University Press), p. 1–63.

Malinowski, B. (1930) 'Kinship', *Man*, 30, pp. 19–29.

Parsons, T. (1951) *The Social System* (Glencoe, Ill., The Free Press).

Parsons, T. (1968) 'Christianity', *The Encyclopedia of the Social Sciences*, 2, pp. 425–447.

Schneider, D. (1968) *American Kinship: A Cultural Account* (Englewood Cliffs, NJ, Prentice-Hall).

18 Ethnic Groups and Boundaries (1969)
Fredrik Barth*

This collection of essays addresses itself to the problems of ethnic groups and their persistence. This is a theme of great, but neglected, importance to social anthropology. Practically all anthropological reasoning rests on the premise that cultural variation is discontinuous: that there are aggregates of people who essentially share a common culture, and interconnected differences that distinguish each such discrete culture from all others. Since culture is nothing but a way to describe human behaviour, it would follow that there are discrete groups of people, i.e. ethnic units, to correspond to each culture. The differences between cultures, and their historic boundaries and connections have been given much attention; the constitution of ethnic groups, and the nature of the boundaries between them, have not been correspondingly investigated. Social anthropologists have largely avoided these problems by using a highly abstracted concept of 'society' to represent the encompassing social system within which smaller, concrete groups and units may be analyzed. But this leaves untouched the empirical characteristics and boundaries of ethnic groups, and the important theoretical issues which an investigation of them raises.

Though the naïve assumption that each tribe and people has maintained its culture through a bellicose ignorance of its neighbours is no longer entertained, the simplistic view that geographical and social isolation have been the critical factors in sustaining cultural diversity persists. An empirical investigation of the character of ethnic boundaries, as documented in the following essays, produces two discoveries which are hardly unexpected, but which demonstrate the inadequacy of this view. First, it is clear that boundaries persist despite a flow of personnel across them. In other words, categorical ethnic distinctions do not

---

* From 'Introduction', in Fredrik Barth, *Ethnic Groups and Boundaries: The Social Organization of Culture Difference* (Bergen: Universitetsforlag and Boston: Little, Brown & Co., 1969), pp. 9–38.

Editor's note: Some of the references in this chapter refer to contributions to the book *Ethnic Groups and Boundaries*.

depend on an absence of mobility, contact and information, but do entail social processes of exclusion and incorporation whereby discrete categories are maintained *despite* changing participation and membership in the course of individual life histories. Secondly, one finds that stable, persisting, and often vitally important social relations are maintained across such boundaries, and are frequently based precisely on the dichotomized ethnic statuses. In other words, ethnic distinctions do not depend on an absence of social interaction and acceptance, but are quite to the contrary often the very foundations on which embracing social systems are built. Interaction in such a social system does not lead to its liquidation through change and acculturation; cultural differences can persist despite inter-ethnic contact and interdependence.

GENERAL APPROACH

There is clearly an important field here in need of rethinking. What is required is a combined theoretical and empirical attack: we need to investigate closely the empirical facts of a variety of cases, and fit our concepts to these empirical facts so that they elucidate them as simply and adequately as possible, and allow us to explore their implications. In the following essays, each author takes up a case with which he is intimately familiar from his own fieldwork, and tries to apply a common set of concepts to its analysis. The main theoretical departure consists of several interconnected parts. First, we give primary emphasis to the fact that ethnic groups are categories of ascription and identification by the actors themselves, and thus have the characteristic of organizing interaction between people. We attempt to relate other characteristics of ethnic groups to this primary feature. Second, the essays all apply a generative viewpoint to the analysis: rather than working through a typology of forms of ethnic groups and relations, we attempt to explore the different processes that seem to be involved in generating and maintaining ethnic groups. Third, to observe these processes we shift the focus of investigation from internal constitution and history of separate groups to ethnic boundaries and boundary maintenance. Each of these points needs some elaboration.

ETHNIC GROUP DEFINED

The term ethnic group is generally understood in anthropological literature (cf. e.g. Narroll, 1964) to designate a population which:

1. is largely biologically self-perpetuating
2. shares fundamental cultural values, realized in overt unity in cultural forms
3. makes up a field of communication and interaction
4. has a membership which identifies itself, and is identified by others,
   as constituting a category distinguishable from other categories of
   the same order.

This ideal type definition is not so far removed in content from the
traditional proposition that a race = a culture = a language and that a
society = a unit which rejects or discriminates against others. Yet, in
its modified form it is close enough to many empirical ethnographic
situations, at least as they appear and have been reported, so that this
meaning continues to serve the purposes of most anthropologists. My
quarrel is not so much with the substance of these characteristics, though
as I shall show we can profit from a certain change of emphasis; my
main objection is that such a formulation prevents us from understanding
the phenomenon of ethnic groups and their place in human society
and culture. This is because it begs all the critical questions: while
purporting to give an ideal type model of a recurring empirical form,
it implies a preconceived view of what are the significant factors in
the genesis, structure, and function of such groups.

Most critically, it allows us to assume that boundary maintenance is
unproblematical and follows from the isolation which the itemized
characteristics imply: racial difference, cultural difference, social separation and language barriers, spontaneous and organized enmity. This
also limits the range of factors that we use to explain cultural diversity: we are led to imagine each group developing its cultural and
social form in relative isolation, mainly in response to local ecologic
factors, through a history of adaptation by invention and selective
borrowing. This history has produced a world of separate peoples, each
with their culture and each organized in a society which can legitimately be isolated for description as an island to itself.

ETHNIC GROUPS AS CULTURE-BEARING UNITS

Rather than discussing the adequacy of this version of culture history for other than pelagic islands, let us look at some of the logical flaws in the viewpoint. Among the characteristics listed above, the sharing of a common culture is generally given central importance. In my view, much can be gained by regarding this very important feature as an implication or result, rather than a primacy and definitional characteristic of ethnic group organization. If one chooses to regard the culture-bearing aspect of ethnic groups as their primary characteristic, this has far-reaching implications. One is led to identify and distinguish ethnic groups by the morphological characteristics of the cultures of which they are the bearers. This entails a prejudiced view-point both on (1) the nature of continuity in time of such units, and (2) the locus of the factors which determine the form of the units.

1. Given the emphasis on the culture-bearing aspect, the classification of persons and local groups as members of an ethnic group must depend on their exhibiting the particular traits of the culture. This is something that can be judged objectively by the ethnographic observer, in the culture-area tradition, regardless of the categories and prejudices of the actors. Differences between groups become differences in trait inventories; the attention is drawn to the analysis of cultures, not of ethnic organization. The dynamic relationship between groups will then be depicted in acculturation studies of the kind that have been attracting decreasing interest in anthropology, though their theoretical inadequacies have never been seriously discussed. Since the historical provenance of any assemblage of culture traits is diverse, the viewpoint also gives scope for an 'ethnohistory' which chronicles cultural accretion and change, and seeks to explain why certain items were borrowed. However, what is the unit whose continuity in time is depicted in such studies? Paradoxically, it must include cultures in the past which would clearly be excluded in the present because of differences in form – differences of precisely the kind that are diagnostic in synchronic differentiation of ethnic units. The interconnection between 'ethnic group' and 'culture' is certainly not clarified through this confusion.

2. The overt cultural forms which can be itemized as traits exhibit the effects of ecology. By this I do not mean to refer to the fact that they reflect a history of adaptation to environment; in a more immediate way they also reflect the external circumstances to which actors must accommodate themselves. The same group of people, with

unchanged values and ideas, would surely pursue different patterns of life and institutionalize different forms of behaviour when faced with the different opportunities offered in different environments? Likewise, we must expect to find that one ethnic group, spread over a territory with varying ecologic circumstances, will exhibit regional diversities of overt institutionalized behaviour which do not reflect differences in cultural orientation. How should they then be classified if overt institutional forms are diagnostic? A case in point is the distributions and diversity of Pathan local social systems, discussed below [see Barth, 1969, pp. 117 ff]. By basic Pathan values, a Southern Pathan from the homogeneous, lineage-organized mountain areas, can only find the behaviour of Pathans in Swat so different from, and reprehensible in terms of, their own values that they declare their northern brothers 'no longer Pathan'. Indeed, by 'objective' criteria, their overt pattern of organization seems much closer to that of Panjabis. But I found it possible, by explaining the circumstances in the north, to make Southern Pathans agree that these were indeed Pathans too, and grudgingly to admit that under those circumstances they might indeed themselves act in the same way. It is thus inadequate to regard overt institutional forms as constituting the cultural features which at any time distinguish ethnic group – these overt forms are determined by ecology as well as by transmitted culture. Nor can it be claimed that every such diversification within a group represents a first step in the direction of subdivision and multiplication of units. We have well-known documented cases of one ethnic group, also at a relatively simple level of economic organization, occupying several different ecologic niches and yet retaining basic cultural and ethnic unity over long periods (cf., e.g., inland and coastal Chuckchee (Bogoras, 1904–9) or reindeer, river, and coast Lapps (Gjessing, 1954)).

In one of the following essays, Blom [see Barth, 1969, pp. 74 ff] argues cogently on this point with reference to central Norwegian mountain farmers. He shows how their participation and self-evaluation in terms of general Norwegian values secures them continued membership in the larger ethnic group, despite the highly characteristic and deviant patterns of activity which the local ecology imposes on them. To analyse such cases, we need a viewpoint that does not confuse the effects of ecologic circumstances on behaviour with those of cultural tradition, but which makes it possible to separate these factors and investigate the non-ecological cultural and social components creating diversity.

ETHNIC GROUPS AS AN ORGANIZATIONAL TYPE

By concentrating on what is *socially* effective, ethnic groups are seen as a form of social organization. The critical feature then becomes item (4) in the list on p. 296 the characteristic of self-ascription and ascription by others. A categorical ascription is an ethnic ascription when it classifies a person in terms of his basic, most general identity, presumptively determined by his origin and background. To the extent that actors use ethnic identities to categorize themselves and others for purposes of interaction, they form ethnic groups in this organizational sense.

It is important to recognize that although ethnic categories take cultural differences into account, we can assume no simple one-to-one relationship between ethnic units and cultural similarities and differences. The features that are taken into account are not the sum of 'objective' differences, but only those which the actors themselves regard as significant. Not only do ecologic variations mark and exaggerate differences; some cultural features are used by the actors as signals and emblems of differences, others are ignored, and in some relationships radical differences are played down and denied. The cultural contents of ethnic dichotomies would seem analytically to be of two orders: (i) overt signals or sign – the diacritical features that people look for and exhibit to show identity, often such features as dress, language, house-form, or general style of life, and (ii) basic value orientations: the standards of morality and excellence by which performance is judged. Since belonging to an ethnic category implies being a certain kind of person, having that basic identity, it also implies a claim to be judged, and to judge oneself, by those standards that are relevant to that identity. Neither of these kinds of cultural 'contents' follows from a descriptive list of cultural features or cultural differences; one cannot predict from first principles which features will be emphasized and made organizationally relevant by the actors. In other words, ethnic categories provide an organizational vessel that may be given varying amounts and forms of content in different socio–cultural systems. They may be of great relevance to behaviour, but they need not be; they may pervade all social life, or they may be relevant only in limited sectors of activity. There is thus an obvious scope for ethnographic and comparative descriptions of different forms of ethnic organization.

The emphasis on ascription as the critical feature of ethnic groups also solves the two conceptual difficulties that were discussed above.

1. When defined as an ascriptive and exclusive group, the nature of continuity of ethnic units is clear: it depends on the maintenance of a boundary. The cultural features that signal the boundary may change, and the cultural characteristics of the members may likewise be transformed, indeed, even the organizational form of the group may change – yet the fact of continuing dichotomization between members and outsiders allows us to specify the nature of continuity, and investigate the changing cultural form and content.

2. Socially relevant factors alone become diagnostic for membership, not the overt, 'objective' differences which are generated by other factors. It makes no difference how dissimilar members may be in their overt behaviour – if they say they are A, in contrast to another cognate category B, they are willing to be treated and let their own behaviour be interpreted and judged as A's and not as B's; in other words, they declare their allegiance to the shared culture of A's. The effects of this, as compared to other factors influencing actual behaviour, can then be made the object of investigation.

THE BOUNDARIES OF ETHNIC GROUPS

The critical focus of investigation from this point of view becomes the ethnic *boundary* that defines the group, not the cultural stuff that it encloses. The boundaries to which we must give our attention are of course social boundaries, though they may have territorial counterparts. If a group maintains its identity when members interact with others, this entails criteria for determining membership and ways of signalling membership and exclusion. Ethnic groups are not merely or necessarily based on the occupation of exclusive territories; and the different ways in which they are maintained, not only by a once-and-for-all recruitment but by continual expression and validation, need to be analysed.

What is more, the ethnic boundary canalizes social life – it entails a frequently quite complex organization of behaviour and social relations. The identification of another person as a fellow member of an ethnic group implies a sharing of criteria for evaluation and judgement. It thus entails the assumption that the two are fundamentally 'playing the same game', and this means that there is between them a potential for diversification and expansion of their social relationship to cover eventually all different sectors and domains of activity. On the other hand, a dichotomization of others as strangers, as members of another ethnic group, implies a recognition of limitations on shared understandings, differences in criteria for judgement of value and performance, and a restriction of interaction to sectors of assumed common understanding and mutual interest.

This makes it possible to understand one final form of boundary maintenance whereby cultural units and boundaries persist. Entailed in ethnic boundary maintenance are also situations of social contact between persons of different cultures: ethnic groups only persist as significant units if they imply marked difference in behaviour, i.e. persisting cultural differences. Yet where persons of different culture interact, one would expect these differences to be reduced, since interaction both requires and generates a congruence of codes and values – in other words, a similarity or community of culture (cf. Barth 1966, for my argumentation on this point). Thus the persistence of ethnic groups in contact implies not only criteria and signals for identification, but also a structuring of interaction which allows the persistence of cultural differences. The organizational feature which, I would argue, must be general for all inter-ethnic relations is a systematic set of rules governing inter-ethnic social encounters. In all organized social life, what can be made relevant to interaction in any particular social situation is prescribed (Goffman, 1959). If people agree about these prescriptions, their agreement on codes and values need not extend beyond that which is relevant to the social situations in which they interact. Stable inter-ethnic relations presuppose such a structuring of interaction: a set of prescriptions governing situations of contact, and allowing for articulation in some sectors or domains of activity, and a set of proscriptions on social situations preventing inter-ethnic interaction in other sectors, and thus insulating parts of the cultures from confrontation and modification.

POLY-ETHNIC SOCIAL SYSTEMS

This of course is what Furnivall (1944) so clearly depicted in his analysis of plural society: a poly-ethnic society integrated in the market place, under the control of a state system dominated by one of the groups, but leaving large areas of cultural diversity in the religious and domestic sectors of activity.

What has not been adequately appreciated by later anthropologists is the possible variety of sectors of articulation and separation, and the variety of poly-ethnic systems which this entails. We know of some

of the Melanesian trade systems in objects belonging to the high-prestige
sphere of the economy, and even some of the etiquette and prescriptions governing the exchange situation and insulating it from other
activities. We have information on various traditional polycentric systems from S.E. Asia [see Izikowitz, in Barth, 1969, pp. 135ff.] integrated both in the prestige trade sphere and in quasi-feudal political
structures. Some regions of S.W. Asia show forms based on a more
fully monetized market economy, while political integration is poly-
centric in character. There is also the ritual and productive cooperation and political integration of the Indian caste system to be considered,
where perhaps only kinship and domestic life remain as a proscribed
sector and a wellspring for cultural diversity. Nothing can be gained
by lumping these various systems under the increasingly vague label
of 'plural' society, whereas an investigation of the varieties of structure can shed a great deal of light on social and cultural forms.

What can be referred to as articulation and separation on the macro-
level corresponds to systematic sets of role constraints on the micro-
level. Common to all these systems is the principle that ethnic identity
implies a series of constraints on the kinds of roles an individual is
allowed to play, and the partners he may choose for different kinds of
transactions.[1] In other words, regarded as a status, ethnic identity is
superordinate to most other statuses, and defines the permissible constellations of statuses, or social personalities, which an individual with
that identity may assume. In this respect ethnic identity is similar to
sex and rank, in that it constrains the incumbent in all his activities,
not only in some defined social situations.[2] One might thus also say
that it is *imperative*, in that it cannot be disregarded and temporarily
set aside by other definitions of the situation. The constraints on a
person's behaviour which spring from his ethnic identity thus tend to
be absolute and, in complex poly-ethnic societies, quite comprehensive; and the component moral and social conventions are made further resistant to change by being joined in stereotyped clusters as
characteristics of one single identity.

THE ASSOCIATIONS OF IDENTITIES AND VALUE
STANDARDS

The analysis of interactional and organizational features of inter-ethnic
relations has suffered from a lack of attention to problems of boundary
maintenance. This is perhaps because anthropologists have reasoned

from a misleading idea of the prototype inter-ethnic situation. One has tended to think in terms of different peoples, with different histories and cultures, coming together and accommodating themselves to each other, generally in a colonial setting. To visualize the basic require- ments for the coexistence of ethnic diversity, I would suggest that we rather ask ourselves what is needed to make ethnic distinctions *emerge* in an area. The organizational requirements are clearly, first, a categor- ization of population sectors in exclusive and imperative status cat- egories, and second, an acceptance of the principle that standards applied to one such category can be different from that applied to another. Though this alone does not explain why cultural differences emerge, it does allow us to see how they persist. Each category can then be as- sociated with a separate range of value standards. The greater the differ- ences between these value orientations are, the more constraints on inter-ethnic interaction do they entail: the statuses and situations in the total social system involving behaviour which is discrepant with a person's value orientations must be avoided, since such behaviour on his part will be negatively sanctioned. Moreover, because identities are signalled as well as embraced, new forms of behaviour will tend to be dichotomized: one would expect the role constraints to operate in such a way that persons would be reluctant to act in new ways from a fear that such behaviour might be inappropriate for a person of their identity, and swift to classify forms of activity as associated with one or another cluster or ethnic characteristics. Just as dichotomizations of male versus female work seem to proliferate in some societies, so also the existence of basic ethnic categories would seem to be a factor encouraging the proliferation of cultural differentiae.

In such systems, the sanctions producing adherence to group-specific values are not only exercised by those who share the identity. Again, other imperative statuses afford a parallel: just as both sexes ridicule the male who is feminine, and all classes punish the proletarian who puts on airs, so also can members of all ethnic groups in a poly-ethnic society act to maintain dichotomies and differences. Where social ident- ities are organized and allocated by such principles, there will thus be a tendency towards canalization and standardization of interaction and the emergence of boundaries which maintain and generate ethnic di- versity within larger, encompassing social systems.

INTERDEPENDENCE OF ETHNIC GROUPS

The positive bond that connects several ethnic groups in an encompassing social system depends on the complementarity of the groups with
respect to some of their characteristic cultural features. Such complementarity can give rise to interdependence or symbiosis, and constitutes the areas of articulation referred to above; while in the fields
where there is no complementarity there can be no basis for organization on ethnic lines – there will either be no interaction, or interaction
without reference to ethnic identity.

Social systems differ greatly in the extent to which ethnic identity,
as an imperative status, constrains the person in the variety of statuses
and roles he may assume. Where the distinguishing values connected
with ethnic identity are relevant only to a few kinds of activities, the
social urbanization based on it will be similarly limited. Complex
polyethnic systems, on the other hand, clearly entail the existence of
extensively relevant value differences and multiple constraints on status combinations and social participation. In such systems, the boundary maintaining mechanisms must be highly effective, for the following
reasons: (i) the complexity is based on the existence of important,
complementary cultural differences; (ii) these differences must be generally standardized within the ethnic group – i.e. the status cluster, or
social person, of every member of a group must be highly stereotyped
– so that inter-ethnic interaction can be based on ethnic identities; and
(iii) the cultural characteristics of each ethnic group must be stable, so
that the complementary differences on which the systems rest can persist in the face of close inter-ethnic contact. Where these conditions
obtain, ethnic groups can make stable and symbiotic adaptations to
each other: other ethnic groups in the region become a part of the
natural environment; the sectors of articulation provide areas that can
be exploited, while the other sectors of activity of other groups are
largely irrelevant from the point of view of members of any one group.

ECOLOGIC PERSPECTIVE

Such interdependences can partly be analysed from the point of view
of cultural ecology, and the sectors of activity where other populations
with other cultures articulate may be thought of as niches to which the
group is adapted. This ecologic interdependence may take several different forms, for which one may construct a rough typology. Where

two or more ethnic groups are in contact, their adaptations may entail
he following forms:

(1) They may occupy clearly distinct niches in the natural environment and be in minimal competition for resources. In this case their
interdependence will be limited despite co-residence in the area, and
the articulation will tend to be mainly through trade, and perhaps in a
ceremonial-ritual sector.

(2) They may monopolize separate territories, in which case they
are in competition for resources and their articulation will involve politics
along the border, and possibly other sectors.

(3) They may provide important goods and services for each other,
i.e. occupy reciprocal and therefore different niches but in close interdependence. If they do not articulate very closely in the political sector, this entails a classical symbiotic situation and a variety of possible
fields of articulation. If they also compete and accommodate through
differential monopolization of the means of production, this entails a
close political and economic articulation, with open possibilities for
other forms of interdependence as well.

These alternatives refer to stable situations. But very commonly,
one will also find a fourth main form: where two or more interspersed
groups are in fact in at least partial competition within the same niche.
With time one would expect one such group to displace the other, or
an accommodation involving an increasing complementarity and interdependence to develop.

From the anthropological literature one can doubtless think of type
cases for most of these situations. However, if one looks carefully at
most empirical cases, one will find fairly mixed situations obtaining,
and only quite gross simplifications can reduce them to simple types.
I have tried elsewhere (Barth, 1964b) to illustrate this for an area of
Baluchistan, and expect that it is generally true that an ethnic group,
on the different boundaries of its distribution and in its different ac-
commodations, exhibits several of these forms in its relations to other
groups.

DEMOGRAPHIC PERSPECTIVE

These variables, however, only go part of the way in describing the
adaptation of a group. While showing the qualitative, (and ideally
quantitative) structure of the niches occupied by a group, one cannot
ignore the problems of number and balance in its adaptation. Whenever

a population is dependent on its exploitation of a niche in nature, this implies an upper limit on the size it may attain corresponding to the carrying capacity of that niche; and any stable adaptation entails a control on population size. If, on the other hand, two populations are ecologically interdependent, as two ethnic groups in a symbiotic relationship, this means that any variation in the size of one must have important effects on the other. In the analysis of any poly-ethnic system for which we assert any degree of time depth, we must therefore be able to explain the processes whereby the sizes of the interdependent ethnic groups are balanced. The demographic balances involved are thus quite complex, since a group's adaptation to a niche in nature is affected by its *absolute* size, while a group's adaptation to a niche constituted by another ethnic group is affected by its *relative* size.

The demographic problems in an analysis of ethnic inter-relations in a region thus centre on the forms of recruitment to ethnic groups and the question of how, if at all, their rates are sensitive to pressures on the different niches which each group exploits. These factors are highly critical for the stability of any poly-ethnic system, and it might look as if any population change would prove destructive. This does not necessarily seem to follow, as documented e.g. in the essay by Siverts [see Barth, 1969, pp. 101 ff], but in most situations the poly-ethnic systems we observe do entail quite complex processes of population movement and adjustment. It becomes clear that a number of factors other than human fertility and mortality affect the balance of numbers. From the point of view of any one territory, there are the factors of individual and group movements: emigration that relieves pressure, immigration that maintains one or several co-resident groups as outpost settlements of larger population reservoirs elsewhere. Migration and conquest play an intermittent role in redistributing populations and changing their relations. But the most interesting and often critical role is played by another set of processes that effect changes of the identity of individuals and groups. After all, the human material that is organized in an ethnic group is not immutable, and though the social mechanisms discussed so far tend to maintain dichotomies and boundaries, they do not imply 'stasis' for the human material they organize: boundaries may persist despite what may figuratively be called the 'osmosis' of personnel through them.

This perspective leads to an important clarification of the conditions for complex poly-ethnic systems. Though the emergence and persistence of such systems would seem to depend on a relatively high stability in the cultural features associated with ethnic groups – i.e. a high degree of rigidity in the interactional boundaries – they do *not* imply a similar rigidity in the patterns of recruitment or ascription to ethnic groups: on the contrary, the ethnic inter-relations that we observe frequently entail a variety of processes which effect changes in individual and group identity and modify the other demographic factors that obtain in the situation. Examples of stable and persisting ethnic boundaries that are crossed by a flow of personnel are clearly far more common than the ethnographic literature would lead us to believe. Different processes of such crossing are exemplified in these essays, and the conditions which cause them are shown to be various. We may look briefly at some of them.

FACTORS IN IDENTITY CHANGE

The Yao described by Kandre (1967b) are one of the many hill peoples on the southern fringe of the Chinese area. The Yao are organized for productive purposes in extended family households, aligned in clans and in villages. Household leadership is very clear, while community and region are autochthonously acephalous, and variously tied to poly-ethnic political domains. Identity and distinctions are expressed in complex ritual idioms, prominently involving ancestor worship. Yet this group shows the drastic incorporation rate of 10% non-Yao becoming Yao in each generation (Kandre, 1967a, 594). Change of membership takes place individually, mostly with children, where it involves purchase of the person by a Yao house-leader, adoption to kinship status, and full ritual assimilation. Occasionally, change of ethnic membership is also achieved by men through uxorilocal marriage; Chinese men are the acceptable parties to such arrangements.

The conditions for this form of assimilation are clearly twofold: first, the presence of cultural mechanisms to implement the incorporation, including ideas of obligations to ancestors, compensation by payment, etc., and secondly, the incentive of obvious advantages to the assimilating household and leader. These have to do with the role of households as productive units and agro-managerial techniques that imply an optimal size of 6–8 working persons, and the pattern of intra-community competition between household leaders in the field of wealth and influence.

Movements across the southern and northern boundaries of the Pathan area [cf. Barth, 1969, 123 ff] illustrate quite other forms and conditions. Southern Pathans become Baluch and not vice versa; this transformation can take place with individuals but more readily with whole households or small groups of households; it involves loss of position in the rigid genealogical and territorial segmentary system of Pathans and incorporation through clientage contract into the hierarchical, centralized system of the Baluch. Acceptance in the receiving group is conditional on the ambition and opportunism of Baluch political leaders. On the other hand, Pathans in the north have, after an analogous loss of position in their native system, settled in and often conquered new territories in Kohistan. The effect in due course has been a reclassification of the settling communities among the congeries of locally diverse Kohistani tribes and groups.

Perhaps the most striking case is that from Darfur provided by Haaland [see Barth, 1969, pp. 58 ff] which shows members of the hoe-agricultural Fur of the Sudan changing their identity to that of nomadic cattle Arabs. This process is conditional on a very specific economic circumstance: the absence of investment opportunities for capital in the village economy of the Fur in contrast to the possibilities among the nomads. Accumulated capital, and the opportunities for its management and increase, provide the incentive for Fur households to abandon their fields and villages and change to the life of the neighbouring Baggara, incidentally also joining one of the loose but nominally centralized Baggara political units if the change has been economically completely successful.

These processes that induce a flow of personnel across ethnic boundaries will of necessity affect the demographic balance between different ethnic groups. Whether they are such that they contribute to stability in this balance is an entirely different question. To do so, they would have to be sensitive to changes in the pressure on ecologic niches in a feed-back pattern. This does not regularly seem to be the case. The assimilation of non-Yao seems further to increase the rate of Yao growth and expansion at the expense of other groups, and can be recognized as one, albeit minor, factor furthering the progressive Sinization process whereby cultural and ethnic diversity has steadily been reduced over vast areas. The rate of assimilation of Pathans by Baluch tribes is no doubt sensitive to population pressure in Pathan areas, but simultaneously sustains an imbalance whereby Baluch tribes spread northward despite higher population pressures in the northern areas. Kohistani assimilation relieves population pressure in Pathan area while maintaining a geographically stable boundary. Nomadization of the Fur replenishes the Baggara, who are elsewhere becoming sedentarized. The rate, however, does *not* correlate with pressure on Fur lands – since nomadization is conditional on accumulated wealth, its rate probably decreases as Fur population pressure increases. The Fur case also demonstrates the inherent instability of some of these processes, and how limited changes can have drastic results: with the agricultural innovation of orchards over the last ten years, new investment opportunities are provided which will probably greatly reduce, or perhaps for a while even reverse, the nomadization process.

Thus, though the processes that induce change of identity are important to the understanding of most cases of ethnic interdependence, they need not be conducive to population stability. In general, however, one can argue that whenever ethnic relations are stable over long periods, and particularly where the interdependence is close, one can expect to find an approximate demographic balance. The analysis of the different factors involved in this balance is an important part of the analysis of the ethnic inter-relations in the area.

THE PERSISTENCE OF CULTURAL BOUNDARIES

In the preceding discussion of ethnic boundary maintenance and interchange of personnel there is one very important problem that I have left aside. We have seen various examples of how individuals and small groups, because of specific economic and political circumstances in their former position and among the assimilating group, may change their locality, their subsistence pattern, their political allegiance and form, or their household membership. This still does not fully explain why such changes lead to categorical changes of ethnic identity, leaving the dichotomized ethnic groups unaffected (other than in numbers) by the interchange of personnel. In the case of adoption and incorporation of mostly immature and in any case isolated single individuals into pre-established households, as among the Yao, such complete cultural assimilation is understandable: here every new person becomes totally immersed in a Yao pattern of relationships and expectations. In the other examples, it is less clear why this total change of identity takes place. One cannot argue that it follows from a universally imputable rule of cultural integration, so that the practice of the politics of one group or the assumption of its pattern of ecologic adaptation in subsistence and economy, entails the adoption also of its other parts and forms. Indeed, the Pathan case (Ferdinand, 1967) directly falsifies this argument, in that the boundaries of the Pathan ethnic group cross-cuts ecologic and political units. Using self-identification as the critical criterion of ethnic identity, it should thus be perfectly possible for a small group of Pathans to assume the political obligations of membership in a Baluch tribe, or the agricultural and husbandry practices of Kohistanis, and yet continue to call themselves Pathans. By the same token one might expect nomadization among the Fur to lead to the emergence of a nomadic section of the Fur, similar in subsistence to the Baggara but different from them in other cultural features, and in ethnic label.

Quite clearly, this is precisely what has happened in many historical situations. In cases where it does *not* happen we see the organizing and canalizing effects of ethnic distinctions. To explore the factors responsible for the difference, let us first look at the specific explanations for the changes of identity that have been advanced in the examples discussed above.

In the case of Pathan borderlands, influence and security in the segmentary and anarchic societies of this region derive from a man's previous actions, or rather from the respect that he obtains from these acts as judged by accepted standards of evaluation. The main fora for exhibiting Pathan virtues are the tribal council, and stages for the display of hospitality. But the villager in Kohistan has a standard of living where the hospitality he can provide can hardly compete with that of the conquered serfs of neighbouring Pathans, while the client of a Baluch leader cannot speak in any tribal council. To maintain Pathan identity in these situations, to declare oneself in the running as a competitor by Pathan value standards, is to condemn oneself in advance to utter failure in performance. By assuming Kohistani or Baluch identity, however, a man may, by the same performance, score quite high on the scales that then become relevant. The incentives to a change in identity are thus inherent in the change in circumstances.

Different circumstances obviously favour different performances. Since ethnic identity is associated with a culturally specific set of value standards, it follows that there are circumstances where such an identity can be moderately successfully realized, and limits beyond which such success is precluded. I will argue that ethnic identities will not be retained beyond these limits, because allegiance to basic value standards will not be sustained where one's own comparative performance is utterly inadequate.[3] The two components in this relative measure of success are, first, the performance of others and, secondly, the alternatives open to oneself. I am not making an appeal to ecologic adaptation. Ecologic feasibility, and fitness in relation to the natural environment, matter only in so far as they set a limit in terms of sheer physical survival, which is very rarely approached by ethnic groups. What matters is how well the others, with whom one interacts and to whom one is compared, manage to perform, and what alternative identities and sets of standards are available to the individual.

ETHNIC IDENTITY AND TANGIBLE ASSETS

The boundary-maintaining factors in the Fur are not immediately illuminated by this argument. Haaland (pp. 65 ff.) discusses the evaluation of the nomad's life by Fur standards and finds the balance between advantages and disadvantages inconclusive. To ascertain the comparability of this case, we need to look more generally at all the factors that affect the behaviour in question. The materials derive from grossly different ethnographic contexts and so a number of factors are varied simultaneously.

The individual's relation to productive resources stands out as the significant contrast between the two regions. In the Middle East, the means of production are conventionally held as private or corporate, defined and transferable property. A man can obtain them through a specific and restricted transaction, such as purchase or lease; even in conquest the rights that are obtained are standard, delimited rights. In Darfur, on the other hand, as in much of the Sudanic belt, the prevailing conventions are different. Land for cultivation is allocated, as needed, to members of a local community. The distinction between owner and cultivator, so important in the social structure of most Middle Eastern communities, cannot be made because ownership does not involve separable, absolute, and transferable rights. Access to the means of production in a Fur village is therefore conditional only on inclusion in the village community – i.e. on Fur ethnic identity. Similarly, grazing rights are not allocated and monopolized, even as between Baggara tribes. Though groups and tribes tend to use the same routes and areas every year, and may at times try in an *ad hoc* way to keep out others from an area they wish to use, they normally intermix and have no defined and absolute prerogatives. Access to grazing is thus an automatic aspect of practising husbandry, and entails being a Baggara.

The gross mechanisms of boundary maintenance in Darfur are thus quite simple: a man has access to the critical means of production by virtue of practising a certain subsistence; this entails a whole style of life, and all these characteristics are subsumed under the ethnic labels Fur and Baggara. In the Middle East, on the other hand, men can obtain control over means of production through a transaction that does not involve their other activities; ethnic identity is then not necessarily affected and this opens the way for diversification. Thus nomad, peasant, and city dweller can belong to the same ethnic group in the Middle East; where ethnic boundaries persist they depend on more subtle and specific mechanisms, mainly connected with the unfeasibility of certain status and role combinations.

ETHNIC GROUPS AND STRATIFICATION

Where one ethnic group has control of the means of production utilized by another group, a relationship of inequality and stratification obtains. Thus Fur and Baggara do not make up a stratified system, since they utilize different niches and have access to them independently of each other, whereas in some parts of the Pathan area one finds stratification based on the control of land, Pathans being landowners, and other groups cultivating as serfs. In more general terms, one may say that stratified poly-ethnic systems exist where groups are characterized by differential control of assets that are valued by all groups in the system. The cultures of the component ethnic groups in such systems are thus integrated in a special way: they share certain general value orientations and scales, on the basis of which they can arrive at judgements of hierarchy.

Obversely, a system of stratification does not entail the existence of ethnic groups. Leach (1967) argues convincingly that social classes are distinguished by different sub-cultures, indeed, that this is a more basic characteristic than their hierarchical ordering. However, in many systems of stratification we are not dealing with bounded strata at all: the stratification is based simply on the notion of scales and the recognition of an ego-centered level of 'people who are just like us' versus those more select and those more vulgar. In such systems, cultural differences, whatever they are, grade into each other, and nothing like a social organization of ethnic groups emerges: Secondly, most systems of stratification allow, or indeed entail, mobility based on evaluation by the scales that define the hierarchy. Thus a moderate failure in the 'B' sector of the hierarchy makes you a 'C', etc. Ethnic groups are not open to this kind of penetration: the ascription of ethnic identity is based on other and more restrictive criteria. This is most clearly illustrated by Knutsson's analysis of the Galla in the context of Ethiopian society [see Barth, 1969, pp. 86 ff.] – a social system where whole ethnic groups are stratified with respect to their positions of privilege and disability within the state. Yet the attainment of a governorship does not make an Amhara of a Galla, nor does estrangement as an outlaw entail loss of Galla identity.

From this perspective, the Indian caste system would appear to be a special case of a stratified poly-ethnic system. The boundaries of castes are defined by ethnic criteria: thus individual failures in performance lead to out-casting and not to down-casting. The process whereby the hierarchical system incorporates new ethnic groups is demonstrated in the *sanscritization of tribals*: their acceptance of the critical value scales defining their position in the hierarchy of ritual purity and pollution is the only change of values that is necessary for a people to become an Indian caste. An analysis of the different processes of boundary maintenance involved in different inter-caste relations and in different regional variants of the caste system would, I believe, illuminate many features of this system.

The preceding discussion has brought out a somewhat anomalous general feature of ethnic identity as a status: ascription[4] is not conditional on the control of any specific assets, but rests on criteria of origin and commitment; whereas *performance* in the status, the adequate acting out of the roles required to realize the identity, in many systems does require such assets. By contrast, in a bureaucratic office the incumbent is provided with those assets that are required for the performance of the role; while kinship positions, which are ascribed without reference to a person's assets, likewise are not conditional on performance – you remain a father even if you fail to feed your child.

Thus where ethnic groups are interrelated in a stratified system, this requires the presence of special processes that maintain differential control of assets. To schematize: a basic premise of ethnic group organization is that every A can act roles, 1, 2 and 3. If actors agree on this, the premise is self-fulfilling, unless acting in these roles requires assets that are distributed in a discrepant pattern. If these assets are obtained or lost in ways independent of being an A, and sought and avoided without reference to one's identity as an A, the premise will be falsified: some A's become unable to act in the expected roles. Most systems of stratification are maintained by the solution that in such cases, the person is no longer an A. In the case of ethnic identity, the solution on the contrary is the recognition that every A no longer can or will act in roles 1 and 2. The persistence of stratified poly-ethnic systems thus entails the presence of factors that generate and maintain a categorically different distribution of assets: state controls, as in some modern plural and racist systems; marked differences in evaluation that canalize the efforts of actors in different directions, as in systems with polluting occupations; or differences in culture that generate marked differences in political organization, economic organization or individual skills.

THE PROBLEM OF VARIATION

Despite such processes, however, the ethnic label subsumes a number of simultaneous characteristics which no doubt cluster statistically, but which are not absolutely interdependent and connected. Thus there will be variations between members, some showing many and some showing few characteristics. Particularly where people change their identity, this creates ambiguity since ethnic membership is at once a question of source of origin as well as of current identity. Indeed, Haaland was taken out to see 'Fur who live in nomad camps', and I have heard members of Baluch tribal sections explain that they are 'really Pathan'. What is then left of the boundary maintenance and the categorical dichotomy, when the actual distinctions are blurred in this way? Rather than despair at the failure of typological schematism, one can legitimately note that people *do* employ ethnic labels and that there are in many parts of the world most spectacular differences whereby forms of behaviour cluster so that whole actors tend to fall into such categories in terms of their objective behaviour. What is surprising is not the existence of some actors that fall between these categories, and of some regions in the world where whole persons do not tend to sort themselves out in this way, but the fact that variations tend to cluster at all. We can then be concerned not to perfect a typology, but to discover the processes that bring about such clustering.

   An alternative mode of approach in anthropology has been to dichotomize the ethnographic material in terms of ideal versus actual or conceptual versus empirical, and then concentrate on the consistencies (the 'structure') of the ideal, conceptual part of the data, employing some vague notion of norms and individual deviance to account for the actual, statistical patterns. It is of course perfectly feasible to distinguish between a people's model of their social system and their aggregate pattern of pragmatic behaviour, and indeed quite necessary not to confuse the two. But the fertile problems in social anthropology are concerned with how the two are interconnected, and it does not follow that this is best elucidated by dichotomizing and confronting them as total systems. In these essays we have tried to build the analysis on a lower level of interconnection between status and behaviour. I would argue that people's categories are for acting, and are significantly affected by interaction rather than contemplation. In showing the connection between ethnic labels and the maintenance of cultural diversity, I am therefore concerned primarily to show how, under varying circumstances, certain constellations of categorization and value orientation have a self-fulfilling character, how others will tend to be falsified by experience, while others again are incapable of consummation in interaction. Ethnic boundaries can emerge and persist only in the former situation, whereas they should dissolve or be absent in the latter situations. With such a feedback from people's experiences to the categories they employ, simple ethnic dichotomies can be retained, and their stereotyped behavioural differential reinforced, despite a considerable objective variation. This is so because actors struggle to maintain conventional definitions of the situation in social encounters through selective perception, tact, and sanctions, and because of difficulties in finding other, more adequate codifications of experience. Revision only takes place where the categorization is grossly inadequate – not merely because it is untrue in any objective sense, but because it is consistently unrewarding to act upon, within the domain where the actor makes it relevant. So the dichotomy of Fur villagers and Baggara nomads is maintained despite the patent presence of a nomadic camp of Fur in the neighbourhood: the fact that those nomads speak Fur and have kinship connections with villagers somewhere does not change the social situation in which the villager interacts with them – it simply makes the standard transactions of buying milk, allocating camp sites, or obtaining manure, which one would have with other Baggara, flow a bit more smoothly. But a dichotomy between Pathan landowners and non-Pathan labourers can no longer be maintained where non-Pathans obtain land and embarrass Pathans by refusing to respond with the respect which their imputed position as menials would have sanctioned.

MINORITIES, PARIAHS, AND ORGANIZATIONAL CHARACTERISTICS OF THE PERIPHERY

In some social systems, ethnic groups co-reside though no major aspect of structure is based on ethnic inter-relations. These are generally referred to as societies with minorities, and the analysis of the minority situation involves a special variant of inter-ethnic relations. I think in most cases, such situations have come about as a result of external historical events; the cultural differentiae have not sprung from the local organizational context – rather, a pre-established cultural contrast is brought into conjunction with a pre-established social system, and is made relevant to life there in a diversity of ways.

An extreme form of minority position, illustrating some but not all features of minorities, is that of pariah groups. These are groups actively rejected by the host population because of behaviour or characteristics positively condemned, though often useful in some specific, practical way. European pariah groups of recent centuries (executioners, dealers in horseflesh and -leather, collectors of night-soil, gypsies, etc.) exemplify most features: as breakers of basic taboos they were rejected by the larger society. Their identity imposed a definition on social situations which gave very little scope for interaction with persons in the majority population, and simultaneously as an imperative status represented an inescapable disability that prevented them from assuming the normal statuses involved in other definitions of the situation of interaction. Despite these formidable barriers, such groups do not seem to have developed the internal complexity that would lead us to regard them as full-fledged ethnic groups; only the culturally foreign gypsies[5] clearly constitute such a group.

The boundaries of pariah groups are most strongly maintained by the excluding host population, and they are often forced to make use of easily noticeable diacritica to advertise their identity (though since this identity is often the basis for a highly insecure livelihood, such over-communication may sometimes also serve the pariah individual's competitive interests). Where pariahs attempt to pass into the larger society, the culture of the host population is generally well known; thus the problem is reduced to a question of escaping the stigmata of disability by dissociating with the pariah community and faking another origin.

Many minority situations have a trace of this active rejection by the host population. But the general feature of all minority situations lies in the organization of activities and interaction: In the total social system, all sectors of activity are organized by statuses open to members of the majority group, while the status system of the minority has only relevance to relations within the minority and only to some sectors of activity, and does not provide a basis for action in other sectors, equally valued in the minority culture. There is thus a disparity between values and organizational facilities: prized goals are outside the field organized by the minority's culture and categories. Though such systems contain several ethnic groups, interaction between members of the different groups of this kind does not spring from the complementarity of ethnic identities; it takes place entirely within the framework of the dominant, majority group's statuses and institutions, where identity as a minority member gives no basis for action, though it may in varying degrees represent a disability in assuming the operative statuses. Eidheim's paper gives a very clear analysis of this situation, as it obtains among Coast Lapps.

But in a different way, one may say that in such a poly-ethnic system, the contrastive cultural characteristics of the component groups are located in the non-articulating sectors of life. For the minority, these sectors constitute a 'backstage' where the characteristics that are stigmatic in terms of the dominant majority culture can covertly be made the objects of transaction.

The present-day minority situation of Lapps has been brought about by recent external circumstances. Formerly, the important context of interaction was the local situation, where two ethnic groups with sufficient knowledge of each other's culture maintained a relatively limited, partly symbiotic relationship based in their respective identities. With the fuller integration of Norwegian society, bringing the northern periphery into the nation-wide system, the rate of cultural change increased drastically. The population of Northern Norway became increasingly dependent on the institutional system of the larger society, and social life among Norwegians in Northern Norway was increasingly organized to pursue activities and obtain benefits within the wider system. This system has not, until very recently, taken ethnic identity into account in its structure, and until a decade ago there was practically no place in it where one could participate *as a Lapp*. Lapps as Norwegian citizens, on the other hand, are perfectly free to participate, though under the dual disability of peripheral location and inadequate command of Norwegian language and culture. This situation has elsewhere, in the inland regions of Finnmark, given scope for Lappish innovators with a political program based on the ideal of ethnic pluralism (cf. Eidheim, 1967), but they have gained no following in the Coast Lapp area here discussed by Eidheim. For these Lapps, rather, the relevance of Lappish statuses and conventions decreases in sector after sector (cf. Eidheim, 1966), while the relative inadequacy of performance in the widest system brings about frustrations and a crisis of identity.

CULTURE CONTACT AND CHANGE

This is a very widespread process under present conditions as dependence on the products and institutions of industrial societies spreads in all parts of the world. The important thing to recognize is that a drastic reduction of cultural differences between ethnic groups does not correlate in any simple way with a reduction in the organizational relevance of ethnic identities, or a breakdown in boundary-maintaining processes. This is demonstrated in much of the case material.

We can best analyse the interconnection by looking at the agents of change: what strategies are open and attractive to them, and what are the organizational implications of different choices on their part? The agents in this case are the persons normally referred to somewhat ethno-centrically as the new elites: the persons in the less industrialized groups with greater contact and more dependence on the goods and organizations of industrialized societies. In their pursuit of participation in wider social systems to obtain new forms of value they can choose between the following basic strategies: (i) they may attempt to pass and become incorporated in the pre-established industrial society and cultural group; (ii) they may accept a 'minority' status, accommodate to and seek to reduce their minority disabilities by encapsulating all cultural differentiae in sectors of non-articulation, while participating in the larger system of the industrialized group in the other sectors of activity; (iii) they may choose to emphasize ethnic identity, using it to develop new positions and patterns to organize activities in those sectors formerly not found in their society, or inadequately developed for the new purposes. If the cultural innovators are successful in the first strategy, their ethnic group will be denuded of its source of internal diversification and will probably remain as a culturally conservative, low-articulating ethnic group with low rank in the larger social system. A general acceptance of the second strategy will prevent the emergence of a clearly dichotomizing poly-ethnic organization, and – in view of the diversity of industrial society and consequent variation and multiplicity of fields of articulation – probably lead to an eventual assimilation of the minority. The third strategy generates many of the interesting movements that can be observed today, from nativism to new states.

I am unable to review the variables that affect which basic strategy will be adopted, which concrete form it may take, and what its degree of success and cumulative implications may be. Such factors range from the number of ethnic groups in the system to features of the ecologic regime and details of the constituent cultures, and are illustrated in most of the concrete analyses of the following essays. It may be of interest to note some of the forms in which ethnic identity is made organizationally relevant to new sectors in the current situation.

Firstly, the innovators may choose to emphasize one level of identity among the several provided by the traditional social organization. Tribe, caste, language group, region or state all have features that make them a potentially adequate primary ethnic identity for group reference, and the outcome will depend on the readiness with which others can be led to embrace these identities, and the cold tactical facts. Thus, though tribalism may rally the broadest support in many African areas, the resultant groups seem unable to stand up against the sanctioning apparatus even of a relatively rudimentary state organization.

Secondly, the mode of organization of the ethnic group varies, as does the inter-ethnic articulation that is sought. The fact that contemporary forms are prominently political does not make them any less ethnic in character. Such political movements constitute new ways of making cultural differences organizationally relevant (Kleivan, 1967), and new ways of articulating the dichotomized ethnic groups. The proliferation of ethnically based pressure groups, political parties, and visions of independent statehood, as well as the multitude of subpolitical advancement associations (Sommerfelt, 1967) show the importance of these new forms. In other areas, cult-movements or mission-introduced sects are used to dichotomize and articulate groups in new ways. It is striking that these new patterns are so rarely concerned with the economic sector of activities, which is so major a factor in the culture contact situation, apart from the forms of state socialism adopted by some of the new nations. By contrast, the traditional complex poly-ethnic systems have been prominently based on articulation in this sector, through occupational differentiation and articulation at the market place in many regions of Asia and Middle America, or most elaborately, through agrarian production in South Asia. Today, contending ethnic groups not infrequently become differentiated with respect to educational level and attempt to control or monopolize educational facilities for this purpose (Sommerfelt, 1967), but this is not so much with a view to occupational differentiation as because of the obvious connection between bureaucratic competence and opportunities for political advancement. One may speculate that an articulation entailing complex differentiation of skills, and sanctioned by the constant dependence on livelihood, will have far greater strength and stability than one based on revocable political affiliation and sanctioned by the exercise of force and political fiat, and that these new forms of poly-ethnic systems are probably inherently more turbulent and unstable than the older forms.

When political groups articulate their opposition in terms of ethnic criteria, the direction of cultural change is also affected. A political confrontation can only be implemented by making the groups similar and thereby comparable, and this will have effect on every new sector of activity which is made politically relevant. Opposed parties thus tend to become structurally similar, and differentiated only by a few clear diacritica. Where ethnic groups are organized in political confrontation in this way, the process of opposition will therefore lead to a reduction or the cultural differences between them.

For this reason, much of the activity of political innovators is concerned with the codification of idioms: the selection of signals for identity and the assertion of value for these cultural diacritica, and the suppression or denial of relevance for other differentiae. The issue as to which new cultural forms are compatible with the native ethnic identity is often hotly contended, but is generally settled in favour of syncretism for the reasons noted above. But a great amount of attention may be paid to the revival of select traditional culture traits, and to the establishment of historical traditions to justify and glorify the idioms and the identity.

The interconnection between the diacritica that are chosen for emphasis, the boundaries that are defined, and the differentiating values that are espoused, constitute a fascinating field for study.[6] Clearly, a number of factors are relevant. Idioms vary in their appropriateness for different kinds or units. They are unequally adequate for the innovator's purposes, both as means to mobilize support and as supports in the strategy of confrontation with other groups. Their stratificational implications both within and between groups are important: they entail different sources and distributions of influence within the group, and different claims to recognition from other groups through suppression or glorification or different forms of social stigmata. Clearly, there is no simple connection between the ideological basis or a movement and the idioms chosen; yet both have implications for subsequent boundary maintenance, and the course or further change.

VARIATIONS IN THE SETTING FOR ETHNIC RELATIONS

These modern variants for poly-ethnic organization emerge in a world of bureaucratic administration, developed communications, and progressive urbanization. Clearly, under radically different circumstances, the critical factors in the definition and maintenance of ethnic boundaries would be different. In basing ourselves on limited and contemporary data, we are faced with difficulties in generalizing about ethnic processes, since major variables may be ignored because they are not exhibited in the cases at our disposal. There can be little doubt that social anthropologists have tended to regard the rather special situation of colonial peace and external administration, which has formed the backdrop of most of the influential monographs, as if this were representative of conditions at most times and places. This may have biased the interpretation both of pre-colonial systems and of contemporary, emergent forms. The attempt in these essays to cover regionally very diverse cases is not alone an adequate defence against such bias, and the issue needs to be faced directly.

Colonial regimes are quite extreme in the extent to which the administration and its rules are divorced from locally based social life. Under such a regime, individuals hold certain rights to protection uniformly through large population aggregates and regions, far beyond the reach of their own social relationships and institutions. This allows physical proximity and opportunities for contact between persons of different ethnic groups regardless of the absence of shared understandings between them, and thus clearly removes one of the constraints that normally operate on inter-ethnic relations. In such situations, interaction can develop and proliferate – indeed, only those forms of interaction that are directly inhibited by other factors will be absent and remain as sectors of non-articulation. Thus ethnic boundaries in such situations represent a positive organization of social relations around differentiated and complementary values, and cultural differences will tend to be reduced with time and approach the required minimum.

In most political regimes, however, where there is less security and people live under a greater threat of arbitrariness and violence outside their primary community, the insecurity itself acts as a constraint on inter-ethnic contacts. In this situation, many forms of interaction between members of different ethnic groups may fail to develop, even though a potential complementarity of interests obtains. Forms of interaction may be blocked because of a lack of trust or a lack of opportunities to consummate transactions. What is more, there are also internal sanctions in such communities which tend to enhance overt conformity within and cultural differences between communities. If a person is dependent for his security on the voluntary and spontaneous support of his own community, self-identification as a member of this community needs to be explicitly expressed and confirmed; and any behaviour which is deviant from the standard may be interpreted as a weakening of the identity, and thereby of the bases of security. In such situations, fortuitous historical differences in culture between different communities will tend to perpetuate themselves without any positive organizational basis; many of the observable cultural differentiae may thus be of very limited relevance to the ethnic organization.

The processes whereby ethnic units maintain themselves are thus clearly affected, but not fundamentally changed, by the variable of regional security. This can also be shown by an inspection of the cases analysed in these essays, which represent a fair range from the colonial to the poly-centric, up to relatively anarchic situations. It is important, however, to recognize that this background variable may change very rapidly with time, and in the projection of long-range processes this is a serious difficulty. Thus in the Fur case, we observe a situation of externally maintained peace and very small-scale local political activity, and can form a picture of inter-ethnic processes and even rates in this setting. But we know that over the last few generations, the situation has varied from one of Baggara – Fur confrontation under an expansive Fur sultanate to a nearly total anarchy in Turkish and Mahdi times; and it is very difficult to estimate the effects of these variations on the processes of nomadization and assimilation, and arrive at any long-range projection of rates and trends.

ETHNIC GROUPS AND CULTURAL EVOLUTION

The perspective and analysis presented here have relevance to the theme of cultural evolution. No doubt human history is a story of the development of emergent forms, both of cultures and societies. The issue in anthropology has been how this history can best be depicted, and what kinds of analyses are adequate to discover general principles in the courses of change. Evolutionary analysis in the rigorous sense of the biological fields has based its method on the construction of phyletic lines. This method presumes the existence of units where the boundaries and the boundary-maintaining processes can be described, and thus where the continuity can be specified. Concretely, phyletic lines are meaningful because specific boundaries prevent the interchange of genetic material; and so one can insist that the reproductive *isolate* is the unit, and that it has maintained an identity undisturbed by the changes in the morphological characteristics of the species.

I have argued that boundaries are also maintained between ethnic units, and that consequently it is possible to specify the nature of continuity and persistence of such units. These essays try to show that ethnic boundaries are maintained in each case by a limited set of cultural features. The persistence of the unit then depends on the persistence of these cultural differentiae, while continuity can also be specified through the changes of the unit brought about by changes in the boundary-defining cultural differentiae.

However, most of the cultural matter that at any time is associated with a human population is *not* constrained by this boundary; it can vary, be learnt, and change without any critical relation to the boundary maintenance of the ethnic group. So when one traces the history of a ethnic group through time, one is *not* simultaneously, in the same sense, tracing the history of 'a culture': the elements of the present culture of that ethnic group have not sprung from the particular set that constituted the group's culture at a previous time, whereas the group has a continual organizational existence with boundaries (criteria of membership) that despite modifications have marked off a continuing unit.

Without being able to specify the boundaries of cultures, it is not possible to construct phyletic lines in the more rigorous evolutionary sense. But from the analysis that has been argued here, it should be possible to do so for ethnic groups, and thus in a sense for those aspects of culture which have this organizational anchoring.

Notes

1. The emphatic ideological denial of the primacy of ethnic identity (and rank) which characterizes the universal religions that have arisen in the Middle East is understandable in this perspective, since practically any movement for social or ethical reform in the poly-ethnic societies of that region would clash with conventions and standards of ethnic character.
2. The difference between ethnic groups and social strata, which seems problematical at this stage of the argument, will be taken up below.
3. I am here concerned only with individual failure to maintain identity, where most members do so successfully, and not with the broader questions of cultural vitality and anomie.

4. As opposed to presumptive classification in passing social encounters – I am thinking of the person in his normal social context where others have a considerable amount of previous information about him, not of the possibilities afforded occasionally for mispresenting one's identity towards strangers.
5. The condemned behaviour which gives pariah position to the gypsies is compound, but rests prominently on their wandering life, originally in contrast to the serf bondage of Europe, later in their flagrant violation of puritan ethics of responsibility, toil and morality.
6. To my knowledge, Mitchell's essay on the Kalela dance (Mitchell, 1956) is the first and still the most penetrating study on this topic.

References

Barth, F. (1964b) 'Competition and Symbiosis in North East Baluchistan', *Folk*, 6, 1.
Barth, F. (1966) *Models of Social Organization*. Royal Anthropological Institute of Great Britain and Ireland, Occasional Papers, No. 23.
Bogoras, W. (1904–9) *The Chickchee*. Anthropological Memoirs, American Museum of Natural History, Vol. II. New York.
Eidheim, H. (1966) 'Lappish Guest Relationships under Conditions of Cultural Change,' *American Anthropologist*, 68.
Eidheim, H. (1968) 'The Lappish Movement and Innovative Political Process', in M. Swartz (ed.) *Local-Level Politics*. Chicago.
Ferdinand, K. (1967) 'Ættelinjestabilitet Blandt Nomader i Øst-Afghanistan', Paper submitted in advance for participants in the Wenner-Gren Symposium on 'Ethnic Groups', Bergen, Feb. 23rd to 26th 1967.
Gjessing, G. (1954) *Changing Lapps: A Study in Culture Relations in Northernmost Norway*. London School of Economics Monographs on Social Anthropology, No. 13.
Kandre, P. (1967a) 'Autonomy and Integration of Social Systems: The Iu Mien (Yao) Mountain Population and their Neighbours', in P. Kunstadter (ed.) *Southeast Asian Tribes, Minorities, and Nations*. Princeton.
Kandre, P. (1967b) 'Om etnisitet hos Iu Mien-Yao i Thailand, Laos och Burma', Paper for Wenner-Gren Symposium on 'Ethnic Groups', Bergen, Feb. 23rd to 26th 1967.
Kleivan, H. (1967) 'Grønlendere og andre dansker: Identitetsunderstrekning og politisk integrasjon', Paper for Wenner-Gren Symposium on 'Ethnic Groups', Bergen, Feb. 23rd to 26th 1967.
Leach, E.R. (1967) 'Caste, Class and Slavery–the Taxonomic Problem', in A. de Reuck and J. Knight (eds.) *Caste and Race: Comparative Approaches*. London.
Mitchell, J.C. (1956) *The Kalela Dance: Aspects of Social Relationships among Urban Africans in N. Rhodesia*. The Rhodes-Livingstone Papers, No. 27. Manchester.
Narroll, R. (1964) 'Ethnic Unit Classification', *Current Anthropology*, 5, 4.
Sommerfelt, A. (1967) 'Inter-etniske relasjoner i Toro', Paper for Wenner-Gren Symposium on 'Ethnic Groups', Bergen, Feb. 23rd to 26th 1967.

19 Insiders and Outsiders: A Chapter in the Sociology of Knowledge (1972)[1]

Robert K. Merton*

The sociology of knowledge has long been regarded as a complex and esoteric subject, remote from the urgent problems of contemporary social life. To some of us, it seems quite the other way.[2] Especially in times of great social change, precipitated by acute social conflict and attended by much cultural disorganization and reorganization, the perspectives provided by the various sociologies of knowledge bear directly upon problems agitating the society. It is then that differences in the values, commitments, and intellectual orientations of conflicting groups become deepened into basic cleavages, both social and cultural. As the society becomes polarized, so do the contending claims to truth. At the extreme, an active and reciprocal distrust between groups finds expression in intellectual perspectives that are no longer located within the same universe of discourse. The more deep-seated the mutual distrust, the more does the argument of the other appear so palpably implausible or absurd that one no longer inquires into its substance or logical structure to assess its truth claims. Instead, one confronts the other's argument with an entirely different sort of question: how does it happen to be advanced at all? Thought and its products thus become altogether functionalized, interpreted only in terms of their presumed social or economic or psychological sources and functions. In the political arena, where the rules of the game often condone and sometimes support the practice, this involves reciprocated attacks on the integrity of the opponent; in the academic forum, where normative expectations are somewhat more restraining, it leads to reciprocated ideological analyses (which often deteriorate into barely concealed *ad hominem* innuendos). In both, the process feeds upon and nourishes collective insecurities.[3]

* From *The American Journal of Sociology*, 78(1) (July 1972), pp. 9–47.

SOCIAL CHANGE AND SOCIAL THOUGHT

This conception of the social sources of the intensified interest in the sociology of knowledge and some of the theoretical difficulties which they foster plainly has the character, understandably typical in the sociology of scientific knowledge, of a self-exemplifying idea. It posits reciprocal connections between thought and society, in particular the social conditions that make for or disrupt a common universe of intellectual discourse within which the most severe disagreements can take place. Michael Polanyi (1958, 1959, 1964, 1967) has noted, more perceptively than anyone else I know,[4] how the growth of knowledge depends upon complex sets of social relations based on a largely institutionalized reciprocity of trust among scholars and scientists. In one of his many passages on this theme, he observes that

> in an ideal free society each person would have perfect access to the truth: to the truth in science, in art, religion, and justice, both in public and private life. But this is not practicable; each person can know directly very little of truth and must trust others for the rest. Indeed, to assure this process of mutual reliance is one of the main functions of society. It follows that such freedom of the mind as can be possessed by men is due to the services of social institutions, which set narrow limits to man's freedom and tend to threaten it even within those limits. The relation is analogous to that between mind and body: to the way in which the performance of mental acts is restricted by limitations and distortions due to the medium which makes these performances possible. (1959, p. 68)

But as cleavages deepen between groups, social strata or collectivities of whatever kind, the social network of mutual reliance is at best strained and at worst broken. In place of the vigorous but intellectually disciplined mutual checking and rechecking that operates to a significant extent, though never of course totally, within the social institutions of science and scholarship, there develops a strain toward separatism, in the domain of the intellect as in the domain of society. Partly grounded mutual suspicion increasingly substitutes for partly grounded mutual trust. There emerge claims to group-based truth: Insider truths that counter Outsider untruths and Outsider truths that counter Insider untruths.

In our day, vastly evident social change is being initiated and funneled through a variety of social movements. These are formally alike in their objectives of achieving an intensified collective consciousness, a deepened solidarity and a new or renewed primary or total allegiance of their members to certain social identities, statuses, groups, or collectivities. Inspecting the familiar list of these movements centered on class, race, ethnicity, age, sex, religion, and sexual disposition, we note two other instructive similarities between them. First, the move- ments are for the most part formed principally on the basis of ascribed rather than acquired statuses and identities, with eligibility for inclusion being in terms of who you are rather than what you are (in the sense of status being contingent on role performance). And second, the move- ments largely involve the public affirmation of pride in statuses and solidarity with collectivities that have long been socially and culturally downgraded, stigmatized, or otherwise victimized in the social sys- tem. As with group affiliations generally, these newly reinforced social identities find expression in various affiliative symbols of distinctive speech, bodily appearance, dress, public behavior patterns and, not least, assumptions and foci of thought.

THE INSIDER DOCTRINE

Within this context of social change, we come upon the contemporary relevance of a long-standing problem in the sociology of knowledge: the problem of patterned differentials among social groups and strata in access to certain types of knowledge. In its strong form, the claim is put forward as a matter of epistemological principle that particular groups in each moment of history have *monopolistic access* to par- ticular kinds of knowledge. In the weaker, more empirical form, the claim holds that some groups have *privileged access*, with other groups also being able to acquire that knowledge for themselves but at greater risk and cost.

Claims of this general sort have been periodically introduced. For one imposing and consequential example, Marx, a progenitor of the sociology of knowledge as of much else in social thought, advanced the claim that after capitalistic society had reached its ultimate phase of development, the strategic location of one social class would en- able it to achieve an understanding of the society that was exempt from false consciousness.[5] For another, altogether unimposing but also consequential example involving ascribed rather than achieved status, the Nazi *Gauleiter* of science and learning, Ernest Krieck (1935), ex- pressed an entire ideology in contrasting the access to authentic scien- tific knowledge by men of unimpeachable Aryan ancestry with the corrupt versions of knowledge accessible to non-Aryans. Krieck could refer without hesitation to 'Protestant and Catholic science, German and Jewish science.' And, in a special application of the Insider doctrine, the Nazi regime could introduce the new racial category of 'white Jews' to refer to those Aryans who had defiled their race by actual or symbolic contact with non-Aryans. Thus, the Nobel Prize physicist, Werner Heisenberg, became the most eminent member of this new race by persisting in his declaration that Einstein's theory of relativity constituted 'an obvious basis for further research.' While another Nobel laureate in physics, Johannes Stark, could castigate not only Heisenberg but his other great scientific contemporaries – Planck, von Laue, and Schrödinger – for accepting what Stark described as 'the Jewish physics of Einstein' (Merton, 1968, pp. 538–41).

For our purposes, we need not review the array of elitist doctrines which have maintained that certain groups have, on biological or social grounds, monopolistic or privileged access to new knowledge. Differing in detail, the doctrines are alike in distinguishing between Insider access to knowledge and Outsider exclusion from it.

SOCIAL BASES OF INSIDER DOCTRINE

The ecumenical problem of the interaction between a rapidly changing social structure and the development of Insider and Outsider doctrines is examined here in a doubly parochial fashion. Not only are my observations largely limited to the United States in our time but they are further limited to the implications of doctrines advocated by spokesmen for certain black social movements, since these movements have often come to serve as prototypical for the others (women, youth, homosexuals, other ethnics, etc.).

Although Insider doctrines have been intermittently set forth by white elitists through the centuries, white male Insiderism in American sociology during the past generations has largely been of the tacit or de facto rather than doctrinal or principled variety. It has simply taken the form of patterned expectations about the appropriate selection of specialities and of problems for investigation. The handful of Negro sociologists were in large part expected, as a result of social selection and self-selection, to study problems of Negro life and relations between the races just as the handful of women sociologists were expected to study problems of women, principally as these related to marriage and the family.

In contrast to this de facto form of Insiderism, an explicitly doctrinal form has in recent years been put forward most clearly and emphatically by some black intellectuals. In its strong version, the argument holds that, as a matter of social epistemology, *only* black historians can truly understand black history, *only* black ethnologists can understand black culture, *only* black sociologists can understand the social life of blacks, and so on. In the weaker form of the doctrine, some practical concessions are made. With regard to programs of Black Studies, for example, it is proposed that some white professors of the relevant subjects might be brought in since there are not yet enough black scholars to staff all the proliferating programs of study. But as Nathan Hare, the founding publisher of the *Black Scholar*, stated several years ago, this is only on temporary and conditional sufferance: 'Any white professors involved in the program would have to be black in spirit in order to last. The same is true for "Negro" professors.'[6] Apart from this kind of limited concession, the Insider doctrine maintains that there is a body of black history, black psychology, black ethnology, and black sociology which can be significantly advanced only by black scholars and social scientists.

In its fundamental character, this represents a major claim in the sociology of knowledge that implies the balkanization of social science, with separate baronies kept exclusively in the hands of Insiders bearing their credentials in the shape of one or another ascribed status. Generalizing the specific claim, it would appear to follow that if only black scholars can understand blacks, then only white scholars can understand whites. Generalizing further from race to nation, it would then appear, for example, that only French scholars can understand French society and, of course, that only Americans, not their external critics, can truly understand American society. Once the basic principle is adopted, the list of Insider claims to a monopoly of knowledge becomes indefinitely expansible to all manner of social formations based on ascribed (and, by extension, on some achieved) statuses. It would thus seem to follow that only women can understand women – and men, men. On the same principle, youth alone is capable of understanding youth just as, presumably, only the middle aged are able to understand their age peers.[7] Furthermore, as we shift to the hybrid cases of ascribed and acquired statuses in varying mix, on the Insider principle, proletarians alone can understand proletarians and presumably capitalists, capitalists; only Catholics, Catholics; Jews, Jews, and to halt the inventory of socially atomized claims to knowledge with a limiting case that on its face would seem to have some merit, it would then plainly follow that only sociologists are able to understand their fellow sociologists.[8]

In all these applications, the doctrine of extreme Insiderism represents a new credentialism.[9] This is the credentialism of ascribed status, in which understanding becomes accessible only to the fortunate few or many who are to the manner born. In this respect, it contrasts with the credentialism of achieved status that is characteristic of meritocratic systems.[10]

Extreme Insiderism moves toward a doctrine of *group* methodological solipsism.[11] In this form of solipsism, each group must in the end have a monopoly of knowledge about itself just as according to the doctrine of *individual* methodological solipsism each individual has absolute privacy of knowledge about him- or her-self. The Insider doctrine can be put in the vernacular with no great loss in meaning: you have to be one in order to understand one. In somewhat less idiomatic language, the doctrine holds that one has monopolistic or privileged access to knowledge, or is wholly excluded from it, by virtue of one's group membership or social position. For some, the notion appears in the form of a question-begging pun: Insider as Insighter, one endowed with special insight into matters necessarily obscure to others, thus possessed of penetrating discernment. Once adopted, the pun provides a specious solution but the serious Insider doctrine has its own rationale.

We can quickly pass over the trivial version of that rationale: the argument that the Outsider may be incompetent, given to quick and superficial forays into the group or culture under study and even unschooled in its language. That this kind of incompetence can be found is beyond doubt but it holds no principled interest for us. Foolish men (and women) or badly trained men (and women) are to be found everywhere, and anthropologists and sociologists and psychologists and historians engaged in study of groups other than their own surely have their fair share of them.[12] But such cases of special ineptitude do not bear on the Insider *principle*. It is not merely that Insiders also have their share of incompetents. The Insider principle does not refer to stupidly designed and stupidly executed inquiries that happen to be made by stupid Outsiders; it maintains a more fundamental position. According to the doctrine of the Insider, the Outsider, no matter how careful and talented, is excluded in principle from gaining access to the social and cultural truth.

In short, the doctrine holds that the Outsider has a structurally imposed incapacity to comprehend alien groups, statuses, cultures, and societies. Unlike the Insider, the Outsider has neither been socialized in the group nor has engaged in the run of experience that makes up its life, and therefore cannot have the direct, intuitive sensitivity that alone makes empathic understanding possible. Only through continued socialization in the life of a group can one become fully aware of its symbolisms and socially shared realities; only so can one understand the fine-grained meanings of behavior, feelings, and values; only so can one decipher the unwritten grammar of conduct and the nuances of cultural idiom. Or, to take a specific expression of this thesis by Ralph W. Conant (1968): 'Whites are not and never will be as sensitive to the black community precisely because they are not part of that community.' Correlatively, Abd-l Hakimu Ibn Alkalimat (Gerald McWorter) draws a sharp contrast between the concepts of 'a black social science' and 'a white social science' (1969, p. 35).

A somewhat less stringent version of the doctrine maintains only that Insider and Outsider scholars have significantly different foci of interest. The argument goes somewhat as follows. The Insiders, sharing the deepest concerns of the group or at the least being thoroughly aware of them, will so direct their inquiries as to have them be relevant to those concerns. So, too, the Outsiders will inquire into problems relevant to the distinctive values and interests which they share with members of *their* group. But these are bound to differ from those of the group under study if only because the Outsiders occupy different places in the social structure.

This is a hypothesis which has the not unattractive quality of being readily amenable to empirical investigation. It should be possible to compare the spectrum of research problems about, say, the black population in the country that have been investigated by black sociologists and by white ones, or say, the spectrum of problems about women that have been investigated by female sociologists and by male ones, in order to find out whether the foci of attention in fact differ and if so, to what degree and in which respects. The only inquiry of this kind I happen to know of was published more than a quarter-century ago. William Fontaine (1944) found that Negro scholars tended to adopt analytical rather than morphological categories in their study of behavior, that they emphasized environmental rather than biological determinants of that behavior, and tended to make use of strikingly dramatic rather than representative data. All this was ascribed to a caste-induced resentment among Negro scholars. But since this lone study failed to examine the frequency of subjects, types of interpretation, and uses of data among a comparable sample of white scholars at the time, the findings are somewhat less than compelling. All the same, the questions it addressed remain. For there is theoretical reason to suppose that the foci of research adopted by Insiders and Outsiders and perhaps their categories of analysis as well will tend to differ. At least, Max Weber's notion of *Wertbeziehung* suggests that differing social locations, with their distinctive interests and values, will affect the selection of problems for investigation (Weber, 1951/ 1922, pp. 146–214).

Unlike the stringent version of the doctrine which maintains that Insiders and Outsiders must arrive at different (and presumably incompatible) findings and interpretations even when they do examine the same problems, this weaker version argues only that they will not deal with the same questions and so will simply talk past one another. With the two versions combined, the extended version of the Insider doctrine can also be put in the vernacular: one must not only be one in order to understand one; one must be one in order to understand what is most worth understanding.

Clearly, the social epistemological doctrine of the Insider links up with what Sumner (1907, p. 13) long ago defined as ethnocentrism: 'the technical name for [the] view of things in which one's own group is the center of everything, and all others are scaled and rated with reference to it.' Sumner then goes on to include as a component of ethnocentrism, rather than as a frequent correlate of it (thus robbing his idea of some of its potential analytical power), the belief that one's group is superior to all cognate groups: 'each group nourishes its own pride and vanity, boasts itself superior, exalts its own divinities, and looks with contempt on outsiders' (p. 13). For although the practice of seeing one's own group as the center of things is empirically correlated with a belief in its superiority, centrality and superiority need to be kept analytically distinct in order to deal with patterns of alienation from one's membership group and contempt for it.[13]

Supplementing the abundance of historical and ethnological evidence of the empirical tendency for belief one's group or collectivity as superior to all cognate groups or collectivities –whether nation, class, race, region, or organization – is a recent batch of studies of what Theodore Caplow (1964, pp. 213–16) has called the aggrandizement effect: the distortion upward of the prestige of an organization by its members. Caplow examined 33 different kinds of organizations – ranging from dance studios to Protestant and Catholic churches, from skid row missions to big banks, and from advertising agencies to university departments – and found that members overestimated the prestige of their organization some 'eight times as often as they underestimated it' (when compared with judgments by Outsiders). More in point for us, while members tended to disagree with Outsiders about the standing of their own organization, they tended to agree with them about the prestige of the other organizations in the same set. These findings can be taken as something of a sociological parable. In these matters at least, the judgments of 'Insiders' are best trusted when they assess groups other than their own; that is, when members of groups judge as Outsiders rather than as Insiders.

Findings of this sort do not testify, of course, that ethnocentrism and its frequent spiritual correlate, xenophobia, fear and hatred of the alien, are incorrigible. They do, however, remind us of the widespread tendency to glorify the ingroup, sometimes to that degree in which it qualifies as chauvinism: the extreme, blind, and often bellicose extolling of one's group, status, or collectivity. We need not abandon 'chauvinism' as a concept useful to us here merely because it has lately become adopted as a vogue word, blunted in meaning through indiscriminate use as a rhetorical weapon in intergroup conflict. Nor need we continue to confine the scope of the concept, as it was in its origins and later by Lasswell (1937, p. 361) in his short, incisive discussion of it, to the special case of the *state or nation*. The concept can be usefully, not tendentiously, extended to designate the extreme glorification of *any* social formation.

Chauvinism finds its fullest ideological expression when groups are subject to the stress of acute conflict. Under the stress of war, for example, scientists have been known to violate the values and norms of universalism in which they were socialized, allowing their status as nationals to dominate over their status as scientists. Thus, at the outset of World War I, almost a hundred German scholars and scientists – including many of the first rank, such as Brentano, Ehrlich, Haber, Eduard Meyer, Ostwald, Planck, and Schmoller – could bring themselves to issue a manifesto that impugned the contributions of the enemy to science, charging them with nationalistic bias, logrolling, intellectual dishonesty and, when you came right down to it, the absence of truly creative capacity. The English and French scientists were not far behind in advertising their own brand of chauvinism.[14]

Ethnocentrism, then, is not a historical constant. It becomes intensified under specifiable conditions of acute social conflict. When a nation, race, ethnic group, or any other powerful collectivity has long extolled its own admirable qualities and, expressly or by implication, deprecated the qualities of others, it invites and provides the potential for counterethnocentrism. And when a once largely powerless collectivity acquires a socially validated sense of growing power, its members experience an intensified need for self-affirmation. Under such circumstances, collective self-glorification, found in some measure among all groups, becomes a predictable and intensified counterresponse to long-standing belittlement from without.[15]

So it is that, in the United States, the centuries-long institutionalized premise that 'white (and for some, presumably only white) is true and good and beautiful' induces, under conditions of revolutionary change the counterpremise that 'black (and for some, presumably only black) is true and good and beautiful.' And just as the social system has for centuries operated on the tacit or explicit premise that in cases of conflict between whites and blacks, the whites are presumptively right, so there now develops the counterpremise, finding easy confirmation in the long history of injustice visited upon American Negroes, that in cases of such conflict today, the blacks are presumptively right.

What is being proposed here is that the epistemological claims of the Insider to monopolistic or privileged access to social truth develop under particular social and historical conditions. Social groups or strata on the way up develop a revolutionary élan. The new thrust to a larger share of power and control over their social and political environment finds various expressions, among them claims to a unique access to knowledge about their history, culture, and social life.

On this interpretation, we can understand why this Insider doctrine does not argue for a Black Physics, Black Chemistry, Black Biology, or Black Technology. For the new will to control their fate deals with the social environment, not the environment of nature. There is, moreover, nothing in the segregated life experience of Negroes that is said to sensitize them to the subject matters and problematics of the physical and life sciences. An Insider doctrine would have to forge genetic assumptions about racial modes of thought in order to claim, as in the case of the Nazi version they did claim, monopolistic or privileged access to knowledge in these fields of science. But the black Insider doctrine adopts an essentially social-environmental rationale, not a biologically genetic one.

The social process underlying the emergence of Insider doctrine is reasonably clear. Polarization in the underlying social structure becomes reflected in the polarization of claims in the intellectual and ideological domain, as groups or collectivities seek to capture what Heidegger called the 'public interpretation of reality.'[16] With varying degrees of intent, groups in conflict want to make their interpretation the prevailing one of how things were and are and will be. The critical measure of success occurs when the interpretation moves beyond the boundaries of the ingroup to be accepted by Outsiders. At the extreme, it then gives rise, through identifiable processes of reference-group behavior, to the familiar case of the converted Outsider validating himself, in his own eyes and in those of others, by becoming even more zealous than the Insiders in adhering to the doctrine of the group with which he wants to identify himself, if only symbolically (Merton 1968, pp. 405–6). He then becomes more royalist than the king, more papist than the pope. Some white social scientists, for example, vicariously and personally guilt ridden over centuries of white racism, are prepared to outdo the claims of the group they would symbolically join. They are ready even to surrender their hard-won expert knowledge if the Insider doctrine seems to require it. This type of response was perhaps epitomized in a televised educational program in which the white curator of African ethnology at a major museum engaged in discussion with a black who, as it happens, had had no prolonged ethnological training. All the same, at a crucial juncture in the public conversation, the distinguished ethnologist could be heard to say: 'I realize, of course, that I cannot begin to understand the black experience, in Africa or America, as you can. Won't you tell our audience about it?' Here, in the spontaneity of an unrehearsed public discussion, the Insider doctrine has indeed become the public interpretation of reality.

The black Insider doctrine links up with the historically developing social structure in still another way. The dominant social institutions in this country have long treated the racial identity of individuals as actually if not doctrinally relevant to all manner of situations in every sphere of life. For generations, neither blacks nor whites, though with notably differing consequences, were permitted to forget their race. *This treatment of social status (or identity) as relevant when intrinsically it is functionally irrelevant constitutes the very core of social discrimination.* As the once firmly rooted systems of discriminatory institutions and prejudicial ideology began to lose their hold, this meant that increasingly many judged the worth of ideas on their merits, not in terms of their racial pedigree.

What the Insider doctrine of the most militant blacks proposes on the level of social structure is to adopt the salience of racial identity in every sort of role and situation, a pattern so long imposed upon the American Negro, and to make that identity a total commitment issuing from within the group rather than one imposed upon it from without. By thus affirming the universal saliency of race and by redefining race as an abiding source of pride rather than stigma, the Insider doctrine in effect models itself after doctrine long maintained by white racists.

Neither this component of the Insider doctrine nor the statement on its implications is at all new. Almost a century ago, Frederick Douglass (1966/1889) hinged his observations along these lines on the distinction between collective and individual self-images based on ascribed and achieved status:

> One of the few errors to which we are clinging most persistently and, as I think, most mischievously has come into great prominence of late. It is the cultivation and stimulation among us of a sentiment which we are pleased to call race pride. I find it in all our books, papers, and speeches. For my part I see no superiority or inferiority in race or color. Neither the one nor the other is a proper source of pride or complacency. Our race and color are not of our own choosing. We have no volition in the case one way or another. The only excuse for pride in individuals or races is in the fact of their own achievements ... I see no benefit to be derived from this everlasting exhortation of speakers and writers among us to the cultivation of race pride. On the contrary, I see in it a positive evil. It is building on a false foundation. Besides, what is the thing we are fighting against, and what are we fighting for in this country? What is the mountain devil, the lion in the way of our progress? What is it, but American race pride; an assumption of superiority upon the ground of race and color? Do we not know that every argument we make, and every pretension we set up in favor of race pride is giving the enemy a stick to break over our heads?

In rejecting the cause of racial chauvinism, Douglass addressed the normative rather than the cognitive aspect of Insiderism. The call to total commitment requiring one group loyalty to be unquestionably paramount is most apt to be heard when the particular group or collectivity is engaged in severe conflict with others. Just as conditions of war between nations have long produced a strain toward hyper-patriotism among national ethnocentrics, so current intergroup conflicts have produced a strain toward hyperloyalty among racial or sex or age or religious ethnocentrics. Total commitment easily slides from the solidarity doctrine of 'our group, right or wrong' to the morally and intellectually preemptive doctrine of 'our group, always right, never wrong.'

Turning from the normative aspect, with its ideology exhorting prime loyalty to this or that group, to the cognitive, specifically epistemological aspect, we note that the Insider doctrine presupposes a particular imagery of social structure.

SOCIAL STRUCTURE OF INSIDERS AND OUTSIDERS

From the discussion thus far, it should be evident that I adopt a structural conception of Insiders and Outsiders. In this conception, Insiders are the members of specified groups and collectivities or occupants of specified social statuses; Outsiders are the nonmembers.[17] This structural concept comes closer to Sumner's usage in his *Folkways* than to various meanings assigned the Outsider by Nietzsche, Kierkegaard, Sartre, Camus (1946) or, for that matter, by Colin Wilson (1956) just as, to come nearer home, it differs from the usages adopted by Riesman, Denny, and Glazer (1950), Price (1965, pp. 83–84), or Howard S. Becker (1963). That is to say, Insiders and Outsiders are here defined as categories in social structure, not as inside dopesters or the specially initiated possessors of esoteric information on the one hand and as social-psychological types marked by alienation, rootlessness, or rule breaking, on the other.

In structural terms, we are all, of course, both Insiders and Outsiders, members of some groups and, sometimes derivatively, not of others; occupants of certain statuses which thereby exclude us from occupying other cognate statuses. Obvious as this basic fact of social structure is, its implications for Insider and Outsider epistemological doctrines are apparently not nearly as obvious. Else, these doctrines would not presuppose, as they typically do, that human beings in socially differentiated societies can be sufficiently located in terms of a single social status, category, or group affiliation – black or white, men or women, under 30 or older – or of several such categories, taken seriatim rather than conjointly. This neglects the crucial fact of social structure that individuals have not a single status but a status set: a complement of variously interrelated statuses which interact to affect both their behavior and perspectives.

The structural fact of status sets, in contrast to statuses taken one at a time, introduces severe theoretical problems for total Insider (and Outsider) doctrines of social epistemology. The array of status sets in a population means that aggregates of individuals share some statuses and not others; or, to put this in context, that they typically confront one another simultaneously as Insiders and Outsiders. Thus, if only whites can understand whites and blacks, blacks, and only men can understand men, and women, women, this gives rise to the paradox which severely limits both premises: for it then turns out, by assumption, that some Insiders are excluded from understanding other Insiders with white women being condemned not to understand white men, and black men, not to understand black women,[18] and so through the various combinations of status subsets.

Structural analysis in terms of shared and mutually exclusive status sets will surely not be mistaken either as advocating divisions within the ranks of collectivities defined by a single prime criterion or as predicting that such collectivities cannot unite on many issues, despite their internal divisions. Such analysis only indicates the bases of social divisions that stand in the way of enduring unity of any of the collectivities and so must be coped with, divisions that are not easily overcome as new issues activate statuses with diverse and often conflicting interests. Thus, the obstacles to a union of women in England and North Ireland resulting from national, political, and religious differences between them are no less formidable than the obstacles, noted by Marx, confronting the union of English and Irish proletarians. So, too, women's liberation movements seeking unity in the United States find themselves periodically contending with the divisions between blacks and whites within their ranks, just as black liberation movements seeking unity find themselves periodically contending with the divisions between men and liberated women within their ranks (Chisholm, 1970; LaRue, 1970).

The problem of achieving unity in large social movements based on any one status when its members are differentiated by crosscutting status sets is epitomized in these words about women's liberation by a black woman where identification with race is dominant: 'Of course there have been women who have been able to think better than they've been trained and have produced the canon of literature fondly referred to as "feminist literature": Anais Nin, Simone de Beauvoir, Doris Lessing, Betty Friedan, etc. And the question for us arises: how relevant are the truths, the experiences, the findings of white women to Black women? Are women after all simply women? I don't know that our priorities are the same, that our concerns and methods are the same, or even similar enough so that we can afford to depend on this new field of experts (white, female). It is rather obvious that we do not. It is obvious that we are turning to each other' (Cade, 1970, p. 9).

Correlatively, the following passage epitomizes the way in which internal differentiation works against unity of the black liberation movement where dominant identification with sex status is reinforced by further educational differentiation:

> Seems to me the Brother does us all a great disservice by telling her to fight the man with the womb. Better to fight with the gun and the mind ... The all too breezy no-pill/have-kids/mess-up-the-man's-plan notion these comic-book-loving Sisters find so exciting is very seductive because it's a clear-cut and easy thing for her to do for the cause since it nourishes her sense of martyrdom. If the thing is numbers merely, what the hell. But if we are talking about revolution, creating an army for today and tomorrow, I think the Brothers who've been screaming these past years had better go do their homework. (Cade, 1970, pp. 167–68)

The internal differentiation of collectivities based on a single status thus provides structural bases for diverse and often conflicting intellectual and moral perspectives within such collectivities. Differences of religion or age or class or occupation work to divide what similarities of race or sex or nationality work to unite. That is why social movements of every variety that strive for unity – whether they are establishmentarian movements whipped up by chauvinistic nationals in time of war or antiestablishmentarian movements designed to undo institutionalized injustice – press for total commitments in which all other loyalties are to be subordinated, on demand, to the dominant one.

This symptomatic exercise in status-set analysis may be enough to indicate that the idiomatic expression of total Insider doctrine – one must be one in order to understand one – is deceptively simple and sociologically fallacious (just as we shall see is the case with the total Outsider doctrine). For, from the sociological perspective of the status set, 'one' is not a man *or* a black *or* an adolescent *or* a Protestant, *or* self-defined and socially defined as middle class, and so on. Sociologically, 'one' is, of course, all of these and, depending on the size of the status set, much more. Furthermore, as Simmel (1908, pp. 403–54 [also Chapter 5 in this volume]) and Coser (1965, pp. 18–20) taught us long ago, the individuality of human beings can be sociologically derived from social differentiation and not only psychologically derived from intrapsychic processes. Thus, the greater the number and variety of group affiliations and statuses distributed among individuals in a society, the smaller, on the average, the number of individuals having precisely the same social configuration.

Following out the implications of this structural observation, we note that, on its own assumptions, the total Insider doctrine should hold only for highly fragmented small aggregates sharing the same status sets. Even a truncated status set involving only three affiliations – WASPS, for example – would greatly reduce the number of people who, under the Insider principle, would be able to understand their fellows (WASPS). The numbers rapidly decline as we attend to more of the shared status sets by including such social categories as sex, age, class, occupation, and so on, toward the limiting case in which the unique occupant of a highly complex status set is alone qualified to achieve an understanding of self. The tendency toward such extreme social atomization is of course damped by differences in the significance of statuses which vary in degrees of dominance, saliency, and centrality.[19] As a result, the fragmentation of the capacity for understanding that is implied in the total Insider doctrine will not empirically reach this extreme. The structural analysis in terms of status sets, rather than in the fictional terms of individuals being identified in terms of single statuses, serves only to push the logic of Insiderism to its ultimate methodological solipsism.

The fact of structural and institutional differentiation has other kinds of implications for the effort to translate the Insider claim to solidarity into an Insider epistemology. Since we all occupy various statuses and have group affiliations of varying significance to us, since, in short, we individually link up with the differentiated society through our status sets, this runs counter to the abiding and exclusive primacy of any one group affiliation. Differing situations activate different statuses which then and there dominate over the rival claims of other statuses.

This aspect of the dynamics of status sets can also be examined from the standpoint of the differing margins of functional autonomy possessed by various social institutions and other social subsystems. Each significant affiliation exacts loyalty to values, standards, and norms governing the given institutional domain, whether religion, science, or economy. Sociological thinkers such as Marx and Sorokin, so wide apart in many of their other assumptions, agree in assigning a margin of autonomy to the sphere of knowledge[20] even as they posit their respective social, economic, or cultural determinants of it. The alter ego of Marx, for example, declares the partial autonomy of spheres of thought in a well-known passage that bears repetition here:

According to the materialist conception of history the determining element in history is *ultimately* the production and reproduction in real life. More than this neither Marx nor I have ever asserted. If therefore somebody twists this into the statement that the economic element is the *only* determining one, he transforms it into a meaningless, abstract and absurd phrase. The economic situation is the basis, but the various elements of the superstructure – political forms of the class struggle and its consequences, constitutions established by the victorious class after a successful battle, etc. – forms of law – and then even the reflexes of all these actual struggles in the brains of the combatants: political, legal, philosophical theories, religious ideas and their further development into systems of dogma – also exercise their influence upon the course of the historical struggles and in many cases preponderate in determining their *form*. There is an interaction of all these elements in which ... the economic movement finally asserts itself as necessary. Otherwise the application of the theory to any period of history one chooses would be easier than the solution of a simple equation of the first degree. (Engels, 1936/1890, p. 381; see also p. 392)

We can see structural differentiation and institutional autonomy at work in current responses of scholars to the extreme Insider doctrine. They reject the monopolistic doctrine of the Insider that calls for total ideological loyalty in which efforts to achieve scholarly detachment and objectivity become redefined as renegadism just as ideological reinforcement of collective self-esteem becomes redefined as the higher objectivity. It is here, to continue with our case in point, that Negro scholars who retain their double loyalty – to the race and to the values and norms of scholarship – part company with the all-encompassing loyalty demanded by the Insider doctrine. Martin Kilson (1969), for example, repudiates certain aspects of the doctrine and expresses his commitment to both the institutionalized values of scholarship and to the black community in these words:

I am opposed to proposals to make Afro-American studies into a platform for a particular ideological group, and to restrict these studies to Negro *students and teachers*. For, and we must be frank about this, what this amounts to is racism in reverse – black racism. I am certainly convinced that it is important for the Negro to know of his past – of his ancestors, of their strengths and weaknesses – and they should respect this knowledge, when it warrants respect, and they should question it and criticize it, when it deserves criticism. But it is of no advantage to a mature and critical understanding or appreciation of one's heritage if you approach that heritage with the assumption that it is intrinsically good and noble, and intrinsically superior to the heritage of other peoples. That is, after all, what white racists have done; and none of my militant friends in the black studies movement have convinced me that racist thought is any less vulgar and degenerate because it is used by black men . . . What I am suggesting here is that the serious study of the heritage of any people will produce a curious mixture of things to be proud of, things to criticize and even despise and things to be perpetually ambivalent toward. And this is as it should be: only an ideologically oriented Afro-American studies program, seeking to propagate a packaged view of the black heritage, would fail to evoke in a student the curious yet fascinating mixture of pride, criticism and ambivalence which I think *is, or ought to be the product of serious intellectual and academic activity*. (pp. 329–30; italics added)

Along with the faults of neglecting the implications of structural differentiation, status sets, and institutional autonomy, the Insider (and comparable Outsider) doctrine has the further fault of assuming, in its claims of monopolistic or highly privileged status-based access to knowledge, that social position wholly determines intellectual perspectives. In doing so, it affords yet another example of the ease with which truths can decline into error merely by being extended well beyond the limits within which they have been found to hold. (There *can* be too much of a good thing.)

A long-standing conception shared by various 'schools' of sociological thought holds that differences in the social location of individuals and groups tend to involve differences in their interests and value orientations (as well as the sharing of some interests and values with others). Certain traditions in the sociology of knowledge have gone on to assume that these structurally patterned differences should involve, on the *average*, patterned differences in perceptions and perspectives. And these, so the convergent traditions hold – their convergence being often obscured by diversity in vocabulary rather than in basic concept – should make for discernible differences, on the average, in the definitions of problems for inquiry and in the types of hypotheses taken as points of departure. So far, so good. The evidence is far from in, since it has also been a tradition in the sociology of scientific knowledge during the greater part of the past century to prefer speculative theory to empirical inquiry. But the idea, which can be taken as a general orientation guiding such inquiry, is greatly transformed in Insider doctrine.

For one thing, that doctrine assumes total coincidence between social position and individual perspectives. It thus exaggerates into error the conception of structural analysis which maintains that there is a *tendency for, not a full determination of*, socially patterned differences in the perspectives, preferences, and behavior of people variously located in the social structure. The theoretical emphasis on tendency, as distinct from total uniformity, is basic, not casual or niggling. It provides for a range of variability in perspective and behavior among members of the same groups or occupants of the same status (differences which, as we have seen, are ascribable to social as well as psychological differentiation). At the same time, this structural conception also provides for patterned differences, *on the whole*, between the perspectives of members of different groups or occupants of different statuses. Structural analysis thus avoids what Dennis Wrong (1961) has aptly described as 'the oversocialized conception of man in modern sociology.'[21]

Important as such allowance for individual variability is for general structural theory, it has particular significance for a sociological perspective on the life of the mind and the advancement of science and learning. For it is precisely the individual differences among scientists and scholars that are often central to the development of the discipline. They often involve the differences between good scholarship and bad; between imaginative contributions to science and pedestrian ones; between the consequential ideas and stillborn ones. In arguing for the monopolistic access to knowledge, Insider doctrine can make no provision for individual variability that extends beyond the boundaries of the ingroup which alone can develop sound and fruitful ideas.

Insofar as Insider doctrine treats ascribed rather than achieved statuses as central in forming perspectives, it tends to be static in orientation. For with the glaring exception of age status itself, ascribed statuses are generally retained throughout the life span. Yet sociologically, there is nothing fixed about the boundaries separating Insiders from Outsiders. As situations involving different values arise, different statuses are activated and the lines of separation shift. Thus, for a large number of white Americans, Joe Louis was a member of an outgroup. But when Louis defeated the Nazified Max Schmeling, many of the same white Americans promptly redefined him as a member of the (national) ingroup. National self-esteem took precedence over racial separatism. That this sort of drama in which changing situations activate differing statuses in the status set is played out in the domain of the intellect as well is the point of Einstein's ironic observation in an address at the Sorbonne: 'If my theory of relativity is proven successful, Germany will claim me as a German and France will declare that I am a citizen of the world. Should my theory prove untrue, France will say that I am a German and Germany will declare that I am a Jew.'[22]

Like earlier conceptions in the sociology of knowledge, recent Insider doctrines maintain that, in the end, it is a special category of Inside – a category that generally manages to include the proponent of the doctrine – that has sole or privileged access to knowledge. Mannheim (1936, pp. 10, 139, 232), for example, found a structural warranty for the validity of social thought in the 'classless position' of the 'socially unattached intellectuals' (*sozialfreischwebende Intelligenz*). In his view, these intellectuals can comprehend the conflicting tendencies of the time since, among other things, they are 'recruited from constantly varying social strata and life-situations.' (This is more than a little reminiscent of the argument in the *Communist Manifesto* which emphasizes that 'the proletariat is recruited from all classes of the population.')[23] Without stretching this argument to the breaking point, it can be said that Mannheim in effect claims that there is a category of socially free-floating intellectuals who are both Insiders and Outsiders. Benefiting from their collectively diverse social origins and transcending group allegiances, they can observe the social universe with special insight and a synthesizing eye.

INSIDERS AS 'OUTSIDERS'

In an adaptation of this same kind of idea, what some Insiders profess as Insiders they apparently reject as Outsiders. For example, when advocates of black Insider doctrine engage in analysis of 'white society,' trying to assay its power structure or to detect its vulnerabilities, they seem to deny in practice what they affirm in doctrine. At any rate, their behavior testifies to the assumption that it is possible for self-described 'Outsiders' to diagnose and to understand what they describe as an alien social structure and culture.

This involves the conception that there is a special category of people in the system of social stratification who have distinctive, if not exclusive, perceptions and understanding in their capacities as *both* Insiders and Outsiders. We need not review again the argument for special access to knowledge that derives from being an Insider. What is of interest here is the idea that special perspectives and insights are available to that category of Outsiders who have been systematically frustrated by the social system: the disinherited, deprived, disenfranchised, dominated, and exploited Outsiders. Their run of experience in trying to cope with these problems serves to sensitize them – and in a more disciplined way, the trained social scientists among them – to the workings of the culture and social structure that are more apt to be taken for granted by Insider social scientists drawn from social strata who have either benefited from the going social system or have not greatly suffered from it.

This reminder that Outsiders are not all of a kind and the derived hypothesis in the sociology of knowledge about socially patterned differences in perceptiveness is plausible and deserving of far more systematic investigation than it has received. That the white-dominated society has long imposed social barriers which excluded Negroes from anything remotely like full participation in that society is now known to even the more unobservant whites. But what many of them have evidently not noticed is that the high walls of segregation do not at all separate whites and blacks symmetrically from intimate observation of the social life of the other. As socially invisible men and women, blacks at work in white enclaves have for centuries moved through or around the walls of segregation to discover with little effort what was on the other side. This was tantamount to their having access to a one-way screen. In contrast, the highly visible whites characteristically did not want to find out about life in the black community and could not, even in those rare cases where they would. The structure of racial segregation meant that the whites who prided themselves on 'understanding' Negroes knew little more than their stylized role behaviors in relation to whites and next to nothing of their private lives. As Arthur Lewis has noted, something of the same sort still obtains with the 'integration' of many blacks into the larger society during the day coupled with segregation at night as blacks and whites return to their respective ghettos. In these ways, segregation can make for asymmetrical sensitivities across the divide.

Although there is a sociological tradition of reflection and research on marginality in relation to thought, sociologists have hardly begun the hard work of seriously investigating the family of hypotheses in the sociology of knowledge that derive from this conception of asymmetrical relations between diverse kinds of Insiders and Outsiders.

OUTSIDER DOCTRINE AND PERSPECTIVES

The strong version of the Insider doctrine, with its epistemological claim to a monopoly of certain kinds of knowledge, runs counter, of course, to a long history of thought. From the time of Francis Bacon, to reach back no further, students of the intellectual life have emphasized the corrupting influence of group loyalties upon the human understanding. Among Bacon's four Idols (or sources of false opinion), we need only recall the second, the Idol of the Cave. Drawing upon Plato's allegory of the cave in the *Republic*, Bacon undertakes to tell how the immediate social world in which we live seriously limits what we are prepared to perceive and how we perceive it. Dominated by the customs of our group, we maintain received opinions, distort our perceptions to have them accord with these opinions, and are thus held in ignorance and led into error which we parochially mistake for the truth. Only when we escape from the cave and extend our visions do we provide for access to authentic knowledge. By implication, it is through the iconoclasm that comes with changing group affiliations that we can destroy the Idol of the Cave, abandon delusory doctrines of our own group, and enlarge our prospects for reaching the truth. For Bacon, the dedicated Insider is peculiarly subject to the myopia of the cave.

In this conception, Bacon characteristically attends only to the dysfunctions of group affiliation for knowledge. Since for him access to authentic knowledge requires that one abandon superstition and prejudice, and since these stem from groups, it would not occur to Bacon to consider the possible functions of social locations in society as providing for observability and access to particular kinds of knowledge.

In a far more subtle style, the founding fathers of sociology in effect also argued against the strong form of the Insider doctrine *without turning to the equal and opposite error of advocating the strong form of the Outsider doctrine* (which would hold that knowledge about groups, unprejudiced by membership in them, is accessible only to outsiders).

The ancient epistemological problem of subject and object was taken up in the discussion of historical *Verstehen*. Thus, first Simmel and then, repeatedly, Max Weber symptomatically adopted the memorable phrase: 'one need not be Caesar in order to understand Caesar.'[24] In making this claim, they rejected the extreme Insider thesis which asserts in effect that one *must* be Caesar in order to understand him just as they rejected the extreme Outsider thesis that one must *not* be Caesar in order to understand him.

The observations of Simmel and Weber bear directly upon implications of the Insider doctrine that reach beyond its currently emphasized scope. The Insider argues that the authentic understanding of group life can be achieved only by those who are directly engaged as members in the life of the group. Taken seriously, the doctrine puts in question the validity of just about all historical writing, as Weber clearly saw (1951/1922, p. 428).[25] If direct engagement in the life of a group is essential to understanding it, then the only authentic history is contemporary history, written in fragments by those most fully involved in making inevitably limited portions of it. Rather than constituting only the raw materials of history, the documents prepared by engaged Insiders become all there is to history. But once the historian elects to write the history of a time other than his own, even the most dedicated Insider, of the national, sex, age, racial, ethnic, or religious variety, becomes the Outsider, condemned to error and misunderstanding.

Writing some 20 years ago in another connection, Claude Lévi-Strauss noted the parallelism between history and ethnography. Both subjects, he observed,

> are concerned with societies *other* than the one in which we live. Whether this *otherness* is due to remoteness in time (however slight) or to remoteness in space, or even to cultural heterogeneity, is of secondary importance compared to the basic similarity of perspective. All that the historian or ethnographer can do, and all that we can expect of either of them, is to enlarge a specific experience to the dimensions of a more general one, which thereby becomes accessible as *experience* to men of another country or another epoch. And in order to succeed, both historian and ethnographer, must have the same qualities: skill, precision a sympathetic approach and objectivity.[26]

Our question is, of course, whether the qualities required by the historian and ethnographer as well as other social scientists are confined to or largely concentrated among Insiders or Outsiders. Simmel (1908), and after him, Schütz (1944), and others have pondered the roles of that incarnation of the Outsider, the stranger who moves on.[27] In a fashion oddly reminiscent of the anything-but-subtle Baconian doctrine, Simmel develops the thesis that the stranger, not caught up in commitments to the group, can more readily acquire the strategic role of the relatively objective inquirer. 'He is freer, practically and theoretically,' notes Simmel (1950), 'he surveys conditions with less prejudice; his criteria for them are more general and more objective ideals; he is not tied down in his action by habit, piety, and precedent' (pp. 404–5). Above all, and here Simmel departs from the simple Baconian conception, the objectivity of the stranger 'does not simply involve passivity and detachment; it is a particular structure composed of distance and nearness, indifference and involvement.' It is the stranger, too, who finds what is familiar to the group significantly unfamiliar and so is prompted to raise questions for inquiry less apt to be raised at all by Insiders.

As was so often the case with Simmel's seminal mind, he thus raised a variety of significant questions about the role of the stranger in acquiring sound and new knowledge, questions that especially in recent years have begun to be seriously investigated. A great variety of inquiries into the roles of anthropological and sociological fieldworkers have explored the advantages and limitations of the Outsider as observer.[28] Even now, it appears that the balance sheet for Outsider observers resembles that for Insider observers, both having their distinctive assets and liabilities.

Apart from the theoretical and empirical work examining the possibly distinctive role of the Outsider in social and historical inquiry, significant episodes in the development of such inquiry can be examined as 'clinical cases' in point. Thus, it has been argued that in matters historical and sociological the prospects for achieving certain kinds of insights may actually be somewhat better for the Outsider. Soon after it appeared in 1835, Tocqueville's *Democracy in America* was acclaimed as a masterly work by 'an accomplished foreigner.' Tocqueville himself expressed the opinion that 'there are certain truths which Americans can only learn from strangers.' These included what he described as the tyranny of majority opinion and the particular system of stratification which even in that time involved a widespread preoccupation with relative status in the community that left 'Americans so restless in the midst of their prosperity.' (This *is* Tocqueville, not Galbraith, writing.) All the same, this most perceptive Outsider did not manage to transcend many of the deep-seated racial beliefs and myths he encountered in the United States of the time.

Having condemned the Anglo–Americans whose 'oppression has at one stroke deprived the descendants of the Africans of almost all the privileges of humanity' (Tocqueville 1945/1858, 1, p. 332);

> having described slavery as mankind's greatest calamity and having argued that the abolition of slavery in the North was 'not for the good of the Negroes, but for that of the whites' (ibid., 1:360–61);

having identified the marks of 'oppression' upon both the oppressed Indians and blacks *and* upon their white oppressors (ibid., vol. 1, chap. 18, passim);

having noted 'the tyranny of the laws' designed to suppress the 'unhappy blacks' in the states that had abolished slavery (ibid., 1:368);

having approximately noted the operation of the self-fulfilling prophecy in the remark that 'to induce the whites to abandon the opinion they have conceived of the moral and intellectual inferiority of their former slaves, the Negroes must change; but as long as this opinion subsists, to change is impossible' (ibid., 1:358, n.);

having also approximated the idea of relative deprivation in the statement that 'there exists a singular principle of relative justice which is very firmly implanted in the human heart. Men are much more forcibly struck by those inequalities which exist within the circle of the same class, than with those which may be remarked between different classes' (ibid., 1:373–74);

having made these observations and judgments, this talented Outsider nevertheless accepts the doctrine, relevant in his time, that racial inequalities 'seem to be founded upon the immutable laws of nature herself' (ibid., 1:358–59); and, to stop the list of particulars here, assumes, as an understandable and inevitable rather than disturbing fact that 'the Negro, who earnestly desires to mingle his race with that of the European, cannot effect it' (ibid., 1:335).[29]

Without anachronistically asking, as a Whig historian might, for altogether prescient judgments from this Outsider who was, after all, recording his observations in the early 19th century, we can nevertheless note that the role of Outsider apparently no more guarantees emancipation from the myths of a collectivity than the role of the Insider guarantees full insight into its social life and beliefs.

What was in the case of Tocqueville an unplanned circumstance has since often become a matter of deliberate decision. Outsiders are sought out to observe social institutions and cultures on the premise that they are more apt to do so with detachment. Thus, in the first decade of this century, the Carnegie Foundation for the Advancement of Teaching, in its search for someone to investigate the condition of medical schools, reached out to appoint Abraham Flexner, after he had admitted never before having been inside a medical school. It was a matter of policy to select a total Outsider who, as it happened, produced the uncompromising Report which did much to transform the state of American medical education at the time.

Later, casting about for a scholar who might do a thoroughgoing study of the Negro in the United States, the Carnegie Corporation searched for an Outsider, preferably one, as they put it, drawn from a country of 'high intellectual and scholarly standards but with no background or traditions of imperialism.' These twin conditions of course swiftly narrowed the scope of the search. Switzerland and the Scandinavian countries alone seemed to qualify, with the quest ending, as we know, with the selection of Gunnar Myrdal. In the preface to *An American Dilemma*, Myrdal (1944, pp. xviii–xiv) reflected on his status as an Outsider who, in his words, 'had never been subject to the strains involved in living in a black-white society' and who 'as a stranger to the problem . . . has had perhaps a greater awareness of the extent to which human valuations everywhere enter into our scientific discussion of the Negro problem.'

Reviews of the book repeatedly alluded to the degree of detachment from entangling loyalties that seemed to come from Myrdal's being an Outsider. J. S. Redding (1944), for one, observed that 'as a European, Myrdal had no American sensibilities to protect. He hits hard with fact and interpretation.' Robert S. Lynd (1944), for another, saw it as a prime merit of this Outsider that he was free to find out for himself 'without any side glances as to what was politically expedient.' And for a third, Frank Tannenbaum (1944) noted that Myrdal brought 'objectivity in regard to the special foibles and shortcomings in American life. As an outsider, he showed the kind of objectivity which would seem impossible for one reared within the American scene.' Even later criticism of Myrdal's work – for example, the comprehensive critique by Cox (1948, chap. 23) – does not attribute imputed errors in interpretation to his having been an Outsider.

Two observations should be made on the Myrdal episode. First, in the judgment of critical minds, the Outsider, far from being excluded from the understanding of an alien society, was able to bring needed perspectives to it. And second, that Myrdal, wanting to have both Insider and Outsider perspectives, expressly drew into his circle of associates in the study such Insiders, engaged in the study of Negro life and culture and of race relations, as E. Franklin Frazier, Arnold Rose, Ralph Bunche, Melville Herskovits, Otto Klineberg, J. G. St. Clair Drake, Guy B. Johnson, and Doxey A. Wilkerson.

It should be noted in passing that other spheres of science, technology, and learning have accorded distinctive and often related roles to both the Insider and the Outsider (Zuckerman and Merton, 1972, pp. 311–14). As long ago as the 17th century, Thomas Sprat, the historian of the Royal Society, for example, took it 'as evident, that divers sorts of Manufactures have been given us by men who were not bred up in Trades that resembled those which they discover'd. I shall mention Three; that of Printing, [Gun]Powder, and the Bow-Dye.' Sprat goes on to expand upon the advantages of the Outsider for invention, concluding with the less-than-science-based observation that 'as in the Generation of Children, those are usually observ'd to be most sprightly, that are the stollen Fruits of an unlawful Bed; so in the Generations of the Brains, those are often the most vigorous, and witty, which men beget on other Arts, and not on their own' (Sprat, 1959, pp. 391–93).

In our own time, Gilfillan (1935, p. 88) reported that the 'cardinal inventions are due to men outside the occupation affected, and the minor, perfective inventions to insiders.' And in a recent and more exacting inquiry, Joseph Ben-David (1960) found that the professionalization of scientific research 'does not in itself decrease the chances of innovation by outsiders to the various fields of science.' For the special case of outsiders to a particular discipline, Max Delbrück (1963, p. 13), himself a founding father of molecular biology, notes that although 'nuclear physics was developed almost exclusively within the framework of academic institutes at universities, molecular biology, in contrast, is almost exclusively a product of outsiders, of chemists, physicists, medical microbiologists, mathematicians and engineers.'

The cumulative point of this variety of intellectual and institutional cases is not – and this needs to be repeated with all possible emphasis – is *not* a proposal to replace the extreme Insider doctrine by an extreme and equally vulnerable Outsider doctrine. The intent is, rather, to transform the original question altogether. We no longer ask whether it is the Insider or the Outsider who has monopolistic or privileged access to social truth; instead, we begin to consider their distinctive and interactive roles in the process of truth seeking.

INTERCHANGE, TRADE OFFS, AND SYNTHESES

The actual intellectual interchange between Insiders and Outsiders – in which each adopts perspectives from the other – is often obscured by the rhetoric that commonly attends intergroup conflict. Listening only to that rhetoric, we may be brought to believe that there really is something like antithetical 'black knowledge' and 'white knowledge,' 'man's knowledge' and 'woman's knowledge,' etc., of a sort that allows no basis for judging between their differing claims to knowledge.

Yet the boundaries between Insiders and Outsiders tend to be far more permeable than this allows. Just as with the process of competition generally, so with the competition of ideas. Competing or conflicting groups take over ideas and procedures from one another, thereby denying in practice the rhetoric of total incompatibility. Even in the course of social polarization, conceptions with cognitive value are utilized all apart from their source. Concepts of power structure, co-optation, the dysfunctions of established institutions and findings associated with these concepts have for some time been utilized by social scientists, irrespective of their social or political identities. Nathan Hare (1967), for example, who remains one of the most articulate exponents of the Insider doctrine, made use of the notion of the self-fulfilling prophecy in trying to explain how it is that organizations run by blacks find it hard to work out.[30] As he put it, 'White people thought that we could not have any institutions which were basically black which were of good quality. This has the effect of a self-fulfilling prophecy, because if you think that black persons cannot possibly have a good bank, then you don't put your money in it. All the best professors leave black universities to go to white universities as soon as they get the chance. The blacks even do the same thing. And this makes your prediction, which wasn't true in the beginning, come out to be true' (p. 65). Such diffusion of ideas across the boundaries of groups and statuses has long been noted. In one of his more astute analyses, Mannheim (1952) states the general case for the emergence and spread of knowledge that transcends even profound conflicts between groups:

> Syntheses owe their existence to the same social process that brings about polarization; groups take over the modes of thought and intellectual achievements of their adversaries under the simple law of 'competition on the basis of achievement' ... In the socially-differentiated thought process, even the opponent is ultimately forced to adopt those categories and forms of thought which are most appropriate in a given type of world order. In the economic sphere, one of the possible results of competition is that one competitor is compelled to catch up with the other's technological advances. In just the same way, whenever groups compete for having their interpretation of reality accepted as the correct one, it may happen that one of the groups takes over from the adversary some fruitful hypothesis or category – anything that promises cognitive gain. ... [In due course, it becomes possible] to find a position from which both kinds of thought can be envisaged in their partial correctness, yet at the

same time also interpreted as subordinate aspects of a higher synthesis. (pp. 221–23)

The essential point is that, with or without intent, the process of intellectual exchange takes place precisely because the conflicting groups are in interaction. The extreme Insider doctrine, for example, affects the thinking of sociologists, black and white, who reject its extravagant claims. Intellectual conflict sensitizes them to aspects of their subject that they have otherwise not taken into account.

SOCIAL SADISM AND SOCIOLOGICAL EUPHEMISM

As a case in point of this sort of sensitization through interaction, I take what can be described as a composite pattern of social sadism and sociological euphemism. 'Social sadism' is more than a metaphor. The term refers to social structures which are so organized as to systematically inflict pain, humiliation, suffering, and deep frustration upon particular groups and strata. This need have nothing at all to do with the psychic propensities of individuals to find pleasure in cruelty. It is an objective, socially organized, and recurrent set of situations that has these cruel consequences, however diverse its historical sources and whatever the social processes that maintain it.

This type of sadistic social structure is readily overlooked by a perspective that can be described as that of the sociological euphemism. This term does not refer to the obvious cases in which ideological support of the structure is simply couched in sociological language. Rather, it refers to the kind of conceptual apparatus that, once adopted, requires us to ignore such intense human experiences as pain, suffering, humiliation, and so on. In this context, analytically useful concepts such as social stratification, social exchange, reward system, dysfunction, symbolic interaction, etc., are altogether bland in the fairly precise sense of being unperturbing, suave, and soothing in effect. To say this is not to imply that the conceptual repertoire of sociology (or of any other social science) must be purged of such impersonal concepts and filled with sentiment-laden substitutes. But it should be noted that analytically useful as these impersonal concepts are for certain problems, they also serve to exclude from the attention of the social scientist the intense feelings of pain and suffering that are the experience of some people caught up in the social patterns under examination. By screening out these profoundly human experiences, they become sociological euphemisms.

Nor is there any easy solution to the problem of sociological euphemism. True we have all been warned off the Whiteheadian fallacy of misplaced concreteness, the fallacy of assuming that the particular concepts we employ to examine the flow of events capture their entire content. No more than in other fields of inquiry are sociological concepts designed to depict the concrete entirety of the psychosocial reality to which they refer. But the methodological rationale for conceptual abstraction has yet to provide a way of assessing the intellectual costs as well as the intellectual gains of abstraction. As Paul Weiss (1971) has put the general issue: 'How can we ever retrieve information about distinctive features once we have tossed it out?' (p. 213).

Consider some outcomes of the established practice of employing bland sociological concepts that systematically abstract from certain elements and aspects of the concreteness of social life. It is then only a short step to the further tacit assumption that the aspects of psychosocial reality which these concepts help us to understand *are the only ones worth trying to understand.* The ground is then prepared for the next seemingly small but altogether conclusive step. The social scientist sometimes comes to act as though the aspects of the reality which are neglected in his analytical apparatus *do not even exist.* By that route, even the most conscientious of social scientists are often led to transform their concepts and models into scientific euphemisms.

All this involves the special irony that the more intellectually powerful a set of social science concepts has proved to be, the less the incentive for trying to elaborate it in ways designed to catch up the humanly significant aspects of the psychosocial reality that it neglects.

It is this tendency toward sociological euphemism, I suggest, that some (principally but not exclusively black) social scientists are forcing upon the attention of (principally but not exclusively white) social scientists. No one I know has put this more pointedly than Kenneth Clark (1965): 'More privileged individuals may understandably need to shield themselves from the inevitable conflict and pain which would result from acceptance of the fact that they *are* accessories to profound injustice. The tendency to discuss disturbing social issues such as racial discrimination, segregation, and economic exploitation in detached, legal, political, socio-economic, or psychological terms as if these persistent problems did not involve the suffering of actual human beings is so contrary to empirical evidence that it must be interpreted as a protective device' (p. 75).

FROM SOCIAL CONFLICT TO INTELLECTUAL CONTROVERSY

Perhaps enough has been said to indicate how Insider and Outsider perspectives can converge, in spite of such differences, through reciprocal adoption of ideas and the developing of complementary and overlapping foci of attention in the formulation of scientific problems. But these intellectual potentials for synthesis are often curbed by social processes that divide scholars and scientists. Internal divisions and polarizations in the society at large often stand in the way of realizing those potentials. Under conditions of acute conflict, each hostile camp develops highly selective perceptions of what is going on in the other. Perspectives become self-confirming as both Insiders and Outsiders tend to shut themselves off from ideas and information at odds with their own conceptions. They come to see in the other primarily what their hostile dispositions alert them to see and then promptly mistake the part for the whole. The initial interaction between the contending groups becomes reduced in response to the reciprocal alienation that follows upon public distortions of the others' ideas. In the process, each group becomes less and less motivated to examine the ideas of the other, since there is manifestly small point in attending to the ideas of those capable of such distortion. The members of each group then scan the outgroup's writings just enough to find ammunition for new fusillades.

The process of increased selective inattention to ideas of the other produces rigidified all-or-none doctrines. Even intellectual orientations that are not basically contradictory come to be regarded as though they were. *Either* the Insider *or* the Outsider has access to the sociological truth. In the midst of such polarized social conflict, there is little room for the third party uncommitted in the domain of knowledge to, for them, situationally irrelevant group loyalties, who try to convert that conflict into intellectual criticism. Typically, these would-be noncombatants are caught in the crossfire between hostile camps. Depending on the partisan vocabulary of abuse that happens to prevail, they are tagged as intellectual mugwumps, pharisees or renegades, or somewhat more generously, as 'mere eclectics' with the epithets making it unnecessary to examine the substance of what is being asserted or to consider how far it holds true. Perhaps most decisively, they are defined as mere middle-of-the-roaders who, through timidity or expediency, will not see that they try to escape the fundamental conflict between unalloyed sociological good and unalloyed sociological evil.[31]

When a transition from social conflict to intellectual controversy is achieved, when the perspectives of each group are taken seriously enough to be carefully examined rather than rejected out of hand, there can develop trade offs between the distinctive strengths and weaknesses of Insider and Outsider perspectives that enlarge the chances for a sound and relevant understanding of social life.

INSIDERS, OUTSIDERS, AND TYPES OF KNOWLEDGE

If indeed we have distinctive contributions to make to social knowl-edge in our roles as Insiders or Outsiders – and it should be repeated that all of us are both Insiders and Outsiders in various social situa-tions – then those contributions probably link up with a long-standing distinction between two major kinds of knowledge, a basic distinction that is blurred in the often ambiguous use of the word 'understand-ing.' In the language of William James (1932, pp. 11–13), drawn out of John Grote (1865, p. 60), who was in turn preceded by Hegel (1961/ 1807),[32] this is the distinction between 'acquaintance with' and 'knowl-edge about.' The one involves direct familiarity with phenomena that is expressed in depictive representations; the other involves more ab-stract formulations which do not at all 'resemble' what has been di-rectly experienced (Merton, 1968, p. 545). As Grote noted a century ago, the distinction has been imbedded in contrasting pairs of terms in various languages as shown below.

'Acquaintance with'	'Knowledge about'
noscere	scire
kennen	wissen
connaître	savoir

These interrelated kinds of understanding may turn out to be dis-tributed, in varying mix, among Insiders and Outsiders. The introspec-tive meanings of experience within a status or a group may be more readily accessible, for all the seemingly evident reasons, to those who have shared part or all of that experience. But authentic awareness, even in the sense of acquaintance with, is not guaranteed by social affiliation, as the concept of false consciousness is designed to remind us. Determinants of social life – for an obvious example, ecological patterns and processes – are not necessarily evident to those directly engaged in it. In short, sociological understanding involves much more than acquaintance with. It includes an empirically confirmable comprehension of the conditions and often complex processes in which people are caught up without much awareness of what is going on. To analyze and understand these requires a theoretical and technical competence which, as such, transcends one's status as Insider or Outsider. The role of social scientist concerned with achieving knowledge about society requires enough detachment and trained capacity to know how to assemble and assess the evidence without regard for what the analysis seems to imply about the worth of one's group.

Other attributes of the domain of knowledge dampen the relevance of Insider and Outsider identities for the validity and worth of the intellectual product. It is the character of an intellectual *discipline* that its evolving rules of evidence are adopted *before* they are used in assessing a particular inquiry. These criteria of good and bad intellectual work may turn up to differing extent among Insiders and Outsiders as an artifact of immediate circumstance, and that is itself a difficult problem for investigation. But the margin of autonomy in the culture and institution of science means that the intellectual criteria, as distinct from the social ones, for judging the validity and worth of that work transcend extraneous group allegiances. The acceptance of criteria of craftsmanship and integrity in science and learning cuts across differences in the social affiliations and loyalties of scientists and scholars. Commitment to the intellectual values dampens group-induced pressures to advance the interests of groups at the expense of these values and of the intellectual product.

The consolidation of group-influenced perspectives and the autonomous values of scholarship is exemplified in observations by John Hope Franklin who, for more than a quarter-century, has been engaged in research on the history of American Negroes from their ancient African beginnings to the present.[33] In the first annual Martin Luther King, Jr., Memorial Lecture at the New School for Social Research, he observes in effect how great differences in social location of both authors and audiences can make for profound differences in scholarly motivation and orientation. Franklin notes that it was the Negro teacher of history, 'outraged by the kind of distorted history that he was required to teach the children of his race,' who took the initiative in the 19th century to undo what one of them described as 'the sin of omission and commission on the part of white authors, most of whom seem to have written exclusively for white children' (1969, p. 4). The pioneering revisionist efforts of W. E. B. Du Bois and others found organized expression in the founding in 1915 of the Association for the Study of Negro Life and History and, a year later, of the *Journal of*

Negro History by Carter G. Woodson and his associates. This institutionalization of scholarship helped make for transfer and interchange of knowledge between Insiders and Outsiders, between black historians and white. In Franklin's words, the study of Negro history became 'respectable. Before the middle of the twentieth century it would entice not only a large number of talented Negro scholars to join in the quest for a revised and more valid American history, but it would also bring into its fold a considerable number of the ablest white historians who could no longer tolerate biased, one-sided American history. Thus, Vernon Wharton's *The Negro in Mississippi*, Kenneth Stampp's *The Peculiar Institution*, Louis Harlan's *Separate But Unequal* and Winthrop Jordan's *White Over Black* – to mention only four – rank among the best of the efforts that any historians, white or black, have made to revise the history of their own country. In that role they, too, became revisionists of the history of Afro-Americans' (1969, pp. 5–6).

These efforts only began to counter the 'uniformed, arrogant, uncharitable, undemocratic, and racist history [which] . . . spawned and perpetuated an ignorant, self-seeking, superpatriotic, ethnocentric group of white Americans who can say, in this day and time, that they did not know that Negro Americans had a history' (1969, p. 9). But much needed counterdevelopments can induce other kinds of departure from scholarly standards. Franklin notes that the recent 'great renaissance' of interest in the history of Negro Americans has found proliferated and commercialized expression. 'Publishers are literally pouring out handbooks, anthologies, workbooks, almanacs, documentaries, and textbooks on the history of Negro Americans. . . . Soon, we shall have many more books than we can read; indeed, many more than we should read. Soon, we shall have more authorities on Negro history than we can listen to; indeed, many more than we should listen to' (1969, pp. 10–11).

Franklin's application of exacting, autonomous and universalistic standards culminates in a formulation that, once again, transcends the statuses of Insiders and Outsiders:

Slavery, injustice, unspeakable barbarities, the selling of babies from their mothers, the breeding of slaves, lynchings, burnings at the stake, discrimination, segregation, these things too are a part of the history of this country. If the Patriots were more in love with slavery than freedom, if the Founding Fathers were more anxious to write slavery into the Constitution than they were to protect the rights of men, and if freedom was begrudgingly given and then effectively denied for another century, these things too are a part of the nation's history. It takes a person of stout heart, great courage, and uncompromising honesty to look the history of this country squarely in the face and tell it like it is. But nothing short of this will make possible a reassessment of American history and a revision of American history that will, in turn, permit the teaching of the history of Negro Americans. And when this approach prevails, the history of the United States and the history of the black man can be written and taught by any person, white, black, or otherwise. For there is nothing so irrelevant in telling the truth as the color of a man's skin. (1969, pp. 14–15)

Differing profoundly on many theoretical issues and empirical claims, Cox (1948; also introduction to Hare, 1970) and Frazier (1957, 1968) are agreed on the relative autonomy of the domain of knowledge and, specifically, that white scholars are scarcely barred from contributing to what Frazier described as a 'grasp of the condition and fate of American Negroes.' Recognition of what has been called 'the mark of oppression,' Frazier notes, 'was the work of two white scholars that first called attention to this fundamental aspect of the personality of the American Negro. Moreover, it was the work of another white scholar, Stanley M. Elkins, in his recent book on *Slavery*, who has shown the psychic trauma that Negroes suffered when they were enslaved, the pulverization of their social life through the destruction of their clan organization, and annihilation of their personality through the destruction of their cultural heritage' (Frazier, 1968, p. 272). And Cox, in his strong criticism of what he describes as 'the black bourgeoisie school' deriving from Frazier's work, emphasizes the distorting effects of the implicitly black nationalist ideology of this school on the character of its work (Cox, 1970, pp. 15–31).

It should now be evident that structural analysis applied to the domain of knowledge provides an ironically self-exemplifying pattern. For just as the union of any other collectivity based on a single status – of Americans or of Nigerians, of blacks or of whites, of men or of women – is continuously subject to the potential of inner division owing to the other statuses of its members, so with the collectivities often described as the scientific community and the community of scholars. The functional autonomy of science and learning is also periodically subject to great stress, owing in part to the complex social differentiation of the population of scientists and scholars that weakens their response to external pressures. The conditions and processes making

for the fragility or resiliency of that autonomy constitute one of the
great questions in the sociology of knowledge.

It is nevertheless that autonomy which still enables the pursuit of
truth to transcend other loyalties, as Michael Polanyi (1959), more
than most of us, has long recognized: 'People who have learned to
respect the truth will feel entitled to uphold the truth against the very
society which has taught them to respect it. They will indeed demand
respect for themselves on the grounds of their own respect for the
truth, and this will be accepted, even against their own inclinations,
by those who share these basic convictions' (pp. 61–62).[34]

A paper such as this one needs no peroration. Nevertheless, here is
mine. Insiders and Outsiders in the domain of knowledge, unite. You
have nothing to lose but your claims. You have a world of understanding to win.

Notes

1. A first edition of this paper was read on November 6 1969 to the semi-
   nar celebrating the 50th anniversary of the department of sociology at
   the University of Bombay, India. A second edition was read at the Cen-
   tennial Symposium of Loyola University (of Chicago) on January 5 1970
   and at the annual meetings of the Southwestern Sociological Association
   in Dallas, Texas, on March 25 1971. This third edition was presented at
   the annual meeting of the American Sociological Association in Denver,
   Colorado, September 1 1971. Any errors I have retained after the critical
   examinations of the paper by Walter Wallace and Harriet Zuckerman are
   of course entirely my own. Aid from the National Science Foundation is
   gratefully acknowledged, as is indispensable help of quite another kind
   provided by Hollon W. Farr, M.D.
2. As witness the spate of recent writings in and on the sociology of knowledge, including far too many to be cited here. Some essential discussions and bibliography are provided by Berger and Luckmann (1966),
   Stark (1958), Wolff (1965), Curtis and Petras (1970). The application of
   the sociology of knowledge to the special case of sociology itself has
   also burgeoned since 1959 when the Fourth World Congress of Sociology held by the International Sociological Association focused on the
   social contexts of sociology. See, for prime examples, Gouldner (1970),
   Friedrichs (1970), Tiryakian (1971).
3. This passage on the conditions making for intensified interest in the sociology of knowledge and for derivative problems of theoretical analysis
   in the field has not been written for this occasion. It is largely drawn
   from my paper in Gurvitch and Moore (1945, but now out of print) and
   reprinted in Merton (1968, pp. 510–14). Since the cognitive orientations
   of group members and nonmembers has long been a problem of endur-

ing interest to me, I shall have occasion to refer to my writings throughout this paper.

4. Polanyi's detailed development of this theme over the years represents a
basic contribution to the sociology of science by providing a model of
the various overlapping cognitive and social structures of intellectual disciplines. Ziman (1968) has useful observations along these lines and
Campbell (1969) has contributed some typically Campbellian (i.e., imaginative and evocative) thinking on the subject, in developing his 'fish-
scale model' of overlapping disciplines.

5. Observations on the advantaged position of the proletariat for the perception of historical and social truth are threaded throughout Marx's writings. For some of the crucial passages, see his *Poverty of Philosophy*
(1847, e.g., pp. 125–26). On Marx's thinking along these lines, Georg
Lukács, in spite of his own disclaimers in the new introduction to his
classic work, *History and Class Consciousness*, remains of fundamental
importance (1971, esp. pp. 47–81, 181–209).

6. Nathan Hare as quoted by Bunzel (1968, p. 32).

7. Actually, the case of age status is structurally different from that of other
ascribed statuses. For although, even in this time of advanced biotechnology,
a few men become transformed into women and vice versa, this remains
a comparatively rare instance of the ordinarily ascribed status of sex
becoming an achieved status. But in contrast to sex and other ascribed
statuses, each successive age status has been experienced by suitably
long-lived social scientists (within the limits of their own inexorably advancing age cohorts). On the basis of a dynamic Insider doctrine, then,
it might even be argued that older social scientists are better able than
very young ones to understand the various other age strata. As context,
see the concept of the reenactment of complementary roles in the life
cycle of scientists in Zuckerman and Merton (1972).

8. As we shall see, this is a limiting type of case that merges into quite
another type, since as a fully acquired status, rather than an ascribed
one, that of the sociologist (or physician or physicist) presumably pre-
supposes functionally relevant expertise.

9. I am indebted to Harriet Zuckerman for these observations on the new
credentialism of ascribed status. The classic source of meritocracy remains Young (1958); on the dysfunctions of educational credentialism,
see Miller and Roby (1970, Chapter 6).

10. But as we shall see, when the extreme Insider position is transformed
from a doctrine of assumptions-treated-as-established-truth into a set of
questions about the distinctive roles of Insiders and Outsiders in intellectual inquiry, there develops a convergence though not coincidence between the assumptions underlying credentials based on ascribed status
and credentials based on achieved status. In the one, early socialization
in the culture or subculture is taken to provide readier access to certain
kinds of understanding; in the other, the component in adult socialization
represented by disciplined training in one or another field of learning is
taken to provide a higher probability of access to certain other kinds of
understanding.

11. As Agassi (1969, p. 421) reminds us, the term 'methodological solip-

sism' was introduced by Rudolf Carnap to designate the theory of knowledge known as sensationalism: 'the doctrine that all knowledge – of the world and of one's own self – derives from sensation.' The belief that all one *really* knows is one's subjective experience is sometimes described as the 'egocentric predicament.'

12. As I have noted in the first edition of this paper, the social scientists of India, for one example, hav long suffered the slings and arrows of outrageously unprepared and altogether exogenous social scientists engaging in swift, superficial inquiries into matters Indian (Merton, 1971, p.465).

13. By introducing their useful term 'xenocentrism' to refer to both basic *and* favorable orientations to groups other than one's own, Kent and Burnight (1951) have retained Sumner's unuseful practice of prematurely combining centrality and evaluation in the one concept rather than keeping them analytically distinct. The analytical distinction can be captured terminologically by treating 'xenocentrism' as the generic term, with the analytically distinct components of favorable orientation to nonmembership groups (as with the orientation of many white middle-class Americans toward blacks) being registered in the term 'xenophilia' and the unfavorable orientation by Pareto's term 'xenophobia.' The growing theoretical interest in nonmembership reference groups (a concept implying a type of Outsider) (Hyman, 1968; Merton and Rossi, 1950) and the intensified spread of both ethnocentrism and xenocentrism in our times have given the term xenocentrism greater relevance than ever and yet, for obscure reasons, it has remained largely sequestered in the pages of the *American Journal of Sociology* where it first appeared 20 years ago. Caplow (1964, p. 216) and Horton (1965) are the only ones I know to have made good use of the term, but their unaccustomed behavior only emphasizes its more general neglect.

14. Current claims of Insiderism still have a distance to go, in the academic if not the political forum, to match the chauvinistic claims of those days. For collections of such documents, see Pettit and Leudet (1916), Duhem (1915), Kellermann (1915), Kherkhof (1933).

15. This is not a prediction after the fact. E. Franklin Frazier (1949, 1957) repeatedly made the general point and Merton (1968, p. 485) examined this pattern in connection with the self-fulfilling prophecy.

16. Heidegger (1927) as cited and discussed by Mannheim (1952, pp. 196 ff.).

17. This is not the place to go into the theoretical problems of identifying the boundaries of groups, the criteria of group membership, and the consequent varieties of members and nonmembers. For an introduction to the complexities of these concepts, see Merton (1968, pp. 338–54, 405–7).

18. The conflicts periodically reported by black women – for example, the debate between Mary Mebane (Liza) and Margaret Sloan (in defense of Gloria Steinem) – between identification with black liberation and the women's liberation movement, reflect this sociological fact of crosscutting status sets. The problem of coping with these structurally induced conflicts is epitomized in Margaret Sloan's (1971) 'realization that I was going to help the brothers realize that as black women we cannot allow

black men to do [to] us what white men have been doing to their women all these years."

19. This is not the place to summarize an analysis of the dynamics of status sets that takes up variation in key statuses (dominant, central, salient) and the conditions under which various statuses tend to be activated, along lines developed in unpublished lectures by Merton (1955–71). For pertinent uses of these conceptions in the dynamics of status sets, particularly with regard to functionally irrelevant statuses, see Epstein (1970, esp. Chapter 3).

20. For a detailed discussion of the partial autonomy of subsystems in the conceptions of Marx and Sorokin, see Merton and Barber (1963, pp. 343–49) and Merton (1968, pp. 521 ff.). On the general notion of functional autonomy as advanced by Gordon W. Allport in psychology, see the discussion and references in Merton (1968, pp. 15–16); on functional autonomy in sociology, see Gouldner (1958, 1959).

21. Wrong's paper is an important formulation of the theoretical fault involved in identifying structural position with individual behavior. But, in some cases, he is preaching to the long since converted. It is a tenet in some forms of structural analysis that differences in social location *make for* patterned differences in perspectives and behavior *between* groups while still allowing for a range of variability *within* groups and thus, in structurally proximate groups, for considerably overlapping ranges of behavior and perspective. On the general orientation of structural analysis in sociology, see Barbano (1968); for some specific terminological clues to the fundamental distinction between social position and actual behavior or perspective as this is incorporated in structural analysis, See Merton (1968, passim) for the key theoretical expressions that '*structures exert pressures*' and structures 'tend' to generate perspectives and behaviors. For specific examples: 'people in the various occupations *tend* to take different parts in the society, to have different shares in the exercise of power, both acknowledged and unacknowledged, and to *see* the world differently' (p. 180). 'Our primary aim is to discover how some *social structures exert a definite pressure upon certain persons in the society to engage in nonconforming rather than conforming conduct.* If we can locate groups peculiarly subject to such pressures, we should expect to find fairly high *rates* of deviant behavior in those groups' (p. 186). And for immediate rather than general theoretical bearing on the specific problems here under review, see Merton (1957): 'In developing this view, I do not mean to imply that scientists, any more than other men [and women] are merely obedient puppets doing exactly what social institutions require of them. But I do mean to say that, like men [and women] in other institutional spheres, scientists tend to develop the values and to channel their motivations in directions the institution defines for them' (p. 640).

22. On the general point of shifting boundaries, see Merton (1968, pp. 338–42, 479–80). Einstein was evidently quite taken with the situational determination of shifts in group boundaries. In a statement written for the London *Times* at a time (November 28 1919) when the animosities of World War I were still largely intact, he introduced slight variations on

the theme: 'The description of me and my circumstances in the *Times* shows an amusing flare of imagination on the part of the writer. By an application of the theory of relativity to the taste of the reader, today in Germany I am called a German man of science and in England I am represented as a Swiss Jew. If I come to be regarded as a *'bête noire'* the description will be reversed, and I shall become a Swiss Jew for the German and a German for the English' (Frank, 1963, p. 144).

23. For further discussion of the idea of social structural warranties of validity, see Merton (1968, pp. 560–62).

24. Thanks to Donald N. Levine (1971, p. xxiii), I learn that in often attributing the aphorism, with its many implications for social epistemology, to Weber, I had inadvertently contributed to a palimpsestic syndrome: assigning a striking idea or formulation to the author who first introduced us to it when in fact that author had simply adopted or revived a formulation that he (and others versed in the same tradition) knew to have been created by another. As it happens, I first came upon the aphorism in Weber's basic paper on the categories of a *verstehende* sociology published in 1913. In that passage, he treats the aphorism as common usage which he picks up for his own analytical purposes: 'Man muss, wie oft gesagt worden ist, "nicht Cäsar sein, um Cäsar zu verstehen."' Alerted by Levine's note, I now find that Weber made earlier use of the aphorism back in 1903–6 (1951, pp. 100–1) as he drew admiringly upon Simmel's *Probleme der Geschichtsphilosophie* to which he attributes the most thoroughly developed beginnings of a theory of *Verstehen*. Properly enough, Weber devotes a long, long note to the general implications of Simmel's use of the aphorism, quoting it just as we have seen but omitting the rest of Simmel's embellished version: 'Und kein zweiter Luther, um Luther zu begreifen.' In his later work, Weber incorporated the aphorism whenever he examined the problem of the 'understandability' of the actions of others.

25. Having quoted the Caesar aphorism, Weber goes on to draw the implication for historiography: 'Sonst wäre alle Geschichtsschreibung sinnlos.'

26. The essay from which this is drawn was first published in 1949 and is reprinted in Lévi-Strauss (1963, p. 16).

27. It is symbolically appropriate that Simmel should have been attuned to the role of the stranger as outsider. For as Lewis Coser (1965, pp. 29–39) has shown, Simmel's style of sociological work was significantly influenced by his role as 'The Stranger in the Academy.'

28. Many of these inquiries explicitly take off from Simmel's imagery of the roles and functions of the stranger. From the large and fast-growing mass of publications on fieldwork in social science, I cite only a few that variously try to analyze the roles of the Outsider as observer and interpreter. From an earlier day dealing with 'stranger value,' see Oeser (1939), Nadel (1939), Merton (1947), and Paul (1953). For more recent work on the parameters of adaptation by strangers as observers, see especially the imaginative analysis by Nash (1963) and the array of papers detailing how the sex role of women anthropologists affected their access to field data (Golde, 1970). On comparable problems of the roles of Insiders and Outsiders in the understanding of complex public bureaucracies, see the

short, general interpretation by Merton (1945) and the comprehensive, detailed one by Frankel (1969).

29. Tocqueville also assumes that 'fatal oppression' has resulted in the enslaved blacks becoming 'devoid of wants,' and that 'plunged in this abyss of evils, [he] scarcely feels his own calamitous situation,' coming to believe that 'even the power of thought . . . [is] a useless gift of Providence' (1, p. 333). Such observations on the dehumanizing consequences of oppression are remarkable for the time. As Oliver Cromwell Cox (1948) observes about part of this same passage, Tocqueville's point 'still has a modicum of validity' (p. 369, n.).

30. Elsewhere, Hare treats certain beliefs of 'Negro dignitaries' as a self-fulfilling prophecy (1970, p. 44). A recent work (Hole and Levine, 1971) on women's liberation movements, both new and old, also observes: 'Feminists argue further that there is a self-fulfilling prophecy component: when one group dominates another, the group with power is, at best, reluctant to relinquish its control. Thus in order to keep woman in "her place,"' theories are propounded which presume that her place is defined by nature'(p. 193).

31. The foregoing two paragraphs are drawn almost verbatim from a not easily accessible source (Merton, 1961, pp. 21–46).

32. Hegel catches the distinction in his aphorism: 'Das Bekannte überhaupt ist darum, weil est bekannt is, nicht erkannt.' Polanyi (1959, 1967) has made a significant effort to synthesize these modes of understanding, principally in his conception of 'tacit knowing.'

33. Perhaps the best known of Franklin's many writings is *From Slavery to Freedom*, now in its third edition.

34. I have taken the liberty of modifying Polanyi's pronouns in this passage in order to preserve his meaning within the context of the subject of this paper.

References

Agassi, Joseph (1969) 'Privileged Access,' *Inquiry*, 12 (Winter), 420–26.

Barbano, Filippo (1968) 'Social Structures and Social Functions: The Emancipation of Structural Analysis in Sociology,' *Inquiry*, 11:40–84.

Becker, Howard S. (1963) *Outsiders: Studies in the Sociology of Deviance* (New York: Free Press).

Ben-David, Joseph (1960) 'Role and Innovations in Medicine,' *American Journal of Sociology*, 65 (May): 557–68.

Berger, Peter L., and Thomas Luckmann (1966) *The Social Construction of Reality*. Garden City: Doubleday.

Bunzel, John H. (1968) 'Black Studies at San Francisco State,' *Public Interest*, 13 (Fall): 22–38.

Cade, Toni (ed.) (1970) *The Black Woman: An Anthology*. New York: New American Library.

Campbell, Donald T. (1969) 'Ethnocentrism of Disciplines and the Fish-Scale

Model of Omniscience,' in Muzafer Sherif and Carolyn W. Sherif (eds), *Interdisciplinary Relationships in the Social Sciences*. Chicago: Aldine.

Camus, Albert (1946) *The Outsider*. London: Hamilton.

Caplow, Theodore (1964) *Principles of Organization*. New York: Harcourt Brace Jovanovich.

Chisholm, Shirley (1970) 'Racism and Anti-Feminism,' *Black Scholar*, 1 (January–February): 40–45.

Clark, Kenneth (1965) *Dark Ghetto*. New York: Harper & Row.

Conant, Ralph W. (1968) 'Black Power in Urban America,' *Library Journal*, 93 (May 15): 1963–67.

Coser, Lewis A. (1965) *Georg Simmel*. Englewood Cliffs, N.J.: Prentice-Hall.

Cox, Oliver Cromwell (1948) *Caste, Class and Race*. New York: Doubleday.

Curtis, James E. and John W. Petras (1970) *The Sociology of Knowledge*. New York and Washington: Praeger.

Delbrück, Max (1963) 'Das Begriffsschema der Molekular-Genetik,' *Nova Acta Leopoldina* 26:9–16.

Douglass, Frederick (1966/1889) 'The Nation's Problem,' speech delivered before the Bethel Literary and Historical Society in Washington, D.C., in Howard Brotz (ed.), *Negro Social and Political Thought*. New York: Basic.

Duhem, Pierre (1915) *La science allemande*. Paris: Hermann.

Engels, Friedrich (1936/1890) 'Letter to Joseph Block,' in V. Adoratsky (ed.), *Karl Marx: Selected Works*, Vol. 1. Moscow: Cooperative Publishing Society.

Epstein, Cynthia (1970) *Woman's Place: Options and Limits in Professional Careers*. Berkeley: University of California Press.

Fontaine, William T. (1944) '"Social Determination" in the Writings of Negro Scholars,' *American Journal of Sociology* 49 (Winter): 302–15.

Frank, Philipp (1963) *Einstein: His Life and Times*. New York: Knopf.

Frankel, Charles (1969) *High on Foggy Bottom: An Outsider's Inside View of the Government*. New York: Harper & Row.

Franklin, John Hope (1967) *From Slavery to Freedom: A History of Negro Americans*. 3d ed. New York: Knopf.

Franklin, John Hope (1969) *The Future of Negro American History*. New York: New School for Social Research.

Frazier, E. Franklin (1949) *The Negro in the United States*. New York: Macmillan.

Frazier, E. Franklin (1957) *Black Bourgeoisie*. New York: Free Press.

Frazier, E. Franklin (1968) 'The Failure of the Negro Intellectual,' in G. Franklin Edwards (ed.), *E. Franklin Frazier on Race Relations*. Chicago: University of Chicago Press.

Friedrichs, Robert W. (1970) *A Sociology of Sociology*. New York: Free Press.

Gilfillan, S. C. (1935) *The Sociology of Invention*. Chicago: Follett.

Goldee, Peggy (ed.) (1970) *Women in the Field*. Chicago: Aldine.

Gouldner, Alvin W. (1958) 'Reciprocity and Autonomy in Functional Theory.' In *Symposium on Social Theory*, edited by L. Z. Gross. Evanston, Ill.: Row, Peterson.

Gouldner, Alvin W. (1959) 'Organizational Analysis.' In *Sociology Today*, edited by Robert K. Merton, Leonard Broom, and L. S. Cottrell, Jr. New York: Basic.

Gouldner, Alvin W. (1970) *The Coming Crisis of Western Sociology.* New York: Basic.

Grote, John (1865) *Exploratio Philosophica.* Cambridge: Deighton, Bell & Co.

Gurvitch, Georges and Wilbert E. Moore (eds) (1945). *Twentieth Century Sociology.* New York: Philosophical Library.

Hare, Nathan (1967) 'Interview with Nathan Hare,' *US News and World Report,* 22 (May): 64–68.

Hare, Nathan (1970) *The Black Anglo-Saxons.* London: Collier-Macmillan.

Hegel, Georg (1961/1807) *The Phenomenology of Mind.* New York: Macmillan, 2nd rev. edn.

Heidegger, Martin (1927) *Sein und Zeit.* Halle: Max Niemeyer.

Hole, Judith and Ellen Levine (1971) *Rebirth of Feminism.* New York: Quadrangle.

Horton, Paul B. (1965) *Sociology and the Health Sciences.* New York: McGraw-Hill.

Hyman, Herbert H. (1968) 'Reference Groups,' *International Encyclopedia of the Social Sciences*, Vol. 13. New York: Macmillan and Free Press.

Ibn Alkalimat, Abd-l Hakimu (Gerald McWorter) (1969) 'The Ideology of Black Social Science.' *Black Scholar* (December): 28–35.

James, William (1932/1885) *The Meaning of Truth.* New York: Longmans Green.

Kellermann, Hermann (1915) *Der Krieg der Geister.* Weimar.

Kent, Donald P. and Robert G. Burnight (1951) 'Group Centrism in Complex Societies.' *American Journal of Sociology* 57 (November): 256–59.

Kherkhof, Karl (1933) *Der Krieg gegen die Deutsche Wissenschaft.* Halle.

Kilson, Martin (1969) 'Black Studies Movement: A Plea for Perspective.' *Crisis* 76 (October): 327–32.

Krieck, Ernst (1935) *Nationalpolitische Erziehung.* Leipzig: Armanen Verlag.

La Rue, Linda (1970) 'The Black Movement and Women's Liberation.' *Black Scholar* 1 (May): 36–42.

Lasswell, Harold D. (1937) 'Chauvinism.' *Encyclopedia of the Social Sciences.* Vol. 3. New York: Macmillan.

Levine, Donald N. (1971) *Georg Simmel: On Individuality and Social Forms.* Chicago: University of Chicago Press.

Lévi-Strauss, Claude (1963) *Structural Anthropology.* New York: Basic.

Lukács, Georg (1971/1923) *History and Class Consciousness: Studies in Marxist Dialectics.* Cambridge, Mass.: M.I.T. Press.

Lynd, Robert S. (1944) 'Prison for Our Genius.' *Saturday Review*, April 22, pp. 5–7, 27.

Mannheim, Karl (1936) *Ideology and Utopia.* New York: Harcourt Brace Jovanovich.

Mannheim, Karl (1952) *Essays on the Sociology of Knowledge.* New York: Oxford University Press.

Marx, Karl (1847) (n.d.) *The Poverty of Philosophy.* Moscow: Foreign Languages.

Merton, Robert K. (1945) 'Role of the Intellectual in Public Bureacracy.' *Social Forces* 23 (May): 405–15.

Merton, Robert K. (1947) 'Selected Problems of Field Work in the Planned Community.' *American Sociological Review* 12 (June): 304–12.

Merton, Robert K. (1957) 'Priorities in Scientific Discovery: A Chapter in the Sociology of Science.' *American Sociological Review* 22 (December): 635–59.

Merton, Robert K. (1961) 'Social Conflict in Styles of Sociological Work.' *Transactions, Fourth World Congress of Sociology* 3:21–46.

Merton, Robert K. (1968) *Social Theory and Social Structure.* Rev. ed. New York: Free Press.

Merton, Robert K. (1971) 'Insiders and Outsiders,' in A. R. Desai (ed.), *Essays on Modernization of Underdeveloped Societies.* Bombay: Thacker.

Merton Robert K. and Bernard Barber (1963) 'Sorokin's Formulations in the Socioiogy of Science,' in Philip J. Allen (ed.), *Pitirim A. Sorokin in Review.* Durham, N.C.: Duke University Press.

Merton, Robert K., and Alice Kitt Rossi (1950) 'Contributions to the Theory of Reference Group Behavior,' in R. K. Merton and P. F. Lazarsfeld (eds), *Continuities in Social Research.* New York: Free Press. (Now out of print and reprinted in Merton, *Social Theory and Social Structure,* 1968.)

Miller, S. M., and Pamela A. Roby (1970) *The Future of Inequality.* New York: Basic.

Myrdal, Gunnar, with the assistance of Richard Steiner and Arnold Rose (1944) *An American Dilemma: The Negro Problem and Modern Democracy.* New York and London: Harper & Bros.

Nadel, S. F. (1939) 'The Interview Technique in Social Anthropology,' in F. C. Bartlett, M. Ginsberg, E. J. Lindgren, and R. H. Thouless (eds), *The Study of Society.* London: Kegan Paul.

Nash Dennison (1963) 'The Ethnologist as Stranger: An Essay in the Sociology of Knowledge.' *Southwestern Journal of Anthropology* 19:149–67.

Oeser, O. A. (1939) 'The Value of Team Work and Functional Penetration as Methods in Social Investigation,' in F. C. Bartlett, M. Ginsberg, E. J. Lindgren, and R. H. Thouless (eds), *The Study of Society.* London: Kegan Paul.

Paul, Benjamin D. (1953) 'Interview Techniques and Field Relationships,' in A. L. Kroeber (ed.), *Anthropology Today.* Chicago: University of Chicago Press.

Pettit, Gabriel, and Maurice Leudet (1916) *Les allemands et la science.* Paris.

Polanyi, Michael (1958) *Personal Knowledge.* London: Routledge & Kegan Paul.

Polanyi, Michael (1959) *The Study of Man.* London: Routledge & Kegan Paul.

Polanyi, Michael (1964) *Science, Faith and Society.* Chicago: University of Chicago Press.

Polanyi, Michael (1967) *The Tacit Dimension.* London: Routledge & Kegan Paul.

Price, Don K. (1965) *The Scientific Estate.* Cambridge, Mass.: Harvard University Press.

Redding, J. S. (1944) 'Review.' *New Republic*, March 20, pp. 384–86.

Riesman, David, with Reuel Denny and Nathan Glazer (1950) *The Lonely Crowd.* New Haven: Yale University Press.

Schütz, Alfred (1944) 'The Stranger: An Essay in Social Psychology.' *American Journal of Sociology* 49 (May): 499–507.

Simmel, Georg (1905) *Die Probleme der Geschichtsphilosophie: eine erkenntnistheoretische Studie* (Leipzig: Duncker und Humblot), 2nd edn.

Simmel, Georg (1908) *Soziologie.* Leipzig: Duncker und Humblot.

Simmel, Georg (1950) *The Sociology of Georg Simmel,* translated, edited, and with an introduction by Kurt H. Wolff. New York: Free Press.

Sloan, Margaret (1971) 'What We Should Be Doing, Sister,' *New York Times,* December 8.

Sprat, Thomas (1959/1667). *History of the Royal Society,* edited by Jackson I. Cope and Harold W. Jones. London: Routledge & Kegan Paul.

Stark, Werner (1958) *The Sociology of Knowledge.* London: Routledge & Kegan Paul.

Sumner, William Graham (1907) *Folkways.* Boston: Ginn.

Tannenbaum, Frank (1944) 'An American Dilemma.' *Political Science Quarterly* 59 (September): 321–40.

Tiryakian, Edward A. (ed.) (1971) *The Phenomenon of Sociology.* New York: Appleton-Century-Crofts.

Tocqueviile, Alexis de (1945/1835) *Democracy in America.* New York: Knopf.

Weber, Max (1913) 'Ueber einige Kategorien der verstehenden Soziologie.' *Logos* 4:254.

Weber, Max (1951/1922) *Gesammelte Aufsatze zur Wissenschaftslehre.* Tubingen: J. C. B. Mohr.

Weiss, Paul A. (1971) 'One Plus One Does Not Equal Two.' In *Within the Gates of Science and Beyond.* New York: Hafner.

Wilson, Colin (1956) *The Outsider.* Boston: Houghton Mifflin.

Wolff, Kurt H. (1965) 'Ernst Grünwald and the Sociology of Knowledge: A Collective Venture in Interpretation.' *Journal of the History of the Behavioral Sciences* 1:152–64.

Wrong, Dennis (1961) 'The Oversocialized Conception of Man in Modern Sociology.' *American Sociological Review* 26 (April): 183–93.

Young, Michael (1968) *The Rise of Meritocracy 1870–2033.* London: Thames & Hudson.

Ziman, John (1968) *Public Knowledge.* Cambridge: Cambridge University Press.

Zuckerman, Harriet A. and Robert K. Merton (1972) 'Age, Aging and Age Structure in Science,' in Matilda W. Riley, Marylin Johnson and Ann Foner (eds), *Aging and Society.* New York: Russell Sage Foundation. Vol. 3, *A Theory of Age Stratification.*

20 The Lesson of Ethnicity (1974)

Abner Cohen*

The papers presented in this volume deal with a number of problems relating to the nature of ethnicity in a variety of situations in different countries. Ethnicity is a ubiquitous phenomenon in both developing and developed countries, past and present. In the Third World the tribes, villages, bands, and isolated communities, which have until recently been our traditional subject-matter, are everywhere today becoming integral parts of new state structures and are thus being transformed into ethnic groupings with varying degrees of cultural distinctivenes. Social anthropologists, whether students of rural or urban areas, are therefore being increasingly forced into dealing with the socio-cultural problems raised by the developing interdependence between these parts and by the processes of socio-cultural change involved in this development. For both heuristic and theoretical considerations, this interest in the phenomenon of ethnicity is likely to become a major pre-occupation in our discipline for many years to come.

Because of its ubiquity, variety of form, scope, and intensity, and of its involvement in psychic, social, and historical variables, ethnicity has been defined in a variety of ways, depending on the discipline, field experience, and interests of the investigators. Many of these definitions are discussed in the papers in this volume. The question is not which definition is the most valid, but which is most helpful in the analysis of certain theoretical problems.

To make a start in this discussion, an ethnic group can be operationally defined as a collectivity of people who (a) share some patterns of normative behaviour and (b) form a part of a larger population, interacting with people from other collectivities within the framework of a social system. The term ethnicity refers to the degree of conformity by members of the collectivity to these shared norms in the course of social interaction. It is obvious that this definition is so wide that it covers collectivities that are not usually described as 'ethnic'. This is

* From 'Introduction: The Lesson of Ethnicity', in Abner Cohen (ed.), *Urban Ethnicity* (London: Tavistock Publications, 1974), pp. ix–xxiv.

a significant point to which I shall return later.

By patterns of normative behaviour I am referring here to the symbolic formations and activities found in such contexts as kinship and marriage, friendship, ritual, and other types of ceremonial. Some anthropologists refer to these patterns as customs or simply as culture. These are not the idiosyncratic habits, hallucinations, or illusions of isolated individuals but largely collective representations, even though they manifest themselves in individual behaviour. They are involved in psychic processes and thus can be subjectively experienced by the actors. They are nevertheless objective in the sense that the symbolic formations representing them, i.e. the stereotypes, mythologies, slogans, 'theories', ideologies, and ceremonials, are socially created and are internalized through continuous socialization. Often it is objective symbolic forms that generate the subjective experience of ethnicity and not the other way round. In terms of observable and verifiable criteria, what matters sociologically is what people actually do, not what they subjectively think or what they think they think. The prophet Muhammad is said to have once remarked that what concerned him was that a good Moslem should go through the act of praying five times a day. As to what went on in the mind of the worshipper, that was between the worshipper and Allah.

Our subjective life is notoriously chaotic, whimsical, vague, shifty, and very largely unconscious. Most people are therefore only too happy to be assisted by 'experts' or 'leaders', parents or teachers, or the culture they inherit, to find definite expressions for their uncertain ideas and feelings. When questioned, though, different men give different reasons for performing certain patterns of behaviour, and the same man may give different reasons for performing the same act at different times.

Symbols are thus essentially objective, not subjective, forms. They may be originally the spontaneous creation of specific individuals going through specific subjective experiences, but they attain an objective existence when they are accepted by others in the course of social interaction within a collectivity. What was originally subjective and individual becomes objective and collective, developing a reality of its own. The symbols become obligatory and thus exercise constraint on the individual. In the field of ethnicity this is manifested, for example, in such a common statement as 'My best personal friends are Jews (or Negroes, Yoruba, Bemba, Catholic) but . . .'. Unlike signs, symbols are not purely cognitive constructs, but are always also emotive and conative. In situations where ethnicity is a relevant issue, labels such as 'Jews', 'Negroes', or 'Catholics' (as the case may be) are not neutral intellectual concepts but symbols that agitate strong feelings and emotions.

The term ethnicity will be of little use if it is extended to denote cultural differences between isolated societies, autonomous regions, or independent stocks of populations such as nations within their own national boundaries. The differences between the Chinese and the Indians, considered within their own respective countries, are national not ethnic differences. But when groups of Chinese and Indian immigrants interact in a foreign land as Chinese and Indians they can then be referred to as ethnic groups. Ethnicity is essentially a form of interaction between culture groups operating within common social contexts.

It is for this reason that the phenomena of ethnicity are so dramatically evident in the cities, in both developing and developed countries. Here the division of labour is usually highly advanced and the struggle for resources, like employment, wages, housing, education, and political following, is intense. But of course ethnicity is not confined to the cities. In both the developed and the developing countries the city is today but a part of the national state. Economically, politically, demographically, and culturally it makes no sociological sense unless we study it within this wider context. Urban anthropology is indeed the anthropology of the complex structure of the new national state.

It is obvious that ethnicity is a complex phenomenon that is involved in psychological, historical, economic, and political factors. A full study of its nature – if this is at all possible – will require giving due weight to these and probably many other factors, and will call for the cooperation of many disciplines. But if we seriously attempt to do this at one and the same time we shall not be able to go far in our analysis. We are therefore forced to concentrate on as few variables as possible at a time, trying to keep the other variables constant in our analysis. This is one of the rudimentary strategies in all research.

ETHNICITY AS A CULTURAL PHENOMENON

Some anthropologists emphasize the cultural nature of ethnicity. One of the earliest and most influential schools of thought in this respect has been that of the former Rhodes Livingstone Institute anthropologists, notably Mitchell (1956), Epstein (1958), and Gluckman (1961), whose views were greatly affected by the special conditions existing in the industrial towns of Northern Rhodesia, now Zambia, during the 1950s. The major social cleavage in those towns ran along racial lines, and the political scene was dominated by a continuous struggle by African workers against White employers. Within the African camp ethnicity, according to this school, was not a live economic or political issue, but essentially an epistemological device developed by the Africans so that they could comprehend, or make sense of, the bewildering complexity and heterogeneity of urban society. They did this by classifying other townsmen in terms of broad tribal categories. In a more recent work, Barth (1969) follows an essentially similar line, seeing ethnic categories as classifying persons in terms of their 'basic most general identity' as determined by their origin and background. Some writers attribute primordiality to this basic identity.

Ethnicity tends to be conceived by this school of thought as an essentially innate predisposition. Barth goes so far as to attribute to it an existence of its own, separate from any social 'content'. He describes ethnic categories as: 'organisational vessels that may be given varying amounts and forms of content in different socio-cultural systems. They may be of great relevance to behaviour, but they need not be; they may provide all social life, or they may be relevant only in limited sectors of activity' (1969, p. 14).

This approach raises a number of logical, methodological, and sociological difficulties. Its central theme is descriptive and its argument is essentially circular. What it says is that people act as the members of ethnic categories because they identify themselves, and are sometimes also identified by others, with these ethnic categories. How do we know this? The actors say so, or so they act. Such statements and arguments will not become more analytical if we attribute identification and categorization to so-called cognition and begin to construct 'cognitive maps' to 'explain' them. At most, what we are establishing by this procedure is the simple fact that ethnic categories exist. This is of course legitimate if it is taken as the starting-point of an investigation, not as its conclusion. For, by itself it generates no hypotheses and leads to no further analysis. This is why nearly all the anthropologists who approach ethnicity from this angle seek to proceed further beyond this starting-point.

But, as Evans-Pritchard (1951, p. 19) points out, a continued preoccupation with problems of culture inevitably leads to psychology or history. Some writers thus end up explaining ethnicity in terms of motivation, primordial ideas, or the psychology of identity. Even when no such explanations are explicitly presented there is a tendency to posit ethnicity as a strategy manipulated by *individuals* to advance their personal interests and maximize their power. The difficulty with this kind of explanation is that it is one sided and cannot account for the potency of the normative symbols which the individual manipulates in his struggle for power. An ethnic group is not simply the sum total of its individual members, and its culture is not the sum total of the strategies adopted by independent individuals. Norms, beliefs, and values are effective and have their own constraining power only because they are the collective representations of a group and are backed by the pressure of that group. An individual can manipulate customs if he becomes part of such a group, adopting its current major symbols. He cannot manipulate others without being ready to be manipulated by them. He must pay the price of membership by participating in the group's symbolic activities and by a measure of adherence to the group's aims.

Other writers, on the other hand, end up explaining ethnicity in terms of process in time. Ethnicity here is often associated with migrancy, and is taken to be a stage in the adaptation of the group to its new environment and in the final assimilation of its members within the new society. One of the difficulties with this approach is that it is often not very clear whether one is concerned with a historical process or a cyclical one. If it is historical, then the process is unique and our account of it is descriptive, being a chronological narrative of a migration. If it is cyclical, then our analysis cannot produce generalizations that apply to all cases of ethnicity. For, while it is true that many migrant communities, or ethnic groupings forming a state, go through a process of mutual adjustment and/or of integration, and in the process lose their cultural identity, there are many situations where the reverse can occur. Here a group adjusts to the new situation by reorganizing its own traditional customs, or by developing new customs under traditional symbols, using traditional norms and ideologies to enhance its distinctiveness within the contemporary situation. As time goes on the group will become more and more distinct, sometimes even reviving old customs. This ethnic continuity or revival can be found in almost all societies, both developed and underdeveloped (Cohen, 1969a). In many situations migrancy is not a developmental phase but a structural status. Among Hausa traders in Yoruba towns, a Hausa man may operate in the same trading community for many years and yet will remain a 'stranger' performing special roles. On the other hand, a Hausa migrant who performs the economic roles of a settler will be regarded as a member of the settled community shortly after joining it.

ETHNICITY AND POWER RELATIONS

Again, we must remember that ethnicity is a matter of degree. There is ethnicity and ethnicity. The constraint that custom exercises on the individual varies from case to case. We may yet lack the techniques for the exact measurement of the magnitude of this constraint, but I think that it is common sense that the ethnicity of a collectivity that manifests itself in the form of an annual gathering of a few of its numbers to perform a dance or a ceremonial is different from the ethnicity manifested by, say, the Catholics in Northern Ireland. In some situations ethnicity amounts to no more than the exchange of jokes between different culture groups at the strange and bizarre nature of one another's customs. In other situations it leads to violence and bloodshed.

The definition of ethnicity as cognition of identity obscures, even nullifies, the conception of differences in degree of ethnicity. Barth's conception of ethnic categories as organizational *vessels* that are fixed, static, always there even when not relevant to behaviour, suffers from the same difficulties. His separation between 'vessel' and 'content' makes it difficult to appreciate the dynamic nature of ethnicity. It also assumes an inflexible structure of the human psyche and implicitly denies that personality is an open system given to modifications through continual socialization under changing socio-cultural conditions. Unless we recognize differences in degree of manifestation we shall fail to make much progress in the analysis of ethnicity. To put it in the idiom of research, ethnicity is a variable.

In any socio-cultural milieu this variable is interdependent with many other variables. But one must tackle one problem at a time, as it is only in this way that the analysis can be developed. For this reason I find the concepts of 'social organization' or 'social structure' difficult to operate with in this kind of analysis because each of them subsumes a large number of variables and is therefore highly ambiguous.

One way to make a start is to analyse ethnicity in terms of interconnections with economic and political relationships, both of which I shall, for brevity, describe as political. One need not be a Marxist in order to recognize the fact that the earning of livelihood, the struggle for a larger share of income from the economic system, including the struggle for housing, for higher education, and for other benefits, and similar issues constitute an important variable significantly related to ethnicity. Admittedly it is not the only relevant variable. What is more, its operation is modified and affected by the processual and psychological factors that I mentioned earlier. But it is a variable that pervades almost the whole universe of social relationships. This holds true of even so-called domestic relationships, which some writers seem to exclude from the realm of politics. Relations like those between father and son or husband and wife have their own aspects of power, and thus form part of the political system in any society. Indeed, in many preindustrial societies the whole political structure is embedded within such 'domestic relationships'. Certainly there are many relationships and activities, such as friendship or recreation, whose aim is mainly the satisfaction of personality needs, and which are thus non-political. But as Marcuse (1964) shows, there is a tendency for the 'big corporations' to exploit such relations and activities for their own ends. The non-political becomes thereby politicized. The youth movements that arose only a few years ago as 'marginal' enterprises striving for the utopianism of 'non-structure' have been rapidly drawn into politics (Farren and Barker 1972). Symbolic activities that are aimed at the solution of such perennial problems of human existence as those of life and death, good and evil, fortune and misfortune are exploited in all societies, whether industrial or preindustrial, by different political interests, and their dominant symbols are thus loaded with a multiplicity of political meanings. Indeed I go so far as to argue that the specialization of social anthropology is this very political interpretation of what are essentially non-political formations and activities (Cohen, 1969b). The cultures of ethnic groups are universes of such formally non-political formations and activities that are politicized in the course of social action.

The relations between ethnicity and politics are discussed, or touched upon, in some of the papers in this volume, and I myself have done some work on them (Cohen, 1965, 1966, 1967, 1968, 1969a, 1971; see also Parkin, 1969, and Caplan, 1970). Some writers in this field stress the political factor and even tend to explain, or rather explain away, the cultural factor as being of trivial importance. Others put their emphasis on the cultural side. A few are more concerned with the systematic interconnections, or dialectical interaction, between the two variables. What I wish to do here is mention briefly a few points that are not discussed in the papers presented below, but which I think bear on our general discussion.

ETHNICITY AND INFORMAL ORGANIZATION

In the course of the organization of economic production, exchange, and distribution, and more particularly through the processes of the division of labour and the competition for greater shares of income between men, a variety of interest groups emerge, whose members have some interests in common. To operate successfully an interest group has to develop basic organizational functions: distinctiveness (some writers call it boundary); communication; authority structure; decisionmaking procedure; ideology; and socialization. Indeed, organization is the group, since we are often dealing here not with a collectivity of total personalities, but with patterns of behaviour developed by a number of people participating with one another in respect of some specific, segmental, roles.

These interest groups can be organized on formal bases. This means that their aims are clearly specified and their organizational functions are rationally planned on bureaucratic lines. As Weber showed, this kind of organization, or association, is the most efficient and effective type of human organization, and in industrial society most groups attempt to make use of it.

But even in the advanced liberal industrial societies there are some structural conditions under which an interest group cannot organize itself on formal lines. Its formal organization may be opposed by the state or by other groups within the state, or may be incompatible with some important principles in the society; or the interests it represents may be newly developed and not yet articulated in terms of a formal organization and accommodated with the formal structure of the society. Under these conditions the group will articulate its organization on informal lines, making use of the kinship, friendship, ritual, ceremonial, and other symbolic activities that are implicit in what is known as style of life.

This strategy of organizing a group on the basis of different types of obligation is likely to be wasteful in time and energy and is not as efficient and effective in achieving the group's end as formal organization. For example, instead of organizing an official meeting for the members of the group to discuss some current problems, the informal group will attend a ceremonial during which these problems are only informally and unsystematically discussed amidst a great deal of what are, for the aims of the group, irrelevant symbolic activities, though these activities may at the same time satisfy some important personality needs.

The use of the term 'informal' to designate group organizations of this type is certainly far from being satisfactory. I have myself been looking for a substitute term for a number of years without much success. The term is highly ambiguous, is negative, and has to be related always to the existence of a formal structure. Some political scientists (see Almond and Powell, 1966, pp. 76–7) have used the term 'non-associational' for such interest groups. But it is obvious that this, too, is a negative term and does not seem to solve the terminological problem.

The members of interest groups who cannot organize themselves formally will thus tend to make use, though largely unconsciously, of whatever cultural mechanisms are available in order to articulate the organization of their grouping. And it is here, in such situations, that political ethnicity comes into being. In my view, unless we make this distinction between formal and informal articulation of interest group organization, we shall not be able to understand or to appreciate the nature of ethnicity in either the developed or the underdeveloped countries.

There are, of course, some conceptual problems that will have to be overcome if we want to push our analysis further. The distinction between formal and informal type of grouping is a matter of degree. Some groups are initially formed on formal lines but develop some informal mechanisms of organization later on. Other groups seek from the start to articulate part of their organization on formal lines and part on informal lines. It may be helpful to conceive of the organization of all groups as having two dimensions, the one formal and the other informal; the one governed by contract, the other by moral or ritual obligations or by what we usually call custom. Few groups are wholly formal or wholly informal. Most are in between on the same continuum.

ETHNICITY IN THE POLITICS OF STRATIFICATION

The literature of social anthropology abounds in cases where we can see the use of ethnicity in articulating the organizational functions of interest groups that for one reason or another cannot organize themselves formally. Examples such as the organization of resistance movements and of trading disporas in underdeveloped countries illustrate the same process.

In order to highlight a few other points in the analysis of this type of organization, I would like to discuss briefly one more situation, this time within the context of such a complex and highly industrialized society as Britain.

I will not choose an apt illustration, such as Protestant and Catholic groupings in Northern Ireland or the formation of ethnic immigrant communities in many parts of the country, but a highly formalized and bureaucratized structure officially governed by purely contractual mechanisms. I am referring here to the now widely known case of the economic elite, or elites, that dominate the City of London, the nerve-centre of the financial system of Britain. No fieldwork by professional anthropologists or sociologists has been carried out in the City, but in recent years, and particularly since the publication of the report of the Bank Rate Tribunal in 1968, some accounts of various features of the organization of business within it have emerged, from a number of publications (see Lupton and Wilson, 1959; Ferris, 1960; Sampson, 1962; Chapman, 1968; Parry, 1969).

From these it is evident that millions of pounds' worth of business is conducted daily in the City without the use of written documents, arranged mainly verbally, in face-to-face conversations or over the telephone. It is claimed that this is necessary if business is to flow. But as the risks involved are formidable, the business is confined to a limited circle of people who trust one another. Such a high degree of trust can arise only among men who know one another, whose values are similar, who speak the same language in the same accent, respect the same norms, and are involved in a network of primary relationships that are governed by the same values and the same patterns of symbolic behaviour.

For these reasons, City men are recruited from exclusive status groups. They are mostly products of the public-school system. The schools in this system achieve two major tasks: they socialize, or rather train, their pupils in specific patterns of symbolic behaviour, including accent, manner of speech, etiquette, style of joking, play; second, they create a web of enduring friendship and comradeship among the pupils, and these relationships are often continued through periodic old-boy reunions, affiliation with the same clubs, and further interaction in other social situations.

The City is thus said to be a village – barely one square mile in territory – in which everyone of importance knows everyone of importance. *Who* you know is more important than what you know. Often, the elite of the City are related to one another not only by a common style of life and by friendship, but also by kinship and affinal relationships. Lupton and Wilson (1959) present a reconstruction of the genealogies of over twenty elite family groupings that are interrelated through marriage and show the connections between top administrative, financial, and industrial 'decision-makers'.

The available reports indicate strongly that the speed and efficiency with which the City conducts its business are made possible mainly by this network of primary, informal, relationships connecting the business elite. This network is governed by archaic norms, values, and codes that are derived from the City's 'tribal past' – as Sampson puts it. It is held together by a complex body of customs that are to an outsider as esoteric and bizarre as those in any foreign culture. Ferris (1960, pp. 58–74) gives a dramatic description of the odd and highly stylized manner in which the stockbrokers – known in the City as the top-hatters because they still wear top hats – make their daily rounds in the City. They queue at a bank sitting on a hard bench, their striped trousers tugged up, exchanging a copy of *The Times* for the *Telegraph*. When they talk to the bank official, they pull up a chair and discuss cricket, television, and politics before mentioning money. This business of 'how-do-you-do', Ferris was told, is to acknowledge: 'we accept the normal rules of society, and we can now start exchanging ideas'. 'If you go to a bank with a top hat they say: "Oh, it's one of the brokers", and you walk right in. If you went in in a homburg there'd be an awful business of "Good gracious me, Mr –, where's your hat this morning?" There'd be a *thing*, which of course you want to avoid at all costs.' For if you behave in an 'abnormal' manner, your bank official will think that there is something 'fishy' about your behaviour, and unless there is an obvious explanation your creditworthiness may suffer – and without unblemished trustworthiness a broker cannot operate.

The Hausa traders in Yoruba towns (Cohen, 1969a) conduct their business in much the same way as the City men, though they operate under different structural circumstances and using different symbolic patterns. A Hausa dealer from Northern Nigeria will entrust his goods and money in the South only to a Hausa broker. No matter how long the Hausa broker has been living in the South he will always be anxious to preserve the symbols of his Hausaism, dressing like a Hausa, speaking and behaving like a Hausa. Hausaism is essential for his livelihood. Just as City men in London make use of a series of customs to overcome technical problems of business, so the Hausa use different Hausa customs to create relationships of trust in the trading network. The customs that are implicit in the life-style of the City men are sovereign in their constraining power, as are the customs implicit in Hausa culture.

THE HEURISTIC SIGNIFICANCE OF ETHNICITY

City men constitute an interest group that is part of the system of the division of labour in our society. They use their connections and the symbolism of their life-style to articulate a corporate organization that is partly formal and partly informal, in order to compete within the wider social system for a greater share of the national income. So do the Hausa use their culture to organize and coordinate their effort in order to maintain their share of the profits. In short, City men are socio-culturally as distinct within British society as are the Hausa within Yoruba society. They are indeed as 'ethnic' as any ethnic group can be. But they are not usually described as an ethnic group because the term is principally social and political, not sociological, even though there is massive sociological literature about it, particularly in the USA. To many people, the term ethnicity connotes minority status, lower class, or migrancy. This is why sooner or later we shall have to drop it or to find a more neutral word for it, though I can see that we shall probably have to live with it for quite a while. This is not because it is difficult to find a substitute, but because the term can be of great heuristic significance for the current phase in the development of the anthropology of complex society. The concept of ethnicity throws into relief, or rather dramatizes, the processes by which the symbolic patterns of behaviour implicit in the style of life, or the 'sub-culture', of a group – even of highly individualistic men like members of an elite – develop in order to articulate organizational functions that cannot be formally institutionalized. It is easy to identify an elite when its men are from an ethnically distinct group like the Creoles in Sierra Leone (Cohen, 1971), the Americo Liberians in Liberia (Liebenow, 1969), or the Tutsi in Rwanda (Maquet, 1961). But it is difficult to do so with an elite whose cultural distinctiveness within the society is not so visible, and whose members appear to the casual observer to be highly independent individualists.

If in a dynamic contemporary complex society a group of second- or third-generation migrants preserve their distinctiveness and make extensive use of the symbolism of their endoculture, then the likelihood that within the contemporary situation they have become an interest group is very strong. When, in a hypothetical case, two culture groups join together and interact politically and economically, and establish a new political system, they will soon become involved in cleavages on economic and political lines running throughout the extent of the new society. If a new line of cleavage, such as that of social class, then cuts across ethnic lines, ethnic identity and exclusiveness will tend to be inhibited by the emerging countervailing alignments. The poor from the one ethnic group will cooperate with the poor from the other ethnic group against the wealthy from both ethnic groups, who will, on their part, also cooperate in the course of the struggle to maintain their privileges. If the situation develops in this way, tribal differences will weaken and eventually disappear. The people will become detribalized. In time, class division will be so deep that two subcultures, with different styles of life, will develop and we may have a situation similar to that of Victorian Britain, to which Disraeli referred as 'the two nations', meaning the privileged and the underprivileged.

But the situation will be entirely different if the new class cleavage, in our hypothetical example, coincides with tribal affiliations, so that within the new system the privileged will tend to be identified with one tribal group and the underprivileged with the other tribal group. In this situation cultural differences between the two groups will become entrenched, consolidated, and strengthened in order to articulate the struggle between the two social groups across the new class lines. Old customs will tend to persist. But within the newly emerging social system they will assume new values and new social significance.

The study of enthnicity will be heuristically important for us also in that it can help us to clarify the nature of socio–cultural change. For it is now clear to us that the formation of an ethnic group in town involves a dynamic rearrangement of relations and of customs, and that it is not the result of cultural conservatism and continuity. The continuity of customs and of some social formations is certainly there, but their functions change dramatically – although to the casual observer it will look as if there is stagnation, conservatism, or a return to the past. This is why a concentration on the study of culture as such will shed little light on the nature of ethnicity.

It is here that the monographs on tribal studies of the 1940s and 1950s can be of immense value. For by the study of the members of those tribes within the context of the developing towns, by either the same or different anthropologists, we shall be able to develop the analysis of the dynamics of cultural and structural changes in response to the complexity of modern society. We shall find out what customs are retained, borrowed, or developed and for what political purposes. More generally we shall be able to develop the dialectical study of socio–cultural interdependence.

Studies of this type will be of immense value in analysis of the more general processes of institutionalization and of symbolization, and will thus provide a unique contribution to social science generally. At the same time they will usher social anthropology into the systematic study of the complexity of contemporary industrial society, without our discipline losing its identity, i.e. without social anthropology becoming sociology, or political science, or history.

References

Almond, G. A. and Powell, G. B. (1966) *Comparative Politics*. Boston: Little, Brown.

Barth, F. (1969) 'Introduction', in F. Barth (ed.), *Ethnic Groups and Boundaries*. London: George Allen & Unwin, 9–38. Now also Chapter 18 of this volume.

Caplan, L. (1970) *Land and Social Change in East Nepal*, Berkeley: University of California Press.

Chapman, R. A. (1968) *Decision-making: A Case Study of the Decision to raise the Bank Rate in September 1957*. London: Routledge & Kegan Paul.

Cohen, A. (1965) 'The Social Organization of Credit in a West African Cattle Market', *Africa*, 35, pp. 8–20.

Cohen, A. (1966) 'Politics of the Kola Trade', *Africa*, 36, pp. 18–36.

Cohen, A. (1967) 'The Hause', in P. C. Lloyd *et. al.* (eds), *The City of Ibadan*, (Cambridge: Cambridge University Press), pp. 117–27.

Cohen, A. (1968) 'The Politics of Mysticism in Some Local Communities in Newly Independent African States', in M. Swartz (ed.), *Local-level Politics*. Chicago: Aldine.

Cohen, A. (1969a) *Custom and Politics in Urban Africa*. London: Routledge & Kegan Paul; Berkeley: University of California Press.

Cohen, A. (1969b) 'Political Anthropology: the Analysis of the Symbolism of Power Relations'. *Man* 4, pp. 217–35.

Cohen, A. (1971) 'The Politics of Ritual Secrecy'. *Man* 6, 427–48.

Epstein, A. L. (1958) *Politics in an Urban African Community*. Manchester: Manchester University Press.

Evans-Pritchard, E. E. (1951) *Social Anthropology*. London: Cohen & West.

Farren, M. and Barker, E. (1972) *Watch Out Kids*, Open Gate Books London: Macmillan.

Ferris, P. (1960) *The City*. Harmondsworth: Penguin.

Gluckman, M. (1961) 'Anthropological Problems arising from the African Industrial Revolution', in A. Southal (ed.), *Social Change in Modern Africa*. London: Oxford University Press.

Liebenow, J. G. (1969) *Liberia: The Evolution of Privilege*. Ithaca and London: Cornell University Press.

Lupton, T. and Wilson, S. (1959) 'Background and Connections of Top Decision-makers. *Manchester University School*.

Maquet, J. (1961) *The Premise of Inequality in Rwanda*. London: Oxford University Press.

Marcuse, M. (1964) *One-Dimensional Man*. Boston: Beacon Press.

Parkin, D. (1969) *Neighbours and Nationals*. London: Routledge & Kegan Paul.

Parry, G. (1969) *Political Elites*. London: George Allen & Unwin.

Sampson, A. (1962) *Anatomy of Britain*. New York and Evanston: Harper & Row; London: Hodder and Stoughton.

21 Ethnic Identity: Its Logical Foundations and its Dysfunctions (1975)

George Devereux*

THE DOUBLE MEANING OF IDENTITY

In the following chapter I propose to show that ethnic identity (and the operations by which it is determined) can be usefully contrasted with other forms of identity (and the operations by which they are determined). A discussion of this contrast lays the foundations for a rigorous analysis of what I term the dysfunctional-dissociative aspects of ethnic identity. Although I analyze mainly the dissociative (differentiating) and the dysfunctional aspects of ethnic identity, I do not deny the associate (dedifferentiating) and functional aspects of identity. In fact, it is precisely the analysis of the former which permits one to grasp more fully the latter – as the study of neurosis helps one to understand the meaning of normality. These terms will be clarified in the course of the discussion. Throughout this study, the term 'class' is used in its mathematical sense only. It is never used in the sense of 'social class;' the term 'Spartan' denotes only the truly free upper stratum of that city-state – the 'equals' (*homoioi*) (Forrest, 1968).

*Identity is the absolute uniqueness of individual A. Non-*identity with any other individual is determined by at least one very precise operation which shows A to be the sole member of a class. The result of such an operation can often be expressed by a cardinal or an ordinal number. A cardinal number expresses A's unique weight in x millionths of a milligram. Nothing else has the same weight (except the aggregate of weights used to weigh him on a scale). An ordinal number (masquerading as a cardinal number), such as a social security number, can also uniquely identify A. Practices such as primogeniture and ultimogeniture prove that this type of identification is ancient (Devereux, 1972b). But it is meaningful and unambiguous only if the class con-

---

* From Chapter 2 in George de Vos and Lola Romanucci-Ross, *Ethnic Identities: Cultural Continuities and Change* (Palo Alto: Mayfield, 1975), pp. 42–70.

tains more than one member. Indeed, if a couple has one child only, that child will in a primogeniture system inherit as 'the first born,' and in an ultimogeniture system as 'the last born.' This kind of identity is of little immediate interest to the student of ethnic identity. But A's uniqueness – his total distinguishability in space and time (Kroeber, 1952b) implemented by the temporal Ego (Devereux, 1967a, 1967b) – is of great importance. For in order to have an ethnic identity, one must first be human. Humanness implies a capacity to be unique, for individuation is more characteristic of man than of the amoeba. But the uniqueness of A is a consequence of the exceptional range of his potential behavioral repertoire, which is at the root of his extreme plasticity. This quality is relevant for the student of ethnic identity in two ways: it permits A to assume an ethnic identity and to maintain it operationally under highly variable conditions; and it permits A to change his ethnic identity, when necessary.

Other problems arising out of the relationship between the exceptionally high degree of the individual's uniqueness and between his collective ethnic identity are analyzed below.

An individual's absolute uniqueness is defined by an induplicable accumulation of imprecise determinations. Each of these operations denies A's uniqueness in one respect sufficient to permit him to be assigned, *in that respect*, to a particular class, which has at least one other member. Such an assignment involves a deliberate imprecision which, in principle, is of a specifiable degree.

Case 1: Some women athletes have a female anatomy and are heterosexual, but are genetically 'less female' than other women. Their genetic anomaly is disregarded in nearly all sociological operations, yet athletic authorities often question their right to compete with 'real' women, for their anomalous genetic make-up appears to give them an unfair advantage in sports.

Case 2: Maria Theresa, quasi-absolute queen of Hungary, Elizabeth II, constitutional queen of England, and Anne of Austria, queen of Louis XIII, can all be assigned to the class 'queens,' but only by operations of considerable imprecision, i.e., by leaving the concept of 'queen' very flexible.

Assigning A to class X by means of a specifiable degree of imprecision – that is, by the affirmation that, in that respect, A is not different from B – *neither affirms nor denies A's total uniqueness* in some *other* respect, such as weight, or the fact that only he discovered the theory of relativity. The identity of A can be unambiguously determined without enumerating all classes to which, within specifiable degrees of imprecision, he may be assigned. The more highly differentiated A is, the fewer of his class memberships need be enumerated in order to identify him uniquely.

Case 3: One can uniquely identify Freud by saying that he is (a) a member of the class (having two members: Freud and Breuer) whose researches made the discovery of psychoanalysis possible; and (b) one member of (the more numerous) class of persons who actually laid the foundations of the science of psychoanalysis. This class includes Freud, Ferenczi, and Abraham, but excludes Breuer.

Certain conventions tend to rank the classes to which A belongs in terms of their relevance for establishing his identity.

Case 4: Euripides was both a member of the class of all playwrights and of the class of all persons having facial warts, but the former class membership is usually considered more relevant than the latter – because, for example, more persons will be able to name the author of the *Bacchae*, than the person who had *x* facial warts.

In times of crisis this hierarchy of classes tends to become scrambled.

Case 5: Before Hitler, Einstein's most relevant class membership was 'physicist.' Under Hitler, at least in Germany, it was 'Jew,' and Einstein had to take this into account.

In times of crisis it can also happen that only one, or a very few, class memberships of A are considered relevant.

Case 6: Under Hitler, the most relevant class memberships were being a 'pure' Aryan and being militarily useful. Initially the Nazi regime did not fully realize the military usefulness of physicists, which led to the flight of many Jewish physicists. By contrast, the military usefulness of generals was recognized: Goering himself declared the half-Jewish general, Milch, an Aryan, while Germany's wartime Japanese allies were honorary Aryans.

These findings give us a first glimpse of the dysfunctional-dissociative aspects of ethnic identity, and of other group identities, but a detailed discussion must be postponed for the moment, in order to contrast 'ethnic personality' with 'ethnic identity.'

ETHNIC PERSONALITY VERSUS ETHNIC IDENTITY

Though in practice ethnic personality and ethnic identity overlap, no satisfactory analysis of ethnic identity is possible unless the two concepts are first sharply defined and carefully contrasted.

Ethnic personality is a conceptual scheme derived inductively from concrete data of two not very distinct types. The first consists of directly observed behavior which, as one's data become more numerous, appear to be typical of and distinctive for a particular group. Such behavior is recognized as not being simply human behavior, since the elements of the total possible human repertoire that it includes are used in a distinctive way. The second type of concrete data is directly observed verbal behavior consisting of generalizations about the ethnic personality by informants acting as self-ethnographers (Devereux, 1972a). Only if such statements are viewed as observable behavior can one lend credence to the Cretan self-ethnographer Epimenides' affirmation that 'All Cretans are liars.' Bertrand Russell (1919) has shown that even though Epimenides was a Cretan, and even though by his own account all Cretans are liars, it is possible to accept Epimenides' self-ethnographic generalization as true, for it is a statement about all Cretan statements and therefore does not apply to itself (Forrest, 1968). In the perspective of ethnic personality, the key word in Epimenides' statement is 'liars.' The statement cannot be turned around and expressed in the form 'All liars are Cretans,' even if it could be shown that only Cretans lie, primarily because this latter formulation – even if it were true – would pertain not to the ethnic personality but to a bastard 'ethnic identity model.' In addition, in Epimenides' statement, the term 'Cretan' *could* be defined without reference to ethnic identity – for example, in purely geographical terms. As to the ethnic personality of Cretans, one predicates about it only the trait 'liar.' This very probably does not suffice to render Cretan ethnic personality distinct from all other ethnic personalities, since it is possible that one could say, also correctly, 'All X's are liars,' where X denotes an ethnic group not identical with the Cretans.

In principle, an *ethnos* could exist which does not enunciate anything whatever about its ethnic personality. An *ethnos* could also exist which does enunciate generalizations about its ethnic personality, but views them as a formulation of human personality, as distinct from animal behavior only. This could happen in an imaginary tribe so cut off from other tribes for so long, that it had lost any knowledge of the existence of other people.

Only an outside observer would realize that his informant enunciated the group's *ethnic* personality. As I understand it, the Cape York Eskimo formerly somewhat approximated this condition. That some tribes call themselves simply 'the people' is also suggestive in this context. But I note the occurrence of an inverse type of 'misapprehension.' In one instance, the Sedang Moi viewed as a typically Sedang (cleverly legalistic) manipulation of Sedang customs, a universally female act of ingratiation performed by a captive Annamese girl, who certainly had no knowledge whatever of Sedang law and custom.

At times, the generalizations enunciated by informants fit but poorly the findings of the competent observer. Such poor fit is often the result of attempts to represent the ethnic personality as congruent with the ethnic identity, treated in such cases as an ideal model of conduct, which it primarily is not. In many such instances the traits ascribed to the ethnic personality, and believed to be part of the ethnic identity, tend to have the quality of a value judgment.

Case 7: When a missionary told the Arunta about original sin, the Arunta indignantly replied, 'All Arunta are good!' And this answer was given even though they occasionally ostracized or punished for badness people whom they recognized to be Aruntas, and who misbehaved in an Arunta manner.

Case 8: There are probably few ethnic personality self-models which do not include the ascription of courage, though manifestly not all *ethnes* are equally warlike.

I will show further on that treating ethnic identity as an ideal self-model, composed of predicative statements is, strictly speaking, an adulterated ethnic identity, already contaminated by the ethnic personality self-model. It is also significant that the logical construct, 'ethnic personality,' pre-supposes the existence of sets of conjugate and well-articulated ethnic sub-personalities.

Case 9: A Spartan man's ethnic personality differed significantly from that of a Spartan woman, but could not have existed without the latter. The Spartan woman, too, was laconic and dour, but she did not fight in battles; she only encouraged her men to fight, mocked inadequate fighters and bore stoically the death of her men on the battlefield. But one notes that not even one of the 27 cases cited in Plutarch's essay *On the Bravery of Women* concerns a Spartan woman.

One can supposedly exhibit the ethnic personality either in a good or a bad way, as in Linton's (1936) 'patterns of misconduct.'

Case 10: According to the Israeli sabras, there is a good (*sabra*) and a bad (ghetto Jew) Jewish ethnic personality. The reverse valuation is ascribed to these patterns by the Chassidic Jews of Israel.

Case 11: The militant and the 'Uncle Tom' Afro-American ethnic personality models contrast in similar ways.

It is inherent in the notion of ethnic personality that members of the ethnos display that ethnic personality both in various ways and to a different degree. This finding leads to the logical problems of 'ethnic typicality,' admirably analyzed by Bertrand Russell (1919, Vajda, 1937): 'How shall I define a "typical Frenchman?" We may define him as one "possessing all qualities that are possessed by most Frenchmen." But unless we confine "all qualities" to such as do not involve a reference to any *totality* (my italics) of qualities, we shall have to observe that most Frenchmen are *not* typical in the above sense, and therefore the definition shows that to be not typical is essential to a typical Frenchman. This is not a logical contradiction, since there is no reason why there should be any typical Frenchman; but it illustrates the need of separating off qualities that involve reference to a totality of qualities from those that do not.' Again, with reference to Napoleon, Russell observes, 'I must define "qualities" in such a way that it will not include what I am now saying, i.e., 'having all the "qualities" that make a great general' must not be itself a quality in the sense supposed.'

A distinction must also be made between the actualization and the exhibition of ethnic personality in behavior. Much ethnic-personality determined behavior is actualized (manifested) unwittingly and at times without an awareness that the behavior manifests the ethnic personality. Roughly speaking, such behavior is actualized because, owing to conditioning, it follows the line of least resistance and involves the smallest amount of effort, at least for the one who performs it.

Case 12: Though displaying *machismo* is easy for a Cuban, a Hopi may view it as singularly strenuous behavior.

When the ethnic personality is consciously implemented in behavior, it tends to be experienced also as an implementation of the kind of ethnic identity model which is logically already contaminated by the ethnic personality model. In many eases, an unwitting, spontaneous actualization of some aspect of ethnic personality is less easily identifiable as such, than is an act which intentionally exhibits it. An analogy may be helpful here.

Case 13: Consider two sets of photographs. One set shows the faces of persons genuinely experiencing extreme grief, pain or stress; the other set shows the faces of good actors mimicking extreme grief, pain or stress. Psychologists have found that subjects misidentify the expression of a genuinely experienced state more often than a mimicked one. Actual laughter may, for example, be identified as 'crying,' while the facial expression of a 'laughing' actor is generally correctly identified.

One last and extremely important characteristic of ethnic personality must now be noted. Ethnic personality may be defined as a set of usually hierarchized sets of positive (positive = ego ideal) predicative statements, such as 'A Spartan is brave, dour, frugal, laconic, etc.' All such adjectives are attributes, even when they are negatively worded: 'A Spartan is not loquacious.' (Super ego.) (Devereux, 1956) One often encounters such seemingly negative statements in such formulations of the ethnic personality as: 'The Spartan is not loquacious' (like the Athenian, whom he does not wish to resemble); 'he is not alcoholic' (like the Helot, whom he despises). I show further on that such negative formulations often reflect historical processes. They highlight the dissociative-differentiating origins of many ethnic personality traits.

Ethnic identity is far more difficult to define in a strictly logical sense than is ethnic personality, because in practice it is so often and so abusively contaminated by the latter. Ethnic identity must first be considered in a rigorously logical manner, even though such a purely logical view of ethnic identity has almost no direct practical applicability. It nonetheless needs to be defined, in order to render understandable both the way in which it becomes contaminated by the ethnic personality and how it functions after being so contaminated.

Ethnic identity is neither logically nor operationally an inductive generalization from data. In the narrowest sense it is not even an ideal model. It is simply a sorting device. It has in principle nothing to do with modes of behavior, be they directly observed by the field worker or enunciated by the informant. But ethnic identity must be enunciable and be enunciated by a self-ethnographer. Let us consider once more Epimenides' statement, 'All Cretans are liars.' We saw that in the framework of the ethnic personality, the key word is 'liars.' But in the framework of ethnic identity, the key word is 'Cretans,' whose existence this statement postulates. In the present frame of reference, 'Cretans are those who inhabit Crete' is the equivalent of 'All Cretans are liars,' for we can can consider here only the postulation of the existence of 'Cretans' – *independently* of any quality we may attribute to Cretans.

Exactly as in the case of the ethnic personality, we can also imagine an ethne whose ethnic identity is identical with its notion of human identity (as distinct from being an animal). But even such a pure ethnic identity can develop only out of a confrontation with and a differentiation from 'others,' to whom a different ethnic identity is ascribed. In logic, the ascription of an ethnic identity to another need not presuppose any performance or predisposition. Where such an ascription is made, the concept is already impure.

Case 14: A baby born to Spartan parents – an even which, for the newborn, was not a performance but a passive experience – was labelled a Spartan. He had a Spartan ethnic identity. But it was recognized from the start that he would have to acquire a Spartan ethnic personality, through an extremely rigorous training, which all ancient studies of Sparta discuss at great length (Plutarch, *The Life of Lycurgus, The Institutions of Laconians; Xenophon, The Constitution of the Lacedaemonians*, etc.). By contrast, a Mohave baby was held to have a Mohave temperament ('predisposition') already in the womb. In cases of obstetrical difficulties, the shaman could appeal to the unborn child's Mohave personality, to persuade him to be born (Devereux, 1948). This belief made even birth a performance of the infant and, moreover, a characteristically Mohave performance.

The ethnic identity, being simply a label or sorting device, does not presuppose, at least in theory, the existence of ethnic sub-identities. Spartan men, women, or children were all equally Spartan with respect to their ethnic identity and, moreover, Spartans in the same sense. This implies that, within the framework of pure ethnic identity, one could not be more or less Spartan, nor Spartan in good or bad, male or female ways. One either was a Spartan on one was not. Ethnic identity is an all-or-nothing proposition, to such an extent that the concept of typicality simply does not intervene at any point of the discourse concerning it. (Similarly, any finite integer is either an even or an odd number: 2 is neither more nor less an even number than 6 or 20, nor more typical of the set of all finite even integers than any other even integer.)

In this framework, then, ethnic identity is operationally a sorting device for oneself and for 'others,' and sociologically, a label which can be attributed or withheld only totally. Hence, it matters not at all, in this frame of reference and at this stage of the analysis, whether A asserts, 'I am a Spartan' (with B concurring or dissenting), or whether B asserts, 'A is a Spartan' (with A concurring or dissenting). In practice, of course, such things do matter:

Case 15: Brasidas asserted that he was a Spartan, and the Athenians concurred.

Case 16: Róheim asserted that he was a Hungarian, but under Nazi influence most Hungarians dissented and drove him into exile.

Case 17: The Hungarians asserted that, though Hungarian-born, Herzl was a Jew and Herzl concurred.

Case 18: The Nazi-influenced Hungarians asserted: Róheim is a Jew Róheim dissented so strongly that he arranged to have his coffin covered with a Hungarian flag when he was buried in New York.

The moment anything is predicated about ethnic identity other than

'A is while B is not, an X' (Spartan, Hungarian, Mohave), ethnic identity
begins to function as an ideal model, akin at its worst to a kind of
superego which is but a residue of traumata that were not mastered
when they were endured (5), and at its best to a kind of ego-ideal.
Like them, the ideal model car variously be implemented and it may
even be quite illegitimately argued that the concept 'typical' can intervene in discussions of ethnic identity. But underneath it all, the all-or-
nothing concept persists. A good example is the difference regularly
made between the concepts 'spy' and 'traitor.' A curious example of
the latter follows.

Case 19: When Rumania was still a kingdom, its laws recognized
the right of a Rumanian to acquire another nationality and even another
ethnic identity. Hence, when a foreign-naturalized ex-Rumanian returned to Rumania on a visit, he was not held to be still sufficiently
Rumanian to be forcibly inducted into military service. But there was
one limitation: he could be penalized, even after his naturalization elsewhere, for service in an army fighting the Rumanian army. Thus we
have the case of a Transylvanian Hungarian who becomes through
conquest a Rumanian citizen in 1919, but who moved to Hungary and
resumed his Hungarian citizenship. If taken prisoner by the Rumanians
while serving in the Hungarian armed forces, he could have been penalized for fighting as a Hungarian citizen against his alleged country
of birth. But this is admittedly a highly unusual situation.

This all-or-nothing element continues to exist even where there are
attempts to postulate partial or hyphenated ethnic identities.

Case 20: The WASP usually claims to have a more genuine American ethnic identity than, let us say, an Italian-American, who also claims
an American ethnic identity. But for the sociologist, what matters is
that WASPness is meaningful only because there also exist non-WASPs.
It is an important characteristic of the American ethnic identity model
that both WASPs and non-WASPs can and do claim it. This flexibility
is inherent in the ideal model of American ethnic identity, and does
not modify, for the logician at least, its all-or-nothing character.

The moment one begins to predicate anything about ethnic identity,
one is faced with the seeming paradox that one can express one's ethnic identity by turning traitor (as distinct from spy), as far as other
members of the *ethnos* are concerned, and that one can even express
one's ethnic identity by not expressing it in a certain way.

Case 21: During the eighteenth and nineteenth centuries, a class of
Catholic Hungarian aristocrats existed, who claimed Hungarian ethnic
identity (conceded by their opponents), but whose entire behavior was

not Hungarian. Many of them spoke no Hungarian, lived in Vienna, were close to the Hapsburg court, and believed a total Austrianization of Hungary to be in Hungary's best interests and in their own, as Hungarian aristocrats. It may even be said that they manifested their Hungarian ethnic identity differently from the way Bohemian (Czech) aristocrats, of similar outlook, manifested their Bohemianness, for similar reasons.

It is also necessary to specify that even though a particular conduct may be felt by the observer to be an instance of A's ethnic personality and his ethnic identity (as an ideal model), it expresses ethnic identity from the point of view of the subject only if the performance is intended, or is retrospectively felt, to express it. Training usually made a Spartan 'spontaneously' laconic (ethnic *personality*). But if he made a show of his laconism, especially in his contacts with an outsider, in such a way as to exhibit his ethnic identity, his performance was logically inseparable from role playing. I cite in this connection a curious observation.

Case 22: Hundreds of typical Spartan sayings (Plutarch, *The Sayings of Kings and Commanders*, of *Spartans*, of *Spartan Women*) have come down to us. Plutarch alone assembled about two hundred of them. All, or nearly all, of them are so typical, or ritualistic, that if one has read twenty or thirty of them, one feels that one has read them all. Allowances must of course be made for Plutarch's selection of these sayings. Nonetheless, I note a curious fact. Though we also possess a number of pithy sayings by such Athenians as Themistocles, Aristides, Pericles, and others, their sayings are not monotonous and are not cited as specimens of typical Athenian wit. They are cited to shed light upon the individual personalities of these great Athenians. In fact, they are typically Athenian precisely by being so very different, for individualism was part of the Athenian ethnic personality and ethnic identity model.

It is also striking that many of the Spartan sayings were addressed to non-Spartans, or concern non-Spartans, or concern Spartans in their relations with foreigners. Since the Spartans themselves were for hundreds of years intellectually unproductive, and since most accounts of Spartan were written by non-Spartans, this finding can be partly explained by assuming that foreigners would hear and report mainly remarks addressed to them by Spartans, or made about them between Spartans. But even when allowances are made for both these factors, it still would seem that Spartans were more laconic in connection with non-Spartans than in daily relations among themselves. I hold, for example, that the extreme and 'typical' laconism of these sayings was to a large extent due to role playing, to an 'exhibiting' of Spartan ethnic identity (see below, *Case 24*).

I must, for clarity's sake, repeat here something already mentioned in connection with the ethnic personality. Consider an activity which, from the viewpoint of the performer, seems easy and natural because it is an expression of his ethnic personality. If the observer views it as an actualization of that person's ethnic identity, he does more than view it as role playing. He (rightly or wrongly) assumes also that the act intentionally involves more effort than the act which the observer would naturally execute under the 'same' circumstances and for the 'same' purpose. The observer may even hold that it entails more effort than an ideally economic act seeking to achieve the 'same' objective would entail. I place the word 'same' in quotes, since owing to cultural evaluations, an activity might not have the same meaning in two cultures. Acquisitive activity in Mohave and in Yurok society is a case in point.

This brings me to the key findings of this paper:

Since the ethnic personality is an inductive generalization from behavioral data and may be held to describe or model accurately some basic aspects of the personality of any X (Mohave, Spartan, etc.), then a particular activity which can be predicted or explained from a knowledge of that ethnic personality must be viewed as a natural manifestation of it. Though the conceptual model of the Spartan ethnic personality was originally constructed out of the observation of certain modes of behavior current in Sparta, those modes of behavior were derivable from it, once that model was constructed. Thus Brasidas was brave because he could not help being brave, given his Spartan ethnic personality. In the framework of ethnic personality he did not act bravely in order to express his Spartan ethnic personality.

Since the ethnic identity is not an inductive generalization from behavioral data, it cannot be held to describe or model accurately any basic aspect of the personality of any X (Mohave, Spartan, etc.). No particular activity can be predicted from a knowledge of the pure ethnic identity (label) or explained in terms of it. No activity can be viewed as a natural actualization of that pure ethnic identity, nor can it be held to express the pure ethnic identity, since, in strict logic, nothing is predicated about ethnic identity except that it exists, or is claimed by or imputed to A. Only when in a logically abusive manner something is predicated about ethnic identity, does it become a model, more or less congruent in its contents with the ethnic personality, but quite distinct from it in terms of its logical status. Once one operates, as one must in practice, with the logically impure ethnic identity model, one can assert that Brasidas was brave in order to instance his Spartan ethnic identity. I note in passing that a number of Spartan sayings, which I cannot cite here, do tend to represent the bravery of some particular Spartan, A, as something which voluntarily expresses his Spartan ethnic *identity*, rather than as something which automatically derives from his Spartan ethnic *personality*.

The explanation which views Brasidas' bravery as an inevitable manifestation of his Spartan personality and the explanation which views it as an intentional expression of his Spartan ethnic identity stand in a relationship of Heisenbergian complementarity to each other. (The nature and socio–psychological importance of complementary explanations cannot be discussed here; they have been analyzed in a series of earlier publication (Devereux, 1967a; 1970, Chapters 4, 5.) Speaking somewhat loosely, the analysis of Brasidas' bravery in terms of his ethnic personality is primarily a psychological one; its analysis in terms of his ethnic identity is primarily a sociological one.

The preceding paragraphs are the core of this essay's argument; I now pass from the concept of pure ethnic identity, to the logically impure concept of the ethnic identity *model*, about which many predicative statements will be made. But the reader must constantly bear in mind that from this point on 'ethnic identity' denotes *not* the pure concept (label), but the impure ethnic identity model, which is more or less congruent, in terms of what is predicated about it, with the inductively formulated ethnic personality.

I conclude this section by citing three types of observations which help one to distinguish fairly easily between behavior voluntarily expressing ethnic identity and behavior which manifests almost automatically the ethnic personality as it really is.

Behavior expressing ethnic identity often disappears as soon as A ceases to be under the eyes of other members of his *ethnos*.

Case 23: An old oracle predicted that 'Sparta would perish through greed.' Spartans were therefore forbidden to own precious metals, and their houses could be searched for it (Xenophon, *The Constitution of the Lacedaemonians*, 7.6). Nonetheless, as soon as a Spartan went abroad – for example, as governor (*harmost*) of a subject city – he displayed notorious greed and corruptibility (Plutarch, *Spartans*, p. 220F ff.). This suggests that impulses incompatible with the ethnic identity (functioning as a superego) were inhibited, but were nonetheless part of the ethnic personality. (Compare the Mohave belief that the ghost of a very generous man is highly acquisitive and possessive, Devereux, 1969.)

Behavior expressive of ethnic identity also tends to disappear when a strong upheaval brings about a state of affairs incompatible with the ethnic identity model.

Case 24: As soon as the previously invincible Spartan army was decisively beaten *on land* by a foreign power (the Thebans) – a state of affairs which destroyed forever Sparta's military supremacy in Greece and which was totally unimaginable in terms of Spartan self-definition – the Spartan negotiators for peace displayed such loquacity that the victors mockingly remarked that they had put an end to Spartan laconicity (Plutarch, *Kings and Commanders*, p. 193D, etc.).'

There is often a tendency to exaggerate, with respect to foreigners, an ethnic identity trait that is less obvious in intra-ethnic relations. Spartan laconism with aliens is an example (*Case 22*). A variant of this process is the exaggeration of the tokens of one's ethnic identity during exile (*Case 18*).

THE FORMATION AND MANIFESTATIONS OF ETHNIC IDENTITY

Logically, ethnic identity involves two symmetrical specifications:

(1) A is an X (Brasidas is a Spartan);

(2) A is not a non-X (Brasidas is not an Athenian).

I have already indicated that an absolutely isolated hypothetical tribe's ethnic identity model is totally congruent with its human identity model. It can cease to overlap with the latter only after the group enters into contact with another group and establishes its difference from the latter.

In the analysis and perhaps in the historical development of the sense of ethnic identity, the statement, 'A is not a non-X ("they"),' is prior to the statement, 'A is an X ("we").' In short, specifications as to what constitutes ethnic identity develop only after an ethnic group recognizes the existence of others who do not belong to the group. At the start, these specifications may conceivably include only certain real (racial, cultural, personality) traits of the group. But it is almost inevitable that these distinguishing traits will eventually acquire also evaluative connotations.

Case 25: The Moi tribes have no generic name for themselves. They differentiate themselves from the non-Moi by referring to themselves both neutrally and accurately as 'those who eat from wooden platters.' They can also differentiate themselves by attributing to themselves a good trait said not to be characteristic of the non-Moi. One such (formerly correct) trait was 'courage in war.' Lastly, they differentiate themselves by the admission that they lack some good trait of others: 'We don't know how to talk to the buffaloes and therefore cannot yoke them.' They even have a myth explaining why they are illiterate.

At times, a tribe may not attribute to themselves a trait which they possess and value, in order to differentiate themselves from others.

Case 26: A Spartan unable to grasp the speech of a Spartan orator would have deemed himself stupid and would have been called stupid by others. Yet, leading Spartans repeatedly and contemptuously professed not to understand the eloquent speeches of non-Spartan envoys (Strabo, *Geography*, 1.86; Plutarch, *Kings and Commanders*, p. 223D, p. 232E, etc.).

I note in this context an unusual fact.

Case 27: Owing no doubt to linguistic isolation in Europe, the Hungarian word 'to explain' actually means 'to Hungarianize,' to put into Hungarian (*magyarazni*).

I will now give some examples of routine items internal to the race and/or culture, terms which had originally probably no relation to ethnic identity, but which acquired that quality when they began to be used as a means of differentiation, of being X by being non-Y.

Examples of physical traits include the following:

Case 28: The realism of Bushman wall paintings makes easy the identification of the animal species they depict. By contrast, the representation of human beings remained quite schematic until after the country of the Bushmen (who are small and yellowish) was invaded by the Bantu (who are tall and black) (D. F. Bleek). Nonetheless, paintings showing *battles* between the two races do not accentuate the *penis rectus* (Schapera, 1930) of the Bushmen (castration anxiety?).[1]

An ordinarily unexploited potential may acquire the quality of a component of ethnic identity and may be arbitrarily held to be ancient.

Case 29: The 'Afro' hairstyle seems to me Melanesian rather than African. It does not appear to be traditional in those parts of Africa where Afro-Americans originated. It seems, rather, to reflect a reaction against the former assimilative use of hair straighteners. But there may be more to it than that. The excessive use of inferior hair-straighteners sometimes caused a considerable, if temporary, loss of hair. What little fuzz remained somewhat resembled a scanty 'Afro' (Devereux, 1967a). Also, the 'Afro' is something most other races cannot duplicate or imitate. It is therefore 'Afro' only in the sense that it is not imitable, except artificially, by non-Africans (and non-Melanesians).

Internal cultural traits at times acquire the value of ethnic identity tokens, differentiating the group members from non-members, especially under conditions of stress.

Case 30: The ancient nomadic Hebrews probably had no pigs because pig-breeding was inconvenient for nomads living in a semi-desert. They may therefore be presumed not to have eaten pork simply because they had no pigs. Once settled in Canaan, however, they were among peoples who not only ate pork, but ate it at times ritually, because in their myths (Adonis, etc.) wild boars played a significant role. Thus for the Hebrews, not eating pork became a token of Hebrew ethnic-religious identity. The custom remained the same all along, but acquired a new meaning related to the implementation of dissociative ethnic identity. I note in passing that, even though the Hebrew dietary laws did not enunciate the taboo in that form, they tabooed in effect the flesh of all polymastic animals, perhaps because their neighbors had a polymastic female deity, such as the Artemis of the Ephesians. To my knowledge, this point has not previously been made.

Case 31: In the ninth and tenth centuries, the pagan Hungarians routinely drank fermented mare's milk, for it was their only alcoholic beverage. But they also drank with pleasure the beer and wine they found in sacked Western cities. However, beginning with Hungary's Christianization and Westernization, the Western priests decided to treat kumys-drinking as a pagan practice (Devereux, 1967a), just as missionaries in Kenya treated Kikuyu clitoridectomy as a pagan practice, though nothing in the Bible forbids either one. (Note that Strabo, *Geography*, 16.4.9, asserts, probably erroneously, that Jewish girls were 'circumcised.') As a result, certain Hungarians who wished to resist both Christianization and Westernization, defiantly began to drink kumys in a new and different spirit. It became a token of their old-fashioned 'pagan Hungarian' ethnic identity. Much the same may be said of obstinate advocacy of clitoridectomy on the part of some educated Kikuyus in response to missionary interference (Kenyatta, 1938).

This brings me to what I believe is an overlooked fact.

Case 32: Marie Bonaparte (1950) divides mankind as a whole into 'friends of the clitoris' and 'enemies of the clitoris.' Now in some areas of Africa, girls are in fact deprived of their clitoris and much of their labia (Bonaparte, 1950; Bryk, 1939). But in certain other African tribes girls are encouraged to manipulate and to tug at their external genitals, so as to increase their length and bulk (Bryk, 1939). To my knowledge, neither of these symmetrical practices has been correlated with the fact that Khoisan women naturally have very long labia, the 'Hottentot apron' (Schapera, 1930). Since the Khoisans formerly lived far to the North of their present habitat, the Hottentot apron of their women may perhaps have inspired both the differentiating (Kikuyu, etc.) practice of female circumcision and the assimilative practice of the artificial lengthening of the labia in other African cultures.

Some of the most striking tokens of the dissociative nature of ethnic identity models are new culture traits that have evolved in the form of an 'antagonistic acculturation,' a process defined and analyzed by E. M. Loeb and myself (Devereux, 1943). I can enumerate only a few striking maneuvers of this kind. For example, total imitation in reverse, while not common, does exist.

Case 33: Adult Spartans forced the despised Helots – a subject population 'neither slave nor free,' as an ancient authority puts it – to get drunk and then exhibited them to Spartan youth as negative models (Plutarch, *The Life of Lyangus*, 28.4–5), to teach the young Spartans sobriety. I note in passing that this did not suffice to teach King Kleomenes I to be sober, for he had learned to drink undiluted wine from (non-despised) Scythian ambassadors (Herodotus, *The Histories*, 6.84, etc.).

Another example of antagonistic acculturation is partially deviative imitation which consists in evolving practices that deliberately deviate from traits held to be part of the ethnic identity of 'others,' and become components of one's own ethnic identity.

Case 34: The Bible repeatedly admonishes the Jews in Canaan not to 'be like unto' the people surrounding them.

Case 35: G. Vajda (1937) has shown that after Mohammed lost hope of converting the 'people of the Book' (Jews and Christians), he devised a whole series of behavior patterns for Mohammedans, the main purpose of which was to differentiate them from the 'unbelievers.'

Alloplastic activities involve either the denial or the imposing of distinctive culture traits on others. The dominant group then treats both as tokens of the ethnic identity of the dominated. The yellow Star of David, which the Nazis forced the Jews to wear, is an obvious case. But it is striking that the forbidden trait can be smuggled into the culture of the oppressed in *disguise* and accepted as a token of ethnic identity. Invidiously imposed culture elements can also turn into such tokens.

Case 36: Some Arab states forbade the Jews to ride camels. According to an informant, the Jews compensated for this by rocking themselves like camel riders while praying, but this may be only folklore.

Case 37: The Manchus imposed the pigtail on the Chinese, for whom it soon became a token of ethnic identity.

Case 38: The Chassidim consider certain garments necessary tokens of Jewish ethnic identity, even though they had been invidiously forced upon them by their former Polish overlords.

Case 39: Between 1926 and 1932, I never once saw a French Jewish youth or girl wear the Star of David as a necklace. In 1946, after the Nazi occupation, I saw many French Jewish girls and even boys wear such pendants, but have seen none since my return to France in 1963.

I note in passing that antagonistic acculturation often involves the borrowing of the 'other's' means, the better to defeat his ends, and to protect one's own ethnic identity. Sometimes it takes the form of what Kroeber called 'stimulus diffusion' (Kroeber, 1952).

Case 40: Sequoya invented the Cherokee alphabet in competition with (and as a result of stimulus diffusion from) the English alphabet.

A particularly interesting example of the implementation of ethnic identity is the acceptance of 'ethnic' psychological traits invidiously attributed to certain oppressed groups.

Case 41: Many formerly warlike groups, forced to become despised merchants and then accused of shrewd practices, tend to take pride in being shrewd and deem it a token of their ethnic identity. This is as true of medieval Jews as it is of Armenians in Mohammedan lands, of Levantine Greeks, etc. The Greek hero Odysseus becomes almost caricaturally Levantine in some Greek tragedies (Euripides, *Hecuba*; Sophocles, *Ajax*, *Philoctetes*), although of the Homeric poems only one scene of the *Iliad* (6.234 ff.) depicts a profitable deal 'pulled off' in a Levantine manner – the scene in which Glaucus exchanges his golden armor, worth 100 oxen, for Diomedes' bronze armor, worth only nine – a naivete which the poet himself highlights and ridicules.

Case 42: Aside from dire necessity, the development of strong military forces on the part of the Israelis is partly a reaction to their millenary intimidation and partly a conscious return to the ethnic identity model of the pre-Diaspora Jews, whose great military prowess was recognized even by their Hellenistic and Roman conquerors.

I note, *in fine*, that a change in one's ethnic self-definition is at times made possible by an undeviating adherence to one ethnic identity trait.

Case 43: A French Jewish acquaintance, who had fought in the Free French army and had considered military skill an important component of his French ethnic identity, began to feel that he had (also) a Jewish ethnic identity only after the Israelis displayed great valor in battle in 1948, 1956 and 1967. (I suspect, however, that part of this shift in his ethnic identity was due to the 1940 French military disaster and to the antisemitic measures of the Petain regime.)

Several more very important aspects of the implementation of ethnic identity may also be mentioned. Behavior expressing ethnic identity tends to be more ritualistic and monotonous than behavior triggered off by the ethnic personality (see *Case 22*). One cannot but think, in this connection, of a remark Dodds (1960) made in another context: history repeats itself, but only ritual repeats itself *exactly*. This ethnic identity ritualism may even become exaggerated in times of decline. The Spartans under Roman domination, for example, seem to have played at being Spartans more consistently than they did at the peak of Spartan power, and this despite the likelihood that earlier Spartan sayings probably lost nothing of their typicality in the telling. In the same sense, only a modern-day millionaire can have a 100 percent Louis XIV salon, for the salons of dukes in the time of Louis XIV assuredly also contained Henri IV or Louis XIII heirlooms and portraits of ancestors. In some cases such ethnic role-playing leads to excesses comparable only to the absurdity of eighteenth Century *castrati* singing passionately sensual operatic *roles*.

Ethnic identity is sometimes maximally implemented by those who, by ordinary standards, would not be expected to possess it.

Case 44: The greatest Hungarian Poet, a patriot who died a hero's death as a volunteer in the revolutionary army of 1848–49, was of Serbian extraction, and had Magyarized his name, Petrovitch, to its Hungarian equivalent of Petöfi (Peter-son).

Case 45: European public opinion forced the Emperor of Austria to dismiss in disgrace the half-demented Austrian general Haynau, notorious for his brutal repressions in Hungary after the 1848 revolution. Upon his dismissal, Haynau purchased an estate in Hungary, affected the Hungarian national costume and went about proclaiming, 'We Hungarians will not allow ourselves to be robbed of our national liberties.' It won him no recognition as a possessor of Hungarian ethnic identity. (Compare with the Athenian, Alcibiades, exiled in Sparta, playing at being more Spartan than the native inhabitants of that city.)

The intellectual awareness that a trait, previously felt to be a manifestation of one's ethnic identity, is actually alien, does not necessarily destroy its capacity to be experienced as ethnic.

Case 46: Until Bartók had shown that gypsy music was not Hungarian, it was thought to be, and, despite Bartók, continues to be experienced as Hungarian. What little I preserve of a 'Hungarian ethnic identity' is more easily aroused by a gypsy *csardas* than by a pentatonic peasant song.

Last, there are very few one-dimensional ethnic identities.

Case 47: I remind the reader once again that in the following discussion the term 'Spartan' denotes only the 'full' Spartans, the 'Equals,' who claimed a Hellenic ethnic identity (as contrasted with that of the Barbarians); at times they also claimed a 'racial' Doric identity, as did King Anaxandridas who called his favorite wife's eldest son 'Dorieus' meaning 'the Dorian.' But at other times the Spartans claimed to be successors of the Achaean Atreids, as did the *ephor* Chilon and the son of his kinswoman (by Anaxandridas), King Cleomenes (Herodotus, *The Histories*, 5.72). They validated the latter claim by 'discovering' abroad and reburying in Sparta the bones of the Achaean, Orestes, son of Agamemnon and nephew, son-in-law, and heir of Menelaus (Herodotus, *The Histories*, 1.67). Thus Spartan expansionism could be justified either by claiming Dorian (conqueror) identity or else Achaean (legal successor) identity.

The Spartans also claimed a Spartan identity as contrasted with the Athenians, with their Helot serfs, and with Sparta's satellites by maintaining that to be Spartan meant to be a soldier, for only the Spartan was not permitted to be anything but a soldier.

Case 48: At a gathering of the armies of Sparta and its satellites, an ally protested that Sparta had contributed too few soldiers. In response, the Spartan leader asked that all potters, smiths carpenters, and so on in the assembled armies stand up in turn. Eventually all the allied warriors stood up. Finally, he asked that the professional soldiers stand up, and only the Spartan contingent rose, for they alone were professional soldiers only. This was held to prove that Sparta had contributed more soldiers than anyone else (Plutarch, *Spartans*, p. 214A).

A last aspect of ethnic identity, areal climax, must now be considered. In certain cases the claim to incarnate the areal climax, in Kroeber's sense (1952b) is part of the ethnic identity of more than one *ethnos*. At least two Greek city-states professed to incarnate the essence of Greece.

Case 49: Athens was called 'the school of Hellas' by Pericles; a poet hailed it as 'the Hellas of Hellas.' It deemed itself typical of Greece in the sense in which the finest race horse may be said to typify the species. How different Athens was from other Greek states is shown by the characterizations of Athens by the Corinthian, Spartan, and Athenian orators at a gathering of Sparta and its allies, who had to decide on peace or war with Athens (Thucydides, *The Peloponnesian War*, 1.68 ff.). In addition, Athens claimed to be the most Greek of all Greek cities because only its people were truly autochthonous, having always lived in Attica (Herodotus, *The Histories,* 1.56; 7.161). This also made them different from other Greek cities, where the pre-Greek (Pelasgian) racial element was minimal. Many of these other cities had, in addition, been overthrown by the invading Dorians at the end of the Achaean period. Yet even Sparta acknowledged at least the eminence, if not pre-eminence, of Athens in Hellas. When Athens lost the Peloponnesian war, one Theban envoy urged that it be dealt with as Athens had dealt with Melos – the city razed, the men slaughtered, the women and children enslaved. At that point, a Phocian envoy, one of Athens' enemies, rose and sang a choral ode from Euripides' *Electra*, and a dour Spartan envoy declared that Sparta was unwilling to destroy the city that had saved Greece during the Persian wars, some 80 years earlier (Plutarch, *The Life of Lycurgus*, 15). At that moment, Athens' ethnic identity, as expressed by its past, became for it a capital reserve.

Sparta – so outlandish by ordinary Greek cultural standards – was also deemed by some to be 'ideal Greece,' on a very different, and possibly even less valid, grounds. The 'real' Spartans were Doric invaders, while most of Greece was *not* Dorian. No Greek state differed more – in qualitative ways – from the rest of Greek states than did Sparta. Athens, on the other hand, differed from the others mainly *quantitatively*: it had *more* good poets, artists, philosophers, craftsmen, sailors, and so on, than the other Greek states. We may note the curious fact that even though it is generally recognized that the Roman conquerors preserved Sparta as a kind of 'reservation for antiquarians,' they also preserved Athens as a kind of 'reservation for students,' as a university town. It is ironic that Sparta became a super-tough reservation when it had ceased to be a military power, and Athens an intellectual reservation when it had ceased to produce first-class minds.

Unlike ethnic personality, ethnic identity nearly always has both a 'self' mystique and an 'ascribed' mystique. Let us examine a highly peculiar example of such a twofold mystique, a town which was in significant respects a product of outsiders.

Case 50: Several aspects of the mystique of Spartan ethnic identity must be considered.

The self mystique and the ascribed mystique converged in some respects: The Spartans deemed themselves invincible on land, and the Athenians, their enemies, concurred. At the outbreak of the Peloponnesian War, Pericles advised Athens to fight only at sea (Thucydides, *The Peloponnesian War*, 1.142 ff.).

The two mystiques may diverge, at least in their evaluation. The

Spartan deemed absolute rectitude a token of his ethnic identity. The Athenians held the Spartan to be totally dishonest, especially when he pretended to be righteous. It suffices to cite here Euripides' characterization of Menelaus, king of Sparta, in his *Andromache*, a characterization based not upon the image of the Achaean Menelaus of the *Iliad*, but upon the Athenian image of the fifth century BC Spartan.

Even where the facts prove both the convergent self mystique and the ascribed mystique to be false, they often continue to be accepted by both in-group and out-group. The myth of Spartan invincibility on land survived their severe defeat by the Athenians at Sphacteria. Plutarch wrote almost 500 years after his own city, Thebes, had forever broken Spartan pre-eminence at Leuctra; yet he too preserved the mystique of the Spartans military superiority to the Theban hoplite; he attributed Sparta's defeat to the genius of a single Theban: Epaminondas (Plutarch, *Spartans*, 214C ff.).

At times an *ethnos* can have a double ethnic-identity self mystique. Thus, Sparta's double (Dorian and Achaean) ethnic identity and mystique led only to alternations in the choice of foes; Sparta remained expansionist. As shown in *Case 47*, the Dorian ethnic mystique justified aggression by a Dorian superiority in arms, while the Achaean mystique sought to give a mythico–legal basis to Spartan expansionism.

In the case of Sparta, much of the mystique of its ethnic identity was manufactured by outsiders, though the Spartans gladly went along with it.

The Spartans did originate a mystique of superiority, what Ollier (1933) calls the 'romance of Sparta,' regarding the antiquity and stability of Sparta's aristocratic constitution. But the 'romance of Sparta' was fully elaborated only by pro-Spartan outsiders, the Spartans themselves being too brutishly uneducated to do it. The real 'romance of Sparta' was written by three Athenians, all of them disciples of Socrates: the ghastly oligarch and traitor Critias, the bright but naive Xenophon, and Plato, who valued systems more than men and deemed abstractions more real than reality.

I must add that much of the mystique of Spartan ethnic identity rested on a misconception assiduously fostered by Spartans. Its 'Lycurgan' constitution was almost certainly less ancient than claimed. But it may well have been the first revolutionary constitution of Greece, because Sparta had earlier and greater inner troubles than the other Greek city-states (Forrest, 1968). Also, the stability of its institutions – on which the ethnic identity of the 'real' Spartans largely depended – was achieved at the appalling cost of turning every free Spartan into a military slave of the state, for Sparta was sitting on a volcano (Devereux, 1965). Other states refused to pay so high a price for stability, especially since the continuity of *their* ethnic identity did not depend on it. They had occasional civil disorders, but of a different nature. In Athens, for example, the Athenian aristocrats clashed with the Athenian democrats. But whoever won was an Athenian. By contrast, in Sparta the overthrow of the free Spartans by the Helots would have impaired and changed Spartan ethnic identity and destroyed the city-state. Solon's law could afford to disenfranchise an Athenian who did not take sides in civil strife (Plutarch, *The Life of Solon*, 20), but the laws of Lycurgus could not afford this.

THE FUNCTIONALITY AND DYSFUNCTIONALITY OF GROUP IDENTITIES

Marcel Mauss (1950) has shown that even though every person is aware of his own identity ('selfhood') many primitive societies do not implement his distinctiveness socially. Sometimes the individual is in some respects functionally interchangeable with other individuals, and he may freely acknowledge this fact (Devereux, 1942).

Case 51: A Sedang man married two cousins, who were also best friends, and therefore called each other by the same (invented) name. One day I asked one of them if she was jealous when her husband cohabited with her co-wife and cousin. She replied: 'Why should I? She is the same person as I' (in this respect). At the same time, this woman knew herself to be a unique and strong personality, who knowingly repudiated many Sedang attitudes and beliefs.

It is convenient to approach the social implementation of individuality from the vantage point of types of relationships. Parsons has outlined three such types (1939): (1) *The functionally specific* (e.g., buyer and seller). All that is not explicitly included is excluded. The demand must be justified. This type of relationship is highly segmental and predominates in complex societies. (2) *The functionally diffuse* (e.g., husband and wife). All that is not explicitly excluded from it is deemed to be included. Not the demand, but the refusal must be justified. (3) *The functionally cumulative* (e.g., employer–lover and secretary–mistress). Such relations tend to cause conflict (Devereux, 1970, Chapter 9). Parsons' scheme omits what I consider to be the type of relationship that predominates in primitive societies: *The functionally multiple*. Abraham, for example, was tribal chief, general, priest, and *pater familias*, and could not have been any one of these without being all the others as well.

But the predominance of functionally multiple relationships in some primitive societies does not necessarily represent an extensive social implementation of a person's uniqueness, for a single attribute may enable a person to accede to many a status in which his relations are functionally multiple. In sororal polygyny, it suffices to be a married woman's sister in order to become a wife, though in that capacity the woman's social relations will certainly be functionally multiple, including sexual partner, mother, and cook. In order to become king, one need only be a king's oldest son. The proclamation: '*Le Roi est mort, vive le Roi!*' affirms the functional interchangeability of the defunct king and his successor.

It is precisely at the top and bottom of the social scale that people are, on the one hand, functionally most interchangeable and at the same time possess – at least in principle – the highest degree of freedom to select from the potential range of behavior those aspects which they choose to actualize at any moment. The law of ancient Persia was that the king was not subject to the law (Herodotus, *The Histories*, 3.31). Under the *ancien regime*, the law was in theory the king's untrammelled will: '*Le Roi le veut;*' '*tel est Notre plaisir.*' Even more relevant is Dollard's (1937) observation that the Southern police often overlooked a Negro's misconduct, though they would have arrested a white for similar behavior.

Evidently, the social recognition and implementation of personal identity resulted from the disintegration of functionally multiple relationships into their components. This appears to have accompanied what Durkheim called 'social polysegmentation,' which permitted a woman, for example, to become A's wife, B's mistress, and C's cook. Historically, the socially implemented individual identity of A seems to have emerged from the recognition that a person could have simultaneously plural class identities with respect to B, and even that each of his class identities (memberships) could be relevant only with regard to a different person and/or in different contexts. At the same time, a number of conditions which a person had to satisfy in order to be assigned to any particular class tended to increase. Though Louis XIV was in principle still commander-in-chief, in practice he entrusted the command of his armies in the field to great generals.

One also observes that in many instances A's membership in class X gains added dimensions by his membership in classes Y and Z, or, conversely, his non-membership in classes M and N. Thus Condé's status as a (Bourbon) Serene Highness greatly increased his authority as a brilliant general. On the other hand, a ruined nobleman of Normandy who wished to restore his fortune by engaging in commerce could temporarily place his nobility 'in escrow' with the parliament of his province.

But the social recognition of A's multiple class memberships can also entail the recognition that he belongs to some class cutting across ethnic lines. Thus a Mohave of the Hipa patrilineal clan would be committing incest if he married a Yuma woman belonging to the same clan. Such multiple class memberships can also lead to the formation of outlooks or character traits cutting across ethnic barriers. Thus some Plains Indian songs and *Fragment 10* of the Spartan poet Tyrtaeus affirm that the corpse of a young man fallen in battle is a beautiful and inspiring sight.

Case 52: A Spartan's 'Spartan-ness' compelled him to implement intensively and exclusively the segment of behavior related to military prowess. Sparta seems to have produced no intellectuals between the time of Alcman and Tyrtaeus (fifth century B.C.) and the unimportant hellenistic antiquarian Sosibius (third century B.C.). The law prohibiting gainful occupations also caused Sparta to enter the Peloponnesian War with only a negligible amount in the treasury (Thucydides, *The Peloponnesian War*, 1.130. etc.). In short, the Spartan's Spartan-ness tended to exclude entirely the implementation of many of his potentialities and to subordinate to his Spartan-ness even those of his potentialities which were deemed compatible with his being a Spartan: he had the right to be a husband and father, but his family life was reduced to a minimum, to give him more time to be a Spartan. By contrast, the Athenian's Athenian-ness also demanded that he be brave, but he was free to and expected to express other aspects of Athenian ethnic identity as well. Sophocles was an industrialist, general and statesman, as well as a dramatic poet. He was, moreover, entitled to a genuine private life, to a meaningful social and personal identity. The flexibility of the Athenian's ethnic identity was probably due to the early establishment of a true unity and equality among the inhabitants of Attica. Attic 'synoecismus' contrasts greatly with the basic disunity of the Spartan state, inhabited by 'true' Spartans, Perioecians ('dwellers about') and Helots – not to speak of a variety of intermediate layers – Partheniae, Neodamodae, and so on – all with very unequal rights. The constant conflicts of these groups were both Sparta's *raison d'être* and curse. (Devereux, 1965).

Of course, in selecting for development only certain aspects of his total repertoire, man theoretically impoverishes and constricts himself. But in practice this loss is more than compensated for by a greater and more satisfying expertness in those aspects selected for development (Devereux, 1970, Chapter 2). Moreover, this selectiveness also has valuable psychological and social consequences. Linton (1938) hinted long ago that the flexibility of man's instincts is so great that they are unable to organize effectively and to render predictable his behavior and personality sufficiently to make life in society possible. In order to organize his personality and render it predictable, man needs to provide himself with an armor of habits and customs.

I now specify that what in one perspective is a necessarily selective custom is in another perspective the selection, for consistent expression, of certain aspects of man's total potential repertoire. In still another perspective, the selection of certain of these aspects for a consistent behavioral expression entails assigning to A a whole series of class memberships, a series of *class identities*, one of which is his ethnic identity.

But, bearing in mind that A's individuality can be made totally unique by enumerating all his class identities, by assembling an unduplicable accumulation of specifiably imprecise informations about him, it becomes apparent that this selectiveness as to the aspects of the repertoire which A manifests makes him unique, as well as exceptionally creative and spontaneous. In short, A becomes unique by his distinctive selection of certain aspects of his potential repertoire, not duplicated by anyone else. Since the selection of certain of these aspects can, in another perspective, be viewed as the self-ascription of a series of class memberships (class identities), A's unique identity can be determined by an enumeration of all his class identities – or at least of a sufficient number of his class identities to make it impossible for any other person to belong also to all these classes.

When an individual has a sufficient number of sufficiently varied class identities, each of them becomes a tool and their totality becomes a kind of 'tool box,' which both actualize and implement socially his unique pattern of personality.

But when one of A's class identities becomes hypercathected to the point of severely conflicting with, or else totally subordinating to it, all the rest of A's class identities, singularly dysfunctional manifestations of class identity begin to appear. One conflict can arise when what is deemed to be the principal class identity is actually less effective in certain circumstances than are other class identities.

Case 53: The Marseillaise appeals to all *enfants* of only *la Patrie*; a

Marxist slogan urges only *workers* of the world to unite. Yet, in order to encourage the Soviet armies to resist the Nazi armies to the utmost, Stalin had to appeal to ethnic identity and represent the struggle as taking place between Russians and Germans.

Turning specifically to ethnic identity, when a hypercathected ethnic identity overrides all other class identities, it ceases to be a tool and becomes, as was shown for Sparta (*Case 52*), a straitjacket. Indeed, the achievement of a collective distinctiveness by means of a hypercathected ethnic identity can, as a simple example will show, lead to an obliteration of individual distinctiveness.

Case 54: The Spartan hoplite wore a red cloak, which distinguished him from all other heavily armed infantrymen. But the redness of his cloak had another function: if he was wounded, the blood he shed did not show on the cloak (Plutarch, *The Institutions of the Laconians*; Kroeber, 1952b; Xenophon, *The Constitution of the Lacedaemonians*, 2.3). Hence the wounded Spartan individual's special condition could neither encourage the foe, nor elicit his compassion (Homer, *Iliad* 12.390 ff.). Glaucus, wounded, withdraws from the battle, so that his wounded state will not encourage the foe.

In short, in implementing one's hypercathected ethnic identity, one increasingly minimizes and even negates one's individual identity. Yet, man's functionally relevant dissimilarity from all others is what makes him human: similar to others precisely through his high degree of differentiation. It is this which permits him to claim a human identity.

A hypercathected ethnic identity's implementation can also become onerous to the point of becoming dysfunctional.

Case 55: A Roman magistrate was sometimes compelled by his Roman ethnic identity to sentence his own son to death – and to do so with a stiff upper lip. By contrast, Pericles could afford to plead in tears with the Athenian assembly to secure the acquittal of his mistress, Aspasia (Plutarch, *The Life of Lycurgus*, 32).

Case 56: The cost at which the Jews preserved their ethnico-religious identity need hardly be recalled. Under Antiochus Epiphanes it was at the risk of their lives that they circumcised their sons.

In short, it may be argued that a hypercathecting of one's ethnic identity leads, in effect, to a drastic reduction of one's relevant class identities and thus to the annihilation of the individual's real identity. The same occurs when only one of a person's class identities is deemed relevant. Under the Nazis the Jews were gradually stripped of all their relevant class identities, save only their Jewish identity, and in the process were denied a personal identity.

It is dysfunctional, indeed catastrophic, to reduce another person to such one-dimensionality. But the contemporary scene abounds in examples of persons stripping themselves of all their potentially meaningful class identities, ceasing to be anything but X's, where X denotes a real or spurious *ethnos*. This process is more impoverishing than ever today, when one's ethnic identity can structure only increasingly limited aspects of one's total potential repertoire. Hence, the moment A insists on being only and ostentatiously an X, 24 hours a day, all those aspects of his behavior which cannot be correlated with his ethnic identity are deprived of any organizing and stabilizing framework. His behavior therefore tends to become increasingly chaotic, particularly when he operates as a member of an actual group.

As a result, there tends to appear, side by side with what little structuring of his behavior his ethnic identity ('being an X') provides – even when it is asserted mainly dissociatively ('not being a Y') – a logically untenable and operationally fraudulent incorporation into the ethnic identity of ideologies based on principles which are, in essence, not only non-ethnic, but outright anti-ethnic. It is, and must be, possible to be an American without being a capitalist, a Russian without being a communist and a Jew without being orthodox. In this latter connection, I note a paradox. Israeli law holds that a gentile can become a Jew only by becoming a convert to orthodox Judaism. But a person born of a Jewish and possibly non-orthodox mother is a Jew even if he is an atheist.

Viewing things from another angle, ethnic identity can be functional only if its scope is substantially expanded and if it is appreciably decathected. It must not be permitted to engulf, nor to become parasitical upon, one's other class identities, whose unduplicable accumulation is, as pointed out earlier, the very basis of an authentic identity.

I now come to a point that is crucial logically as well as in practice. Even though ethnic identity (and practically every other class identity) is logically and historically the product of the assertion that 'A is an X because he is not a Y,' and of the differentiating implementation of this distinctiveness, it is truly functional only if it involves the uninvidious appreciation of 'B is a Y by being a non-X.' The currently fashionable slogan, 'black is beautiful,' for example, can be true and functional only if it subsumes that 'white is also beautiful,' albeit in a different way. The reverse is needless to say, also true (Devereux, 1967a).

Any *ethnos* incapable of recognizing this elementary fact condemns itself dissociatively to a slow drift, as a closed system, toward total meaninglessness, and thereby brings itself – and mankind – to a standstill, and gradually annihilates the individual claiming exclusively such a *purely dissociative* ethnic identity by reducing him to one-dimensionality.

I was not quite twenty years old, and had not as yet taken an interest in the human sciences when, in an open letter to a famous German regional periodical, the now extinct *Böttcherstrasse*, I affirmed that human civilization depended on the diversity of cultures and ethnic identities. I reached this conclusion solely on the basis of my early studies in theoretical physics, for the second law of thermodynamics teaches that a totally homogenous closed system ceases to produce externally perceptible work. As Bertrand Russell expressed this law, the law of entropy, in one of his more popular books: 'Things left to themselves tend to get into a mess.' That mess mankind cannot afford.

I therefore hold that an insistent and even obsessive stressing of and clinging to one's ethnic (or any other 'class') identity reveals a flaw in one's self-conception as a unique multidimensional entity. The Nazi SS member who pleaded that in performing atrocities he only obeyed commands implicitly affirmed that his SS status took precedence over all his other group identities, including his membership in the human estate. Sane and mature persons do not hypercathect their ethnic identity or any other class identity. An overriding emphasis on one of a person's several 'class' identities, such as ethnic identity, simply seeks to shore up a flawed self and an uncertain awareness of one's identity as a person. The current tendency to stress one's ethnic or class identity, its use as a crutch, is *prima facie* evidence of the impending collapse of the only valid sense of identity: one's differentness, which is replaced by the most archaic pseudo-identity imaginable. I do not think that the 'identity crisis' of our age can be resolved by recourse to the artificial props of collective identities: of ethnic, class, religious, occupational or any other 'assistant identity.' I have said elsewhere that this can lead only to a renunciation of identity, in order to fend off what is apprehended as a danger of total annihilation (Devereux, 1967b). I consider the evolving of any massive and dominant 'class' identity as a first step toward such a 'protective' renunciation of true identity. If one is nothing but a Spartan, a capitalist, a proletarian, or a Buddhist, one is next door to being nothing and therefore even to not being at all.

Note

1. I am not altogether certain of the second half of this statement. One fairly reliable novel and one not altogether reliable informant affirmed that these battle scenes *did* emphasize the *penis rectus*. A specialist, consulted by mail, did not know the answer. My own examination of reproductions in the Rhodes Library, Oxford, yielded negative results, but the books I consulted dated from an age where 'obscene' details were obliterated even in some scientific works.

References

Bonaparte Marie (1950) 'Notes on Excision,' in G. Róheim (ed.), *Psychoanalysis and the Social Sciences*, Vol. 2, pp. 67–83.

Bryk, Felix (1939) *Dark Rapture* (New York).

Devereux, G. (1942) 'Social Structure and the Economy of Affective Bonds,' *Psychoanalytic Review*, 29, pp. 303–314.

Devereux G. (1948) 'Mohave Indian Obstetrics,' *American Imago*, 5, pp. 95–138.

Devereux, G. (1956) *Therapeutic Education*. New York.

Devereux, G. (1958) 'The Significance of the External Female Genitalia and of Female Orgasm for the Male,' *Journal of the American Psychoanalytic Association*. 6:278–286.

Devereux, G. (1965) 'La Psychanalyse et l'Histoire: Une Application à l'Histoire de Sparte,' *Annales: Economies, Sociétés, Civilisations*. 20:18–44.

Devereux, G. (1961) 'Two Types of Modal Personality Models,' in B. Kaplan (ed.), *Studying Personality Cross-Culturally*. Evanson, Ill. Devereux G. (1966) 'Transference Screen Memory and the Temporal Ego,' *Journal of Nervous and Mental Disease*. 143:318–323.

Devereux, G. (1967a) *From Anxiety to Method in the Behavioral Sciences*. Paris and The Hague.

Devereux, G. (1967b) 'Le Renonciation à l'Identité! Défense contre l'Anéantissement.' *Revue Française de Psychanalyse*. 31:101–142.

Devereux, G. (1969) *Mohave Ethnopsychiatry* (Washington, D.C.), 2nd edn.

Devereux, G. (1973) *Essais d'Ethnopsychiatrie Generale*. Paris (2nd edn, 1973).

Devereux, G. (1972a) *Ethnopsychoanalyse Complémentariste*. Paris.

Devereux, G. (1972b). 'Quelques Traces de la Succession par Ultimogeniture en Scythie,' *Inter-Nord* 12:262–270.

Dodds, E. R. (1960) Introduction to *Euripides: Bacchae* Oxford.

Dollard, John. (1937) *Caste and Class in a Southern Town*. New Haven.

Euripides. *Andromache*.

Euripides. *Hecuba*.

Forrest, W. G. (1968) *A History of Sparta*. London.

Herodotus. *The Histories*.

Homer. *The Iliad*.

Kenyatta, Jomo. (1938) *Facing Mount Kenya*. London.

Kroebel, A. L. (1952a) 'Stimulus Diffusion,' in *The Nature of Culture*. Chicago, pp. 344–357.

Kroeber, A. L. (1952b) 'Cultural Intensity and Climax,' in *The Nature of Culture.* Chicago, pp. 337–343.

Lenzen, V. F. (1937) 'Individuality in Atomism,' in *The Problem of the Individual.* Vol. 20, University of California Publications in Philosophy, pp. 31–52.

Linton, Ralph. (1936) *The Study of Man.* New York.

Linton, Ralph. (1938) 'Culture, Society and the Individual.' *Journal of Abnormal and Social Psychology.* 33:425–436.

Mauss, Marcel. (1950) 'Une Categorie de l'Esprit Humain: La Notion de Personne, Celle de "Moi".' In *Sociologie et Anthropologie Paris*, pp. 336–362.

Ollier, F. (1933) *Le Mirage Spartiate.* (2 vols) Paris.

Parsons, Talcott. (1939) 'The Professions and Social Structure.' *Social Forces.* 17:457–467.

Plutarch. *The Life of Lycurgus.*

Plutarch. *The Life of Pericles.*

Plutarch. *The Life of Solon.*

Plutarch. *On the Bravery of Women.*

Plutarch. *The Institutions of the Laconians.*

Plutarch. *The Sayings of Kings and Commanders.*

Plutarch. *The Sayings of Spartans.*

Plutarch. *The Sayings of Spartan Women.*

Russell, Bertrand, (1919) *Introduction to Mathematical Philosophy.* London.

Schapera, I. (1930) *The Khoisan Peoples of South Africa.* London.

Sophocles. *Ajax.*

Sophocles. *Philoctetes.*

Strabo. *Geography.*

Thucydides. *The Peloponnesian War.*

Tyrtaeus. *Fragment 10.* ((ed.) Edmunds)

Vajda, G. (1937) 'Juifs et Musulmans selon le Hadit.' *Journal Asiatique.* 229:57–127.

Whitehead, A. N. and Russell, Bertrand. (1925) *Principia Mathematica 1.* Cambridge, 1925.

Xenophon, *The Constitution of the Lacedaemonians.*

22 Some Comments on the Anthropology of Ethnicity in the United States (1976)

Ulf Hannerz*

A well-known theologian has remarked that he who marries the spirit of the age soon finds himself a widower. Some people, however, will soon be ready to marry again, as Peter Berger (1972) has recently shown in an essay on 'The liberal as fall guy,' where he gives some examples of recent reversals of opinion among American liberal intellectuals. After preaching economic growth, they find that a nongrowth economy is necessary for world survival. After working for equality between the sexes on the assumption that men and women are basically alike, they find that this is only a more refined form of sexism, and that true equality must be based on our acceptance of the differences between male and female. Turning to our concern here, after telling each other and everybody else that minority group members are just like everybody else, they must now start to convince themselves that minority peoples are really quite unique.[1]

Social scientists form a considerable part of the constituency for these rather flighty opinions and do much to provide the arguments for them, and consequently it seems useful to begin these brief comments on tendencies and opportunities in the anthropological study of ethnicity in the United States with some reflections on its ideological component.

CLASS, ETHNICITY, AND POLITICAL IMPLICATIONS

It is not so many years ago that one particular version of the 'just like everybody else' view of American minorities, that which saw the

---

* From Frances Henry (ed.), *Ethnicity in the Americas*, World Anthropology Series (The Hague and Paris: Mouton, 1976), pp. 429–38.

roots of most peculiarities of behavior in lower class status rather than in historically based cultural differences, was clearly dominant among anthropological and sociological commentators. A small and rather quiet opposition insisted that there were also cultural differences, but to a great extent even it accepted the emphasis on factors of class as a useful basis for social activism. If the 'power structure' could be persuaded that whatever seemed objectionable about the life of the people in the ghettos and on the reservations was the consequence rather than the cause of their being poor, a case would exist for a national mobilization against poverty.

We now know that to a great extent such hopes were thwarted. In the meantime, however, a reaction emerged against the strategy which was based on them. There had been more emphasis on what what wrong than on what was right with the minorities; and the idea that they would be helped by revealing their conditions of life to the wider society was contrary to notions of group integrity. Well-meaning as the researchers and policy-makers may have been in trying to draw attention to the results of class injustices, they could also be seen by minorities to be involved in unwarranted intervention.

As one significant part of current anthropological study of American ethnic groups, we now witness the academic wing of this reaction. There is a new emphasis on the unique cultural wealth of the minority group, with the implication that its distinctiveness gives it the right to determine its own future and to be treated as the equal of any other group, and on its strengths, largely derived from the historical heritage, rather than on weaknesses which may be due to low social and economic status. To some degree, certainly, these new emphasis must be applauded. They contribute to a full picture of what minority group life is really like, by complementing or qualifying the view resulting from the earlier emphasis. One may find it easy enough also to sympathize with the political goals which are implicitly expected to go with them.

On the other hand, there are some reasons why one might be somewhat critical of the new emphasis. By pointing to ethnic strengths and by undercommunicating the difficulties inherent in existing conditions of life they could just possibly undermine more active social policies, playing into the hands of an attitude of 'benign neglect' (where the stress seems to be on the noun rather than on the adjective). Furthermore, they are some sometimes expressed with a lack of nuance which might create problems of credibility. For that segment of popular opinion which was slowly and hesitatingly accepting the socioeconomically oriented analysis as the most enlightened view 'based on scientific research,' the new switch could be disconcerting and lead to increasing skepticism toward what supposedly is intellectual leadership. As Abraham Lincoln aptly noted, 'you can fool some of the people all the time and all the people some of the time, but you cannot fool all the people all the time.'

There seems to have been an element of rhetoric (in the pejorative sense), then, in some of the recent anthropological writings on American ethnic groups – a concern with making one particular point as strongly as possible, accompanied by a neglect of the complexity of many issues. If our first commitment as anthropologists is to descriptive and analytic exactness rather than political expediency (relative to our objectives), we should be concerned with this, and even if we feel strongly about political commitments we should beware lest expediency becomes counterproductive. Probably many of the anthropologists who have at one time or other made facile statements on 'socioeconomic' or 'ethnic' tendencies would agree, in a more reflective mood, that the interplay between socioeconomic stratification and cultural heritage is a complex one, and that it leaves room for considerable diversity of life-styles within any one ethnic group. When we have come further in our mapping of this interplay and this diversity, and in learning to communicate about it with a wider audience, we might still earn a greater credibility with people in general and with those minority group members who are sometimes heard wondering who on earth we are describing.

There are a couple of other points involving the impact on ethnic studies of the relationship between anthropologists and American society which may be worth mentioning. One is that anthropologists (like other social scientists) seem generally to have been very willing to accept the WASP definition of ethnicity. It is thus a quality which is absent among Anglo-Saxons; which, apart from this, increases among Americans of European descent as you pass over the map of Europe from the northwest toward the southeast: and which is very strong among people of non-European ancestry. This, of course, is ethnocentric nonsense. If we are to use concepts of ethnicity analytically, no people is any more or any less ethnic than any other people, although their relationships to the common societal arena might differ. This brings us directly to the other point which should be made: if we accept a stricter anthropological definition of ethnicity, many of the recent so-called ethnic studies hardly seem to deal with it at all. Instead, they are fairly general studies of the cultures of those groups which the American majority have chosen to call ethnic. Naturally, there need be nothing wrong with such studies. The use of one term to cover two quite different things can cause some confusion, however, and the acceptance of the folk definition might blind anthropologists to the fact that there is a vast field of study of American ethnicity in the stricter anthropological sense where relatively little work seems to be going on. This field could in fact be a laboratory for the development of theoretical insights into ethnicity, because of the richness of American materials. I doubt that it could be validly argued that it is less 'relevant,' as a general enlightenment on the nature of group relationships in American society could probably serve the general public as well as an inside scoop on the strangers next door.

ETHNICITY AS AN ORGANIZATIONAL PHENOMENON

The stricter definition to which I am referring, of course, is that which holds ethnicity to be primarily a social–organizational phenomenon, a matter of drawing boundaries between groups on the basis of a combination of criteria of ascription and diacritical cultural markers and thus channeling interaction. Which cultural forms will be used as ethnic markers by the people of a society cannot be predicted from first principles, as Barth (1969, p. 14) rightly points out: the distinctions are made on an emic level, and an 'objective' ethnographic inventory of traits may reveal nothing about where boundaries are drawn as people in the society may disregard great diversity within an ethnic as well as great similarity between groups. This is why many recent studies of ethnic groups may tell us little about ethnicity. It is not made clear whether the people concerned themselves use the cultural forms described as ethnic markers, and the studies tend to deal internal group organization without explicit attention to the ways in which the contrast with nongroup members is recognized as a facet of life within the group. Conceivably such studies could contribute to building the strength of ethnicity as an organizational form, if there is the kind of feedback from the researcher to the society by which the former could identify to the latter unique cultural forms with a potential as ethnic markers. This would resemble the kind of culture-building in the service of ethnic solidarity to which Blauner (1970) has drawn attention and may well be a worthy intellectual task. But it must not confused with the analysis of what cultural forms are in actual use as ethnic markers.

What kinds of questions, then, have anthropologists more or less neglected in the study of ethnicity in the United States? Elsewhere (Hannerz 1974), I have tried to conceptualize ways in which American data may be used to follow up some of the leads concerning the use of ethnic solidarity in the pursuit of individual or group interests which emerge for example from Cohen's study (1969) of a trading minority in an African city. Here I would like to draw attention to some issues concerning the definition of ethnic boundaries and markers in American society.

THE VARIETIES OF BOUNDARY DEFINITIONS

The multiethnic situation which we tend to regard as 'normal,' and for which our analytical models are thus most immediately constructed, is perhaps one largely characterized by stable, unambiguous. and consensual ethnic definitions. Members of all ethnic groups agree on where boundaries are drawn, members and nonmembers of a group agree on what are its markers, and the ethnic identity of any particular individual is clearcut. Furthermore, the situation does not seem to be significantly affected by change over time. In the United States, however, we may find exceptions to each of these points, and more systematic inquiries into these variations could conceivably enrich both our picture of American society and our theoretical understanding of ethnicity.

As far as ambiguity of boundaries is concerned, for example, the American experience might provide a view of how a dominant group has a power of definition which could overwhelm competing understandings. During the period of immigration, northern Italians showed some tendency to draw a line between themselves and southern Italians (at a time when the conception of a national identity was very weakly developed in Italy itself), and Jews of German origin similarly maintained some distance from the later Jewish arrivals from Eastern Europe. Yet these splits conflicted with a tendency on the part of other Americans toward lumping all Jews together and all Italians together. An intensive analysis of the interaction between these different boundary conceptions over time might throw new light on facts which may be well known but poorly understood. Similarly, white Americans are generally little aware of ethnic distinctions between different groups of black Americans. Although such groups as Creoles and Geechees may be numerically a minor part of the total black population, their separate identity is a significant factor in the social map of some regions. One might hope also that the growing interest among anthropologists and social historians in the backstage life of the old Southern slave quarter could lead to an increased understanding of the melting together of various African ethnic groups into one American black group, in a process to which Singer (1962) may have been the first to attach the term ethnogenesis.

There is another kind of lack of mutuality of boundary concepts which is theoretically possible and to which some American cases may bear some resemblance. This is where the ethnic boundary is recognized on one side of it but not on the other; more exactly, where the outside society is largely unaware of the existence of a group whose members have a shared identity among themselves. Among Euro-American ethnic groups, most Americans are probably only aware of those whose boundaries are congruent with those of contemporary European nationalities. Yet Eastern Europe in particular has a great many smaller ethnic minorities, and the representatives of some of these groups in America have maintained some measure of ethnic cohesion. The implications of a form of ethnicity which is visible inwards but hardly noticeable to the outside may be interesting to explore further.

UNDERSTANDINGS OF ETHNIC MARKERS

Let us turn now to the ways in which the understandings of the markers of ethnic identity may be less than clearcut, and the ways in which cultural processes in a society may be influenced by interpretations of certain phenomena in terms of ethnicity.

Barth (1969, pp. 12–13), in his analysis of ethnicity, points out that ethnic markers are generally presumed to be cultural forms which are historically transmitted within the group.[2] This, he suggests, is why not all distinct overt forms of behavior can serve as markers, as they may exhibit the effects of ecology. It should be emphasized in this context, however, that current ecological adaptations are most likely to be disregarded as possible ethnic markers where there is effective communication between groups concerning the determinants of distinctive behavior. If nonmembers are free to interpret ecologically determined behavior forms as due to a cultural heritage, it is quite possible that they will also consider them ethnic markers. And in the long run, of course, members of the group may also take on similar definitions.

This is relevant to the discussions of 'ethnicity versus class' in the study of American minority group life. These two terms are in themselves hardly useful opposites for analytical purposes, of course, since the former is based on an emic perspective while we tend to use 'class' in this context within the framework of an etic analysis. The proper dichotomy, rather, in an outside observer's analytical terms, is 'historically transmitted culture' versus 'contemporary socioeconomic constraints' as determinants of behavior. Phrased in these terms, it is easier to see how modes of behavior which are matters of class in an etic analysis can be matters of ethnicity in an emic analysis. This is the point made by Bennett Berger (1967) as he notes that several of the components of the black American 'soul' concept are inside interpretations of an adaptation to poverty. Switching to the nonmember's perceptions, it is also clear that many of the ethnic stereotypes which the dominant group has seen as markers of minority membership have not always been so much untrue in an absolute sense as due to a lack of understanding of the pressures of poverty. At various times this has affected for example the Irish, the Italians, and the blacks; to take another example, it is obvious that the notion of what is characteristically Jewish has changed considerably at least in some circles in the last half-century as members of the group have been mobile between niches in the American social structure (cf. van den Haag, 1969).

This takes us to questions involving changes of ethnic markers coupled with persistence of ethnic groups. Ecological change, as we have seen, is one facet of this; but it is also possible that an interplay of cultural diffusion between groups and the interpretation of ethnic characteristics may have an impact on markers. Generally, one might assume that cultural forms which are strongly associated with stigmatized groups will not spread from them to dominant groups. At one time, American fashion designers had to be concerned over the conspicuous acceptance of a new development by blacks, as this could effectively kill its attractiveness to other groups, but this is apparently no longer so (cf. Ephron, 1973, p. 123). In particular cases, however, more widely accepted standards of ethnic excellence in certain fields, even on the part of low-status groups, might lead to the appropriation by nonmembers of cultural forms which members have used as ethnic markers. LeRoi Jones has a vivid example of this in his book *Blues People* (1963: 220 ff.), where he suggests that black music has been undergoing a continuous revitalization as a reaction to the equally continuous assimilation of its forms into mainstream music. To generalize from this model, then, one might set forth the hypothesis that the desire to maintain ethnic boundaries despite cultural diffusion may be a source of cultural vitality in a multiethnic society. This could be one area of investigation where Bateson's neglected concept (1935) of schismo-genesis might prove useful. I am not sure what other examples of such processes could be found in American cultural history, but pre-sumably its diversity can give us many new insights into the ways in which ethnic boundaries and markers are created and recreated.

TOWARD A WIDER SCOPE

The kinds of topics of study I have hinted at may be of a rather different sort from those currently dominant in American ethnic studies. They are not necessarily more important than the latter, but I believe that they may tell us more about ethnicity as a SOCIAL phenomenon. In much of the recent work, we find that only lip service is paid to theoretical understandings of ethnicity; I would like to see more studies which use the opportunities provided by American society for the systematic testing and expansion of these understandings. Conflict over definitions of markers or boundaries, or – less dramatically – absence of shared definitions between group members and nonmembers is one area of study with potential for such new developments, changes in definition over time is another. A third might be the use of alternative identities by persons of multiethnic background, a category which is probably larger in the United States than in most societies (cf. Bram, 1965).

Obviously studies of this type will partially be historical and com-parative in nature, to a greater extent than most current ethnic studies in American anthropology. Undoubtedly the restricted scope and ahistorical character of these studies have in part been the result of the strong orientation toward fieldwork on the part of the anthropol-ogists involved.[3] We hear occasionally nowadays of the evils of field workism: I am certainly not about to join the small choir singing this tune by suggesting that those concerned with ethnic studies should withdraw totally from the real world into libraries and archives. Par-ticipant observation is still the foundation of the anthropological en-terprise; neighboring disciplines are celebrating their rediscovery of it. But masses of data which have been accumulated over the years by historians, sociologists, journalists, and others, deserve the attention of anthropologists familiar with the analytical understandings of eth-nicity which have evolved in their discipline. These anthropologists may be best able to make use of the data available if they do not confine themselves solely to the perspective of one single ethnic group, as they tend to do in fieldwork, but try to develop a picture of the interaction over matters of ethnic organization in a wider social field. For this reason, too, they should not take too seriously the suggestions we sometimes hear that the situation of some ethnic groups 'cannot be compared' with others, for to compare situations is not to suggest that they are identical, and it is only by comparison that one can find out how and why they differ. Light's study (1972) of *Ethnic Enterprise in America* may not be flawless, but it certainly provides an example of how original research on ethnicity in the United States can proceed within a comparative framework. Anthropologists may well try to work more often on a similar scale as they make their contributions to a kaleidoscopic view of American culture and society.

Notes

1. Berger evidently uses 'liberal' in the conventional American sense of 'moderately left' on the national political spectrum; it might be another example of recent reversals that many within the group now prefer the label 'radical' and use their old self-designation as an epithet although it is uncertain whether the change in terminology has been accompanied by a basic change in ideology or behavior.
2. This argument has been presented in a slightly different form in Hannerz (1974).
3. This is not to say that the standards of fieldwork among all those anthropologists who have engaged in the study of American ethnic groups have been consistently high. I have commented on this elsewhere (cf. Hannerz, 1972; also Szwed 1972, p. 171).

References

Barth, Fredrik (1969) 'Introduction', in Fredrik Barth (ed.), *Ethnic Groups and Boundaries* (Berger and Oslo: Universitetsforlag). Now also Chapter 18 of this volume.

Bateson, Gregory (1935) 'Culture Contact and Schismogenesis', *Man* 35: 178–183.

Berger, Bennett M. (1967) Soul searching. *Trans-action* 4(7):54–57

Berger, Peter L. (1972) 'The liberal as fall guy,' in *Don't Just do Something*. Santa Barbara: Center for the Study of Democratic Institutions.

Blauner, Robert (1970) 'Black culture: myth or reality?' in Norman E. Whitten,

Jr. and John F. Szwed (eds), *Afro-American Anthropology*. New York: Free Press.

Bram, Joseph (1965) 'Change and choice in ethnic identification', *Transactions of the New York Academy of Sciences* series II, 28, pp. 242–248.

Cohen, Abner (1969) *Custom and Politics in Urban Africa*. London: Routledge and Kegan Paul.

Ephron, Nora (1973) *Wallflower at the Orgy*. New York: Ace.

Hannerz, Ulf (1972) 'Comment on Charles A. Valentine, racism and recent anthropological studies of U.S. blacks', *Human Organization* 31:99–100.

Hannerz, Ulf (1974) 'Ethnicity and opportunity in urban America,' in Abner Cohen (ed.), *Urban Ethnicity* (ASA 12) London: Tavistock.

Jones, Leroi (1963) *Blues People*. New York: William Morrow.

Light, Ivan H. (1972) *Ethnic Enterprise in America*. Berkeley and Los Angeles: University of California Press.

Singer, L. (1962) 'Ethnogenesis and Negro-Americans Today', *Social Research* 29: 419–432.

Szwed, John F. (1972) 'An American anthropological dilemma: the politics of Afro-American culture,' in Dell Hymes (ed.), *Reinventing anthropology* New York: Pantheon.

Van den Haag, Ernest (1969) *The Jewish Mystique*. New York: Stein and Day.

23 Symbolic Ethnicity: The Future of Ethnic Groups and Cultures in America (1979)

Herbert J. Gans*

INTRODUCTION

One of the more notable recent changes in America has been the renewed interest in ethnicity which some observers of the American scene have described as an ethnic revival. This paper argues that there has been no revival, and that acculturation and assimilation continue to take place. Among third- and fourth-generation 'ethnics' (the grandchildren and great-grandchildren of Europeans who came to America during the 'new immigration'), a new kind of ethnic involvement may be occurring, which emphasizes concern with identity, with the feeling of being Jewish or Italian, etc. Since ethnic identity needs are neither intense nor frequent in this generation, however, ethnics do not need either ethnic cultures or organizations; instead, they resort to the use of ethnic symbols. As a result, ethnicity may be turning into symbolic ethnicity, an ethnicity of last resort, which could, nevertheless persist for generations.

Identity cannot exist apart from a group and symbols are themselves a part of culture, but ethnic identity and symbolic ethnicity require very different ethnic organizations and cultures than existed among earlier generations. Moreover, the symbols third-generation ethnics use to express their identity are more visible than the ethnic cultures and organizations of the first- and second-generation ethnics. What appears to be an ethnic revival may therefore be only a more visible form of long standing phenomena, or of a new stage of acculturation and assimilation. Symbolic ethnicity may also have wider ramifica-

---

* Chapter 9 in Herbert Gans *et al.* (eds), *On the Making of Americans: Essays in Honor of David Riesman* (Philadelphia, University of Pennsylvania Press, 1979), pp. 193–220.

tions, however, for David Riesman has suggested that 'being American has some of the same episodic qualities as being ethnic.'[1] In effect, both kinds of being are also new ways of striving for individualism.

ACCULTURATION AND ASSIMILATION[2]

The dominant sociological approach to ethnicity has long taken the form of what Neil Sandberg aptly calls 'straight-line theory,' in which acculturation and assimilation are viewed as secular trends that culminate in the eventual absorption of the ethnic group into the larger culture and general population.[3] Straight-line theory in turn is based on melting pot theory, which implies the disappearance of the ethnic groups into a single host society. Even so, it does not accept the values of the melting pot theorists, since its conceptualizers could have used terms like cultural and social liberation from immigrant ways of life, but did not.

In recent years, straight-line theory has been questioned on many grounds. For one thing, many observers have properly noted that even if America might have been a melting pot early in the twentieth century, the massive immigration from Europe and elsewhere has since then influenced the dominant groups, summarily labeled 'WASP,' and has also decimated their cultural, if not their political and financial, power, so that today America is a mosaic, as Andrew Greeley has put it, of subgroups and subcultures.[4] Still, this criticism does not necessarily deny the validity of straight-line theory, since ethnics can also be absorbed into a pluralistic set of subcultures and subgroups, differentiated by age, income, education, occupation, religion, region, and the like.

A second criticism of straight-line theory has centered on its treatment of all ethnic groups as essentially similar, and its failure, specifically, to distinguish between religious groups, like the Jews, and nationality groups, like the Italians, Poles, etc. Jews, for example, are a 'peoplehood' with a religious and cultural tradition of thousands of years, but without an 'old country' to which they owe allegiance or nostalgia, while Italians, Poles, and other participants in the 'new immigration' came from parts of Europe that in some cases did not even become nations until after the immigrants had arrived in America.

That there are differences between the Jews and the other 'new' immigrants cannot be questioned, but at the same time, the empirical evidence also suggests that acculturation and assimilation affected them quite similarly. (Indeed, one major difference may have been that Jews were already urbanized and thus entered the American social structure at a somewhat higher level than the other new immigrants, who were mostly landless laborers and poor peasants.) Nonetheless, straight-line theory can be faulted for virtually ignoring the fact that immigrants arrived here with two kinds of ethnic cultures sacred and secular; that they were Jews from Eastern– and Western–Europe, and Catholics from Italy, Poland, and elsewhere. (Sacred cultures are, however, themselves affected by national and regional considerations; for example, Italian Catholicism differed in some respects from German or Polish, as did Eastern European Judaism from Western.)

While acculturation and assimilation have affected both sacred and secular cultures, they have affected the latter more than the former, for acculturation has particularly eroded the secular cultures that Jews and Catholics brought from Europe. Their religions have also changed in America, and religious observance has decreased, more so among Jews than among Catholics, although Catholic observance has begun to fall off greatly in recent years. Consequently, the similar American experience of Catholic and Jewish ethnics suggests that the comparative analysis of straight-line theory is justified, as long as the analysis compares both sacred and secular cultures.

Two further critiques virtually reject straight-line theory altogether. In an insightful recent paper, William Yancey and his colleagues have argued that contemporary ethnicity bears little relation to the ancestral European heritage, but exists because it is functional for meeting present 'exigencies of survival,' particularly for working-class Americans.[5] Their argument does not invalidate straight-line theory but corrects it by suggesting that acculturation and assimilation, current ethnic organizations and cultures, as well as new forms of ethnicity, must be understood as responses to current needs rather than departures from past traditions.

The other critique takes the opposite position; it points to the persistence of the European heritage, argues that the extent of acculturation and assimilation have been overestimated, and questions the rapid decline and eventual extinction of ethnicity posited by some straight-line theorists. These critics call attention to studies indicating that ethnic cultures and organizations are still functioning, that exogamous marriage remains a practice of numerical minorities, that ethnic differences in various behavior patterns and attitudes can be identified, that ethnic groups continue to act as political interest groups, and that ethnic pride remains strong.[6]

The social phenomena that these defenders of ethnicity identify exist; the only question is how they are to be interpreted. Straight-line theory postulates a process, and cross-sectional studies do not pre-empt the possibility of a continuing trend. Also, like Yancey and his co-authors, some of the critics are looking primarily at poorer ethnics, who have been less touched by acculturation and assimilation than middle-class ethnics, and who have in some cases used ethnicity and ethnic organization as a psychological and political defense against the injustices that they suffer in an unequal society.[7] In fact, much of the contemporary behavior described as 'ethnic' strikes me as work-ing-class behavior, which differs only slightly among various ethnic groups, and then largely because cf variations in the structure of oppor-tunities open to people in America, and in the peasant traditions their ancestors brought over from the old country, which were themselves responses to European opportunity structures. In other words, ethnicity is largely a working-class style.[8]

Much the same observation applies to ethnic political activity. Ur-ban political life, particularly among working-class people, has always been structured by and through ethnicity, and while ethnic political activity may have increased in the last decade, it has taken place around working-class issues rather than ethnic ones. During the 1960s, urban working-class Catholic ethnics began to politicize themselves in re-sponse to black militancy, the expansion of black ghettoes, and govern-ment integration policies that they perceived as publicly legitimated black invasions of ethnic neighborhoods, but which threatened them as working-class homeowners who could not afford to move to the suburbs. Similarly, working- and lower-middle-class Catholic ethnics banded together in the suburbs to fight against higher public school taxes, since they could not afford to pay them while they also had to pay for parochial schools. Even so, these political activities have been *pan-ethnic*, rather than ethnic, since they often involved coalitions of ethnic groups that once considered each other enemies but were now united by common economic and other interests. The extent to which these pan-ethnic coalitions reflect class rather than ethnic interests is illustrated by the 1968 election campaign of New York City's Mario Procaccino against John Lindsay. Although an Italian, he ran as a 'candidate of the little people' against what he called the 'limousine liberals.'

The fact that pan-ethnic coalitions have developed most readily in conflicts over racial issues also suggests that in politics, ethnicity can sometimes serve as a convenient mask for antiblack endeavors, or for political activities that have negative consequences for blacks. While attitude polls indicate that ethnics are often more tolerant racially than other Americans, working-class urban ethnics are also more likely to be threatened, as homeowners and jobholders, by black demands, and may favor specific antiblack policies, not because they are 'racists,' but because their own class interests force them to oppose black demands.

In addition, part of what appears as an increase in ethnic political activity is actually an increase in the visibility of ethnic politics. When the pan-ethnic coalitions began to copy the political methods of the civil rights and antiwar movements, their protests became newsworthy and were disseminated all over the country by the mass media. At about the same time, the economic and geographic mobility of Catholic ethnic groups enabled non-Irish Catholic politicians to win important state and national electoral posts for the first time, and their victories were defined as ethnic triumphs, even though they did not rely on ethnic constituents alone and were not elected on the basis of ethnic issues.

The final, equally direct, criticism of straight-line theory has questioned the continued relevance of the theory, either because of the phenomenon of third-generation return, or because of the emergence of ethnic revivals. Thus, Marcus Hansen argued that acculturation and assimilation were temporary processes, because the third generation could afford to remember an ancestral culture that the traumatic Americanization process forced the immigrant and second generations to forget.[9] Hansen's hypothesis can be questioned on several grounds, however. His data, the founding of Swedish and other historical associations in the Midwest, provided slender evidence of a widespread third-generation return, particularly among nonacademic ethnics; in addition, his theory was static, for Hansen never indicated what would happen in the fourth generation, or what processes were involved in the return that would enable it to survive into the future.[10]

The notion of an ethnic revival has so far been propounded mostly by journalists and essayists, who have supplied impressionistic accounts or case studies of the emergence of new ethnic organizations and the revitalization of old ones.[11] Since the third- and fourth-generation ethnics who are presumably participating in this revival are scattered all over suburbia, there has so far been little systematic research among this population, so that the validity of the revival notion has not yet been properly tested.

The evidence I have seen does not convince me that a revival is taking place. Instead, recent changes can be explained in two ways, neither of which conflicts with straight line theory: (1) today's ethnics have become more visible as a result of upward mobility; and (2) they are adopting the new form of ethnic behavior and affiliation I call 'symbolic ethnicity.'

THE VISIBILITY OF ETHNICITY

The recent upward social, and centrifugal geographic, mobility of ethnics, particularly Catholics, has finally enabled them to enter the middle and upper-middle classes, where they have been noticed by the national mass media, which monitor primarily these strata. In the process they have also become more noticeable to other Americans. The newly visible may not participate more in ethnic groups and cultures than before, but their new visibility makes it appear as if ethnicity had been revived.

I noted earlier the arrival of non-Irish Catholic politicians on the national scene. An equally visible phenomenon has been the entry of Catholic ethnic intellectuals into the academy and its flourishing print culture. To be sure, the scholars are publishing more energetically than their predecessors, who had to rely on small and poverty-stricken ethnic publishing houses, but they are essentially doing what ethnic scholars have always done, only more visibly. Perhaps their energy has also been spurred in part by the need, as academics, to publish so that they do not perish, as well as by their desire to counteract the anti-ethnic prejudices and the entrenched vestiges of the melting pot ideal that still prevail in the more prestigious universities. In some cases, they are also fighting a political battle, because their writings often defend conservative political positions against what they perceive – I think wrongly – as the powerful liberal or radical academic majority. Paradoxically, a good deal of their writing has been nostalgic, celebrating the immigrant culture and its Gemeinschaft at the same time that young Catholic ethnics are going to college partly in order to escape the restrictive pressures of that Gemeinschaft. (Incidentally, an interesting study could be made of the extent to which writers from different ethnic groups, of both fiction and nonfiction, are pursuing nostalgic, contemporary, or future-oriented approaches to ethnicity, comparing different ethnic groups, by time of arrival and position in the society today, on this basis.)

What has happened in the academy has also happened in literature and show business. For example, although popular comedy has long been a predominantly Eastern European Jewish occupation, the first generations of Jewish comic stars had to suppress their ethnicity and even had to change their names, much as did the first generation of academic stars in the prestigious universities. Unlike Jack Benny, Eddie Cantor, George Burns, George Jessel, and others, the comics of today do not need to hide their origins, and beginning perhaps with Lenny Bruce and Sam Levinson, comics like Buddy Hackett, Robert Klein, Don Rickles, and Joan Rivers have used explicitly Jewish material in entertaining the predominantly non-Jewish mass media audience.[12]

Undoubtedly, some of these academics, writers, and entertainers have undergone a kind of third-generation return in this process. Some have re-embraced their ethnicity solely to spur their careers, but others have experienced a personal conversion. Even so, an empirical study would probably show that in most cases their ethnic attitudes have not changed; either they have acted more publicly and thus visibly than they did in the past, or in responding to a hospitable cultural climate, they have openly followed ethnic impulses that they had previously suppressed.

A similar analysis may explain the resurgence of traditionalism among some Jews and Protestants. In both instances largely middle-class young people are perceived as having become newly orthodox (or fundamentalist) and in some cases this is undoubtedly true. Religious conversions may have increased in the last decade, partly because of the ideological and other turbulence of the 1960s, but also because the postwar affluence spawned a cohort of parents who were so upwardly mobile that they were too busy to pay attention to their children. These children developed a strong need for substitute parental guidance, which later manifested itself by their joining the theocratic Gemeinschafts that can be found among virtually all of the recent neotraditional movements. Converts are, however, also the most visible, since they tend to be leaders and are thus most often monitored by the mass media. At the same time, they have been joined by less visible young people who were already orthodox, but perhaps quiescently so, either because orthodoxy was in disrepute among their peers while they were growing up, or because they were uncomfortable in orthodox groups dominated by old people.[13] Only empirical research can indicate the proportions of third-generation returnees and already orthodox people in these groups, but in any case, it seems wrong on the part of enthusiastic observers of a religious revival to group the neotraditionalists with earlier traditional groups, such as the Chassidim, the non-Chassidic Orthodox Jews living in such enclaves as New York City's Boro Park, and rural groups like the Amish.[14] These groups have survived by insulating themselves from the larger society, rarely take in converts, and thus have also insulated themselves from the neotraditionalists.

ETHNICITY IN THE THIRD GENERATION

The second explanation for the changes that have been taking place among third-generation ethnics will take up most of the rest of this paper; it deals with what is happening among the less visible population, the large mass of predominantly middle-class third- and fourth-generation ethnics, who have not been studied enough either by journalists or by social scientists.[15]

In the absence of systematic research, it is difficult even to discern what has actually been happening, but several observers have described the same ethnic behavior in different words. Michael Novak has coined the phrase 'voluntary ethnicity'; Samuel Eisenstadt has talked about 'Jewish diversity'; Allan Silver about 'individualism as a valid mode of Jewishness'; and Geoffrey Bock about 'public Jewishness.'[16] What these observers agree on is that today's young ethnics are finding new ways of being ethnics, which I shall later label 'symbolic ethnicity.'

I start my analysis with the assumption, taken from straight-line theory, that acculturation and assimilation are continuing among the third and fourth generations.[17] If these concepts were quantified, one might find that upwardly mobile working-class groups are moving out of ethnic cultures and groups faster than other ethnics as they try to enter the middle class, whereas those already in the middle class are now acculturating and assimilating at a slower rate, partly because they have already moved out of ethnic cultures and groups to a considerable extent, but also because they are finding that middle-class life is sufficiently pluralistic and their ethnicity sufficiently cost-free that they do not have to give it up deliberately.

In any case, for the third generation, the secular ethnic cultures that the immigrants brought with them are now only an ancestral memory, or an exotic tradition to be savored once in a while in a museum or at an ethnic festival. The same is true of the 'Americanization cultures,' the immigrant experience and adjustment in America, which William Kornblum suggests may have been more important in the lives of the first two generations than the ethnic cultures themselves. The old ethnic cultures serve no useful function for third-generation ethnics who lack direct and indirect ties to the old country, and neither need nor have much knowledge about it. Similarly the Americanization cultures have little meaning for people who grew up without the familial conflict over European and American ways that beset their fathers and mothers: the second generation that fought with and was often ashamed of immigrant parents.

Assimilation is still continuing, for it has always progressed more slowly than acculturation. If one distinguishes between primary and secondary assimilation, that is, movement out of ethnic primary and secondary groups, the third generation is now beginning to move into nonethnic primary groups.[18] Although researchers are still debating just how much intermarriage is taking place, it is rising in the third generation for both Catholic ethnic groups and Jews, and friendship choices appear to follow the same pattern.[19]

The departure out of secondary groups has already proceeded much further. Most third-generation ethnics have little reason, or occasion, to depend on, or even interact with, other ethnics in important secondary-group activities. Ethnic occupational specialization, segregation and self-segregation are fast disappearing, with some notable exceptions in the large cities. Since the third generation probably works like other Americans, largely for corporate employers, past occupational ties between ethnics are no longer relevant. Insofar as they live largely in the suburbs, third-generation ethnics get together with their fellow homeowners for political and civic activities, and are not likely to encounter ethnic political organizations, balanced tickets, or even politicians who pursue ethnic constituencies.

Except in suburbs where old discrimination and segregation patterns still survive, social life takes place without ethnic clustering, and Catholics are not likely to find ethnic subgroups in the Church. Third-generation Jews, on the other hand, particularly those who live in older upper-middle-class suburbs where segregation continues, if politely, probably still continue to restrict much of their social life to other Jews, although they have long ago forgotten the secular divisions between German (and other Western) and Eastern European Jews, and among the latter, between 'Litwaks' and 'Galizianer.' The religious distinction between German Reform Judaism and Eastern European Conservatism has also virtually disappeared, for the second generation that moved to the suburbs after World War II already chose its denomination on the basis of status rather than national origin.[20] In fact, the Kennedy-Herberg prediction that eventually American religious life would take the form of a triple melting pot has not come to pass, if only because people, especially in the suburbs, use denominations within the major religions for status differentiation.

Nevertheless, while ethnic ties continue to wane for the third generation, people of this generation continue to *perceive* themselves as ethnics, whether they define ethnicity in sacred or secular terms. Jews continue to remain Jews because the sacred and secular elements of their culture are strongly intertwined, but the Catholic ethnics also retain their secular or national identity, even though it is separate from their religion.

My hypothesis is that in this generation, people are less and less interested in their ethnic cultures and organizations – both sacred and secular – and are instead more concerned with maintaining their ethnic identity, with the feeling of being Jewish or Italian or Polish, and with finding ways of feeling and expressing that identity in suitable ways. By identity, I mean here simply the sociopsychological elements that accompany role behavior, and the ethnic role is today less of an ascriptive than a voluntary role that people assume alongside other roles. To be sure, ethnics are still identified as such by others, particularly on the basis of name, but the behavioral expectations that once went with identification by others have declined sharply, so that ethnics have some choice about when and how to play ethnic roles. Moreover, as ethnic cultures and organizations decline further, fewer ethnic roles are prescribed, thus increasing the degree to which people have freedom of role definition.

Ethnic identity can be expressed in either action or feeling, or combinations of these, and the kinds of situations in which it is expressed are nearly limitless. Third-generation ethnics can join an ethnic organization or take part in formal or informal organizations composed largely of fellow ethnics, but they can also find their identity by 'affiliating' with an abstract collectivity that does not exist as an interacting group. That collectivity, moreover, can be mythic or real, contemporary or historical. On the one hand, Jews can express their identity as synagogue members, or as participants in a consciousness-raising group consisting mostly of Jewish women. On the other hand, they can also identify with the Jewish people as a long-suffering collectivity that has been credited with inventing monotheism. If they are not religious, they can identify with Jewish liberal or socialist political cultures, or with a population that has produced many prominent intellectuals and artists in the last hundred years. Similar choices are open to Catholic ethnics. In the third generation, Italians can identify through membership in Italian groups, or by strong feelings for various themes in Italian or Neapolitan or Sicilian culture, and much the same possibilities exists for Catholics whose ancestors came over from other countries.

Needless to say, ethnic identity is not a new or a third-generation phenomenon, for ethnics have always had an ethnic identity, but in the past it was largely taken for granted, since it was anchored to groups and roles, and was rarely a matter of choice. When people lived in an ethnic neighborhood, worked with fellow ethnics, and voted for ethnic politicians, there was little need to be concerned with identity except during conflict with other ethnic groups. Furthermore, the every-day roles people played were often defined for them by others as ethnic. Being a drygoods merchant was often a Jewish role; restaurant owners were assumed to be Greek, and bartenders, Irish.

The third generation has grown up without assigned roles or groups that anchor ethnicity, so that identity can no longer be taken for granted. People can of course give up their identity, but if they continue to feel it, they must make it more explicit than it was in the past, and must even look for ways of expressing it. This has two important consequences for ethnic behavior. First, given the degree to which the third generation has acculturated and assimilated, most people look for easy and intermittent ways of expressing their identity, for ways that do not conflict with other ways of life. As a result, they refrain from ethnic behavior that requires an arduous or time-consuming commitment, either to a culture that must be practiced constantly, or to organizations that demand active membership. Second, because people's concern is with identity, rather than with cultural practices or group relationships, they are free to look for ways of expressing that identity which suits them best, thus opening up the possibility of voluntary, diverse, or individualistic ethnicity. Any mode of expressing ethnic identity is valid as long it enhances the feeling of being ethnic, and any cultural pattern or organization that nourishes that feeling is therefore relevant, providing only that enough people make the same choices when identity expression is a group enterprise.

In other words, as the functions of ethnic cultures and groups diminish and identity becomes the primary way of being ethnic, ethnicity takes on an expressive rather than instrumental function in people's lives, becoming more of a leisure-time activity and losing its relevance, say, to earning a living or regulating family life. Expressive behavior can take many forms, but it often involves the use of symbols – and symbols as signs rather than as myths.[21] Ethnic symbols are frequently individual cultural practices that are taken from the older ethnic culture; they are 'abstracted' from that culture and pulled out of its original moorings, so to speak, to become stand-ins for it. And if a label is useful to describe the third generation's pursuit of identity, I propose the term 'symbolic ethnicity.'

SYMBOLIC ETHNICITY

Symbolic ethnicity can be expressed in a myriad of ways, but above all, I suspect, it is characterized by a nostalgic allegiance to the culture of the immigrant generation, or that of the old country; a love for and a pride in a tradition that can be felt without having to be incorporated into everyday behavior. The feelings can be directed at a generalized tradition, or at specific ones: a desire for the cohesive extended immigrant family, or the obedience of children to parental authority or the unambiguous orthodoxy of immigrant religion, or the old-fashioned despotic benevolence of the machine politician. People may even sincerely desire to 'return' to these imagined pasts, which are conveniently cleansed of the complexities that accompanied them in the real past, but while they may soon realize that they cannot go back, they may not surrender the wish. Or else they displace that wish on churches, schools, and the mass media, asking them to recreate a tradition, or rather, to create a symbolic tradition, even while their familial, occupational, religious, and political lives are pragmatic responses to the imperatives of their roles and positions in local and national hierarchical social structures.

All of the cultural patterns that are transformed into symbols are themselves guided by a common pragmatic imperative: they must be visible and clear in meaning to large numbers of third-generation ethnics, and they must be easily expressed and felt, without requiring undue interference in other aspects of life. For example, Jews have abstracted *rites de passage* and individual holidays out of the traditional religion and given them greater importance, such as the *bar mitzvah* and *bas mitzvah* (the parallel ceremony for thirteen-year-old girls that was actually invented in America). Similarly, Chanukah, a minor holiday in the religious calendar, has become a major one in popular practice, partly since it lends itself to impressing Jewish identity on the children. Rites de passage and holidays are ceremonial, and thus symbolic to begin with; equally importantly, they do not take much time, do not upset the everyday routine, and also become an occasion for reassembling on a regular basis family members who are rarely seen. Catholic ethnics pay special attention to the feast days of saints affiliated with their ethnic group, or attend ethnic festivals that take place in the area of first settlement or in ethnic churches.

Consumer goods, notably foods, are another ready source for ethnic symbols, and in the last decades the food industry has developed a large variety of easily cooked ethnic foods, as well as other edibles that need no cooking – for example, chocolate matzohs that are sold as gifts at Passover. The response to symbolic ethnicity may even be spreading into the mass media, for films and television programs with ethnic characters are on the increase. The characters are not very ethnic in their behavior, and may only have ethnic names – for example, Lieutenant Colombo, Fonzi, or Rhoda Goldstein – but in that respect they are not very different from the ethnic audiences who watch them.

Symbolic ethnicity also takes political forms, through identification or involvement with national politicians and international issues that are sufficiently remote to become symbols. As politicians from non-Irish ethnic backgrounds achieve high national or state office, they become identity symbols for members of their group, supplying feelings of pride over their success. For example, Michael Dukakis, ex-governor of Massachusetts, and John Brademas, congressman from Indiana, may currently serve this function for Greeks, being the first members of the ethnic group to be elected to high office – other than Spiro Agnew, who, however, changed both his name and his religion before entering politics. That such politicians do not represent ethnic constituencies, and thus do not become involved in ethnic political disputes, only enhances their symbolic function, unlike local ethnic politicians, who are still elected for instrumental bread-and-butter reasons and thus become embroiled in conflicts that detract from their being symbols of ethnic pride. Thus, there was little pride in New York's Jewish community when Abe Beame was elected the first Jewish mayor of the city in 1973; in fact, some New York Jews opposed his election on the ground that any new difficulties facing the city during his administration would be blamed on the Jews. As it happened, the city's financial crisis turned disastrous while Beame was in office, and although he was widely criticized for his role in it, he was not attacked as a Jew, and was in fact succeeded by another Jewish mayor, Ed Koch.

Symbolic ethnicity can be practiced as well through politically and geographically even more distant phenomena, such as nationalist movements in the old country. Jews are not interested in their old countries, except to struggle against the maltreatment of Jews in Eastern Europe, but they have sent large amounts of money to Israel, and political pressure to Washington, since the establishment of the state. While their major concern has undoubtedly been to stave off Israel's destruction, they might also have felt that their own identity would be affected by such a disaster. Even if the survival of Israel is guaranteed in the future, however, it is possible that as allegiances toward organized local Jewish communities in America weaken, Israel becomes a substitute community to satisfy identity needs. Similar mechanisms may be at work among other ethnic groups who have recently taken an interest in their ancestral countries – for example, the Welsh and the Armenians – and among those groups whose old countries are involved in internal conflict – for example, the Irish, and Greeks and Turks since the Cyprus war of 1973.

Old countries are particularly useful as identity symbols because they are far away and cannot make arduous demands on America ethnics; even sending large amounts of money is ultimately an easy way to help, unless the donors are making major economic sacrifices. Moreover, American ethnics can identify with their perception of the old country or homeland, transforming it into a symbol, which leaves out those domestic or foreign problems that could become sources of conflict for Americans. For example, most American Jews who support Israel pay little attention to its purely domestic policies; they are concerned with its preservation as a state and a Jewish homeland, and see the country mainly as a Zionist symbol.

The symbolic functions of old countries are facilitated further when interest in them is historical, when ethnics develop an interest in their old countries as they were during or before the time of the ancestral departure. Marcus Hansen's notion of third-generation return was actually based on the emergence of interest in Swedish history, which suggests that the third-generation return may itself be only another variety of symbolic ethnicity. The third generation can obviously attend to the past with less emotional risk than first- and second-generation people, who are still trying to escape it, but even so, an interest in ethnic history is a return only chronologically.

Conversely, a new symbol may be appearing among Jews: the Holocaust, which has become a historic example of ethnic-group destruction that can now serve as a warning sign for possible future threats. The interest of American Jews in the Holocaust has increased considerably since the end of World War II; when I studied the Jews of Park Forest in 1949–1950, it was almost never mentioned, and its memory played no part whatsoever in the creation of a Jewish community there. The lack of attention to the Holocaust at that time may, as Nathan Glazer suggests, reflect the fact that American Jews were busy with creating new Jewish communities in the suburbs.[22] It is also possible that people ignored the Holocaust then because the literature detailing its horrors had not yet been written, although since many second-generation American Jews had relatives who died in the Nazi camps, it seems more likely that people repressed thinking about it until it had become a more historical, and therefore a less immediately traumatic, event. As a result, the Holocaust may now be serving as a new symbol for the threat of group destruction, a symbol required, on the one hand, by the fact that rising intermarriage rates and the continued decline of interest and participation in Jewish religion are producing real fears about the disappearance of American Jewry altogether; and on the other hand, by the concurrent fact that American anti-Semitism is no longer the serious threat to group survival that it was for first- and second-generation Jews. Somewhat the same process appears to be taking place among some young Armenians who are now reviving the history of the Turkish massacre of Armenians some sixty years later, at a time when acculturation and assimilation are beginning to make inroads into the Armenian community in America. Still, good empirical data about the extent of the concern both with the Holocaust and the Turkish massacre are lacking, and neither may be as widespread among third-generation Jews and Armenians as among their professional and voluntary organizational leaders. Conversely, the 1978 NBC miniseries 'The Holocaust' may be both an effect of rising interest in the tragedy and a cause of further interest, even if NBC commissioned the series in the hope of duplicating the earlier success of 'Roots.'

Most of the symbols used by third-generation ethnics are, however, more prosaic. Jews who take vacations in Israel and Catholic ethnics who go back to their ancestral countries may make these visits in part to satisfy identity needs. Some agnostic Jewish college students appear to have transformed Yom Kippur into a symbol of their Jewishness and stay away from classes even though they do not go to synagogue. It is even possible that the recent public emergence of Polish and other ethnic jokes serves some symbolic functions. Sandberg found that his Polish respondents were not particularly upset by Polish jokes, and perhaps third-generation Poles tell them to each other as negative symbols, which indicate to them what Polishness is not, and concurrently enable them to express their distaste for the butts of these jokes: Poles of an earlier generation or lower socioeconomic status.[23]

I suggested previously that ethnicity per se had become more visible, but many of the symbols used by the third generation are also visible to the rest of America, not only because the middle-class people who use them are more visible than their poorer ancestors; but because the national media are more adept at communicating symbols than the ethnic cultures and organizations of earlier generations. The visibility of symbolic ethnicity provides further support for the existence of an ethnic revival, but what appears to be a revival is probably the emergence of a new form of acculturation and assimilation that is taking place under the gaze of the rest of society.

Incidentally, even though the mass media play a major role in enhancing the visibility of ethnicity and communicating ethnic symbols, they do not play this role because they are themselves ethnic institutions. True, the mass media, like other entertainment industries, continue to be dominated by Jews (although less so than in the past), but for reasons connected with anti-Semitism, or the fear of it, they have generally leaned over backwards to keep Jewish characters and Jewish fare out of their offerings, at least until recently. Even now, a quantitative analysis of major ethnic characters in comedy, drama, and other entertainment genres would surely show that Catholic ethnics outnumber Jewish ones. Perhaps the Jews who write or produce so much of the media fare are especially sensitive to ethnic themes and symbols; my own hypothesis, however, is that they are, in this case as in others, simply responding to new cultural tendencies, if only because they must continually innovate. In fact, the arrival of ethnic characters followed the emergence and heightened visibility of ethnic politics in the late 1960s, and the men and women who write the entertainment fare probably took inspiration from news stories they saw on television or read in the papers.

I have suggested that symbolic ethnicity must be relatively effortless, but while this is probably true for the majority of third-generation ethnics, it is possible that more intense identity needs may produce a more intense form of symbolic ethnicity. Thus, Paul Ritterband has suggested that some aspects of the contemporary neotraditional movement among Jews may be in part symbolic, in that the movement is more concerned with strengthening feelings of Jewish identity and a sense of historic continuity than with perpetuating an Orthodox culture. Drawing on the distinction between *Halachah* (law) *Aggadah* (myth), he suggests that such leading figures of the movement as Martin Buber and Abraham Heschel developed what he calls a new mythic culture, which manifests little relationship or allegiance to the existing law-centered Orthodox Judaism. Consequently, it would be useful to study the members of this movement to discover to what extent they are pursuing new ways of being good Jews, and to what extent they want to perpetuate the laws and other dictates of Orthodoxy.

I noted earlier that identity cannot exist apart from a group and that symbols are themselves part of a culture, and in that sense, symbolic ethnicity can be viewed as an indicator of the persistence of ethnic groups and cultures. Symbolic ethnicity, however, does not require functioning groups or networks; feelings of identity can be developed by allegiances to symbolic groups that never meet, or to collectivities that meet only occasionally and exist as groups only for the handful of officers that keep them going. By the same token, symbolic ethnicity does does not need a practiced culture, even if the symbols are borrowed from it. To be sure, symbolic culture is as much culture as practiced culture, but the latter persists only to supply symbols to the former. Indeed, practiced culture may need to persist, for some, because people do not borrow their symbols from extinct cultures that survive only in museums And insofar as the borrowed materials come from the practiced culture of the immigrant generation, they make it appear as if an ethnic revival were taking place.

Then, too, it should be noted that even symbolic ethnicity may be relevant for only some of the descendants of the immigrants. As inter-marriage continues, the number of people with parents from the same secular ethnic group will continue to decline, and by the time the fourth generation of the old immigration reaches adulthood, such people may be a minority. Most Catholic ethnics will be hybrid, and will have difficulty developing an ethnic identity. For example, how would the son of an Italian mother and Irish father who has married a woman of Polish-German ancestry determine his ethnicity, and what would he and his wife tell their children? Even if they were willing, would they be able to decide on their, and their children's, ethnicity; and in that case, how would they rank or synthesize their diverse backgrounds? These questions are empirical, and urgently need to be studied, but I would suggest that there are only three possibilities. Either the parents choose the single ethnic identity they find most satisfying, or they encourage the children to become what I earlier called pan-ethnics, or they cope with diversity by ignoring it, and raise their children as non-ethnics.

THE EMERGENCE OF SYMBOLIC ETHNICITY

The preceding observations have suggested that symbolic ethnicity is a new phenomenon that comes into being in the third generation, but it is probably of earlier vintage and may have already begun to emerge among the immigrants themselves. After all, many of the participants in the new immigration were oppressed economically, politically, and culturally in their old countries, and could not have had much affec-tion even for the villages and regions they were leaving. Consequently, it is entirely possible that they began to jettison the old culture and to stay away from ethnic organizations other than churches and unions the moment they came to America, saving only their primary groups, their ties to relatives still left in Europe, and their identity. In small-town America, where immigrants were a numerically unimportant minority, the pressure for immediate acculturation and assimilation was much greater than in the cities, but even in the latter, the seeds for symbolic ethnicity may have been sown earlier than previously thought.

Conversely, despite all the pressures toward Americanization and the prejudice and discrimination experienced by the immigrants, they were never faced with conditions that required or encouraged them to give up their ethnicity entirely. Of course, some of the earliest Jewish arrivals to America had become Quakers and Episcopalians before the end of the nineteenth century, but the economic conditions that persuaded the Jamaican Chinese in Kingston to become Creole, and the social isolation that forced Italians in Sydney, Australia, to abolish the traditional familial male-female role segregation shortly after arriving, have never been part of the American experience.[24]

Some conditions for the emergence of symbolic ethnicity were present from the beginning, for American ethnics have always been characterized by freedom of ethnic expression, which stimulated both the ethnic diversity and the right to find one's own way of being ethnic that are crucial to symbolic ethnicity. Although sacred and secular ethnic organizations that insisted that only one mode of being ethnic was legitimate have always existed in America, they have not been able to enforce their norms, in part because they have always had to compete with other ethnic organizations. Even in ethnic neighborhoods where conformity was expected and social control was pervasive, people had some freedom of choice about ethnic cultural practices. For example, the second-generation Boston Italians I studied had to conform to many family and peer-group norms, but they were free to ignore ethnic secondary groups, and to drop or alter Italian cultural practices according to their own preference.

Ethnic diversity within the group was probably encouraged by the absence of a state religion and national and local heads of ethnic communities. For example, American Jewry never had a chief rabbi, or even chief Orthodox, Conservative, and Reform rabbis, and the European practice of local Jewish communities electing or appointing local laymen as presidents was not carried across the ocean.[25] Catholic ethnics had to obey the cardinal or bishop heading their diocese, of course, but in those communities where the diocese insisted on an Irish church, the other ethnic groups, notably the Italians, kept their distance from the church, and only in the parochial schools was there any attempt to root out secular ethnic patterns. The absence of strong unifying institutions thus created the opportunity for diversity and freedom from the beginning, and undoubtedly facilitated the departure from ethnic cultures and organizations.

Among the Jews, symbolic ethnicity may have been fostered early by self-selection among Jewish emigrants. As Liebman points out, the massive Eastern European immigration to America did not include the rabbis and scholars who practiced what he calls an elite religion in the old countries; as a result, the immigrants established what he calls a folk religion in America instead, with indigenous rabbis who were elected or appointed by individual congregations and were more permissive in allowing, or too weak to prevent, deviations from religious orthodoxy, even of the milder folk variety.[26] Indeed, the development of a folk religion may have encouraged religious and secular diversity among Jews from the very beginning.

Still, perhaps the most important factor in the development of symbolic ethnicity was probably the awareness, which I think many second-generation people had already reached, that neither the practice of ethnic culture nor participation in ethnic organizations was essential to being and feeling ethnic. For Jews, living in a Jewish neighborhood or working with Jews every day was enough to maintain Jewish identity. When younger second-generation Jews moved to suburbia in large numbers after World War II, many wound up in communities in which they were a small numerical minority, but they quickly established an informal Jewish community of neighborly relations, and then built synagogues and community centers to formalize and supplement the informal community. At the time, many observers interpreted the feverish building as a religious revival, but for most Jews the synagogue was a symbol that could serve as a means of expressing identity without requiring more than occasional participation in its activities.[27] Thus, my observations among the second-generation Jews of Park Forest and other suburbs led me to think, as far back as the mid-1950s, that among Jews, at least, the shift to symbolic ethnicity was already under way.[28]

Suburban Jews also built synagogues and centers to help them implant a Jewish identity among their children, and to hold back primary assimilation, particularly intermarriage. Jewish parents sent their teenagers into Jewish organizations so that they would date other Jews, and then to colleges where they would be most likely to find Jewish spouses. Rising intermarriage rates suggest, however, that their efforts were not always successful, but also that their fears of the consequences of intermarriage were exaggerated. By now, many Jewish parents realize that intermarriage need not inevitably lead to surrender of Jewish identity. Non-Jewish spouses of third-generation Jews sometimes convert to Judaism, more frequently adopt some trappings of Jewish culture and pay homage to Jewish symbols, and even raise their children as Jews, thus suggesting that even with third-generation intermarriage, the next generation will still consider itself to be Jewish.[29]

Actually, if being Jewish need only mean feeling Jewish and attending to Jewish symbols, the transmission of Jewish identity to the next generation is fairly easily achieved, even by non-Jewish parents. Although little is known about socialization for Jewish identity, it may require only a minimum of parental action, no cultural or organizational affiliation, and perhaps not even a Jewish education for the children. Some evidence suggests that at about age five, children begin to ask themselves, their peers, and their parents what they are, and being told that they are Jewish may be sufficient to plant the seeds of Jewish identity.[30]

Needless to say, a person's ethnic identity is not firmly established at five and can weaken or disappear in later years. Even when this does not happen, adolescents and adults often develop doubts about their ethnic identity, and particularly about their ability to pass it on to their children.[31] I have the impression that ambivalence about one's identity is weaker among third-generation Jews than it was among their parents, if only because ethnic identity is now not burdensome or beset with major social and economic costs. Still, unless strong incentives or pressures develop to encourage Jews to give up their identity, it seems likely that they will retain it in the fourth generation, especially since the demands of symbolic ethnicity are light enough not to cause conflict with other, more highly valued, identities and activities.

Some of these observations apply equally well to third-generation Catholic ethnics, especially those who live in the suburbs. They still attend church more frequently than Jews attend synagogue, generally marry Catholics, and are unlikely to give up their Catholic identity. They do not, however, feel a strong need to perpetuate their secular ethnicity, so that, for example, Italian parents do not press their adolescent children to date other Italians. Even so, it is possible that identity may also be transmitted to children by others besides parents, for example, grandparents and peers. In any case, Sandberg has shown that fourth-generation Poles still retain their Polish identity, and Crispino has found the same among Italians.[32]

As intermarriage increases, however, it will be important to discover which ethnic identity, if any, is transmitted to children by intermarried Catholic ethnics; whether mothers and fathers play different roles in identity transmission; and how grandparents and close friends act in this connection. Similar questions could be asked of hybrid ethnics, although it seems unlikely that they could even decide which of their many ancestries they should pass on to their children.

THE FUTURE OF ETHNICITY

The emergence of symbolic ethnicity naturally raises the question of its persistence into the fifth and sixth generations. Although the Catholic and Jewish religions are certain to endure, it appears that as religion becomes less important to people, they, too, will be eroded by acculturation and assimilation. Even now synagogues see most of their worshipers no more than once or twice a year, and presumably the same trend will appear, perhaps more slowly, among Catholics and Protestants as well.

Whether the secular forms of ethnicity can survive beyond the fourth generation is somewhat less certain. One possibility is that symbolic ethnicity will itself decline as acculturation and assimilation continue, and then disappear as erstwhile ethnics forget their secular ethnic identity to blend into one or another subcultural melting pot. The other possibility is that symbolic ethnicity is a steady-state phenomenon that can persist into the fifth and sixth generations.

Obviously this question can only be guessed at, but my hypothesis is that symbolic ethnicity may persist. The continued existence of Germans, Scandinavians, and Irish after five or more generations in America suggests that in the larger cities and suburbs, at least, they have remained ethnic because they have long practiced symbolic ethnicity.[33] Consequently, there is good reason to believe that the same process will also take place among ethnics of the new immigration.

Ethnic behavior, attitudes, and even identity are, however, determined not only by what goes on among the ethnics, but also by developments in the larger society, and especially by how that society will treat ethnics in the future: what costs it will levy and what benefits it will award to them as ethnics. At present, the costs of being and feeling ethnic are slight. The changes that the immigrants and their descendants wrought in America now make it unnecessary for ethnics to surrender their ethnicity to gain upward mobility, and today ethnics are admitted virtually everywhere, provided they meet economic and status requirements, except at the very highest levels of the economic, political, and cultural hierarchies. Moreover, since World War II, the ethnics have been able to shoulder blacks and other racial minorities with the deviant and scapegoat functions they performed in an earlier America, so that ethnic prejudice and 'institutional ethnism' are no longer significant, except, again, at the very top of the societal hierarchies.

To be sure, some ethnic scapegoating persists at other levels of these hierarchies; American Catholics are still blamed for the policies of the Vatican, Italo-Americans are criticized for the Mafia, and urban ethnics generally have been portrayed as racists by a sometime coalition of white and black Protestant, Jewish, and other upper-middle-class cosmopolitans. But none of these phenomena, however repugnant, strike me as serious enough to persuade anyone to hide his or her ethnicity. White working-class men, and perhaps others, still use ethnic stereotypes to trade insults, but this practice serves functions other than the maintenance of prejudice or inequality.

At the same time, the larger society also seems to offer some benefits for being ethnic. Americans increasingly perceive themselves as undergoing cultural homogenization, and whether or not this perception is justified, they are constantly looking for new ways to establish their differences from each other. Meanwhile, the social, cultural, and political turbulence of the last decade and the concurrent delegitimation of many American institutions have also cast doubt on some of the other ways by which people identify themselves and differentiate themselves from each other. Ethnicity, now that it is respectable and no longer a major cause of conflict, seems therefore to be ideally suited to serve as a distinguishing characteristic. Moreover, in a mobile society, people who often find themselves living in communities of strangers tend to look for commonalities that make strangers into neighbors, and shared ethnicity may provide mobile people with at least an initial excuse to get together. Finally, as long as the European immigration into America continues, people will still be perceived, classified, and ranked at least in part by ethnic origin. Consequently, external forces exist to complement internal identity needs, and unless there is a drastic change in the allocation of costs and benefits with respect to ethnicity, it seems likely that the larger society will also encourage the persistence of symbolic ethnicity.

Needless to say, it is always possible that future economic and political conditions in American society will create a demand for new scapegoats, and if ethnics are forced into this role, so that ethnicity once more levies costs, present tendencies will be interrupted. Under such conditions, some ethnics will try to assimilate faster and pass out of all ethnic roles, while others will revitalize the ethnic group socially and culturally, if only for self-protection. Still, the chance that Catholic ethnics will be scapegoated more than today seems very slight. A serious economic crisis could, however, result in a resurgence of anti-Semitism, in part because of the affluence of many American Jews, in part because of their visibly influential role in some occupations, notably mass communications.

If present societal trends continue, however, symbolic ethnicity should become the dominant way of being ethnic by the time the fourth generation of the new immigration matures into adulthood, and this in turn will have consequences for the structure of American ethnic groups. For one thing, as secondary and primary assimilation continue, and ethnic networks weaken and unravel, it may be more accurate to speak of ethnic aggregates rather than groups. More importantly, since symbolic ethnicity does not depend on ethnic cultures and organizations, their future decline and disappearance must be expected, particularly those cultural patterns that interfere with other aspects of life and those organizations that require active membership.

Few such patterns and organizations are left in any case, and leaders of the remaining organizations have long been complaining bitterly over what they perceive as the cultural and organizational apathy of ethnics. They also criticize the resort to symbolic ethnicity, identifying it as identifying it as an effortless way of being ethnic that further threatens their own persistence. Even so, attacking people as apathetic or lazy and calling on them to revive the practices and loyalties of the past have never been effective for engendering support, and reflect instead the desperation of organizations that cannot offer new incentives that would enable them to recruit members.

Some cultural patterns and organizations will survive. Patterns that lend themselves to transformation into symbols and easy practice, such as annual holidays, should persist. So will organizations that create and distribute symbols, or 'ethnic goods' such as foodstuffs or written materials, but need few or no members and can function with small staffs and low overhead. In all likelihood, most ethnic organizations will eventually realize that in order to survive, they must deal mainly in symbols, using them to generate enough support to fund other activities as well.

Symbols do not arise in a vacuum, however, but are grounded in larger cultures. Moreover, insofar as ethnicity involves the notion of a heritage and an actual or imagined gloried past, contemporary symbols depend on older cultures. What kinds of symbols future generations of ethnics will want can hardly be predicted now, but undoubtedly some will want nostalgia, while others will use ethnicity as a substitute or indicator for other goals or purposes. Even now, ethnicity has served as an intentional or unintentional cover for racism, conservative political and economic ideologies, and the defense of familial and local structures and values against national forces and tendencies that drive American society further from Gemeinschaft and closer to a nationally homogeneous Gesellschaft.[34]

The demand for current ethnic symbols may require the maintenance of at least some old cultural practices, possibly as hobbies, and through the work of ethnic scholars who keep old practices alive by studying them. It is even possible that the organizations that attempt to maintain the old cultures will support themselves in part by supplying ethnic nostalgia, and some ethnics may aid such organizations if only to assuage their guilt at having given up ancestral practices.

Still, the history of religion and nationalism, as well as events of recent years, should remind us that the social process sometimes moves in dialectical ways, and that acculturative and assimilative actions by a majority occasionally generate revivalistic reactions by a minority. As a result, even ethnic aggregates in which the vast majority maintains its identity in symbolic ways will probably always bring forth small pockets of neotraditionalism – of rebel converts to sacred and secular ways of the past. They may not influence the behavior of the majority, but they are almost always highly visible, and will thus continue to play a role in the ethnicity of the future.

SYMBOLIC ETHNICITY AND STRAIGHT-LINE THEORY

The third and fourth generations' concern with ethnic identity and its expression through symbols seems to me to fit straight-line theory, for symbolic ethnicity cannot be considered as evidence either of a third-generation return or of a revival. Instead, it constitutes only another point in the secular trend that is drawn, implicitly, in straight-line theory, although it could also be a point at which the declining secular trend begins to level off and perhaps to straighten out.

In reality, of course, the straight line has never been quite straight, for even if it accurately graphs the dominant ethnic experience, it ignores the ethnic groups who still continue to make small bumps and waves in the line. Among these are various urban and rural ethnic enclaves, notably among the poor; the new European immigrants who help to keep these enclaves from disappearing; the groups that successfully segregate themselves from the rest of American society deliberately enclosed enclaves; and the rebel converts to sacred and secular ways of the past who will presumably continue to appear.

Finally, even if I am right to predict that symbolic ethnicity can persist into the fifth and sixth generations, I would be foolish to suggest that it is a permanent phenomenon. Although all Americans, save the Indians, came here as immigrants and are thus in one sense ethnics, people who arrived in the seventeenth and eighteenth centuries, and before the mid-nineteenth-century old immigration, are, except in some rural enclaves, no longer ethnics even if they know where their emigrant ancestors came from. Admittedly, in recent years some upper-class WASPs have begun to consider themselves to be ethnics, but they have done so as a reaction to their loss of cultural power, and the feeling of being a minority that has accompanied this loss, and they have not identified themselves by their European origins.

The history of groups whose ancestors arrived here seven or more generations ago suggests that, eventually, the ethnics of the new immigration will be like them; they may retain American forms of the religions that their ancestors brought to America, but their secular cultures will be only a dim memory, and their identity will bear only the minutest trace, if that, of their national origins. Ultimately, then, the secular trend of straight-line theory will hit very close to zero, and the basic postulates of the theory will turn out to have been accurate – unless, of course, by then America, and the ways it makes Americans, have altered drastically in some now unpredictable manner.

Notes

This paper was stimulated by S. H. Eisenstadt's talk at Columbia University in November 1975 on 'Unity and Diversity in Contemporary Jewish Society.' I am grateful to many people for helpful comments on an earlier draft of the paper, notably Harold Abramson, Richard Alba, James Crispino, Nathan Glazer, Milton Gordon, Andrew Greeley, William Kornblum, Peter Marris, Michael Novak, David Riesman, Paul Ritterband, Allan Silver, and John Slawson.

1. Personal communication. Incidentally, David Riesman is now credited with having invented the term 'ethnicity' as it is currently used. (Hereafter, I shall omit personal communication notes, but most of the indi-

viduals mentioned in the text supplied ideas or data through personal communication.)

2. For the sake of brevity, I employ these terms rather than Gordon's more detailed concepts. Milton Gordon, *Assimilation in American Life* (New York: Oxford University Press, 1964), chap. 3.

3. Neil C. Sandberg, *Ethnic Identity and Assimilation: The Polish–American Community* (New York: Praeger, 1974). The primary empirical application of straight-line theory is probably still W. Lloyd Warner and Leo Srole, *The Social Systems of American Ethnic Groups* (New Haven: Yale University Press, 1945).

4. See, for example, Andrew Greeley, *Ethnicity in the United States* (New York: Wiley, 1974), Chapter 1.

5. W. Yancey, E. Ericksen, and R. Juliani, 'Emergent Ethnicity: A Review and Reformation,' *American Sociological Review*, 41 (1976), pp. 391–403; words quoted at p. 400.

6. The major works include Greeley, *Ethnicity in the United States*; Harold J. Abramson, *Ethnic Diversity in Catholic America* (New York: Wiley, 1973); and Nathan Glazer and Daniel P. Moynihan, *Beyond the Melting Pot 2nd ed.* (Cambridge: MIT Press, 1970) 2nd edn.

7. Class differences in the degree of acculturation and assimilation were first noted by Warner and Srole, *Social Systems*; for some recent data among Poles, see Sandberg, *Ethnic Identity*.

8. Herbert J. Gans, *The Urban Villagers* (New York: Free Press, 1962), chap. 11. See also Dennis Wrong, 'How Important is Social Class,' in Irving Howe (ed.), *The World of the Blue Collar Worker* (New York: Quadrangle, 1972), pp. 297–309; William Kornblum, *Blue Collar Community* (Chicago: University of Chicago Press, 1974); and Stephen Steinberg, *The Academic Melting Pot* (New Brunswick: Transaction Books, 1977).

9. Marcus L. Hansen, *The Problem of the Third Generation Immigrant* (Rock Island, Ill.: Augustana Historical Society, 1938); and 'The Third Generation in America,' *Commentary*, 14 (1952): 492–500.

10. See also Harold J. Abramson, 'The Religioethnic Factor and American Experience: Another Look at the Three-Generations Hypothesis,' *Ethnicity*, 2 (1975): 163–77.

11. One of the most influential works has been Michael Novak, *The Rise of the Unmeltable Ethnics* (New York: Macmillan, 1971).

12. See Phil Berger, *The Last Laugh* (New York: Morrow, 1975).

13. Similarly, studies of the radical movements of the 1960s have shown that they included many people who themselves grew up in radical families.

14. See, for example, Egon Mayer, 'Modern Jewish Orthodoxy in Post-Modern America: A Case Study of the Jewish Community in Boro Park' (Ph.D. diss., Rutgers University, 1974).

15. Perhaps the first, and now not sufficiently remembered, study of third-generation Jews was Judith Kramer and Seymour Leventman, *The Children of the Gilded Ghetto* (New Haven: Yale University Press, 1961).

16. Geoffrey Bock, 'The Jewish Schooling of American Jews', Ph.D. dissertation (Harvard University, 1976).

17. I also make the assumption that generation is an important determinant of ethnic behavior, but I am aware that it is less important than I some-

times imply; that there are large differences in the experience of a generation within and between ethnic groups; and that the immigrants' age of arrival in the United States affected both their acculturation and that of their descendants.

18. The notion of primary assimilation extends Gordon's concept of marital assimilation to include movement out of the extended family, friendship circles, and other peer groups. In describing marital assimilation, Gordon did, however, mention the primary group as well. Gordon, *Assimilation in American Life*, p. 80.

19. The major debate at present is between Abramson and Alba, the former viewing the amount of intermarriage among Catholic ethnics as low; and the latter, as high. See Abramson, *Ethnic Diversity in Catholic America*; and Richard Alba, 'Social Assimilation of American Catholic National-Origin Groups,' *American Sociological Review* 41 (1976): 1030–46.

20. See, for example, Marshall Sklare and Joseph Greenblum, *Jewish Identity on the Suburban Frontier* (New York: Basic Books, 1967); Herbert J. Gans, 'The Origin and Growth of a Jewish Community in the Suburbs: A Study of the Jews of Park Forest,' in Marshall Sklare (ed.), *The Jews: Social Pattern of an American Group* (New York: Free Press, 1958), pp. 205–48; and Herbert J. Gans, *The Levittowners* (New York: Pantheon, 1967), pp. 73–80. These findings may not apply to communities with significant numbers of German Jews with Reform leanings. There are few Orthodox Jews in the suburbs, except in those surrounding New York City.

21. My use of the word 'symbol' here follows Lloyd Warner's concept of symbolic behavior. See W. Lloyd Warner, *American Life: Dream and Reality* (Chicago: University of Chicago Press, 1953), chap. 1.

22. See Nathan Glazer, *American Judaism* (Chicago: University of Chicago Press, 1972), 2nd edn pp. 114–15.

23. Sandberg, *Ethnic Identity*, Table 5-20. Understandably enough, working class Poles felt more offended by these jokes. Table 5-19.

24. On the Jamaica Chinese, see Orlando Patterson, *Ethnic Chauvinism* (New York: Stein Day, 1977), chap. 5; on the Sydney Italians, see Rina Huber, *From Pasta to Pavlova* (St. Lucia: University of Queensland Press, 1977), part 3.

25. For a study of one unsuccessful attempt to establish a community presidency, see Arthur A. Goren, *New York Jews and the Quest for Community* (New York: Columbia University Press, 1970).

26. Charles S. Liebman, *The Ambivalent American Jews* (Philadelphia: Jewish Publication Society and America, 1973), Chapter 3. Liebman notes that the few elite rabbis who did come to America quickly sensed they were in alien territory and returned to Eastern Europe. The survivors of the Holocaust who came to America after World War II were too few and too late to do more than influence the remaining Jewish Orthodox organizations.

27. Gans, 'The Origin of a Jewish Community in the Suburbs.'

28. See Herbert J. Gans, 'American Jewry: Present and Future,' *Commentary*, 21 (1956): 422–30, which includes a discussion of 'symbolic Judaism.'

29. Fred S. Sherrow, 'Patterns of Religious Intermarriage among American

College Graduates', Ph.D. dissertation Columbia University, 1971.
30. See, for example, Mary E. Goodman, *Race Awareness in Young Children* (Cambridge: Addison-Wesley, 1952).
31. Sklare and Greenblum, *Jewish Identity on the Suburban Frontier*, p. 331.
32. Sandberg, *Ethic Identity*; and James Crispino, *The Assimilation of Ethnic Groups: The Italian Case* (New York: Center for Migration Studies, 1979).
33. Unfortunately, too little attention has been devoted by sociologists to ethnicity among descendants of the old immigration.
34. The Ethnic Millions Political Action Committee (EMPAC), founded by Michael Novak, described itself as a 'national civil rights committee, dedicated to a politics of family and neighborhood, to equality and fairness, to a new American.' Conversely, Patterson sees ethnicity as a major obstacle to the achievement of a universalist, and socialist, humanism. Patterson, *Ethnic Chauvinism*.

EPILOGUE (1995)

Nearly two decades have gone by since I first published this paper, and many new, then unpredictable phenomena, have taken place, including the growth of the global economy and its weakening of the American economy, the extent of the post-1965 immigration and its illegal portion, as well as the just beginning negative reaction of economically - squeezed and culturally – threatened native-born Americans to it. Some of the trends discussed in the paper have persisted or have increased, for example the Jewish reactions, symbolic and otherwise, to the Holocaust. Other trends, important in 1979, like the so-called ethnic revival among European ethnics, have been forgotten. Although I do not lack for temptation to update everything I wrote then, I do lack space, and I will limit myself to seven issues from the original paper that I feel are of importance in 1995. Many of these concern ethnic and straight-line theory more than the concept of symbolic ethnicity.

First, symbolic ethnicity seems to have become a useful concept. While I have not tracked its use, over the years a number of scholars have verified its existence empirically.[1] To be sure, the concept has been repeatedly criticized as representing an inauthentic, trivial, or shallow kind of ethnicity, and authors have criticized me as well for appearing to advocate that kind of ethnicity.[2] Nonetheless, when I wrote this paper, I intended the term to be purely descriptive and analytic, making no value judgment about its desirability. This intention continues.

Indeed, I was surprised how often I was misread, even by social scientists, for while I can understand an advocate of ethnic organizations disapproving the concept, I was a bit nonplussed by authors writing in this vein as social scientists. However, ethnic research has never been noted for its interest in empirical objectivity, and too many ethnic researchers write as defenders of ethnic groups and traditions they are studying, without indicating, or perhaps even being aware, that they are taking a stand.[3]

In addition, I was misunderstood, but that is a normal experience in an author's life. Some of the misunderstandings might have been avoided if the original article had emphasized the symbolic element as merely a *necessary* factor in symbolic ethnicity, symbols being ever present in all forms of ethnicity. However, the lack of involvement in organized ethnic groups or cultures is the *sufficient* factor without which symbolic ethnicity as I conceive it is impossible.

Second, my formulation of symbolic ethnicity was also a statement about 'straight-line theory.' Originally, I viewed symbolic ethnicity as a stage in that theory, and ended the paper by raising the possibility that the secular trend of straight-line theory would end with the final disappearance of the ethnic groups I was discussing, that is, the white Europeans. Although I was not alone, I failed to realize that other groups might have had different experiences because while they also had distinctive ethnic cultures and organizations, they were also racial groups.[4]

In the late 1970s, straight-line theory was still the reigning paradigm in ethnic studies, though its hegemony was clearly declining.[5] Today, straight-line theory is not only no longer dominant, but it is thought to be empirically invalid as well as being normatively undesirable. Instead, the reigning paradigm argues that, ethnicity being a constructed notion, people are able to construct, reconstruct, or invent a variety of ethnicities that can follow any 'line,' or none at all.[6]

I have never been persuaded by this total rejection of straight line theory. While people *can* construct or invent their own ethnicity, the materials which they use in doing so have to come from what they know about their own or another ethnicity. Moreover, since acculturation and assimilation continue to take place, what they know differs from what their parents or other ancestors knew. It is therefore unlikely, if not impossible, for them to reconstruct even pale imitations of the ethnic groups or cultures of their immigrant ancestors, except perhaps as museum exhibits, or as events at an ethnic festival.

Likewise, no one can invent an ethnic group or culture not their own. The many intermarried ethnics now to be found in America can borrow from the ethnicity of their spouses and in-laws, but such borrowings are apt to be meager, since exogamous spouses are usually marginal to their own ethnic origins.[7]

Third, despite the decline of straight-line theory in social science thought, the theory seems to be applicable to the post-1965 immigrants for, with some exceptions, the children of the new immigrants are acculturating in much the same way as did the Europeans decades earlier.[8] Concurrently, these children are also constructing and inventing ethnic patterns that fit their perception of the economy and society they live in, and are inventing ethnic identities that earlier immigrants may not have needed. If current conditions continue, the spread and intensity of 'identity politics' may increase for some, particularly the immigrants who must deal concurrently with their ethnicity and their racial origins, and with the reactions of white non-immigrant America to them. However, it may still be possible that the old patterns of straight-line theory, as well as the symbolic ethnicity I saw among the European third generation, will occur among the third generation of the new immigrants.

Indeed, it is even possible that by the time the third generation becomes adult, the bipolar redefinition of race into black and non-black that is now beginning in those parts of the country that have been the main hosts for immigrants will have become fully established, and that what are now perceived as racial differences between, for example, Asian-Americans and Caucasian-Americans will no longer be noted, at least when class differences are minimal.[9]

Still, the notion that ethnicity would someday end in a totally melted American pot is not considered possible by anyone in the last decade of the twentieth century, although half a century from now straight-line theory may be once again on top of the heap. But we know now, more than we did 50 years ago, how much the requirements of national economies, polities and ideologies influence the struggles between theories, including empirically-grounded ones. And no one can predict what disasters or persecutions, or the now unpredictable arrivals of new and distinctive immigrants will do to ethnicity and theories about it.

Fourth, the current, and long overdue, study of the economic roles of immigrants and ethnic groups raises new issues about the future of straight-line theory. For example, Alejandro Portes' and Min Zhou's notion of segmented assimilation not only calls attention to the variety of scenarios, particularly economic ones, currently experienced by different immigrant groups, but it also raises questions for the future.[10]

One question concerns the fate of ethnic economic enclaves, niches and the ethnic markets created by immigrant languages and immigrant food habits, as well as the likelihood of persistence over several generations. Although some ethnic economic niches that began early in the twentieth century have survived nearly 100 years later, no one can predict what the new global economy will do to them, and to new ones. For example, the children of some poorer immigrants, especially dark-skinned ones may not even have work, joining poor native-born blacks and Hispanics in unemployment and on welfare, should the latter survive the 1995 onslaught on it.[11]

Most likely, economic segmentation in production will coexist with acculturation and the beginning of social assimilation in consumption. Thus, many members of the second generation may still work with fellow ethnics but their lifestyles will be predominantly American, and many non-black and non-poor children of immigrants may join mainstream suburban American society.[12]

Fifth, with the new and desirable emphasis on agency and choice in ethnicity and thus on the construction of ethnicity, it is possible that my speculations in the original article (pp. 441–43) about the resort to symbolic ethnicity before the third generation may be supported by new historical research. Even immigrants who do not like their fellow immigrants, or who resign from the power struggles and other conflicts that beset ethnic organizations, or want nothing to do with the religious institutions which control ethnic culture among some immigrant groups, could develop the distanced ethnicity possible via symbolic ethnicity, and that can come at any time.[13] Here, too, however, race cannot be ignored, for as long as whites perceive immigrants or their children as non-white, the latter will be forced to maintain some contact with their fellows, if only for reasons of security.

Sixth, I wish I could add more here about the development of symbolic ethnicity and especially its persistence, but it is too early to answer such questions, since adult fourth-generation European ethnics do not yet show up in studies. Moreover, the research among fifth, sixth, seventh and later generations, for example of Germans and Scandinavians that I had advocated in the original article still remains to be undertaken. Pockets of German and Scandinavian communities continue to exist in various parts of the country, however, and obviously they must act or feel ethnically in some respect to be visible to the rest of the population. Conversely, the rising intermarriage rates in all third generations, their meager connections to any single ethnicity, and the increasing scarcity of 'pure' ethnics reported by Alba and others also means that pockets of the other European immigrant populations, especially those not supplemented by newcomers after 1965, will be shrinking continually.[14]

Bakalian reminds us, however, that symbolic ethnicity can persist independently of any immediate demand for symbolic products. She observes that ethnic groups now preserve some of their cultural heritage through what she calls 'knowledge banks' such as university chairs in ethnic studies, ethnic museums, or wings at larger museums, although such banks are apt to preserve ethnic high and elite national culture rather than popular, everyday or even peasant culture.[15] Nonetheless, her observation suggests that symbolic ethnicity does not require a living ethnic group or culture, and can be pursued through ethnic 'museum culture' whether it flourishes in museums, research monographs or CD-Roms, data banks, and their yet unknown technological descendants.

Perhaps the most interesting innovation in symbolic ethnicity since I first wrote in 1979 stems from the widespread marketing of ethnic products and even ideas all over America. As a result, Americans can now indulge in being or feeling ethnic in many ethnic groups, and can change from one ethnic group to another when they so choose. Whether they opt to eat in Ethiopian restaurants or buy Peruvian crafts in import stores, and then shift to Vietnamese restaurants and Indian crafts the next time, even the descendants of immigrants who arrived on the Mayflower, can enjoy ethnic symbols. To be sure, this phenomenon is 'symbolic multiethnicity' and probably differs from the more typical symbolic ethnicity discussed in the original article.[16]

Seventh, I hope, naturally, that future ethnic researchers will undertake more systematic studies of symbolic ethnicity.[17] Such studies should move beyond verifying the existence, and persistence of symbolic ethnicity, and determine how it operates, sociologically, intellectually and emotionally, with an eye also to understanding its functions and dysfunctions, i.e. consequences for different people and strata, and its prerequisites, e.g. what kind of ethnic group or culture it requires to sustain it, if any. Later in the twenty-first century, similar studies can be conducted among the descendants of the various post-1965 immigrants. Perhaps some researchers can also use these and other data to identify new bumps in straight line theory, or new lines that are no longer even straight, and speculate about the likelihood of an ending of ethnicity, if there should be one, as predicted by classical straight-line theory.

Such an ending could probably not occur in the twenty-first century, even if no further immigration took place. But if it did occur, the outcome might even resemble the 'new American', albeit one more more heterogeneous in class and race, and less godlike in morality than the new American about whom Crevecoeur and Zangwill wrote so long ago.[18]

Notes

1. Those who found it useful include James Crispino, *The Assimilation of Ethnic Groups: The Italian Case* (Staten Island, NY: Center for Migration Studies, 1980); Richard Alba, *Ethnic Identity:The Transformation of White America* (New Haven, CT.: Yale University Press, 1990); Mary C. Waters, *Ethnic Options* (Berkeley: University of California Press, 1990; and Anny Bakalian, *Armenian-Americans: From Being to Feeling Armenian* (New Brunswick, NJ: Transaction Publishers, 1993).

   The only study I know of that did not find the concept relevant was Peter Kivisto and Ben Nefzger, 'Symbolic Ethnicity and American Jews: The Relationship of Ethnic Identity to Behavior and Group Affiliation,' *Social Science Journal* 30 (1993): 1–12. However, the two researchers studied a well-organized Jewish community in a small town, where for social control reasons alone, I would imagine practicing symbolic ethnicity to be impossible.

2. I have not kept track of such critics either. Conversely, Jenna Joselit wrote of my parallel notion of 'symbolic Judaism' in an almost celebratory tone, describing this form of Judaism as 'an inchoate and at times ineptly rendered but consistently heartfelt and deeply intended emotional and cultural sensibility.' Jenna W. Joselit, *The Wonders of America: Reinventing Jewish Culture 1880–1950* (New York: Hill & Wang, 1994), p. 133.

3. Most of the time, I suspect they assume the desirability of the ethnic group or culture *a priori*, ignoring that other value judgments are possible. After all, why would they study their own ethnic group if not to help assure its survival and persistence.

4. I failed to do so in 1979, but now, ethnic researchers must follow the lead of Ruben Rumbaut and Mary Waters, among others, and pay special attention to the many non-white immigrants who must also deal with racism as they maintain, or give up, their ethnic cultures.

   I did at least note that some white ethnics also had distinctive religions, but even today, some ethnic researchers still conflate such groups, for example Jews and various Eastern Orthodox groups, with mainstream Protestant or Catholic ethnic groups. The more recent arrival or visibility of Buddhists, Hindus, Moslems and others may finally end this conflation, and perhaps someone will even study ethnics who are also atheists. On some similarities between ethnic and religious acculturation, see my 'Symbolic Ethnicity and Symbolic Religiosity: Toward a Comparison of

Ethnic and Religious Acculturation,' *Ethnic and Racial Studies* 17 (1994): 577–92.

5. Actually, the interest I expressed in straight-line theory in the original paper also reflected the fact that in the mid-1950s, I had already written about 'symbolic Judaism,' an earlier version of symbolic ethnicity, and at that time, straight-line theory had no real competition in the academy. The earlier articles appeared in *Commentary*; for citations, see note 20 of the original paper.

6. See e.g. Werner Sollors, (ed.), *The Invention of Ethnicity* (New York: Oxford University Press, 1989); and Kathleen N. Conzen, *et al.*, 'The Invention of Ethnicity: A Perspective from the US' *Journal of American Ethnic History* 12 (1992): 3–41. I defended what I now called 'bumpy-line theory' in an invited comment: 'Comment: Ethnic Invention and Acculturation: A Bumpy-Line Approach,' pp. 43–52.

7. Today, Americans can also choose their own religions, save those not accepting converts, and in each case the converts have to learn as much of the secular ethnic cultures that are practiced by these religions so as to prevent being socially isolated. Still, new Moslems do not have to, and cannot become Arab-Americans. However, it is surely no coincidence that ethnic groups lack institutions to encourage and manage conversions.

8. Unfortunately, there is so far mainly anecdotal data, much of which is personal observations of researchers among their students. For early evidence of acculturation among the children of the first (pre 1965) Cuban immigrants, see Eleanor Rogg, *The Assimilation of Cuban Exiles: The Role of Community and Class* (New York: Abingdon, 1974).

9. This would not be entirely novel, since native born WASPs originally opposed the poor Jews, Catholics and others who came to America from Eastern and Southern Europe after the Civil War as different, i.e., 'swarthy,' races. They stopped doing so, however, once the newcomers spoke English and earned sufficient incomes from respectable jobs. In the process, old differences in hair color, head shapes or other physical details originally defined as racial were no longer visible, and now the descendants of these newcomers are 'white ethnics' who feel entitled to oppose those of different 'race.' Actually, the swarthy immigrants were anti-black even before native-born whites began to treat them as whites.

10. Alejandro Portes and Min Zhou, 'The New Second Generation: Segmented Assimilation and its Variants,' *Annals of the American Academy of Political and Social Science* 530 (1993): 74–96.

11. Herbert J. Gans, 'Second-generation Decline: Scenarios for the Economic and Ethnic Futures of the post-1965 American Immigrants,' *Ethnic and Racial Studies* 15 (1992): 173–92.

12. In this connection, Mary Waters rightly wonders whether middle class West Indian immigrants who now use Caribbean cultures and dialects to prevent their being confused with African-Americans will be able to pass this pattern on to the second generation, since this requires the latter's being willing, and more important, able, to maintain the immigrant dialects. Mary C Waters, 'Ethnic and Racial Identities of Second Generation Black Immigrants in New York City,' *International Migration Review* (Special issue: The New Second Generation' ed. by Alejandro Portes) 23

(1994): 795–820. Of course, second-generation West Indians may invent new ways of distinguishing themselves from African Americans, if they choose to do so.

13. Joselit's *The Wonders of America* is full of examples of the early construction of Jewish symbols and the invention of symbolic products. However, these appear to be Americanized European-Jewish practices and products, or Jewish version of American ones, but they were intended for use in Jewish groups, and thus fail to meet the sufficient factor in my definition of symbolic ethnicity.

14. Alba, *Ethnic Identity.*

15. Bakalian, *Armenian-Americans*, pp. 439–40.

16. I say probably because too little is still known about the subjective aspects of symbolic ethnicity. In any case, symbolic multi-ethnicity is a worthy research topic of its own. Nor should it be forgotten that all the symbols involved create jobs for someone, either in the old country or an immigrant in the United States, in the latter case supporting some kind of ethnic economic niche.

17. Actually, it is the fourth generation of the later European immigration, since the descendants of the Europeans who came around the middle of the nineteenth century, and even of the first of the Eastern and Southern Europeans who arrived in 1870 and 1880 must now be of a later generation. However, they do not seem to be visible, and thus difficult for researchers to study.

18. On these two writers see Werner Sollors, *Beyond Ethnicity: Consent and Descent in American Culture* (New York: Oxford University Press, 1986) especially pp. 66–81. Both writers were indulging in nationalist teleology reflecting both the chauvinism and idealism of American exceptionalism. When I raise the possibility of the end of ethnicity, I see it as one of several alternative cultural–structural extrapolations, modeled on that done by demographic forecasters but based on the data on acculturation and assimilation that social scientists have accumulated during this century.

24 Identifying Identity: A Semantic History (1983)

Philip Gleason*

Today we could hardly do without the word *identity* in talking about immigration and ethnicity. Those who write on these matters use it casually; they assume the reader will know what they mean. And readers seem to feel that they do – at least there has been no clamor for clarification of the term. But if pinned down, most of us would find it difficult to explain just what we do mean by identity. Its very obviousness seems to defy elucidation: identity is what a thing is! How is one supposed to go beyond that in explaining it? But adding a modifier complicates matters, for how are we to understand identity in such expressions as 'ethnic identity,' 'Jewish identity,' or 'American identity'?

This is a question to which the existing writings on ethnicity do not provide a satisfactory answer. There are helpful discussions, to be sure, but none seems altogether adequate, at least not from the historian's viewpoint. The historically minded inquirer who gains familiarity with the literature, however, soon makes an arresting discovery – *identity* is a new term, as well as being an elusive and ubiquitous one. It came into use as a popular social science term only in the 1950s. The contrast between its handling in two standard reference works dramatizes its novelty. The *International Encyclopedia of the Social Sciences*, published in 1968, carries a substantial article on 'Identity, Psychosocial,' and another on 'Identification, Political.' The original *Encyclopedia of the Social Sciences*, published in the early 1930s, carries no entry at all for *identity*, and the entry headed 'Identification' deals with fingerprinting and other techniques of criminal investigation.[1]

So striking a shift demands investigation. In the following pages I will attempt to show that the semantic history of the word *identity* casts useful light on its ambiguities of meaning and also upon certain aspects of recent American thought. The investigation proceeds in three phases. Part one, which traces the emergence and diffusion of the term, is brief and descriptive. In the second section of the essay, I have singled out the work of Erik H. Erikson and of certain sociologists as

* From *The Journal of American History*, 69(4) (March 1983), pp. 910–31.

the principal sources of interest in identity and have analyzed some of the complications that arise from the differing interpretations of the concept that they advance. The final section is more interpretive in the historical sense, since it focuses on those aspects of recent American cultural history that seem to me most relevant in explaining why the term *identity* caught on so quickly.

Identity comes from the Latin root *idem*, the same, and has been used in English since the sixteenth century. It has a technical meaning in algebra and logic and has been associated with the perennial mind-body problem in philosophy since the time of John Locke. The meaning of *identity* in this philosophical context is close to its meaning in ordinary usage, which is given as follows by the *Oxford English Dictionary* (OED):

> the sameness of a person or thing at all times or in all circumstances; the condition or fact that a person or thing is itself and not something else; individuality, personality.
>
> *Personal identity* (in *Psychology*), the condition or fact of remaining the same person throughout the various phases of existence; continuity of the personality.[2]

The *OED*'s first two usage citations illustrating psychological 'personal identity' are from Locke's *Essay Concerning Human Understanding* (1690) and David Hume's *Treatise on Human Nature* (1739). This tends to corroborate Robert Langbaum's assertion that identity did not take on psychological connotations until the empiricist philosophers called into question what he calls 'the unity of the self.' The unity of the self was not a problem so long as the traditional Christian conception of the soul held sway, but it became a problem when Locke declared that a man's 'Identity . . . consists in nothing but a participation of the same continued Life, by constantly fleeting Particles of Matter, in succession vitally united to the same organized Body.' Langbaum argues that Locke and Hume 'use the word *identity* to cast doubt on the unity of the self,' and he has written a book to show how writers from William Wordsworth to D. H. Lawrence reacted to this challenge to the integrity of 'the self.'[3]

This tradition of usage is obviously very important; it invested identity with great intellectual significance and moral seriousness. But it was a restricted, quasi-technical tradition. Most of the time people who used the word *identity* in reference to personality or individuality did so in a looser, more informal manner. The *OED* gives two examples of this vernacular usage, as we might call it: 'He doubted his own identity, and whether he was himself or another man' (from Washington Irving's *Sketch Book*, 1820); and 'Tom . . . had such a curious feeling of having lost his identity, that he wanted to reassure himself by the sight of his little belongings' (from E. Garrett's *At Any Cost*, 1885).[4]

Identity was sometimes casually employed in this vernacular manner by writers discussing immigration, but it did not represent an important analytical concept. Oscar Handlin's classic *The Uprooted* (1951) is perhaps the last major work in the field of which that could be said. Handlin used *identity* or *identify* a half-dozen or so times, but it was not a key term and the contexts suggest that he was employing it in an unself-conscious manner as part of the ordinary vocabulary of common discourse. A particularly telling example is the passage in which he contrasts the immigrant's loneliness and isolation in the New World to his secure niche in the ancestral village: 'In the Old Country, this house in this village, these fields by these trees, had had a character and identity of their own. They testified to the peasant's *I*, had fixed his place in the visible universe.' Here the word refers, not directly to the peasant's psyche, but to the distinctive physical surroundings of his once-familiar world. The connection with psychological identity is very clear – indeed, the passage reminds us of Tom and his little belongings – but Handlin does not use the term in the way that contemporary usage has led us to expect. On the contrary, in looking back at the book one is struck at its virtually complete absence. The book's themes are expressed, and its tone established, not by *identity*, but by words like *uprootedness*, *alienation*, and *loneliness*.[5]

With Will Herberg's *Protestant–Catholic–Jew* (1955) we have turned a corner. Not only do the words recur again and again, but identity and identification are, in a sense, what the book is all about. They are central to the interpretation of the problem Herberg set out to explore, namely, the place of organized religion in American life in the 1950s. Religion, he said, had become the most satisfactory vehicle for locating oneself in society and thereby answering the 'aching question' of identity: 'Who am I?' Ethnic identity figured prominently in the discussion because Herberg argued that the ethnic identities of an immigrant-derived population had transformed themselves into religious identification with organized Protestantism, Catholicism, or Judaism through the workings of Hansen's Law ('What the son wants to forget, the grandson wants to remember') and the triple melting pot. In short, Herberg interpreted the whole situation in terms of what was already being called 'the search for identity.'[6]

C. Vann Woodward's essay, 'The Search for Southern Identity,' published in 1958, used the term without enclosing it in quotation marks or explicitly defining it, but it carried the new weight of meaning that *identity* was acquiring in the mid-1950s. W. L. Morton's *The Canadian Identity*, published a few years later, likewise regarded the word as entirely unproblematic.[7] A rash of other publications used *identity* in title or subtitle in the late 1950s, and in 1960 the editors of an anthology entitled *Identity and Anxiety* drew attention to a marked shift from concern over conformity to concern with identity.[8] Three years later the editor of another volume of readings could introduce the opening section, headed 'Identity,' with the remark: 'It is common knowledge that identity becomes a problem for the individual in a rapidly changing dynamic and technological society such as we have in America.' The collection included a selection by Kenneth Keniston in which he listed *identity* among 'the most appealing moral terms of our time.'[9]

Robert Penn Warren highlighted the importance identity had assumed by the mid-1960s in his *Who Speaks for the Negro* (1965):

> I seize the word *identity*. It is a key word. You hear it over and over again. On this word will focus, around this word will coagulate, a dozen issues, shifting, shading into each other. Alienated from the world to which he is born and from the country of which he is a citizen, yet surrounded by the successful values of that new world, and country, how can the Negro define himself?[10]

Negroes were far from being alone in having identity problems. American Catholics fairly luxuriated in them. Martin Marty remembers being told by some Catholic collegians who were enthusiastically applauding a priest who had just renounced his priesthood: 'You'll never understand what an identity crisis the Catholic Church gave each one of us.' Others managed to preserve a better humor in their travail – at Harvard University notices were posted facetiously announcing that Catholic students were holding an 'Identity Crisis' at a specified time and place.[11]

By the early 1970s Robert Coles could lament that the terms *identity* and *identity crisis* had become 'the purest of clichés.' A 1972 book, *The Identity Society*, which stated among other things that Vietnam was the first war fought by an 'identity society,' offered corroborative evidence for that judgment. *Identity* had reached the level of generality and diffuseness that A. O. Lovejoy complained of many years earlier in respect to the word *romantic*: it had 'come to mean so many things that, by itself, it means nothing. It has ceased to perform the function of a verbal sign.'[12] There is little point in asking what *identity* 'really means' when matters have reached this pass. The more pertinent questions are, What can we find out about the specific channels through which the word passed into such widespread use? and What elements in the intellectual background of its emergence help explain its extraordinary popularity? To the first of these questions we now turn.

Erikson was the key figure in putting the word into circulation. He coined the expression *identity crisis* and did more than anyone else to popularize *identity*. In his usage identity means something quite definite, but terribly elusive. In fact, the subtlety of Eriksonian identity helps account for the vagueness that soon enveloped the term, for his ideas are of the sort that cannot bear being popularized without at the same time being blunted and muddied.

Erikson admits that identity, as he conceives it, is hard to grasp because it concerns 'a process "located" *in the core of the individual* and yet also *in the core of his communal culture*, a process which establishes, in fact, the identity of those two identities.'[13] What he seems to mean by this delphic deliverance is that identity involves an interaction between the interior development of the individual personality, understood in terms derived from the Freudian id–ego–superego model, and the growth of a sense of selfhood that arises from participating in society, internalizing its cultural norms, acquiring different statuses, and playing different roles. As the individual passes through the eight stages of the life cycle distinguished by Erikson, the ego undergoes certain experiences, and confronts various tasks, distinctive to each stage. These experiences and tasks are related to biological maturation, but they are also intrinsically linked through social interaction to the milieu in which the individual finds himself; the features of that milieu are in turn conditioned by the historical situation of the culture that shapes the social world in which the individual and his fellows exist. An identity crisis is a climactic turning point in this process; it is the normal occurrence of adolescence, but it can also be precipitated by unusual difficulties further along in the life cycle.

This conception of identity developed from Erikson's clinical experience as a psychoanalyst working chiefly with children, and from reflection upon his own life experience as a European refugee intellectual who traveled widely in the United States and was acquainted with some of the leading social scientists of his generation. The rise of Adolf Hitler and World War II contributed to his interest in the interaction between large-scale historical movements and the development of individual personality, and it was against the background of World War II that Erikson first began to use the term *identity*.

Knowledge of his work was at first confined to professionals in psychology and related fields, but by the late 1950s his reputation began to reach a larger public. The appearance in 1963 of a second edition of *Childhood and Society* (originally published in 1950) was a major event. As other books followed in quick succession over the next few years, Erikson and his ideas became something of a cultural phenomenon. His study of Mahatma Gandhi won both a Pulitzer Prize and a National Book Award. These honors, plus a biography by Coles in 1970, provided the occasion for extensive treatment of Erikson in mass-circulation magazines. His being selected in 1973 to deliver the prestigious Jefferson Lectures in the Humanities testified to Erikson's high standing among intellectual opinion leaders.[14]

Erikson's influence was crucial, but his writings were not the only source from which the terminology of identity passed into general circulation. On the contrary, Erikson was concerned as early as 1958 to distinguish his version of identity from other usages; the following year he insisted that identity formation, as he understood it, began where the notion of 'identification' left off. By the late 1960s the terminological situation had gotten completely out of hand, and Erikson tried once more to set the record straight. Identity was not the same as role playing, he wrote; it was not just self-conception or self-image, and it was not simply an answer to the faddish question, 'Who am I?'[15]

The mentions of identification and role playing provide useful clues to follow up in searching for other sources of interest in identity. The term *identification* was introduced by Sigmund Freud to designate the process by which the infant assimilates to itself external persons or objects. It became a key element in psychoanalytical explanations of socialization in children; through the 1940s its use was confined almost exclusively to psychologists.[16] Gordon W. Allport was still using identification primarily in connection with childhood development in his influential *The Nature of Prejudice* (1954), but his discussion is significant because it implied a more general applicability for the concept and linked it with ethnicity. Conceding that the term was loosely defined, Allport said that it conveyed 'the sense of emotional merging of oneself with others.' Then he illustrated its operation:

> One of the areas where identification may most easily take place is that of social values and attitudes. . . . Sometimes a child who confronts

a social issue for the first time will ask his parent what attitude he should hold. Thus he may say, 'Daddy, what are we? Are we Jews or gentiles; Protestants or Catholics; Republicans or Democrats?' When told what 'we' are, the child is fully satisfied. From then on, he will accept his membership and the ready-made attitudes that go with it.[17]

Identification understood in this sense is very closely related to role theory and reference-group theory. That is, identification is involved in the process by which a person comes to realize what groups are significant for him, what attitudes concerning them he should form, and what kind of behavior is appropriate. Both role theory and reference-group theory were new; they were also gaining rapidly in acceptance among sociologists and social psychologists. As they did so, the theoretical relevance of identification – and the inseparably linked notion of identity – was brought home to other social scientists besides the psychologists who had first used these terms.[18]

Ralph Linton's *The Study of Man* (1936) introduced role theory, showed how the concept of social role was intimately linked with that of social status, and made it possible for these two concepts to be 'systematically incorporated into a developing theory of social structure.'[19] Role theory quickly became a major conceptual perspective for sociology, but as Nelson N. Foote pointed out in 1951, it lacked 'a satisfactory account of motivation.' To explain why people were willing to be cast in certain roles, accepting the statuses that accompanied those roles, Foote proposed identification as the basis for a theory of motivation in social interaction.[20]

Explicitly distinguishing his use of the term from Freud's, Foote defined *identification* as 'appropriation of and commitment to a particular identity or series of identities' on the part of an individual. Identification 'proceeds by *naming*,' he added, for to appropriate and be committed to an identity meant that one accepted the name (that is, assignment to a certain category) given by others on the basis of family lineage, religion, work activity, and other attributes. Appropriation of these identities by an individual transformed social ascriptions into elements of an evolving sense of selfhood and was experienced as a process of self-discovery and self-actualization. But identities of this sort were not imposed by society in an absolute way, and as one grew older and was exposed to a greater variety of social situations, one could combine and modify identities by conscious choice more effectively than was possible for a child or young person.[21]

Foote's article firmly linked identification with role theory; in doing so it laid great stress on a kind of 'identity' that was different from Erikson's and closer to what I have called the vernacular meaning of the word. Foote did not mention reference-group theory, perhaps because it was so new when he wrote. It was, however, quite compatible with his analysis since it dealt with the way in which a person's attitudes, values, and sense of identity were shaped by alignment with, or rejection of, 'reference groups' that had significance for the individual, either positively or negatively. The expression *reference group* was coined only in 1942, and for the first few years its use was confined to social psychologists. In 1950 Robert Merton and Alice S. Kitt (later Alice S. Rossi) brought the concept to the attention of the larger sociological community in a path-breaking essay. Seven years later this discussion, revised and enlarged, was given much greater visibility in the second edition of Merton's very influential *Social Theory and Social Structure*, which devoted no fewer than 161 pages to reference groups. Being primarily interested in systematic structural analysis, Merton did not lay much emphasis on identity or identification. He did, however, point out the relevance of reference-group theory to these matters, and by so greatly augmenting the prestige of a sociological approach to which they were intimately related, he contributed importantly to popularizing the terminology of identity.[22]

Identity eventually gained an even more prominent place in the vocabulary of the sociological school known as symbolic interactionists. Emerging as a self-conscious group around 1940, the symbolic interactionists were especially interested in the way social interaction, mediated through shared symbolic systems, shaped the self-consciousness of the individual. They did not at first use the word *identity* in analyzing this sort of interaction because the founding fathers of the approach, Charles Horton Cooley and George Herbert Mead, had spoken instead of 'the self,' and that continued to be the preferred term through the 1960s. By that time, however, *identity* had also become a 'stock technical term' for symbolic interactionists.[23] Erving Goffman and Peter L. Berger played important roles in popularizing this sociological understanding of identity since their works reached a more general audience than that constituted solely by academic specialists. Goffman shifted from the terminology of 'the self' to that of 'identity' in his 1963 work, *Stigma*. In the same year, Berger's popular *Invitation to Sociology* featured identity quite prominently in its treatment of role theory and reference-group theory, dramaturgical sociology, and the phenomenological approach.[24]

By the mid-1960s, the word *identity* was used so widely and so loosely that to determine its provenance in every context would be impossible. But enough has been said to show that sociological traditions of usage in role theory, reference-group theory, and symbolic interactionism constituted important feeder streams supplementing the principal source of popularization, Eriksonian psychology. Besides helping to popularize the term, sociological usage also contributed to its uncertainty of meaning because the kind of identity that sociologists had in mind was not the same as that contemplated by Erikson.

The two approaches differ most significantly on whether identity is to be understood as something internal that persists through change or as something ascribed from without that changes according to circumstance. For Erikson, the elements of interiority and continuity are indispensable. Working within the Freudian tradition, he affirms that identity is somehow 'located' in the deep psychic structure of the individual. Identity is shaped and modified by interaction between the individual and the surrounding social milieu, but, change and crisis notwithstanding, it is at bottom an 'accrued confidence' in the 'inner sameness and continuity' of one's own being.[25]

The sociologists, on the other hand, tend to view identity as an artifact of interaction between the individual and society – it is essentially a matter of being designated by a certain name, accepting that designation, internalizing the role requirements accompanying it, and behaving according to those prescriptions. Foote is explicit here, and Berger asserts not only that identities are 'socially bestowed' but that they 'must also be socially sustained, and fairly steadily so.' He adds pointedly that this sociological view of personality challenges the assumption of continuity in the self. 'Looked at sociologically, the self is no longer a solid, given entity. . . . It is rather a process, continuously created and re-created in each social situation that one enters, held together by the slender thread of memory.'[26] Another sociologist, acknowledging Goffman's influence, goes even further by equating identity with social relationship. 'We have treated social relationship and identity as merely different terms for referring to the same phenomena: the establishment of mutually recognized, expected sequences of behavior in a transaction. Identity refers to the individual's sequence of acts; relationship refers to the ensemble of acts made up by the sequences of all the parties involved.'[27]

Obviously we are back at the problem of 'the unity of the self,' the emergence of which Langbaum associates with the writings of Locke and Hume. Indeed, it is striking how closely the formulation just quoted parallels Locke's contention that 'Identity ... consists in nothing but a participation of the same continued Life, by constantly fleeting Particles of Matter.' The reappearance in new form of what we might call the philosophical problem of the soul is of considerable interest in itself, but it is also related to an issue more immediately relevant to students of ethnicity, namely, whether ethnic identity is something primordially given or optionally cultivated.

The distinction between these two interpretations emerged only recently; it has not, to my knowledge, been systematically explored.[28] Briefly, the difference between the two approaches is that primordialists regard ethnicity as a given, a basic element in one's personal identity that is simply there and cannot be changed, while optionalists hold that ethnicity is not an indelible stamp impressed on the psyche but a dimension of individual and group existence that can be consciously emphasized or de-emphasized as the situation requires. This disagreement obviously involves a fundamental issue concerning ethnic identity, and it just as obviously parallels the difference between the Eriksonian and the sociological understanding of identity itself.

The parallel rests on the fact that the question of continuity or permanence is central to both sets of contrasting interpretations. In the case of identity, Erikson insists that an inner continuity of personality perdures through all the changes the individual undergoes in passing through the stages of the life cycle, while the interactionists envision a flickering succession of identities adopted and shed according to the requirements of different social situations. In respect to ethnicity, the primordialists plump for permanence, whereas the optionalists believe that ethnicity can, within certain limits, be assumed or put aside by conscious choice.

The analogy between these two sets of interpretations is striking. But since it has never been pointed out before, much less studied in detail, its implications are not wholly clear. One might ask, for example, whether a person who accepts the Eriksonian version of personal identity is thereby committed to a primordialist position on ethnic identity. The two positions are beautifully congruent, but I would not be prepared to argue that the one logically entails the other. On the other hand, consistency would surely require an interactionist on personal identity to adopt the optionalist view of ethnicity. The key point for the present discussion, however, is that the analogy brings out clearly the basic equivocation embedded in discussions of identity (including ethnic identity) as a result of the fact that different users assign different meanings to the term. For Eriksonians/primordialists, identity is deep, internal, and permanent; for interactionists/optionalists, identity is shallow, external, and evanescent. It is bad enough that, in many contexts of usage, one cannot tell which of these very different interpretations is intended. Much worse is the likelihood that many who speak of identity are completely oblivious of the equivocation and hence do not themselves know which of the interpretations they intend.

Confusion arising from this source and from other perplexities of terminology bedevils discussion at every level from popular journalism to scholarly analysis.[29] Hearings recently held by the Civil Rights Commission on 'Civil Rights Issues of Euro-Ethnic Americans' furnish an instructive example from the broad area of debate over social policy. The 'consultation,' as it was officially designated, took place in 1979 and provided a sounding board for white ethnic spokesmen unhappy about programs of the affirmative-action type. Several of the witnesses likewise expressed misgivings about the label 'Euro–ethnic,' which led Geno Baroni to observe: 'We argue about terminology – even the name of this meeting . . . We don't have the language to describe ourselves, and America has no national sense of identity.'[30] Irving M. Levine, like Baroni a pioneer of the new ethnicity, was equally troubled about Americans' inability to understand the nature of identity. The situation was not helped by the careless way terms relating to race and ethnicity are used, even by judges, and Levine suggested that it was time for the Civil Rights Commission 'to clear up some of the definitions.'[31]

Especially interesting were the remarks of Francis X. Femminella. Noting that other witnesses had 'talked about ethnic identity,' Femminella delivered a brief disquisition on 'ethnic *ego* identity . . . a very special kind of a concept.' His purpose was not merely to clarify the ambiguities left by other testimony, but also to refute the claim that ethnic groups could not perpetuate themselves without some degree of self-segregation. Invoking Erikson's authority, he argued that a person internalizes the social heritage of his or her group at so deep a level that it is 'damn close' to being 'genetically inheritable.' For that reason, ethnic communities need not seal themselves off from others; rather, 'if that heritage is there, then the ethnic communities will go on irrespective of whether they have a locale.'[32]

These observations illustrate the affinity between Eriksonian identity and primordialist ethnicity. The linkage has important implications from the viewpoint of advocacy, for the intimate association thus established between personal identity and ethnic heritage makes plausible the argument that ethnic cultures require some sort of official recognition if the self-esteem of individuals is not to suffer damage. The respect for the dignity of the individual demanded by the democratic ideology is thereby extended to cover ethnic cultures that sustain the sense of personal self-worth.[33] Femminella did not develop this aspect of the matter, but his remarks suggest another strategic use of this perspective in controversy. For the Eriksonian theoretical framework, 'where,' as Femminella put it, 'you can get something going,' made it possible for him to avoid the taint of racialism while asserting that ethnicity would perdure indefinitely without any need for potentially divisive group self-segregation.

But of course every position has the defect of its virtues. The defect here is that so strong a primordialist argument inevitably suggests the conclusion that, if ethnicity is bound to persist anyhow, there is no great need for new social policies designed to foster or protect it. The optionalist view is much better adapted for arguing in favor of new social policies because it stresses the role of situational factors in shaping ethnic identity. Since the participants in the Euro-ethnic consultation were overwhelmingly in favor of changes in policy, it is not surprising that they also made use of the optionalist argument. Paul J. Asciolla was most explicit: he said that 'the concept of ethnicity as a factor in American culture' would 'diminish or indeed vanish' if it were not 'kept alive consciously.'[34]

No one pointed out the contradiction between Femminella's position and that of Asciolla. Very likely it was not even noticed; we are so accustomed to hearing ethnic identity talked about in both ways that the contradictory implications pass us by. From the viewpoint of advocacy, it would not have been very adroit to call attention to the equivocation of terminology anyhow, for it is clearly advantageous to be able in certain contexts to argue that ethnic identity is fixed and in others to affirm that it is malleable. But much as the controversialist may like having terms that mean whatever the rhetorical situation requires, equivocation of this sort is fatal to efforts to achieve a clear theoretical grasp of the issues. It is likewise a grievous handicap to the forging of sound social policy through rational debate. On that account, bringing such equivocation out into the open is of more than purely academic interest.

Having sketched the popularization of the term and having investigated its provenance and some of its complexities, we turn now to the matter of causes, seeking to answer the question, Why did *identity* so quickly become an indispensable term in American social commentary?

A full answer would take more space than is available here, but some comments are required to round out the semantic history of identity. We will first consider the mystique of the social sciences and the vogue of national-character studies, which are best thought of as mediating conditions that contributed to the popularization of the term. Then we will look briefly at more substantive causes for concern with identity.

The mystique of the social sciences is relevant to the popularization of identity because the new usage derived from the technical vocabulary of psychology and sociology; for that reason, it shared in the aura of cognitive authority surrounding the social sciences at midcentury. Although they had emerged as autonomous disciplines around 1900, the social sciences only came into their own after World War I. They developed a strong corporate sense in the 1920s and created a major support institution in the Social Science Research Council (SSRC), which quickly attracted large-scale funding from philanthropic foundations. By the end of the decade, the social scientific disciplines had matured sufficiently to make possible the publication of a monumental collaborative work, the *Encyclopedia of the Social Sciences*, which appeared between 1930 and 1935. The New Deal opened new opportunities for public service for economists and other social scientists. Then came World War II. That really brought the social scientists out of their ivory towers and set them to work for their country, as Stuart Chase observed in an admiring survey of the wartime accomplishments and postwar prospects of the social sciences.[35]

Chase's book, *The Proper Study of Mankind* (1948), illustrates the way the war enhanced the prestige of the social sciences. It was undertaken at the suggestion of officials of the SSRC and Carnegie Corporation, who 'followed the project step by step' and provided financial support. The roll call of scholars who encouraged Chase and provided information on the 'mine of fresh material accumulated during the war' constituted a veritable who's who of the social sciences. The book itself explained the scientific method and reviewed its achievements – many of which were war-related – in such fields as human relations, public-opinion polling, and learning theory. Reviewers hailed the book as a valuable reconnaissance that indicated directions for future research, and it sold well enough to justify a revised edition in 1956. By that time the intellectual authority of the social sciences seemed to Chase so well established that he said 'an intelligent layman' would hesitate to form a judgment on 'complicated questions about, crime or sex or the federal budget without some background in social science – perhaps a course or two in college, or in the extension field.'[36]

As supporting evidence for this dictum Chase might have cited the role played by social-scientific evidence in the fight for racial desegregation. He might likewise have pointed to the vast readership enjoyed by David Riesman's *The Lonely Crowd* (1950) and the almost equal success of William H. Whyte, Jr.'s *The Organization Man* (1956). With the publication in 1959 of Vance Packard's *The Status Seekers*, 'pop sociology' had come of age as a literary genre with mass appeal.[37]

These developments testify to the belief, widely held by laymen as well as by academic intellectuals, that the social sciences could unlock the secrets of the human condition.[38] This belief goes a long way toward explaining why identity caught on so quickly in the 1950s. Although the word had been used in the vernacular sense for a long time, the kind of identity talked about by psychologists and sociologists seemed to refer to something deeper, more mysterious, and more important. It was a matter of universal concern, since everyone had an identity, but to fathom its involvement in harrowing 'searches' and agonizing 'crises' one had to call on the special expertise of the social scientist. The association of the term *identity* with the social sciences thus added to its intellectual cachet, making it part of the conceptual equipment of the approach that offered the best hope of solving the problems besetting American society.

Among the many problems facing American society in the years after World War II, understanding the national character would probably not strike us today as one meriting high priority. Yet self-understanding is always important, and in that era the study of national character was regarded as one of the most exciting frontier areas of the social sciences.[39] The vogue of national-character studies is particularly relevant for us because Erikson had close connections with the group of social scientists who pioneered a new approach to the subject, and it was against the background of national-character studies that he began to put the term *identity* into circulation.

The belief that different human groups are marked by distinctive characteristics is at least as old as Herodotus, but it had fallen into disrepute in the 1930s as a result of its association with racialism. The new era of scientifically respectable study of national character was inaugurated in World War II by a group of scholars who were called upon by agencies of the United States government to apply their skills to such questions as how civilian morale could best be maintained or what kind of propaganda could be most effectively employed against the enemy. Margaret Mead was the best-known scholar involved, and she led the way in applying to these questions the methods worked out in the 1930s by the culture-and-personality school of anthropologists. She was one of the founders of this school, which combined psychological assumptions and ethnographic observation in the effort to discover how group norms and attitudes were stamped on the personalities of individuals belonging to different cultures. From this mode of investigation to the study of national character was only a short step, and Margaret Mead later stated explicitly that what were called culture-and-personality studies in the 1930s 'would today [1961] be called . . . "national character" [studies].'[40] The degree of scientific prestige attained by this approach is best illustrated in the postwar Tensions Project, an ambitious collaborative investigation initiated by the United Nations Educational, Scientific, and Cultural Organization and supported by the SSRC, which relied heavily on the national-character perspective in its effort to find ways of reducing 'tensions affecting international understanding.' And in 1954 the historian of nationalism Louis L. Snyder spoke respectfully of the developing 'science of national character.'[41]

There were national-character studies of other peoples–Ruth Benedict's book on the Japanese, *The Chrysanthemum and the Sword* (1946), being especially notable – but American-character studies were the most popular. Margaret Mead's *And Keep Your Powder Dry* (1942) opened the era in which studies of the American character became a leading growth sector of the knowledge industry, and almost the reason for being of the new discipline (or disciplinary holding company) of American Studies.[42] The key point for us is that American-character studies dealt directly with the relationship of the individual and society and explored the problem of whether, to what extent, or how the individual's personality, character, or 'identity' was shaped by the culture in which he or she was a participant.

A direct connection can be shown between this general development and the introduction of the term *identity*, since Erikson was closely associated with the social scientists engaged in wartime national-character studies. He prepared memoranda for the Committee for National Morale on the stresses of life on submarines, on interrogating German prisoners of war, and on the feasibility of making psychological observations in internment camps. His major contribution was an inquiry into Hitler's success in winning the loyalty of German youth by embodying in himself the anxieties and fantasies of a generation that experienced national humiliation, cultural crisis, and economic collapse. Margaret Mead cited this study in *And Keep Your Power Dry*, and Coles has stressed its importance when discussing the impact of the war on Erikson's thinking about identity.[43]

Erikson knew and admired Margaret Mead's work on the American character, and he first worked out his ideas on the interaction between 'ego identity' and 'group identity' in the context of the wartime investigation of national character.[44] The 1946 article 'Ego Development and Historical Change' was published in a specialized psychoanalytical journal and was clinically oriented, but it also showed marked affinities with national-character studies since Erikson was concerned with the way in which the individual's social heritage (group identity) affected the development of his or her personality (ego identity). It was essential, he wrote, 'to correlate a patient's childhood history with the history of his family's sedentary residence in prototypical areas (East), in 'backward' areas (South), or in 'forward' areas (Western and Northern frontier), as these areas were gradually incorporated into the American version of the Anglo-Saxon cultural identity.' In emphasizing polarities in the American group identity, Erikson was taking over an insight first elaborated by one of his wartime co-workers, Gregory Bateson, in a paper on 'Morale and National Character.' As heir to a history of extreme contrast and abrupt changes, said Erikson, the 'functioning American . . . bases his final ego-identity on some tentative combination of dynamic polarities such as migratory and sedentary, individualistic and standardized, competitive and cooperative, pious and free-thinking, etc.' Touching on the challenges of the war experience, Erikson spoke of the 'subliminal panic' that accompanied 'the large scale testing of the American identity' in the war. 'Historical change,' he declared, 'has reached a coercive universality and a global acceleration which is experienced as a threat to the emerging American identity.'[45]

Erikson reworked much of this material for the chapter of *Childhood and Society* (1950) entitled, 'Reflections on the American Identity.' This chapter marks a milestone in the semantic history of identity because it was the first major publication in which the expression 'American identity' was used as the equivalent of 'American character.' Reverting again to the subject of polarities, Erikson began by observing that virtually all characteristically American traits have opposites likewise characteristically American. 'This, one suspects,' he continued in the second sentence of the chapter, 'is true of all 'national characters' or (as I would prefer to call them) national identities.'[46] Although distinctive in being based primarily on Erikson's clinical experience as a psychoanalytical therapist, the chapter was clearly in the tradition of commentaries on the American character. Thus Erikson made reference to Vernon Louis Parrington's work, alluded to the legacies of Puritanism and the frontier, and touched on many other familiar themes of national-character commentary.[47]

The fact that *identity* could be used alternatively for *character* in an era when national-character studies were extremely popular doubtless helped to smooth the way for its rapid acceptance. But that is surely not a sufficient explanation for the enormous success of the term. *Identity*, after all, gained much greater currency than *character* ever had, and its popularity continued long after the vogue of national-character studies was forgotten. Its having been launched in the favorable climate created by the interest in national character studies and its prestige as a term taken from the technical vocabulary of social science must therefore be understood as factors that mediated its popularization rather than being regarded as decisive causes.

What then *was* the decisive cause? The most important consideration, I would say, was that the word *identity* was ideally adapted to talking about the relationship of the individual to society as that perennial problem presented itself to Americans at midcentury. More specifically, *identity* promised to elucidate a new kind of conceptual linkage between the two elements of the problem, since it was used in reference to, and dealt with the relationship of, the individual personality and the ensemble of social and cultural features that gave different groups their distinctive character.

The relationship of the individual to society has always been problematic for Americans because of the surpassing importance in the national ideology of the values of freedom, equality, and the autonomy of the individual. Alexis de Tocqueville analyzed in classical fashion how democratic principles and equalitarian social conditions gave rise to an 'individualism' (a word he effectively introduced into the language) that tended to shrivel a man's consciousness of solidarity with his fellows, throwing him forever back upon himself alone and threatening to 'shut [him] up in the solitude of his own heart.'[48] He did not, of course, use the term *identity* in this connection, but it is impossible for today's reader not to think of 'identity problems' on encountering Tocqueville's uncannily modern diagnosis of the psychological strains created by uncertainties of status and his description of the strange restlessness that made Americans 'serious and almost sad even in their pleasures.'[49] It is also easy to understand why there was in the 1950s an admiration for Tocqueville that approached veneration, for 'the isolation of the individual and the atomization of society' that he described in Jacksonian times anticipated the discovery of mass society that loomed so large in the landscape of American social commentary at midcentury.[50]

The post-World War II critique of mass society drew on a variety of sources, but what gave it compelling urgency and made it a matter of general concern was undoubtedly the frightening rise of totalitarianism followed by the catastrophe of world war. Refugee intellectuals, who had special reason to abhor totalitarianism, were important contributors to the mass-culture critique, and one influential group – the so-called Frankfurt School whose 'dialectical method' fused Marxist and Freudian perspectives – saw in American society tendencies that could well eventuate in totalitarianism and that were already producing 'authoritarian personalities' susceptible to fascism.[51] The relation of the individual to society was the crucial issue for critics of mass society, who discussed it in terms of 'alienation,' 'anxiety,' 'anomie,' 'ethnocentrism,' 'status consciousness,' 'conformity,' and 'the need for belonging.' Riesman introduced 'other-directedness,' and the title of his book – *The Lonely Crowd* – epitomized the central problem: personal isolation in a mass society. Handlin's *The Uprooted*, published a year after Riesman's volume, explored a different dimension of American social experience, but it also put into circulation a term – *uprootedness* – that added a new strain of poignance to the interpretation of the relation of the individual to American society.

In these circumstances the questions, 'Who am I?' and 'Where do I belong?' became inevitable. Identity was, in a sense, what the discussion was all about. As Erikson noted in 1950, 'we begin to conceptualize matters of identity at the very time in history when they become a problem.' The study of identity, he believed, was 'as strategic in our time as the study of sexuality was in Freud's time.'[52] Understood as a concept of the social sciences, *identity* thus gained its original currency because of its aptness for discussing one of the issues that dominated the American intellectual horizon of the 1950s, 'the survival of the person in mass society.[53] In those days the characteristic problem centered around 'the search for identity,' which was thought to arise primarily from the individual's feeling of being rootless and isolated in a swarming, anonymous throng. In the next decade the cultural climate changed drastically and the mass-society problem receded far into the background. But *identity* did not decline with the fading interest in the problems that first called for employment of the concept; on the contrary, it gained even greater popularity. The problem of the relation of the individual to society assumed new forms in the turmoil of the 1960s, but identity was more relevant than every – only now it was of 'identity crises' that one heard on every hand.

Few who lived through that troubled time would deny that the expression 'identity crisis' spoke with greater immediacy to the American condition than the formula 'search for identity.' For the nation did go through a profound crisis – social, political, and cultural – between the assassination of John F. Kennedy and the resignation of Richard Nixon. The ingredients of the crisis – racial violence, campus disruptions, antiwar protests, cultural upheaval, and the abuse of official power and betrayal of public trust – need no elaboration. The point is that the national crisis translated itself to the ordinary citizen as a challenge to every individual to decide where he or she stood with respect to the traditional values, beliefs, and institutions that were being called into question, and with respect to the contrasting interpretations being offered of American society, American policies, and the American future. In other words, the national crisis brought about a reexamination on a massive scale of the relationship between the individual and society. That was the relationship with which identity dealt, and in innumerable cases the reexamination was sufficiently intense to make the expression 'identity crisis' seem very apt.

Within the context of cultural crisis, the revival of ethnicity deserves special attention as perhaps the most important legacy of the 1960s so far as usage of *identity* is concerned. There is in the nature of the case a close connection between the notion of identity and the awareness of belonging to a distinctive group set apart from others in American society by race, religion, national background, or some other cultural marker. As a matter of fact, Erikson alluded to the acculturation of immigrants immediately after drawing attention in 1950 to the timeliness of identity as an analytical concern. Looking back twenty years later, he underscored his own experience as an immigrant in tracing the developing of his thinking about identity. 'It would seem almost self-evident now,' he wrote, 'how the concepts of 'identity' and 'identity crisis' emerged from my personal, clinical, and anthropological observations in the thirties and forties. I do not remember when I started to use these terms; they seemed naturally grounded in the experience of emigration, immigration, and Americanization.'[54]

That is certainly plausible. But the connection between Erikson's personal experience and his sensitivity to identity problems doubtless seemed clearer by 1970 because of the growth of interest in ethnicity in the intervening years and because of the new respectability gained by ethnic consciousness. In the late 1940s, assimilation was thought to have eroded immigrant cultures almost entirely, and the lingering vestiges of group consciousness seemed not only archaic but also potentially dysfunctional as sources of ethnocentrism, anti-intellectualism, and isolationist sentiment.[55] Even Herberg, who first stressed the linkage between ethnicity and the search for identity, believed ethnic identities were being replaced by religious identities. The black revolution of the 1960s, and the subsequent emergence of the new ethnicity, changed all that. These movements affirmed the durability of ethnic consciousness, gave it legitimacy and dignity, and forged an even more intimate bond between the concepts of ethnicity and identity. And these developments not only took place against the background of the national identity crisis, they were also dialectically related to it – that is, ethnic or minority identities became more appealing options because of the discrediting of traditional Americanism brought about by the racial crisis and the Vietnam War.[56] As Nathan Glazer pointed out in 1975, a situation had by then developed in 'the ecology of identities' in which, for the first time in American history, it seemed more attractive to many individuals to affirm an ethnic identity than to affirm that one was simply an American.[57] The evidence cited earlier from the consultation on Euro-ethnics indicates that ethnic identity is still perceived to be closely related to group concerns and social policy, which supports the contention that the ethnic revival has had the most enduring effect on usage of the term *identity*.

Thus far the semantic history of identity. What can we conclude from it? Three reflections of special relevance for historians suggest themselves. The first is simply a plea for wider application of the historical approach as a method for clarifying ambiguous concepts. Not many American historians have undertaken investigations of this sort, although there are a few outstanding examples.[58] Without claiming to have cleared up all the problems associated with identity, I would argue that the present study has brought to light much that was not known about it before and that could never have been discovered by purely systematic conceptual analysis.

Second, I would suggest that historians interested in problems involving identity acquaint themselves with the sociological writings about the subject in addition to resorting to the works of Erikson. There are, as we have seen, important differences between the two interpretations. Erikson's is by far the better known; for certain purposes, however, the sociological perspective may offer a more useful conceptual framework for analyzing socio-historical influences on identity than Erikson's primarily psychological approach.[59] In any case, familiarity with both brings into sharper focus the distinctive assumptions of each and thereby assists the historian in reaching his or her own conclusions as to how the concept of identity should be handled.

The final point to be emphasized is the obvious one that historians need to be very careful in talking about identity and highly critical in assessing the way others talk about it. The term can legitimately be employed in a number of ways. It may, for example, mean no more than that a person or group is known by a certain name, but it may also be used in reference to the distinguishing characteristics marking whatever is known by that name or to the ensemble of cultural features that collectively constitutes the larger reality with which a person or group is identified through a certain name.[60] Erikson seems at times to encompass all of these senses in his notion of identity, but his characteristic emphasis is on a crucial psychic ingredient, something within the personality of the individual that makes it possible 'to experience one's self as something that has continuity and sameness, and to act accordingly.'[61] Adding to the already great likelihood of confusion arising from this array of possible meanings is the ambiguity stemming from the fact that the sociologists most apt to talk about identity understand it in a quite different way.

For these reasons, responsible use of the term demands a lively sensitivity to the intrinsic complexities of the subject matter with which it deals, and careful attention to the need for precision and consistency in its application. But of course its enormous popularization has had just the opposite effect: as *identity* became more and more a cliché, its meaning grew progressively more diffuse, thereby encouraging increasingly loose and irresponsible usage. The depressing result is that a good deal of what passes for discussion of identity is little more than portentous incoherence, and the historian need not be intimidated into regarding it as more than that.[62] What is called for, rather, is confidence in the traditional critical skills of the historical craft. By applying them with care, historians can make a contribution to better understanding of a significant problem in contemporary American culture.

Notes

1. David L. Sills (ed.), *International Encyclopedia of the Social Sciences* (18 vols., New York, 1968–1979), VII, 57–65; Edwin R. A. Seligman and Alvin Johnson (eds), *Encyclopedia of the Social Sciences* (15 vols., New York, 1930–1935), VII, 573–74. A discussion that is opaque to the reader not well versed in the tradition of continental philosophical psychology is David J. de Levita, *The Concept of Identity* (New York, 1965). More useful is Arnold Dashefsky (ed.), *Ethnic Identity in Society* (Chicago, 1976), esp. 5–9. Examples of recent discussions by social scientists are Frank A. Salomone and Charles H. Swanson, 'Identity and Ethnicity: Ethnic Groups and Interactions in a Multi-Ethnic Society,' *Ethnic Groups*, 2 (May 1979), 167–83; and Kwen Fee Lian, 'Identity in Minority Group Relations,' *Ethnic and Racial Studies*, 5 (January 1982), 42–52.

2. The definition quoted in the text is the second given for *identity*. The first, not germane here, is: 'The quality or condition of being the same in substance, composition, nature, properties, or in particular qualities under consideration; absolute or essential sameness; oneness.' *Oxford English Dictionary*, s.v. 'identity.'

3. *Ibid.*, Robert Langbaum, *The Mysteries of Identity: A Theme in Modern Literature* (New York, 1977), 25.

4. *Oxford English Dictionary*, s.v. 'identity.'

5. Oscar Handlin, *The Uprooted: The Epic Story of the Great Migrations That Made the American People* (Boston, 1951), 105, 185, 188, 194, 239, 280, 304. *Identity* is not used as a technical term in William Carlson Smith's synthesis of the sociological literature on immigrant assimilation. William Carlson Smith, *Americans in the Making: The Natural History of the Assimilation of Immigrants* (New York, 1939).

6. Will Herberg, *Protestant-Catholic-Jew: An Essay in American Religious Sociology* (Garden City, 1956), 24–31, 40–44.

7. C. Vann Woodward, 'The Search for Southern Identity,' *Virginia Quarterly Review*, 34 (Summer 1958), 321–38; W. L. Morton, *The Canadian Identity* (Madison, 1961).

8. Allen Wheelis, *Quest for Identity* (New York, 1958), Helen Merrell Lynd, *On Shame and the Search for Identity* (New York, 1958); Erik H. Erikson, *Identity and the Life Cycle: Selected Papers* (New York, 1959); Anselm Strauss, *Mirrors and Masks: The Search for Identity* (Glencoe, Ill., 1959); Maurice R. Stein, Arthur J. Vidich, and David Manning White (eds.), *Identity and Anxiety: Survival of the Person in Mass Society* (Glencoe, Ill., 1960), 25.

9. Hendrik M. Ruitenbeek (ed.), *Varieties of Modern Social Theory* (New York, 1963), 3, 100. Elsewhere Hendrik M. Ruitenbeek asks, 'Who, thirty years ago, would have thought that the problem of identity would become one of the most crucial issues for the searching individual in our society?' *Ibid.*, xii–xiii. See also Roger L. Shinn (ed.), *The Search for Identity: Essays on the American Character* (New York, 1964).

10. Robert Penn Warren, *Who Speaks for the Negro?* (New York, 1965), 17.

11. Martin E. Marty, *By Way of Response* (Nashville, 1981), 19. The Harvard University episode is reported in Erik H. Erikson, *Identity: Youth and*

Crisis (New York, 1968), 15–16.

12. Robert Coles, review of *Dimensions of a New Identity* by Erik H. Erikson, *New Republic*, June 8 1974, p. 23; William Glasser, *The Identity Society* (New York, 1972), 43; Arthur O. Lovejoy, *Essays in the History of Ideas* (Baltimore, 1948), 232.

13. Erikson, *Identity*, 22. For the best introduction to Erik H. Erikson's writings, see *ibid.*; Erikson, *Identity and the Life Cycle*; and Erik H. Erikson, *Childhood and Society* (New York 1950). See also Chapter 15 in this volume.

14. An informative biography that provides extensive commentary on Erikson's writings is Robert Coles, *Erik H. Erikson: The Growth of His Work* (Boston, 1970). See also Erik H. Erikson, 'Autobiographic Notes on the Identity Crisis,' *Daedalus*, 99 (Fall 1970), 730–59; and H. Stuart Hughes, *The Sea Change: The Migration of Social Thought, 1930–1965* (New York, 1975), 217–32. For journalistic coverage, see David Elkind, 'Erik Erikson's Eight Stages of Man,' *New York Times Magazine*, April 5 1970, pp. 25–27, 84, 87, 89, 90, 92, 110, 112, 114, 117, 119; Robert Coles, 'Profiles: The Measure of Man – I,' *New Yorker*, November 7 1970, pp. 51–131; Robert Coles, 'Profiles: The Measure of Man – II,' *ibid.*, November 14 1970, pp. 59–138; Webster Schott, 'Explorer of Identity,' *Life*, November 27 1970, p. 24; review of *Erik H. Erikson* by Robert Coles, *Time*, November 30 1970, p. 51–52; and 'Erik Erikson: The Quest for Identity,' *Newsweek*, December 21 1970, pp. 84–89. The Jefferson Lectures were published as Erik H. Erikson, *Dimensions of a New Identity: The 1973 Jefferson Lectures in the Humanities* (New York, 1974).

15. Erik H. Erikson, 'Identity and Uprootedness in Our Time,' in *Varieties of Modern Social Theory* (ed.) Ruitenbeek, 59–60; Erikson, *Identity and the Life Cycle*, 112–13; Erikson, *Identity*, 23, 314.

16. Jack Rothman, *Minority Group Identification and Intergroup Relations: An Examination of Kurt Lewin's Theory of Jewish Group Identity* (New York, 1965), 14–19; Gordon W. Allport, 'The Historical Background of Modern Social Psychology,' in *Handbook of Social Psychology*, (ed.) Gardner Lindzey (12 vols., Cambridge, Mass., 1954), I, 24.

17. Gordon W. Allport, *The Nature of Prejudice* (Reading, Mass., 1954), 293–94.

18. In 1950 a sociologist associated with the Menninger Clinic began an article by asking: 'What concern can sociology have, one might ask, with such a strictly psychological phenomenon as identification?' Louisa P. Holt, 'Identification: A Crucial Concept for Sociology,' *Bulletin of the Menninger Clinic*, 14 (September 1950), 164–73.

19. Ralph Linton's paternity of role theory as a systematic conceptual perspective is categorically asserted by Robert Merton, *Social Theory and Social Structure* (Glencoe, Ill., 1957), 368 n. See also Ralph Linton, *The Study of Man: An Introduction* (New York, 1936), 113–31.

20. Nelson N. Foote, 'Identification as the Basis for a Theory of Motivation,' *American Sociological Review*, 16 (February 1951), 14–21.

21. *Ibid.*, 17–19. See also Everett Cherrington Hughes and Helen MacGill Hughes, *Where Peoples Meet: Racial and Ethnic Frontiers* (Glencoe, Ill., 1952), 102.

22. Robert K. Merton and Alice S. Kitt, 'Contributions to the Theory of

Reference Group Behavior, ' in *Continuities in Social Research. Studies in the Scope and Method of 'The American Soldier,'* (ed.) Robert K. Merton and Paul P. Lazarsfeld (Glencoe, Ill., 1950), 40–105; Merton, *Social Theory and Social Structure*, 225–386. For allusions to identification and the introduction of the term 'reference group,' see *ibid.*, 269, 275–76, 277.

23. Andrew J. Weigert, 'Identity: Its Emergence within Sociological Psychology,' unpublished typescript, 1982 (in possession of Andrew J. Weigert). For general treatments, see Bernard N. Meltzer, John W. Petras, and Larry T. Reynolds, *Symbolic Interactionism: Genesis, Varieties and Criticism* (London, 1975); and Paul Elliott Rock, *The Making of Symbolic Interactionism* (Totowa, N.J., 1979).

24. Erving Goffman, *The Presentation of the Self in Everyday Life* (Garden City, 1959); Erving Goffman, *Stigma: Notes on the Management of Spoiled Identity* (Englewood Cliffs, 1963); Peter L. Berger, *Invitation to Sociology: A Humanistic Approach* (Garden City, 1963). The importance of Anselm Strauss's *Mirrors and Masks* in putting the word *identity* into the working vocabulary of symbolic interactionists is stressed by Weigert, 'Identity,' 10–11.

25. For discussion of the evolution of Erikson's concept of identity, see Coles, *Erik H. Erikson*, 165–79, 265.

26. Foote, 'Identification,' 14–21; Berger, *Invitation to Sociology*, 100–06.

27. Thomas J. Scheff, 'On the Concepts of Identity and Social Relationship,' in *Human Nature and Collective Behavior: Papers in Honor of Herbert Blumer*, (ed.) Tamotsu Shibutani (Englewood Cliffs, 1970), 205. See also the discussion of Erving Goffman's term 'identity kit,' which refers to 'the assortment of role identities that each individual carries with him,' in William M. Newman, 'Multiple Realities: The Effects of Social Pluralism on Identity,' in *Ethnic Identity in Society* (ed.) Dashefsky, 40.

28. The distinction was, I believe, first broached by Nathan Glazer and Daniel P. Moynihan in commenting on the contributions to a volume of essays that they edited. See Nathan Glazer and Daniel P. Moynihan (eds), *Ethnicity: Theory and Experience* (Cambridge, Mass., 1975), 19–20. They called the two approaches 'primordialist' and 'circumstantialist,' but the term 'optionalist' was substituted for 'circumstantialist' in Peter K. Eisinger, 'Ethnicity as a Strategic Option: An Emerging View,' *Public Administration Review*, 38 (January–February 1978), 89–93. See also Pierre L. van den Berghe, *The Ethic Phenomenon* (New York, 1981), 17–18, 256, 261.

29. Calling for 'deobfuscation' of identity, Carlos H. Arce says that the scholarly literature on Chicano identity 'demonstrates the confused commingling of disparate phenomena and the failure to develop consistent conceptual definitions.' He also speaks of the 'conceptual morass' of earlier work on Mexican-American communities Carlos H. Arce, 'A Reconsideration of Chicano Culture and Identity,' *Daedalus*, 110 (Spring 1981), 182–83.

30. *Civil Rights Issues of Euro-Ethnic Americans in the United States: Opportunities and Challenges. A Consultation Sponsored by the United States Commission on Civil Rights, Chicago, Illinois, December 3, 1979* (Washington, 1980), 590. For other observations about the term 'Euro-ethnic,' see *ibid.*, 76, 584.

31. *Ibid.*, 12, 8.

32. *Ibid.*, 284.

33. As John W. Briggs has noted, it is 'the central tenet of the "new ethnicity" movement that group identity and roots are vitally important to personal identity, character, and psychological well-being.' See John W. Briggs, review of *Old Bread, New Wine* by Patrick J. Gallo, *American Historical Review*, 87 (April 1982), 544. This theme recurs frequently in the 1970 hearings on the bill to establish ethnic heritage studies centers. See U.S. Congress, House, Committee on Education and Labor, *Ethnic Heritage Studies Centers: Hearings before the General Subcommittee on Education of the Committee on Education and Labor, House of Representatives. Ninety-First Congress, Second Session, on H.R. 14910*, 91 Cong., 2 sess., 1970, pp. 1, 22, 23–24, 129, 135, 175–76, 255, 256, 263, 267.

34. *Civil Rights Issues of Euro-Ethnic Americans*, 284, 569.

35. Stuart Chase, *The Proper Study of Mankind* (New York, 1956), x. Another observer stated at the time: 'During World War II the social scientist took his place, with dignity, alongside the medical and physical scientist. To the contributions of the physicist, the chemist, and the technologist were added the contributions of the anthropologist, economist, political scientist psychologist, psychiatrist, and sociologist . . . This phenomenal acceleration in the development and productivity of the social sciences, though occurring under the compulsion of war, may yet prove at least one great boon to mankind.' Charles E. Hendry, 'Foreword,' in Goodwin Watson, *Action for Unity* (New York, 1947), x. For a more recent survey of the subject, see Gene M. Lyons *The Uneasy Partnership: Social Science and the Federal Government in the Twentieth Century* (New York, 1969), 80–123.

36. For the role of the Social Science Research Council and Carnegie Corporation, and for the listing of social science informants, see Stuart Chase, *The Proper Study of Mankind* (New York, 1948), xv–xx; for the quotation, see Chase, *Proper Study* (1956), 307.

37. David Riesman, *The Lonely Crowd: A Study of the Changing American Character* (New Haven, 1950); William H. Whyte, Jr., *The Organization Man* (New York, 1956); Vance Packard, *The Status Seekers: An Explanation of Class Behavior in America and the Hidden Barriers That Affect You, Your Community, Your Future* (New York, 1959). For the role of social scientific evidence in the struggle for desegregation, see Kenneth B. Clark, 'The Social Scientist as an Expert Witness in Civil Rights Litigation,' *Social Problems*, 1 (June 1953), 5–10; *Brown* v. *Board of Education of Topeka*, 347 US 483; and Richard Kluger, *Simple Justice: The History of Brown* v. *Board of Education and Black America's Struggle for Equality* (New York, 1976), 315–45, 556–57.

38. Still another indication of this belief was the 1950 decision of the Ford Foundation 'to throw its great financial resources behind the effort 'to advance human welfare' through the application of scientific methods and techniques to the study of human behavior.' Heinz Eulau called this 'a milestone in the development of modem social science' and 'an act of faith . . . that social Science is ready to contribute to the solution of the manifold problems which vex mankind.' Heinz Eulau, 'Social Science at the Crossroads,' *Antioch Review*, 11 (March 1951), 117–28.

39. Cf. Alex Inkeles and Daniel J. Levinson, 'National Character: The Study of Modal Personality and Sociocultural Systems,' in *Handbook of Social Psychology*, (ed.) Lindzey, II, 977–1020; and Milton Singer, 'A Survey of Culture and Personality Theory and Research,' in *Studying Personality Cross-Culturally*, (ed.) Bert Kaplan (New York, 1961), 43–57.

40. Margaret Mead, 'National Character and the Science of Anthropology,' in *Culture and Social Character: The Work of David Riesman Reviewed* (ed.) Seymour Martin Lipset and Leo Lowenthal (New York, 1961), 17.

41. Louis L. Snyder, *The Meaning of Nationalism* (New Brunswick, N.J., 1954), 162–87. On the Tensions Project, see Otto Klineberg, *Tensions Affecting International Understanding: A Survey of Research* (New York, 1950); and Morroe Berger, '"Understanding National Character" – and War: The Psychological Study of Peoples,' *Commentary*, 11 (April (1951), 375–86.

42. Ruth Benedict, *The Chrysanthemum and the Sword: Patterns of Japanese Culture* (Boston, 1946); Margaret Mead, *And Keep Your Powder Dry: An Anthropologist Looks at America* (New York, 1942). See also Chapter 14 of this volume. For a useful guide to the immense literature on American character, see Michael McGiffert, 'Selected Writings on American National Character,' *American Quarterly*, 15 (Summer 1963), 271–88. Other illuminating discussions are Thomas L. Hartshorne, *The Distorted Image: Changing Conceptions of the American Character since Turner* (Cleveland, 1968); E. Adamson Hoebel, 'Anthropological Perspectives on National Character,' *Annals of the American Academy of Political and Social Science*, 370 (March 1967), 1–7; and David E. Stannard, 'American Historians and the Idea of National Character: Some Problems and Prospects,' *American Quarterly*, 23 (May 1971), 202–20.

43. Mead, *And Keep Your Powder Dry*, 274; Coles, *Erik H. Erikson*, 84–100, 421.

44. Erik Homburger Erikson, 'Childhood and Tradition in Two American Indian Tribes,' *Psychoanalytic Study of the Child*, 1 (1945), 348n. In 1950 Erikson stated: 'It would be impossible for me to itemize my over-all indebtedness to Margaret Mead.' Erikson, *Childhood and Society* (1950), 13.

45. Erik Homburger Erikson, 'Ego Development and Historical Change,' *Psychoanalytic Study of the Child*, 2 (1946), 373–74, 378, 388. Gregory Bateson, 'Morale and National Character,' in *Civilian Morale: Second Yearbook of the Society for the Psychological Study of Social Issues*, ed. Goodwin Watson (Boston, 1942), 71–91. There is a strong likelihood that Erikson was acquainted with Gregory Bateson's polarities approach, since the latter was at the time married to Mead and his general assistance is acknowledged in Erikson, *Childhood and Society* (1950), 14.

46. Erikson, *Childhood and Society* (1950), 244; see Chapter 16, p. 232, this volume.

47. Erikson did not change this chapter in the 1963 edition of the book, but he added a rather murky endnote. Erik H. Erikson, *Childhood and Society* (New York, 1963), 324–25.

48. Alexis de Tocqueville, *Democracy in America*, (ed.) Jacob Peter Mayer (Garden City, 1969), 506–08.

49. *Ibid.*, 536. Two recent critics of 'the prevalent American piety toward

the self' who cite Alexis de Tocqueville's discussion are Philip Rieff, *The Triumph of the Therapeutic: Uses of Faith after Freud* (New York, 1966), 62, 69–70; and Christopher Lasch, *The Culture of Narcissism American Life in an Age of Diminishing Expectations* (New York, 1978), 9.

50. The quotation is from Yehoshua Arieli, *Individualism and Nationalism in American Ideology* (Cambridge, Mass., 1964), 196. For interest in Tocqueville in the 1950s, see John Higham, Leonard Krieger, and Felix Gilbert, *History* (Englewood Cliffs, 1965), 221–22. For an introduction to the discussion of mass society, see Daniel Bell, 'Modernity and Mass Society: On the Varieties of Cultural Experience,' in *Paths of American Thought*, (ed.) Arthur M. Schlesinger, Jr., and Morton White (Boston, 1963), 411–31, 547–77.

51. Martin Jay, *The Dialectical Imagination: A History of the Frankfurt School and the Institute of Social Research 1923–1950* (London, 1973), 212–52. See also Hughes, *Sea Change* 134–88.

52. Erikson, *Childhood and Society* (1950), 242.

53. This was the subtitle of Stein, Vidich, and White (eds), *Identity and Anxiety*. See also Winston White, *Beyond Conformity* (Glencoe, Ill., 1961), 50–52.

54. Erikson, *Childhood and Society* (1950), 242; Erikson, *Life History and the Historical Moment* (New York, 1975), 43. The wording here varies slightly from Erikson's first published autobiographic reflections, in Erikson, 'Autobiographic Notes on the Identity Crisis,' 747–48. Interestingly, Erikson did not say in the 1970 version that the connection between immigration and his interest in identity problems 'seem[ed] almost self-evident.'

55. Philip Gleason, 'Americans All: World War II and the Shaping of American Identity,' *Review of Politics*, 43 (Oct. 1981), 498, 509–11.

56. This interpretation is developed more fully in Philip Gleason, 'American Identity and Americanization.' in *Harvard Encyclopedia of American Ethnic Groups*, ed. Stephan Thernstrom, Ann Orlov, and Oscar Handlin (Cambridge, Mass., 1980), 52–55. See also Arthur Mann, *The One and the Many: Reflections on the Identity* (Chicago, 1979), 1–45.

57. Nathan Glazer, *Affirmative Discrimination: Ethnic Inequality and Public Policy* (New York, 1975), 177–78.

58. Arthur E. Bestor, Jr., 'The Evolution of the Socialist Vocabulary,' *Journal of the History of Ideas*, 9 (June 1948), 259–302; Donald Fleming, 'Attitude: The History of a Concept,' *Perspectives in American History*, 1 (1967), 287–365; John Higham, 'Ethnic Pluralism in Modern American Thought' in John Higham, *Send These to Me: Jews and Other Immigrants in Urban America* (New York, 1975), 196–230; and Job L. Dittberner, *The End of Ideology and American Social Thought: 1930–1960* (Ann Arbor, 1979), 1–101, on the introduction and early diffusion of the concept of ideology among American intellectuals.

59. For an impressive example, see Peter Berger, 'Modern Identity: Crisis and Continuity,' in *The Cultural Drama: Modern Identities and Social Ferment*, (ed.) Wilton S. Dillon (Washington, 1974), 158–81.

60. Thus in some contexts 'American identity' has the same meaning as 'American character,' while in others it is equivalent to 'American nationality.' C. Vann Woodward uses *identity* to designate a distinctive regional her-

itage in Woodward, 'Search for Southern Identity,' 321–38; and identity
is synonymous with nationality in Morton, *Canadian Identity.*
61. Erikson, *Childhood and Society* (1950), 38.
62. See, for example, Vine Deloria, Jr., 'Identity and Culture,' *Daedalus,*
110 (Spring 1981), 13–27.

Index